Palgrave Series in African Borderlands Studies

Series Editors
Gregor Dobler
Institute for Ethnology
Freiburg University
Freiburg, Germany

William Miles
Professor of Political Science
Northeastern University
Boston, MA, USA

Wolfgang Zeller
Centre of African Studies
University of Edinburgh
Edinburgh, UK

African borderlands are among the continent's most creative and most rapidly changing social spaces. Because their unique position offers more flexibility to social actors, they reflect changes on the national level more quickly and more radically than most inland locations. The Palgrave Series in African Borderlands Studies is the first series dedicated to the exploration and theoretical interpretation of African borderlands. It contributes to core debates in a number of disciplines and provides vital insights for practical politics in border-related issues, ranging from migration and regional integration to conflict resolution and peace-building.

More information about this series at
http://www.palgrave.com/gp/series/14666

Lotje de Vries
Pierre Englebert • Mareike Schomerus
Editors

Secessionism in African Politics

Aspiration, Grievance, Performance,
Disenchantment

Editors
Lotje de Vries
Wageningen University & Research
De Bilt, Utrecht, The Netherlands

Pierre Englebert
Pomona College
Claremont, CA, USA

Mareike Schomerus
Overseas Development Institute
London, UK

Palgrave Series in African Borderlands Studies
ISBN 978-3-319-90205-0   ISBN 978-3-319-90206-7   (eBook)
https://doi.org/10.1007/978-3-319-90206-7

Library of Congress Control Number: 2018948197

Cover design: Hajo Schomerus

Printed on acid-free paper

This Palgrave Macmillan imprint is published by the registered company Springer International Publishing AG part of Springer Nature.
The registered company address is: Gewerbestrasse 11, 6330 Cham, Switzerland

PRAISE FOR *SECESSIONISM IN AFRICAN POLITICS*

"*Secessionism in African Politics* navigates through highly contested and charged terrain of secessionism and self-determination. The concepts still invoke strong feelings. The anthology challenges our theoretical, legal and empirical perceptions of the field. It will certainly generate well-deserved debate. A valuable reading for scholars, students, policymakers, NGOs and civil society organisations."
—Redie Bereketeab, *Senior Researcher, Nordic Africa Institute, Sweden, and Editor,* "Self-determination and Secessionism in Africa: The Post-colonial State"

"With secessionist sentiment on the rise in Cameroon, Ethiopia, and Kenya – to name but a few – this book could not be more timely or significant. Combining in-depth case studies with theoretical rigour and an illuminating comparative perspective, it will be essential reading for years to come."
—Nic Cheeseman, *Professor of Democracy, University of Birmingham, UK*

"The survival, over fifty years after independence, of the African states haphazardly established by European colonialism, questions basic assumptions about viable statehood. Only in north-east Africa – in Eritrea, South Sudan and arguably Somaliland – has the territorial integrity of these states successfully been challenged, and even there only within boundaries already laid down under colonialism. This book examines the sources of secessionism and the obstacles to it, and its troubled legacies even in those cases where it has succeeded. It makes a vital contribution to the understanding, not only of secessionism, but also of the continuing bases of African statehood."
—Christopher Clapham, *Professor, Centre of African Studies, University of Cambridge, UK*

"Secessionism is currently receiving global attention and this edited volume, comparing fifteen on-going African secessionist claims, is timely and welcome. The book reminds us that despite the limited success stories of African secessionist movements, secessionism is very much a dream, discourse, argument, and activity across the continent. Through the rich and nuanced case-studies, we are reminded that secessionism is a complex political phenomenon; the call for a redefinition of state boundaries is linked to political grievances, sentiments of marginalization, historical narratives, and economic projects that operate outside the boundaries of the territorial state. The chapters of the book list an array of reasons for the secessionist claims, and bring up vital questions of identity and history, marginalization, or ideology.

This volume provides a comprehensive study of contemporary African secessionist movements exploring its roots, changing relations to the territorial state, and the international community. The volume's main contribution is the richness in its coverage and the systematic comparison of the root causes of the myriad of ambitions and complexities of secessionism."

—Lise Rakner, *Professor of Comparative Politics, University of Bergen, Norway*

"This book is the most comprehensive volume on secessionist movements in Africa to date. For five decades, Africa's borders were, with a few exceptions, kept intact by an agreement made at the 1963 Organisation of African Unity meeting where African countries committed to working to preserve colonial borders after independence. Nevertheless, secessionist movements have continued to exist, buoyed by the failures of postcolonial African states to live up to their promises, as this book effectively demonstrates. The remarkable range and depth of cases in this collection, in addition to its broad historical, comparative, and legal perspectives, makes this a volume an important contribution to our understanding of the contemporary African state."

—Aili Mari Tripp, *Wangari Maathai Professor of Political Science and Gender & Women's Studies, University of Wisconsin-Madison, USA*

"This is an important book on a surprisingly under-studied topic in contemporary Africa. Far from being a rare and predominantly historical phenomenon, this volume demonstrates the salience of secessionism across a wide range of cases in Africa and the distinct varieties in which it can be divided. With an impressive cast of well-known authors, this volume presents a significant step forward in our understanding of past and present secessionism in Africa, its inherent challenges and contradictions. But the book is also indispensable reading for anyone interested in statehood, state-society relations and armed conflict in Africa."

—Denis Tull, *researcher at the Institute for Strategic Research (IRSEM), France*

"A well-qualified team of contributors produced this thorough exploration of a key theme of African politics."

—Crawford Young, *Professor Emeritus of Political Science, University of Wisconsin-Madison, USA*

Sponsor Series Acknowledgment

The African Borderlands Research Network (ABORNE) is an interdisciplinary network of researchers interested in all aspects of international borders and trans-boundary phenomena in Africa. The network held its inaugural meeting in Edinburg in 2017 and has since grown to over 300 members worldwide. ABORNE's core funding is provided by membership fees and, from 2009 to 2014, by the Research Network Programme of the European Science Foundation.

The European Science Foundation (ESF) was established in 1974 to provide a common platform for its Member Organizations to advance European research collaboration and explore new directions for research. It is an independent organization, owned by 78 Member Organizations, which are research funding and research performing organizations, academies, and learned societies from 30 countries. ESF promotes collaboration in research itself, in funding of research, and in science policy activities at the European level.

Advisory Board

David Coplan (University of the Witwatersrand)
Pierre Englebert (Pomona College)
Jan-Bart Gewald (University of Leiden)
Thomas Hüsken (University of Bayreuth)
Georg Klute (University of Bayreuth)
Paul Nugent (University of Edinburgh)
Cristina Udelsmann Rodrigues (Nordic Africa Institute, Uppsala)

Published by Palgrave Macmillan

Namibia's Red Line: The History of a Veterinary and Settlement Border (2012)
By Giorgio Miescher
Violence on the Margins: States, Conflict, and Borderlands (2013)
Edited by Benedikt Korf and Timothy Raeymaekers
The borderlands of South Sudan: Governance and Power in Contemporary and Historical Perspective (2013)
Edited by Christopher Vaughan, Mareike Schomerus, and Lotje de Vries

Acknowledgments

This book would not exist without Wolfgang Zeller and Jordi Tomas, who spotted the need to reflect on the phenomenon of African secessionism through a collection of case studies. Wolfgang and Jordi shepherded the book and its authors through many of its stages. We are grateful for their work, insights, and most of all their trust in handing this task over to us. In addition, we thank Laura Major, who helped in the early stages of the book.

We would like to express our gratitude to the contributors to this volume. We much appreciated their patience throughout the process.

An edited volume of this size and diversity requires a small nation-state of peer reviewers: Thank you for all your time and expertise from us as editors and from all the authors. Our respective institutions—Wageningen University, Pomona College, and Overseas Development Institute (ODI)—deserve our gratitude for allowing us the time and space to work on this volume and for their financial contributions to its copy editing.

Palgrave Macmillan guided us through the many stages of publication.

Bill Miles' benevolent oversight allowed us to bring this book to light; a kind reviewer of the proposal helped pave the way.

Hajo Schomerus designed the cover.

Many thanks to all of you.

CONTENTS

A Note on Maps

Disputes over territory and borderlines and how both link to identity, belonging, and resources are at the heart of many of the cases discussed in this volume. And yet, we offer no detailed maps to show the exact location of the secessionist struggles. Maps can be both tremendously helpful and extraordinarily powerful in capturing attention.

Often, the presence of a map—of what seems like a visualized snapshot of a complicated situation—means that the map takes power of authority over the many nuances that are crucial to all the cases of secessionist struggle presented here. Often, reducing a secessionist aspiration to a line on paper also fuels debates merely focused on where the line has been drawn.

We have thus taken the decision to offer detailed discussions without the distraction of a detailed map that goes beyond a sketch in the concluding chapter of what Africa might look like if all current secessionist movements succeeded. Maps with varying levels of detail are readily available to anyone interested in more specific locations.

Notes on Contributors

Heather Byrne is a US Fulbright researcher at the Centre for Policy Research in New Delhi, India, where she studies nonalignment, US-India relations, and energy security. She has a BA in International Relations from Pomona College and received her MPhil in International Relations from the University of Oxford, where she worked on the role of intelligence in UN Peacekeeping.

Greg Cameron is Associate Professor of Political Science and Rural Studies in the Faculty of Agriculture, Dalhousie University, Canada. Prior to joining in 2007, he taught political science at the University of Asmara, Eritrea, from 2002 to 2006. During the 1990s, he worked in Tanzania with the co-operative movement on the islands of Zanzibar and then with pastoralist NGOs in Arusha. His fieldwork and research in Eastern Africa have focused on rural development, the developmental state, and democratization transitions. His thesis at the School of Oriental and African Studies, London, UK, was on the Zanzibar co-operative movement.

Lotje de Vries is Assistant Professor at the Sociology of Development and Change Group of Wageningen University, The Netherlands. Her research focuses on local dynamics of (in)security, transnational security governance in peripheries and at borders, and state-society relations in (post-)conflict settings. Before joining Wageningen, she worked at the Centre for International Conflict-Analysis and Management (CICAM) of the Nijmegen School of Management, Radboud University, and as a

Postdoctoral Research Fellow at the German Institute of Global and Area Studies (Institute of African Affairs) (GIGA) in Hamburg, Germany. As a practitioner, she worked in Senegal with the development organization Enda Diapol.

Alexandra Dias is assistant professor at the Department of Political Studies of Nova, University of Lisbon, and a researcher at the Portuguese Institute of International Relations at the same University (NOVA IPRI). As the principal investigator of several research projects, she has done fieldwork in various Horn of Africa countries. She is working on the community of Portuguese-speaking African countries and on the prevention of radicalization across regional international societies, using European and African case studies. She has worked on the International Electoral Observation Mission of the Somaliland Presidential Elections in June 2010 and November 2017.

Gregor Dobler is Professor of Social and Cultural Anthropology at Freiburg University, Germany. His main fields are economic and political anthropology of Southern African and Western European countries. Before moving to Freiburg in 2010, Dobler worked at the Universities of Basel and Bayreuth. He is a co-founder of the African Borderlands Research Network (ABORNE), and his works on the anthropology of borders and borderlands have appeared in many journals like *Africa*, *The Journal of Modern African Studies*, *The China Quarterly*, *The Journal of the Royal Anthropological Institute*, and the *Journal of Southern African Studies*.

Sara Dorman is Senior Lecturer in African Politics at the University of Edinburgh. Her research focuses on postliberation states and the politics of nationalism, citizenship, state building, and urban politics in the Horn of Africa and Southern Africa. She is senior editor of the *Journal of Southern African Studies* and was co-editor of *African Affairs* from 2005 to 2011. Her monograph *Understanding Zimbabwe: From Liberation to Authoritarianism* was published in 2016.

Pierre Englebert is the H. Russell Smith Professor of International Relations at Pomona College, USA. His publications include *State Legitimacy and Development in Africa* (2000), *Africa: Unity, Sovereignty and Sorrow* (2009) and *Inside African Politics* (2013, with Kevin Dunn).

Joseph Figueira Martin is based in Kinshasa, Democratic Republic of Congo, as the chief of Party at African Parks Network, a nonprofit organization that takes on direct responsibility for the rehabilitation and long-term management of national parks and protected areas in partnership with governments and local communities. Previously EU Advocacy & Research Analyst at International Crisis Group, a conflict resolution think tank, his research focuses primarily on Portuguese-speaking African countries (PALOP) and conflicts linked to extractive resources. He is a graduate from the University of Manchester and holds a master's degree from the Brussels School of International Studies.

Vincent Foucher is a Senior Research Fellow of the French Centre national de la recherche scientifique based at the research centre *Les Afriques dans Le Monde*, Sciences-Po Bordeaux, France. He obtained his PhD in Political Science at the School of Oriental and African Studies, London. His research deals with armed conflict, identity politics, and state formation in West Africa. He has worked in Senegal, Guinea, and Guinea-Bissau and has more recently begun work on Boko Haram. He served as the editor-in-chief of the journals *Politique Africaine* and *Afrique Contemporaine*.

Johannes Harnischfeger (1954–2015) was associated with the Universities of Frankfurt and Cologne, Germany. His articles on ethnic and religious conflict in Nigeria, state collapse and militias, prophets and the occult, and independent African churches have appeared in many publications. His perhaps best-known work focuses on Nigeria's vigilante "Bakassi Boys" (*Journal of Modern African Studies*, 2003). Teaching positions or visiting professorships included the universities of Kobe, Japan; Zululand and University of Natal, South Africa; University of Nigeria; University of Heidelberg and Saarland, Germany; Kenyatta University; and University of Nairobi, Kenya. He held a master's degree in Anthropology and two PhDs in Literature and Political Science.

Markus Virgil Hoehne is lecturer at the Institute of Social Anthropology at the University of Leipzig, Germany. He works on conflict, identity, state formation, borderlands, transitional justice, and forensic anthropology in Somalia and Peru. He co-edited *The State and the Paradox of Customary Law in Africa* (Routledge 2018) and *Borders and Borderlands as Resources in the Horn of Africa* (James Currey, 2010), among other volumes, and he is the author of *Between Somaliland and Puntland: Marginalization, Militarization and Conflicting Political Visions* (Rift Valley Institute 2015).

Erik Kennes is associate professor at the *Institut Supérieur d'Etudes Sociales* in Lubumbashi, Democratic Republic of the Congo (DRC) and research associate at the Institute for Development Policy and Management of the University of Antwerp, Belgium, and the Africa Museum in Tervuren, Belgium. His publications include "The Katangese Gendarmes and War in Central Africa" (with Miles Larmer, 2016) and "Essai Biographique sur Laurent Désiré Kabila" (with Crispin Kalumba Nsanki, 2003). His research interests and publications focus on Congolese political history, comparative politics, and the DRC political economy of the mining sector.

Georg Klute is Professor of Anthropology at the University of Bayreuth, Germany. Since 2005, he has also tutored at the *Ecole Nationale d'Administration*, France. As a visiting professor at Addis Ababa University, Ethiopia, he has been teaching an annual course since 2012. He chaired the German African Studies Association (2012–2014) and remains part of its steering committee. His memberships include the German Anthropological Association, the Executive Board of ABORNE, and the Bayreuth Academy of Advanced African Studies. He is principal investigator of Bayreuth International Graduate School of African Studies and co-edits the journal *Modern Africa*.

Piet Konings used to be a senior researcher at the African Studies Centre in the University of Leiden until his retirement in 2008. He remains as an Honorary Fellow at the Centre. He has done extensive research on socioeconomic and political developments in Ghana and Cameroon, and his work has appeared in many publications.

Miles Larmer is Professor of African History at the University of Oxford and Research Fellow in the Department of Historical and Heritage Studies at the University of Pretoria. He has written extensively on the social and political history of Central Africa. His most recent book is *The Katangese Gendarmes and War in Central Africa: Fighting their way home*, co-authored with Erik Kennes (Indiana University Press, 2016).

Baz Lecocq is Professor of African History at the Humboldt University of Berlin, Germany. He specializes in the contemporary late colonial and postcolonial history of the continent, studying a broad set of social-political and cultural topics, including nationalism and post-slavery in the contemporary Sahara and Sahel. His recent focus is on the global connectivity of the continent, which he approaches by looking at transport technology and religious identity. His articles on the conflict between the Tuareg and the Malian State have appeared in many publications.

Henning Melber is senior research associate of the Nordic Africa Institute in Uppsala, Sweden; extraordinary professor at the Department of Political Sciences, University of Pretoria and professor extraordinary at the Centre for Africa Studies at the University of the Free State in Bloemfontein, both South Africa; and Senior Research Fellow at the Centre for Commonwealth Studies/School for Advanced Study at the University of London in the UK. He was Executive Director of the Dag Hammarskjöld Foundation in Uppsala (2006–2012), Research Director of the Nordic Africa Institute (2000–2006), and Director of the Namibian Economic Policy Research Unit (1992–2000) in Windhoek, Namibia.

Francis B. Nyamnjoh is Professor of Social Anthropology at the University of Cape Town, South Africa, having joined in 2009 from the Council for the Development of Social Science Research in Africa (CODESRIA), Senegal, where he was Head of Publications. He has taught sociology, anthropology, and communication studies at universities in Cameroon and Botswana—two countries on which he has published extensively. He is a B1-rated professor and researcher by the South African National Research Foundation (NRF) as well as a Fellow of the Cameroon Academy of Science, the African Academy of Science, and the Academy of Science of South Africa.

Matthew Porges is a doctoral student in Social Anthropology at the University of St Andrews, Scotland. His research interests are wide ranging but focus on the relationships between people, power, and ecology in North Africa. He has undertaken fieldwork in Morocco, Algeria, Mauritania, and Western Sahara.

Mareike Schomerus is a Senior Research Fellow at Overseas Development Institute (ODI), UK, and the Research Director of the Secure Livelihoods Research Consortium (SLRC). A former broadcast journalist, she received her doctorate in international development from the London School of Economics and Political Science. She has published on the resolution of violent conflict in Uganda and South Sudan; border management and conflict; civilian-military relations; armed groups; use of information technology, media, and evidence in situations of conflict and political contestation; provision of civilian security; as well as (mis)readings of violent extremism and how to counter it.

Sarah Vaughan is an Honorary Fellow in Political Science and International Relations at the University of Edinburgh, UK, where she completed a PhD in 2004. She has worked and written on Ethiopia and the Horn of Africa for 30 years. Her research interests include the political economy of development, federalism and nationalism, conflict, and power. She is an associate of The Policy Practice and a member of Ethiopia WIDE, which is a team studying longitudinal change in a series of Ethiopian communities (EthiopiaWIDE.net).

Wolfgang Zeller is a Senior Research Fellow at the Centre of African Studies in the University of Edinburgh, UK, and has a PhD in Development Studies from the University of Helsinki. He is a founding member and the coordinator of the ABORNE. His work as the co-initiator of the African Governance and Space (AFRIGOS) project researching transport corridors, border towns, and port cities in Namibia, Zambia, DRC, Ghana, and Burkina Faso continues his long-term interest in cross-border governance and movement of people and goods in the grey zones of (in)formality and (il)legality.

List of Figures

Africa's Secessionism: A Breakdance of Aspiration, Grievance, Performance, and Disenchantment

Mareike Schomerus, Pierre Englebert, and Lotje de Vries

The photograph, taken inside Cameroon's parliament, shows the bloodied face of a member of the ruling Cameroon People's Democratic Movement. He is clutching his head after an object, likely a shoe, was thrown at him in anger. That this parliamentary budget debate in late 2017 was not going to go as planned became clear when members of the main opposition party, the Social Democratic Front (SDF), chanted and blew vuvuzela horns. Then the object came hurling.

M. Schomerus (✉)
Overseas Development Institute, London, UK
e-mail: m.schomerus@odi.org

P. Englebert
Pomona College, Claremont, CA, USA
e-mail: penglebert@pomona.edu

L. de Vries
Wageningen University & Research, De Bilt, Utrecht, The Netherlands
e-mail: lotje.devries@wur.nl

1

At the heart of this turmoil lay "the Anglophone problem"—a perceived pattern of discrimination against Cameroon's two Anglophone provinces and the subsequent secessionist ambitions of some among their population. The turmoil in parliament marked the latest wave of secessionist tensions; this last wave had started in October 2016 when strikes and protests brought public life in the Anglophone provinces to a standstill.[1]

Cameroon is far from alone in facing secessionist agitation of late. Namibia continues to grapple with the high-treason trial over the failed 1999 secession of the Zambezi Region, formerly known as the Caprivi Strip. The trial entered its 13th year in 2017 with an appeal trial expected for June 2018. Morocco, meanwhile, is pushing within the African Union (AU) to have Namibia's jurisdiction over the Zambezi Region investigated because of Namibia's stance in the past over Morocco's own challenges linked to Western Sahara. Kenya's high court was asked to rule on whether to allow an independence referendum in its Western Province, formerly part of Uganda's Eastern Province, which had been merged with the British East African Protectorate in 1962.[2] In November 2017, South Africa's Institute for Security Studies felt compelled enough to ask about a country whose political crises are not usually associated with territorial challenges: "Could Parts of Kenya Really Secede?"[3]

Colonial history proves to be a continuous inspiration for legitimizing such claims in contemporary political arenas. In the last five years alone, Tuareg separatists (briefly) controlled and declared the independence of Azawad, the part of Mali north of Mopti, which they claim as historically theirs;[4] the Front for the Liberation of the Enclave of Cabinda (FLEC) has increased armed attacks against Angolan forces;[5] the Association for Islamic Mobilization and Propagation (UAMSHO) has demanded a referendum on the separation of Zanzibar from Tanzania; and Boko Haram has called

---

[1] Cameroon MP Injured by Flying Debris (2017) and Pommerolle and Heungoup (2017).

[2] The petitioners claimed the merger had happened without the consent of the people, who had been "a distinct, cohesive, homogeneous, and a united community." Merging it with the British East Africa Protectorate had been "illegal" and a violation of the UN Charter and UN Resolution No. 1514 (XV) that laid out the principles of equal rights and self-determination of all peoples, they further argued (Akwei September 19, 2017).

[3] Allison (November 3, 2017).

[4] See Lecocq and Klute (2018) in this volume.

[5] See Martin (2018) in this volume.

for the restoration of an Islamic Caliphate in Northern Nigeria. Meanwhile, Somaliland—unrecognized by all since its breakup from Somalia in 1990— endures as a "de facto" state, and also as one of Africa's few democracies, having completed its presidential election in November 2017.[6]

Secessionist narratives, aspirations, and activities have been a permanent, if changing, feature of African politics. The continent's first independent decade saw the secession of Katanga a mere few days after Congo acquired sovereignty (1960–63), followed shortly thereafter by the humanitarian disaster of the Biafra War, which cost about one million lives from 1967 to 1970.[7] More than 50 years later, secessionist discourse and activism remain alive in Katanga, where a self-described separatist insurgency, Kata Katanga ("cut off Katanga"), briefly marched into Lubumbashi in 2013,[8] and in Biafra, where several groups, not least the Movement for the Actualization of the Sovereign State of Biafra (MASSOB), continue to keep the dream of independence alive and regularly clash with the Nigerian armed forces.[9]

These are more than unrelated anecdotes from past and present. They are emblematic of the larger picture of increased alienation and pushback against the African post-colonial state. And there are many more, albeit often smaller, similar instances. Throughout the continent, including in places where it would not be expected, secessionism has reemerged on political agendas.

Secessionism has been high on the agenda in other continents, too, with the 2014 referendum on Scottish independence from the UK, and Catalonia, which unilaterally declared independence from Spain on October 27, 2017, after a referendum in which 92% voted in favor of secession. The aspirations of certain Kurdish groups for a united and independent Kurdistan are also well known. Although throughout the world secessionism continues to be a powerful source of mobilization and a popular way to channel political grievances, there is, however, a distinct African dimension to the issue on which we elaborate in this volume.

---

[6] See Walls and Pegg (November 10, 2017).
[7] Harnischfeger (2018).
[8] See Larmer and Kennes (2018) in this volume.
[9] BBC Focus on Africa (September 11, 2017).

THE MANY FACES OF SECESSIONISM IN AFRICA OR
THE MYTH OF THE SIMPLE SOLUTION

Contemporary African secessionism extends far beyond the purview of historic cases. Recent claims suggest that South Sudan's catastrophic first few years as an independent nation do not appear to have tempered the secessionist aspirations of others on the continent. If anything, we discern a small uptick in the public currency of African separatist grievances.[10] Despite the argument that Africa experiences fewer secessionist conflicts than one would expect, given that many African states struggle to deliver on a state's expected duties and the heterogeneity of their societies,[11] secessionism—as dream, discourse, argument, and activity—remains a fundamental theme of African politics.

Yet, despite its aspirational simplicity—Give us a new nation!—secessionism is a complex political phenomenon. At its core, it is a subnational group's demand for the separate sovereignty of a piece of a country's territory. This claim is often legitimized by invocations of the right to self-determination.[12] But while the basic material consequence of a call for secessionism is territorial—a redefinition of boundaries of the space upon which state power is projected—the foundations for such claims lie in political grievances, sentiments of marginalization, historical narratives, and economic projects that are engineered by members of the subnational group often operating from far beyond the stated spatial claims. The consequences of such claims vary greatly—including whether or not the claim is supported violently—and yet the effects almost always resonate transnationally and in regional and international political arenas.

THE SHIFTING LEGAL INTERPRETATIONS OF SECESSIONISM

Discussions about secessionism in Africa are particularly intriguing because the phenomenon is essentially outlawed. The Organisation of African Unity (OAU) famously settled in 1963 on maintaining colonial borders at independence.[13] Its 1964 Cairo Declaration affirmed the principle of *uti possidetis*—the notion that borders would be maintained as they were—as

---

[10] See Byrne and Englebert (2018) in this volume.
[11] Englebert (2009).
[12] de Vries and Schomerus (2017).
[13] Organisation of African Unity (1963).

a way of avoiding future border conflicts. With a few notable exceptions, this approach of avoiding border conflicts has largely helped African states endure. But while the borders have lasted, problems have continued to fester for people living within, without, or across the *uti possidetis* borders. Paradoxically, the maintenance of territorial integrity and rejection of identity-based territorial claims promoted by *uti possidetis* have crystallized arbitrary colonial borders in a manner that has continued to feed identity-based secessionist grievances. Along with the OAU, the international community, in general, has never been keen to confer the entitlements that come with sovereignty on peoples that aspired to it. Where one might hope that international law dealing with the subject of self-determination would offer clarity on the matter, the opposite is true.

The UN's stance at first glance seems clear—until it is not. The 1960 UN General Assembly (UNGA) Resolution 1514 (XV)—also known as the Declaration on the Granting of Independence to Colonial Countries and Peoples—is often referenced throughout this volume. It states the right to self-determination but also stresses that "any attempt aimed at the partial or total disruption of the national unity and the territorial integrity of a country is incompatible with the purposes and principles of the Charter of the United Nations."[14] Article 1 of the International Covenant on Civil and Political Rights restates that "All peoples have the right of self-determination," but fails to define what constitutes a people and whether the right to "freely determine their political status and freely pursue their economic, social and cultural development" necessarily implies sovereignty.[15]

Yet, the Declaration on Principles of International Law concerning Friendly Relations and Co-operation among States in accordance with the Charter of the United Nations (1970), of weaker legal status than a Resolution, enshrined that "the establishment of a sovereign and independent State, the free association or integration with an independent State or the emergence into any other political status freely determined by a people constitute modes of implementing the right of self-determination by that people."[16] Castellino argues that the emphasis in UN documents highlights that self-determination was "the vehicle of choice for decolonization"—which also meant that the term "people" simply captured "colonial

---

[14] United Nations General Assembly (1960).
[15] Office of the United Nations High Commissioner for Human Rights (1966, 1976).
[16] United Nations General Assembly (1970).

peoples."[17] It seems that the UN simply did not expect self-determination claims to outlast decolonization, hence it saw no necessity to develop a document that would stand a more complex set of secessionist endeavors.

When it was becoming clear that secessionist claims would remain in the post-colonial age, the 1993 Vienna Declaration and Programme of Action, signed by 171 states, thus stated that a commitment to self-determination

> shall not be construed as authorizing or encouraging any action which would dismember or impair, totally or in part, the territorial integrity or political unity of sovereign and independent States conducting themselves in compliance with the principle of equal rights and self-determination of peoples and thus possessed of a Government representing the whole people belonging to the territory without distinction of any kind.[18]

While not necessarily illegal, it was hence clear that African secessionism was removed from the realm of the thinkable. Then South Sudan's independence happened, throwing a wrench in what little there was of UN and AU doctrine. Scholars such as Bereketeab have even questioned whether the AU was "aware of the gravity of its action" with regard to allowing South Sudan to secede,[19] fearing that it might become a watershed moment of encouragement for other secessionists. That international law leaves room for a variety of interpretations and remains negotiable is most notable in the many different ways claims to self-determination and secession have been received and treated. In this collection alone, South Sudan (and to a certain extent Eritrea) stands in stark contrast to how the international community has been dealing with claims for independence in Western Sahara or Somaliland. Political legitimacy in Africa is often conditioned in part by the capacity to share the bounties of power[20] and underwritten by relatively shallow "permissive" social contracts.[21] When redistribution dries up or authoritarianism rises, territorially grounded alternatives offer powerful mobilization potential. The diminished mobilization of movements opposed to the Sudanese regime in the wake of the

---

[17] Castellino (2014: 31).
[18] World Conference on Human Rights (1993).
[19] Bereketeab (2015: 229).
[20] Bayart (1993).
[21] Nugent (2010).

South's departure has brought this lesson home painfully to northern opposition groups lacking such a plausible claim to self-determination.

Bereketeab also argues that the AU clearly prioritizes "state integrity over people's rights."[22] He offers theories for how South Sudan managed to become the African exception: theories of suffering, remedial theory, and theory of distance—which highlight that cultural distance may warrant secession—offered the international community the alternative justifications for accepting South Sudan's claim. Legally, however, the main argument that makes secession possible is when both separatist entity and mother state agree to separate.[23] Yet, even in that case, the dreams and realities of secessionism in Africa are not adequately captured with a legal lens, and international law is not the clear guiding light to make sense of secessionism.

Yet, most legal theories fail to adequately acknowledge that self-determination is more than secessionism. Self-determination also includes the primacy of the individual will, as well as political participation when decisions are made on how to be governed and through what kind of system. In the case of South Sudan, for instance, the emphasis on secession has somewhat reduced the meaning of the much more nuanced, long-term and politically ambitious concept of self-determination.[24]

Secessionism in Africa thus presents itself as a veritable dance around a wide range of issues, including many layers of political maneuvering, shifting positions and identities, loyalties and disloyalties, betrayals and promises—a breakdance.

Dancing to Break Away?

The chapters in this volume list an array of reasons or arguments that underpin secessionist claims or their rejections. Some ascribe responsibility to colonial/ex-colonial powers, post-colonial regimes, or the international community. Others stress more inward-looking reasons, such as (at times essentialized) cultural differences or an unwillingness to engage with the state. Many cases presented here offer a combination of arguments.

Secessionism brings up vital questions of identity, regularly cited as one of its driving forces. But where does identity begin? Through previous

---

[22] Bereketeab (2015: 229).
[23] Bereketeab (2015: 229) and Dobler (2018).
[24] de Vries and Schomerus (2017).

rulers, as in the case of Cameroon where German rule "created" the notion of Kamerun?[25] Is it based on language, borders, or political affiliation? While many cases of secessionist struggles are too nuanced to foreground ethnicity as the driving force of the wish to separate, the notion of "one people" claiming its right to govern itself naturally shines a light on questions of ethnicity. The same light, however, immediately highlights the precarious nature of using ethnicity as an explanation for secessionist struggle—too diverse are the secessionist claims, too divided the groups claiming secession for the same territory. Maybe identity—whether based on ethnicity, language, or culture—is created when, as Dobler argues for the case of Anjouan, secessionist movements "re-interpret cultural contents, privilege differences with other groups and overstate inner homogeneity" in order "to offer a narrative which makes a different political organization plausible."[26]

Most cases discussed in this volume are rooted in questions of identity and history. Another theme that many of the cases have in common is marginalization. Secessionist claims are sometimes rooted in an active experience of marginalization, citing lack of political representation, weakening language identities or cultural institutions, or targeted underdevelopment as the reason for the desire to go it alone. Such marginalization might be the most measurable way to link secessionist claims to the lived experience of having a "hostile" mother government. At times, this marginalization might be perceived or feared.

Secessionists can be freedom fighters or political entrepreneurs; they can seek to protect a territory from environmental exploitation or seek to gain authority over it to exploit it. Some areas with separatist ambitions are wealthy in resources, such as oil, minerals, but also tradable agricultural goods or valuable land and water or access to waterways. Often—but not always—resource wealth and its inadequate sharing underpins separatist claims and forms the main reason why they are rebutted.[27]

Borders play a crucial role in the way secessionism is presented; they are the physical manifestation of the less visible aspects such as identity, belonging, or marginalization. Border studies have highlighted the nature of borders as identity givers, obstacles, areas of strategic importance, or, generally speaking, as a space for opportunity.[28]

[25] In this volume, Konings and Nyamnjoh (2018).
[26] In this volume, Dobler (2018).
[27] Horowitz (2001, 2nd ed.).
[28] Anthony I. Asiwaju (2016), A.I. Asiwaju and Nugent (1996), Nugent and Asiwaju (1996) and C. Vaughan, Schomerus, and De Vries (2013).

Only few secessionist claims seek to depart entirely from the state as it continues to be imagined on the African continent—broadly modeled on the European administrative structures, with adjustments based on cultural identifiers, understandings of tradition, or a realpolitik approach to governing that has set in since post-colonial times. Recent calls for new Islamic Caliphates—even though these are also, as Miles argues, deeply rooted in history[29]—however, might mark a much starker departure from what the post-colonial map left behind.

Whether based on identity, marginalization, or ideology, secessionist movements are rarely homogenous. If consensus about ownership and vision could be established among separatists, Africa's map today might look very different indeed, as Byrne and Englebert show in this volume.[30] That it does not signifies also that the suggested stability, which stems from a largely unchanged map of Africa, in reality paints over many areas of conflict. These conflicts are between groups but often also fueled by internal divisions within groups laying claim to the same secessionist identity—Cabinda, the Tuareg, Casamance, and others discussed in this book offer only a brief glimpse of how challenging it is to be united in a cause.

Governments and secessionist movements dance around (and, eventually, with) each other, finding ever new ways of expressing separatist ambitions or rebutting these. The secessionist repertoire is broad, ranging from nonviolent protest (including associative action, cyberspace militantism, legal proceedings, songs, and poetry) to armed struggle (e.g., attacks on government installations and civilians, guerrilla tactics, full-fledged warfare, or coups). Some simply throw their hat in the ring through unilateral declarations of independence, accompanied with a display of national sovereignty involving flags, anthems, and identity documents. Other ways are more surprising, such as posing as an independent police force to project the presence of a new state security force.

The government response repertoire is equally impressive in its diversity. Variations on crackdowns, arrests of leaders or diaspora activists, controlling access to natural resources or the media are the least surprising; creating their own factions of secessionist movement to cause division, offering improved development in secessionist areas or political appointments for secessionists are more unusual.

---

[29] Miles (2018).
[30] Byrne and Englebert (2018).

The breakdance is both lively and syncopated because secessionism is more than simply an ambition toward independence; it is also an effective political threat used as needed to contest election results, oust unwanted political leaders, rewrite history, or avoid external muddling in internal affairs. State sovereignty remains a strong argument to keep international interests at bay.

Several chapters in this volume highlight the importance of international actors ready to support or oppose separatist ambitions based on their own geostrategic interests or moral claims. International support does not guarantee success, but lack thereof can thwart even effective independence, as Somalilanders can so readily attest. Altogether, there is no unified international stance. Interpretation of international law is fickle, due to the many divergent interests and might result in backing a principled AU-driven antiseparatist stance or sending troops or weapons to support a secession.

Other international links, just as vital, are more easily overlooked: a strong diaspora, with its material resources, can make or break a secessionist claim. Remittances or infrastructure investment have also proven critical to sovereignty claims.

UNDERSTANDING FOUR CATEGORIES OF SECESSIONISM

As the dramatic cases of Eritrea and South Sudan illustrate, secession and its associated dreams of freedom might seem like a *panacea ex ante* but hardly addresses the issues that feed local grievances or ambitions—In fact, secession barely seems to even work as a corrector of historical narratives. Wars and conflict can continue after part of a country breaks away as well as when a part of a country stays inside the union or secedes against its will. Being able to impute a territorial dimension to one's grievances or aspirations allows, however, for a somewhat stronger position from which to challenge authorities. Groups without such territorial claim may well feel marginalized too but need to draw on different registers to challenge the political establishment. Darfur's call about genocide, the spread of violence to the center of the country in Mali's conflict, and the declaration of the Caliphate in Northern Nigeria, are just a few examples. Questioning the fundamental legitimacy and universality of the post-colonial state, a terrain on which few if any of Africa's elites stand firmly, was and has continued to be a powerful register to draw upon.

This line of reasoning is not to suggest that secessionism does not have substance per se. It often does. However, the subnational territorial claim is multilayered, both fundamental and instrumental. It is one of this book's main contributions, we hope, that it deconstructs secessionism into distinct analytical categories, thereby helping to make sense of the varieties of African secessionism. We distinguish four categories. Of course, there are few if any "pure" cases, where causality is so straightforward as to be so easily imputable. Nevertheless, a dominant motivation or practice usually prevails.

In some cases, secessionism is aspiration; it seems to truly represent ambitions for a nation of one's own, a rejection of the colonial legacy based on a deeper regional sense of belonging. In other cases, secessionism is the expression of a grievance, at times rooted in a post-colonial muddle, which in some cases represents, somewhat ironically, the very opposite of self-determination. Here, the language of secession is used to backup decolonization demands, claims for statehood based on allegedly distinct colonial regimes—reaching as far as the demand to be "recolonized" by the colonial power, as in the case of Comoros Islands.[31] Of course, the colonial period generated new "selves" in Africa.[32] But the principle invoked here is that colonial rather than subnational identity should confer rights. Secession can also be theatrical and performance-based—a useful threat or a mobilizing discourse that facilitates bargaining for other goals, be they local autonomy, greater access to existing sovereign resources, or political representation in the central government. Finally, in our fourth category, we revisit "successful" secessionist cases. As is clear, however, success at obtaining independence does not guarantee success at being independent.

Secessionism as Aspirations or Dreams of a Solution

When aspirational, secessionism is understood as the solution to a broader crisis underwritten by marginalization, identity, or representation, as is at least in part the case with the Tuareg in Mali and Niger, the Anglophone movements in Cameroon, and Ethiopia's (or not) Ogaden.

The Tuareg, spread over five states, are a case study in aspiration and imagined solution to marginalization but also in the challenging practicalities of identity-based secessionism. Formal claims for Tuareg independence

---

[31] Dobler (2018).
[32] Young (1994).

have been minimal, but the notion of a Tuareg state is culturally prominent, romanticized as a unifying factor in poetry and music. In reality, Tuareg aspirations are more concretely expressed in smaller secessionist claims, such as Tuareg states of Agadez within Niger and Azawad in Mali, rather than through the pursuit of a bigger Tuareg nation.[33]

Cameroon's "Anglophone Problem" stems from the Anglophone minority's marginalization since the reunification with Francophone Cameroon. Language (another colonial legacy that has produced a powerful identity) serves here as the obvious marker of the secessionist ambition. The aspiration is thus more comfortably couched in the language of a solution: an Anglophone Cameroon is understood to build its own existence on a powerful history and identity.[34]

The Ogaden, currently in Ethiopia's territory with Somalia also laying claim on it, is a case of aspiration of establishing a stronger identity. A history of governments seeking to level identity differences with their main territory has meant that secession here has become the imagined solution to being an identity under threat, including the economic and religious marginalization such leveling of identity brings.[35]

Secessionism as Grievance or Post-colonial Metastasis

Colonial and post-colonial history is one of promises made and broken, imprinting itself on today's political developments, as highlighted by five cases in this volume. These cases also show the political, human, and time cost involved in seeking governance systems that work, may these be systems of federalism or autonomy.

Western Sahara and Morocco might arguably not belong in a volume on secessionism, with the legal arguments sitting firmly on the side of a decolonization that never happened. And yet, the case serves as a reminder of how interpretation of a situation is fluid and at times removed from seemingly clear international standards. Western Sahara's emphasis on culture shows how *uti possidetis* failed to instill an identity that would easily surpass other measures of cultural identity. Yet, the Sahrawi struggle also confirms that establishing a seemingly clear case is a challenge unless a leadership approaches it with a clear vision.[36]

---

[33] Lecocq and Klute (2018).
[34] Konings and Nyamnjoh (2018).
[35] Vaughan (2018).
[36] Porges (2018).

When big powers choose to get involved, the secessionist dynamics change. Despite UN calls for Mayotte's reintegration into the Comoros, France has maintained its claim of authority over the island. At the same time, the former (and somewhat reinstated) colonial power was reluctant to accept Anjouan when it became obvious that overseas territories are politically difficult to justify, unless they deliver obvious payoff. Mayotte also highlights how identity can become instrumentalized: claiming self-determination of a *people*, rather than a less identity-based definition of *population*, shifts the political argument toward a less contestable rights-based approach, even if the claimed cultural identity was created as part of the political argument.[37]

In Zanzibar, secessionism is also an expression of the search for the best governance system after federalism failed to deliver on the promise of autonomy with inclusion. Much like Western Sahara, Zanzibar might not strictly be a secessionist case but one of seeking the most representative governance system after post-colonial allegiances were forged. Whether this system can be found through the continuing search for a history that is acceptable for both mainland Tanzania and Zanzibar, with a political leadership that represents the different post-colonial experiences, and whether grievances that stem from economic differences can be addressed remain Zanzibar's challenge.[38]

Angola's secessionist movements in Cabinda—a dizzying array of actors operating under variations of the FLEC moniker, including running their own branches from European capitals—embodies the international dimension of the post-colonial Cold War muddle, with foreign (Cuban) troops defending US interests in the forests of Angola, fighting off South African forces that were also backed by the USA.[39]

Somaliland's case—which, in different ways from South Sudan, challenges the notion of a clear framework on African secessionism—shows the many paths of achieving independence without officially achieving it. Now a peaceful de facto state, its roots lie in the voluntary handover of power by the victorious guerrilla movement to a civilian government. The departure from a militarized administration toward a civilian one anchored in clan-based governance structures—albeit one with a huge annual security budget—might be the crucial reason for Somaliland's unacknowledged

---

[37] Dobler (2018).
[38] Cameron (2018).
[39] Martin (2018).

success story. But even within Somaliland, the diversity of experience is greater than what the secessionist narrative suggests; the post-colonial muddle and the layers of identities it brings about are not entirely clarified once a core achieves a status akin to independence.[40]

Somaliland again highlights, *a contrario*, that resources can complicate the picture—a resource-poor area like Somaliland was largely spared internal and external resource wars. Finding a political order that works—possibly due to a lack of international interest to intervene—took time but has ultimately created a situation in which governance mechanisms are more stable and suitable than in many other parts of Africa. Yet, while no intervention took place to stifle Somaliland's secession, no recognition has been forthcoming either. Thus, the post-colonial muddle is both: a departure from international templates as well as an attempt to remain close to them to be admitted into the international community that perpetuates the templates.

Secessionism as Performance and Posturing

The secessionist breakdance can be most prominently identified when secessionism is used for political leverage. Senegal's Casamanche is driven by a redefinition of a narrative that casts one group against the central state, but it is not obvious that it is the ultimate ambition of the *Casamançais* to establish their own state. Instead, the secessionist agenda is used to gain a better position under the umbrella of Senegal. Access to formal education and the knock-on effects of having received such education play a hugely important role in the way the *Casamançais* continue to navigate their precarious, but also well-established, performative relationship with the Senegalese state.[41]

With the Lozi of Namibia and Zambia, identity is a marker of secessionist ambition that obscures more than it reveals in multiple and overlapping political dynamics. The Lozi case also illustrates how a moment in history—the 1964 Barotseland Agreement—can become the marker against which all future political developments and posturing are projected.[42]

---

[40] Hoehne (2018).
[41] Foucher (2018).
[42] Zeller and Melber (2018).

Nigeria's Biafra, imprinted in memories as the quintessential prototype of the secessionist war, reminds us that political performance can happen along ethnic or religious lines, depending on what motivation is usefully considered the stronger factor to mobilize public support and to put pressure on a central government keen to maintain the unity of a federation. Since arguably the secessionist entity would benefit little from losing its role in the federation, Biafran separatism is also an expression of political frustration that needs to be understood and addressed without the secessionist ultimatum coloring all analysis.[43]

Katanga, the other prominent and early case of secessionism in Africa, still painfully dismantles the myth of Congolese state coherence in Democratic Republic of the Congo (DRC) and reveals the state for what it is: a mere posturing. Katangese secessionism shows both how the imagination of the post-colonial state is misleading and how operating within its boundaries can have benefits to regional elites that at the same time occasionally suggest to aspire self-determination. The case of Katanga also highlights the limits of shaping African political institutions according to Western models, with political organization falling too easily along ethnic lines, in turn recreating the very same political marginalization such organization sought to address.[44]

Secessionism as Disenchantment: Plus ça change, plus c'est la même chose

Previous sections have shown how secessionism is too easily considered as the answer to a wide variety of political problems. The two states that managed to secede in post-colonial Africa serve as stark reminders that the separation from a mother state does not necessarily bring about a solution to one's problems. Both cases also highlight that what made a rebel movement successful might be exactly what makes it a less-than-convincing independent government.

In the case of Eritrea, the principle of self-reliance served to establish a strong identity against the Ethiopian state. But it has created an Eritrean state that is the most isolated of all African states, governing a population desperate to leave in high numbers and an inward-looking extreme interpretation of identity as the only marker of credible collaboration. Eritrean

---

[43] Harnischfeger (2018).
[44] Larmer and Kennes (2018).

national identity is strong to the level of absolute exclusion of others, which does not work well with a state that—in subscribing to an international model of a sovereign state—seeks admission into an international construct of states that make up an international community.[45]

South Sudan's disenchantment is of a different nature: it is more a matter of recognition that a South Sudanese identity was strongly and convincingly imagined in the run-up to the internationally supported referendum on independence, but that it did not exist for much longer afterwards as political power struggles quickly took on an overtly ethnic tone. South Sudan's secessionist success continues to puzzle analysts. Yet, it was the implausibility that made it possible, as the secessionist claim was so subdued until a very late stage when international alliances were too strong for the international community to back off and maintain credibility.[46] The "successful" cases of Eritrea and South Sudan remind us that the often wide array of grievances cannot be solved by one solution—secession.

SECESSIONISM'S CONTRADICTION: A PERMANENT HOPE FOR CHANGE

The many cases discussed here—and the many facets on which they touch—show one thing clearly: African secessionism is inherently contradictory. It expresses a permanent hope for change. It seeks to change the nature of African states, develop or confirm group identities, and change or clarify resource governance. Yet, African secessionism, caught as it is in the post-colonial state system, in most cases does so by reinventing the same structures from which it seeks to depart, the very same structures that have created grievances now expressed in a desire to quit the existing state. In the notion of secessionism—of going it alone—is embedded the idea that things will need to change.

Yet the desire for change is not unique to those aspiring to secede but a widely felt sentiment across the continent. Urban youth all over Africa aspire to political inclusion, as do the inhabitants of peripheries of the Horn and Central Africa, as well as African migrants in Southern Africa. Certain groups are willing to express their grievances violently, as the conflicts in Eastern DRC, South Sudan, and Mali demonstrate. Secessionism offers a more powerful register for the call for change, but

[45] Dias and Dorman (2018).
[46] Schomerus and de Vries (2018).

the frustrations that underpin the cases in this book are found throughout the continent.

The question on how to handle secessionist claims thus lies not only in legal frameworks and procedures to deal with dreams of independence. Continuing secessionist aspirations require broad national, regional, and international engagement with the key challenge of many African nations: how can people's frustrations and grievances with the post-colonial politics be justly addressed?

The notion that the sovereign territorial state is the answer to Africa's problems, rather than one of its roots, is not challenged in many secessionist claims. Secessionism continues to express a dream of a brighter and more reliable future without endless political negotiation. And yet, governing does not work like that. The secessionist dream is thus condemned to become an uncompromising response to unsteady and ever-shifting situations. The two are unlikely to ever work well together; how they dance around each other is discussed in great detail in the following chapters.

REFERENCES

Akwei, I. (2017). Kenya's high court to hear case on secession of western region. *Africa News*. http://www.africanews.com/2017/09/19/kenya-s-high-court-to-hear-case-on-secession-of-western-region/

Allison, S. (2017). *Could parts of Kenya really secede?* Retrieved from Pretoria: https://issafrica.org/iss-today/could-parts-of-kenya-really-secede?utm_source=BenchmarkEmail&utm_campaign=ISS+Today&utm_medium=email

Asiwaju, A. I. (2016). Scars of partition: Postcolonial legacies in French and British borderlands. *Journal of Borderlands Studies, 31*(4), 565–566. https://doi.org/10.1080/08865655.2015.1067825

Asiwaju, A. I., & Nugent, P. (Eds.). (1996). *African boundaries: Barriers, conduits and opportunities*. London/New York: Frances Pinter.

Bayart, J. F. (1993). *The state in Africa: the politics of the belly*. London: Longman.

BBC Focus on Africa. (2017). *Clashes between soldiers and Biafra protesters*. https://www.bbc.co.uk/programmes/w172vg34x0268ny

Bereketeab, R. (2015). Self-determination and secession: African challenges. In R. Bereketeab (Ed.), *Self-determination and secession in Africa: The post-colonial state*. London/New York: Routledge.

Byrne, H., & Englebert, P. (2018). Shifting grounds for African secessionism? In L. de Vries, P. Englebert, & M. Schomerus (Eds.), *Secessionism in African politics: Aspiration, grievance, performance, disenchantment*. New York: Palgrave.

Cameron, G. (2018). Zanzibar in the Tanzania Union. In L. de Vries, P. Englebert, & M. Schomerus (Eds.), *Secessionism in African politics: Aspiration, grievance, performance, disenchantment*. New York: Palgrave.

Cameroon MP Injured by Flying Debris. (2017, December 10). *The Guardian*.

Castellino, J. (2014). International law and self-determination. In C. Walter, A. von Ungern-Sternberg, & K. Abushov (Eds.), *Self-determination and secession in international law*. Oxford: Oxford University Press.

de Vries, L., & Schomerus, M. (2017). Fettered self-determination: South Sudan's narrowed path to secession. *Civil Wars, 19*(1), 1–20. https://doi.org/10.1080/13698249.2017.1342442

Dias, A., & Dorman, S. (2018). We didn't fight for this: The pitfalls of state and nation building in Eritrea. In L. de Vries, P. Englebert, & M. Schomerus (Eds.), *Secessionism in African politics: Aspiration, grievance, performance, disenchantment*. New York: Palgrave.

Dobler, G. (2018). Anjouan and secessionism in the Comoros: Internal dynamics, external decisions. In L. de Vries, P. Englebert, & M. Schomerus (Eds.), *Secessionism in African politics: Aspiration, grievance, performance, disenchantment*. New York: Palgrave.

Englebert, P. (2009). *Africa: Unity, sovereignty, and sorrow*. Boulder: Lynne Riener.

Foucher, V. (2018). The mouvement des Forces Démocratiques de Casamance: The illusion of separatism in Senegal? In L. de Vries, P. Englebert, & M. Schomerus (Eds.), *Secessionism in African politics: Aspiration, grievance, performance, disenchantment*. New York: Palgrave.

Harnischfeger, J. (2018). Biafra and secessionism in Nigeria: An instrument of political bargaining. In L. de Vries, P. Englebert, & M. Schomerus (Eds.), *Secessionism in African politics: Aspiration, grievance, performance, disenchantment*. New York: Palgrave.

Hoehne, M. V. (2018). Against the grain: Somaliland's secession from Somalia. In L. de Vries, P. Englebert, & M. Schomerus (Eds.), *Secessionism in African politics: Aspiration, grievance, performance, disenchantment*. New York: Palgrave.

Horowitz, D. L. (2001). *Ethnic groups in conflict* (Updated 2nd ed.). Berkeley: University of California Press.

International Covenant on Civil and Political Rights, adopted and opened for signature, ratification and accession by General Assembly resolution 2200A (XXI) of 16 December 1966/entry into force 23 March, in accordance with Article 49 C.F.R. (1966/1976).

Konings, P., & Nyamnjoh, F. B. (2018). Anglophone secessionist movements in Cameroon. In L. de Vries, P. Englebert, & M. Schomerus (Eds.), *Secessionism in African politics: Aspiration, grievance, performance, disenchantment*. New York: Palgrave.

Larmer, M., & Kennes, E. (2018). Katanga's secessionism in the Democratic Republic of Congo. In L. de Vries, P. Englebert, & M. Schomerus (Eds.), *Secessionism in African politics: Aspiration, grievance, performance, disenchantment*. New York: Palgrave.

Lecocq, B., & Klute, G. (2018). Tuareg separatism in Mali and Niger. In L. de Vries, P. Englebert, & M. Schomerus (Eds.), *Secessionism in African politics: Aspiration, grievance, performance, disenchantment.* New York: Palgrave.

Martin, J. F. (2018). The front(s) for the liberation of Cabinda in Angola: A phantom insurgency. In L. de Vries, P. Englebert, & M. Schomerus (Eds.), *Secessionism in African politics: Aspiration, grievance, performance, disenchantment.* New York: Palgrave.

Miles, W. F. S. (2018). Jihads and borders: Social networks and spatial patterns in Africa, present, past and future. In O. J. Walther & W. F. S. Miles (Eds.), *African border disorders: Addressing transnational extremist organizations.* London/New York: Routledge.

Nugent, P. (2010). States and social contracts in Africa. *New Left Review, 63,* 35–68.

Nugent, P., & Asiwaju, A. I. (Eds.). (1996). *African boundaries: Barriers, conduits and opportunities.* London: Pinter.

Organisation of African Unity. (1963). *Charter of the OAU.*

Pommerolle, M. E., & Heungoup, H. D. M. (2017). The "Anglophone crisis": A tale of the Cameroonian postcolony. African Affairs, *116*(464), 526–538. doi: https://doi.org/10.1093/afraf/adx021

Porges, M. (2018). Western Sahara and Morocco: Complexities of resistance and analysis. In L. de Vries, P. Englebert, & M. Schomerus (Eds.), *Secessionism in African politics: Aspiration, grievance, performance, disenchantment.* New York: Palgrave.

Schomerus, M., & de Vries, L. (2018). A state of contradiction: Sudan's unity goes south. In L. de Vries, P. Englebert, & M. Schomerus (Eds.), *Secessionism in African politics: Aspiration, grievance, performance, disenchantment.* New York: Palgrave.

United Nations General Assembly. (1960). *Declaration on the granting of independence to colonial countries and peoples.* Adopted by General Assembly Resolution 1514 (XV) of 14 December 1960.

United Nations High Commissioner for Human Rights. (1966). International Covenant on Civil and Political Rights [entered into force 1976]. http://www.ohchr.org/EN/ProfessionalInterest/Pages/CCPR.aspx

United Nations General Assembly. (1970). *2625 (XXV). Declaration on principles of international law concerning friendly relations and co-operation among states in accordance with the Charter of the United Nations.*

Vaughan, S. (2018). Ethiopia, Somalia and the Ogaden: Still the running sore at the heart of the Horn of Africa? In L. de Vries, P. Englebert, & M. Schomerus (Eds.), *Secessionism in African politics: Aspiration, grievance, performance, disenchantment.* New York: Palgrave.

Vaughan, C., Schomerus, M., & De Vries, L. (Eds.). (2013). *The borderlands of South Sudan: Authority and identity in contemporary and historical perspectives.* New York: Palgrave Macmillan.

Walls, M., & Pegg, S. (2017, November 10). *Somaliland votes next week. Its biggest challenges come after the election.* https://www.washingtonpost.com/news/monkey-cage/wp/2017/11/10/somalilands-presidential-elections-takeplace-oct-13-after-many-delays/?utm_term=.4d1f6ffa6ccb

World Conference on Human Rights. (1993). *Vienna Declaration and Programme of Action.* Adopted by the World Conference on Human Rights in Vienna on 25 June 1993.

Young, C. (1994). *The African colonial state in comparative perspective.* New Haven: Yale University Press.

Zeller, W., & Melber, H. (2018). United in separation? Lozi secessionism in Zambia and Namibia. In L. de Vries, P. Englebert, & M. Schomerus (Eds.), *Secessionism in African politics: Aspiration, grievance, performance, disenchantment.* New York: Palgrave.

PART I

Aspiration: Dreams of Independence

CHAPTER 2

Tuareg Separatism in Mali and Niger

Baz Lecocq and Georg Klute

INTRODUCTION

Following independence, colonial boundary and state making has left the Tuareg divided over five sovereign countries: Algeria, Burkina Faso, Libya, Mali, and Niger. There are three particularities to the Tuareg desire for an independent state. The first is that the lands they inhabit were colonized by only two European powers—France, which conquered the largest part of Tuareg land, and Italy—but their homeland has, nevertheless, been carved up between five different postcolonial states. Second, while secessionism is strong enough among the Tuareg of Mali and Niger to have resulted in armed rebellions in these countries, irredentist claims to unite all Tuareg into one territorial state have never been formally made, let alone been supported. Third, while ideals of national independence have been expressed explicitly internally within Tuareg poetry, pop songs, pamphlets, and political discourse, this ideal has never been raised externally in official negotiations with the states against which the Tuareg fought to

B. Lecocq (✉)
Humboldt University of Berlin, Berlin, Germany
e-mail: baz.lecocq@hu-berlin.de

G. Klute
University of Bayreuth, Bayreuth, Germany

23
L. de Vries et al. (eds.), *Secessionism in African Politics,*
Palgrave Series in African Borderlands Studies,
https://doi.org/10.1007/978-3-319-90206-7_2

gain independence. Until the most recent creation of the *Mouvement national de libération de l'Azawad* (MNLA), the independence movement in Mali in 2012, no Tuareg movement has ever formally expressed pursuit of independence.

In this chapter, we take these particularities as a point of departure, explaining them in their historical context and from the viewpoint of Tuareg political thought and organization. We describe how Tuareg nationalism gained shape during the decolonization process of French West Africa in the 1950s, finding its first expression in the early 1960s and evolving further during the droughts in the 1970s and 1980s. It then found larger and better-organized expression in the rebellions of the 1990s, changed toward new political claims in the new political context of the War on Terror, and finally erupted again as a fully fledged war of independence in 2012.

Tuareg Political Systems and the Imposition of the Colonial State

Historically, the Tuareg inhabit the Central Saharan mountain ranges— the Ajjer, Hoggar, Aïr and Adagh n Ifoghas, the adjacent Sahel-Saharan plains on the southern edge of the desert, and the interior bend of the Niger River. The oldest sources describing Saharan populations that could clearly be identified as Tuareg ancestors date from the tenth century AD.[1] The Tuareg call themselves *Imajeghan* (the free born) or *Kel Tamasheq* (those who speak Tamasheq, or Tamahaq or Tamajeq, as dialectical variations), making their language a primary source of collective identity. Tamasheq is part of the Berber languages group. Tuareg are Muslims without exception, but Islam is not central to the identity of all. Prior to the second half of the twentieth century, many lived a pastoral nomadic existence, engaging in animal husbandry and caravan trade. The droughts of the 1970s and 1980s changed Tuareg economy and lifestyle, away from pastoralism to agriculture or to an urban wage-earning existence in adjacent countries.[2]

Historically, Tuareg political unity took shape in a constellation of a number of similarly structured and organized tribal federations ruling particular parts of the Tuareg world and, prior to colonial conquest, neighboring populations such as the Hausa in today's Niger or Songhay in

[1] Ibn Hauqal (1964).
[2] Klute (2013a) and Lecocq (2004).

today's Mali.[3] Some of the subdued groups remember their life under Tuareg rule as a slave-like existence.[4] These federations competed with each other over economic and political resources, therewith creating an internal political hierarchy of tribes and social groups within Tuareg society,[5] as well as neighboring peoples, with the subjected neighbors at the bottom and particular noble Tuareg lineages at the top. This political space was among the last parts of Africa to be colonized.

The French approached from two sides: from Algeria in the north and from French Sudan in the southwest. Most Tuareg groups put up heavy resistance and were able to defeat French expeditions a number of times. Although all federations surrendered at the beginning of the twentieth century, a series of revolts broke out during World War I[6] and continued resistance from smaller groups of fighters meant that the Pax Gallica was only complete in 1934.[7] However, after conquest and pacification, the Tuareg came to occupy a privileged place in the French colonial imagination. The orientalist vision on the Tuareg was based on particularities in race and gender relations structuring internal social power, the hierarchical power relations between tribes, and a certain military prowess.

This "colonial privilege" was ambiguous in its effects. The Tuareg were exempted from forced labor and military conscription but also from Western education, before the mid-1940s.[8] Probably the most enduring legacy came by their neighbors as "colonial darlings," and later as "neo-colonial henchmen of the French."[9] The Tuareg viewpoint, on the other hand, is most ambivalent. Though there actually existed friendly feelings toward their colonial masters, the memory of the resistance against the Western "unbelievers" is vivid up until today.

DECOLONIZATION

The establishment and subsequent decolonization of the colonies of French West Africa, Algeria, and the Italian colony of Libya left the Tuareg divided between the postcolonial states of Mali, Niger, Burkina Faso, Algeria, and Libya. The borders between and within these countries were

[3] Bernus (1981) and Nicolaisen and Nicolaisen (1997).
[4] Olivier de Sardan (1976).
[5] Berge (2000).
[6] Grémont (2010) and Triaud (1993).
[7] Aouad-Badoual (1993).
[8] Blanguernon (1983).
[9] Clauzel (1992, 1963), Henry (1996), Lecocq (2010) and Hall (2011).

gradually enforced by these states. Borders presented both opportunities, for example for tax evasion and smuggling, and obstacles to mobility. Eventually, the Tuareg internalized the borders as the prevailing logic of political and administrative organization or a framework of collective identity.[10] The logic of territorial demarcation and political freedom or subjection played an important role in the shaping of Tuareg ideas on national independence.

Tuareg political leaders first expressed these ideas in debates surrounding the decolonization of French West Africa in the 1950s. As mineral wealth, most importantly oil, was discovered in the hitherto worthless Sahara during this period, conflicts broke out over attempts to redraw the Saharan borders. In 1957, the French Assembly voted for the creation of the *Organisation Commune des Régions Sahariennes* (OCRS). This was a barely concealed French attempt to restructure the colonial territories in such a way that Saharan resources would remain under French control after the imminent independence of the West African States. Likewise, in 1957, the Moroccan Liberation Army invaded the Spanish Sahara and Mauritania to bring them into the Moroccan Kingdom. The Moroccans were driven back by French and Spanish forces in 1958, but Morocco did not give up its claims.[11]

Algeria was ravaged by a ferocious colonial war of independence in which the Tuareg inhabited Saharan territories—and from 1960 onwards, the Tuareg-inhabited Malian Sahara—served as a hinterland for the Algerian Front de Libération Nationale (FLN). The inchoate and politically charged decolonization of the Sahara led to competition over power between old and new political elites in the region and finally to the creation of competing expressions of nationalism: that of the leaders of political parties and that of the Tuareg. Whereas Libyan and Algerian Tuareg had taken part in the struggle for independence and hence became, to a greater or lesser extent, integrated into the political structures of both states,[12] a number of Malian and Nigerien Tuareg politicians strongly supported the OCRS. Inclusion in the OCRS meant inclusion in an administrative territory. This would then remain under French tutelage but with large autonomy to its inhabitants and perhaps independence outside the existing African polities that were already taking shape.[13]

[10] Lecocq (2003).
[11] Correale (2009) and Lecocq (2010). See also Porges (2018) in this volume.
[12] Badi (2010).
[13] Boilley (1993) and Lecocq (2010).

Through these debates, Tuareg nationalism took a particular outlook: it expressed what Saharans did not want for their political future. First and foremost, Tuareg did not want to be part of a sub-Saharan or "black" Africa. One problem in the creation of the OCRS was how to delimit its southern border. On one side of the argument, the supporters of Saharan unification believed the Sahara ended where the Sudan started. Here, Sudan meant the original Arabic *bilâd es-sudân*—"land of the blacks." All parties involved, themselves included, saw the Tuareg as racially "white." Accordingly, it was felt that those areas inhabited by the Tuareg were Saharan and areas inhabited by "black" populations were not. Tuareg nationalism thus became linked to racial perceptions of African populations supposedly divided over a "white" Arab and Berber North Africa and a "black" sub-Saharan Africa. The racial distinction now came to partly define the otherness of the Tuareg in their own eyes and in those of the West African political elite.[14]

From its inception, the OCRS received political opposition from French Sudanese politicians, who did not want to see future independent Mali robbed of "national" territory and potential mineral riches. However, most Nigerien politicians did not oppose the project. Thus, Niger benefited from development projects within the OCRS framework. By 1959, the OCRS had been watered down to a kind of development agency. It was finally dismantled upon Algeria's independence in 1962.[15] After independence, ties between France and Niger remained strong.[16] The Diori government relied on "traditional" authorities, including those of the Tuareg. The economic development cooperation, the mining of coal, tin, and uranium in the Tuareg-inhabited north of the country, assured some economic progress and co-optation of the Tuareg within the state. That the Tuareg formed about 10% of Niger's population and inhabited about two thirds of the country helped their further integration in the fabric of the Nigerien nation.

INDEPENDENCE AND THE FIRST TUAREG UPRISING: MALI

In independent Mali however, government-Tuareg relations quickly deteriorated after an already bad start. The Malian government took a socialist course and set out on an active policy to modernize society by undoing parts

---

[14] Lecocq (2010) and Hall (2011).
[15] Lecocq (2010) and Boilley (1993, 1995).
[16] Fluchard (1995).

of the colonial heritage. A patronizing attitude of the regime toward the Tuareg, informed by stereotypical ideas on the Tuareg as "white, slave-raiding nomads" or "neo-colonial agents of France," built up tensions between the state and its Saharan population. The regime's lack of under-standing of local work ethics, gender relations, social dynamics, and power structures led to a wavering modernization policy that sought to "civilize" the Tuareg through sedentarization projects, the promotion of agriculture, enrollment of children in school and pioneer scout groups, curtailing of the powers of tribal leaders, and all kinds of discursive practices promoted the idea of Tuareg feudal backwardness.[17] These policies were much resented among a population that saw itself as superior to the new Malian rulers, and which had previously already sought national independence outside Mali.

The tensions between the regime and the Tuareg came to a head in May 1963, when a group of Tuareg started a revolt against the state. This first Tuareg rebellion after independence became known as *Alfellaga*, a North African Arabic term designating a fighter for independence, which was taken up by the Tuareg. The Tuareg fighters were small in number, 200 at maximum, and ill prepared. Most came from the *Adagh n Ifoghas* Mountains on the Malian-Algerian border, complemented by some Tuareg from other areas. The rebels had no modern means of communication or vehicles. They were mostly armed with rifles of World War II stock. In the first months of the rebellion, the Malian government deployed local mili-tary police forces recruited from within Tuareg society. As these could not quell the revolt, the army deployed regular units, many of whom were veterans from the French colonial army with combat experience in Algeria or Indochina. These too were unable to suppress the rebellion.

The Tuareg fighters knew the terrain better, the heavy material used was inefficient in the Adagh Mountains, and the logistics of provision were beyond the capacity of the Malian army. In retaliation, the army resorted to brutal reprisal tactics against the civilian population. The exact number of victims is unknown. Estimates range from several hundreds to several thousands.[18] Aided by the rebels, large parts of the population of then about 20,000 people[19] fled to Algeria where most stayed after the end of the conflict.

The rebels set hopes on French and Algerian intervention in the conflict if it drew out long enough, but this hope was a grave miscalculation of

---

[17] Lecocq (2010).
[18] Boilley (1999).
[19] Kaufmann (1964).

international relations. Algeria supported Mali, a fellow socialist state, in its fight against the rebels. France would not risk its strategic interests and atomic bases in Southern Algeria in support for its former colonial *amour*. In October 1963, the main political leaders of the rebellion, who were trying to garner support in Algeria and Morocco, were arrested by the armed forces of the respective countries and extradited to Mali. In February 1964, the Malian army obtained a right of pursuit of rebel forces into Algeria, which meant that the rebels and the fleeing civilians lost their safe haven. In August 1964, the rebellion was over.[20]

Although an ill-prepared and ill-conceived rebellion, it expressed Tuareg nationalist aspirations. Malian rule was partly resented as illegitimate. At the turn of the century, the Tuareg political leadership had surrendered to the French by treaty. These treaties were seen as legitimate and binding, but they had been struck with France and not with any successor state to French rule. Hence, in Tuareg's opinion, new treaties were needed. According to Tuareg nationalist historical memory, the leaders of the Malian state had promised not to touch the relative autonomy they had enjoyed under indirect French rule.[21] But these new rulers engaged in policies of direct rule, interfering in local politics, and violating local customs. This is in short the narrative of "promises broken" by the French on the eve of independence (the creation of the OCRS) and by the Malian government on becoming independent (autonomy for the Tuareg within Mali). This narrative now forms the basis of a nationalist history of relations with outside forces and today still justifies Tuareg national resistance. Especially *Alfellaga* would have a lasting and crucial legacy in Tuareg history and their vision on the state and independence. Narratives of the bloody repression of the 1963 rebellion would become a central part of Tuareg nationalist discourse from the 1970s onwards.

HEALING OLD WOUNDS, PREPARING A NEW UPRISING: 1970s–1990s

Those Tuareg who had fled from repression in Mali during *Alfellaga*, especially the leaders of that rebellion, formed the nucleus of a new informal nationalist organization in exile called *Tanekra*: uprising.[22] This movement would form the basis of the secessionist rebel movement of the

---

[20] Lecocq (2010).
[21] Klute (2013a) and Lecocq (2010).
[22] Lecocq (2010).

1990s. The number of Tuareg in Algerian and Libyan exile increased dramatically during the Sahel drought of the 1970s. The *Tanekra* organization revived the solidarity funds system they had set up to support *Alfellaga*, to help Tuareg newcomers from Mali and Niger to travel North in search of jobs.[23] In the second half of the 1970s, this loose network transformed into a structured organization with the aim to struggle for the creation of a Tuareg state. Practically, however, almost only Tuareg from Mali and Niger were involved.

In 1979, the Libyan regime offered support to the Tuareg organization. The background for Libya's engagement was Gaddafi's policy to extend Libyan influence southwards, particularly toward Niger. In August/September 1980, the Tuareg organized a conference in the Libyan town of Al-Khums with the support of the Libyan regime. The most important result of the meeting was the foundation of a formal resistance organization, the Popular Front for the Liberation of the Arab Central Sahara (PFLACS). This organization has to be considered to a large part a Libyan initiative. The name hints at Gaddafi's ideal vision of the Sahara as an Arab space, denying Berber or other cultural differences, to be united under Libyan guidance. The Tuareg were invited to become Libyan citizens.

Following the Al-Khums conference, Libya offered the PFLACS the opportunity for military training. In December 1980, about 1000 Tuareg entered military training camps, some in order to prepare a new uprising back home, most, however, because this was a good job opportunity. Largely due to his support for the Tuareg movement, Algeria and Niger broke all relations with Gaddafi's regime in 1981[24] while Gaddafi needed a good press for the upcoming OAU conference in Tripoli in 1982.[25] Thus, in late 1981, the training camps were closed, and the PFLACS was dissolved. Those PFLACS members who had received training were invited to join the regular Libyan army or a volunteer force in support of the Palestinians in Lebanon—about 200 fighters did. These men gained fighting experience in the Bekaa Valley and Beirut until Israel ousted the PLO from Lebanon in 1982, after which they returned to the Sahara. From 1986 onwards, Gaddafi also deployed Tuareg soldiers, trained in newly opened training camps, in the conflict with Chad.[26]

---

[23] Klute (2013a).
[24] Salifou (1993).
[25] Boilley (1999).
[26] Lecocq (2010) and Klute (2013a).

The campaigns in Lebanon and Chad had reinforced and deepened Tuareg political solidarity and understanding. Their experiences with the Palestinians in particular served as example for their own political project. In 1987, a group of Malian Tuareg veterans from the Lebanon and Chad campaigns living in Libya founded a new clandestine organization, which set as its task to prepare the armed fight for secession from Mali and the erection of a new state: *Azawad*.[27] This organization had no formal Libyan support. Tuareg veterans of Libyan campaigns from Niger looked reluctantly upon their Malian colleagues' project. Instead, they aimed at using nonviolent political means to improve integration of the Tuareg into Nigerien society. This option for a nonviolent political project was strengthened by the death of Nigerien dictator Seyni Kountché in 1987. Kountchés successor, General Ali Saibou, launched his regime under the slogan *décrispation*: an opening up of political life in Niger.

The Rebellions of the 1990s: Mali

The Tuareg rebellion in Mali was a small war, or low-intensity conflict.[28] From the perspective of its Tuareg proponents, it was the revenge for many defeats and injuries, most importantly the bloody retaliation against civilians during *Alfellaga*, and the economic, social, and political neglect of their land by the respective postcolonial regimes.

Logistical preparations for this uprising had started in earnest in the late 1980s with the organization of arms depots within Mali. At the beginning of 1990, the Malian secret service had precise knowledge of the existence of the Tuareg organization and arrested some of its members and confiscated the amassed arsenal.

At the end of June 1990, a group of barely armed rebels attacked the town of Menaka in Northern Mali, freed the arrested, captured weaponry from the Malian Armed Forces' barracks, and confiscated some

---

[27] A similar name for an independent land, Azawagh, which essentially means the same as Azawad, was adopted by Tuareg movements in Niger in the 1990s. This topographical indicator—the word essentially means "prairie" or "steppe"—would become a strong issue between Tuareg nationalists and Malian patriots. Leo Africanus' Description of Africa (1550) already indicates the Timbuktu region as Azawad, and from his description, the name found its way to European maps of the late sixteenth century. Yet most Malian patriots deny the term any historical validity and maintain that the only name the region has historically been known under is as part of the Malian empire.

[28] Klute and von Trotha (2000).

four-wheel-drive vehicles. The rebels organized themselves as the *Mouvement Populaire pour la Libération de l'Azawad* (MPLA). Its primary leadership consisted of a number of men who would remain key players in many events to come, including the 2012 rebellion. Among these were Iyad ag Ghali, Cheick ag Aoussa, Ahmada ag Bibi, Elhajji ag Gamou, and Ibrahim ag Bahanga. The MPLA gained a number of victories over the Malian army during this phase. About 200 experienced guerrillas deployed high-speed motorized guerrilla tactics, based on so-called "technicals" (open four-wheel-drive vehicles mounted with heavy machine guns and a combat group of about a dozen men), fully adapted to desert warfare,[29] which they had learned during their deployment in Chad. The Malian Armed Forces were forced to deploy at least two thirds of their total strength in defense: around 4000 men. As during *Alfellaga*, civilians were the main victims of army retaliation, which led civilians to take the rebels' side with many young men joining the MPLA.

Apart from the Tuareg rebellion, the Malian regime under Moussa Traoré faced a democratic opposition movement in the capital Bamako, which grew bolder as elite troops were sent from the capital to the North. To solve at least one of these conflicts, Traoré signed a ceasefire with the MPLA under the mediation of Algeria in January 1991. In the Treaties of Tamanrasset, the signatories agreed to a "special status" for the north of Mali, which was practically equivalent to autonomy for the Tuareg. Moreover, the north was granted economic concessions, which would prove to be a heavy mortgage on future peace negotiations. This did not save the regime. Traoré was toppled in a coup on March 26, 1991, following days of demonstrations and violence in Bamako.

The successful fight against Mali and disagreement about the Tamanrasset Agreement unleashed social and political dynamics within Tuareg society. From January 1991 onwards, the rebel movement splintered under violent internal conflicts that were to last until October 1994. The divisions between movements occurred along tribal lines, reflecting power dynamics internal to Tuareg society, which can be traced back to alliances and hostilities formed within the context of colonial penetration.[30] They also reflected internal political conflicts about the future structure of Tuareg society, based on existing internal social divisions, notably the divisions between noble (*amajegh*), free and powerful (*ellelu*), dependent (*imhgad*), and

---

[29] Klute (2009).
[30] Klute (1995).

former slave (*iklan, ighawelen*). This opposed traditionalists in favor of tribal structures and progressives promoting an egalitarian society.

Additionally, some disputed the validity and content of the Tamanrasset Agreement. The dissidents, organized from January 1991 as the *Front Populaire pour la Libération de l'Azawad* (FPLA) under leadership of Ghissa ag Sidi Mohamed and Elhajji ag Gamou, came from those groups who had suffered most severely at the hands of the army and from lower-status groups in Tuareg society. A few months later, the *Armée Révolutionaire pour la Libération de l'Azawad* (ARLA), led by Abderrahmane ag Galla was founded, which represented tribes in opposition to the dominance of particular tribes in the Adagh n Ifoghas Mountains. The Arab nomadic groups of Mali had already created their own organization in late 1990—the *Front Islamique Arabe de l'Azawad* (FIAA) led by Zahabi ould Sidi Mohamed. The leaders of the MPLA, under command of Iyad ag Ghali, then changed the name of what was left of their movement to *Mouvement Populaire de l'Azawad* (MPA).

In order to coordinate negotiations with the Malian government, the movements created an umbrella structure called *Mouvements et Fronts Unifiés de l'Azawad* (MFUA), which was largely manned by Tuareg who had made a career as civil servants or NGO employees in Mali, with few links to the militant movement in exile of the 1980s. Prominent among these was MFUA coordinator Zeidane ag Sidalamine. These men were inclined to peace and especially to cooptation within the Malian political structure.

The fall of dictator Traoré had led to the installation of a democratic government in Mali under an elected President, Alpha Oumar Konaré. The latter signed a new peace agreement, the National Pact, in April 1992, under the mediation of France and Mauritania. The National Pact stipulated, among many things, the creation of Kidal as a new administrative region in Northern Mali, the integration of former rebels in the Malian Armed Forces, and special economic programs for the North. The latter never materialized, while the integration of former rebels in the Malian Armed Forces proved problematic. Subsequently, many former rebels "deserted" the movement and joined existing movements refractory to the National Pact or created new movements with ill-defined goals.

Between January 1993 and October 1994, Tuareg rebels kept fighting among themselves in an evermore splintered field of movements. The main conflict pitted the MPA against the ARLA and FPLA. The conflicts mainly reflected social and tribal differences between members of both armies, with the FPLA and ARLA representing lower social strata and politically subordinate tribes, while the MPLA represented the Ifoghas tribe that strove for (and gained) political supremacy within the tribal hierarchy.

With the logistical support of the Malian army, the MPA defeated the ARLA by the end of 1994, and therewith won regional power. Eventually, the MPA managed to get most rebel movements under its control. Meanwhile, armed bands of former rebels operated on their own initiative, beyond the control of the rebel movements, robbing travelers and commercial transports. In April 1994, in reaction to the uncontrolled raids of the former Tuareg rebels against settlements along the Niger River and the infighting between the movements, merchants and military of the Songhay population mobilized a militia with the support of some parts of the army and perhaps with the consent of the government.[31]

This new movement, called *Ganda Koy*, Masters of the Land in the Songhay language, carried out pogroms against Tuareg and Arab inhabitants of the major cities in Northern Mali. These pogroms resulted in the mass flight of around 100,000 Tuareg and Arabs to neighboring countries. This full-scale ethnic conflict, with *Ganda Koy* fighting the Tuareg movements and harassing Tuareg civilians, and the Tuareg movements fighting each other and taking revenge for *Ganda Koy* actions by retaliating against Songhay civilians, lasted until October 1994.

By this time, the civilian population of Northern Mali had become so war weary that traditional leaders of the Songhay communities along the river, in collaboration with Tuareg tribal and religious leaders, initiated reconciliatory meetings between all ethnic groups of North Mali. This led to the Bourem Pact: an entirely local initiative taken outside any state structures or rebel movement. The Bourem Pact became the example for similar initiatives, which were supported by the few international NGOs still left in the area, notably the Norwegian Church.[32] These local initiatives culminated in a solemn ceremony on March 26, 1996, in Timbuktu, *La Flamme de la Paix*, which sealed a peace that, however fragile, lasted for about a decade.

THE REBELLIONS OF THE 1990S: NIGER

In May 1990, the inhabitants of a transit camp for repatriated Tuareg from Algeria and Libya near the hamlet of Tchin Tabaraden in northwestern Niger protested violently against conditions in the camp and the arrest of

---

[31] Klute (2013a).
[32] Poulton and ag Youssouf (1998).

persons suspected of participation in Tuareg resistance movements. The paratroopers sent in by the government with the order to suppress the upheaval arrested, tortured, and killed a great number of innocent civilians. Estimates of the number of victims range between 70 and over 600.

While the events of Tchin Tabaraden were met with indifference from the side of the new democratic government that replaced the military ruler Ali Saibou in 1991, and from the larger population, it led to a general Tuareg outrage. In September 1991, the *Front pour la Libération de l'Aïr et de l'Azawaq* (FLAA) took up the armed struggle for the liberation of the Tuareg area in Niger. *Azawaq* is the name for the region between the Aïr Mountains and the Niger River, which, like *Azawad* in Mali, would become the term for the Tuareg homeland to be separated from Niger. The word *Azawad* or *Azawaq* in fact simply means "prairie" or "grass steppe" in Tamasheq. While being a symbol for Tuareg resistance in both countries, the events of Tchin Tabaraden nonetheless failed to become a unifying moment, bringing Tuareg from both countries together in a united struggle.

In January 1992, the government finally acknowledged that Niger was facing a Tuareg rebellion that the Nigerien army was unable to control, despite deploying up to two thirds of its forces. Making use of the terrain, climate, and their fighting experiences in Chad, the FLAA rebels remained undefeated, inflicting severe losses on the Nigerien army. The resulting frustration among the troops led to the extra-legal arrest and torture of nearly 300 leading Tuareg politicians and civil society leaders. This, however, did not stop the FLAA offensive.[33]

In June 1993, France intervened, proposing a three-month ceasefire followed by French-mediated negotiations between the warring parties. The French efforts were undermined by the foundation of a new resistance movement, the *Armée Révolutionnaire de Libération du Nord-Niger* (ARLNN), and a mutiny in some garrisons directed against any negotiation with the Tuareg rebels, with the mutineers proceeding to arrest government officials. These and similar phenomena, together with fights between Tuareg rebel movements, would become recurrent in the years to come.

A new rebel movement, the *Front de Libération Temoust* (FLT) was founded in July 1993. *Temoust* is the Tamasheq term for nation. This movement received strong logistical support from the French secret service, the *Direction Générale de la Sécurité Extérieure* (DGSE).[34] The

[33] Klute (2013a).
[34] Klute (2013a).

French were hoping that FLT would take leadership within the rebellion, and that the conflict could then be ended with a lasting peace treaty under French supervision.[35] Security in Northern Niger was a key concern for the French, as the rebellion hampered the exploitation of uranium at the French-operated mines in the Arlit area in Northern Niger, considered indispensable for both French nuclear energy and the French atomic "*Force de Frappe*." The FLT signed a renewable three-month ceasefire with the Nigerien government in September 1993.

Early 1994 saw the creation of yet another rebel movement, the *Front Populaire de Libération du Sahara*, FPLS, led by Mohammed Anako, now president of the council of the region of Agadez in Northern Niger. Shortly afterwards, the four rebel movements united under the leadership of FLT leader Mano Dayak as the *Coordination de la Résistance Armée* (CRA). The CRA immediately took up negotiations with the Niger government, demanding political, economic, and administrative autonomy for the northern part of the country. The government responded by proposing an administrative reform. In a second round of negotiations in Paris in June 1994, both parties agreed on administrative decentralization and local elections.

Negotiations continued in Ouagadougou in the fall of 1994. Although both parties apparently wanted peace, they nonetheless continued military actions in order to strengthen their respective positions for future negotiations. At the same time, the Tuareg rebels split further along tribal lines, with each new movement laying claims to the benefits that were to be distributed in a final peace agreement. Subsequently, in March 1995, a new common structure was created: The *Organisation de la Résistance Armée* (ORA). The ORA supplanted the CRA and continued negotiations with the government, which led to a ceremonially celebrated peace agreement in the capital Niamey, in April 1995. In all, the government signed peace agreements with ten different Tuareg resistance movements and a further two movements of the nomadic Tubu who, like the Tuareg, inhabit Northern Niger and Chad.[36] Apart from these 12 officially recognized movements, several armed militias organized on an ethnic basis, especially of the Arab and Fulani populations in the region, operated in the country by the mid-1990s.

---

[35] Silberzahn (1995).

[36] Ethnographic literature on the Tubu is scanty. See in particular Baroin (1985), Chapelle (1982), Kronenberg (1958), and Le Coeur (1950). The historian of Chad's Civil War, Robert Buijtenhuijs, has also elucidated the role of the Tubu therein (1978, 1987a, b, 1988).

Despite the peace ceremony, there was no peace on the ground. Several rebel factions continued the attacks, mostly for mere particularistic and pecuniary reasons. The small war in Niger's north, interrupted by periods of relative calmness, continued until August 1998 when the last Tubu resistance movement signed peace agreements in Chad's capital N'Djamena.

THE LATE-1990S TO MID-2000S: MALI AND NIGER

Administrative decentralization and the implementation of local democracy in both Mali and Niger meant that the Tuareg could arrange their political life more freely. A number of Tuareg men and women rose to the ranks of ministers in various governments. Violence remained an integral part of the political process, though. The possession of firearms had slowly become an integral part of Tuareg daily life. Old and new local conflicts about pastures and tribal hierarchy were fought out both in the new game of decentralized administration and democracy and in intertribal armed clashes and raids. In Northern Mali, the combination of violence and democracy was mockingly dubbed *demokalashi*.[37]

At the start of the twenty-first century, the geostrategic and economic importance of the Sahara had increased dramatically. Tourism, as well as migrants on their passage to Europe, generated new income. Furthermore, it became center stage in the new scramble for Africa between petrol companies in search of hydrocarbons. Some infrastructure was put in place with development money liberated for the postwar reconstruction. Bridges, tarmac roads, and electronic communication infrastructure were built. International traffic and commerce, including the transport of African migrants across the Sahara, and a range of smuggled goods, from Algerian foodstuffs to Moroccan hashish and Colombian cocaine, renewed the old trans-Saharan trade.[38]

Most important is the geopolitical dimension. As part of their post-9/11 "War on Terror," the USA turned its attention to the outer reaches of the Muslim world, including the Sahel and Sahara. It shared this focus of attention with its adversaries, the propagators of worldwide Jihad. Around 2000, the Algerian *Groupe Salafiste pour la Prédication et le Combat* (GSPC) had established itself in the Algerian Sahara under the leadership of a local *emir* Mokhtar Belmokhtar; it spread out to Northern

---

[37] Lecocq (2010).
[38] Brachet (2009) and Scheele (2012).

Mali and Niger, especially during the 2003 hostage crisis. The GSPC kidnapped 32 European tourists in the Algerian Sahara, who were subsequently released on ransom payments through the mediation of the Malian government and Tuareg leaders.[39]

In 2007, the GSPC rebaptized itself as al-Qaeda in the Lands of the Islamic West (al-Qaeda in the Islamic Maghreb—AQIM).[40] By that time, the US army had installed itself in the region to hunt Muslim "terrorists." The US Armed Forces initiatives started in 2002 under the name Pan-Sahel Initiative (PSI), encompassing Mauritania, Mali, Niger, and Chad. In 2005, the PSI was continued by the Trans-Saharan Counter Terrorism Initiative (TSCTI), which had a wider range than its predecessor. The aim was to set up antiterrorism units in each of these countries, as well as semi-permanent bases of operations for American troops, established in Tamanrasset (Algeria), Tessalit (Mali), and Assamaka (Niger). The Global War on Terror would become an important factor in the conflict in Northern Mali enmeshing an international conflict with local political issues between Tuareg and Arab Saharans.

Strictly speaking, however, the political claims made by Islamist movements in the Sahel fall outside the scope of this chapter, which deals with nationalist and separatist claims. These are not part of the Salafi or Wahhabi-inspired ideological political positions of the Islamist movements. While separatist movements act within the logic of the international state order, defying only the legitimacy of existing states, Islamists contest the very legitimacy and existence of the international state order.

THE CONFLICTS OF THE MID-2000S: MALI AND NIGER

In 2006, a decade after the rebellions of the 1990s had come to an end, conflicts flared up again in both Mali and Niger. These renewed conflicts centered around dynamics of Tuareg internal politics in Mali and economic and ecological demands in Niger, rather than around Tuareg nationalism. Internal power struggles within the Tuareg communities of Northern Mali,

[39] Lecocq and Schrijver (2007).

[40] The Arabic name of the movement, *at-Tanzîm al-Qâeda fi Bilâd al-Maghreb al-Islâmi-yya* is generally translated as al-Qaeda in the Islamic Maghreb, abbreviated as AQIM. The correct translation would be The al-Qaeda Chapter in the Islamic Lands of the West. Translating al-Maghreb to "The West," referring to both North Africa and Western Europe, would do more justice to the global intentions of this movement.

related to the conflicts between MPA and ARLA described earlier, led to the creation of a new rebel movement in May 2006: the *Alliance Démocratique du 23 Mai pour le Changement* (ADC). The movement was led by a number of former leaders of the MPA who had come to occupy higher ranks in the Malian army. The demands of the movement remained rather vague, evoking an unequal development between Northern and Southern Mali and the lack of implementation of the National Pact of 1992.

President Amadou Toumani Touré handled the crisis with resolve, determined not to let the violence spiral out of control, despite widespread criticism for not choosing the military option. Negotiations through the intermediary of Algeria led to the Algiers Agreement between the rebels and the Malian government in June 2006. This, however, did not end the conflict. Mali's National Assembly adopted the Algiers Agreement in early 2007, leading to the dismantling of the ADC in March of that year. However, some Tuareg renegades led by Ibrahim ag Bahanga did not agree with the settlement and founded the *Alliance Touarègue du Nord Mali pour le Changement* (ATNMC) in September 2007.

Neither the ADC nor the ATNMC received general approval in the Tuareg world. Both were seen as the expressions of local power politics at the expense of peace and post-conflict reconstruction. This vision was strengthened by the fact that the army unit fighting the new movements was led by Elhajji ag Gamou, a former Tuareg rebel officer of the FPLA who had joined the Malian army. With the tacit support of the Malian Armed Forces, he recruited a special unit, called Delta Force (in humorous reference to the US army), consisting solely of Tuareg soldiers of his own tribal affiliation and social group: men of politically subordinate *imghad* tribes. Delta Force won the military struggle with the ATNMC in February 2009, therewith ending the conflict for the time being, and altering internal power relations in Tuareg society in favor of the *imghad*, against the Ifoghas tribe.[41]

As in Mali, new fighting had broken out in Northern Niger in February 2007. Here, a number of key issues led to renewed violence. The first was the lack of application of the various peace agreements of the late 1990s, together with political tensions around former rebel leader (and then minister in various governments) Rhissa Boula, and general dissatisfaction with the government of President Mamadou Tandja. More important

---

[41] Lecocq (2010).

were tensions over the possible discovery of new mineral riches. With oil prices staggering to new heights and the search for other energy sources becoming more urgent, uranium prices likewise rose and so did international interest in Niger's uranium and petroleum deposits. The carving up of the entire northern part of the country into prospection and exploitation blocks for crude oil and uranium raised great concerns among the Tuareg about environmental issues, the possible loss of access to pastures, and, not least, the distribution of the revenues of these new riches.

Contrary to the Tuareg of the ADC or ATNMC, the *Mouvement des Nigériens pour la Justice* (MNJ) made no public claims to more autonomy, let alone independence. They claimed to defend the rights of all inhabitants of Northern Niger, regardless of ethnic background, and the presence among their ranks of a few Fulani, Arabs, and, especially, a group of defected army officers gave these claims some credibility. In July 2007, the Malian ATNMC entered into an alliance with the MNJ, called the *Alliance Touarègue Niger-Mali pour le Changement* (ATNMC, which was, unsurprisingly, the same abbreviation as for this movement in Mali). The alliance was short lived. Fighting between the MNJ and the Nigerien Armed Forces led to a full rupture of tourism, one of the sources of revenue for the Tuareg of the Aïr Mountains, as the region was declared a no-go area for all foreigners by the Nigerien government in 2008.[42]

In 2009, the MNJ split in three factions. Starting March 2009, these factions negotiated with the Nigerien government under Libyan mediation. A ceasefire came into effect in May 2009, followed by disarmament. The political stage in Niger changed dramatically with a coup d'état in February 2010 that ousted President Tandja, who had tried to remain in power despite the formal ending of his mandate in December 2009. The MNJ declared itself in support of the coup and the military transition government. Since then, political developments within Niger have left the "Tuareg problem" unattended. Even the return of several 100 Libyan soldiers of Nigerien origin and thousands of migrant workers from Libya to Niger in the second half of 2011 did not bring the "Tuareg problem" back on the agenda. This only changed with the upheaval of Tuareg rebels in neighboring Mali in January 2012.

---

[42] Lecocq (2010).

INDEPENDENT AZAWAD

In October 2010, some young and well-educated Tuareg in Northern Mali founded the *Mouvement National de l'Azawad* (MNA), a political movement striving for autonomy in Mali through political activity.[43] The movement's political demands were ignored and two of its leaders arrested.

The MNA drew inspiration from the then imminent independence of South Sudan,[44] a region that has much in common with Northern Mali in its own history of conflict with a postcolonial state.[45] The Arab spring and especially the Libyan Revolution had further impacts on this movement. In the 1980s and 1990s, a number of Tuareg of Malian and Nigerien origins had already taken Libyan nationality and joined the Libyan Armed Forces. In early 2011, Tuareg fighters from the ATNMC joined the Libyan army against the Libyan revolutionaries. In that same period, Gaddafi recruited Tuareg, along with other Malians, and Nigeriens and Chadians, as mercenaries. After the defeat of the Gaddafi regime in August 2011, many of these men—former Malian ATNMC rebels, mercenaries, and former soldiers of the Libyan armed forces—returned to Mali, bringing along personal and heavy arms, as well as many Tuareg labor migrants traveling along for protection from Libyan xenophobic pogroms.

While the majority of the returnees who had served in the Libyan Armed Forces demanded (and received) integration into the Malian army, making it clear that they had not come to fight the government, the former members of the ATNMC rebel movement joined the MNA to form the *Mouvement National pour la Libération de l'Azawad* (MNLA). A number of other returnees from Libya joined as well, as did some Tuareg politicians. This new Tuareg nationalist movement thus comprised both a well-equipped military wing and a well-educated and media and Internet-experienced political wing. The latter expressed the movement's demands

---

[43] For more details on the foundation of the MNA and the profile of its first leaders, see Morgan, Andy (February 6, 2012). "The Causes of the Uprising in Northern Mali". Think Africa Press. Retrieved February 10, 2012. [http://thinkafricapress.com/mali/causes-uprising-northern-mali-tuareg; last accessed 28/11/2012] and http://www.maliweb.net/category.php?NID=82864 (last accessed November 6, 2011).

[44] See also Schomerus and de Vries (2018) in this volume.

[45] This was the reasoning of Ahmeyede Ag Ilkamassene, one of MNA's leading figures, in an article published in its press release website Toumast Press on 23 December 2011 "Azawad, it's now or never!" [http://toumastpress.com/autres/analyse/196-azawad-maintenant-ou-jamais.html; last accessed November 27, 2012].

of self-determination, human rights, and the rights of indigenous peoples, using English, French, and Arabic as its languages of communication on various electronic media, including the MNLA's own website.[46]

In November 2011, the MNLA organized a number of protests in cities in Northern Mali, demanding self-determination or independence for Azawad.[47] The MNLA was the first Tuareg separatist movement that openly declared to fight for an independent state of Azawad, donning itself in explicitly nationalist symbols: a national flag (black, red, and green fesses with a yellow chevron), a national emblem (the map of Azawad with the letters M.N.L.A. and two crossed traditional Tuareg swords), and creed ("Unity, Justice, Liberty," written in French, Arabic, and Tamasheq on the emblem). The MNLA stated its demand for independence on the movement's website (www.mnlamov.net) until late 2012, when negotiations in Ouagadougou with the international community led to the withdrawal of this demand.

On January 17, 2012, the MNLA started attacks in the northern regions of Mali. The success of the rebels was advanced by two factors: on March 21, a group of junior officers staged a coup d'état ousting president Touré. The putschists criticized Touré's dealing with the Tuareg upheaval as ambivalent, too soft, and professionally incompetent—all of which they argued had led to repeated defeats of the Malian army.

Instead of improving the military situation, however, the coup broke down chains of command, and as a consequence, logistical support failed to reach army units fighting in the north. A number of units, abandoned to fend for themselves, simply retreated in the face of advancing rebels. The second factor explaining the rebels' success is the tacit military alliances the MNLA had forged with other armed groups of Islamist orientation in Northern Mali, in particular, with *Gamá'at Ansár ud-Dín*: Society of the Companions of the Religion, which fought for Muslim rule in Azawad, or even in the whole of Mali. The adoption of an Arabic name only referring to religion, instead of a French name referring to the national homeland Azawad, is significant for the movement's Islamist orientation that however, it mixed with Tuareg nationalist ideology.

Ansár ud-Dín was attractive locally mainly because it seemed to fulfill an Islamic claim. Whereas *Ansár ud-Din* explicitly promoted Islam, the

[46] http://www.mnlamov.net/ (last accessed March 23, 2012).

[47] http://www.youtube.com/watch?v=-IrCUoBUMWM&context=C461258fADvjVQa 1PpcFOiaSz-oISwGTTz67955NwvoxwVCKX6uVw= (last accessed March 23,2012).

MNLA proclaimed Azawad as a secular state, displeasing large parts of the predominantly Muslim local population.[48] Most attacks claimed by the MNLA were carried out by *Ansâr ud-Dîn* in alliance with AQIM. It participated in the siege and conquest of the region's capital Kidal and the strategically important town of Tessalit, which was conquered despite the reinforcement of the Malian army with helicopter gunships, fighter jets, and armored vehicles and despite further support from the US army.[49]

On the side of the Malian army, Tuareg army units (among them returnees from Libya) spearheaded operations against Tuareg rebels; Tuareg were fighting on both sides. By the end of March, the coalition of fighters had evicted the Malian army from all of the north, establishing a frontline from Douentza close to the Burkina/Mali border to Léré on the Mauritania/Mali border, hence occupying some two thirds of the Malian state territory.

On April 6, the MNLA declared the independence of Northern Mali, announcing the creation of a new state: "The Republic of Azawad," governed by a transitory state council.[50] The new republic found no international recognition and was heavily contested by the MNLA's tacit Jihadi allies from early 2012 onwards, as well as by the majority of non-Tuareg and non-Arab populations of the declared Azawad republic.

However, the MNLA drew significant support from Tuareg populations and leaders, notably Intallah ag Attaher and Ambeiri ag Rhissa. Intallah ag Attaher, *amenokal* or "traditional" chief of the Ifoghas, counted among the most influential Tuareg leaders in Mali. From his accession to the position of *amenokal* in 1962, to his formal retreat from that position in 2011, through three uprisings organized mainly by his kin and clansmen, Intallah has taken a pro-Malian position, remaining loyal to the government in Bamako. In 2012, Intallah declared his open support for the MNLA and the Azawad Republic. Leaving the MNLA in 2013 to join the HCUA, Intallah did not retract his new-found position on Tuareg independence. In one of his last interviews before his death in December 2014, he advocated the separation of Mali and the founding of a new Tuareg state.[51]

---

[48] Klute (2013b).
[49] Lecocq and Belalimat (2012).
[50] http://www.mnlamov.net/ (last accessed Novermber 28, 2012).
[51] Sahelien.com. "Intalla Ag Attaher: « La seule manière de garantir la paix définitive, c'est. la division du pays » December 14, 2014. https://www.youtube.com/watch?v=E34iBeHArd4 (last accessed March 18, 2017).

Ambeiri ag Rhissa is among the most influential intellectuals and thinkers in the Kidal region. Educated in French schools, Ambeiri has fulfilled various public positions in Kidal in government. In 1963, he was the only Tuareg, or even Malian, to publish an article in national newspaper *l'Essor* on the 1963 rebellion and its goals, taking a nuanced but clear position against the objectives of the rebels. During the rebellion of the 1990s, Ambeiri remained an outspoken critic and adversary of the separatist movements, leading to his abduction. He recounted his experience of being held hostage for six months by rebel movement FPLA in a now famous poem lambasting the nationalist ideology of Tuareg separatism. In 2012, Ambeiri joined the MNLA's Transitory Council of the Azawad Republic. The support for and adherence to the MNLA of these two men should be regarded as indicative for significant shifts in favor of a nationalist political outlook in the Kidal region.

THE RENEWED SPLINTERING OF THE NATIONALIST MOVEMENT

The alliances between the MNLA and groups of Islamist orientation were concluded for pragmatic purposes only, as both sides follow divergent ends. Their cohabitation proved to be short lived. As early as September 2012, the MNLA was driven out of Gao, the largest city it had conquered and had declared the capital of the Azawad Republic, by the *Mouvement pour l'Unicité (Divine) et le Jihad en Afrique de l'Ouest* (MUJAO), a splinter group of AQIM, founded in 2011. The MNLA had lost popular support in Gao due to the undisciplined behavior of its fighters, committing theft, robbery, plunder, and rape in the territories they occupied.[52] The MNLA either had no interest in or did not dispose of the capacities necessary to build up administrative structures and to guarantee order, some sort of justice, and most important of all, protection from violence, therewith losing what has been conceptualized as the crucial form of legitimacy of political power.[53] Barely six months after its declaration of independence, the Azawad Republic and all dreams of independence seemed to have come to an end.

The MNLA now was limited to its last strongholds, the towns of Menaka and Léré, in the extreme western and eastern peripheries of

---

[52] Amnesty International (May 2012).
[53] Bellagamba and Klute (2008).

Azawad. In November 2012, the MUJAO chased the MNLA from Menaka, leaving Léré under the threat of *Ansâr ud-Dîn*. In December 2012, *Ansâr ud-Dîn*, which had so far been left out of negotiations between the MNLA and the Malian government, exerted military pressure on the Malian Armed Forces at the frontline around the village of Konna in order to have its presence felt and to fight its way to the negotiation table. Their offensive led to the total collapse of the Malian army units at the front.

Interim President Dioncounda Traoré formally asked French military support to counter the Islamist forces. Thus, under the name of "Operation Serval," an alliance of French and Chadian forces landed in Mali in January 2013, advancing on the Islamist coalition of *Ansâr ud-Dîn*, MUJAO, and AQIM. Within a number of weeks, the French-Chadian forces conquered the major cities of Northern Mali. The French/Chadian forces were assisted by Malian army units consisting of military men of northern origins, mostly Tuareg, under the command of the former 1990s Tuareg rebel officer Lieutenant-Colonel Elhajji ag Gamou. These men guided the Franco/Chadian forces through Northern Mali, therewith strengthening their own position vis-à-vis the Ifoghas tribe, the majority of which had fought for *Ansâr ud-Dîn* or the MNLA.

The collapse of Islamist rule led to the temporary retreat of most foreign Islamist fighters from Mali and a regrouping of those Tuareg fighters with Islamist views in the Islamic Movement of Azawad (MIA) which, after further regroupings, renamed itself the High Council for the Unity of Azawad (HCUA). These political moves reflected attempts by the Ifoghas tribe to salvage their power, under threat by the new political developments, especially the position of pro-Malian forces under Elhajj ag Gamou.

THE ISLAMIC CLAIM AND THE INTERNATIONALIZATION OF THE CONFLICT

The Franco-Chadian forces, formally fighting to restore Malian territorial integrity and to stem the tide of Jihadi Islam in Mali, did not engage in combat with the MNLA, to the contrary. In mid-2013, the MNLA reemerged from its weak position, attracting former Tuareg Islamist fighters to its ranks and occupying the city of Kidal, with the tacit agreement of the French command of Operation Serval, which hoped to be able to use MNLA knowledge of the north to flush out the last vestiges of AQIM's foreign Islamist fighters.

The French government left the MNLA as a player in the political field to send a clear signal to the Malian political elite that France was not there to solve the decades-old political problem of the Tuareg nationalist minority and that "Bamako" had to find a solution to this problem through negotiations with a negotiation partner in its strength.[54] Between May and July 2013, a small number of Malian troops reentered the north, including the city of Kidal, while MNLA fighters remained armed and present, next to Serval Forces. Tensions and occasional clashes between the MNLA and the Malian army remained checked against the foreign military presence.

The reconquest of Northern Mali through Operation Serval ended in June 2013 but was followed in August 2014 by Operation Barkhane: a French military operation explicitly formulated as a fight against terrorist organizations in the entire Sahel (Chad formally retreated its offensive troops in 2014 but deployed most of these within the Multidimensional Integrated Stabilization Mission in Mali [MINUSMA] in which Chadian troops have formed the bulk of the peacekeeping mission). Despite Operation Barkhane, Islamist military presence remains strong in Mali, having spread from the north to the central and southern Mopti and Sikasso regions of the country. Islamist military initiatives in Mali follow well-known guerrilla tactics of Global Jihad.

The combative Franco/Chadian Operation Serval was partly complemented and partly succeeded by larger international interventions. More than the separatist efforts of the MNLA, the conquest of two thirds of Mali by Islamist forces and the subsequent imposition of their interpretation of Shari'a law stirred up international attention on an African and global level. A host of African and Western states; the African and the European Union; the Economic Community of West African States (ECOWAS); United Nations (UN) organizations; and the UN security council, diplomats, or (self-declared) mediators of any provenance engaged with the conflict in various roles as facilitators of negotiation, negotiating partners, supporters of the Malian government, and active military party in the conflicts on the ground.

Early October 2012, the UN Security Council approved a resolution to support an ECOWAS force in support of the Malian army. Before the African-led International Support Mission to Mali (AFISMA) could even

---

[54] No formal statement of this kind has of course ever been issued, but anonymous French diplomats at the EU confirmed so much to one of the authors as well as to some other colleagues.

be fully deployed, it was transformed into the UN's MINUSMA: a peace-keeping mission with an extensive mandate created in April 2013. Under the terms of its founding resolution

> the mission would support the political process and carry out a number of security-related stabilization tasks, with a focus on major population centres and lines of communication, protecting civilians, human rights monitoring, the creation of conditions for the provision of humanitarian assistance and the return of displaced persons, the extension of State authority and the preparation of free, inclusive and peaceful elections.[55]

MINUSMA was complemented by the European Union Training Mission to Mali (EUTM), active since April 2013, which tries to rebuild the Malian Armed forces.[56] Yet, despite its extensive mandate, MINUSMA has not been able to establish peace between the Malian government and the MNLA and other Tuareg movements. At the advent of MINUSMA, no peace agreement was even signed, making the peacekeeping mandate both dubious and impossible to maintain. Since its deployment, MINUSMA has risen from an original mandate of more than 12,500 staff to more than 15,000 staff in 2017. So far, MINUSMA has proven to be among the UN's most deadly peacekeeping missions with more than 150 casualties by early 2018.[57]

INTERNATIONAL MEDIATION AND PEACE NEGOTIATIONS

With the start of Operation Serval, the international community pressured the Malian government into organizing elections, in order to restore political order and to give constitutionally and internationally valid spokes partners to the MNLA, but especially to the international community invested in Mali. The elections took place in two rounds on July 28 and August 11, with former Prime Minister Ibrahim Boubakar Keita the victor.[58]

Under the auspices of the international community, the newly elected Keita government and the HCUA and MNLA, complemented by a growing

---

[55] http://www.un.org/en/peacekeeping/missions/minusma/background.shtml (last accessed May 15, 2017).

[56] http://www.eutmmali.eu/ (last accessed July 22, 2013).

[57] Lecocq (2013).

[58] United Nations Peacekeeping: fatalities by Mission and Appointment Type up to March 31, 2017. http://www.un.org/en/peacekeeping/fatalities/documents/stats_3mar.pdf (last accessed 05/15/2017).

body of smaller movements, most notably *Le Groupe autodéfense touareg Imghad et alliés* (GATIA), engaged in peace negotiations. The Ouagadougou Agreement of June 2013 constituted a preliminary agreement, facilitating the July 2013 elections and setting the context for further peace talks.[59] Mediation between the various parties was provided by ECOWAS and Algeria, with a number of other organizations and countries involved or taking an interest, among which the Organization of Islamic Cooperation, France, and the USA, and general oversight being given by the United Nations.

International pressure also led the Malian government to create a Transitional Justice and Reconciliation infrastructure. This has changed the name and status a number of times since its inception in March 2013 as the *Commission Dialogue et Réconciliation*, having been transformed into the *Ministère de la Réconciliation et du Développement des Régions du Nord* in September 2013, which under its mandate created the *Commission Vérité, Justice et Réconciliation* in April 2014. As the conflicts in Northern Mali continue, the effect of the work of any of these commissions has remained very limited.

Despite (or perhaps because of) these numerous facilitators and the international interest, peace negotiations were slow, in part due to unwillingness from the side of all belligerents and the continued fighting in the north between HCUA, MAA, GATIA, MAA, Operation Barkhane, and various Islamist movements. On May 15, 2015, the Malian government signed a peace agreement (*Accord pour la Paix et la Réconciliation au Mali*) in the presence of various international representatives and dignitaries but without countersigning by the representatives of the *Coordination des Mouvements de l'Azawad*, representing the various Tuareg secessionist and autonomist movements. Further international meditation led to the signing by both the Malian government and the Tuareg movements of two further documents. The first is entitled "Relevé de conclusions des consultations préparatoires à la mise en oeuvre de l'Accord pour la paix et la réconciliation au Mali, issu du processus d'Alger," which means as much as a review of the negotiations but without an explicit outcome upon which peace terms are agreed. A second document functions as a ceasefire between the various Tuareg groups and the Malian Armed Forces.

---

[59] Accord Préliminaire a l'élection présidentielle et aux pourparlers inclusifs de paix au Mali. Ouagadougou June 2013.

Although these two documents, signed on June 20, 2015, and referred to as the Algiers Agreements (a confusing name as the agreements signed between the Malian government and the Tuareg movements in June 2006 are also known under this name), are generally considered to be a peace agreement, they are not to the letter of their text. Since the signing of these agreements, internecine strife between HCUA, MNLA, MAA, and GATIA, Islamist attacks, and intercommunal violence have continued in Northern Mali, while Islamist attacks and the proliferation of Islamist movements has spread to the central and southern parts of the country. For the foreseeable future, Mali will most likely remain a divided country, with a small yet determined Tuareg minority struggling for independence.

INTERNAL FACTIONALISM AND CONTINUED FIGHTING THREATENS THE PEACE PROCESS

The military intervention of Franco/Chadian troops in the north of the country followed by the increasing presence of external actors,[60] military, and civilians alike, set in motion a process of creation of a number of militias and political movements of various kinds and differing political orientations. Some of them are spinoffs of existing groups; others are entirely new creations. These groupings fight militarily and politically—often in fast-shifting alliances among them or with external power groups—for different objectives that likewise may change quickly as well. As the Malian state has lost its monopoly on violence—at least in the northern parts of the country—and with it much of its legitimacy, the government can be considered one of several political-military groups in the area.

The resulting complexity of the political field seems to present huge challenges to political analysis.[61] To come to terms with this heterogeneity and for the sake of analysis, we have divided the various groups into the following categories—bearing in mind, however, that these categories represent only types. There is as much overlap in political orientations between the groups as there is internal political diversity.

[60] See Klute (2013b), where global actors in the region, their objectives and ideologies are discussed in more detail.
[61] For example, Bøås and Torheim (2013).

Pro-Malians or "loyalists": Composed of various ethnic and political organizations, the loyalists signed the Agreement of Algiers[62] and are organized in a "platform." Although each member of the platform follows its own agenda, they share loyalty to the central government and hostility towards the pro-Azawadian movement. The groups organized in the platform are politically and militarily dominated by a militia of Imghad-Tuareg named GATIA (*Groupe d'Auto Défence Touareg-Imghad et Alliés*) led currently by General Elhajji ag Gamou. A second member group calls itself *Coordination des Mouvements et Fronts Patriotiques de Résistance* (CMFPR), an acronym for the *Gandy Koy* and *Ganda Izo* militias, whose social base is the ethnic group of the Songhay joined by some Tuareg of slave descent. The last member of the platform is a spinoff of a militia of Malian Bidân Arabs, organized as MAA (*Mouvement Arabe de l'Azawad*). Because of its loyalty to the Malian government, it calls itself MAA pro-Bamako.

Traditionalists: These are composed of traditional chieftaincies and their various tribal allies. The ultimate goal of their politics seems to be the reinforcement or at least the preservation of their respective positions. Following their "intermediary tradition,"[63] they present themselves as go-betweens between the various actors in the region and between themselves and the central government in Bamako. It is noteworthy that some chieftaincies ally with existing militias or participate in the founding of new ones. This is the case, for instance, of the Menaka- and the Timbuktu-Tuareg. Some former MNLA- and HCUA-members, all of Menaka origins, founded a new militia MSA (*Mouvement pour le Salut de l'Azawad*) in September 2016. The leading figure of MSA, Moussa ag Acharatoumane, declared to the news outlet *Jeune Afrique* that the MSA is composed of traditional chiefs (of the Menaka Région) as well as of fighters, likewise from the region.[64] Despite Moussa ag Acharatoumane's declaration that the MSA continues to pursue the original goal of the MNLA to fight for independence or autonomy for the whole of Northern Mali, it is clearly a regional militia molded on the model of the traditional federacy of Tuareg tribes. This became evident in early 2017, when the MSA started to join military patrols of the Malian army and the French forces in the Menaka region. A similar evolution took place in the Timbuktu region, which is the revitalization

---

[62] Despite long months of negotiations in Algiers between the Malian government and movements fighting for independence or autonomy of Northern Mali, they failed to conclude a peace agreement. Under the pressure of the international community, the Malian government and militias of the "platform" loyal to the government's cause then signed a peace agreement in May 2015, which the movements struggling for independence joined one month later. [http://www.aps.dz/monde/24902-la-signature-de-l-accord-d-alger-par-la-cma-fortement-salu%C3%A9e-%C3%A0-bamako,-hommage-%C3%A0-l-alg%C3%A9rie].

[63] Klute (2013a).

[64] *Jeune Afrique*, September 9, 2016.

and reorganization of traditional forms of Tuareg political rule. Here, a splinter group of the MNLA, the CJA (*Congrès pour la Justice dans l'Azawad*), composed of politicians and fighters from the region, opposed—even with military means—in spring 2017, the insertion of intermediate administrative authorities in the region foreseen in the Algiers' agreement. The CJA advocates an equitable repartition of political positions and benefices, determined in the agreements, between the various regions in Northern Mali, regardless of their share in the struggle.

Civilian organizations: Some civil organizations of the north attempt playing the role of intermediaries between the populace, the central government of Bamako and even foreign actors in similar ways to the "traditional" chieftaincies, which puts civil society in competition with those chieftaincies. The actors here are a number of NGOs and grassroot organizations as well as the platform of the Kel Tamashek and the Northern National Coordination (COREN). COREN is one of the privileged interlocutors of the central government on issues related to the north.

Contenders: These are ethno- or regional-political movements composed of the secular MNLA (mostly Tuareg), the CPA (a splinter group of MNLA), the ethno-religious HCUA (Tuareg), and the MAA-coordination (Malian Bidân Arabs), organized in the "*Coordination des Mouvements de l'Azwad*" (CMA). The contenders struggle for the independence of Azawad or at least for a strong autonomy, possibly within the framework of a (future) federal state of Mali. Politically, the CMA asks for the strict application of the Algiers agreements. Ideologically, however, it is deeply divided about which political project to pursue in the future. While the MNLA strives for a secular mode of societal organization, the HCUA aims at organizing society according to Islamic principles, including the application of Shari'a law.[65] In contrast to the other Islamist groups in Mali, however, it limits its "Islamic claim" to Northern Mali and refuses the use of violent means to pursue this goal.

Local(ized) Islamists and Jihadists: Around the new millennium, jihadists in Northern Mali were quasi exclusively non-Malians (see above). Since then, a process of localization of jihadi Salafism has taken place. There are several reasons for this: Firstly, some local networks of the Pakistani Islamic movement of Tablighi Jama'āt seem to have converted into jihadist Salafism.[66] Secondly, non-Malian jihadists established marital ties with local groups, in

---

[65] This was recently confirmed by Hassan ag Fagaga, President of the intermediate administrative authorities in the Kidal region in an interview to Jeune Afrique. http://www.tamoudre. org/geostrategie/hassan-ag-fagaga-jihadiste-nest-quun-homme-autres-kalach/ (last accessed May 274, 2017).

[66] Lecocq et al. (2013).

particular within the Ifoghas tribe. Some of their children born in the 1990s might well be today's fighters. Thirdly, non-Malian jihadi fighters seemed to have suffered heavy losses (up to 600 casualties) during the French Intervention Operation Serval, which were compensated by increased local recruitment in the following years. This localization process was seemingly completed when leaders of all jihadist groups in Mali announced the foundation of a new jihadi movement: *Nusrat al-Islam*, also known as Al-Qaida in Mali (AQM) in a video (the official name is: *Jama'a Nusrat ul-Islam wa al-Muslimín*: Union for the Support of Islam and Muslims). *Nusrat al-Islam* unites all Malian jihadi movements, namely, MUJAO, al-Murabitun, AQIM, and the Liberation Front of Macina in Central Mali (apparently a branch of Ansâr ud-Dîn) in this alliance, pledging allegiance to (global) al-Qaeda. It is remarkable that Nusrat al-Islam is led by the Tuareg Iyad ag Ghali, the leader of Ansâr ud-Dîn. It is likewise remarkable that Nusrat al-Islam seems to seek to increase its "strategic depth" by extending its military actions to central Mali and even to the border regions of neighboring Burkina Faso and Niger.

While a number of military clashes occurring since the French intervention in 2013 are due to the political and ideological differences existing between the various groups, other clashes are not as easily identified. Pro-Bamako militias ("loyalists") and "contenders" are struggling for divergent ends and hence have clashed violently on a number of occasions. Jihadists, for example, fight foreign powers (French forces and MINUSMA) as well as all those who ally with or support them.[67] There are, however, clashes that do not seem to be caused by political or ideological divergences at all. We explain these clashes by the attempts of the various groups to reproduce themselves politically, socially, economically, and materially.

Obviously, some groups ally with foreign power groups or collaborate with aid organizations in order to tap material resources as well as political support. Others play regional and/or ethnical identity cards to gain adherents, enabling them to blackmail the Bamako government for support of all kinds. All this brings the various militias into competition with one

---

[67] The most spectacular jihadist strike against "supporters" of foreign powers present in Northern Mali was a kamikaze attack by al-Murabitun in January 2017. The attack targeted a camp of fighters of various militias (pro- and anti-Bamako) in Gao. The concentration and training of ex-fighters, foreseen in the Algiers agreement, is meant to prepare them to patrol Northern Mali together with units of the Malian army. The Gao attack caused about 200 casualties, mostly among fighters of the CMA (https://fr.wikipedia.org/wiki/Attentat_de_Gao, last accessed 04/06/2017).

another, adding to or despite their political-ideological differences over which they occasionally fight using military means. In the current situation, long existing economic and social connections across state borders and within borderlands are revitalized, despite increasing efforts by the French, Algerian, Nigerien, and Mauritanian armed forces to better control national borders.

OUTLOOK

As mentioned earlier, we have retraced Tuareg secessionist political projects since the start of the decolonization process of African colonies. Despite the fact that ideals of national independence have since been expressed in Tuareg internal discourses, these ideals were only recently transformed into formal claims to independence by the MNLA in Mali. A second aspect is remarkable: there has never been a common secessionist project encompassing all Tuareg groups of the five postcolonial states they live in. This may point toward either the constancy of the tribal federacies that make up the Tuareg political system or, to put it more generally, at a particular vitality of traditional forms of political order in Africa.[68] Or it may hint at what the impact of (postcolonial) national identities actually has been on the political thinking of the various Tuareg groups in the respective postcolonial states. Islamist and jihadist projects seem to have supplanted secessionist ideas and any utopia of an independent Tuareg state.

This, however, may be a premature judgment. In Northern Mali, an "Islamic claim," or more precisely, a claim to promote Islam and to install an Islamic mode of societal organization, exists since the independence of the country besides, or at times in opposition to, the claim for independence or autonomy.[69]

REFERENCES

Amnesty International. (2012). *Mali: retour sur cinq mois de crise. Rébellion armée et putsch militaire.* London: Amnesty International report reference Afr 37/001/ 2012. Retrieved from http://www.amnesty.org/en/library/asset/AFR37/ 001/2012/en/35f18828-e1f3-4557-a09c-41a1cd584190/afr370012012fr.pdf

[68] Forrest (2003).
[69] Klute (2013b).

Aouad-Badoual, R. (1993). Le rôle de 'Abidine el Kounti dans la résistance nomade à la conquête française de la boucle du Niger (1894–1902). *Les Cahiers de l'IREMAM, 4,* 35–48.

Badi, D. (2010). Les relations des Touaregs aux Etats: le cas de l'Algérie et de la Libye. *Note de l'Ifri, 2010, Programme "Le Maghreb dans son environnement régional et international".* Paris: IFRI.

Baroin, C. (1985). *Anarchie et cohésion sociale chez les Toubous. Les Daza Kéšerda (Niger).* Paris: Éditions de la Maison des Sciences de l'Homme/Cambridge University Press.

Bellagamba, A., & Klute, G. (2008). Tracing emergent powers in contemporary Africa – Introduction. In A. Bellagamba & G. Klute (Eds.), *Beside the state. Emergent powers in contemporary Africa* (pp. 7–21). Köln: Köppe Verlag.

Berge, G. (2000) *In defense of pastoralism. Form and flux among Tuaregs in Northern Mali.* Doctoral Dissertation. Oslo: Oslo University.

Bernus, E. (1981). *Touaregs Nigériens. Unité culturelle et diversité régionale d'un peuple Pasteur.* Paris: Éditions de l'Office de la Recherche Scientifique et Technique outre-mer.

Blanguernon, C. (1983). *Le Hoggar.* Paris: Arthaud.

Bøås, M., & Torheim, L. E. (2013). The international intervention in Mali: "Desert blues" or a new beginning? *International Journal, 68*(3), 417–423.

Boilley, P. (1993). L'organisation Commune des Régions Sahariennes (OCRS): une tentative avortée. In E. Bernus, P. Boilley, J. Clauzel, & J.-L. Triaud (Eds.), *Nomades et commandants: administration et sociétés nomades dans l'ancienne A.O.F* (pp. 215–239). Paris: Karthala.

Boilley, P. (1995). OCRS/Royaume sanussi de Libye: deux tentatives pour durer? In C.-R. Ageron & M. Michel (Eds.), *L'ère des décolonisations* (pp. 359–368). Paris: Karthala.

Boilley, P. (1999). *Les Touaregs Kel Adagh. Dépendances et révoltes: du Soudan français au Mali contemporain.* Paris: Karthala.

Brachet, J. (2009). *Migrations transsahariennes: vers un désert cosmopolite et morcelé, Niger.* Croquant: Bellecombe-en-Bauges.

Buijtenhuijs, R. (1978). *Le Frolinat et les revoltes populaires du Tchad, 1965–1976.* Den Haag: Mouton.

Buijtenhuijs, R. (1987a). *Le Frolinat et les révoltes populaires du Tchad. 1965–1976.* The Hague/Paris/New York: Mouton.

Buijtenhuijs, R. (1987b). *Le Frolinat et les guerres civiles du Tchad (1977–1984).* Paris: Karthala.

Buijtenhuijs, R. (1988). Les Toubous et la rébellion tchadienne. In C. Baroin (Ed.), *Gens du roc et du sable: les Toubou. Hommage à Charles et Marguerite Le Cœur* (pp. 73–86). Paris: Presses du CNRS.

Chapelle, J. (1982). *Nomades noirs du Sahara. Les Toubous.* Paris: Harmattan.

Clauzel, J. (1963). L'évolution contemporaine de l'économie et de la société chez les Touaregs. *Institut National de la Statistique et des Etudes Economiques: Actualités d'Outre-mer, No. 24,* Juillet.

Clauzel, J. (1992). L'administration coloniale française et les sociétés nomades dans l'ancienne Afrique occidental française. *Politique africaine, 46,* 99–116.

Correale, F. (2009). Le Sahara espagnol: histoire et mémoire du rapport colonial. Un essai d'interprétation. In S. Caratini (Ed.), *La question du pouvoir en Afrique du Nord et de l'Ouest* (pp. 103–152). Paris: Harmattan.

Fluchard, C. (1995). *Le PPN-RDA et la décolonisation du Niger: 1946–1960.* Paris: l'Harmattan.

Forrest, J. (2003). *Lineages of state fragility. Rural civil society in Guinea-Bissau.* Oxford/Athens: James Currey/Ohio University Press.

Grémont, C. (2010). *Les Touaregs Iwellemmedan (1647–1896).* Paris: Karthala.

Hall, B. (2011). *A history of race in Muslim West Africa 1600–1960.* Cambridge: Cambridge University Press.

Henry, J.-R. (1996). Les Touaregs des Français. *Les cahiers de l'IREMAM, 7*(8), 249–268.

Ibn Hauqal. (1964). *Configuration de la terre (Kitab surat al-'ard)* (trans: Kramers, J. H., & Wiet, G.). Collection Unesco D'oeuvres Représentatives Série Arabe. Paris: Maisonneuve & Larose.

Kaufmann, H. (1964). *Wirtschafts- und Sozialstruktur der Iforas Tuareg.* Dissertation, Köln.

Klute, G. (1995). Hostilité et alliances: archéologie de la dissidence des Touaregs au Mali. *Cahiers d'Études africaines, 137*(XXXV-1), 55–71.

Klute, G. (2009). The technique of modern chariots: About speed and mobility in contemporary small wars in the Sahara. In J. Bart, S. Luning, & K. van Walraven (Eds.), *The speed of change. Motor vehicles and people in Africa, 1890–2000* (pp. 192–211). Leiden: Brill.

Klute, G. (2013a). *Tuareg-Aufstand in der Wüste. Ein Beitrag zur Anthropologie der Gewalt und des Krieges.* Köln: Koeppe Verlag.

Klute, G. (2013b). Post-Gaddafi Repercussions, global Islam or local logics? In L. Koechlin, & T. Förster (Eds.), *Mali – Impressions of the current crisis Mali – impressions de la crise actuelle, Basel Papers on Political Transformations No. 5* (pp. 7–13). Basel: Institute of Social Anthropology.

Klute, G., & von Trotha, T. (2000). Wege zum Frieden. Vom Kleinkrieg zum parastaatlichen Frieden im Norden von Mali. *Sociologus, L*(1), 1–37.

Kronenberg, A. (1958). *Die Teda von Tibesti, (Wiener Beiträge zur Kulturgeschichte und Linguistik, Band XII).* Wien: Verlag Ferdinand Berger.

Le Coeur, C. (1950). *Dictionnaire ethnographique Téda précédé d'un lexique français-téda.* Paris: Mémoires de l'Institut français d'Afrique Noire.

Lecocq, B. (2003). This country is your country: Territory, borders and decentralisation in Tuareg politics. *Itinerario: European Journal of Overseas History,* *27*(1), 58–78.

Lecocq, B. (2004). Unemployed intellectuals in the Sahara: The Teshumara nationalist movement and the revolutions in Tuareg society. *International Review of Social History, 49*(Suppl. 12), 87–109.

Lecocq, B. (2010). *Disputed desert: Decolonisation, competing nationalisms and Tuareg rebellions in Northern Mali.* Leiden: Brill.

Lecocq, B. (2013). Mali: This is only the beginning. *Georgetown Journal of International Affairs, 14*(summer/fall), 59–69.

Lecocq, B., & Belalimat, N. (2012). The Tuareg: Between armed uprising and drought. *African arguments.* London: Royal African Society. http:// africanarguments.org/2012/02/28/the-tuareg-between-armed-uprising-and-drought-baz-lecocq-and-nadia-belalimat/

Lecocq, B., & Schrijver, P. (2007). The war on terror in a haze of dust: Potholes and pitfalls on the Saharan front. *Journal of Contemporary African Studies, 25*(1), 141–166.

Lecocq, B., Mann, G., Whitehouse, B., Dida, B., Pelckmans, L., Belalimat, N., Hall, B., & Lacher, W. (2013). One hippopotamus and eight blind analysts: A multivocal analysis of the 2012 political crisis in the divided Republic of Mali. *Review of African Political Economy, 40*(137), 343–357.

Nicolaisen, J., & Nicolaisen, I. (1997). *The pastoral Tuareg. Ecology, culture and society* (Vol. I + II). Copenhagen/London/New York: Rhodos International Science and Art Publishers/Thames and Hudson/Thames and Hudson.

Olivier de Sardan, J.-P. (1976). *Quand nos pères étaient captifs… Récits paysans du Niger. (Traduits et édités par Jean-Pierre Olivier de Sardan).* Paris: Nubia.

Porges, M. (2018). Western Sahara and Morocco: Complexities of resistance and analysis. In L. de Vries, P. Englebert, & M. Schomerus (Eds.), *Secessionism in African politics: Aspiration, grievance, performance, disenchantment.* New York: Palgrave.

Poulton, R., & ag Youssouf, I. (1998). *A peace of Timbuktu – Democratic governance, development and African peacemaking.* Geneva/New York: UNIDIR, 1998.

Salifou, A. (1993). *La question touarègue au Niger.* Paris: Karthala.

Scheele, J. (2012). *Smugglers and saints of the Sahara: Regional connectivity in the twentieth century.* Cambridge: Cambridge University Press.

Schomerus, M., & de Vries, L. (2018). A state of contradiction: Sudan's unity goes south. In L. de Vries, P. Englebert, & M. Schomerus (Eds.), *Secessionism in African politics: Aspiration, grievance, performance, disenchantment.* New York: Palgrave.

Silberzahn, C. (avec J. Guisnel). (1995). *Au cœur du secret. 1500 jours aux com-mandes de la DGSE (1989–1993)*. Paris: Fayard.

Triaud, J.-L. (1993). Un mauvais départ: 1920, l'Air en ruines. In E. Bernus, P. Boilley, J. Clauzel, & J.-L. Triaud (Eds.), *Nomades et commandants: Administration et sociétés nomades dans l'ancienne AOF* (pp. 93–100). Paris: Karthala.

CHAPTER 3

Anglophone Secessionist Movements in Cameroon

Piet Konings and Francis B. Nyamnjoh

INTRODUCTION

The "Anglophone problem" in Cameroon is a byword for a secessionist claim that has posed a major challenge to the post-colonial state's efforts to forge national unity and integration. Anglophone Cameroonians in the country and in the diaspora widely feel that reunification with Francophone Cameroon in 1961 has led to the marginalization of their minority group in the post-colonial nation-state project. They allege that this project is controlled by the Francophone political elite and endangers Anglophone cultural heritage and identity. Although Anglophone resistance has been a permanent feature of Cameroon's post-colonial biography,[1] it was not until political liberalization in the early 1990s that the Anglophone elite began to mobilize the wider population. They claimed self-determination

[1] Konings and Nyamnjoh (2003).

P. Konings
African Studies Centre, University of Leiden, Leiden, The Netherlands

F. B. Nyamnjoh (✉)
University of Cape Town, Cape Town, South Africa

© The Author(s) 2019   59
L. de Vries et al. (eds.), *Secessionism in African Politics*,
Palgrave Series in African Borderlands Studies,
https://doi.org/10.1007/978-3-319-90206-7_3

and autonomy, first, as a return to a federal state, and later, after persistent refusals by the Biya regime to discuss the federal option, called for outright secession. The Anglophone secessionist movement has, however, maintained that its agenda is to achieve an independent Anglophone state through peaceful negotiations rather than force. This option is not facilitated by the resolute determination of the Francophone-dominated state to approach every attempt by Anglophone Cameroonians to draw attention to their predicaments in the manner of a workman whose only tool is a hammer and to whom every problem is a nail.[2]

Since the Biya government has continued to uphold the unitary state and dismissed the secessionist option, the Anglophone leadership has adopted two main strategies to achieve its aim. On the one hand, it is trying to gain international recognition for its cause. On the other hand, it is sensitizing the Anglophone population to its objectives and mobilizing it against the Francophone-dominated unitary state. Increasingly, given the Biya government's predictable high-handedness, even mainstream Francophone Cameroonians initially indifferent to or ignorant of the Anglophone condition are gradually waking up to the idea of an Anglophone problem in Cameroon, becoming sympathetic to it, and investing in understanding the merits of decentralization beyond political rhetoric.[3] Such consciousness reached a peak in late 2016 when protests by Anglophone teachers and lawyers disrupted the school year and the administration of justice and resulted in generalized protests in the two regions—a situation that attracted international condemnation.[4]

Our chapter shows why the prospects of Anglophone secession to succeed are rather bleak, despite some signs of promise. The relevant international organizations continue to favor territorial integrity, and the Francophone-dominated state has successfully employed divisive and repressive tactics to contain the Anglophone problem. One immediate consequence has been that Anglophone nationalists have resorted to less visible and controllable forms of protest and Anglophones in the Diaspora have taken to the Internet to promote their cause. However, it is unclear that this cybernationalism will have much impact, especially considering

---

[2] Anyangwe (2008, 2009) and Ndi (2014a, b).

[3] Gwaibi (2016).

[4] See, for example, http://www.iuaes.org/statement/letter_on_%20Cameroon.pdf, and http://www.rfi.fr/emission/20170219-comprendre-question-anglophone-cameroun (last accessed April 15, 2017).

the Internet blackout enforced by the government in the Anglophone regions since January 2017.[5] There are also multiple internal divisions among the leadership of the various Anglophone movements. One major fault line is the ethno-regional division between the South West Region (the coastal forest) and the inland savannah (the so-called Grassfields), today's North West Region. This questions not only the likelihood of separatism but undermines the goals of separatism should it be achieved.

This chapter is divided into five sections. The first provides an insight into the Anglophone problem, the second describes the Anglophone historical trajectory to secessionist claims in the political liberalization era, the third deals with the Anglophone leadership's struggle for international recognition of its secessionist stand, the fourth documents the leadership's sensitization and mobilization campaign. Finally, the fifth section explores the future prospects for Anglophone secessionist claims.

THE ANGLOPHONE PROBLEM

The roots of the so-called Anglophone problem[6] can be traced back to the partitioning between the French and British of the German Kamerun Protectorate (1884–1916) after the First World War, first as mandates under the League of Nations and then as trusts under the United Nations (UN). As a result, the British acquired two narrow and noncontiguous regions in the western part of the country bordering Nigeria. The southern part, which is the focus of our study, was named Southern Cameroons, and the northern part became known as Northern Cameroons.[7] Significantly, the British territory was much smaller than the French one, comprising only about 20% of the total area and population of the former German colony.

The partitioning of the territory into British and French spheres established the historical and spatial foundations for the construction of Anglophone and Francophone identities in the territory. The populations in each region came to see themselves as distinct communities defined by differences in language and inherited colonial traditions of education, law,

[5] Cameroon Anglophone Civil Society Consortium, https://www.ca-csc.org (last accessed April 14, 2017).

[6] cf. Konings and Nyamnjoh (1997, 2003), Eyoh (1998), Jua (2003), Anyangwe (2008, 2009), and Ndi (2014a, b).

[7] For the history of Northern Cameroons, see Le Vine (1964) and Welch (1966). Northern Cameroons voted in the 1961 plebiscite for integration into the Federation of Nigeria.

and public administration. While French Cameroon was incorporated into the French colonial empire as a distinct administrative unit separate from neighboring French Equatorial Africa, the British Cameroons was administered as an integral part of the Eastern Region of Nigeria. This led to the neglect of its socioeconomic development and the increasing of Nigerians, notably the Igbo, to Southern Cameroons, where they came to dominate the regional economy.[8] Britain intended to integrate Southern Cameroons into Nigeria, in spite of its distinct status as a trust territory.[9] The dominant position of the Igbo in the regional economy and administration was deeply resented by the local population and resulted in an explosive situation after the Second World War when regional politicians started exploiting the "Igbo scare" in nationalist struggles.[10] It was therefore not surprising that the nationalist struggles in Southern Cameroons had more of an anti-Nigerian than an anti-colonial character.

Southern Cameroonian nationalists decried their subordinate position in the British-Nigerian colonial system and the domination of the Igbo. They initially claimed a larger representation of the Southern Cameroonian elite in the Nigerian administration, and later regional autonomy. The British authorities gradually yielded to these demands. They granted Southern Cameroons a quasi-regional status and limited degree of self-government in 1954 and full regional status within the Federation of Nigeria in 1958.[11] Part of the Southern Cameroonian elite, organized by Dr. E.M.L. Endeley in the South West-based Kamerun National Congress (KNC) party consequently adopted a more positive view of Nigeria. From their perspective, regional status seemed a satisfactory answer to the problem of Nigerian domination, the lack of Southern Cameroonian participation in the Nigerian political system, and economic stagnation.

From the late 1940s onwards, the question of reunification had cropped up in the programs of various Southern Cameroonian pressure groups and newly created parties. This raised the possibility of an alternative option for Southern Cameroons to escape from its subordinate position in the colonial system and Igbo domination. A number of factors underpinned their reunification campaign. There was the emergence of the "Kamerun idea" among some members of the Southern Cameroonian elite and the belief

---

[8] Konings (2005a).
[9] Awasom (1998).
[10] Amazee (1990).
[11] Ngoh (2001).

that the period of German rule had created a Cameroon identity or nation.[12] It has been pointed out that irredentist feelings of one Cameroon under German administration hardly corresponded with reality since German colonial rule had been too short to create a Cameroonian identity among the territory's multiplicity of ethnic groups.[13] However Kofele-Kale argued that it was not the reality of the German experience but memories and myths (factual or otherwise) that inspired the Southern Cameroonian elite to start advocating reunification.[14] To strengthen their arguments, the elite referred to the close relationship between ethnic groups straddling the British-French Cameroon border. This boundary, they stressed, was regarded as an unnecessary inconvenience in the area because it restricted the free movement of people belonging to the same ethnic group.

The idea of reunification was much more popular among Francophones than among Anglophones.[15] Its loyal flag bearers were from the *Union des Populations du Cameroun* (UPC), the radical nationalist party in French Cameroon,[16] and among Francophone immigrants in Southern Cameroons who saw reunification principally as a way of removing their second-class citizenship and discrimination by the British Administering Authority.[17] Significantly, the Southern Cameroonian elite initially regarded the propagation of reunification as an effective strategy that would encourage the British administration to grant their territory either a larger measure of autonomy within the Nigerian Federation or separation from Nigeria altogether. Dr. Endeley's rejection of this idea in 1954 attests to the fact that it was not a genuine concern among the people. Even John Ngu Foncha, the leader of the North West-based Kamerun National Democratic Party (KNDP) which was championing reunification, had picked up the reunification idea merely as an electoral slogan to combat Endeley's new position. More importantly, he saw reunification not as an immediate goal but as an issue to be negotiated after the territory's separation from Nigeria and a period of continued trusteeship or independence. Besides being a slogan in Anglophone Cameroon, the idea of reunification had been rejected by the French colonial administration and most of the Francophone political elite.

[12] Welch (1966: 158–88) and Johnson (1970: 42).
[13] Ardener (1967), Chem-Langhëë and Njeuma (1980), and Ebai (2009).
[14] Kofele-Kale (1980).
[15] Awasom (2000).
[16] Joseph (1977) and Mbembe (1996).
[17] Amazee (1994) and Njeuma (1995).

With Nigeria approaching independence in 1960, the population of the British trust territory needed to decide on its own political future. The majority of Southern Cameroonians favored joining neither Nigeria nor Francophone Cameroon, which became independent in 1960 under the new name of the Republic of Cameroon. They wanted to form an independent state.[18] That this expressed wish was not honored must be attributed to two factors: first, internal divisions within the Anglophone political elite prevented them from rallying behind the majority option in the territory. Second, the United Nations (UN) refused, with the complicity of the British, to put the option of an independent Southern Cameroons state to the vote in the UN-organized plebiscite on February 11, 1961,[19] on the grounds that the creation of another tiny state was likely to contribute to a further "Balkanization" of Africa and economically unviable.[20] Three Southern Cameroonian parties—the Kamerun United Party (KUP) led by Paul Kale, the Cameroons Commoners' Congress (CCC) led by Chief Stephen Nyenti, and the Cameroons Indigenes Party (CIP) under Jesco Manga Williams—insisted on the inclusion of an independent Southern Cameroons state as a third plebiscite option. They sent several petitions to the UN and threatened to boycott the plebiscite, but they were unsuccessful.[21]

In the end, the majority of Southern Cameroonians voted for what they considered the lesser of two evils. Their vote in favor of reunification appeared to be more a rejection of continuous ties with Nigeria, which had proved detrimental to Southern Cameroonian development, than a vote for union with Francophone Cameroon, a territory with a different cultural heritage that was then involved in a violent civil war.[22] As Susungi observed, reunification was far from being the reunion of two prodigal sons who had been unjustly separated at birth but was more like a loveless UN-arranged marriage between two people who hardly knew each other.[23]

[18] Awasom (2000) and Konings and Nyamnjoh (2003).

[19] Percival (2008).

[20] The British had informed the United Nations that the Southern Cameroons would not be economically viable as an independent state. This was based on the Phillipson Report (1959) commissioned by the Foncha government in 1959.

[21] Ngoh (1990: 179–80).

[22] Joseph (1977).

[23] Susungi (1991); For similar ideas, see Victor Epie Ngome's excellent novel *What God Has Put Asunder* (1992).

The Anglophone elite had hoped to enter a loose federal union as a way of protecting their territory's minority status and cultural heritage.[24] The Francophone leadership, however, wanted a highly centralized, unitary state, and they were in a stronger position to impose their vision. The Republic of Cameroon was already a much larger newly independent state, and its leadership received strong support from the French during constitutional negotiations. The Anglophone leadership, in contrast, was virtually abandoned by the British, who deeply resented the Southern Cameroons option for reunification with Francophone Cameroon.[25]

During constitutional talks in July 1961, the Francophone leadership insisted on a centralized federation, which they regarded merely as a transitional phase toward the formation of a unitary state. Pierre Messmer,[26] one of the last French high commissioners in Cameroon and a close advisor to President Ahmadou Ahidjo, pointed out that he and others knew at the time that the so-called federal constitution provided merely a "sham federation," which was "safe for appearances, an annexation of West Cameroon" (the new name of the former Southern Cameroons).[27] The final version of the constitution was only approved by the Parliament of the Republic of Cameroon on September 1, 1961, just one month prior to reunification. For this reason, the present Anglophone movements declared in 1993 "the union between the Southern Cameroons and the Republic of Cameroon had proceeded without any constitutional basis."[28]

Under its new constitution, West Cameroon lost most of the limited autonomy it had enjoyed as part of the Nigerian federation.[29] A few months after reunification, President Ahidjo created a system of regional administration in which West Cameroon was designated as one of six regions, basically ignoring the country's federal system. Powerful federal inspectors headed the regions, who, in the case of West Cameroon, overshadowed the prime minister.[30] The West Cameroon government was fiscally dependent on the federal government, which was its major source of revenue.[31]

---

[24] Konings and Nyamnjoh (2003).
[25] Awasom (2000), Milne (1999: 432–48), and Gaillard (1994).
[26] Messmer (1998: 134–35).
[27] Anyangwe (2009).
[28] All Anglophone Conference (1993: 12).
[29] Ardener (1967) and Stark (1976).
[30] Stark (1976).
[31] Benjamin (1972).

To achieve his objective of integrating the Anglophone minority into a strongly centralized, unitary state, Ahidjo used several tactics. One was to play Anglophone political factions off against each other and eventually integrate them into a single party, the Cameroon National Union (CNU). Another was to eliminate from positions of power any Anglophone leaders who remained committed to federalism, replacing them with others who favored a unitary state. Ahidjo also created "clients" among the Anglophone elite, granting top positions in federal institutions and the single party to representatives of significant ethnic and regional groups in the Anglophone region. Finally, he did not stop short of using repressive force. Ahidjo finally abolished the federation in 1972, directly contravening constitutional provisions. His justification for this "glorious revolution" was that federalism fostered regionalism and impeded economic development.

A growing number of Anglophones were, however, inclined to attribute the emergence of regionalism and the lack of economic development not to federalism *per se* but to the hegemonic tendencies of the Francophone-dominated state. For them, the nation-state project after reunification was driven by the firm determination of the Francophone political elite to dominate the Anglophone minority and erase the cultural and institutional foundations of Anglophone identity.[32] Several studies have shown that Anglophones have regularly been relegated to inferior positions in the national decision-making process and have been constantly underrepresented in ministerial as well as senior- and middle-management positions in the administration, the military, and parastatals.[33] There is also general agreement that Anglophones have been exposed to a carefully considered policy aimed at eroding their language and institutions. Low socioeconomic development of the Anglophone region stands in contrast to its rich agricultural potential and its oil resources. Oil revenues were alleged to have been used by those in power to feed "the bellies" of their allies[34] and to stimulate the economy in other regions. Among the Anglophone population, this created feelings of being recolonized and marginalized in all spheres of public life and thus of being citizens in their own country.

---

[32] Eyoh (1998).
[33] Kofele-Kale (1986) and Takougang and Krieger (1998).
[34] Bayart (1989).

To reduce the danger of united Anglophone action against the Francophone-dominated state, Ahidjo decided, after the "revolution" of May 20, 1972, to divide the Anglophone territory into the South West and North West Provinces (subsequently renamed) Regions. When making this decision, he was well aware of the internal contradictions within the Anglophone community between the coastal-forest people in the south and the Grassfields people in the north. A major reason for these was the transfer of political power from the South West to the North West elite at the end of the 1950s. Following this, the North West elite began to assert its newly acquired position of power, something that soon became ubiquitous in higher levels of government and in senior nongovernmental positions. They took up for themselves the top jobs and best lands in the South West, causing resentment among southwesterners.[35] Another root for this divide was the 1961 UN plebiscite when the South West showed considerable sympathy for alignment with Nigeria, while the choice for Cameroon prevailed, mainly on the strength of the northwestern votes. A final source of tension was the massive labor migration from the North West to southwestern plantations and the subsequent settlement of northwestern workers in the South West.[36]

Lack of unity and growing repression precluded the Anglophone elite from openly expressing its grievances about Francophone domination until 1982 when Paul Biya took power. Following the limited degree of liberalization introduced by the new president,[37] the Anglophone elite began to voice their long-standing grievances.[38] There was vehement Anglophone protest when the new president changed the country's official name from the "United Republic of Cameroon" to simply the "Republic of Cameroon" in February 1984. The new name was not only similar to that of independent Francophone Cameroon prior to reunification but also appeared to ignore the fact that the Cameroonian state was composed of two distinct entities. In Anglophone circles, Biya's unilateral name change gave rise to two interpretations: some Anglophones considered this action as the boldest step yet taken toward their assimilation and disappearance as a distinct founding community. For them, the new name was clear evidence that, as far as Biya was concerned, the Anglophone territory and its people had

---

[35] Kofele-Kale (1981) and Rowlands (1993).
[36] Konings (2001).
[37] Takougang and Krieger (1998).
[38] Konings and Nyamnjoh (2003).

become an indistinguishable part of the former Republic of Cameroon, fulfilling Ahidjo's designs for absorbing and assimilating the Anglophone minority into the Francophone-dominated state.[39] Other Anglophones argued that, by this action, *La République du Cameroun* had unilaterally seceded from the union and thus lacked any constitutional base from which to continue ruling the former Southern Cameroons.[40] They are inclined to appeal to the UN to assist its former trust territory in peacefully separating from *La République*.[41] Fon Gorji Dinka, the eminent Anglophone lawyer and first president of the Cameroon Bar Association, first expressed this view. On March 10, 1985, Dinka addressed a memorandum to Paul Biya entitled "The New Social Order,"[42] in which he declared the Biya government to be unconstitutional and called for Southern Cameroons to become independent and be renamed the Republic of Ambazonia.[43] Dinka was arrested and imprisoned without trial until January 1986, which earned him the status of martyr for the Anglophone cause.

The Biya government stepped up repression in a situation of deepening economic and political crisis during the 1980s, and it was only after political liberalization set in during the early 1990s that Anglophones openly started to organize in defense of their interests.

POLITICAL LIBERALIZATION AND THE ANGLOPHONE MOVEMENT'S STRUGGLE FOR SECESSION

Anglophones have not only played a leading role in accomplishing political liberalization in Cameroon but have also used the liberalization of political space to create or reactivate various organizations to represent

[39] Biya (1987), Nyamnjoh and Akum (2008).

[40] Reference to the incumbent regime as the government of *La République du Cameroun*, the name adopted by Francophone Cameroon at independence, has become a key signifier in the replotting of the nation's constitutional history as a progressive consolidation of the recolonization of Anglophone Cameroon by the post-colonial Francophone-dominated state. See Eyoh (1998: 264).

[41] Anyangwe (2008).

[42] "The New Social Order" by Fon Gorji Dinka, March 20, 1985, reproduced in Mukong (1990: 98–99).

[43] The name is derived from Ambas Bay at the foot of Mount Cameroon, which was the area of permanent British settlement in the present-day Anglophone region. In 1858, the British Baptist missionary, Alfred Saker, purchased land from the King of Bimbia and became the de facto governor of the small colony of Victoria that was named after the British Queen. See Ardener (1968).

their interests. Given Anglophone frustration with the Francophone-dominated state, it is not surprising that the country's first opposition party the Social Democratic Front (SDF) emerged in 1990 in Bamenda, the capital of North West Region. Its chairman was John Fru Ndi who enjoyed widespread popularity among the urban masses because of his courage and populist style of leadership.[44] A massive rally to launch the SDF on May 26, 1990, ended in the deaths of six young Anglophones.[45] Anglophone students at the University of Yaoundé, who demonstrated in support of the SDF and political liberalization on the same day, were falsely accused by the regime of having marched in favor of the reintegration of Anglophone Cameroonians into Nigeria and of singing the Nigerian national anthem and raising the Nigerian flag.[46] Anglophones were called "Biafrans" and "enemies in the house" and the Minister of Territorial Administration, Ibrahim Mbombo Njoya, suggested they should "go elsewhere." Indignant at his own party's behavior, John Ngu Foncha, the principal Anglophone architect of the federal state, resigned as the Cameroon People's Democratic Movement (CPDM's) first vice-president in June 1990. He lamented that the provisions that had protected Anglophones in the 1961 federal constitution had been discarded and their voices drowned out, while the rule of the gun had replaced the dialogue that Anglophones so cherished.[47]

Under considerable internal and external pressure, the Biya government eventually introduced a measure of political liberalization. In December 1990, it declared multipartyism as well as a degree of freedom in mass communication, association, and the holding of public meetings and demonstrations. As a result, several political parties, associations, pressure groups, and private newspapers were established in Anglophone Cameroon. SDF's influence spread from North West Region to South West Region, soon becoming the major opposition party in Anglophone Cameroon. The South West elite nevertheless continued to be suspicious of the aspirations of SDF leaders, fearing renewed North West domination.

The leaders of the SDF helped turn the Anglophone region into a hot-bed of rebellion, leading to several fierce confrontations with the regime

[44] Krieger (2008).
[45] Nyamnjoh (2005).
[46] Konings (2002).
[47] Konings and Nyamnjoh (2003: 77–78).

in power.[48] Biya's self-declared victory in the October 1992 presidential elections was a traumatic experience in Anglophone Cameroon and resulted in violent protests against the "theft of Fru Ndi's victory" throughout North West Region. Despite its contribution to Anglophone consciousness and action, the party began presenting itself as a national rather than as an Anglophone party. This was evidenced by its growing membership of Bamileke who live in the Francophone part of the Grassfields and are ethnically related to groups in North West Region. Since the SDF adopted a half-hearted stand toward the Anglophone problem,[49] Anglophone interests came to be first and foremost represented by associations and pressure groups created and reactivated by the Anglophone elite with the introduction of political liberalization in 1990. Some of them, such as the Free West Cameroon Movement (FWCM) and the Ambazonian Movement (AM) of Fon Gorji Dinka, advocated outright secession. Most, however, initially championed a return to the federal state, especially the Cameroon Anglophone Movement (CAM). This was the only Anglophone association operating legally in the country and the most important Anglophone pressure group for some time. In addition to these associations aiming to represent broad-based Anglophone interests, numerous other associations representing specialized interest groups have emerged, along with intellectuals, journalists, and church leaders championing the Anglophone agenda.[50]

A major challenge to the Francophone-dominated state was the All Anglophone Conference (AAC). It was held in Buea, the former capital of Southern Cameroons, on April 2–3, 1993, "for the purpose of adopting a common Anglophone stand on constitutional reform and of examining several other matters relating to its welfare of ourselves, our posterity, our territory and the entire Cameroon nation."[51] Its conveners were the four Anglophone members of a committee that was to determine the outline of a new constitution in accordance with the resolutions of the Tripartite Conference held between October 30 and November 18, 1991. Three members, Benjamin Itoe, Simon Munzu, and Sam Ekontang Elad came from South West Region, while the fourth, Carlson Anyangwe, was the only northwesterner in the group. The AAC turned out to be a landmark in the

---

[48] Mbu (1993).
[49] Konings (2004).
[50] Konings and Nyamnjoh (2003: 142–48).
[51] All Anglophone Conference (1993: 8).

history of Anglophone Cameroon. It brought together more than 5000 members of the Anglophone elite and all the Anglophone associations and organizations were represented. After two days of deliberations, the conference issued the Buea Declaration listing the multiple Anglophone grievances about Francophone domination. It called for a return to the federal form of government, arguing the cultural differences between Anglophones and Francophones had not been bridged more than 30 years after reunification.

The AAC emerged as the leading Anglophone association and became responsible for the representation of Anglophone interests in general. All existing and newly emerging Anglophone associations became auxiliary organizations of the AAC and under its umbrella they continued to carry out their own specific responsibilities. They were represented in the 65-member Anglophone Standing Committee created by the AAC, which submitted a draft federal constitution to the Biya government on May 27, 1993.[52] This was simply ignored by the regime and, in a series of interviews in Cameroon and France, Biya stated that federalism was inappropriate for a country like Cameroon.

The government's persistent refusal to enter into negotiations on the federal option created a growing radicalization among the Anglophone movements. The Bamenda Proclamation adopted by the AAC II, which was held in Bamenda from April 29 to May 1, 1994, stipulated: "should the government either persist in its refusal to engage in meaningful constitutional talks or fail to engage in such talks *within a reasonable time*," the Anglophone Council should "proclaim the revival of the independence and sovereignty of the Anglophone territory and take all measures necessary to secure, defend and preserve the independence, sovereignty and integrity of the said country."[53] After the AAC II, the Anglophone movements provocatively reintroduced the name of Southern Cameroons when referring to the Anglophone territory to "make it clear that our struggles are neither of an essentially linguistic character nor in defense of an alien colonial culture...but are aimed at the restoration of the autonomy of the former Southern Cameroons which has been annexed by *La République du Cameroun*."[54] The Anglophone movements' umbrella organization was subsequently named the Southern Cameroons National Council (SCNC).

---

[52] Konings (1999).

[53] All Anglophone Conference (1994).

[54] See SCNC press release reprinted in Cameroon Post, August 16–23, 1994: 3. See also Anyangwe (2008).

The Biya government continued its refusal of the federal proposal and pushed the SCNC to consider the possibility of outright secession. The SCNC leadership consequently set October 1, 1996, as the date to declare the independence of Southern Cameroons. However, nothing happened on that day except an "Independence Day" address by the new SCNC chairman, Ambassador (retired) Henry Fossung, who called upon Southern Cameroonians to use their national day as a "day of prayer," asking God "to save us from political bondage." He reiterated that independence was "irreversible and non-negotiable."[55]

After embracing a secessionist stand, the SCNC adopted the motto "the force of argument, and not the argument of force." This emphasized their pursuit of independence for Southern Cameroons through peaceful negotiation and not through armed struggle. Given the Francophone-dominated state's unitary approach to the post-colonial nation-state project and its condemnation of any secessionist claims, the SCNC leadership developed two strategies for the peaceful establishment of Southern Cameroons: to seek international recognition and to sensitize and mobilize the Anglophone population.

SEEKING INTERNATIONAL RECOGNITION

The SCNC leadership has made strenuous efforts to gain formal international recognition of the Anglophone cause through diplomatic and legal channels.[56] Only the most important undertakings are mentioned here. On May 19, 1995, the SCNC sent a nine-man delegation to the UN in New York. This included two of the main Anglophone architects of reunification, John Ngu Foncha and Solomon Tandeng Muna. This mission was to file a petition against "the annexation of the Southern Cameroons by *La République du Cameroun* and to commit the international community to the Southern Cameroons" and search for a peaceful solution to head off the dangerous conflict that was brewing between *La République du Cameroun* and Southern Cameroons.[57] After this mission, the SCNC delegation stated that following the Republic of Cameroon's unilateral secession from the union in 1984, the Southern Cameroons

---

[55] Cameroon Post, October 8–14, 1996 and The Witness, November 12–18, 1996.
[56] Konings and Nyamnjoh (2003) and Anyefru 2010).
[57] See SCNC, "Petition against the Annexation of the Southern Cameroons." Buea, May 1995 (mimeo).

question was no longer an internal problem of *La République du Cameroun* since there were now two distinct de facto entities that were no longer bound by any legal or constitutional ties, with Southern Cameroons having reverted to its pre-independence situation, that is, as a UN Trust Territory.[58] In these circumstances, Southern Cameroons demanded that the UN terminate its annexation to *La République du Cameroun* and grant full independence to its Trust Territory, in accordance with Article 76 of the UN Charter. It was only after gaining full independence that Southern Cameroons would enter into negotiations with *La République du Cameroun* on future constitutional and bilateral links under the auspices of the UN.

The various missions by Anglophone leaders to the UN contributed to a growing awareness of the Anglophone problem in UN circles. There is sufficient evidence that UN leaders had become increasingly concerned about the possible outbreak of another violent ethno-regional conflict in West-Central Africa, but they appear not to have supported SCNC secessionist claims. During his visit to Cameroon in May 2000, then UN Secretary-General Kofi Annan pleaded for dialogue between Francophone and Anglophone leaders, and at a press conference shortly before leaving Cameroon, he said:

> I leave Cameroon with the impression that there is only one Cameroon, multilingual and multi-ethnic. I encourage a dialogue of these stakeholders. In every country there are problems of marginalization. The way it has to be solved is by dialogue and not by walking away.[59]

The SCNC has since then succeeded in approaching the UN through an intermediary channel. In 2004, it became a member of the Unrepresented Nations and Peoples Organization (UNPO)in The Hague, an international organization of "nations, peoples and minorities striving for recognition and protection of their identity, culture, human rights and their environment."[60] The organization provides a legitimate and established international forum for members to present their grievances at an international level and through the UNPO, SCNC leaders have been able to address certain UN organs regarding the plight of Anglophones. For

[58] SCNC, "The London Communiqué." London, June 22, 1995 (mimeo).
[59] See "Annan Ends African Tour, Seeks Cameroon Dialogue" on sncforum website, May 4, 2000.
[60] See http://www.unpo.org

example, in 2005 Anglophone leaders made a first representation to the 61st session of the United Nations Commission on Human Rights (UNCHR).[61]

SCNC leaders also engaged in intensive lobbying to forestall the Republic of Cameroon's admission to the Commonwealth and to instead file an application for Commonwealth membership for Southern Cameroons. However, on October 16, 1995, the Republic of Cameroon was admitted into the Commonwealth. The SCNC denounced the decision and blamed Britain for its "second treachery" toward the Southern Cameroons cause. The SCNC then pleaded for a Quebec-style referendum on independence for Southern Cameroons and for separate Commonwealth membership.[62] The decision by the Nigerian and Cameroonian governments to submit their dispute over the oil-rich peninsula of Bakassi to the International Court of Justice (ICJ) for adjudication in 1994 offered Anglophone leaders the opportunity to assess the legality of their defense of Southern Cameroons statehood.[63] They claimed that Bakassi was neither a part of Cameroon nor a part of Nigeria, but that it belonged to Southern Cameroons.[64]

In 2001, the Southern Cameroons People's Organization (SCAPO) was formed under the banner of the SCNC, with the specific goal of pursuing legal avenues to address "the claims of the peoples of Southern Cameroons to self-determination and independence from *La République du Cameroun*." It soon filed a lawsuit against the Nigerian government in the Federal High Court in Abuja for its continuing disregard of the statehood and sovereignty of Southern Cameroons.[65]

In March 2002, SCAPO felt they scored a major victory when the Nigerian Federal High Court ruled that "the Federal Republic of Nigeria shall be compelled to place before the ICJ and the UN General Assembly and ensure diligent persecution to the conclusion the claims of the people of Southern Cameroons to self-determination and their declaration of independence." It also placed a permanent injunction restraining "the government of the Federal Republic of Nigeria from treating the Southern

---

[61] Anyefru (2010: 94–99) and Nfor (2016).
[62] Konings and Nyamnjoh (2003: 96–99).
[63] Jua and Konings (2004), Gumne (2006), and Anyefru (2010).
[64] Kinni (2013).
[65] Jua and Konings (2004: 624).

Cameroons and all the people of the territory as an integral part of *La República du Cameroun*."[66] This ruling was considered by the Anglophone leadership as a significant step toward international recognition of the Anglophone secessionist claims. However, Nigeria had a vested interest in the court's ruling considering the Bakassi case at the ICJ. This became obvious when the Nigerian Federal High Court ordered the Nigerian government to ask the ICJ to rule on whether it was Southern Cameroons or the Republic of Cameroon that shared a maritime boundary with the Federal Republic of Nigeria.

This victory inspired the SCNC and SCAPO to start another legal action at African Union (AU) level. They made a formal complaint against the Republic of Cameroon to the African Commission on Human and Peoples' Rights (ACHPR) in Banjul in 2003.[67] It claimed that Anglophones were a "separate and distinct" people who deserved not only the right to development but also to self-government.

In its 2009 ruling, the ACHPR affirmed Anglophone grievances against the Biya government and recognized Southern Cameroons as a distinct "people," but it did not support Southern Cameroons secessionist claims. It was bound by Article 4(b) of the AU's Constitutive Act that calls for respect of existing borders at the time of independence. Consequently, it recommended "comprehensive national dialogue."[68]

The SCNC has also failed to enlist the support of Cameroon's former colonial masters in its secessionist claims.[69] Generally speaking, France has continued to support the Francophone-dominated regime in Cameroon. Paris regarded the growing popularity of the Anglophone movements as detrimental to French interests in Cameroon: they fuelled existing anti-French sentiments and threatened its stake in the oil industry in Anglophone Cameroon. While the British government has shown more sympathy than France for the Anglophone cause, it has consistently rejected the SCNC's secessionist claims.[70]

---

[66] Jua and Konings (2004: 624–25).
[67] Dicklitch (2010).
[68] Ebai (2009).
[69] Konings and Nyamnjoh (2003: 99–101).
[70] See Star Headlines, 19 March 2006, "The British Government Condemns Anglophone Secession."

SENSITIZING AND MOBILIZING THE ANGLOPHONE POPULATION

From the start, the Anglophone leadership made considerable efforts to transform Anglophone organizations from elitist movements into mass movements. To this end, the leadership of the various Anglophone movements organized frequent meetings and rallies, strikes, demonstrations, and boycotts. Some of these were directed at the myths and symbols of the unitary state. For example, Anglophone nationalists have refused to recognize the government's designation of May 20, the date of the inauguration of the unitary state in 1972, as the country's national day. Since the early 1990s, they have boycotted these celebrations, declaring it a "Day of Mourning" and a "Day of Shame." They have also indicted the regime for declaring February 11, the day of the 1961 plebiscite, as Youth Day, seeing the continued failure of the government to highlight the historical significance of this day as a conscious attempt to reconfigure the nation's history. They have therefore called upon the Anglophone population to mark February 11 as the "Day of the Plebiscite" and October 1 as the "Day of Independence" as alternative days of national celebration. Anglophone activists have attempted to hoist federation, UN, or independent Southern Cameroons flags on these days, but the security forces usually challenged their attempts.

The Anglophone leadership's sensitization campaign was quite successful between 1992 and 1995. A sense of euphoria spread through Anglophone Cameroonians when the SCNC delegation returned from its mission to the UN in 1995. At rallies attended by large crowds in various Anglophone towns, the delegation displayed a huge UN flag, claiming it had received it from the UN itself to show that Southern Cameroons was still a UN trust territory, and that independence was only a matter of time.[71]

From 1996 to late 2016, however, the Anglophone leadership's campaign lost its momentum. Following the resignation of the founding fathers of the SCNC, the new leadership under its Chairman Henry Fossung appeared incapable of devising a strategy to counteract the government's increasingly divisive and repressive tactics. Given this leadership problem and the government's persistent reluctance to enter into negotiations, a conflict developed within the Anglophone movements between the doves—those who continued to adhere to a negotiated separation

---

[71] Jua and Konings (2004).

from *La République du Cameroun*—and the hawks—those who had concluded that the independence of Southern Cameroons could only be achieved through armed struggle. The Southern Cameroons Youth League (SCYL), in particular, opted for the latter strategy, as is manifest in its motto: "The argument of force."

The SCYL emerged in the mid-1990s as one of the many Anglophone associations operating under the umbrella of the SCNC. Composed of "young people who do not see any future for themselves and would prefer to die fighting than continue to submit to the fate imposed on Southern Cameroons by *La République du Cameroun*,"[72] the Biya government quickly judged the SCYL as the most dangerous Anglophone movement. The government's reaction to an ill-planned SCYL attack on military and civil establishments in North West Region between March 27 and March 31, 1997, was ruthless. Several local men and women were killed, tortured, raped, arrested, or forced into exile. Some SCYL members died while in prison, and others were not brought to trial until they were charged with criminal offences in 1999. Realizing that their organization lacked the necessary weapons and training to engage in guerrilla warfare against the large and well-equipped Cameroonian armed forces, SCYL leaders resorted to less easily controlled forms of action, in particular, the use of the Internet and the organization of symbolic actions.

Following the 1997 revolt, the SCNC leadership appeared less inclined to sensitize and mobilize the Anglophone population, leading to a general lethargy and internal divisions among the leadership. With a sense of despair, Justice Frederick Alobwede Ebong, chairman of the SCNC's High Command Council, took over the Cameroon Radio and Television (CRTV) station in Buea on December 30, 1999, proclaiming the restoration of the independence of the Federal Republic of Southern Cameroons (FRSC). He was subsequently detained in Yaoundé. At an SCNC meeting on April 1, 2000, Ebong was nominated as chairman of the SCNC and the first head of state of the FRSC.

With a view to endowing the FRSC with all the attributes of statehood as well as guaranteeing state continuity, the FRSC Constituent Assembly meeting in Bamenda in May 2000 adopted resolutions on a coat of arms, a flag, and a national anthem.[73] These developments gave new impetus to the Anglophone struggle. After years of vehement con-

---

[72] Konings (2005b: 176).
[73] The Post, November 13, 2000: 3.

flict about policies and strategies, four of the major Anglophone organizations, namely the SCNC, the SCYL, the AM, and the Southern
Cameroons Restoration Movement (SCARM),[74] agreed to form an
alliance to achieve the independence of the territory of the ex-British
Southern Cameroons in 2001. At a summit in Washington in June
2001, representatives of the territory adopted the so-called Washington
Proclamation of the Statehood of the ex-British Southern Cameroons,
"confirming the declaration of separate independence already made by
Justice Ebong in Buea on December 30, 1999," and decided to set up
the British Southern Cameroons Provisional Administration.[75]

Under its subsequent leadership, the SCNC has done much to reignite
its secessionist ambitions,[76] which have received a boost from protesting
lawyers and teachers that commenced in late 2016. Chief Ayamba Ette
Otun succeeded Henry Fossung as national chairman of the SCNC. When
the chief died in June 2014, Ayah Paul Abine, allegedly elected in absentia
in December 2014, was supposed to succeed him as national chairman. It
is unclear whether he accepted the role, as he declined to say much on the
matter in an interview sometime in January 2015 in which he discussed his
appointment as advocate-general of the Cameroon Supreme Court.[77] In
relation to this appointment, people wondered whether he was betraying
the SCNC or opting to work from within as he has publicly questioned
the legality of reunification. In a later interview with the *Recorder
Newspaper* in April 2015, Abine defended his reluctance to accept SCNC
leadership. In the interview, he asserted that he is not even a member of
the SCNC.[78] However, the fact that Ayah Paul Abine was arrested and
detained in connection with the 2016–2017 protests by Anglophone lawyers and teachers indicated that the Francophone-dominated state that
appointed him to the Supreme Court does not trust that he has severed
whatever links he may have had with the SCNC prior to his appointment.

---

[74] SCARM was the successor of the Cameroon Anglophone Movement (CAM), which was
originally the most important Anglophone movement.

[75] See "British Southern Cameroons Summit, Resolutions." Washington, June 17, 2001
(mimeo); and "Washington Proclamation of the Statehood of Ex-British Southern
Cameroons." Washington, June 17, 2001 (mimeo).

[76] Nfor (2016).

[77] See http://bamendaonline.net/blog/hon-ayah-speaks-out-after-supreme-court-
appointment/ (last accessed April 2015).

[78] See http://www.cameroonvoice.com/news/article-news-18398.html (last accessed
April 15, 2017).

Judging from his writings[79] and a press release[80] by the SCNC commenting on the 2016–2017 civil unrest and government repression signed by him, Nfor Ngala Nfor is the current chairman of the SCNC.[81]

Anglophone Cameroonians in the diaspora are playing an important role in the SCNC sensitization and mobilization campaign. They have contributed financially for the Anglophone movements' activities and promoted online activism at times when Anglophone voices critical of the government have been largely silenced in Cameroon.[82] They are maintaining a plethora of websites such as the homepages of the SCNC, the SCYL, the AM, and the FRSC. Their online activities, however, clearly demonstrate the considerable differences in their political agendas and ideologies, which have resulted in very little cooperation between the various cyber communities.

Prospects for Anglophone Secessionist Claims

The SCNC has, in recent years, continued to adhere to its two-pronged strategy to seek international recognition and to sensitize and mobilize the Anglophone population. Having opted for a peaceful solution of the "Anglophone problem," the SCNC leadership has persistently argued that the Anglophone rights to self-determination and autonomy had been disregarded in national and international law. Consequently, it has been in the habit of blaming the UN, the ex-colonial masters, and the Cameroonian post-colonial regime for this situation.

The Anglophone movements have booked several successes in their attempts to gain international recognition of their secessionist claims and in their regional sensitization and mobilization campaign. Nevertheless, the prospects for their ultimate aim, that is, the independence of Southern Cameroons, presently appear bleak. In addition to the fact that the principal international organizations, like the UN, the Commonwealth and the AU, are inclined to reject secessionist claims on the grounds of their respect for the sovereignty and integrity of member states, there are a number of other factors that are hampering Anglophone chances of success. These include the Cameroonian government's persistent refusal to

---

[79] Nfor (2016).
[80] January 2017.
[81] See https://www.facebook.com/scncsoutherncameroonsnationalcouncil/posts/592013517662909 (last accessed April 2015).
[82] Jua and Konings (2004), Nyamnjoh (2005), and Anyefru (2008).

negotiate with secessionist movements and its tactics to contain the Anglophone danger as well as the internal divisions among the Anglophone leadership and the elite.

The Biya government has managed to neutralize the Anglophone movements by employing divide-and-rule tactics, co-opting ethno-regional leaders into the regime, and the use of severe repression in some cases. Its main strategy has been to divide the Anglophone elite by capitalizing on existing rivalries between the South West and North West elites. Seeing themselves as having suffered in the distribution of state power, the South West elite have been inclined to see more political capital in the promotion of regional identity and organization than in working to consolidate an Anglophone identity and organization.[83] The government has found it increasingly worthwhile to tempt the South West elite away from Anglophone solidarity with strategic appointments and the idea that the North West elite rather than the Francophone-dominated state is their primary enemy.[84] Following the 1996 constitution that provided state protection to autochthonous minorities, it became instrumental in cementing an alliance between the South West elite and the ethnically related Francophone coastal elite. The so-called Sawa movement is an alliance that transcends the Francophone-Anglophone divide.[85] It is further argued that even if secession were to become a reality, the internal contradictions would actually undermine the desired outcome of socio-spatial and political autonomy.[86]

In addition to its divisive strategies, the government has enhanced its repressive tactics after the SCNC's adoption of a secessionist program. It is worth noting that the SCNC pattern of pursuing international recognition on Anglophone marginalization has always involved detailed accounts of the gross human rights abuse by the Republic of Cameroon.[87] In October and November 2016, Anglophone lawyers and teachers engaged in strike action around the Anglophone problem. However, they were met with heavy-handed repression.[88] In the wake of civil unrest brought about

---

[83] Nyamnjoh and Rowlands (1998).

[84] Eyoh (1998), Mbile (2000), and Fonchingong (2005).

[85] Geschiere and Nyamnjoh (2000), Konings and Nyamnjoh (2003).

[86] Awoh and Nkwi (2015).

[87] Anyefru (2010), and Nfor (2016).

[88] See Cameroon Concord, http://cameroon-concord.com/headlines/item/7265-cameroon-lawyers-protest-police-injure-dozens-raid-law-offices-american-diplomat-steps-in (last accessed April 14, 2017).

by the aforementioned strike action, the government enforced an Internet ban in the two Anglophone regions on January 17, 2017. This ban remains in force as we submit the revised version of this chapter (April 14, 2017). The Cameroon Anglophone Civil Society Consortium maintains that the Internet blackout serves to undermine the spread of information regarding human rights violations that include extrajudicial killings, as well as arbitrary abduction and detention.[89]

The Anglophone secessionist stand is not only strongly opposed by the Biya regime but also faces a great deal of resistance in the Anglophone community itself. While most Anglophones tend to support the Anglophone movements' grievances about Francophone domination, they are deeply divided over which path to take to resolve the problem. Besides the Anglophone movements advocating peaceful secession with an agreement about the sharing of assets, there are a considerable number in the Anglophone elite who favor federalism, albeit with differing views on the number of states. Since the 1996 constitution, the Cameroonian government appeared to be willing to concede to a certain degree of decentralization. As a consequence, pro-government Anglophone voices that are in favor of decentralization based on the country's ten existing regions have emerged.

There are clear differences within and between the various Anglophone movements. Since the founding fathers (Sam Ekontang Elad, Simon Munzu, and Carlson Anyangwe) resigned from the SCNC leadership, growing factionalization has plagued the organization. At times, the leaders appear to be more concerned with contesting each other's position of power than promoting the Anglophone cause. Currently, there are at least four factions in the SCNC, with each one claiming to be authentic.[90] Chief Ayamba Ette Otun from the Manyu Division in South West Region chairs the main faction, but because of his advancing age and relatively low level of education, the real holder of power is its North West Vice-President Nfor Ngala Nfor. Curiously, the Biya government has created its own SCNC faction to counter the Southern Cameroons struggle. This pro-government faction is led by Chief Isaac Oben, another chief from the Manyu Division, and was rewarded by the regime for trying to challenge the SCAPO representation during the ACHPR sessions in Banjul.

---

[89] See https://www.ca-csc.org (last accessed April 2017).
[90] Owono (2010).

There has also been a lot of infighting over the control of the SCNC's relatively scarce financial resources. Apart from the traditional financial contributions from the diaspora, some among the SCNC leadership seem to have devised another income-generating activity. They offer (allegedly for money) Cameroonian emigrants, regardless of whether they have actually participated in the Anglophone struggles, certificates claiming they are SCNC activists in order to make them eligible for political asylum in the host countries. Nfor Ngala Nfor and one of his lieutenants, Prince Mbinglo Hitler, have regularly been accused by other SCNC leaders of having appropriated part of the organization's income for personal use.[91]

In addition, there are regular problems of disunity among the Anglophone organizations and a certain ambiguity in their objectives. Subsidiary organizations are developing objectives and strategies different from those of the SCNC, the umbrella organization. Although most of them nowadays champion the independence of Southern Cameroons, some appear never to have altogether dropped the idea of the return to a federal state.

With their tendency to make the entire Francophone community responsible for the Anglophone predicament, the Anglophone movements have alienated the Francophones who had shown sympathy for their cause. It must, however, be admitted that Francophone sympathizers with the Anglophone struggles form only a tiny minority group among the Francophone population. The majority of the population is inclined to deny the very existence of an "Anglophone problem" and strongly condemns any Anglophone agitation. Two factors appear to be largely responsible for this situation. First, most Francophones have no idea what Anglophones are complaining about. They often stress that some Francophone regions are more marginalized than the Anglophone region and that there are close links between the ethnic groups on both sides of the Anglophone-Francophone divide that transcend any Anglophone-Francophone cleavage. Second, Francophones are constantly exposed to their leadership's official pronouncements in defense of the unitary state and hostile reactions toward the Anglophone movements.

The predominantly hostile Francophone attitude tends to reinforce mutual distrust, suspicion, and stereotypes. Francophone scholars and politicians tend to attribute the emergence of Anglophone nationalism in the public sphere to the mobilization efforts of a few discontented elites

[91] Owono 2010).

who were denied a place at the "dining table" during political liberaliza-tion.[92] Their explanation in terms of opportunist entrepreneurs in search of a political market comes close to the government position on Anglophone nationalism.

Given all those grave obstacles to the achievement of an independent Southern Cameroons state, there are growing doubts in Anglophone Cameroon that the SCNC's secessionist claims will ever be realized. One desperate SCNC member has made the following complaint to the authors: "With no money, no foreign support, no arms, little grassroots support and most of the fighting and activism taking place on the Internet instead of on the ground, are we not wasting our time?"

CONCLUSION

The Anglophone call for secession and the concomitant establishment of an independent state has a long history. It appears to have been the most popular option in Southern Cameroons in the period preceding reunifica-tion, but the local population was never given the chance to vote for it in the 1961 plebiscite. The Anglophone call for secession reemerged in the mid-1980s when a prominent Anglophone chief and lawyer, Fon Gorji Dinka, demanded the immediate promulgation of an independent Anglophone state, which he called the Republic of Ambazonia.

Anglophone movements renewed this call during political liberalization in the early 1990s, but unlike the pre-reunification period, the renewed pursuit of an independent state was initially a minority option, with most Anglophone movements striving for the return to a federal state. It was not until the Biya government refused to discuss the federal option that the leadership of the Anglophone movements started championing the separa-tion between Anglophone and Francophone Cameroon into two sovereign states. It was envisaged that this kind of peaceful separation could be accompanied by an equitable sharing of assets and liabilities and be sup-ported by the establishment of other cross-border confidence-building institutions. Most of the leaders of the Anglophone movements now agree that this solution holds the best chance for peace in the long run because any attempts to engage belatedly in democratic and institutional reforms just to placate Anglophones and preserve international appearances will only postpone the day of reckoning and prolong the misery.

---

[92] Sindjoun (1995), Ndjana (1996), Nkoum-Me-Ntseny (1999), and Owono (2010).

The question, however, remains as to whether there is sufficient support for the Anglophone secessionist call. Contrasting their leadership's claim of widespread regional support, we found evidence that many among the Anglophone elite favor a form of federation.[93] Even some SCNC leaders, like the late John Ngu Foncha and Solomon Tandeng Muna, who were Anglophone architects of reunification, appear never to have abandoned their federalist ideal although they continued to support the SCNC line for strategic reasons.

It is unlikely that the Anglophone movements' call for an independent Southern Cameroons state will receive any support from the Francophone leadership and the international community. The majority of the Francophones are clearly in favor of a decentralized unitary state and are determined to keep control of Anglophone Cameroon's rich natural resources in an area that has become the country's breadbasket and the source of considerable oil wealth. Nigeria handing over the final parts of Bakassi to Cameroon on August 14, 2008, and the October 2012 announcement by the China Petroleum and Chemical Corporation that it has discovered new oil and gas resources in the Bakassi region, would seem to have cemented this stance for the foreseeable future.

Anglophone initiatives for international recognition offer little prospect of success. International organizations continue to respect the territorial integrity of member states and disapprove moves toward any further Balkanization. During his visit to Cameroon in 2000, the then UN Secretary-General Kofi Annan made the Anglophone movements understand in no uncertain terms that dialogue and reconciliation rather than separation would be instrumental to solving the Anglophone problem. A similar appeal was made in the 2009 ACHPR ruling.

Although the struggle for an independent Southern Cameroons state remains alive, especially as a result of the financial contributions and Internet activities of Anglophones in the diaspora, the prospects of success, if measured in terms of achieving a sovereign state, remain extremely remote. This notwithstanding, in the light of 2016–2017 high-handed response of the Francophone-dominated state to the legitimate concerns of teachers and lawyers of the two Anglophone regions, and in view of repeated provocations of systematic marginalization of Anglophone Cameroonians since 1961, it would hardly surprise anyone if the popula-

---

[93] Konings (1999).

tion of these regions were finally to say enough is enough and opt for secession as the last resort.

If this were to happen, it would echo the words of the late Bernard Fonlon. This pioneer Anglophone intellectual and one of the foremost architects of reunification warned, in a secret memo addressed to President Ahmadou Ahidjo in 1964, that the newly founded federation could only survive if it lived and grew according to definite principles arrived at not by whim, caprice, or arbitrariness but through careful stock taking and commitment to the founding ideals of the federation. He challenged the then leaders of the federation, President Ahidjo and his Francophone compatriots at the helm of the state, in particular, to be like "a traveler on the road" who "stops from time to time to look back and see the ground he has covered," like "merchants" who "close shops at intervals to take stock," and like "users of machines" who "are bound to service and over-haul them now and again." It was only natural, he argued, that those involved with the project of building a lasting federation in Cameroon "to halt, once in a while, to see how much ground has been covered, to draw up their balance sheet, to service or overhaul, if need be, the machinery of the State."[94]

REFERENCES

All Anglophone Conference. (1993). *The Buea declaration*. Limbe: Nooremac Press.

All Anglophone Conference. (1994). *The Bamenda proclamation*. Bamenda (mimeo).

Amazee, V. B. (1990). The 'Igbo scare' in the British Cameroons, c. 1945–61. *Journal of African History, 31*, 281–293.

Amazee, V. B. (1994). The role of the French Cameroonians in the unification of Cameroon, 1916–1961. *Transafrican Journal of History, 23*, 195–234.

Anyangwe, C. (2008). *Imperialistic politics in Cameroon: Resistance and the inception of the restoration of the statehood of Southern Cameroons*. Bamenda: Langaa RPCIG.

Anyangwe, C. (2009). *Betrayal of too trusting a people: The UN, the UK and the trust territory of the Southern Cameroons*. Bamenda: Langaa RPCIG.

Anyefru, E. (2008). Cyber-nationalism: The imagined Anglophone Cameroon community in cyberspace. *African Identities, 6*(3), 253–274.

[94] See Bernard Fonlon, http://www.alafnet.com/cameroon-a-secret-memo-by-bernard-fonlon-to-ahmadou-ahidjo/ (last accessed April 2017).

Anyefru, E. (2010). Paradoxes of internationalisation of the Anglophone problem in Cameroon. *Journal of Contemporary African Studies, 28*(1), 85–101.

Ardener, E. (1967). The nature of the reunification of Cameroon. In A. Hazlewood (Ed.), *African integration and disintegration: Case studies in economic and political union* (pp. 285–337). Oxford: Oxford University Press.

Ardener, S. G. (1968). *Eye-witness to the annexation of Cameroon 1883–1887.* Buea: Ministry of Primary Education and West Cameroon Antiquities Commission.

Awasom, N. F. (1998). Colonial background to the development of autonomist tendencies in Anglophone Cameroon, 1946–1961. *Journal of Third World Studies, 15*(1), 168–183.

Awasom, N. F. (2000). The reunification question in Cameroon history: Was the bride an enthusiastic or a reluctant one? *Africa Today, 47*(2), 91–119.

Awoh, L. E., & Nkwi, G. W. (2015). A disease of will among African states: The separatist agenda of Southern Cameroon National Council (SCNC), c. 1995–2004. *Conflict Studies Quarterly, 12*, 3–17.

Bayart, J.-F. (1989). *L'État en Afrique: La Politique du Ventre.* Paris: Fayard.

Benjamin, J. (1972). *Les Camerounais Occidentaux: La Minorité dans un État Bicommunautaire.* Montréal: Les Presses de l'Université de Montréal.

Biya, P. (1987). *Communal liberalism.* London/Basingstoke: Macmillan.

Chem-Langhëë, B., & Njeuma, M. Z. (1980). The Pan-Kamerun movement, 1949–1961. In N. Kofele-Kale (Ed.), *An African experiment in nation building: The bilingual Cameroon republic since reunification* (pp. 25–64). Boulder: Westview Press.

Dicklitch, S. (2010). *The Southern Cameroons and minority rights in Cameroon.* Unpublished paper.

Ebai, E. S. (2009). The right to self-determination and the Anglophone Cameroon situation. *International Journal of Human Rights, 13*(5), 631–653.

Eyoh, D. (1998). Conflicting narratives of Anglophone protest and the politics of identity in Cameroon. *Journal of Contemporary African Studies, 16*(2), 249–276.

Fonchingong, C. C. (2005). Exploring the politics of identity and ethnicity in state reconstruction in Cameroon. *Social Identities, 11*(4), 363–380.

Gaillard, P. (1994). *Ahmadou Ahidjo (1922–1989).* Paris: Jalivres.

Geschiere, P., & Nyamnjoh, F. B. (2000). Capitalism and autochthony: The see-saw of mobility and belonging. *Public Culture, 12*(2), 423–452.

Gumne, K. (2006). *Comprehensive road map for the settlement of the Bakassi conflict.* Bamenda (mimeo).

Gwaibi, N. (2016). *Decentralisation and community participation: Local development and municipal politics in Cameroon.* Bamenda: Langaa RPCIG.

Johnson, W. R. (1970). *The Cameroon federation: Political integration in a fragmentary society.* Princeton: Princeton University Press.

Joseph, R. (1977). *Radical nationalism in Cameroun: Social origins of the U.P.C. rebellion*. Oxford: Oxford University Press.

Jua, N. (2003). Anglophone political struggles and state responses. In J.-G. Gros (Ed.), *Cameroon: Politics and society in critical perspectives* (pp. 87–110). Lanham: University Press of America.

Jua, N., & Konings, P. (2004). Occupation of public space: Anglophone nationalism in Cameroon. *Cahiers d'Études Africaines, XLIV*(3), 175, 609–33.

Kinni, F. K.-Y. (2013). *Bakassi: Or the politics of exclusion and occupation?* Bamenda: Langaa RPCIG.

Kofele-Kale, N. (1980). Reconciling the dual heritage: Reflections on the 'Kamerun idea'. In N. Kofele-Kale (Ed.), *An African experiment in nation building: The bilingual Cameroon republic since reunification* (pp. 3–23). Boulder: Westview Press.

Kofele-Kale, N. (1981). *Tribesmen and patriots: Political culture in a poly-ethnic African state*. Washington, DC: University Press of America.

Kofele-Kale, N. (1986). Ethnicity, regionalism, and political power: A postmortem of Ahidjo's Cameroon. In M. G. Schatzberg & I. W. Zartman (Eds.), *The political economy of Cameroon* (pp. 53–82). New York: Praeger.

Konings, P. (1999). The Anglophone struggle for federalism in Cameroon. In L. R. Basta & J. Ibrahim (Eds.), *Federalism and decentralisation in Africa* (pp. 289–325). Fribourg: Institut du Fédéralisme.

Konings, P. (2001). Mobility and exclusion: Conflicts between autochthons and allochthons during political liberalization in Cameroon. In M. de Bruijn, R. van Dijk, & D. Foeken (Eds.), *Mobile Africa: Changing patterns of movement in Africa and beyond* (pp. 169–194). Leiden: Brill.

Konings, P. (2002). University students' revolt, ethnic militia, and violence during political liberalization in Cameroon. *African Studies Review, 45*(2), 179–204.

Konings, P. (2004). Opposition and social-democratic change in Africa: The social democratic front in Cameroon. *Commonwealth and Comparative Politics, 42*(3), 289–311.

Konings, P. (2005a). The Anglophone Cameroon-Nigeria boundary: Opportunities and conflicts. *African Affairs, 104*(415), 275–301.

Konings, P. (2005b). Anglophone university students and Anglophone nationalist struggles in Cameroon. In J. Abbink & I. van Kessel (Eds.), *Vanguard or vandals: Youth, politics and conflict in Africa* (pp. 161–188). Leiden: Brill.

Konings, P., & Nyamnjoh, F. B. (1997). The Anglophone problem in Cameroon. *Journal of Modern African Studies, 35*(2), 207–229.

Konings, P., & Nyamnjoh, F. B. (2003). *Negotiating an Anglophone identity: A study of the politics of recognition and representation in Cameroon*. Leiden: Brill.

Krieger, M. (2008). *Cameroon's social democratic front: Its history and prospects as an opposition party (1990–2011)*. Bamenda: Langaa RPCIG.

Le Vine, V. T. (1964). *The Cameroons: From mandate to independence*. Berkeley/Los Angeles: University of California Press.

Mbembe, A. (1996). *La Naissance du Maquis dans le Sud-Cameroun, 1920–1960*. Paris: Karthala.

Mbile, N. N. (2000). *Cameroon political story: Memories of an authentic eye witness*. Limbe: Presbyterian Printing Press.

Mbu, A. N. T. (1993). *Civil disobedience in Cameroon*. Douala: Imprimerie Georges Freres.

Messmer, P. (1998). *Les Blancs s'en Vont: Récits de Décolonisation*. Paris: Albin Michel.

Milne, M. (1999). *No telephone to heaven*. Stockbridge: Meon Hill Press.

Mukong, A. (Ed.). (1990). *The case for the Southern Cameroons*. Uwani-Enugu: Chuka Printing Company.

Ndi, A. (2014a). *Southern West Cameroon revisited volume two. North-South West nexus 1858–1972*. Bamenda: Langaa RPCIG.

Ndi, A. (2014b). *Southern West Cameroon revisited (1950–1972) volume one. Unveiling inescapable traps*. Bamenda: Langaa RPCIG.

Ndjana, M. (1996). Le Dépassement Ethnique: Esquisse d'une Théorie de l'Identité. *Epasa Moto, 1*(3), 51–65.

Nfor, N. N. (2016). *The urgency of a new Dawn: Prison thoughts and reflections*. Bamenda: Langaa RPCIG.

Ngoh, V. J. (1990). *Constitutional developments in Southern Cameroons, 1946–1961: From trusteeship to independence*. Yaoundé: CEPER.

Ngoh, V. J. (2001). *Southern Cameroons, 1922–1961: A constitutional history*. Aldershot: Ashgate.

Ngome, V. E. (1992). *What god has put asunder*. Yaoundé: Pitcher Books.

Njeuma, M. Z. (1995). Reunification and political opportunism in the making of Cameroon's independence. *Paideuma, 41*, 27–37.

Nkoum-Me-Ntseny, L.-M. (1999). Question Anglophone, libéralisation Politique et Crise de l'État-Nation: Les Ennemis dans la Maison? In L. Sindjoun (Ed.), *La Révolution Passive au Cameroun: État, Société et Changement* (pp. 157–229). Dakar: Éditions Démocraties Africaines.

Nyamnjoh, F. B. (2005). *Africa's media: Democracy and the politics of belonging*. London/New York: Zed Books.

Nyamnjoh, F. B., & Akum, R. F. (Eds.). (2008). *Cameroon GCE crisis: A test of Anglophone solidarity*. Bamenda: Langaa RPCIG.

Nyamnjoh, F. B., & Rowlands, M. (1998). Elite associations and the politics of belonging in Cameroon. *Africa, 68*(3), 320–337.

Owono, F. M. (2010). *Une culture Protestaire entre local et transnational: Trajectoires des mobilisations Anglophones du Cameroun*. PhD dissertation, University of Bordeaux.

Percival, J. (2008). *The 1961 Cameroon plebiscite: Choice or betrayal.* Bamenda: Langaa RPCIG.

Phillipson, S. S. (1959). *Report on the financial, economic and administrative consequences to Southern Cameroons of separation from the federation of Nigeria.* Buea: Prime Minister's Office, Southern Cameroons.

Rowlands, M. (1993). Accumulation and the cultural politics of identity in the Grassfields. In P. Geschiere & P. Konings (Eds.), *Itinéraires d'Accumulation au Cameroun* (pp. 71–97). Paris: Karthala.

Sindjoun, L. (1995). Mobilisation Politique du Pluralisme Culturel et Crise de l'État-Nation au Cameroun. In I. Mane (Ed.), *État, Démocratie, Sociétés et Culture en Afrique* (pp. 87–115). Dakar: Éditions Démocraties Africaines.

Stark, F. M. (1976). Federalism in Cameroon: The shadow and the reality. *Canadian Journal of African Studies, 10*(3), 423–442.

Susungi, N. N. (1991). *The crisis of unity and democracy in Cameroon.* No publisher mentioned.

Takougang, J., & Krieger, M. (1998). *African state and society in the 1990s: Cameroon's political crossroads.* Boulder/Oxford: Westview Press.

Welch, C. E. (1966). *Dreams of unity: Pan-Africanism and political unification in West Africa.* Ithaca: Cornell University Press.

CHAPTER 4

Ethiopia, Somalia, and the Ogaden: Still a Running Sore at the Heart of the Horn of Africa

Sarah Vaughan

INTRODUCTION

If Africa has a "secessionist deficit,"[1] the Horn of Africa has surely done more than its share to redress this imbalance. With Somaliland still unrecognized,[2] and South Sudan in chronic crisis for most of its short period of independence,[3] it is worth remembering that the two largest and bloodiest wars between African states in contemporary times have both been intimately connected with secessionism in the region. The Ethio-Eritrean War of 1998–2000 erupted only a few years after a 30-year conflict resulted in Eritrean independence de facto in 1991 and *de jure* in

---

[1] Englebert and Hummel (2005).

[2] See Hoehne (2018) in this volume; I am also grateful for his comments on an earlier draft of this chapter.

[3] See Schomerus and de Vries (2018) in this volume.

S. Vaughan (✉)
University of Edinburgh, Edinburgh, UK

© The Author(s) 2019
L. de Vries et al. (eds.), *Secessionism in African Politics*,
Palgrave Series in African Borderlands Studies,
https://doi.org/10.1007/978-3-319-90206-7_4

1993.[4] The Ethio-Eritrean War shattered the much-vaunted peace dividend, reopened depths of bitterness in and between both countries, and refuelled the long-standing regional catechism that "my enemy's enemy is my friend." The Ethio-Somali war of 1977–78, meanwhile, represented the high-water mark of Somali irredentism,[5] the spectacular attempt to wrest by force almost a third of the territory Ethiopia sees as indisputably its own: it centered on areas of the Ethiopian Somali National Regional State (SNRS), commonly referred to as the Ogaden.[6] The Ethio-Somali war drove tens of thousands from their homes to remain as refugees over decades, poured new poison into the suspicion between the two states, and scarred the military and political elites of both. Civilian, military, and insurgent deaths during these two wars, and the multiple other conflicts that blazed in the period in between in other parts of Ethiopia, have been estimated as in excess of a million.[7]

If Eritrea provides a rare example of an African secessionist movement that succeeded in its goal of winning national independence, conflict over the fate of the Ogaden, on which this chapter focuses, has continued to fester. Over more than a century of violence in the modern period, this variously defined territory has been the object of state-sponsored Somali irredentism, of secessionist dreams of independence, and of attempts to win qualitatively—even spatially—different forms of "self-determination" or autonomy, within or beyond the Ethiopian state. Characterizing conflict in the Ogaden as necessarily or consistently "secessionist" is, as this chapter discusses, undoubtedly an oversimplification: but the notion of secession—threat or aspiration—runs like a toxic current throughout. The profound incompatibilities among the deeply held views of different Ethiopians, Somalis, and Ethiopian Somalis over the rightful disposal and governance of this area have proved a consistent and effective stumbling

---

[4] See Diaz and Dorman (2018) in this volume.

[5] Gebru Tareke (2000).

[6] The term "Ogaden," usually associated with the period of British Military Administration during and after World War II, was historically ill-defined, referring roughly to the central areas of the current Ethiopian Somali Region, but importantly excluding the Haud grazing areas, along its north-eastern border with Somaliland and Puntland, and (apparently) some other non-Ogaadeeni-inhabited areas to the north and south. Following common convention, I use "Ogaden" to refer to the territory, and "Ogaadeen" or "Ogaadeeni" of the clan or its members. Somali orthography is not followed, with names rendered in forms in which they are commonly found in English.

[7] Gebru Tareke (2009) and de Waal (2009).

block, vitiating and curtailing attempts at a solution and perhaps even limiting what is written.[8]

On April 24, 2007, the Ogaden National Liberation Front (ONLF) hit the headlines with an audacious attack on an oil exploration facility at Abole in the northeast of the Ethiopian Somali Region, killing 65 Ethiopians and 9 Chinese. The military crackdown that ensued, coincident with Ethiopia's military operations in Somalia itself, drew international condemnation. An aggressive counter-insurgency strategy on the part of the government from 2007–2009 limited the military scope of the ONLF, at the cost of heavy disruption of Ethiopian Somali livelihoods, and widespread human rights violations. It was a stark reminder of how far things had changed since the optimism of the early 1990s, when, under a new federal dispensation, politics in the SNRS were briefly described as the country's most open, even democratic.[9] As exceptionally high levels of violence settled into lower-level norms of brutality, a number of peace deals with lesser groups were engineered in 2010. Several rounds of face-to-face peace talks brokered by Kenya in 2012 and again in early 2015 came to nothing, and violence has rumbled on. At the time of writing in 2017, the conflict is increasingly invisible, an assumed and intractable feature of the context, as international attention focused again on the devastating impact of drought across the Somali arena. Any prospect of a sustainable overall settlement has receded again, governance remains poor, and the citizens of the region continue to pay a heavy price for these failures, with the anger and frustrations of a diverse Ogaadeen diaspora smoldering and flaring with events.[10]

Violent disputes over the rightful fate of the Ogaden—as an integral part of Ethiopia, a natural Ogaadeen homeland within Somalia, or an

---

[8] It goes, almost without saying, that this makes the grail of "objective, analytical and balanced" discussion of this issue particularly fraught. With accounts seen to be "Somali-influenced" regularly dismissed in Addis Ababa, and vice versa, there is little or no consensus on what is "reasonable." An Ethiopian interlocutor recently told me ruefully that "reading your work gave me a stomachache." I can only regret—very much—that this chapter may have the same effect on some readers, including a number of those who have been generous with their time and ideas over the years.

[9] Markakis (1997).

[10] The social media storm which erupted in early September 2017 over the Somali Government's handover to Ethiopia of Abdikarim Sheikh Muse, a key ONLF leader who had been living in Mogadishu, is a case in point. Ogaden secessionism may not be as prominent as it was in the minds of Somali nationalists, but sensitivities over the perceived "betrayal" of its principles remain extremely deep. This is alluded to again below.

independent entity—is of long duration, and the current protagonists (the Ethiopian Federal and Regional Governments and the contemporary ONLF) are only its most recent placeholders. This chapter sketches the politics and rhetoric of the area since its forcible incorporation within the Ethiopian Empire state by Menelik II at the end of the nineteenth century. It examines how this toxic colonial legacy in the heart of the Horn of Africa has poisoned domestic and transnational politics under successive regimes. The first section looks at historical resources; the second outlines more recent experiences, as the federal period after 1991 added new interests, actors, resources, and complexities to the picture.

James Mayall and Mark Simpson argue that ethnic difference per se does not explain prolonged secessionism. Differential treatment of groups within a single territory during the colonial process and subsequent government attempts to "eliminate cultural diversity and monopolize access to power" are key drivers, which may be reinforced by economic grievances and confessional divisions. Mayall and Simpson also stress the seminal importance of a regional environment that is "strongly supportive of separatist nationalism."[11] While the prevailing balance of power (Cold War or post-Cold War international relations) is antipathetic to secession, more fundamental is the local "pattern of power—in which geographical contiguity leads naturally to hostility":

> The evidence of the Horn of Africa suggests that for the pattern of power to provide a life-line of support for secession, there needs to be a historical confrontation at its heart, not merely of states but of cultures and world views. In other words, it is not merely that ethnicity is not enough to explain protracted secessionism, nor is geography.[12]

Talk of "historical confrontations" can often seem unfortunately resonant of Huntington's "clash of civilizations" discourse; these notions have been effectively critiqued in a collection of articles, which includes several on the Horn.[13] In line with their critical emphasis on local empirical nuance, this chapter traces and problematizes the historical resources and experiences that shape the dynamics and variety of the confrontations in play in and around the Ogaden. There is no need to resort to millennial

---

[11] Mayall and Simpson (1992: 10).

[12] Mayall and Simpson (1992: 22).

[13] Huntington (1996), Prunier (2009), Ostebo (2009), Hansen (2009), all in Hansen, Mesoy, and Kardas (eds) (2009).

notions of a civilization clash. There is more than enough complex and brutal political history—that has in turn spawned incompatible and unforgiving nationalisms—to account for the extreme polarization and shifting and complex fragmentation of contending perspectives. Violence, including state violence, has not only persisted but "in many ways become normalized."[14]

HISTORICAL RESOURCES: CONQUEST, COLONIES, AND SOMALIA IRREDENTA

Ahmad Gran is for the Somalis a symbol of their past conquests; similarly, Muhammad Abdullah has become for modern Somalis a symbol of a national unity transcending tribal lines but true to Islam and the Somali's love of independence.[15]

The Adal Emirate and Ahmed ibn Ibrahim al-Ghazi

Modern Ethiopia's relations with its eastern periphery and neighbors are profoundly influenced by the telling and retelling of the history of the sixteenth-century invasion by Imam Ahmed ibn Ibrahim al-Ghazi of the Adal Emirate at Harar, more commonly known in the Ethiopian highlands as Ahmed "Gragn," or "Gurey" in the Somali areas.[16] While Imam Ahmed and his force seem to have gone to war with Christian Abyssinia primarily as Muslims, they are widely identified as ethnic Somalis.[17] Ahmed's army destroyed a series of churches across a wide area of the highlands, reaching Lalibella, Axum, and the island monasteries of Hayk and Tana, and was defeated only with the help of a Portuguese expedition of 400 musketeers. Attitudes toward this history are often treated as a litmus test of the incompatibility of Somali and Ethiopian nationalisms: while in the lowlands Ahmed "Gurey" is a Somali national hero, for many in the highlands Ahmed "Gragn" represents the archetype of the "Muslim threat" to Ethiopia. As always with national symbols, the historicity of the story is less important than the contours and considerable power of its ubiquitous—and polarized—retelling.[18]

---

[14] Hagmann (2014: 13) and Hagmann and Korf (2012).
[15] Hess (1964: 415).
[16] "Left-handed" in Amharic and Somali.
[17] Muth (2003).
[18] Henze (2000).

Imperial Incorporation of the Somali Lands

What is now the Ethiopian SNRS was forcibly incorporated into the expanding Ethiopian Empire state by Menelik II in the 1880s, part of a process that was explicitly competitive with European scrambles in the region. The area had strategic and economic significance as buffer,[19] trade corridor, and livestock reservoir.[20] The imperial process was cemented in a series of agreements, concluded under pressure (commercial and territorial) from Ethiopia's colonial neighbors. The Anglo-Ethiopian treaty of 1897 delimited the boundary between British Somaliland and Ethiopia.[21] Whether or not the British intended to cede the strategic Haud dry season grazing lands to Ethiopia,[22] this was the effect of the demarcation of the treaty boundary in 1934. Meanwhile the Italo-Ethiopian Treaty of 1928, which established the border between Ethiopian and Italian Somali areas as parallel to the coast at "21 leagues" (73.5 miles) from the sea, was rapidly undermined when Italy constructed and manned a garrison at Wal Wal in 1930, well within Ethiopian territory. Ethiopian protests and clashes in December 1934 saw discussion of the "Abyssinia crisis" at the UN.

The Dervish Movement: A "Prototype" of Resistant Somali Nationalism?

As a result of these competitive colonial processes in the late nineteenth century, the other Somali-inhabited areas were parceled between France (Djibouti), Britain (Somaliland Protectorate, Northern Frontier District of Kenya), and Italy (Somalia). Reunification of these territories has been a flickering undercurrent of Somali nationalism ever since, and in its first iteration from 1900, the Ogaadeen/Bah Geri Sayyid Mohammed Abdilleh Hassan led a 20-year Somali rebellion, the Dervish movement, against both Ethiopians and Europeans (Hess 1964). Early in the century, the movement had disrupted trade in the Ogaden and in British Somaliland. Although most of its followers were Dhulbahante, the movement also drew support from the Ogaadeen clan, and their involvement was consolidated by the Sayyid's judicious marriage alliance (among more than ten others) with a powerful Mohammed Zubeir clan family. By 1913 and the

---

[19] Tibebe (1994).
[20] Hagmann (2014).
[21] Bahru Zewde (1991: 119).
[22] Lewis (2002: 59).

death of Menelik, Mohammed Abdilleh had consolidated a wider area of control, moving south across British, Ethiopian, and Italian Somali areas and building forts at Wardheer and Korahe in the Ogaden. By 1916, the Italians reported with alarm that he was negotiating a marriage alliance with the recent Muslim convert, the new Ethiopian Emperor *Lij* Iyasu, months before the latter's downfall.

When the British finally routed the so-called Dervish forces in 1920, the Sayyid escaped to the Ogaden, and, in a refuge taken by many subsequent Ogaadeen insurgents, camped near Korahe on the Fafan River.[23] He is remembered regionally as the "forerunner of contemporary Somali nationalism."[24] In the Ogaden, meanwhile, the selective memory of his Ogaadeen nationalist and Mohammed Zubeir credentials also resonates, with the recollection of his expansion of Ogaadeen raiding well into Isaaq areas of the British Somaliland protectorate. Following the defeat of the Sayyid in 1920 and his death in 1921, British Isaaq clans in turn moved deep into Ogaden, where they were increasingly seen by the Ogaadeen as "sub-imperialists."[25] Their effective penetration was a further indication of the weakness of the Ethiopian state, even in the Jijiga region, and its abject failures of border protection. "During the twenties and thirties the British and the Italian territorial administrations were first and foremost rivals for the economic and political returns of Somali clans. Moreover, when Hayla-Sellase's government failed, Somali clans were quick to capitalize."[26]

Internal and External Challenges to Ethiopian Rule in the Ogaden

In a nuanced and original investigation of the extent to which "Ethiopia was able to 'rule' the very unruly Somali periphery," Cedric Barnes investigated the effects of "the subversive influence of surrounding European

---

[23] I am grateful to Markus Hoehne for noting that the contemporary Ogaadeen credentials of Mohammed Abdilleh Hassen, who had a complicated relationship with his paternal clan, and of the Dervish movement overall should not be overstated, with prominent involvement of Dhulbahante and other groups, who moved east and north after defeat. Cf. Samatar, S. (1982: 99ff), and Sheikh-Abdi (1993). Subsequent nationalist reworking, meanwhile, does not always reflect this historical nuance.

[24] Hess (1964: 433).

[25] Barnes (2000: 117).

[26] Ibid.: 166.

rule of other Somalis...on Somali clans under Ethiopian rule."[27] While the characterization of Menelik's state as "military-fiscal"[28] has been widely discussed and critiqued, "military-fiscal" nevertheless identifies the enduring locus of its internal tension: the forceful consolidation of a peripheral tax base to feed the center simultaneously entrenched decentralized (military) centers of authority. Ras Mekonnen established the garrison town of Jijiga in 1891, on the northern flanks of the escarpment near the strategic Marda Pass. Few highland settlers followed the army into the Somali lowlands, contenting themselves with land in the higher altitudes and lucrative grain belt around Jijiga. With the exception of small garrisons at Kebridehar and Degahabur, the state had little presence south of the town, an urban concentration that persisted into the twenty-first century. Externally, meanwhile, the eastern periphery was vital to the modern Ethiopian state's political and economic communications with the outside world, and key to the consolidation of its sovereignty.[29] Barnes writes that the "increasing political and economic articulation of the eastern periphery with neighboring colonial states, especially the growth of markets and improvement in infrastructure there, progressively weakened Ethiopian sovereignty and precipitated the Italian invasion."[30]

1936–1940 Italian Imperial East Africa

On May 4, 1936, Haile Selassie left Djibouti aboard a British vessel bound for Europe. The following day, Mussolini declared in Rome that "Ethiopia is Italian: Italian in fact...Italian in law."[31] The Ethiopian Somali areas with the exception of Jijiga, which were separately incorporated with Harar, were united with Italian Somaliland. The border between the two areas had always been nominal[32] and now disappeared entirely, further facilitating movement and trade. Roads between Harar, Dire Dawa, and Jijiga, as well as from Jijiga to the British Somaliland border and toward Mogadishu, were greatly improved by the Italians. This notably reinforced the links between Darood clan families and territories, including in what is now southern and central Somalia, those of the Ogaadeen among them.

[27] Ibid.: 16.
[28] Tsegaye (1994).
[29] Bahru Zewde (1991) and Barnes (2000).
[30] Barnes (2000: 1).
[31] Steiner (1936).
[32] Barnes (2010).

Many Somalis had fought with the Italian invading force, and Italian imperial policies favored Muslim areas, which were likely to support them against the Christian Ethiopian Emperor. Concessions included the reduction of taxation and the return of land taken by highland settlers. Their initial popularity, however, was mitigated by bureaucratic restrictions that strangled trade in Jijiga, Dire Dawa, and Harar and muzzled exports to the coast.[33] While the occupation of Ethiopia was neither a colonial nor an economic success for Italy, Barnes argues that, ironically, it did "much to achieve...the transition of Ethiopia into a modern centralized bureaucratic and above all 'national' state." The occupation "underlined" the extent to which the national state had failed.[34]

1941–48: The British Military Administration and the "Reserved Areas"

When the Italians were expelled in 1941, the areas they had occupied and colonized were placed under British Military Administration. The nominal northern border with the British Somaliland Protectorate was also abolished, formalizing an existing de facto situation. At this point, the balance of power in the long-standing rivalry between the Isaaq clans dominant in British Somaliland, and the Ogaadeen to the south shifted again: between 1943 and 1944, the British pursued an aggressive campaign of disarmament against the Ogaadeen and others.[35] From an Ethiopian perspective, extended British administration gave multiple causes for concern. Little economic support was forthcoming for post-occupation reconstruction or consolidation. The designation of the railway line, Harar, a corridor to Jijiga, and the area along the border as a "reserved area" was particularly galling: this period saw a dramatic increase in grain prices, and the lucrative grain trade around Jijiga remained outside the control of the Ethiopians. Although Anglo-Ethiopian agreements in 1942 and 1944 explicitly recognized Ethiopian sovereignty in the Ogaden and the reserved area, and although the British never denied Ethiopian sovereignty of the Ogaden, Barnes argues that "by virtue of its continuing

---

[33] Barnes (2000).
[34] Barnes (2000: 173).
[35] Notably against Warsangeeli and Dhulbahante.

government from Mogadishu, [the Ogaden's] future became implicitly bound up with the disposal of ex-Italian Somaliland."[36]

The British presence and ongoing administrative arrangements rendered explicit the coexistence of two different notions of the future of Somali-inhabited areas in Ethiopia. While the integration of the periphery—both in the north and in the east—was increasingly important to the nationalism of the restored imperial government, the Ogaden was also a key location of Somali political, economic, and ultimately national aspirations.[37] These were soon to be further fuelled by the British.

The Bevin Plan for a Greater Somalia

The issue of the fate of the Ogaden came to a head in June 1946 when British Foreign Secretary Ernest Bevin proposed that British Somaliland, Italian Somaliland, and the Ogaden be united in one UN trusteeship under British administration. The proposal was controversial for two reasons: firstly because of Britain's legal recognition of Ethiopia's rights in the Ogaden in 1942 and 1944 and secondly because the Four Power Commission that had been established in April 1946 had a mandate only to consider the disposal of Italy's former colonial possessions (namely Eritrea and Italian Somalia). Haile Selassie had lobbied for the return of the Ogaden and of Eritrea to Ethiopia in 1945, and the other three of the Four Powers—France, the USA, and the USSR—immediately opposed the plan. Nevertheless, British administrators in the region continued to endorse the idea. It also resonated with the Somali Youth Club (SYC) driving its popularity, politicization, expansion, and reincarnation the following year as the Somali Youth League (SYL).[38]

Somali Youth League

The SYC was founded under British rule in Mogadishu on May 15, 1943. A broadly and culturally nationalist organization, it was dedicated to the idea of "Somalia for Somalis" but seeking close relations with the British Military Administration in order to achieve this. A particular focus of friction with the British related to the SYC's determination to break down clan

---

[36] Barnes (2000: 174).
[37] Barnes (2000).
[38] Barnes (2007) and Lewis (1958, 2002).

barriers between Somalis, and its resentment of the British use of clan divisions in their approach to "indirect rule" in the region. SYC became abruptly politicized and politically active in 1946 when the Bevin plan for the unification of all Somali areas was put forward. Its membership grew from around 1000, primarily in Mogadishu, to more than 25,000 across the region in a matter of months, as the Greater Somalia issue galvanized the public mood.[39]

In early 1947, the SYC changed its name to the SYL and became explicitly politically nationalist and anti-Ethiopian. Of particular concern to the Ethiopian state center was the rapid spread of SYL popularity in what Ethiopia regarded as the much better-integrated Ethiopian towns of Dire Dawa and Harar. SYL leaders, including its head in Jijiga, Garad Makhtal Tahir, as well as others, seem to have continued their ambivalent attitude toward the British and the Ethiopians, shifting ground according to their audience and often apparently playing a double game against both. While Makhtal himself refused to co-operate with the Ethiopians, many of the Ogaadeen clans preferred the return to weak Ethiopian rule over unification under the British.[40]

1948 and 1954: Restoration of Ethiopian Rule

The Ogaden was returned to Ethiopian rule in 1948. Only the Haud and a small corridor "reserved area" to Jijiga were retained under the British Military Administration. This last part was finally returned to Ethiopia in 1954—an event that then became a focus of limited northern Somali/Somaliland nationalist resentment. Already in the early 1950s, "a first generation of clandestine activists…mobilized Somali nationalists in the Ogaden and Eastern Harerghe provinces against the imperial government."[41] Other observers commented that Somalis living in Ethiopia at that time seemed to have relatively little commitment to Somali nationalism as compared with their neighbors.[42] Most apparently acquiesced in the return of Ethiopian rule and were more concerned to secure their unhindered movement than about which state claimed their territory—although it seems likely that nationalism was bubbling beneath the surface. In 1956, the Ethiopian government created a new Ogaden

---

[39] Barnes (2007).
[40] Barnes (2000).
[41] Hagmann (2014: 16) citing Tibebe (1991: 23).
[42] Touval (1963) and Lewis (1958).

Administrative Region centered on Kebridehar. When the Emperor visited in 1957, 8 million Ethiopian Birr—then a significant sum—was allocated for public service improvements.[43] Hoping to increase clan loyalty as neighboring Somalia moved toward independence, in 1960, the Ethiopian government appointed Somali administrators in four *awraja* (sub-provinces) and 23 *wereda* (districts). One Somali was made a Deputy Minister in the Ethiopian Government.

1960 and After: Somali Independence and Irredentism

In 1960, Somalia became independent with the union of the former British and Italian Somali territories, and one of the first steps of the new government was to grant citizenship to all ethnic Somalis across the Horn of Africa. The five-pointed star on the new Somali national flag declared its irredentist intent to unite all five Somali-inhabited territories: those considered in the Bevin plan (British, Italian, and Ethiopian Somali areas, the latter now referred to as *soomaali galbeed* or "Western Somalia") with the Issa areas of Djibouti, and the Kenyan Northern Frontier District Radio Mogadishu provided strong irredentist encouragement broadcasting the popular song "I shall not feel well until we go to war to unite the Somali."[44] Somalis from Ethiopia who visited the Somali Republic for trade or education came under the influence of the irredentist rhetoric.

In 1963, an organization called Nasrullah (Nasir Allah, sacrifice for the sake of Allah) was established in the Ogaden to fight for independence from Ethiopia.[45] Among its leaders were highly respected clerics; they drew on religious tropes already familiar from the conceptualization by Ahmed Gragn/Gurey and Mohammed Abdilleh. "Somalis" and "Ethiopians" increasingly began to consider each other as the primary enemy, and religion became more prominent in how the two sides framed each other.[46]

---

[43] Markakis (1987).

[44] Markakis (1987) and Legum (1963: 505).

[45] Markakis (1987) Markakis also mentions a second organization, the Ogaden Company for Trade and Industry that emerged around the same time (2011): "in reality a clandestine group lobbying for Ogaadeeni self-determination" Hagman (2014: 16), drawing on Schroeder (1998).

[46] Seid (2009).

A rebellion in Ethiopia's Bale province, to the southwest of the Wabe Shebelle River, was triggered by the abrupt imposition of new taxes.[47] As the conflict dragged on, it became enmeshed with the irredentist agenda of the Somali Republic, which offered limited cross-border support. The Somali and Ethiopian military clashed on the border in 1964 until a settlement was mediated by the Organisation of African Unity (OAU). In early 1965, Wako Gutu, a leader of the Bale rebellion remembered as the "father of Oromo separatism" obtained weapons from Somalia.[48]

The Western Somali Liberation Front

The Western Somali Liberation Front (WSLF) took shape in 1973. The "creeping coup," which saw the removal of the Ethiopian imperial regime in 1974, and establishment of the *Dergue*[49] military government in 1975 "stirred Somali nationalism to a unique irredentist opportunity."[50] In 1975, the Somali Government reorganized the WSLF, putting it under the command of the National Army in Hargeisa, and organized military training in Somalia and North Korea. Six months later, the Somali Government also established the Somali Abo Liberation Front (SALF) designed to operate west of the Wabe Shebelle (under the Somali Army Command in Baidoa), with its more ambivalent Somali-Oromo identity, and the involvement of Wako Gutu and Sheikh Hussein among other veterans from the 1960s. "Trained, armed, organized and otherwise supported by the Somalia State, the fronts were ancillaries of the Somali army," argues Gebru Tareke.[51]

As a result, the goals of the WSLF remained unclear, oscillating between independence for the Ogaden/Western Somalia, and autonomy within a wider Somalia. The SALF, meanwhile, seems to have been established primarily to counter the emergent Oromo Liberation Front (OLF), whose territorial claims crossed those of the WSLF and Somali Government. The lack of autonomy of the WSLF from the Somali government was to haunt the organization and the various strands of Ogaden nationalism for decades. From 1975 to 1977, the two organizations

---

[47] Gebru Tareke (1991).
[48] Ottaway and Ottaway (1978: 92ff).
[49] "Committee" in Amharic: shorthand for Provisional Military Administrative Committee.
[50] Markakis (2011: 210).
[51] Gebru Tareke (2000: 340).

pursued a guerrilla strategy, pressuring the Ethiopians to negotiate and wearing down Ethiopian troops before the intervention of the regular Somali Army. The WSLF was, according to Gebru Tareke, "universally and enthusiastically welcomed in Somali areas,"[52] while the highland settlers fled, leaving a significant proportion of the eastern rural population under the WSLF already by late 1976.

1977–78: The Ethio-Somali Ogaden War

Analysts have commented that the political and military circumstances in which Somalia invaded Ethiopia in 1977 could not have been more alluring: although Ethiopia's forces outnumbered Somalia's 47,000 to 35,000, they were logistically and organizationally disadvantaged, and already heavily stretched in Eritrea. Meanwhile, what looked like an unstable new government was riven by factionalism as the Red Terror peaked.[53] The Somali invasion began on July 13, 1977, and on September 12 (the third anniversary of the Dergue's Ethiopian "Revolution"), Jijiga fell to the Somalis.

However, the rapid Somali advance in the lowlands slowed as assaults on the towns of the plateau failed and Harar and Dire Dawa held out. Ethiopian resistance proved resilient and the Soviets and their allies came in support of Ethiopia in January 1978 in a dramatic *volte face*. By the time Jijiga was retaken on March 5, 1978, the war was almost over. Somalis of Eastern Ethiopia, however, had welcomed the invasion almost universally.[54] Forty years later, many still talk with enthusiasm of life in Jijiga during this period,[55] before tens of thousands of Somalis fled to Somalia ahead of the returning Ethiopians.

Ethiopia might have won the war, but it lost the peace.[56] Operation Lash[57] was launched in mid-1980, in an attempt to eradicate insurgents (the OLF, Islamic Front for the Liberation of Oromia (IFLO), and Sidama Liberation Movement (SLM) as well as the WSLF and SALF), and expel the Somali army. While villagization became a mechanism of control in

---

[52] Gebru Tareke (2000: 641).
[53] Gebru Tareke (2000: 638).
[54] Gebru Tareke (2000: 607).
[55] Interviews Addis Ababa and Jijiga (2009, 2010, 2017).
[56] Gebru Tareke (2002).
[57] "Ringworm" in Amharic: designed to consume the insurgents as ringworm consumes human hair.

agricultural and highland areas, the use of proxies was a strategy in the Somali lowlands. The Majerteen-based Somali Salvation Democratic Front (SSDF), established in 1979 with Ethiopian support to fight Siad Barre's regime, also attacked the WSLF and the Ogaadeen in support of the Ethiopian military. The military occupation of the Ogaden was brutal and total. In April 1988, each faced with growing internal threats, Mengistu Haile Mariam and Barre signed an opportunistic (and by then irrelevant) Peace Accord, in which the government of Somalia renounced its claims on the Ogaden. Yet the region remained under Emergency Military Rule from Harar (Hurso) and Kebridehar (Iz) until 1991 and the collapse of the *Dergue* regime.

1984: The Formation of the Ogaden National Liberation Front

In the wake of the rout in the Ogaden war, frustration at the WSLF's dependence on Mogadishu and its manipulation by the Somali government fuelled a reappraisal among the organization's Ogaadeen nationalists. The invasion by the Somali Army was itself seen as an attempt to undermine the WSLF's effective campaign of popular liberation. Siad Barre's execution of 14 WSLF commanders following an abortive military coup in Mogadishu a month after the withdrawal from the Ogaden precipitated a further attempt to loosen the regime's grip on the organization: the second congress in 1982 claimed the right and goal of "self-determination," and briefly replaced its chairman. Nevertheless, in May 1982, the Somali government integrated all of its armed units within the Somali Defense Force, and by the time of its 20th anniversary on June 16, 1983, the WSLF was already a "phantom organization."[58]

The dissident Ogaadeen nationalist faction emerged from the WSLF youth wing, established in 1979 and led by Mohammed Sirad Dolal. In August 1984, a leadership of six (Abdullahi Mohammed Saadi, Sheikh Ibrahim Abdellah, Mohammed Ismail Omar, Abdurahman Yusuf Magan, Abdurahman Mahdi, and Abdi Gelle) secretly formed the ONLF, only declaring its existence in March 1986, in Kuwait. The organization defined the issue of the Ogaden as one of "unfinished decolonization," committing itself to "liberating Ogadenia" by all possible means. It denounced the notion of Greater Somalia, asserting that by turning the issue into one of irredentism or secession the Somali Government had

---

[58] Markakis (2011: 213).

undermined the potential for international and continental support. The ONLF, then led by Abdurahman Yusuf Magan, denounced the 1988 Ethio-Somali Peace Accord as "treachery." The definitions of "Ogadenia" (it is not clear if this includes all Ethiopian Somali territories or only Ogaadeen clan lands) and of "liberation" (secession for independence or irredentism for unity with other Somali territories?) remain matters of great controversy to this day.

MORE RESOURCES: FEDERALISM, SELF-DETERMINATION, AND DECOLONIZATION

1991–94 Ethnic Federalism and the Ogaden National Liberation Front in Government

Dramatic political changes followed the collapse of the military governments in Somalia and (a few months later) Ethiopia in the first half of 1991. As the Somali State disintegrated, the Ethiopian Peoples' Revolutionary Democratic Front (EPRDF) sought to usher in a federal system based on the principle of self-determination of Ethiopia's nations, nationalities, and peoples, up to and including secession. It made strenuous efforts to persuade the ethno-national groups that had opposed the *Dergue* to participate in the new political system.[59] WSLF leaders, led by Sheikh Abdinasser Aden, were discovered hiding from "Hawiye vengeance" in a Mogadishu basement.[60] With Sudanese assistance, they were brought to Addis Ababa where they accepted the new Charter, renamed the Front the Western Somali Democratic Party (WSDP) and were given two seats in parliament. Wako Gutu and his colleagues agreed to divide the SALF into two: an Oromo and a Somali organization.

The ONLF proved more recalcitrant: reluctant, ambivalent, and divided about participation in the new Ethiopian federal dispensation. Meetings with the EPRDF in London and Khartoum had reportedly resulted in an agreement not to enter one another's territory; when EPRDF forces then moved to Jijiga, some elements of the diaspora-based ONLF leadership called for the continuation of armed struggle and to "merge with the WSLF."[61] In January 1992, the ONLF held its first national congress in

[59] Vaughan (1994).
[60] Markakis (2011: 306).
[61] Interviews, London and Addis Ababa (2009).

Gerbo in the newly established Ethiopian SNRS and elected Sheikh Ibrahim Abdellah as Chairman. He was known for his sophisticated Islamic education, strong religious views, and uncompromising resistance to Ethiopian rule in the Ogaden. The ONLF congress voted to participate in the forthcoming regional elections, citing the rights of self-determination and secession afforded by the Charter. The organization's position was seen as "ragged and confused."[62] A London-based representative in 1993 announced that ONLF would not participate in elections—only weeks before it did so.

As pre-electoral competition advanced, two key fault lines emerged among more than a dozen political organizations: between the dominant Ogaadeen and the other smaller Ethiopian Somali clans for overall control of the SNRS,[63] and among the Ogaadeen clans over the issue of secession from Ethiopia, with the ONLF for and the WSDP against it. ONLF won the vote in early 1993 but without an outright majority.[64] The new regional assembly changed the region's name from Ogaden to Somali and settled on Gode deep in the Ogaadeen heartland as its capital, after the federal government rejected its first choice (Dire Dawa).[65] Although the ONLF seemed in the ascendant, internal ambivalence about the Ethiopian federal arrangement and toward recognition of Ethiopian sovereignty continued to dog the organization. ONLF founding member Abdillahi Mohammed Saadi became the first regional president but was forced to resign seven months later amidst inter-clan and federal maneuvering and allegations of corruption and criminality.[66] Repeated removals of regional presidents soon became the regular pattern, leaving the SNRS effectively in limbo for the next 15 years.[67]

The ONLF's Return to Armed Struggle in 1994

On January 26, 1994, the ONLF with the support of eight other Ethiopian Somali organizations declared themselves in favor of "self-determination

---

[62] Interview, regional analyst, Nairobi (2009).

[63] Markakis (1997).

[64] Markakis (2011: 309).

[65] Neighboring Oromia also claimed it; Dire Dawa thus remains a city under federal charter, with the positions of Mayor and senior members of the administration revolving between representatives of the two groups.

[66] See UN (2003) and Samatar (2004).

[67] Markakis (2011: 310) and Hagmann (2005).

for Ogadenia." A month later, when Sheikh Ibrahim was due to address a rally in Wardheer, rising tension erupted into violence, and many were killed including senior members of the ONLF. The Sheikh escaped, and other ONLF members went into hiding or were killed by security forces. Regardless of the violence, the ONLF-led SNRS assembly resolved on March 24, 1994, to negotiate a referendum on secession with the federal government, which swiftly rejected the proposal. A month later, the SNRS president and nine others were imprisoned. From that point on, the ONLF was split between those who were willing to co-operate with the Ethiopian Government and those in favor of returning to armed struggle. This division was sealed when on May 27, 1995, the ONLF "legal wing" denounced the leadership in exile, and on June 6, that leadership signed an agreement in London to co-operate with the OLF against the EPRDF. Some argue that the division was a result of federal manipulation,[68] but this was clearly not the only factor.[69] The "legal wing" of the ONLF now found it increasingly difficult to compete with the newly formed and centrally backed Ethiopian Somali Democratic League (ESDL), astutely renamed to try to draw on historical sentiment toward the SYL. At the elections in June 1995, the rump ONLF "legal wing" won 30 out of 139 seats in the SNRS assembly but continued to hemorrhage frustrated members overseas. Another round of heavy federal intervention amalgamated the rump ONLF to form the new Somali People's Democratic Party (SPDP) in June 1998. The same year, the main ONLF held its second congress, replacing Sheikh Ibrahim Abdellah with the current chairman, "Admiral" Mohammed Omar Osman; and bringing into leadership alongside him a series of other former Generals of the Somali Republic's Defence Force.

Tadamun al Islaam and al-Itihaad al-Islaamiyya

Three Islamic organizations, which drew mainly on support from the Ogaadeen clans, had also been established in the region in 1991: the radical militant Ogaden Islamic Union, the Ethiopia branch of al-Itihaad al-Islaamiyya (AIAI), and the more traditionalist Islamic Solidarity Party—Western Somalia—Ogaden, also known as "Tadamun" (solidarity).[70] Abdirahman Yusuf Magan, one of the six founder members of the ONLF in

---

[68] Interviews, Addis Ababa, London (2009).
[69] Samatar (2004), Bryden (1995), and Hagmann (2005).
[70] Markakis (1997).

1984, and Mohammed Moalim Osman led Tadamun Al Islaam. Unlike AIAI, Tadamun did participate in elections in 1992, winning seven seats.[71] Tadamun was mostly composed of religious traditionalists[72] and represented conservative rather than radical Islam. It joined ranks with the WSLF/WSDP in 1994. AIAI was by far the largest Somali Islamist armed organization in the early 1990s, with an agenda reaching beyond the Ogaden.[73] It was invited into the political process by the ONLF but refused to participate in elections in 1992, in line with the teaching of the wider international movement dedicated to the promotion of so-called "Wahabbism." AIAI fragmented into different groups, of which the Ethiopian branch was the most radical. It endorsed a more militant "jihadi" stance against the Ethiopian regime and in this period of the 1990s, seems to have enjoyed a warm relationship with the ONLF.[74] Although even the Ogaden-based wing of AIAI was far from being an Ogaadeen nationalist grouping, once again different strands of "struggle" overlapped and became confused and conflated. At least this is what it looked like to outsiders—much to the frustration of many Ogaadeeni nationalists—as reflected in this US analysis of the period.

"Heightened militarism on the part of the Ethiopian wing of the AIAI was no doubt linked to the fact that the AIAI in Ethiopia was fighting for very different objectives than the AIAI wing inside Somalia. The Ethiopian wing of AIAI was part of a long-standing irredentist armed insurgency by Somali Ethiopians. The movement's aim of imposing an Islamist state over all of Somali-inhabited East Africa required armed violence against one of Africa's largest and most seasoned militaries. By contrast, the AIAI wings inside Somalia were preoccupied with expanding their control in a country where they faced no government at all."[75]

Less than a month after the July 1996 attempt on the life of Ethiopian Somali federal minister and then Chairman of the ESDL, Abdul Meijid Hussein, the Ethiopian military ousted AIAI from the area around Luuq,

---

[71] Markakis (1997: 567).

[72] Perouse de Montclos (2000).

[73] Marchal writes: "Set up in 1983 by the merger of four groups, it already had developed due to the mobilization of the Somali diaspora and its ideological agenda was reshaped by the internal conditions in Somalia [...] and the growing influence of Salafi ideology, due to the involvement of many migrants established in the Gulf who generously funded the movement." Marchal (2009: 5).

[74] Marchal (2009).

[75] Counter Terrorism Centre at West Point (n.d.: 43).

killing many of its members.[76] The mid-1990s period of bombings in Addis Ababa and Dire Dawa and mining of rural roads in SNRS came to an end. From January 1997, AIAI turned its attention to political and welfare activities and the emerging Islamic Courts movement in Somalia. It retained a presence where it could but was not very evident on the Ethiopian side of the border. In 2004–05, some of those involved with the AIAI branch in Ethiopia re-emerged in a new guise, allied with former WSLF personnel within the United Western Somali Liberation Front (UWSLF).

Intensification and Regionalization of Conflict Post-2000

In the "cold-war" period that followed the Ethio-Eritrean conflict of 1998–2000, the Eritrean government intensified its support to a number of movements fighting the Ethiopian government, including the ONLF. Internally, the scope and depth of the ONLF's new alliance with Asmara was controversial, notably for a generation of leaders scarred by the experience of the manipulation of the WSLF by Mogadishu. Relations with Eritrea seem to have been central to the division that developed after 2001 between Chairman Admiral Osman and Dr Mohammed Sirad Dolal, then Foreign Spokesperson in London. Although this view is contentious,[77] Dr. Dolal was widely seen as more critical of the alliance with Eritrea fearing that it could threaten to undermine the struggle for an independent Ogadenia by complicating it with other regional dynamics—as Siad Barre's patronage of the WSLF had done. The split became irrevocable when it was agreed at a meeting in Asmara in June 2006 (at which Dolal was not present) to remove him from the leadership. The removal was sealed in 2007 when the two factions made separate claims to represent the ONLF, each denouncing the other.

Eritrean and other support significantly boosted the military capacity of the ONLF in the region. With the government in Addis Ababa distracted by post-election security in 2005 and 2006, ONLF consolidated its forces and incorporated newly trained recruits, some flown in through Dusamareeb, while the cross-border airstrip was controlled by the Islamic Courts Union in mid-2006. By early 2007, even Ethiopian official sources put numbers of armed and trained ONLF fighters in the region at

---

[76] It is reported that the bodies of a number of foreign fighters, with passports, were discovered in this operation.

[77] Interviews, Addis Ababa, London, and Jijiga (2009).

2500–3000 at the peak, over and above the irregular support of clan mili-tia.[78] In April 2007, after more than a decade of low-intensity conflict, the scale of violence abruptly increased with the ONLF's lethal attack on the Chinese oil exploration facility at Abole. This highlighted the rebels' opposition to the government's facilitation of natural resource explora-tion—and the rebels' new capability. The ONLF explicitly articulated its objective of ensuring that commercial companies working under license with the government did not begin to extract oil and gas and other resources from the region. The ONLF's spokespersons at the time said: "If Ethiopia gets the oil and becomes self-sufficient they are 80 million and we are only 5–6 million. It will be our death warrant. So we are very adamant about this: we will not allow our oil to be exploited."[79]

The Ethiopian military crackdown that ensued throughout 2007–09 coincided with its military operations against the Islamic Courts Union (and its perceived Eritrean backers) in southern Somalia from December 2006 onward. Both drew sharp international condemnation and boosted Ogaadeeni diaspora and wider Somali support for the ONLF's resistance to the "Christian invader." A report, the following year, graphically set out the fears of international observers about the strategies pursued by the contending parties, and the brutal impact of the conflict on the population of the region.[80] The human rights concerns about the SNRS, which had been evident for more than a decade,[81] now escalated sharply.[82]

Indigenizing and Intensifying Counter-Insurgency After 2007

After a decade and a half of the widely ridiculed political instability and recy-cling of SNRS politicians, a younger generation of Ethiopian Somali elite had been brought to power. Trained in the Ethiopian Civil Service College, familiar with highland ways of doing business, and with apparently stronger loyalties to the center, they included a number of Ogaadeeni SPDP politi-cians. Notably, these were Dawd Mohammed (Makahil), Regional president in 2009 and 2010, and Abdi Mohammed Omar (Mohammed Zubeir/Reer Abdilleh), who took over the position in 2010, and—with remarkable

[78] Interviews, Addis Ababa, Harar (2009).
[79] Interview, London (2009).
[80] Human Rights Watch (2008).
[81] Khalif and Doornbos (2002).
[82] Hagmann and Korf (2012).

longevity—remains in post at the time of writing in 2017.[83] The increasing assertiveness, stability, and loyalty of the SNRS government brought new affordances to the Ethiopian counter-insurgency strategy bringing to bear a sophisticated, and increasingly ruthless, "internal" knowledge of clan politics, which had been lacking from ENDF-led activities.

In January 2009, Ethiopian troops in Denaan killed Dr. Dolal. He had returned to the region in November 2008. At the time of his killing, he was in the company of fighters of the UWSLF, with whom he was reported to be co-operating. UWSLF and government sources have subsequently claimed that the military was tipped-off by informants associated with Admiral Osman's ONLF. The Ethiopian and SNRS governments used these suspicions to exacerbate divisions between the two important Ogaadeen Mohammed Zubeir sub-clans: Dr. Dolal's Rer Abdilleh and the Admiral's Rer Isaaq. Ethiopian politicians explicitly articulated this strategy in August 2010, infuriating many Somalis inside and outside the region.

The second, highly controversial, change to counter-insurgency strategy of this period was the formal replacement of the (largely highland) Ethiopian National Defense Forces with newly established SNRS "Special Forces" or *liyu* police responsible for regional security on the ground. This was a significant step. It was the first time that the Ethiopian state had "delegated" responsibility for security on the ground in the Ethiopian SNRS to an ethnic-Somali regional force—albeit one under the close tutelage of federal security structures that continued to be stationed in significant numbers in this sensitive border region. The change transformed the dynamics of conflict, pitting Somali against Somali, and conflating the settling of local social and sub-clan scores with state-sanctioned counter-insurgency. Most observers agree that the activities of the *liyu* police increased the brutality of the conflict. By driving up the stakes, removing the highland-lowland, Christian-Muslim constellation, and sowing division, the strategy succeeded in increasing concomitant community and diaspora pressure for peace.[84] Over time, this markedly reduced the operational military capacity of the ONLF within the region, with many of its

---

[83] Two other non-Ogaadeen SPDP politicians of this generation remain ministers at the federal level.

[84] This chapter does not discuss the influential role of the large, articulate, and influential Ogaadeeni diaspora on this conflict. Hagmann (2014) notes that it has become divided between pro- and anti-government blocs, and over its attitude to the potential for peaceful political settlement.

fighters reportedly withdrawing to refugee camps and the Garissa region of Kenya by 2010. Meanwhile, a number of smaller organizations and splinter groups began to sue for peace.

The UWSLF and the 2010 Peace Negotiations

Little was known about the UWSLF before the organization entered into negotiations with the Ethiopian government in 2010. It had surfaced in 2006, when two aid workers were briefly taken hostage, apparently unintentionally,[85] and in November 2008, pledged to co-operate with the ONLF and a Front for the Independence of Oromia.[86]

The organization was led by Sheikh Ibrahim Dheere, and maintained an active Foreign Relations Spokesman in Scandinavia. It combined former rank-and-file fighters of the WSLF with a leadership drawn primarily from those previously involved with AIAI. In June 2010, the organization signed an agreement with the Ethiopian Government, renouncing its commitment to armed struggle. While still committed to the implementation of Ethiopian constitutional Article 39, giving the right to secession "when the time is appropriate," the organization became rapidly engaged in economic investment, development, and religious proselytism in the region, rather than joining the government or political campaigning.[87] In the wake of the deal, UWSLF became actively involved in humanitarian and developmental activities, import-export businesses, and commercial irrigation in the area around Gode. Half a decade later, its economic influence and sphere of activities was widely seen as having been curtailed.[88] Even less successful was the return of a small ONLF faction led by Salahaddin Ma'o, which also signed a peace deal with the government in 2010, but which quickly encountered difficulties in its attempts to involve itself in regional political activity, and was either swallowed up or marginalized by regional government actors.

---

[85] Human Rights Watch (2008).

[86] In February 2009, it was mentioned in connection with the detention of two Italian nuns who had been kidnapped in El Waq in November 2008 Corriere della Sera (2009). UWSLF, ONLF, et al. (2008).

[87] Interviews, UWSLF representatives, Jijiga, Addis Ababa (2009, 2011).

[88] Interviews, Jijiga, Addis Ababa (2017).

Failed Peace Talks: And a New Regional Environment?

A few months after the sudden death of Ethiopian Prime Minister Meles Zenawi in August 2012, the first official face-to-face talks between the ONLF and the Addis Ababa Government in more than a decade failed abruptly in Nairobi. The parties were divided over a formal commitment to hold a referendum on secession within 15 years, but there was considerable doubt as to the real potential of those negotiations to trigger lasting or sustainable change in the situation.[89] Many saw the fact that they were held at all as evidence of the weakness of the ONLF, with the Ethiopian government widely seen as unlikely to offer substantive concessions, and the gulf between the two sides as wide as ever.

An increasingly assertive SNRS government has played up a series of subsequent defections and/or alleged abductions from Kenya over the past five years as additional evidence of the weakening of the ONLF, although this is moot. Further talks were reported in early 2015 but these too collapsed. In August 2015, ONLF reiterated its commitment to armed struggle. It also joined—alongside the OLF, SLM, and others—the Asmara-backed Peoples' Alliance for Freedom and Democracy, which was formally established in Norway in October 2015. An upsurge in fighting in the SNRS was also widely reported to have flared up around the same time. The Ethiopian PM reportedly requested Turkey's President Erdogan to intervene to promote a peace process but little is known to have come of this. Between November 2016 and August 2017, Ethiopia was preoccupied with an internal state of emergency.[90]

Other important shifts and complications have resulted from wider regional dynamics. Of particular importance is the growth of Gulf-Horn linkages and investment. A close relationship between Ethiopia and Somaliland had already begun to reduce ONLF access to the SNRS from 2010, and this dynamic has continued. In September 2010, for instance, senior Somaliland officials reported that they had surrounded 200–300 ONLF rebels. The Somaliland officials claimed they had evidence that these rebels had been trained in Eritrea and had been transported by boat to Somaliland, from where they were attempting to cross into Ethiopia to

---

[89] Interviews, Addis Ababa, London; Hagmann (2014).

[90] Since January 2017, the SNRS government has been embroiled in a series of violent border clashes with neighboring Oromia. Many of the flashpoints are longstanding areas of controversy, not resolved under a series of border referenda held in October 2004.

pursue their struggle against the government.[91] While the ONLF denied the accusations,[92] the president of the SNRS, Abdi Mohamoud Oumer, endorsed them, adding the further claim that 123 ONLF fighters had been killed and another 90 surrounded.[93]

Landlocked Ethiopia has long been interested in the diversification of its port access from Djibouti, and concrete plans to develop a strategic trade corridor from Berbera inland through the SNRS emerged during 2016–17, with Ethiopia taking a 19% stake in a joint venture with the authorities in Hargeisa and Dubai Ports World. A violent attack at Gashamo on the Somaliland border in March 2016 threatened to derail these close relations. The reported killing of civilians drew outraged criticism of the SNRS government and *liyu* police, resonant with echoes of historical Ogaadeeni-Isaaq antipathy. With the national stakes so high, Ethiopian federal and regional government bodies were under pressure to be publicly seeking quick damage control.

At the broader level, there has been an increase in the global geostrategic attention paid to the Red Sea, Gulf of Aden, and Horn of Africa, described by Prunier as a new "pivot of the world,"[94] and growing interest on the part of a wide range of powers to maintain a strategic—often military—presence. The USA, China, France, and Japan all have operational bases in Djibouti, with Russia and Turkey developing a presence in different regional locations. The activities of the Gulf Co-operation Council since 2015 against Houthi rebels in Yemen have escalated the region's geostrategic significance, with an important GCC base established at Assab in Eritrea in late 2015, and the Emirates, Saudi Arabia, Qatar, and Egypt, all seeking additional influence around the coasts of the Horn. "The politics of the Middle East are spilling over into Somalia in a way we have never seen before," observes Bryden,[95] and during 2017, this became (arguably belatedly) an important new driver of Ethiopian regional foreign and security strategy. The continuing role of Eritrea as an active and public backer of the ONLF (and other Ethiopian opposition groups) ensures that the issue is high on the Ethiopian government agenda. Meanwhile, it seems clear that an influx of Gulf money is creating new incentives—for

[91] Garowe Online (2010).
[92] Malone (2010).
[93] BBC (2010).
[94] Prunier (2016).
[95] Bryden (2016).

investment rather than conflict—across the region. Throughout the Somali areas, inflows of investment money and new infrastructure are also having an effect on the decision-making of a range of actors. Chinese oil and gas exploration in the Ogaden basin has again come to the fore during 2016–17, with a sixth well drilled at the beginning of 2017, and investment in pipelines to the coast at Doraleh now planned.

If changing relations to the north have an impact on the shape of politics in the Ogaden, so too does the constellation of power in southern Somalia. In particular, the establishment of Jubbaland has provided Darood clans with a territorial base and investment focus around Kismayu that many saw as providing an alternative to the Ogaden. Its administration by Ahmed Madobe has further reduced Ethiopian anxieties about the establishment of a "back door into the Ogaden," with joint activities exploiting antipathies between Madobe and the ONLF seen in Addis Ababa as creating a buffer on the border.[96]

Meanwhile, at the end of August 2017, a key ONLF leader, Abdikarim Sheikh Muse—who had been living in Mogadishu—was arrested by Somali authorities and handed over to Ethiopia. This provoked an outcry on Somali social media platforms, where it was discussed as a betrayal of pan-Somali principles, drawing comparison with the 1988 agreement between Addis Ababa and Mogadishu. The arrest provoked demonstrations in the Somali region, Kenya, and London. The Somali Cabinet finally confirmed on September 6, 2017, that it had acted in accordance with 2015 and 2016 agreements between the two states. The incident is indicative of the changed pattern of interests according to which the current Somali government leadership operates, as well as how divided members of the government and parliament are on this issue. Further, it points to the extreme volatility and sensitivity of the issue across the Somali world. The issue of the Ogaden remains unresolved and toxic in both administrative practice and rhetoric potential.

CONCLUSION

Mayall and Simpson have identified what makes a chronic conflict with a secessionist undercurrent.[97] This chapter sought to establish that these dynamics continue to be in place in the Horn of Africa in relation to the

[96] Interviews, Addis Ababa, Nairobi 2011, 2017; Hagmann (2014: 53–4).
[97] Mayall, J. and Simpson, M. (1992).

Ogaden. Ethiopian Somalis have in the past and present experienced differential treatment at the hands of the Ethiopian state. Ethiopian centralism under imperial and military regimes explicitly sought to eliminate cultural diversity. While this seemed to shift to a degree under Ethiopian federalism since 1991, questions remain over the pattern of access to power.

Economic grievances and confessional divisions have emerged as clear drivers of Ogaden secessionism, morphing, and reforming under different historical circumstances. The over-riding importance of the regional environment, including patterns of economic integration and disintegration, emerges with particular clarity in this pastoral context. The practical prospect of *Somalia irredenta* may have diminished with the collapse of the Somali Republic in the wake of Siad Barre but the resentment of perceived Ethiopian policy toward Somalis has not. Likewise, new "enemy's enemies" have become friends, as regional relationships shift and strain.

The ongoing low-level conflict between the ONLF and the Government of Ethiopia is only the latest round in a century-old conflict between highland rulers of Ethiopia and Somali/Ogaadeeni separatists. Viewed from this longer-term perspective, Ethiopia's ruling EPRDF and federal government is only the current post-holder in a series of highland governments. As such, writes the UN, "it is in charge of and logically interested in maintaining Ethiopian cohesion and uses its armed forces to that end."[98] At the nub of the ONLF's shifting and disparate aims and objectives has always been the desire for a referendum on the Ethiopian Somali or Ogaadeen political dispensation. It was the dispute over a referendum on independence in 1994 that pushed the core of the ONLF back into armed struggle in 1995; it broke up talks in 2012 and apparently again in 2015. If there is ever to be a shift from violent to political means of addressing the issue, shifts and consensus in the pattern of popular opinion will have to be part of the process.

Addis Ababa would find it hard to reconcile a secessionist popular vote with the over-riding impetus to maintain Ethiopian cohesion. In the early 1990s, an EPRDF-led government facilitated Eritrean independence and introduced constitutional Article 39 in the teeth of vigorous resistance. By the end of the decade, Ethiopia found itself in a brutal war with its newly independent neighbor; the Ethiopian government was also stunned by the vigor and violence of urban opposition to the system of multinational federalism that crystallized in 2005. As a result of these developments, and

[98] UN (2003: 21).

with Ethiopian nationalism and ethno-nationalisms more sensitive than ever, a sustainable political solution to the situation in the Ogaden requires political courage, creativity, and conviction. These qualities have not been in evidence for some years—particularly in the periods after the 2005 poll, and the 2016–17 state of emergency.

Until 2011, it had seemed unlikely that either the Government of Ethiopia or the ONLF would push for a full negotiated settlement. The military crackdown that followed the 2007 Awole attack, coincident with Ethiopia's military operations in Somalia itself, drew international condemnation. Both sides were publicly committed to seeking a military victory. In 2009 and 2010, SNRS and federal officials repeated that the ONLF had been defeated over the period since early/mid-2007, and that what remained was only a "mopping up" operation against a number of small, scattered, acephalous guerrilla groups. ONLF sources meanwhile asserted—with even less credibility—that because their numbers and support had grown exponentially over the same period, they were confident of "comprehensively defeating" the military forces of the Ethiopian state within the next five years.

Neither of these claims is realistic. Instead there is reason to believe that without an inclusive and comprehensive settlement underpinned by shifts in economic integration and popular support, this conflict could continue, at significant if lower levels of violence, for a long time. The state of what the UN calls "neither peace nor all-out war"[99] has been the best achieved for more than a century. The conflict continues to undermine Ethiopia's attempts at social and political transformation, blighting the lives of its citizens, and shaming the ideals of all of those involved.

Although contemporary conflict in the Ogaden is, at one level, a straightforward secular nationalist struggle (secessionist or not) between different visions of "self-determination" of the Somali-inhabited—or Ogaadeen-inhabited—areas of Ethiopia, it is not just that. First, those involved construct their perceptions of the struggle amidst other complicating dynamics including demographics, clans, territory, natural resources, trade, histories of Abyssinian colonialism and pan-Somali irredentism, human rights violations, Islamism, terrorism, and the regional balance of power. Second, as had always been the case in the histories described in this chapter, the conflict has not been fought between two disciplined, monolithic, and consistent parties—whether thought of as Government

[99] UN (2003: 29).

and Front, clan and "colonizer," Christian and Muslim—each with a stable base of popular support lined up behind it. There are intricate ranges of interests, influences, factions and alliances on both sides and moving between them. They are in continuous flux temporally and spatially, and their shifting constellations look very different at local, regional, national, and international levels.[100]

Thus while it seems clear that widespread assumptions about the macro-level "historical confrontations" in play in this case do indeed fuel chronic secessionism, nevertheless these confrontations perhaps do rather less to account for the micro-sociology of conflict and the desire for peace, as experienced by communities and individuals. The changing pattern of conflict on the ground correlating with changes in the security responsibilities of the SNRS government after 2009 and in the relations with neighboring Somali areas to the north and south since then, demonstrates this point.

Amidst all the claims and counter claims, lurid rumors, frank fabrications, and extravagant propaganda associated with the struggle for the Somali-inhabited areas of Ethiopia, only a few things are known for sure. One is that this conflict will be resolved only by some kind of political settlement, and not through military or violent means. Another is that, in the meantime, over and above those killed or injured, it is the poorest stratum of the inhabitants of the SNRS who are being further impoverished and marginalized by the continuation of conflict.

References

Bahru Zewde (1991). *A history of modern Ethiopia*. Oxford: James Currey.

Barnes, C. (2000). *The Ethiopian state and its Somali periphery, c.1888–1848*. DPhil Thesis, Trinity College, Cambridge University, Faculty of History, Cambridge.

Barnes, C. (2007). The Somali youth league, Ethiopian Somalis, and the greater Somalia idea, c.1946–1948. *Journal of Eastern African Studies, 1*(2), 277–291.

Barnes, C. (2010). The Ethiopian-British Somaliland boundary. In Dereje Feyissa & M. V. Hoehne (Eds.), *Borders and borderlands as resources in the Horn of Africa* (pp. 103–122). Oxford: James Currey.

BBC. (2010, September 15). *Ethiopia 'kills 123' ONLF rebels and surrounds 90 more*. Retrieved from BBC http://www.bbc.co.uk/news/world-africa-11315967

---

[100] Hagmann has made a similar point about the multiple levels of interests in play during the Ogaden war in the late 1970s (2014: 18).

Bryden, M. (1995). *Peace and unity conference of the Somali nation of region 5.* Addis Ababa: UN-EUE.

Bryden, M. (2016). *The race against time in Somalia.* Seminar at the Centre for Strategic and International Studies, posted online 24 March 2016. https://www.youtube.com/watch?v=lZmWu2Yf57I. Accessed 6 Oct 2016.

Counter Terrorism Centre at West Point. (n.d.). *Al Quaeda's (mis)adventures in the Horn of Africa.* Counter Terrorism Centre at the US Military Academy, West Point. Retrieved from http://www.ctc.usma.edu/aq/pdf/Al-Qa%27ida%27s%20MisAdventures%20in%20the%20Horn%20of%20Africa.pdf

de Waal, A. (2009). *The rage of numbers: Recalling Ethiopia's wars.* Retrieved from http://blogs.ssrc.org/darfur/2009/08/16/the-rage-of-numbers-recalling-ethiopias-wars/

Diaz, A., & Dorman, S. R. (2018). We didn't fight for this: The pitfalls of state- and nationbuilding in Eritrea. In L. de Vries, P. Englebert, & M. Schomerus (Eds.), *Secessionism in African politics: Aspiration, grievance, performance, disenchantment.* New York: Palgrave.

Englebert, P., & Hummel, R. (2005). Let's stick together: Understanding Africa's secessionist deficit. *African Affairs, 39*(1), 399–427.

Garowe Online. (2010, September 13). *Somalia: '200 ONLF rebels secretly land in Somaliland,' says govt minister.* Retrieved from http://www.garoweonline.com/artman2/publish/Somalia_27/Somalia_200_ONLF_rebels_secretly_land_in_Somaliland_says_Govt_minister.shtml

Gebru Tareke (1991). *Ethiopia power and protest: Peasant revolts in the twentieth century.* Cambridge: Cambridge University Press.

Gebru Tareke (2000). The Ethiopia-Somalia War of 1977 revisited. *The International Journal of African Historical Studies, 33*(3), 635–667.

Gebru Tareke (2002). From lash to red star: The pitfalls of counter-insurgency in Ethiopia, 1980–1982. *Journal of Modern African Studies, 40*(3), 465–498.

Gebru Tareke (2009). *The Ethiopian Revolution: War in the Horn of Africa.* New Haven: Yale University Press.

Hagman, T. (2014). *Talking peace in the Ogaden: The search for an end to conflict in the Somali Regional State in Ethiopia.* Nairobi: Rift Valley Institute.

Hagmann, T. (2005). Beyond clannishness and colonialism: Understanding political disorder in Ethiopia's Somali region, 1991–2004. *Journal of Modern African Studies, 43,* 509–536.

Hagmann, T., & Korf, B. (2012). Agamben in the Ogaden: Violence and sovereignty in the Ethiopian-Somali frontier. *Political Geography, 31,* 205–214.

Hansen, S. J. (2009). Somalia – Grievance, religion, clan and profit. In S. J. Hansen, A. Mesoy, & T. Kardas (Eds.), *The borders of Islam: Exploring Samuel Huntington's faultlines from Al-Andalus to the virtual umma* (pp. 127–138). New York: Hurst/Columbia University Press.

Hansen, S. J., Mesoy, A., & Kardas, T. (2009). *The borders of Islam: Exploring Samuel Huntingon's faultlines from Al-Andalus to the virtual umma*. New York: Hurst/Columbia University Press.

Henze, P. (2000). *Layers of time: A history of Ethiopia*. London: Hurst.

Hess, R. (1964). The 'Mad Mullah' and northern Somalia. *Journal of African History, 5*(3), 415–433.

Hoehne, M. V. (2018). Against the grain: Somaliland's secession from Somalia. In L. de Vries, P. Englebert, & M. Schomerus (Eds.), *Secessionism in African politics: Aspiration, grievance, performance, disenchantment*. New York: Palgrave.

Human Rights Watch. (2008). *Collective punishment: War crimes and crimes against humanity in the Ogaden area of Ethiopia's Somali Regional State*. New York: Human Rights Watch.

Huntington, S. P. (1996). *The clash of civilizations and the remaking of world order*. New York: Simon & Schuster.

Khalif, M. H., & Doornbos, M. (2002). The Somali region in Ethiopia: A neglected human rights tragedy. *Review of African Political Economy, 29*(91), 73–94.

Legum, C. (1963). Somali liberation songs. *Journal of Modern African Studies, 1*(4), 503–519.

Lewis, I. (1958). Modern political movements in Somaliland. *Africa, 28*(3–4), 244–261.

Lewis, I. (2002). *A modern history of the Somali* (4th ed.). Oxford: James Currey.

Malone, B. (2010, September 15). *Ethiopia rebels deny standoff with Somaliland forces*. Retrieved from http://af.reuters.com/article/topNews/idAFJOE68 E03U20100915

Marchal, R. (2009). A tentative assessment of the Somali Harakat Al-Shabaab. *Journal of East African Studies, 3*(3), 381–404.

Markakis, J. (1987). *National & class conflict in the Horn of Africa*. Cambridge: Cambridge University Press.

Markakis, J. (1997). The Somali in Ethiopia. *Review of African Political Economy, 24*, 567–570.

Markakis, J. (2011). *Ethiopia: The last two frontiers*. Oxford: James Currey.

Mayall, J., & Simpson, M. (1992). Ethnicity is not enough: Reflections on protracted secessionism in the third world. *Journal of Comparative Sociology, 33*(1/2), 5–25.

Muth, F. C. (2003). Ahmad b. Ibrahim al-Ghazi. In S. v. Uhlig, B. Yimam, D. Crummey, & D. Goldenberg (Eds.), *Encylopaedia Aethiopica: A-C* (Vol. 1). Wiesbaden: Harrassowitz Verlag.

Ostebo, T. (2009). Ethiopia – On the borders of Christianity. In S. J. Hansen, A. Mesoy, & T. Kardas (Eds.), *The borders of Islam: An exploration of Samuel Huntingon's faultlines from Al-Andalus to the virtual umma* (pp. 139–154). New York: Hurst/Columbia University Press.

Ottaway, M., & Ottaway, D. (1978). *Ethiopia: Empire in revolution*. New York: Africana Publishing Company/Homes & Meier Publishers.

Perouse de Montclos, M. A. (2000). Des ONG sans gouvernement: Mouvements islamiques et velléités de substitution à l'État dans la Somalie en guerre. Retrieved from http://www.unesco.org/most/perouse.doc

Prunier, G. (2009). Sudan – Trying to understand its multiple marginality. In S. J. Hansen, A. Mesoy, & T. Kardas (Eds.), *The borders of Islam: Exploring Samuel Huntington's faultlines from Al-Andalus to the virtual umma* (pp. 155–168). New York: Hurst/Columbia University Press.

Prunier, G. (2016, September 17). Horn of Africa: Pivot of the world. *Le Monde Diplomatique*. Posted in English translation on Middle East Online. Retrieved from http://www.middle-east-online.com/english/?id=78711

Samatar, S. (1982). *Oral poetry and Somali nationalism*. Cambridge: CUP.

Samatar, A. I. (2004). Ethiopian federalism: Autonomy versus control in the Somali region. *Third World Quarterly, 25*(6), 1131–1154.

Schomerus, M., & de Vries, L. (2018). A state of contradiction: Sudan's unity goes south. In L. de Vries, P. Englebert, & M. Schomerus (Eds.), *Secessionism in African politics: aspiration, grievance, performance, disenchantment*. New York: Palgrave.

Schroeder, G. (1998). *Von Aethiopisch-Somaliland zum Somalistaat Aethiopiens*. Addis Ababa, unpublished manuscript.

Seid, M. M. (2009, January 26). *The role of religion in the Ogaden conflict*. Retrieved July 16, 2009, from http://hornofafrica.ssrc.org/mealin/printable.html

Corriere della Sera. (2009, February 20). *Kidnapped nuns freed in Kenya*. Retrieved from Corriere della Sera. Retrieved from http://www.corriere.it/english/09_febbraio_20/nuns_freed_c6707708-ff51-11dd-a1d5-00144f02aabc.shtml

Sheikh-Abdi, A. (1993). *Divine madness: Mohammed Abdulleh Hassan (1856–1920)*. London: Zed Books.

Steiner, A. (1936). The government of Italian East Africa. *American Political Science Review, 30*(5), 884–902.

Tibebe Eshete (1991). The root causes of political problems in the Ogaden, 1942–1960. *Northeast African Studies, 13*(1), 9–28.

Tibebe Eshete (1994). Towards a history of the incorporation of the Ogaden: 1887–1935. *Journal of Ethiopian Studies, 27*(2), 69–87.

Touval, S. (1963). *Somali nationalism: International politics and the drive for unity in the Horn of Africa*. Cambridge, MA: Harvard University Press.

Tsegaye Tegenu (1994). *The evolution of Ethiopian absolutism: The genesis and making of the fiscal military state, 1696–1913*. Los Angeles/Addis Ababa: Tsehai Publisher.

United Nations. (2003). *Confidential internal report*. Addis Ababa: UN.

UWSLF, ONLF, FIO, etc. (2008, November 19). *Joint press release of ONLF, FIO, UWSLF* etc. Retrieved from http://www.fidoqeyroo.org/Joint_Press_Release. html

Vaughan, S. (1994). The Addis Ababa transitional conference of July 1991: Its origins, history and significance. In *Occasional papers* (Vol. 51). Edinburgh: University of Edinburgh, Centre of African Studies.

PART II

Grievance: Postcolonial Confusion

CHAPTER 5

Western Sahara and Morocco: Complexities of Resistance and Analysis

Matthew Porges

INTRODUCTION

On June 26, 2014, in Curitiba, Brazil, Algeria faced Russia in the group stage of the FIFA World Cup. On the day of the match, I was in El Aaiun, Western Sahara, conducting interviews in the home of one of my translators. My translator was an avid football fan and had been excited about the match all day, so we stopped our interviews shortly before the match began so he could watch. At his insistence, we drove to a café where the match was shown on satellite TV. The café was small, crowded, and noisy, with about 60 people inside cheering loudly for Algeria. When the screen showed a Polisario flag in the Algerian section, the response in the café was deafening.

The scene was familiar, but with high stakes. El Aaiun is the nominal capital of Western Sahara, a territory that has been largely under Moroccan occupation since a 1975 invasion that followed Spain's withdrawal from its former colony. Since 1991, a listless and sometimes tenuous ceasefire has held—with some exceptions—between Morocco and the pro-independence Polisario Front, which is based in nearby Tindouf, Algeria. The Algerian government's support for Polisario, and for

M. Porges (✉)
University of St Andrews, St Andrews, UK

© The Author(s) 2019
L. de Vries et al. (eds.), *Secessionism in African Politics*,
Palgrave Series in African Borderlands Studies,
https://doi.org/10.1007/978-3-319-90206-7_5

Western Sahara, is a curious historical phenomenon. It may be as much a case of solidarity with another victim of clumsy European decolonization as a geopolitical lever against Algeria's regional rival, Morocco, which claims Western Sahara as part of its pre-colonial territory. No country officially recognizes Morocco's claim, but the occupation persists.

Russia scored early in the match, but the mood remained upbeat. My research partner and I were the only non-Sahrawis in the café, and many people came by to introduce themselves and shake our hands. Our host had a number of friends in the crowd, and by halftime we were part of a large group, sitting together and joking about the game and the conflict. "If Algeria wins the game, there's going to be a riot," our host warned. "If they win the tournament," somebody else joked, "Western Sahara will gain independence."

About halfway through the match, a man in street clothes approached us and asked for our passports. Our host pulled him aside, and after a quick exchange, the man sat down at the back of the café, staring at us. Our host explained that he was a Moroccan intelligence officer: "I told him you will show him your passports, but he has to wait until the end of the match."

Algeria scored to tie late in the game, to another explosion of cheers in the café, and held on for a single point and placement in the quarterfinals. When the match ended, Sahrawis poured out of the café—the door was crowded, and several jumped out of the street-level windows—chanting "1-2-3...*Vive Algerie!*"

El Aaiun was dark, and the streets were flooded with people chanting and yelling. On every corner, Moroccan security vehicles were parked, unloading police in riot gear or plainclothes officers carrying radios. Crouched in the back seat of our host's car, we could see a gathering crowd of Sahrawis. Our host rolled down his window and yelled "1-2-3...*Vive Algerie!*" The crowd responded in kind and moved away from us, toward a cluster of Moroccan military vehicles at an intersection ahead. Our host jerked the car off the road, cutting through a network of derelict structures and away from the riot.

Some time after we got home, there was a knock on our host's door. The Moroccan police had apparently tracked us to his house, and demanded to see our passports. They asked what we were doing in Western Sahara—we said, as always, that we were tourists—and after a quick conversation with our host, they left. "We will be smart," our host told us afterwards. "We will play the game of Tom and Jerry."

The arrival of the police at our door, and their abrupt departure, was a message, a symbol of the reach of Moroccan intelligence in Western Sahara. Our host was a Sahrawi, living in a Sahrawi neighborhood—much of El Aaiun is segregated into Moroccan and Sahrawi areas—but he warned us not to go outside, or even to go near the windows. We had first arrived at his house at around five in the morning in a taxi and had left it only to walk a few feet to a waiting car each time we went to the Sahrawi café or to the home of one of his friends. The point of the visit, of course, was to let us know—and to let our host know—that despite our precautions, we were being watched.

This incident was instructive in a number of ways. The most obvious was the visible, performative surveillance by Moroccan security forces. Its impact on Sahrawi life is difficult to overstate. Many Sahrawis told me that they felt the police presence everywhere—that nothing could protect them from the police, who seemed to know about demonstrations before they even began. Another was the fact that hundreds of security forces appeared to have been mobilized for the football riot. This required several assumptions on the part of Moroccan security officials: first, that at least a large percentage of Sahrawis wanted independence. Second, that independence was associated with Polisario. Third, that Polisario was associated with Algeria. Fourth, that the resulting support for Algeria would be so intense that a strong performance by Algeria's football team would inevitably result in pro-independence demonstrations in El Aaiun. And that is exactly what happened.

The football match and subsequent demonstrations were also an illustration of the contested narratives of the Western Sahara conflict. From the perspective of many Sahrawis—certainly from the perspective of Polisario, the independence movement—and the Sahrawi Arab Democratic Republic (SADR), the state-in-exile of which Polisario functions as the major political party, the case is fairly simple. Spanish colonialism, and later Moroccan irredentism, have prevented self-determination for an indigenous population. The Moroccan perspective considers Western Sahara a historical part of Greater Morocco, meaning that Polisario can be written off as an Algerian client, propped up by the Algerian government as leverage in a long-standing regional rivalry. While international law heavily favors the Sahrawi case, the geopolitical reality has left Morocco in control of most of the territory, with no resolution in sight to the stalemate.

This chapter explores some of the ways in which narratives of the Western Sahara conflict have been framed, and how scholars and analysts of Western Sahara can move past some paradoxes and complexities in discussing and studying the conflict. The case is not merely fraught with political partisanship and contested histories but is also in many ways unique in International Relations. Parallels exist between Western Sahara and Palestine, East Timor, the situation of indigenous peoples of North America and Australia, and several other cases. Often, the insights gained from such comparisons are useful, but there are elements of the case of Western Sahara that are all its own; it is neither a case of true secessionism nor simple decolonization. In the sections that follow, I will explore what we can learn from applying several different lenses to Western Sahara, and how we might move beyond simple ontologies of conflict and resistance.

A Brief Political History of Western Sahara

Human and Physical Geography

The territory now known as Western Sahara is located on the west coast of Africa, with a large Atlantic coastline. It shares a land border with Morocco to the north and Mauritania to the south and east, and a very short border with Algeria in the northeast. Its surface area is approximately 266,000 km² —slightly larger than the United Kingdom, and comparable to the state of Colorado—with a population of a little over 500,000, making it one of the most sparsely populated regions on Earth. The terrain consists mainly of low, flat desert, with some small mountains and very limited arable land. The territory is fairly rich in phosphates and iron ore, with potential for oil exploration off the coast. It also features some of the richest coastal fishing grounds in the world.[1]

Western Sahara is divided by a 2,700-kilometer militarized sand wall, or berm, constructed by Morocco during the 1975–1991 war between Morocco and the pro-independence Polisario Front. Often referred to as "defensive," the wall was initially conceived as an offensive tool, expanded in progressively larger concentric semi-circles as a way of slowing raids upon Moroccan positions. Much of the wall is guarded by millions of landmines, and there are unmarked mines scattered throughout both the Moroccan-controlled zone and the Polisario-controlled zone. Approximately two-thirds to three-quarters of the territory of Western Sahara lies west of the wall and is occupied by Morocco (the "Occupied Zone"). The SADR, of which Polisario now functions as the governing party, administrates the remaining section to the east (which Polisario calls the "Liberated Zone" or

---

[1] CIA World Factbook: Western Sahara (n.d.).

"Free Zone"). Morocco does not recognize SADR, frequently and incorrectly derides Polisario as a terrorist group, and administers the Occupied Zone as a part of Morocco's "Southern Provinces," although it maintains what may be among the densest military occupation in the world. SADR administers the area east of the wall, as well as several refugee camps in Tindouf Province, Algeria. The Polisario/SADR zone is home to around 40,000 Sahrawi nomads,[2] while the camps house at least 100,000 refugees.

Western Sahara's inhabitants are primarily Sahrawis, a group with a complex definition and history. Part of the complexity derives from the historic practice of nomadism, which complicates a population's relationship with states and borders. Thus, the correspondance between "Sahrawis" and "Western Sahara" defies simplistic explanations. Stephen Zunes and Jacob Mundy, who have written the definitive history of the conflict, describe the relationship in this way:

> The term *Sahrawi*...is often used to mean "indigenous Western Saharan," although this equivalent is not accurate. Indeed, it is sufficient on most accounts that an "ethnic" Sahrawi only has to claim descent from one of the recognized major or minor social groupings—"tribes" or "confederations"—in or overlapping the former Spanish Sahara.... The most pragmatic definition of Sahrawis is that they are the Hassaniyyah-speaking peoples who claim membership among at least one of the social groupings found in and around the area now known as Western Sahara.[3]

Before Spain began its colonial administration of the area, Sahrawi culture was largely predicated on nomadic pastoralism and trading. Camels, sheep, and goats were the most common livestock, herded between oases and small patches of arable land. Sahrawi social structure, religion, and military strategy are all usefully understood partly through the lens of nomadism and the transition from a nomadic to a semi-urban organization that began under Spanish colonialism and accelerated during the war with Morocco. For Sahrawis and Sahrawi culture, this transition was enormously significant. The political implications of Sahrawi nomadism will be considered in more detail later, but readers should bear in mind that nomadic practice remains meaningful even for sedentarized Sahrawis living in, for instance, Western Saharan cities and towns or the Tindouf refugee camps.

---

[2] Sevillano (2010).
[3] Zunes and Mundy (2010: 92–93).

Accurate and up-to-date demographic statistics for Sahrawi populations in both the Occupied Zone and the Liberated Zone are sparse due to both challenging research conditions and the dynamic definitions in some of the ethnographic categories. A broad sociological survey of the population of Western Sahara would go a long way toward clearing up some major research *lacunae*. Demography is one area where the significance of nomadism becomes evident. The population of the Tindouf camps, for instance, is contested, with Morocco seeking to minimize population estimates for geopolitical gain; Polisario is typically reluctant to allow population census research. The best estimates of camp population typically come from[4] either satellite photography (an estimate based on satellite data came up with 90,000 residents) or aid distribution/consumption (Oxfam, for instance, tends to use 120,000 as a population estimate when distributing food aid).[5]

Any such "snapshot" survey is likely to be incomplete. Many of the Sahrawi residents of Tindouf camps also spend time practicing semi-nomadic pastoralism in the pasturelands in either Tindouf Province or the Liberated Zone; many also spend part of the year in Mauritania or Europe. The population of the Liberated Zone may be around 40,000, but this figure represents a population mostly composed of nomads, whose resistance to being counted and measured is a recurring theme in the scholarship on mobility. Estimates of population, therefore, are provisional, dynamic, and lacking formal consensus in the literature.

Another complicating factor for demographers is the presence of hundreds of thousands of settlers introduced by Morocco into Western Sahara since 1975. This settlement began with the Green March, an episode in which Moroccan civilians crossed into Spanish Sahara ahead of the Moroccan military, taking Spain by surprise. During the war between Morocco and Polisario, more settlers arrived in an attempt to skew the results of a future referendum on independence. The settlers are a mix of Moroccan Arabs, Berbers from the Atlas and Rif, and Sahrawis living in southern Morocco. This demographic engineering reached its apex during the registration process for the referendum in the 1990s, when many of the non-Sahrawi settlers received instruction in Sahrawi culture and in the Hassaniyya dialect of Arabic. The plan was for these "constructed" Sahrawis to vote for integration with Morocco and offset the expected near-unanimous vote in favor of independence by "real" Sahrawis. Although no referendum has yet

[4] UNHCR (2010).
[5] Interview (2016).

been held, the settlement policy has had its desired effect: settlers may now outnumber indigenous Sahrawis in the Occupied Zone.

Colonialism and War in the Sahara

Parts of what is now Western Sahara were occasionally connected in various ways and to varying degrees by regional powers, but the history of the region as a geographically cohesive unit began with Spanish colonization in the late nineteenth century. The region had never existed as an independent state, and state-centralized control was difficult to exert over the sparsely populated, inhospitable territory and the people inhabiting it.

Spanish colonialism in the Sahara officially began in 1884. Spain's administrative control over the territory was often somewhat limited and inconsistent, but by the 1970s, Spain had worn out its welcome and was facing increasing resistance from the population. The Polisario Front (from the Spanish acronym *Frente Popular de Liberación de Saguía el Hamra y Río de Oro*, the original Spanish name of the territory) was established in 1973 and rapidly mobilized much of the population. Spain's strategy of mollifying Sahrawi leaders with gifts of food or automobiles and tying nomads to the cities with promises of jobs had not secured the colonial regime's legitimacy in the eyes of the population.

By the mid-1970s, Spain was considering withdrawing and handing over governance of the territory to the indigenous population. Both Morocco and Mauritania had designs upon the territory, claiming it was part of their historical lands. Morocco based this largely on the irredentist narrative of a Greater Morocco that included parts of Western Sahara, Algeria, and Mauritania, as well as the Spanish (to this day) cities of Ceuta and Melilla. In Mauritania, the connection was predicated largely on a shared dialect and cultural history, as well as geopolitical expediency. An investigation in 1975 by the International Court of Justice (ICJ) produced the following Advisory Opinion:

> [T]he Court's conclusion is that the materials and information presented to it do not establish any tie of territorial sovereignty between the territory of Western Sahara and the Kingdom of Morocco or the Mauritanian entity. Thus the Court has not found legal ties of such a nature as might affect the application of General Assembly resolution 1514 (XV)—in the decolonization of Western Sahara and, in particular, of the principle of self-determination through the free and genuine expression of the will of the peoples of the Territory.[6]

[6] ICJ (n.d.).

Nevertheless, King Hassan II of Morocco declared victory, claiming that the ICJ had decided in his favor. Shortly after, to Spain's surprise, hundreds of thousands of Moroccan civilians marched into Western Sahara. Within days, Spain signed the Madrid Accords, dividing the territory between Morocco and Mauritania. Polisario, still determined to achieve independence, now found itself fighting not a Spanish colonial force, but rather two separate and coordinated invasions.

From the beginning, military and political disparities between the two sides shaped strategies and counterstrategies. Polisario—vastly outnumbered and outgunned but with better knowledge of the deep desert and support from much of local population—relied on hit-and-run guerilla warfare. Sahrawis had employed such tactics for centuries, but now they replaced camels with Spanish-built Land Rovers (in the Tindouf camps, such Land Rovers are still sometimes referred to as *dreimissa*—"short-horned goat").[7] Initially, the emphasis on speed and dispersal worked well for Polisario, allowing attacks on targets well behind the nominal "front line" and making it difficult for Morocco to hold territory. Following Moroccan napalm attacks on Sahrawi civilian targets in Tifariti, Polisario withdrew large numbers of Sahrawi civilians across the border into Tindouf by 1976.

A series of attacks deep into Mauritania, combined with internal instability in the country, led to Mauritania's withdrawal from the war by 1979. Polisario now found itself facing an unusual counterinsurgency strategy. Instead of attempting to defeat Polisario outright, Morocco began to consolidate its control over urban centers and resource-rich areas such as the phosphate mines at Bou Craa, expanding outwards in a series of concentric semi-circles. The barriers thus erected moved over time, functioning essentially as both an offensive territorial weapon and an early-warning system against Polisario raids; guerilla attacks could now hit only the wall itself. This strategy left the territory littered with landmines, and came at tremendous expense for Morocco—but it did render the war a stalemate by the mid-1980s. At that point, Morocco controlled most of the territory (including some originally claimed by Mauritania) but was unable to expand much further into the desert.

With the prospect of significant military progress remote for either side, a UN-brokered ceasefire was signed in 1991, with a referendum on independence to follow in a shift to diplomacy that Zunes and Mundy have

---

[7] Sulaiman and Berkson (2014).

called "a continuation of war by other means."[8] The end of the Western Sahara War kept Spain out of Africa (except for Ceuta and Melilla) while it legally maintained administrating power. Morocco gained control of about two-thirds of the territory, with a dense and costly military occupation looming. Polisario controlled about a third of the territory, as well as a series of refugee camps in Tindouf, Algeria, which existed with the permission of the Algerian government.

Western Sahara Since 1991

The referendum—the condition of the ceasefire negotiations—has yet to happen, and the prospects of it happening in the near future appear slim. The UN mission in the territory, MINURSO, (from the French Mission des Nations Unies pour l'Organisation d'un Référendum au Sahara Occidental) was originally tasked with organizing it, but now functions mainly as a ceasefire monitor. The journalist Jeremy Harding, reviewing Toby Shelley's excellent work on the diplomatic history of the conflict, described the process this way:

> The ceasefire was possible only because of the intervention of other parties, notably the UN. It insisted, as did the Organisation of African Unity, that the fate of the disputed territory should be resolved by a vote. The result would either confirm the annexation or return the Western Sahara to the Sahrawis. ...But who was entitled to take part? The Sahrawis felt that the only fair way to determine this was to look at the census drawn up by Spain before it left. According to their calculations, there would be about 75,000 people who could vote, some in the territory itself, others in exile; most of them, if not all, would favour independence. King Hassan did not see eye to eye with the Sahrawis. There were many more, in the royal view, who lived within the legal borders of his kingdom but who had originated in the annexed slab of desert: these, he was sure, would favour 'integration'.... The royal stratagem was quite clearly to bog down the identification process to such an extent that the UN lost patience and the Sahrawis lost hope.[9]

By progressively introducing new voters into MINURSO's voter census, Morocco stalled the referendum. Raising processual questions throughout

---

[8] Zunes and Mundy (2010). This inverts Clausewitz's dictum that war is "politics by other means".

[9] Harding (2006).

the 1990s, Morocco entrenched its territorial interests while accumulating diplomatic capital in the West. As the referendum has yet to take place, and now appears more complicated than ever, the strategy seems to have been largely successful. Morocco has simply out-waited the various diplomats and negotiators involved, relying heavily on the support of the United States and France at the UN Security Council, both of whom possess geopolitical interests in Morocco.

Meanwhile, a return to war also seems unlikely. Though Polisario retains a standing army, the Sahrawi People's Liberation Army (SPLA), the disparity in military power has widened since 1991. Polisario had previously capitalized on Morocco's inability to comprehensively monitor a vast desert. Yet Moroccan surveillance abilities have improved considerably. During the war, Algeria supported Polisario; Polisario also used captured equipment from Morocco and Mauritania. Morocco has since modernized its forces, while Polisario has had less opportunity to upgrade its military technology. Morocco's continuous efforts to depict Polisario as a terrorist organization have furthermore set up a rhetorical ploy whereby any violence in Western Sahara can be cast as terrorism; indeed, much of Morocco's diplomatic capital in the West comes from its perceived willingness to cooperate in the War on Terror.

The independence movement thus found itself in a dire position, yet support for a Sahrawi state has not significantly waned.[10] As Polisario grew more and more diplomatically beleaguered, resistance shifted from the international diplomatic sphere to the streets of the Occupied Zone. Younger Sahrawis, raised under occupation or in exile, are exploring new modes of nonviolent resistance, manifesting in protests and demonstrations but also in assertions of cultural survival such as the inculcation of nomadic skills to children, use of the Hassaniyya dialect, or even the construction of tents indoors or on rooftops following their prohibition by Morocco. In both the Occupied Zone and the refugee camps, this resistance includes the use of digital communications, journalism by and about Sahrawis, and a large body of resistance poetry and music. Activist groups such as *Asociación Saharaui de Víctimas de Violaciones Graves de los Derechos Humanos Cometidas por el Estado Marroquí* (ASVDH), *Colectivo Saharaui de Defensores de los Derechos Humanos* (CODESA), and *Comité de Defensa del Derecho de Autodeterminacion del Pueblo del Sahara Occidental* (CODAPSO) document human rights abuses and work toward

---

[10] Porges and Leuprecht (2016).

self-determination. In the refugee camps, there is a museum detailing many of the forced disappearances, assassination, and torture of Sahrawi activists. Organizations like ARTifariti and Screams Against the Wall provide creative outlets for resistance in both the physical and digital sphere. Virtually all of this resistance has been remarkably peaceful.

There is a single substantiated potential exception to the nonviolent strategy. In October 2010, at Gdeim Izik, near El Aaiun, thousands of Sahrawis gathered in a protest camp to demonstrate against the Moroccan occupation. The camp quickly became a tent city for more than 20,000 Sahrawis, eventually including a hospital and a prison. On October 24, Moroccan security forces fired on a Sahrawi vehicle entering the camp, killing a 14-year-old boy.[11] Just over two weeks later, on November 8, the security forces attacked and destroyed the camp, triggering violent clashes throughout El Aaiun that spread into other cities in Western Sahara. The rioting left at least 11 Moroccan security forces dead. Although the violence by Sahrawis was self-defensive, international perception of the protest did not help the independence movement.

What exactly transpired at Gdeim Izik, and how best to classify it, is not clear. Violence in practice tends to be quite complicated; self-defensive violence does not necessarily deviate from a nonviolent resistance strategy. A study of Sahrawi nonviolence observed that:

> In the aftermath of Gdeim Izik, young Sahrawi men did engage in violent acts in response to the incitement and brutality of the Moroccan security forces. The range of intensity included physical attacks against security forces, intentionally hitting a security officer with a car, throwing rocks, and setting fire to buildings. While the response from the Moroccan security forces was equal or greater in its brutality and violence, the acts of violence undertaken by Sahrawis were harmful to the message and the success of the largely peaceful movement by playing into the continuing cycle of violence. ...While the original demonstration was meant to be fully nonviolent, the violence perpetrated against the demonstrators did produce a violent response.[12]

Similarly, Mundy and Zunes have written:

> [T]he most serious challenge facing the resistance is the apparent lack of serious strategic thinking on the part of the leadership, something that they freely acknowledge...their appreciation of nonviolent action comes more

[11] All Africa (2010).
[12] Dann (2014).

from a sense that nothing else has worked so far and that armed resistance is unrealistic than a real understanding of how and why it works. Nor does there seem to be adequate understanding of how even very limited violence (throwing rocks and bottles at police) can be used by occupation authorities as an excuse to escalate the repression, lessen sympathy among potential allies, and thereby harm the movement.[13]

CONFLICTING PERSPECTIVES

Bias, Ethics, and Research Challenges

In any conflict as protracted and brutal as that of Western Sahara, both sides will inevitably have entrenched ideological positions. For Sahrawis, the experience of displacement, oppression, occupation, and violence are often extremely painful. The violence has been meted out not just against Sahrawi individuals, but also against Sahrawi identity, which has been subject to a sort of erasure over the course of the conflict. Significantly, the Moroccan use of pro-government "surrogate Sahrawis" is a direct challenge to Sahrawi assertions of agency and identity, while allegations that Polisario or Sahrawi nationalists are Algerian clients without popular support is also harmful. The contradiction between an international legal consensus that favors self-determination and tacit international support for the Moroccan occupation alienates and frustrates many Sahrawis.

The Moroccan case is also often framed in moral terms, though rarely humanitarian ones. Moroccan narratives highlight the historical reaches of Moroccan territory, the significance of decolonization, the role of Algeria, or the supposed nonviability of an independent Western Saharan state. Some vigorously pro-Moroccan commentators in the West have emphasized this latter point—though it should be noted that the UN Declaration on the Granting of Independence to Colonial Countries and Peoples, also known as General Assembly resolution 1514, stipulates that "Inadequacy of political, economic, social or educational preparedness should never serve as a pretext for delaying independence."[14]

---

[13] Mundy and Zunes (2015: 35).
[14] Declaration on the Granting of Independence to Colonial Countries and Peoples (1960).

At the same time, an activist focus on human rights and self-determination can insulate Polisario from internal and external criticism. It is understandable that scholars who have witnessed the brutality of the occupation or the plight of the refugees in Tindouf may become frustrated and angry; indeed, it would be strange to leave such a situation with no moral position at all. This is, of course, no excuse for deliberate bias. Zunes and Mundy noted that "Seduced by the camps' highly self-sufficient organizational structure, the wide deployment of women, and Polisario's lofty rhetoric...some Western observers have tended to blur the lines between members of the nationalist vanguard elite and Polisario as a multifaceted popular movement—between the government in exile and daily self-managed life in the camps."[15] But, within academia, the most significant scholars of the conflict—Toby Shelley, Pablo San Martin, Jacob Mundy, and Stephen Zunes—are by and large very good models of how to write about a morally charged issue without allowing bias to cloud analysis.

Part of the reason that such disparate views of the conflict can flourish is the difficulty of carrying out research in the Occupied Zone. Morocco routinely expels scholars from the territory, or simply denies them entry; scholars and their interview subjects face harassment. Good empirical academic work from the Occupied Zone exists, but there are significant gaps due to barriers to free movement. Research is much easier in the Tindouf refugee camps, although the remoteness of the camps and the occasional opacity of the Polisario leadership (especially concerning population figures) are problematic in their own right.

Violence and Nonviolence

The remarkable transition from a violent guerilla movement to nonviolent resistance in the Occupied Zone is one of the most interesting features of the Western Sahara conflict. A significant subset of the literature examines this nonviolence and the portrayal of Sahrawi nationalism as a nonviolent movement. There are works dedicated to the strategy and tactics of nonviolent resistance in Western Sahara,[16] to the portrayal of the Tindouf

---

[15] Zunes and Mundy (2010: 113).
[16] Dann (2014).

refugee camps as "ideal,"[17] to largely nonviolent Sahrawi protests, and to the possible transgression of the nonviolent norm in Gdeim Izik.

In examining nonviolence, one might begin by asking what its limits are. It is not at all clear that there is a definitive binary distinction between violent and nonviolent resistance. Are stone-throwing protestors violent? What about sabotage to industrial equipment? Are cases of self-defensive violence meaningfully considered under a violence-nonviolence rubric?

Such questions are further complicated by disaggregating Polisario's adherence to the ceasefire from the individual or collective nonviolence of Sahrawi protestors in the Occupied Zone, whose actual connection to Polisario itself may be unclear. Polisario's insistence on the ceasefire has a significant influence even on Sahrawis who have never lived under Polisario administration. Although the ceasefire agreement is specifically between Polisario and the Royal Moroccan Army, some of my interview subjects in the Occupied Zone considered Moroccan violence against protestors to be in violation of the ceasefire, or claimed that their own rejection of violent resistance strategies stemmed from a loyalty to Polisario's focus on the diplomatic track. The precise relationship between the Polisario leadership and Sahrawis living under Moroccan occupation is often unclear, and merits further investigation.[18]

Scholars of nonviolence such as Gene Sharp have much to offer here. Sharp's conception of effective nonviolent resistance imagines an occupied population withdrawing its support for the regime, or actively obfuscating "politics as usual."[19] In Western Sahara, the influx of Moroccan settlers has changed the basis for this model, write Mundy and Zunes:

> The problem for Western Saharan nationalism is the demographic imbalance between Sahrawis in the occupied territory versus the Moroccan military and security apparatus, and the majority settler population. For Western Saharan nationalism to engage in a sustained nonviolent resistance campaign of a higher intensity and duration than [Gdeim Izik] would implicitly tempt the Moroccan regime into committing the very types of abuses that won Western Sahara attention in 2009 and 2010. …If Western Saharan nationalists used nonviolent resistance strategically, this would tempt Morocco to escalate its repression to levels that could easily decimate Western Saharan resistance for a generation. Indeed, most of the activist leaders of the [Gdeim Izik] protest camp will be imprisoned for years, if not decades, unless inter-

---

[17] Fiddian-Qasmiyeh (2014).
[18] Porges and Leuprecht (2016).
[19] Sharp (1973).

national pressure for their release increases. The most likely effect of nonviolent Sahrawi escalation and mass Moroccan repression will not be defection in Morocco or its allies on the UN Security Council. It will be Sahrawis in the refugee camps who see no value in remaining true to the 1991 ceasefire. The challenge for Western Saharan nationalism vis-à-vis strategic nonviolent resistance is to find ways of causing international allegiance shifts without putting hundreds, if not thousands, of civilians in danger.[20]

Strategic nonviolent resistance depends upon a demographic base broad enough to disrupt normal political, economic, and social conditions. The presence of hundreds of thousands of Moroccan settlers in Western Sahara has effectively reduced the proportional efficacy of Sahrawi civil resistance. Whether Sahrawi nonviolence is a tactical/strategic choice or one forced upon the population by circumstance, its utility in this context is severely reduced by Morocco's demographic engineering since 1975.

Sahrawi violent/nonviolent resistance can also be usefully contrasted with Moroccan repression/restraint. There have been several cases of Morocco crossing the berm: in 2001, Morocco routed the annual Paris-Dakar Rally across the berm, nearly triggering a resumption of war. In February of 2016, Moroccan soldiers murdered a Sahrawi nomad named Schmad July after he allegedly wandered close to the berm in pursuit of lost camels. Then-UN Secretary-General Ban Ki-Moon described this incident in a report to the Security Council as a "potential violation of the ceasefire."[21] Relations between the UN and Morocco turned sour when Ban used the word "occupation" to describe Morocco's presence in Western Sahara. Although in line with international legal consensus, this infuriated Morocco and led to the expulsion of some UN staff.[22]

While the case of the murdered nomad is unusual, perhaps unique, Moroccan soldiers kill dozens of Sahrawi livestock each year from their positions on the berm, and occasionally kill activists within the Occupied Territory as well. Nevertheless, as described in the anecdote at the beginning of this chapter, Moroccan security forces exercise some of what has been called "reciprocal restraint," committing far less violence than they potentially could. An uneasy, and continually renegotiated, tension exists in the Occupied Zone, with both sides declining to regularly escalate the conflict outside of its "normal" bounds.

---

[20] Mundy and Zunes (2015: 42).
[21] Porges (2016).
[22] Reuters (2017).

Theoretical Lenses: Decolonization and Secessionism

One might consider the case of Western Sahara through a number of theoretical lenses: decolonization and secessionism, which I will briefly touch on here, are only two possibilities. Rather than arguing for a particular lens, I am seeking to emphasize the complexity of the conflict and the insufficiency of any single nomothetic or disciplinary lens to accurately capture a unique case study. I have previously examined the conflict from a civil war perspective (which it emphatically is not in any meaningful sense); this is a useful approach despite its apparently tangential relevance. Much can be gained from exploring Western Sahara as a case of indigenous resistance, and future work could focus on demographic comparisons between the case of Western Sahara's Sahrawis and the historical case of North America's indigenous population, as both are cases of resistance movements marginalized by extreme demographic changes (this comparison is further examined in the next section).

Western Sahara is frequently referred to as "Africa's last colony" or a case of "decolonization interrupted." Decolonization is a dynamic process that can follow several different pathways, from India's nonviolent Gandhian struggle to lengthy and brutal wars of independence, as in Algeria's case. Most such struggles involve a combination of pathways, or a "continuum of resistance," combining violent and nonviolent struggle, working both inside and outside of existing colonial institutions.

Western Sahara's struggle for independence predates Moroccan involvement. By 1973, Polisario sought to break free from Spain, the existing colonial power, having grown from a movement of Sahrawi students attending Moroccan universities. Some of the earliest resistance took the form of armed raids against Spanish military units, and state-evasion in the desert interior. While the ICJ provided the previously mentioned legal opinion on the matter, that opinion is frequently oversimplified. Alice Wilson has elaborated on its relationship to the Sahrawi tribal system:

> As regards Western Sahara's classification as a decolonization case, Moroccan claims to the territory, as presented to the ICJ, have drawn on the idea that present-day Western Sahara fell within the sultan's realm even when the ties between the sultan and tribes in Western Sahara did not correspond to what the ICJ could recognize as territorial sovereignty. Morocco argued that the precolonial Moroccan state was unique. Even when the sultan lacked temporal authority over and area and its people…the sultanate claimed still to have enjoyed and enacted the authority to appoint officials, collect taxes,

and receive oaths of allegiance...the ICJ, however, found that "oaths of fealty were personal and not indicative of sovereign control" and that, "despite the accepted uniqueness of the Moroccan state at the moment of Spanish colonial occupation, religious ties did not constitute sovereignty." The ICJ finding was a blow to the international legitimacy of Morocco's claims, yet it did not deter Morocco from insisting on its claims and acting on them to annex part of the territory. From Morocco's point of view, the findings of the ICJ confirmed its claims, these claims merely corresponding to a different conception of sovereignty from the territorial control on which international relations, and decolonization, rested.[23]

Western Sahara may therefore be considered a case of decolonization interrupted, or a sort of decolonization-and-recolonization. Morocco's post-1991 occupation of the territory certainly meets the definition of a colonial power. The history of Western Sahara, from Spanish involvement in the 1880s to Moroccan occupation in the present, constitutes both two separate narratives of directly subsequent colonialism, and a single, uninterrupted narrative of foreign occupation now lasting nearly a century and a half. In either case, the story is not simple.

Secessionism is an even more fraught lens. Colloquially, secessionism for our purposes refers to the process of a territory exiting a whole country. Insofar as a large portion of Western Sahara is administrated by Morocco as if it were an integral part of the country, there are some similarities between the Sahrawi struggle for self-determination and those of other secessionist movements. But to classify Western Sahara as *only* or *literally* a case of secessionism would be to tacitly admit that Western Sahara is part of Morocco. Much Sahrawi resistance to the occupation, outside of the official channels of Polisario and SADR, rests on tangible assertions to the contrary: the use of Hassaniyya Arabic rather than Maghrebi Arabic, the construction of banned tents indoors or on the roofs of houses, the inculcation of the Sahrawi struggle in children and youths, and the practice of nomadic heritage as a performative reinforcement of cultural and national identity. Moreover, the legal analysis quite clearly rests on Western Sahara as a case of decolonization rather than secessionism.

Yet short- and medium-term goals for the self-determination movement tend to look very much like those of other secessionist movements,

---

[23] Wilson (2016: 42–43).

and there is value to considering the Sahrawi struggle through the lens of secessionism despite the danger of erasure or confusion. Polisario's insistence on a referendum and Morocco's obfuscation of it have parallels in other secessionist cases. While MINURSO's presence in Western Sahara is a complicating factor, parallels to East Timor exist: another case of not precisely seccessionism, but rather a reversal of an occupation that displayed characteristics of a secessionist movement.

Much can be learned as well from Morocco's attempt to cast the conflict as a case of mere secessionism or separatism. Drawing on Buchanan's typology of arguments against separatism, we can see Morocco's use of common arguments against self-determination. Buchanan lists the "Threat of Anarchy" as a frequently deployed argument against secessionism.[24] The "threat of anarchy" could be used to argue against Western Saharan independence *if* the self-determination struggle was a case of secessionism, positioned either as a moral or pragmatic case, or some combination of the two. If it is a case of decolonization, the UN's Resolution 1514 highlights why such arguments are irrelevant.

Buchanan outlines two normative theories on secessionism, the first being the "Remedial Right Only Theories" that "assert that a group has a general right to secede if and only if it has suffered certain injustices, for which secession is the appropriate remedy of last resort," and for which the particular injustices which qualify may vary from theory to theory.[25] The other category, "Primary Right Theories", "assert that certain groups can have a (general) right to secede in the absence of any injustice."[26] Here, secession is a right irrespective of injustice; to deny the right to secede is itself an injustice.

Within each category, Buchanan offers a number of qualifications and critiques. Applied to Western Sahara, Primary Right Theories are an extension of the democratic will of the people for which the UN's continuously postponed referendum would seem to be the correct solution— although Buchanan's analysis offers some questions about the degree to which such a right could be considered automatic. Remedial theories of secession would require a further framework to assess which sorts of grievances qualify; Buchanan suggest either threats to "the physical survival" of a population (or other extensive human rights abuses), or "previously

---

[24] Buchanan (1991).
[25] Buchanan (1991).
[26] Buchanan (1991).

sovereign territory...unjustly taken by the state," either of which might potentially be applied to Western Sahara.[27]

There is also the more general question of what to do about the hundreds of thousands of Moroccan settlers who have arrived in the territory since 1975. Polisario has suggested that they be allowed to remain in an independent Western Sahara. While there are occasionally clashes between Moroccan settlers and Sahrawis in the Occupied Territory (notably the Wakkala Riots at Dakhla in 2011), there are also cases of Moroccan settlers joining Sahrawi-initiated protests against the territory's administration by Morocco. The question of who would be eligible to vote in the independence referendum was already disastrously complicated in 1991; the question now of whether any Moroccan settlers would be eligible to vote, or what would happen to the territory's new Moroccan-installed infrastructure in the case of independence, remains open.

As one long-time (neither Sahrawi nor Moroccan) resident of the territory put it to me: if a thief steals a car, and then paints it and refurbishes the interior at great expense, whose car is it? Surely the answer cannot be that Morocco has earned the right to legitimize its occupation via infrastructure investment, but the question of what would happen to that infrastructure, which Buchanan echoes as "Preventing Wrongful Taking," remains open as well.[28]

Comparative Case Studies

Although Western Sahara has some unique features, it is frequently compared to other cases of occupation, colonization, and self-determination movements. Palestine and East Timor are the two cases most frequently invoked, although neither is a precise analogue. Khoury, in contrasting Western Sahara and Palestine, has pointed out that "Morocco and Israel each maintain their occupations...utilizing similar means of control and eluding continual resistance from their occupied populations. International politics has contributed to the protracted nature of the conflicts, in the form of military and moral support from the United States to the occupying powers."[29]

---

[27] Buchanan (1997).
[28] Buchanan (1997).
[29] Khoury (2011).

East Timor is particularly useful as a comparison in its orientation to decolonization. Both East Timor and Western Sahara were former European colonies, invaded almost immediately following decolonization by an adjacent country—in fact, both invasions took place in 1975, about one month apart. Where Polisario and Morocco ceased overt hostilities in 1991 and transitioned to a diplomatic struggle, East Timor maintained a low-level guerilla insurgency more or less continuously until the 1999 referendum on independence.

Zunes and Mundy compare Western Sahara to East Timor, noting that Polisario "was able to score a series of diplomatic victories, including formal recognition of the RASD by over eighty countries, full membership in the African Union, and endorsements by the Non-Aligned Movement and in other international forums. The East Timorese, by contrast, had virtually no governments or inter-governmental organizations backing their cause, and instead focused on developing grassroots international solidarity networks."[30] Ultimately, they argue that the key to East Timor's strategy was the ability to garner international support from international human rights activists lobbying their own governments.

A sustained and multinational Palestine solidarity movement has so far failed to resolve the Israeli-Palestinian conflict. Yet Israel has always been able to rely on a few key allies—notably the United States—just as Morocco has been able to rely on the United States and France, who rely on Moroccan support in, for instance, the War on Terror or to control migration flows from Sub-Saharan Africa. Some effective human rights activism around Western Sahara does occur, but a broad-based activist movement putting effective pressure on key Moroccan allies does not yet exist. Israel's reliance on the United States for diplomatic support is instructive here. Israel's leverage in the United States is framed as both a matter of political expediency (as, e.g., the "Middle East's only democracy" or as an ally in the War on Terror) and as a moral case (positing Israel as a beleaguered small nation surrounded by enemies, or invoking a common theological heritage with American Evangelicals). Morocco cannot effectively invoke narratives of victimization or easily make common cause with interest groups in American politics; nor could Indonesia. But Morocco's support in the War on Terror is a recurring theme, as are Moroccan control of the global phosphate market (partly due to exports from Morocco itself, and partly from Bou Craa in Western Sahara) as well

---

[30] Mundy and Zunes (2015).

as the Moroccan monarchy's repeated invocation of itself as a bulwark against regional chaos—*Après moi, le déluge*.

There is no obvious Western Saharan parallel for the Australian and Portuguese public's support for East Timorese independence. Spain, the former colonial power, has more numerous and vocal Sahrawi solidarity groups than elsewhere, but the Spanish government is dependent on Morocco to control refugee flows through the land borders at Ceuta and Melilla; it seems unlikely to bow to the current level of civil society pressure.

The role of settler colonialism and the resulting demographic shifts are among the most salient aspects of the Western Sahara conflict, and they suggest another comparative case: the situation of First Nations in North America (or Australia, or South America). Indigeneity, and indigenous resistance, is therefore another potentially useful theoretical lens to draw upon. Indigeneity is not simply the state of having been there first; it is constructed in relation to colonization, and is therefore a relationship of political power.

A 2011 census determined that 4.3% of Canadians are of aboriginal descent; (National Household Survey 2011) the figure is slightly lower in the United States. Although First Nations populations are often concentrated in areas where they may exert politically significant demographic force, the overwhelming demographic majority represented by the settler-colonial population in North America somewhat precludes politically and economically disruptive nonviolent resistance of the sort typologized by Gene Sharp, or of electorally significant weight outside of heavily indigenous constituencies.

The comparison does not bode well for Sahrawis in Western Sahara, who make up significantly more than 4.3% of the population but are, nevertheless, a minority population and therefore also find their options for resistance somewhat foreclosed. The best hope for Western Saharan nationalism may now lie in bringing disaffected Moroccan settlers into the fold. Indeed, Sahrawi demonstrations in El Aaiun in 2011 included a number of Moroccan settlers expressing their dissatisfaction with the government in Rabat. Polisario has indicated that, in the event of Western Saharan independence, Moroccan settlers could be allowed to remain in Western Sahara in some circumstances. How this would play out in practice is not exactly clear, but as one Sahrawi activist told me in the Tindouf refugee camps, Moroccan civil society may hold the key to an eventual resolution of the conflict.

CONCLUSION

This chapter has aspired to do two things: first, it lays out the political and historical background of the Western Sahara conflict, aiming to contextualize arguments about the conflict's legal and theoretical status, potential future developments, and ethical perspectives. Second, it suggests potential theoretical lenses or bodies of literature that may be useful—though not individually constitutive—for analyzing aspects of the conflict. Among these, secessionism and decolonization are the most prominent, though neither fully captures the unique history of Western Sahara. Other perspectives, such as the literature on indigeneity, civil war, nonviolent resistance, and political violence in general, are also useful perspectives, though each is limited in its own way. This list is by no means exhaustive of either potentially valuable sub-disciplines or the literature and frameworks within the sub-disciplines considered.

As a case study that is both obscure and contested, Western Sahara and its attendant scholarly literature can be difficult to navigate. I have aimed here to point at ways through some common pitfalls, and to draw attention to areas requiring more investigation. Of these, I am particularly interested in the relationship between demographics and resistance strategies, the role of international civil society solidarity groups in self-determination struggles, and the political dimensions of nomadism and nomadic heritage in Western Sahara. There is much about Western Sahara that remains understudied, and in cases where the existing literature is itself contested and subjected to a partisan discourse, there is no substitute for fieldwork.

REFERENCES

AllAfrica. (2010, October). Western Sahara: Donald Payne expresses concern over killing of 14 -year-old boy in Western Sahara by Moroccan soldiers. *AllAfrica*.

Buchanan, A. (1991). *Secession: The morality of political divorce from Fort Sumter to Lithuania and Quebec*. New York: Basic Books.

Buchanan, A. (1997). Theories of secession. *Philosophy and Public Affairs, 26*(1), 31–61.

CIA World Factbook: Western Sahara. (n.d.). Retrieved August 15, 2017, from https://www.cia.gov/library/publications/the-world-factbook/geos/wi.html

Dann, N. (2014). Nonviolent resistance in Western Sahara. *Peace Review: A Journal of Social Justice, 26*(1), 46–53.

Declaration on the Granting of Independence to Colonial Countries and Peoples, General Assembly Resolution 1514 (XV) (United Nations General Assembly December 14, 1960).

Fiddian-Qasmiyeh, E. (2014). *The ideal refugees: Gender, Islam, and the Sahrawi politics of survival.* Syracuse: Syracuse University Press.

Harding, J. (2006, February 23). Behind the sandwall. *London Review of Books, 28*(4).

International Court of Justice. (n.d.). Advisory opinion of 16 October 1975. Retrieved from http://www.icj-cij.org/files/case-related/61/6197.pdf

Interview. (2016, September). Oxfam staff member. (I. b. Author, Interviewer).

Khoury, R. (2011). Western Sahara and Palestine: A comparative study of colonialisms, occupations, and nationalisms. *New Middle Eastern Studies, 1,* 1–20.

Mundy, J., & Zunes, S. (2015). Western Sahara: Nonviolent resistance as a last resort. In V. Dudouet (Ed.), *Civil resistance and conflict transformation: Transitions from armed to nonviolent struggle.* New York: Routledge.

National Household Survey. (2011). *Aboriginal peoples in Canada: First Nations people, Metis, and Inuit.*

Porges, M. (2016, November 5). The death of a nomad. *Jadaliyya.* Retrieved from http://www.jadaliyya.com/Details/33705/The-Death-of-a-Nomad

Porges, M., & Leuprecht, C. (2016). The puzzle of nonviolence in Western Sahara. *Democracy and Security, 12*(2), 65–84.

Sevillano, E. (2010, December 18). Vivir sin nubes. *El Pais.*

Sharp, G. (1973). *The politics of nonviolent action, Volume 1: Power and struggle.* Boston: Porter Sargent.

Sulaiman, M., & Berkson, S. (2014). *Settled wanderers: The poetry of a landless people.* London: Influx Press.

United Nations High Commissioner for Refugees. (2010). UNHCR Algeria Factsheet.

Wilson, A. (2016). *Sovereignty in exile: A Saharan liberation movement governs.* Philadelphia: University of Pennsylvania Press.

Zunes, S., & Mundy, J. (2010). *Western Sahara: War, nationalism, and conflict irresolution.* Syracuse: Syracuse University Press.

CHAPTER 6

Secessionism in Anjouan, Comoros: Internal Dynamics, External Decisions

Gregor Dobler

INTRODUCTION

The Comoros are four small islands in the Indian Ocean, situated at the northern end of the Mozambique channel: Grande Comore, Anjouan, Mohéli, and Mayotte.[1] They have fewer than one million inhabitants and collectively cover little more than 2200 km^2, which is slightly smaller than Luxembourg. About 200,000 people live on Mayotte, 345,000 on Grande Comore, 240,000 on Anjouan, and 40,000 on Mohéli.[2]

The islands get little international political or academic attention. Their recent history, however, offers one of the most pertinent cases for the

---

[1] I use the French designations for the four islands, calling them Mayotte, Grande Comore, Anjouan, and Mohéli. The Shikomor names are Maore, Ngazidja, Nzwani, and Mwali. My use of the colonial names does not reflect any preference for imperialist designations; I simply adapt myself to English usage, just as I would call my own native country Germany, not Deutschland.

[2] UNDP (Comoros) (2010: 12).

G. Dobler (✉)
Institute for Ethnology, Freiburg University, Freiburg, Germany
e-mail: gregor.dobler@ethno.uni-freiburg.de

© The Author(s) 2019
L. de Vries et al. (eds.), *Secessionism in African Politics,*
Palgrave Series in African Borderlands Studies,
https://doi.org/10.1007/978-3-319-90206-7_6

151

study of secessionism in Africa. When the Comoros became independent in 1975, France allowed its colony to split up and kept one of the islands, Mayotte, under its tutelage as an overseas territory. The independent Comoros Republic experienced a history of troubled statehood with a record number of coups (culminating in the state's privatization by French mercenary Bob Denard). Encouraged by the Mayotte precedent and by the central state's inefficiency, the two smaller islands, Anjouan and Mohéli, tried at various times to secede from the Republic. The most dramatic of these crises was only resolved by an external military intervention under the aegis of the African Union (AU) in 2008.

This chapter traces the history of secessionist attempts on the Comoros, analyzes the factors contributing to those attempts, and asks what they can teach us about secessionism and about political identity in general. It concentrates on the secessionist attempts on Anjouan and only treats Mohéli's similar, but less successful, movement in passing.

Background: The Contingency of Colonial Boundaries

For a contemporary observer, islands far off the African shore appear as remote, out-of-the-way places. A few centuries back, however, the Comoros were essential stops in one of the world's busy thoroughfares. Trade routes between the Swahili Coast, Madagascar, India, and Arabia met here, and the regular trade winds made sea voyages in the Indian Ocean cheaper and more reliable than overland travel.

The Comoros were first populated from the Swahili Coast. It is likely that Islam reached the islands in the eighth century and became more firmly established when Persian Shirazi traders settled there in the twelfth century. From alliances between local families and immigrant traders emerged a system of sultanates that dominated the islands over the next centuries. The most powerful dynasties lived on Anjouan and managed to establish varying degrees of overlordship over the islands of Mayotte and Mohéli.

In the sixteenth century, Malagasy Sakalava immigrated mainly to Mayotte. They did not entirely merge with the populations of Shirazi and African descent but remained linguistically, socially, and culturally distinct from mainstream Comoros society. Among the elites of Arab, Malagasy, or Swahili origin lived people whose origins lay farther inland in Africa. They were often descendants of slaves. Shirazian traders had arrived with their slaves, and between the sixteenth and nineteenth centuries, the islands became an *entrepôt* in the Indian Ocean slave trade. The slave trade was also one of the reasons why Malagasy pirates attacked, increasingly frequently over the course of the eighteenth and early nineteenth centuries, weakening the islands enough to succumb to French colonial expansion in the mid-nineteenth century.

For the French, the islands were a means to establish a stronger hold in the Indian Ocean. Having lost Mauritius, Rodriguez, and the Seychelles to Britain in 1814, only La Réunion, whose harbor was unsuitable for permanent anchorage, remained under French control. To counterbalance the English presence in this strategically and economically important trade hub, France annexed Nosy-Be (Madagascar) in 1840 and bought the island of Mayotte from its Malagasy ruler, Andrian Souly, in 1841. Over the following years, France slowly extended its influence to the remaining three Comorian islands. Anjouan became a protectorate in 1866, Mohéli and Grande Comore in 1886. From 1892, the three protectorates were governed by French representatives under the formal authority of the French governor in Mayotte. Only in 1904 were the three remaining islands officially attached to the colony of Mayotte, before—in 1912—collectively becoming part of Madagascar. With the new French constitution of 1946, the four Comoro Islands were transformed into a *Territoire d'Outre-Mer* (TOM) of their own, governed from Dzaoudzi on Mayotte and represented in the French parliament.

The TOM became formally self-governing in 1961 after the population had adopted the French Fifth Republic constitution in 1958. The president of the Governing Council, Said Mohammed Cheik, moved the capital from Dzaoudzi to Moroni on Grande Comore. This decision foreshadowed independence and was an important step toward a "Comorianization" of the state, as the French presence was strongest on Mayotte; it alienated the population of Mayotte, however.[3] Many people on Mayotte feared that with independence, they would come under the overlordship of Grande Comore, simply acquiring more closely situated and less affluent masters.

---

[3] UNDP (Comoros) (2010: 48).

NEGOTIATING POSTCOLONIAL STATEHOOD BY SECESSIONISM

Comorian Independence Without Mayotte

Mahorais fears of Comorian dominance created the conditions for a first "secessionist" moment: When the Comoros became an independent Republic in 1975, Mayotte remained a French colony. This is almost the only case of partial independence in Africa and a clear contravention of the 1960 United Nations (UN) *Declaration on the Granting of Independence to Colonial Countries and Peoples*, the 1963 Organisation of African Unity (OAU) Charter, and the *OAU resolution on border disputes between African States* in 1964.[4] It merits a closer analysis both in its own right and as the background to the 1997 secession of Mohéli and Anjouan.

The briefest look at their history shows that as an administrative unit, the Comoros were a colonial invention—yet "invention" is too friendly a word for a haphazard process of colonial boundary shuffling more dependent on metropolitan power games and problems with individual administrators than on any coherent colonial vision. Colonial boundaries *between* the Comorian islands were, over the course of time, at least as relevant as the outer boundaries. The islands were only defined as one distinct territorial unit in 1946. On Mayotte, the colonial presence, including of French settlers, was much more marked than on the other islands. Very simply put, Anjouan and Grande Comore were the old centers of power in which the political organization linked to the sultanates was strongest, whereas Mayotte was the center of colonial domination and had closer ties with France. Due to Malagasy influences, Christianity was perceived as being stronger on Mayotte; women claimed they had a stronger public status there and criticized patriarchal structures in the other islands.

When the leaders of the TOM recentered island politics on Grande Comore in the 1960s, these political, cultural, and social differences ignited Mayotte's fears of marginalization in an independent state. The

---

[4] UN GA Res. 1514. It states that "any attempt aimed at the partial or total disruption of the national unity or territorial integrity of a country is incompatible with the purposes and principles of the Charter of the United Nations."—Art. 3 of the Charter of the Organisation of African Unity called upon all members "to respect the borders existing on the achievement of national independence." (Zacher 1979:129) The only other case I am aware of is that of Chagos Archipelago and the three Seychelles islands Aldabra, Farquhar, and Desroches, which Britain excised from Mauritius and Seychelles as British Indian Ocean Territory in 1965 to make room for US military bases (see Houbert 1992).

notion of Mahorais independence from independence gained ground—either in the form of a small independent state or as a fully fledged *Département d'Outre-Mer* within the French state. This second solution was favored by the *Mouvement Populaire Mahorais* (founded in 1966) and by its leaders Marcel Henry and Adrien Giraud.

France, in the meantime, was not exactly sure what it thought of Comorian plans for independence. Since this was the mid-1970s, and Comoros was a latecomer for independence anyway, the French government could not very well deny the legitimacy of steadily more vocal Comorian claims on independence. French President Georges Pompidou and his successor Valéry Giscard d'Estaing seemed to favor the transition of all four islands to one independent state, whereas Prime Minister Pierre Messmer was in favor of a continuing French presence on the islands.[5] At the height of the Cold War and its proxy conflicts in Eastern and Southern Africa, many Gaullist politicians were reluctant to lose an important base in the Indian Ocean. The stakes were high, even though US Senator Goldwater slightly exaggerated them when he justified the need for a US military base on Diego Garcia: "He who controls the Indian Ocean is going to control the economy of the world as long as oil is needed to run the economy of the world."[6]

After Pompidou died in April 1974, the weight of opinion shifted in favor of a partition of the Comoros. Intensive lobbying by Henry and Giraud in Paris contributed to an anti-unitarian climate in the Senate. The government's draft law on Comorian independence was changed in a small, but important, way before it became the Act of November 23, 1974: It stated that instead of "*la population comorienne,*" "*les populations comoriennes*" were consulted on their wishes regarding possible independence—not the "population" but the "populations." Six months after a referendum, the French Parliament would have to deliberate on the consequences of the popular vote. This was a typical parliamentarian compromise: It made a separate count of the votes on the four islands possible without explicitly ordering it. After the vote, the French parliament would have to see what to make of it.

Predictably enough, a vast majority of 94.65% of "*les populations comoriennes*" favored independence in the referendum of December 22,

---

[5] Messmer had already told the Comorian *Chambre des Députés* in 1972: "Je dois vous prévenir que rien ne saurait être fait s'il s'agissait de modifications profondes, sans un référendum où chaque île serait appelée à décider de son propre avenir." (Ibrahime 2002: 25).

[6] Wiseberg and Nelson (1977: 12).

1974. Of the roughly 14,000 voting Mahorais, however, 64% opted to remain with France. The French parliament, undecided, did not declare its position on Comorian independence but instead asked for a constitution to be developed and adopted by each of the four islands separately. Faced with this provocation, which bounded Comorian independence as a whole to Mahorian goodwill, the Comorian *Chambre des Députés*, under Ahmed Abdallah, unilaterally declared the independence of the Republic of the Comoros.

Abdallah, who was a representative of the old Comorian establishment and had only reluctantly sided with the independence movement in the early 1970s, hoped to force the hand of France to accept undivided Comorian independence. Instead, he gave a welcome excuse to the French authorities to get rid of the three islands, whose independence was readily accepted, and to organize a second referendum on Mayotte in 1976. With a surprising 99.4% of the votes, the population of Mayotte voted to remain French (and thus to separate from the three other islands). Paris terminated its subsidies to the Republic of the Comoros, which had amounted to 18.5 million USD annually, a quarter of the new country's budget, and, when asked by the new government to withdraw French troops, recalled all development workers and technical advisers as well.[7]

In December 1976, Mayotte became a French "*Collectivité Territoriale*" (a somewhat ambiguous status as an integral part of France, in which laws passed by the central state do not automatically apply). Its citizens were French citizens voting in French elections and represented in the National Assembly and the Senate; its schools, roads, and hospitals were built with subsidies from Paris. Under the *Droit du sol*, children born on Mayotte become French by birth. The state's institutions have since been firmly in place on Mayotte, and public life follows the same order as that of France—only it is warmer in winter and more humid in spring.

Independent Comoros claimed Mayotte as an integral part of its territory and asked for its integration into the Republic—a demand that met stern resistance not only from France, but also from the population of Mayotte. Recalling its Resolution 1514 of 1960, the UN General Assembly passed relevant resolutions no less than 13 times, demanding the reintegration of Mayotte into the Republic of the Comoros. These demands were studiously ignored by France and by Mayotte politicians. The only time the issue made it to the Security Council, immediately prior

[7] Wiseberg and Nelson (1977: 21f).

to the referendum in 1976, France used its veto to prevent an otherwise unanimous decision in favor of the Republic.[8]

Most political parties in Mayotte lobbied instead for a transformation of the island into a fully fledged *Département d'Outre-Mer*. In the face of Comorian resistance (and the likely financial consequences), France was long reluctant to grant this status to the island. Only after the second secessionist crisis and the constitutional reform in independent Comoros, a referendum on *Départementalisation* was organized in Mayotte in March 2009. All of 95.4% of voters supported *Départementalisation*. Since March 2011, Mayotte has been the 101st *Département* of the French state.

Is Mayotte's a case of secessionism at all? From the perspective of the Comoros, Mayotte deserted the independent state with France's help. But when Mahorais declared themselves against independence, there was no independent state from which to secede. Mayotte is indeed a very peculiar case, oscillating between secessionism, irredentism, and territorial expansion: Mahorais challenged the territorial integrity of a new independent state (secessionism); they wanted to join a country that had colonized them and indeed succeeded in transforming their status from colonized to citizens (irredentism), and France successfully acquired new territory, integrating a former colony with precarious international status into their internationally recognized territory (territorial expansion).

Whatever we call it, Mayotte teaches some important general lessons about the possibilities of secession. First, if a powerful Western state backs a territorial rearrangement in a weak colonial state, AU and UN conventions might be less of an obstacle than the rhetoric of international diplomacy suggests. Defining a seceding group as *a people* grants political legitimacy to their wish for self-determination and secession. This is what France attempted to do by asking the *populations*, not the *population*, of the Comoros to vote on independence.

Second, colonialism rarely offers only one relevant set of borders. Each colonized state in Africa has seen internal divisions that, at one point or another, have formed the basis of colonial partition. Divisions might not be as clear-cut as on the Comoros, but boundaries, capitals, classifications, and degrees of structural integration often changed dramatically during colonial times. The status quo at the moment of independence thus often

---

[8] On February 6, 1976, Benin, Guyana, Lybia, Panama, and Tanzania had drafted the resolution. See S/ 11967 and S/ PV 1888, para. 247. The question has not been explicitly addressed by the General Assembly since 1994 but has each year been adjourned to the next.

hides many different earlier status quo ante. According to the doctrine of territorial continuity, the boundaries set up by the colonial powers should have remained unchanged. But had Comorian independence happened at a different moment, today's Comoro Islands might have ended up as a part of Madagascar or as four separate republics.

Third, and linked to the second point: Every secession movement can point to uncontested facts to support contested essentialism. Mahorais came to believe in cultural differences between themselves and the rest of the Comoros: They were better educated, more Westernized, less religious, more gender egalitarian, and wealthier than the rest and therefore belonged to France much more than to their poor cousins. As is to be expected, there are a few truths in this, but generally speaking, it is a caricature based on othering. "Essential facts" about culture or society are not the reason for secessionism; they are its outcome. I will come back to this point later.

Mayotte's precedent played an important role in the later secessionist attempts in independent Comoros. It provided a template to follow and proof that secession was possible in practice; it also formed an example of relatively successful statehood against which Comorian failures seemed all the more glaring.

Postcolonial Secessionism on Anjouan and Mayotte

The Union of the Comoros—the independent islands—are only separated from French soil by a strip of sea, which in clement weather a small boat can easily negotiate in a few hours, but they have experienced a rather different brand of statehood. Since independence, the islands have become the theater of more than 20 coups and coup attempts (most of which I cannot even mention in this overview). One month after independence, Ahmed Abdallah was ousted by a coalition led by the young, modernist, secularist, and anti-French Ali Soilih, who then enlisted the help of French mercenaries under Bob Denard.[9] Three years later, the same Denard helped to reinstate Abdallah and execute Soilih. He became head of the small, but well-equipped and influential Presidential Guard and controlled important business ventures, even though international pressure temporarily forced him to forego permanent residence in favor of frequent visits after 1978.

---

[9] Interestingly enough, Denard had fought in Biafra for the secessionist government, and was paid by the French government, trying to destabilize Nigeria (French 1997: 113).

Abdallah's regime was sustained by commercial and political links with apartheid South Africa, France, and by increasingly multilateral international aid.

The regime became increasingly autocratic, leading to popular unrest. After trying to bring the Presidential Guard back in line, Abdallah was shot dead in 1989 under circumstances that remain unclear. To quell popular unrest that held Denard responsible for the killing, France forced Denard to retire to South Africa (and when things began to change there, to France in 1993). In September 1995, he was back, "invading" the islands with a band of 30 European colleagues who, with the help of parts of the Comorian army, quickly gained power from President Said Muhammad Djohar. As international opinion reacted strongly against Denard's coup, France sent paratroopers, who whisked Denard off to a short stay in a French prison, and showed its capacity as an ordering power. It soon transpired, however, that Paris had at least been a silent accomplice in the coup, fearing increasing Comorian links with Iran.[10]

Faced with a difficult economic situation, increasing centralization, and a progressively autocratic central government, secessionist opposition parties in Anjouan became more active and vocal. On August 3, 1997, 7000 protesters—more than a quarter of the town's population—took to the streets in Anjouan's capital, Mutsamudu. Not content with demanding independence, they declared Anjouan's accession to France instead and hoisted both the French Tricolore and *Faute de Mieux*, the flag of Anjouan's last sultan, on the government palace.[11]

France found this rather embarrassing. Anjouan's demand for recolonialization drew new international attention to the status of Mayotte, and the old sin of organizing secession came back to haunt the French government. Paris made sure to quickly and firmly reject Anjouanais' claims and to stress Comorian unity. Officials of Jospin's socialist government (feeling, it is hoped, slightly sanctimonious) invoked the principle of territorial integrity and the OAU's declarations against secessionism, generally siding with the Comorian government.

This rediscovery of the principle of territorial integrity corresponded with French tangible interests. Paris had no wish at all to add Anjouan to

---

[10] French (1997: 117).

[11] Cornwell (1998: 51). On August 11, Mohéli followed with similar declarations, but the island returned to the Republic in 1998 (Ben Mohadji 2005: 129).

its overseas territories. Apart from concerns about legality and international reputation, the geopolitical situation had changed since 1975. Cold War struggles for predominance were forgotten, pundits had long declared that, in the struggle for influence and raw materials, territory no longer mattered, and China was not yet visible as a new competitor in the scramble for Africa's resources. Many in France thought that even Mayotte was no longer worth the cost of subsidies. Immigration, too, was increasingly seen as a problem; from January 1995, the French government enforced strict visa requirements for Comorian citizens who wanted to visit Mayotte. Nobody wanted to increase the load by adding a second, politically much more problematic, island to the French empire.

Anjouanais were not easily discouraged, however. On August 5, 1997, Abdallah Ibrahim was named the first State President of Anjouan. When Comorian troops tried to invade the self-declared republic in September 1997, Anjouan's gendarmerie easily defeated them and forced them to flee the island. The new government declared that a referendum held on October 26 showed that 99.8% of the population supported independence.[12] A new constitution was adopted, and Anjouan declared an independent republic on February 25, 1998.[13]

While Anjouan was busy organizing its newfound statehood, the Comoros and the international community denounced the secession as illegal. Not a single state recognized Anjouan, and many states and international bodies rejected the island's claim for statehood. UN Secretary-General Kofi Anan exhorted "all Comorian parties to abstain from any act aiming at questioning the territorial integrity, the sovereignty and the national unity of the Comoros Federal Republic," and the OAU strongly condemned the secessionist attempts.[14] Contrary to Mayotte, whose secession was successful at least in practical terms, Anjouan independence remained fictitious outside the island.

Even though international recognition, let alone admission into the fold of the French state, quickly looked unattainable, the new authorities continued their attempts to set up state institutions. Due to its interna-

---

[12] Ougergouz and Tehidrazanarivelo (2006: 269ff). The accuracy of that number was contested on good grounds by the Comorian government, but nobody doubted the support for independence by a majority of Anjouanais.

[13] Ben Mohadjii (2005: 129).

[14] Pahlavi (2001).

tional isolation, the island's financial situation became more and more precarious. Comorian President Taki's death (from natural causes) in November 1998 removed a figure with whom the secessionists found negotiations difficult, but it also led to a new constitutional crisis. The secessionist government no longer saw itself as part of the Comorian Republic and refused to take part in presidential elections. The central authorities could not very well organize elections without Anjouan's participation, and no new president was elected within the limit set by the constitution. In consequence, the Comorian opposition denounced the caretaker government as unconstitutional.

Meanwhile, rifts began to show within the Anjouan secessionist movement. The more rural and younger faction led by Chamasse Said Omar continued to fight for accession to France, while Abdallah Ibrahim had given up on that idea and instead organized the institutions of independent Anjouan. Violent clashes between the factions erupted in December 1998, leaving several dead and many injured.[15] From April 19 to 23, 1999, still under a caretaker central government, Anjouan took part in the inter-island conference in Antananarivo, which reached an agreement between the central state and the island of Mohéli: Through a new constitution, the islands would gain more autonomy within a new federal state now called "Union des Comores." In exchange, Anjouan and Mohéli would abandon their secession attempts.

The delegation from Anjouan had agreed to the principles of the declaration, but it refused to sign the document and asked for a popular vote. Abdallah Ibrahim reiterated that Anjouan's independence was irrevocable.[16] Although the agreement thus found no immediate application, it would later serve as the blueprint for the new federal constitution of 2001.

Amidst increasing bitterness with the state's incapacitated institutions, violence against Ajouanais residents erupted on Grande Comore. Colonel Assoumani Azali, Chief of Staff of the Comorian Army, used this as an excuse for a new military coup on April 30, 1999. Azali declared the constitution null and void, dissolved all institutions emanating from it, including the parliament, and replaced them with a committee of 12,

---

[15] Lehtinen (2002: 60). See also http://www.comores-online.com/Comores-infosweb/Debat/Dossier4.htm, accessed March 31, 2012.

[16] Ben Mohadji (2005: 129) and Ougergouz and Tehidrazanarivelo (2006: 269ff).

headed by himself. The coup was condemned internationally, and the OAU declared Azali to be unwelcome at OAU meetings.[17]

From now on, the central government had almost as little claim to international legitimacy as the secessionists. Over the next two years, however, it became clear that the international community, most of all the OAU, considered the secessionist denial of state sovereignty a more serious threat to the international order than one more military regime. The octogenarian Abdallah Ibrahim resigned in August 1999 and passed power on to Said Abéid Abdérémane, who continued to implement the secession with the help of Mohamed Bacar, commander of Anjouan's gendarmerie. Pressure on Anjouan increased and culminated on March 21, 2000, in an OAU-imposed embargo on mineral fuels, food, maritime and aerial transport, and telecommunication, which, although not completely implemented, brought the island's economy to its knees.[18]

In spite of these hardships, it took some more time to convince Anjouan's leaders that their attempt at secession would not be successful; it did not help that Azali had meanwhile broken his promises of democratization and continued to govern autocratically. Only in February 2001 was a framework agreement on national reconciliation finally signed by representatives from the central government, Mohéli, and Anjouan. It approved "the organization of a New Comorian Commonwealth, only subject to international law, founded on the respect of national unity, territorial integrity and sovereignty of the Comoros within their internationally recognized boundaries"[19] and set up a tripartite commission to prepare a new federal constitution, to be subject to a federal referendum in July 2001. This schedule was again not met, but in December 2001, the new constitution of what was now called *Union des Comores* was accepted by popular vote; 95% of voters on Anjouan but only 62% on Grande Comore voted in its favor. In the meantime, Colonel Bacar had used the gendarmerie forces to oust Said Abéid and become Anjouan's president. He was confirmed as island president in the elections of 2002.[20]

---

[17] "South Africa's OAU mandated role in respect of the Federal Islamic Republic of the Comoros," http://www.dfa.gov.za/foreign/Multilateral/profiles/como.htm, accessed March 31, 2012.

[18] Ougergouz and Tehidrazanarivelo (2006: 270).

[19] http://www.comores-online.com/Comores-infosweb/Debat/Accord4.htm, accessed March 31, 2012. "New Comorian Commonwealth" is my translation of "Nouvel Ensemble Comorien."

[20] Cour National du Droit d'Asile (2009: 90).

With the new constitution, Anjouan's first attempt at secession was over—but the crisis was not. The new arrangement of power sharing between the islands seemed straightforward. It established four presidents and four parliaments (one for the Union, one for each island) and stipulated that the Union presidency should rotate between the islands, starting with Grande Comore. To achieve an agreement, however, the parties had left crucial questions to negotiations between the islands and Union governments. Most importantly, there were no regulations in place on how to allocate taxes, customs duties, and external aid to the central government and the islands.

If the international delegations involved in drafting the constitution had hoped that practical necessities would force the parties to compromise once the framework was in place, they were quickly disappointed. The ensuing power struggle was complicated by an unequal treatment of the three islands: Anjouan and Mohéli had clear internal structures with a president, a government, and a parliament, but the constitution did not establish the similar island institutions on Grande Comore—just an elected island president, whose division of power with the Union presidency, the parliament, and the other institutions of the central state was totally unclear.

Over the next five years, the different institutions became stuck in a deadlock that finally resulted in Anjouan's renewed declaration of secession in 2007.[21] Most importantly, the central government and the island governments, suspicious of each other, could not agree on a revenue-sharing formula. On Anjouan, people were convinced that Grande Comore and the central government received too high a portion of the customs duties, a major source of state income. The central government, in turn, tried to get access to taxes paid on Anjouan that the island government claimed for itself.

Even though international aid resumed, Anjouan's state institutions, which had never been very strong, lost much of their remaining relevance in the power crisis. When I visited Anjouan for two months in early 2003, the Chamber of Commerce and the taxi driver association on the island had just declared they would no longer pay any taxes as long as the different authorities did not agree on whether they were owed to the government of the island or the Union. Wages for government employees were,

---

[21] For an excellent overview, see Rolf Hofmeier's annual chronicle in the Africa Yearbook (Hofmeier 2005–2011).

on average, paid every third month only; teachers were on strike because arrears in their wages had reached 30 months, and students had just launched violent protests because the government had declared that no final exams would be held that year. Just as the hospitals, most schools outside the capital were run by Islamic foundations or by NGOs.

The only institutions that continued to be properly financed were the security forces. When a revenue-sharing formula was finally adopted in January 2005 (giving 33.8% to the Union, 30.7% to Grande Comore, 26.8% to Anjouan, and 8.8% to Mohéli),[22] control of the armed forces became the next bone of contention. Since 2004, the islands had gradually gained control over their gendarmerie forces and transformed them into separate armies, a measure that Union President Assoumani regarded as illegal. In 2006, a compromise was reached between Anjouan and the newly elected Union President Ahmed Abdallah Sambi (who, in accordance with the power-sharing agreement, came from Anjouan): The islands would be responsible for the local security forces, but heavy weapons would remain the Union's prerogative. However, the parties could not agree on the types of weapons defined as "heavy." In December, Anjouan's increasingly autocratic president, Bacar, unsuccessfully tried to forbid Sambi access to the island.

In this tense political climate, new presidential elections for the three islands were scheduled for April 2007. Due to problems on Anjouan, the elections were postponed to June, and Union President Sambi ordered the island presidents to step down in favor of caretaker governments when their term expired in April. On Grande Comore and Mohéli, the incumbents complied, and new presidents were elected in June without problems. On Anjouan, Bacar refused to resign, which led to a short military confrontation between the Union's "Armée Nationale de Développement" (AND) and Anjouan's new "Forces de Sécurité Intérieure" (FSI). The FSI defeated the AND, but under international pressure, Bacar resigned on May 11, two days after an AU decision to send 280 policemen from South Africa and Indian Ocean neighbors to the Comoros to supervise and provide security for the elections.

One week before the election date of June 10, the Union President ordered a one-week postponement to allow the AU mission to deploy units to the island. Bacar did not comply. In a show of force, he prevented Union President Sambi from entering Anjouan for a family funeral on

[22] Hofmeier (2006).

June 5. Then, using locally printed ballot papers, he had himself elected for a second term in a ballot boycotted by all opposition candidates. He used secessionist rhetoric to justify his election and increase his legitimacy in the eyes of the population of Anjouan, but the secessionist vigor among Anjouan's population had mostly ebbed away in the years since 2001. While the 2001 attempt at secession had been backed by a large part of the population, whose aim was the establishment of a new state, the 2007 "secession" was rather the attempt of an autocratic ruler to avoid external interference.

Not surprisingly, the election was declared null and void by the central state and by the AU's subregional ministerial meeting.[23] When Bacar showed no inclination to compromise, the AU reluctantly imposed sanctions, including a travel ban on 145 Anjouan politicians and a partial naval blockade. The inefficiency of these measures and Bacar's renewed talk of secession finally triggered an AU military intervention on March 25, 2008. The 450 Comorian AND soldiers were supported by 750 Tanzanian and 600 Sudanese soldiers who landed on Anjouan and seized the island, while Bacar fled to Mayotte.[24] In elections under AU supervision, Moussa Toybou (Sambi's preferred candidate) was elected as Anjouan's President on June 29.

With this new power constellation, and due to general exhaustion with the permanent institutional crisis, Sambi managed to find approval for a new and much more centralized constitution in a referendum in May 2009. Although the voter turnout of 51.8% was low, 93.9% of the votes were in favor of the new constitution, which downgraded the island presidents and ministers to governors and commissioners, gave the president the right to dissolve parliament, and created a unified public service. Some power struggles over the control of security forces and the appointment of senior civil servants ensued, but popular enthusiasm for divisive

---

[23] Hofmeier (2008).

[24] France later turned down his application for political asylum but refused to extradite him to the Comoros; he found refuge in Benin on the condition that he renounced politics. (Mohamed Bacar en exil au Bénin. Nouvel Observateur, July 20, 2008). The French Cour National de Droit d'Asile turned down Bacar's asylum application on the grounds that, due to numerous human rights violations, such as torture, arbitrary detention, extrajudicial executions, extortions, and the use of fire arms against civilians, the Geneva convention was not applicable to him and the French asylum law did not offer him protection. An extradition to the Comoros was excluded since it was possible he would face the death penalty there (Cour National du Droit d'Asile 2009, 90f.).

action was clearly at ebb. In the parliamentary elections of December 2009, Sambi's centralist camp carried away a clear victory. While the opposition won three of the four constituencies on Mohéli, it did not gain a single seat on Anjouan and only one on Grand Comore.[25] One year later, Sambi's Mohélian Vice President Ikililou Dhoinine was elected his successor. In 2015, 40 years after the Comoros became independent, the political climate seemed at its calmest and secessionism was no longer on the table.

UNDERSTANDING ANJOUAN'S SECESSIONISM

What are the reasons for Anjouan's attempt at secession, and what can we learn from them? I concentrate on four points here: Culture and national cohesion, economic factors, the institutional setting, and the role of international actors.

Culture and National Cohesion

Secessionist movements routinely claim that cultural differences between themselves and the majority population make it impossible, in a common state, to live according to their own values. Such arguments often center on religion, ethnicity, or language, and they are surprisingly similar to some scholarly arguments about the link between colonial boundaries and state failure. Drawn without respect for cultural differences, the argument goes, colonial boundaries confine very different groups into a state, which consequently command less solidarity than the socio-cultural groups within it. Particularized solidarities were strongest if colonial rule was organized along ethnic lines. Moral obligations underlying ethnicity can then form a basis of strong in-group solidarity, but they prevent the emergence of nationhood or citizenship.[26]

Both the secessionist claim and the scholarly argument suggest that socio-cultural unity would make it easier to live together in one state. Iain Walker has recently used the Comorian example to refute this link.[27] He finds important socio-cultural similarities between the four Comorian

---

[25] Hofmeier (2011).

[26] For some of the more sophisticated versions of this argument, see Berman (1998), Chabal and Daloz (1999), and Mamdani (1996).

[27] Walker (2007: 605).

islands. Language, social organization, customs seen as defining traditional society, religion, kinship ties, and even cuisine do not show large differences. They would, Walker argues, form an ideal basis for the development of national consciousness—but they are systematically denied by Comorians, as the only unit conferring meaning to them is a state perceived as foreign and empty. The nation is not rejected due to cultural differences, but cultural differences are overemphasized out of an unwillingness to engage with the state.

Walker's argument can be generalized: National belonging cannot be explained as the natural outcome of cultural homogeneity. In any given situation, many different links between culture and identity are possible. If an existing state offers a form for identity, one possible set of social boundaries may become privileged in the actors' perspective, so that cultural contents can be linked to—and later serve as proof of—national unity. In a different political situation, boundaries drawn in an entirely different way could make as much sense to the actors. In the Comorian case, many similarities are not "Comorian": Some are shared with the Swahili coast, others with Madagascar, and still others situate the island on different points in a sliding scale of differing patterns in the region.

Secessionist movements, and of course nationalist movements without a state in general, reinterpret cultural contents, privilege differences with other groups, and overstate inner homogeneity. In doing so, they strive to offer a narrative that makes a different political organization plausible. If they achieve statehood, the new form can create more efficient conditions for the reproduction of a specific set of identities. As sedimentation of identity is closely linked to everyday practices, however, such establishment of one predominant narrative is limited by the capacity and will of a state's institutions to influence everyday life. Heinrich Popitz called this capacity of an institution to be relevant its "basic legitimacy": A state may not be seen as ideologically legitimate, but it has "legitimacy" in practice because its presence cannot be ignored.[28]

---

[28] The history of European national states shows that even in countries with a very low degree of socio-cultural homogeneity, a measure of national unity can emerge from a state's practical relevance. See, for example, Eugen Weber's classic study on France in the late nineteenth century "Peasants into Frenchmen" (Weber 1976). He clearly shows that administrative unity preceded, and was largely responsible for, national consciousness. Popitz's theory of power and domination, unfortunately not yet translated into English, can be found in his "Phänomene der Macht" (Popitz 1992).

In short: State failure does not occur because people are too heterogeneous. Instead, a state that fails to influence daily life cannot create the conditions of its own ideological reproduction. So, if we are to judge on the Comorian example alone: People are not opting for secession because they are culturally different; the reasons for political secessionism are political. Culture is relevant after the fact. It can serve as a link between political ideas and identity. Culture and politics can then merge in the powerful essentialist claim that lies at the heart of secessionism: If we only had a state of our own, we could organize public life in coherence with who we are.

If we accept this, we have to ask in what ways the state has been relevant on the Comoros. In what ways has it failed to shape public life to become linked to identity as a matter of course—and why has it been salient enough to seek secession? I come back to this point after a closer look at economic reasons for secessionism.

Economic Factors

Secessionist claims are often linked to economic arguments. Some richer regions think they could do better on their own (Italy's Lega Nord wants to get rid of the poor south; Puntland or Cabinda secessionists do not want oil revenue generated in their territory to flow to the distant capital). Some poorer regions feel treated unfairly by the centers (Namibia's Caprivi, e.g., or Mali's northern regions). In some cases (as in the Niger Delta), resource endowment and poor treatment combine. Secessionists ask for a fairer, or simply larger, share of existing wealth. But to be successful, they also need to argue that the new state would be economically viable on its own. Resource endowment helps with this, just as a deep-sea harbor or a transport hub does. A high degree of functional economic integration with the country at large, on the other hand, makes secession more difficult. With Mayotte, as with Anjouan, several factors combined to create an impression of unfair treatment by the capital, and the specific economic structure of the islands made it difficult to see what the islands would lose by seceding.

Mayotte (by virtue of colonial investment) and Anjouan (through its plantation economy and political unity) had been the strongest of the four Comoro Islands' economies before independence. Mayotte's economic benefits from staying with France are easier to see: Political dependence on France came with the silver lining of infrastructure investment, government employment, development aid, and direct transfer payments. The Mahorais' economy was already fairly dependent on, and integrated with, the French, while it had few links with the other islands. A separation from France would have cut through economic ties, whereas the new boundary to the neighboring islands gave Mahorais' plantations a competitive advantage over structurally similar Comorian ones. The transfer of the colonial capital to Moroni and the gradual appropriation of state resources by an elite from Grande Comore and Anjouan made people feel that, in an independent state, they would still be dominated, but no longer by a rich master.

In the case of Anjouan, a more careful analysis is needed to understand the economic lure of independence. Anjouan used to be the wealthiest of the Comoro Islands. Since slave trade was abandoned, its economy lived on spices and later on perfume oils—mainly vanilla, cloves, and ylang-ylang.[29] This agriculture contributes to about 40% of the island's GDP today and employs 80% of the population. Services (another 47% of GDP) account for much of the rest; formal service jobs are often in the public sector, which has a virtual monopoly on the employment of well-qualified people.[30]

In 1982, the new constitution of the Comoros Republic concentrated powers with the central government. Anjouanais gained the impression that transfers from their rich island financed government jobs in the capital and increasingly saw the capital as a dysfunctional center of power only intent on siphoning funds generated elsewhere. To make things worse, world market prices for Anjouan's main exports slumped in the early 1990s. Vanilla, clove, and ylang-ylang prices, which had doubled in real terms in the late 1970s and allowed more government spending through the 1980s, went back to their previous level.[31] At the height of the export crisis, the Comorian Franc, which was pegged to the French Franc, was devalued by 33% in 1994. Per capita gross national income decreased from 600 USD to 400 USD between 1994 and 1996.[32]

---

[29] Voeltzkow (1914). Ylang-ylang was introduced in 1909 from the Philippines (cf. http://www.comores-online.com/epices/ylang.htm, accessed April 10, 2012).

[30] www.anjouangov.com/economy.html (accessed April 10, 2012).

[31] Melo et al. (2000) and Menz and Fleming (1989: 7). Prices for both commodities rose after 1998—by 200% for vanilla, 500% for cloves, and 40% for ylang-ylang (International Monetary Fund 2004a, 14). They have been very volatile since then, losing much of their worth in the 2010s.

[32] World Bank (2004: 6).

With the plantation economy declining, more people competed for fewer public sector jobs, and good connections became ever more important for securing one. Such connections, however, were gained via networks concentrated in the federal capital. Jobs became scarcer for better-qualified people from Anjouan, especially if they belonged to an opposition party. Those already in government employment struggled to make ends meet. Worsening terms of trade and public mismanagement had corrupted state finances to a degree that wages in the public sector were paid irregularly. By the mid-1990s, wage arrears for teachers and other government personnel had accumulated to anything between 12 and 24 months.

No other economic sector on the Comoros Islands was able to make up for the loss of income from agricultural exports. What kept public finances from ruin were transfer payments: Development aid and remittances from Comorian migrants mainly in France.[33] Today, remittances officially amount to around 18% of GDP—half the total cost of all imports to the country.[34] Development aid and remittances, however, were unevenly distributed on the three islands. Headquarters of development agencies, of national implementation agencies, and of most NGOs are situated in the capital, and a higher percentage of aid was spent there. Grande Comore also received a much higher share of remittances than its population size would make plausible in the late 1990s and early 2000s. Independence, secessionists argued, would bring aid and remittances closer to the population.[35]

This adds up to an economic situation strongly favorable to secession, all the more since transaction costs for Anjouan's main economic activities would not change much with secession. Agricultural goods could as efficiently be exported from a smaller country, and services were already very localized on the respective islands. Industrial production, in which supply chains would suffer from an additional border, is almost absent. International trade would become slightly more awkward for an

---

[33] World Bank (2004: 22).

[34] Hofmeier (2011).

[35] World Bank (2004: 22). World Bank statistics claim that Grande Comore received 91% of total remittances, compared to 7% for Anjouan. I am rather sceptical toward these figures; they are based on Western Union data, which probably show the venue where the money was collected rather than the place of residence of the recipient.

independent Anjouan without access to the international airport on Grande Comore, but this would not be a prohibitive disadvantage.

So the costly exercise of building up a new state and its institutions seemed feasible. Why, though, did people think it was worth the trouble to have their own state?

Institutional Setting

I have argued earlier that a sense of national belonging does rather emerge from the relevance of a state's institutions in real life than from cultural unity. Many states are culturally diverse without generating thoughts of secession; others, like the Comoros, are relatively homogeneous in cultural terms but have known strong secessionist movements. After all, secession is not about culture, it is about the state. If we want to understand secession, we have to look at the role a state's institutions play in public life.

The first defining feature of Comorian postcolonial statehood seems to be a combination of autocracy and instability. More governments were ousted by coups than by elections. Once in power, most national and island leaders clung to it by means foul or fair, until the next president hopeful staged a coup of his own. He then denounced the old regime as autocratic, promised reforms, and the cycle continued.

Instability, erratic regime changes, and autocratic self-centeredness have certainly made the state's institutions weaker and worsened its image in the population. But it would be mistaken to see them as the root causes of state dysfunction. Rather than causes, they are symptoms of a specific mode of governance.[36] One main element of that mode of governance is the state's ineffectiveness. In the late 1990s and early 2000s, the Comorian state fulfilled very few of the functions it officially had. Hospitals outside the capital were understaffed and externally funded. Teachers often went unpaid and were frequently on strike. Roads, public buildings, and water and electricity supply were slowly decaying. Only the judiciary and the security forces continued to work reasonably well. Few Comorian people experienced the central state as real, unless in the guise of a tax collector or a gendarme.

---

[36] I use governance in its widest sense: As both the mode of allocation of public goods (be it through state agents or not) and as the normative system underlying it. For a more general discussion, see Förster and Köchlin (2011).

Furthermore, Comorian society is small enough that almost everybody has access to somebody who works for the state. Government ministers host people from their village in their homes in the capital; they travel to "grand marriage" or funeral ceremonies of their extended families; they often have to show their respect to notables at home. Kin and friendship networks extend from the villages through all levels of the state's administration. If people think about officials, it is often in terms of personal relations, not of anonymous office bearers. Power, by definition, is exclusive. In the small society of the Comoros, remoteness of office bearers is not the main governance problem. To the contrary: officials have to limit the claims others (family members, friends, age group peers, party colleagues) have on them. The distribution effect of such claim management may be the same as in any system of patronage. But since all claims are seen as legitimate in the actors' perspective, they are more strongly felt by those whose access is denied.[37]

These two features of Comorian statehood are crucial to understand the role of the state at the time of Anjouan's secession: Increasing irrelevance for the provision of public goods coupled with personalized access and its necessary partial blockade by office bearers. In the late 1990s, the state was seen as important enough to warrant secession, but its importance rested much rather on its economic functions than on its role as a provider of public goods.

For educated urban Comorians, access to the state was almost the only chance of formal employment on the islands. When the economic situation worsened in the 1990s, fewer people found jobs. The number of state employees shrunk from around 9000 in the late 1980s to 6400 in 1998.[38] Those who decided upon employment had to limit their patronage to ever-closer circles. This closure was exacerbated by the fact that the central government found itself under increasing pressure to relinquish its autocratic powers and became more and more suspicious toward outsiders. People farther removed from the capital had very few chances to have expectations fulfilled that they saw as legitimate. The resulting frustration was one of the major causes for the popularity of Anjouan's secession.

---

[37] This interpretation of Anjouan's secession mainly rests on conversations and interviews I had during two months on Grande Comore and Anjouan in March and April 2003. It is consistent, though not identical with existing explanations (cf. Said Omar-Hilali 2000; Baker 2009; Walker 2007).

[38] International Monetary Fund (2004b) (Statistical Appendix): 93.

The Comorian state of the 1990s was not predominantly a provider of public goods—it was a provider of private benefits. As a consequence, secessionists did not worry whether they would be able to replicate its public functions in the new borders; they worried about privatizing its benefits. Secession for them was an extreme form of gerrymandering. For rural people on Anjouan, this logic did not hold. They were largely in favor not of secession but of accession to France. To them, Mayotte and its cornucopia of central state transfers seemed the most attractive model. This explains the rift between the two factions within the secessionist movement. Put very simply, one faction hoped to get better access to state employment, the other hoped for higher transfers from a rich European power. For both factions, the state did not matter as a working institution but as access to resources. Ultimately, Anjouanais secession was an outcome and an expression of the real workings of the Comorian state: By bluntly appropriating the remaining functions of the state, secessionists unmasked its irrelevance in most other fields.

The Role of International Actors

Politicized identity, grievances about distribution of wealth and income, and the particular Comorian variant of statehood go a long way to explain the emergence of secessionism as a social movement and a political campaign. To achieve *secession*, however, a secessionist movement has to convince international actors to acknowledge its legitimacy. In the world of international law, no political body is a state unless recognized as such by "the international community"—that is, the governments of political bodies already recognized as states and the international organizations that represent them. Acknowledgment can only happen after secession has been declared, but its perceived likelihood has strong effects on the chances of secessionist movements. International actors thus play a crucial role both before and after an attempt at secession. To shed more light on the role of international actors, I discuss the legal differences between Mayotte's and Anjouan's separation from the Comoros, sum up the attitude of France, and analyze the interests the AU had when deciding on its military intervention.

Anjouan's secessionists can be forgiven for perceiving their own secession and Mayotte's break with its sister islands as analogous. If the international community tolerated a territorial rearrangement in 1975, why should it not do so in 1997? But seen from the perspective of international law, there were crucial differences between the two situations.

In 1975, Mayotte had evoked the population's right to self-determination, a fundamental principle of international law. It is quite doubtful whether the claim would have stood up to a legal challenge before the International Court of Justice, but in colonial situations, the right to self-determination has at least a likelihood of legal standing. Even if Mayotte's irredentism from the nascent Comorian state went against the principle of *uti possidetis*, it might have been found justified through the competing right to self-determination. After all, according to the French legal text, *the populations,* not *the population,* had to determine whether they wanted to live in an independent state.

Within sovereign postcolonial states, however, the dominant opinion in international law does not accept the right to self-determination as legitimate ground for a right to secession. In the case of Anjouan, "normal" international law applied, which strongly privileges the sovereignty of states.[39] This gave good arguments to the opponents of secession. The reason these arguments were actually used, however, lay in the field of politics much more than of international law. The few cases of successful secession outside of colonial contexts clearly show that the political reality created when the international community acknowledges a new state can be stronger than the opinions legal scholars have about it.

I have already mentioned crucial differences in French interests between 1975 and 1997. The Cold War and the need for a strong base in the Indian Ocean were over, and territorial domination had come to play a different role. Mayotte had shown itself to be quite a costly part of the territory, and in France, immigration from Africa was perceived as a nuisance or a threat. France, in short, had no interest to get Anjouan back. It would probably not have minded much whether Anjouan was part of the Comoros or an independent state, but since Mayotte's status was still contested, Paris made a point not to be perceived as guided by its own interests. Instead, the French government, at least officially, sided with the

---

[39] In its 2010 "Advisory Opinion on Kosovo," partially revising the old consensus, the International Court of Justice (ICJ) declared that nothing in international law explicitly prohibits secession, if the means used to bring it about were not in themselves in breach of international law. But the Court avoided opinion on the question of whether any regulation in international law authorizes secession. The majority of legal scholars continue to deny any such right. See Christakis (2011) for a discussion of the ICJ Opinion and its implications, and, for example, Brilmayer (1991), Crawford (1998), Kohen (2006), Naldi (1998), and Oraison (2001) on the legal arguments surrounding secessionism.

OAU and the Comorian state and (somewhat contradictory) stressed the principle of territorial integrity, in both 1997 and 2007.

The policy of the OAU and its successor since 2002, the AU regarding Anjouan was shaped not by territorial interests but by an obsession with state sovereignty. Many of the leading AU states themselves had, or had previously had, problems with secessionist movements; in others, insurgencies, civil wars, or weak institutions challenged sovereignty. In the 1990s and 2000s, when major international development institutions saw African statehood as failing and showed clear paternalistic tendencies toward African sovereign states, AU leaders were preoccupied with ascertaining their sovereignty and showing efficiency. The Comoros were doubly relevant to that agenda: The ongoing French occupation of Mayotte questioned African sovereignty, and Anjouan's secession threatened it. While the OAU-AU was powerless against the first, it could at least show its might by quelling the second.

How it chose to do so between 1997 and 2008 is an indicator of the organization's evolving role in conflict resolution. The sanctions against Anjouan after 1997 were slow to take effect and only gradually eroded the island's economy. In 2008, the AU's role was much more decisive. It had new mechanisms of intervention in place, and after the failures of its missions to Darfur in 2006 and Somalia in 2007, it was keen to show its capacity in a less difficult environment. The ensuing military victory and political settlement were perhaps small compared to the continent's problems, but they allowed the AU to prove its willingness and capacity to act. The AU contingent that landed on Anjouan was not by chance made up of troops from states that had a history of secessionist movements themselves: Tanzania and Sudan.[40]

Just like a medieval guild, the international community of states controls who should be granted access to insider status and the rights, duties, and sinecures attached to it. As secession is detrimental to the sovereignty of an existing guild member, and thus dangerous to the foundation on which the guild's exclusivity rests, very strong arguments are needed to convince existing states that secession is justified. Perhaps the only real chance for secessionist movements are international constellations of interest that create windows of opportunity. France's political interests made Mayotte's irredentism possible. Due to a different constellation of interests and power, Anjouan's secession remained a dream.

---

[40] See Cameron (2018) and Schomerus and de Vries (2018) in this volume.

REFERENCES

Baker, B. (2009). Comoros: The search for viability. *Civil Wars, 11*(3), 215–233.

Ben Mohadji, F. (2005). Comoros (Union of the Comoros). In J. Kincaid (Ed.), *Handbook of federal countries* (2nd ed., pp. 121–134). Ottawa: McGill-Queen's University Press.

Berman, B. (1998). Ethnicity, patronage and the African state: The politics of uncivil nationalism. *African Affairs, 97*, 305–341.

Brilmayer, L. (1991). Secession and self-determination: A territorial interpretation. *Yale Journal of International Law, 16*, 177–202.

Cameron, G. (2018). Zanzibar in the Tanzania Union. In Secessionism in African politics: Aspiration, grievance, performance, disenchantment, de Vries, Lotje, Pierre Englebert, and Mareike Schomerus. New York: Palgrave, 2018.

Caminade, P. (2003). *Comores-Mayotte: Une histoire neocoloniale.* Marseille: Agone.

Chabal, P., & Daloz, P. (1999). *Africa works: Disorder as political instrument.* Oxford: James Currey.

Chouzour, S. (1994). *Le pouvoir de l'honneur: Tradition et contestation en Grande Comore.* Paris: l'Harmattan.

Christakis, T. (2011). The ICJ advisory opinion on Kosovo: Has international law something to say about secession? *The Leiden Journal of International Law, 24*, 73–86.

Cornwell, R. (1998). Anjouan: A spat in the Indian Ocean. *African Security Review, 7*(3), 51–61.

Cour Nationale du Droit d'Asile. (2009). *Contentieux des réfugiés: Jurisprudence du Conseil d'État et de la cour national du droit d'asile année 2008.* Montreuil-sous-Bois: CNDA. Retrieved from http://www.refworld.org/docid/4dad9d6f2.html

Crawford, J. (1998). State practice and international law in relation to secession. *British Yearbook of International Law, 69*(1), 85–117.

Förster, T., & Köchlin, L. (2011). *The politics of governance: Power and agency in the formation of political order in Africa.* Basel Papers on Political Transformation no 1. Basel: Institute for Social Anthropology.

French, H. (1997). The mercenary position. *Transition, 73*, 110–121.

Hofmeier, R. (2005–2011). Comoros. In A. Mehler, H. Melber, and K. van Walraven (Eds.), *Africa yearbook. Politics, economy and society South of the Sahara in 2004.* Leiden, Brill (Online), 2005–2011.

Houbert, J. (1992). The Indian Ocean creole islands: Geo-politics and decolonisation. *Journal of Modern African Studies, 30*(3), 465–484.

Ibrahime, M. (2002). Les Comores: La marche vers l'indépendance (1972–1975). *Yamkobe, 8*(9), 23–33.

International Monetary Fund. (2004a). Union of the Comoros: 2004 Article IV consultation—staff report; staff statement; and public information notice on the executive board discussion. *Country Report 04/259*. Washington: IMF.

International Monetary Fund. (2004b). Union of the Comoros: Selected issues and statistical appendix. *Country Report 04/233*. Washington: IMF.

Kohen, M. G. (2006). *Secession. International law perspectives*. Cambridge: Cambridge University Press.

Lehtinen, T. (2002). Comoros islands. In T. Kivimäki & L. Lasko (Eds.), *Agents, motives and instruments: An Atlas of African conflicts* (pp. 57–68). Copenhagen: Conflict Transformation Service.

Mamdani, M. (1996). *Citizen and subject: Contemporary Africa and the legacy of late colonialism*. Princeton: University Press.

Massey, S., & Baker, B. (2009). *Comoros: External involvement in a small island state*. Chatham House Programme Paper AFP 2009/1. London: Chatham House.

Melo, J., Oalrreaga, M., & Takacs, W. (2000). Market power and the pricing of commodities imported from developing countries: The case of US vanilla bean imports. *Review of Development Economics, 4*(1), 1–20.

Menz, K. M., & Fleming, E. M. (1989). *Economic prospects for vanilla in the South Pacific*. Canberra: Australian Centre for International Agricultural Research.

Naldi, G. (1998). Separatism in the Comoros: Some legal aspects. *Leiden Journal of International Law, 11*, 247–256.

Oraison, A. (2001). Réflexions sur la double conception française du droit des peuples à disposer d'eux-mêmes à la lumière du cas mahorais. Les problèmes posés à Mayotte sur le plan interne et au niveau international. *Annuaire des Pays de l'Océan Indien, 17*, 235–313.

Ougergouz, F., & Tehidrazanarivelo, D. L. (2006). La problématique de la sécession en Afrique. In M. G. Kohen (Ed.), *Secession. International law perspectives* (pp. 258–296). Cambridge: Cambridge University Press.

Pahlavi, Pierre Cyrill: The Comoros: „The Federation of the Quarrelsome Sultans". In: Gateway. An Academic Journal on the Web, 2001/5. http://archive.is/819Xx (Accessed May 19, 2018).

Popitz, H. (1992). *Phänomene der Macht*. Tübingen: Mohr/Siebeck.

Said Omar-Hilali, T. (2000). Les Comores, la question de l'état nation. Retrieved from http://www.comores-online.com/mwezinet/histoire/nation.html

Schomerus, M., & de Vries, L. (2018). A state of contradiction: Sudan's unity goes south. In L. de Vries, P. Englebert, & M. Schomerus (Eds.), *Secessionism in African politics: Aspiration, grievance, performance, disenchantment*. New York: Palgrave.

United Nations Development Program (Comoros). (2010). *Rapport national sur le développement humain. Cohésion sociale et développement humain en Union des Comores*. Moroni: UNDP.

Vérin, P. (1994). *Les Comores*. Paris: Karthala.

Voeltzkow, A. (1914). *Die Comoren. Nach eigenen beobachtungen, älteren und neuen reiseberichten und amtlichen quelle.* (Reise in Ostafrika in den Jahren 1903–1905, Vol. 1/1). Stuttgart: Schweizerbart.

Walker, I. (2007). What came first, the nation or the state? Political process in the Comoro islands. *Africa, 77*(4), 582–605.

Weber, E. (1976). *Peasants into Frenchmen. The modernisation of rural France, 1870–1914.* Stanford: Stanford University Press.

Wiseberg, L. S., & Nelson, G. F. (1977). Africa's new island republics and U.S. foreign policy. *Africa Today, 24*(1), 6–30.

World Bank. (2004). Memorandum of the president of the International Development Association to the executive directors on a transitional support strategy update for the Union of Comoros. *Report No. 27893-COM.* Washington: World Bank.

Zacher, M. W. (1979). *International conflicts and collective security, 1946–77: The United Nations, Organization of American States, Organisation of African Unity, and Arab League.* New York: Praeger.

CHAPTER 7

Zanzibar in the Tanzania Union

Greg Cameron

INTRODUCTION

The Zanzibar Archipelago in the Indian Ocean is 25–50 km off the coast of the African mainland. It consists of numerous small islands and two large ones: Unguja, where the capital Zanzibar City is located, and Pemba. The United Republic of Tanzania (URT) consists of the territory of the former colony of Tanganyika and the entire Zanzibar Archipelago.

The union of Tanganyika and Zanzibar was made between two previously existing sovereign states that subsequently adopted a (semi-)federal model of constitutional government, the only such case still extant in post-colonial Africa. In a rapid sequence of events, Tanganyika and Zanzibar sealed their union on April 26, 1964, on the back of the Zanzibar Revolution of January 1964, which was itself triggered by Zanzibar's formal independence on December 10, 1963.

Since then, this experiment in African unity has had a turbulent history. The union remains resilient, having outlasted momentous political changes: intra-party conflict over the union itself, the end of the Cold War, the collapse of Tanzanian socialism, the ascendancy of neo-liberalism, and

G. Cameron (✉)
Faculty of Agriculture, Department of Business and Social Sciences,
Dalhousie University, Truro, NS, Canada
e-mail: Gregory.Cameron@Dal.Ca

© The Author(s) 2019
L. de Vries et al. (eds.), *Secessionism in African Politics*,
Palgrave Series in African Borderlands Studies,
https://doi.org/10.1007/978-3-319-90206-7_7

the introduction of multiparty politics. Nevertheless, Zanzibar nationalism continues to challenge the historical and contemporary legacies of the revolution and the union. Zanzibari nationalists argue that Zanzibar is, in fact, not a secessionist question and that their sovereignty was not fully surrendered when the Articles of Union were signed in 1964.

This chapter investigates why a significant number of Zanzibaris oppose the union in its current form. The failure to undertake true restitution and reconciliation after the 1964 revolution, the limited impact of agrarian reforms and other structuralist policies during the socialist period, Pemba's regional marginalization, the ruling party's intolerance of intra- and inter-party challenges, corruption and nepotism, and the social effects of neo-liberal reforms have led Zanzibaris to demand, at a minimum, the reform of the union. Their alienation is articulated through various forms of identity politics, whether regional, racial, religious, or ethnic, depending on political trends and global dynamics. But at the core of this dissent is the reality that after half a century, the union as a "lived experience" has not delivered a better life for the majority of Zanzibaris, especially in the rural areas where most eke out their livelihoods.

In the first section, I outline how the colonial experience influenced the creation of class and other social fractures in Zanzibar. The second section examines the decolonization process and highlights the failure of pre-independence political parties to unify Zanzibaris across the various social divisions, in the run up to the revolution and union. The third section covers the creation of Tanzania and the constitutional provisions of the union. The fourth section describes how the new pan-union party, *Chama cha Mapinduzi* (CCM, or in English, Revolutionary Party), alienated Zanzibaris through its tendency towards political centralization, political bias against the people of Pemba, and the failure of its structuralist economic policies. The fifth section examines the turn to economic and political liberalization. The sixth section covers the electoral landscape up to the government of national unity before turning to more recent developments. Zanzibar reached a critical juncture in October 2015 when the Zanzibar Electoral Commission abruptly canceled elections the ruling CCM was poised to lose. The seventh section argues that opposition in Zanzibar against the union is broadening, and that it is the failed promise of development that largely underlies this sentiment rather than the resurrection of identity politics. It further argues that memory production at the elite level not only fuels identity politics but also obscures a proper evaluation of the whole (post-)revolutionary period. The chapter concludes by arguing that the durability of the union depends on whether Zanzibar's lack of socioeconomic development can be overcome.

COLONIAL ZANZIBAR AND THE INDIAN OCEAN TRADING SYSTEM

The URT consists of Tanganyika on the African mainland and of Zanzibar, comprising the two primary islands of Unguja and Pemba. Zanzibar fell under the control of the Sultan of Oman in 1698, ending two centuries during which the islands had been of Portuguese possession, following the visit of Vasco da Gama in 1499, though there were never more than isolated settlements on the Isles, which existed alongside indigenous rulers. By then, most Zanzibaris were Bantu Swahili speakers with some Persian, but mainly Arab, influence. Agriculture and fishing were the main subsistence activities of the Isles' peasantry. A lucrative trade in slaves and ivory thrived, along with an expanding plantation economy based on cloves. Extensive colonization of Zanzibar by the Omani Busaidi dynasty started in the 1780s. In 1832, the Sultan transferred his capital from Muscat to Zanzibar. Zanzibar and Oman remained an empire until Sultan Seyyid Said's death in 1856, when it was divided among his two sons, and Zanzibar declared its independence from Oman. Under Sultan Seyyid, Zanzibar was also an imperial state due to its possessions on the East African mainland coast, which had been set in train after the expulsion of the Portuguese in 1698 with the capture of Fort Jesus by the Omani Arabs.[1] These comprised a ten-mile deep coastal strip stretching from Witu in Kenya to Portuguese East Africa.[2] This same strip is also the territorial point of reference of current claims for the secession of Coastal Kenya. Zanzibar became the main conduit between the Indian Ocean trading networks and the African hinterland in East Africa, including the slave trade.[3]

European interests in the area that now forms the URT go back to the seventeenth century. The Omani-controlled caravan trade from Zanzibar into eastern Congo and Buganda presented various mercantile opportunities

[1] Gray (1963) and Martin (1978).
[2] Flint (1963).
[3] Freeman-Grenville (1963: 157).

to European powers.[4] British trading interests in Zanzibar, along with its then extensive coastal possessions, expanded rapidly after 1841. Tanganyika itself was declared a German protectorate in 1885. In 1890, following a series of political developments in the region that threatened the security of the sultanate, Great Britain reached an agreement with the Sultan to create a protectorate. Key here was the Anglo-German Agreement of 1890[5] that transferred the island of Heligoland from Great Britain to Germany, who in turn recognized Great Britain's protectorate of Zanzibar.

Other provisions in this treaty included German access in southwest Africa to the Zambezi River via the Caprivi Strip (the basis of secessionist claims in that region from Namibia),[6] Germany renouncing its claim over Witu and Uganda, and the demarcation of the Kenya-Tanganyika frontier, among other border adjustments on the African continent. Britain thus imposed its protectorate on the islands in order to face the German colonization of Tanganyika. The German imperial government soon bought out the Sultan's Tanganyika coastal strip territory in 1890, while the British government took control of the Sultan's Kenya strip in 1895.[7]

In 1920, following Germany's defeat in the First World War, Tanganyika was placed under a League of Nations mandate, with Britain as the administering power. In 1946, it became a UN trust territory, still under British administration.

In 1929, the politicization of indigenous Africans had found an early expression with the formation of the Tanganyika African Association. This evolved in 1954 into the Tanganyika African National Union (TANU) under the leadership of Julius Nyerere.[8] In the general elections of September 1960, TANU won 70 of the 71 seats in the National Assembly. Internal self-government was achieved in May 1961 and Nyerere became Prime Minister. Tanganyika became independent within the Commonwealth on December 9, 1961.

In contrast to mainland Tanganyika, a clear division corresponding to race and class existed early on in pre-manumission Zanzibar, a colony consisting of a wealthy elite of Arab descent ruling over black African slaves,

---

[4] Jennings (2011).
[5] Also known as the "Heligoland-Zanzibar Treaty."
[6] See Zeller and Melber (2018).
[7] Flint (1963) and (Martin 1978).
[8] Jennings (2011).

peasants, and urban workers.[9] The population that had preceded both the Omanis and the mainland Africans comprised the bulk of the indigenous peasantry.[10] In 1897, Britain abolished slavery and granted gradual manumission to those slaves residing on Zanzibar. In 1914, Britain tightened its control over the Sultan's government. It replaced the position of Consul-General with that of British Resident and designated the governor of its colony of Kenya to be High Commissioner of Zanzibar.[11]

The Sultan remained the symbolic head of state, while the British took charge of defense and foreign affairs and eventually all the key political and administrative powers of the protectorate.[12] This represented the consolidation and adaptation of the existing pre-European colonial system through Indirect Rule and meant that Arab "rule" on Zanzibar was purely nominal well before 1964.[13] Nevertheless, Zanzibar, a century-old center of Islamic and Swahili learning had a deeply rooted identity distinct from mainland Tanganyika. This was in part due to its relative isolation as an island archipelago as well as the impacts of Omani colonization and the diffusion of Sunni Islam among the great majority of the Isles' population prior to British colonization.

ZANZIBAR'S FRACTURED DECOLONIZATION PROCESS

Zanzibar was deeply divided on the eve of decolonization. This section sketches the nature of these divisions as well as the alliances established between Tanganyika and pro-unionist political forces in Zanzibar. Both class and racial fault lines characterized the Zanzibar struggle. Differences between the agrarian political economy of Unguja and Pemba are central to an understanding of both its pre-independence nationalist politics and subsequent developments after 1964. The Unguja peasantry was confined to remote coastal areas of poor-quality soil where many were compelled to work on Arab plantations, initially as forced laborers and later as seasonal workers. Furthermore, the descendants of slaves and Christian migrants from the mainland, arriving as plantation labor, would later comprise a significant and staunch pro-unionist constituency.

[9] Brown (2010: 618).
[10] Sheriff (1991).
[11] Lofchie (1965: 53–58).
[12] Bakari (2001: 47–48) and Flint (1963: 383–384).
[13] Bakari (2001: 48) and Sheriff (1987).

On Pemba, the greater abundance of fertile soils buffeted land alienation somewhat. Moreover, the introduction of cloves in the late nineteenth century provided lucrative opportunities for a Pemba peasant smallholder movement to emerge, a class which was in less conflict with the Arab planters than their Unguja peasant counterparts.[14]

Nationalist politics on Zanzibar emerged gradually in line with legislative, judicial, and executive reforms undertaken by the British.[15] The four main parties were the Afro-Shirazi Party (ASP) led by Abeid Karume, the Zanzibar Nationalist Party (ZNP) led by Ali Mushin, the Zanzibar and Pemba People's Party (ZPPP) led by Mohammed Shamte, and the *Umma* (The Masses) Party led by Abdulrahman Babu. The ASP, ZNP, and ZPPP precursors were ethnic associations based on the resident mainlander population, the Arab elite, and the indigenous Shirazi peasantry (subdivided regionally on Unguja, Tumbatu Island, and Pemba), who traced their lineage to the city of Shiraz in medieval Persia. The *Umma* Party represented a leftist breakaway faction of the ZNP; it had a cross-ethnic membership, including Babu who was of Comorian descent, but no real mass support base comparable to the three other parties. The Arab Sultanate was the defining entity of political allegiance for the ZNP and ZPPP. No single leader who could unite all anticolonial forces in a broad nationalist movement emerged from the competing Zanzibar parties, despite concerted efforts.[16] Instead, intense and bitter competition between the ZNP and the ASP characterized the series of colonial elections culminating in the independence poll of July 1963.

The ASP's social base comprised African urban workers, the African Association, and the Unguja section of the Shirazi Association, which merged with the African Association in 1957. The ZNP's core social base on Unguja was the Arab plantation class in western Unguja, together with the civil service and Stone Town dwelling elite. On Pemba, the majority of the indigenous peasantry opted for the ZNP or the ZPPP. The contest centered on the ZNP and ASP trying to win the vote of the indigenous Shirazi peasantry. The pro-Arab ZNP could not make headway on Unguja, nor could the anti-Arab racialism of the ASP make decisive inroads in

---

[14] Sheriff (1991).

[15] Lofchie (1965).

[16] For a firsthand account of an important pan-African initiative seeking to forge an Afro-Shirazi Party-Zanzibar Nationalist Party (ASP-ZNP) united front, see A. M. Babu (1991: 228).

Pemba where Arabs and Pembans lived cheek by jowl and where there were fewer Zanzibaris of recent African descent.[17]

Crucially, the ZPPP failed to chart a course independent of either the ASP or ZNP and formed an alliance with the latter. The preference of Pemban clove growers for the ZPPP-ZNP coalition was a response to the ASP seeking land redistribution in favor of "Africans," a possible threat to their farms. The ZNP program offered no significant land reform to the poorer peasants. The failure of the nationalist parties to resolve such a monumental impasse led to social disaster.

The ZNP-ZPPP won the 1963 election based on constituency seats, though with a lower percentage of the popular vote than the ASP. Mohammed Shamte, leader of the ZPPP and a Pemban, became the Prime Minister of Zanzibar's first independent government formed on December 10, 1963, in coalition with the ZNP. For the ASP, the independence conferred by Britain was seen as "Arab" independence. The ZNP-ZPPP government was thereafter obliterated by the events known as the Zanzibar Revolution of January 12, 1964.[18]

The Zanzibar Revolution was a confused and murky affair. A hitherto unknown Ugandan by the name of John Okello seized power by leading a force of mainland Africans and ASP youth against the Sultan's government. Okello was subsequently expelled from Zanzibar and Tanganyika, by Karume and Nyerere, respectively.[19,20] It appears that the two principal opposition parties, the ASP and *Umma*, played no direct role.

For a few days after the overthrow of the Sultan's government, many people, mainly rural-based lower-class Manga Arabs, were systematically killed in the Unguja countryside. Leaders of the "revolution" downplayed the number of those killed in the terror that followed, but it is commonly accepted that the death toll approximated 10,000, a very high percentage for a population of fewer than 300,000 at the time. By death, deportation, or departure, the Arab population, numbering 50,000 in 1963, fell between 12,000 and 15,000 people by the end of 1964.[21] The leaders of the ZNP-ZNNP government were either deported or imprisoned. The Sultan,

---

[17] Sheriff (1991).
[18] Cameron (2002b: 41).
[19] Martin (1978: 58–59).
[20] Okello eventually disappeared in his native Uganda during the Idi Amin years.
[21] Clayton (1981: 90, 99).

fleeing with his coterie, was forever banned from Zanzibar and went into exile in the United Kingdom. The ASP justified the ethnic violence against Arabs and the indigenous Shirazi as the glorious overthrow of a slave holding feudal regime by an oppressed African majority.[22]

The fact that a democratically elected government was toppled is nowadays rarely recognized in the literature. Past and current governments are also not morally, let alone legally, held to account for the sheer scale of the systematic killing, which for all intents and purposes was one sided, much of it personal or criminal.[23] The insurgents, moreover, appear to have been aided or armed by elements from Tanganyika.[24] The violence of 1964 cowered and crushed the anti-union opposition anchored in the ZNP-ZPPP coalition.[25]

Approximately half of the population of Zanzibar was politically disenfranchised through the banning of the ZNP-ZPPP by an ASP government that would brook no political opposition. The subsequent union, coupled with the post-revolutionary violence of the Karume years, buttressed the pro-union ASP against its domestic opponents, albeit in an increasingly uneasy relationship with the Tanzanian union government. Zanzibari nationalism would not recover for more than 30 years. Yet the memories of the January 1964 bloodletting, the forceful integration of Zanzibar into a union with Tanganyika, the absence of restitution and reconciliation, and the persistence of chronic underdevelopment would infect the Isles' political life for decades to come and eventually destabilize the newly constituted state known as "Tanzania."

The Creation of Tanzania

In April 1964, the Republic of Tanganyika and the People's Republic of Zanzibar formerly united to form the United Republic of Tanganyika and Zanzibar by signing an Act of Union. In October 1964, the union state was named "Tanzania," a portmanteau of Tanganyika and Zanzibar. A new constitution, introduced in July 1965, provided for a one-party state, although, until 1977, TANU and the ASP remained the respective official parties of mainland Tanzania and Zanzibar. Controversially, there was

---

[22] Mapuri (1996) and Okello (1973).
[23] Ayany (1970: 126–127) and Cameron (2004b: 105).
[24] Bakari (2001: 104–106).
[25] Cameron (2002b).

never a clear promise made in any party platform of ASP or TANU for such a union before 1964. The decision to unify with the mainland was made by Nyerere and Karume.

For the people of Zanzibar, there was no referendum, only an agreement between the Government of Tanganyika and some members of the Zanzibar Revolutionary Council (ZRC). Karume most likely sought the union to reinforce his position in Zanzibar against the Zanzibar Left. For example, Babu was overseas when the union was announced. More charitable interpretations would posit that Nyerere may have also sought a means to bring stability to Zanzibar and/or to unite two countries that had close historic links. Internationally, the British sought to support the union as a means of promoting stability and reducing communist influence. The Commonwealth Relations Office even contemplated the preemptive deployment of Nigerian troops to Zanzibar in order to bolster pro-union elements. Likewise, American policymakers, applying their domino-theory logic to the continent, tended to view the loss of an *Umma* Party-dominated Zanzibar to Soviet communism as being disastrous for the future stability of East and Southern Africa. There is also evidence that the Central Intelligence Agency (CIA) encouraged Nyerere in undertaking the union project.[26]

The 1964 Articles of Union classified the URT's areas of jurisdiction as follows: external affairs, defense, police, emergency powers, citizenship, immigration, external trade and borrowing, the public service of the United Republic, income tax, corporation tax, customs and excise duties, harbors, civil aviation, and telegraph.[27] Areas such as health, primary and secondary education, agriculture, cooperatives, and any other residual powers were the constitutional prerogatives of Zanzibar, initially vested in the ZRC.[28]

Shivji infers from the fact that the 1964 Articles of Union had provisions for two vice presidents—one meant for a Tanganyika government and the other for the Zanzibar government—that the original intent was for a three-government federal structure rather than the actually existing two-government system that combined the union with Tanganyika

---

[26] Speller (2007: 294) and Wilson (1989).

[27] Lofchie (1965: 285–287) and Shivji (1990: 21–22).

[28] The constitutional divisions of power and three-government arrangement were strikingly similar to the Ethiopia-Eritrea Federation of 1952. The failure of the Halie Sellasie regime to enforce the federal provisions unleashed the 30-year Eritrean war of liberation. See G. Cameron (2004a: 41).

governments.[29] Zanzibari nationalists would continue to interpret the Articles of Union as stipulating a three-government structure. Offsetting this absence of a popular mandate for a union, and assuaging Zanzibari fears of outright annexation, was the constitutional provision in the 1964 Articles of Union that allocated the posts of president and vice president between the mainland and the Isles. This constitutional provision meant that, in 1964, Abeid Karume became the vice president while Julius Nyerere became president of the URT. Nyerere was elected president of the URT in September 1965 and was subsequently re-elected in 1970, 1975, and 1980 before retiring from government service in 1985.

Zanzibari domestic politics after 1964 were largely an intra-party struggle between Zanzibar nationalists and unionists, first with the Left in the 1960s and then with the Right in the 1980s and 1990s, with neither wing being enthusiastic about the union. I will first address the high politics with the Left.

Zanzibar politics after the union remained radical and subject to relatively little control from the mainland.[30] The Karume regime, its social composition largely urban based and African nationalist, and also including the peasantry of Unguja, moved quickly to marginalize the ASP Left and ex-*Umma* members. The union/British Westminster institutions became platforms for the co-optation of radical Zanzibari nationalists, like Babu and Kassim Hanga, who were conveniently transferred to the mainland and given less-than-prominent union cabinet posts. The astute Karume also strengthened military and economic cooperation with the Eastern Bloc, including China.[31]

Roughly a decade into the Tanzania union, Zanzibari autonomy remained intact, a reflection of the staying power of Zanzibari nationalism, union government respect for the union provisions, as well as Karume's skillful balancing act between union and domestic forces. The inherent instability of this adroit strategy soon became apparent after Karume's assassination in 1972 when weaker Zanzibari leaders would give away additional constitutional powers to the union government.[32] The assassination may have been an attempt by the Zanzibari Left to reassert control of the post-revolutionary process. Instead, "the devouring of the revolution's

---

[29] Shivji (1990: 27–28).

[30] Speller (2007: 293).

[31] Clayton (1981).

[32] For a harrowing account of an *Umma* member who survived Karume's East-German-trained security services, see T. G. Burgess (2010a).

children"—Karume's demise, the smashing of the former *Umma*, and the physical liquidation of left-wing ASP members—paved the way for greater integration into the union.

THE BIRTH OF CCM AND CONSTITUTIONAL CENTRALIZATION

Growing encroachment on Zanzibar's autonomy became evident with the controversial constitutional changes of 1977. These established the supremacy of a new pan-union party, CCM (Revolutionary Party), following the merger of ASP and TANU.[33] TANU and ASP had hitherto only ruled in Tanzania mainland and in Zanzibar, respectively. With the birth of CCM, Nyerere was elected chairman and Aboud Jumbe, Karume's successor, was elected vice chairman. The newly-minted party in turn paved the way for the union government's assertion of additional administrative powers. CCM was envisioned by its drafters in the party to be constitutionally supreme over the organs of state for both Zanzibar and mainland Tanzania.[34] This potentially meant that CCM had authority over non-Union matters.[35] Shivji argues that the 1977 constitution sought undemocratically—through closed sessions of the National Executive Committee (NEC) and without any other fora for debate—to impose mainland party supremacy over the 1964 Articles of Union.[36]

Between 1965 and 1977, new items were added to the list of union matters, giving the union parliament and executive more powers. These included: unilaterally ceding authority over currency, banks, and foreign exchange (1965); industrial licensing and statistics; higher education; matters related to the Treaty for East African Cooperation (1967); oil, petroleum, and natural gas (1968); civil aviation; and post-1977, the Court of Appeal of the Union Republic (1984).[37]

The 1977 constitutional changes also heralded "guided" democratic reforms on the Isles. The 1979 Zanzibar constitution gave Zanzibaris the

---

[33] From the 1977 merger onwards, I refer to the former ASP as *Chama Cha Mapinduzi*—"CCM Zanzibar," the governing party of Zanzibar, and Tanganyika African National Union (TANU) as "CCM Dodoma," the governing party at the union level.

[34] Jumbe (1994: 53).

[35] McHenry (1994: 196).

[36] Shivji (1990: 56–68).

[37] For a recent summary, see F. Jjuuko and G. Muruiuki (2010).

right to directly elect their president within the CCM single-party system in 1980. It also established the House of Representatives (HRP, *Baraza la Wawakilishi* in Swahili) to replace the legislative body that had been abolished in 1964 and then replaced by the ZRC.[38] Representing a real democratic advance for the Isles, Karume's successor as Zanzibar president, Aboud Jumbe, may have been seeking to undercut the hard-line ASP factions, as well as give relief to Zanzibaris weary of over a decade of Karume's autocratic rule.

The first presidential and HRP elections in 1980 were not direct elections.[39] A new constitution for Zanzibar came into force in January 1985 providing for the HRP to be directly elected by universal adult suffrage. In April that year, to enable Zanzibari participation in the union structures, the National Assembly (*Bunge*, in Swahili) approved a new constitution for Tanzania. This provided for the election to the National Assembly in Dodoma (capital of the URT) of representatives from Zanzibar, in addition to those from mainland Tanzania. These reforms to the Zanzibari executive and legislature, and to the union Parliament (*Bunge*), would lay the basis for the political challenge mounted by Zanzibari nationalist forces in the 1990s.

CCM's creation as a constitutionally supreme party, and its encroachment upon Zanzibar's constitutional jurisdiction, triggered a growing political perception in the 1980s that Zanzibar was slowly being "swallowed" by the union government. This perception was due in great part to mainlander dominance in the ranks of CCM, as well as to the curtailment of Zanzibar's relative autonomy in foreign affairs. The mainland population of roughly 44 million has always greatly outnumbered that of Zanzibar's 1.3 million, reinforcing many Zanzibaris' feelings of being dominated. Compounding the political anxieties of many Zanzibaris was the union government's intolerance of factions within CCM Zanzibar over constitutional affairs.

A critical case in point was the fall of Zanzibar President Jumbe after 12 years in office. Chaired by President Nyerere, a special session of CCM's NEC was held in the union capital, Dodoma, to discuss the "polluted political atmosphere" in Zanzibar.[40] The controversy led to Jumbe's forced resignation from the Zanzibar Presidency in January 1984. The crux of the crisis was Jumbe's attempt to reconcile popular discontent on the Isles over Zanzibar's diminished constitutional status within the union.

---

[38] For an in-depth treatment of constitutional and party reforms during this period, see H. Othman and A. Mlimuka (1990, 58–169).

[39] Othman and Mlimuka (1990: 169).

[40] Bakari (2001: 121–122).

By the 1980s, the failures of the structuralist economic policies of the union and Zanzibar governments were apparent to all but the most stalwart of CCM leaders and cadres. Balance of payment difficulties, as well as industrial and agricultural stagnation, deepened throughout Tanzania. A decade after the 1967 socialist Arusha Declaration, agrarian *Ujamaa* had degenerated into forced villagization devoid of any collective content. *Ujamaa* largely bypassed rural Zanzibar apart from a brief and failed collectivization campaign.

Certainly, Karume's left-wing populist policies had made serious efforts to redistribute wealth, status, and opportunity to the rural majority, especially with the 1964 land reform.[41] Yet clove prices remained abysmally low as a government monopsony exploited Pemba clover producers and pickers alike. After 1977, the CCM Zanzibar government, likewise, was unable to revive the Zanzibar economy as import costs soared and agricultural production declined.[42] In short, despite some laudable policies and projects, the inherited colonial agrarian structure remained largely intact. The political and ideological limitations of the ASP- and CCM-era governments, and their failure to effect a new agrarian socialist paradigm with the peasantry, would leave Zanzibar vulnerable to the global shift in development policies of the 1980s.

The Era of Economic and Political Liberalization

The socialist era in Tanzania came to an end in 1985 with the imposition of International Monetary Fund (IMF) Structural Adjustment Policies (SAPs) and World Bank programs.[43] When President Nyerere retired in November 1985, Ali Hassan Mwinyi succeeded him as union president, remaining in office until 1995.[44] Mwinyi presided over sweeping economic liberalization as signified in the Zanzibar Declaration of 1991 that formally spelt the end of the Arusha Declaration of 1967. During this early period of economic liberalization, burgeoning patrimonial networks appear to have emerged in mainland Tanzania and Zanzibar. These may

---

[41] See T. G. Burgess (2010b: 430) and Loimeier (2006: 16–17).

[42] Shao (1993: 84).

[43] Campbell and Stein (1991).

[44] A Muslim and Zanzibari, Mwinyi is widely perceived to have gone some way to redressing religious imbalance in the civil service by promoting Muslims in the union government. While to some extent popular in Zanzibar as union President, Mwinyi also presided over the repression of many Zanzibari nationalists during the transition to multiparty politics.

have bolstered the determination of some CCM Zanzibar leaders to pre-serve the status quo of the union in order to tap into networks that had an income from aid and investment flows. Zanzibar had originally enacted such open-door economic policies when Mwinyi had succeeded Jumbe as Zanzibar president in 1984, with Seif Sharif Hamad, a Pemban, as his chief minister.

Many Zanzibaris fondly remember the times under Mwinyi when goods became more available, and they expected that the popular Hamad, then a staunch unionist, would become Zanzibar's next president in 1985 after Mwinyi became union president (1985–1995). Instead, the CCM political establishment, the mainlander-dominated NEC, selected a politi-cal lightweight to become president of Zanzibar: Idris Abdul Wakil from Unguja (the former Speaker of the Zanzibar HRP and a member of the ASP old guard). The political crisis deepened with the subsequent removal of Hamad as Chief Minister, who was jailed for two years in 1988 after adopting an anti-union stance. Hamad, who would later in the 1990s lead the formal multiparty opposition to CCM Zanzibar, articulated, in part, a regional discourse about Pemba's marginalization within Zanzibar.

By early 1988, tensions were on the rise again in Zanzibar, reflecting underlying rivalries between supporters and opponents of unity with mainland Tanzania.[45] McHenry argues that Zanzibari "sub-nationalism" tends to be unprincipled, and that factions merely employ the "sub-nationalist card" to position themselves in the union's political establish-ment.[46] This explains to some extent the behavior of the Zanzibari political elite but downplays Zanzibari nationalism as a social movement and political force. Hamad's removal was a seminal moment in Zanzibar's post-revolutionary history. It revealed the abysmal failure of the CCM regime to accept Pemba into the revolutionary fold. This historical moment is paramount in making sense of Zanzibar's contemporary seces-sionist sentiment.

Zanzibar and Tanzania held the last single-party elections in October 1990. Dr. Salmin Amour, Wakil's successor, became Zanzibar's president, while Mwinyi was re-elected for a second term as union president. The purges in CCM Zanzibar during the twilight of the single-party era ensured that the Zanzibar nationalist movement would pursue its political program outside of the monolithic CCM.

[45] Brown (2010).
[46] McHenry (1994: 189–213).

In the final years before the first multiparty elections since 1963, cracks began to appear within CCM itself over the union. In 1993, the CCM Zanzibar government attempted to join the Organization of the Islamic Conference (OIC). The initiative was ruled unconstitutional by the union government because a non-sovereign entity (i.e., Zanzibar) could not join such a body. The episode illustrated the growing estrangement between Zanzibar and the Tanzanian mainland, in which religion also played a role. A group of mainland Christian parliamentarians, labeled the "G55," subsequently lobbied for a constitutional reform to limit Zanzibar's budget subsidies and other perceived privileges within the union.[47] Nyerere, continuing to wield considerable power as chairman of CCM until 1990, and later in his role as "Father of the Nation," entered the fray and had the "G55" motion quashed in the Dodoma National Assembly.[48] The disproportionately large number of Zanzibar MPs in the Dodoma union parliament also became an issue of debate, but union President Benjamin Mkapa (1995–2005) made the point repeatedly that the higher share of Zanzibar seats was a consequence of constitutional compromise and was there to stay.

THE RESURGENCE OF ZANZIBARI NATIONALISM

In 1992, the union government proposed constitutional amendments to establish a multiparty political system; the constitutions of both the URT and Zanzibar were amended accordingly. The new electoral law stipulated that to protect national unity, all new political organizations should command support in both Zanzibar and mainland Tanzania, and should be free of tribal, religious, and racial bias. Several political organizations were officially registered from mid-1992 onwards.

Zanzibari nationalism found its institutional expression in the Civic United Front (CUF), formed in 1992 from a merger of a Zanzibari entity called the *Kamati ya Mageuzi Huru* (the Committee of Free Change), and the mainland-based *Chama cha Wananchi* (Citizens' Party). CUF represented a broad alliance of urban intellectuals (many of whom received their higher education while in CCM), business interests connected to the import/export sector on the Isles, Zanzibar Stone Town, the majority of the rural peasantry on Pemba, as well as growing rural support on Unguja.

---

[47] Maliyamkono (2000: 213–244).
[48] McHenry (1994: 198).

After being released from incarceration, Hamad was selected as CUF Zanzibar presidential candidate.

During the single-party era, the clandestine Zanzibar opposition had called for a referendum on the union. With the new multiparty framework, CUF adopted a more reformist course that advocated for a federal structure split three ways: a government of Zanzibar, a Tanganyika government, and an overarching union government based on the original 1964 Articles of Union. The three-government proposal stemmed from the recommendations of the Nyalali Commission—a presidential commission appointed in 1993—but which CCM rejected.

Significantly, the mainland Tanzania opposition parties also endorsed the commission's recommendation for a three-government structure. CUF's party program generally advocated for a free-market economy. CUF repeatedly said it had no intention to break the union but only wished to renegotiate the issues that were added to the union's prerogatives unilaterally in 1977. They argued that, otherwise, Zanzibar's status could eventually be downgraded to an administrative region like Mafia Island off Tanzania's Swahili Coast.

CUF also accused the union government of coveting hidden offshore oil reserves, one of the items constitutionally added to the union government in 1977. Suspicions were confirmed when Mkapa unilaterally declared offshore natural resources to be a union matter and granted exploration rights without consulting Zanzibar.[49] CUF also called for the restitution of those lands seized by the Karume-era land reforms as well as compensation to those victimized by the 1964 massacres. These demands fuelled suspicions in CCM circles that CUF was in the pay of exiled counter-revolutionary Arabs.

The mainstream Zanzibar nationalist movement follows a non-violent parliamentary path. CUF made significant legislative inroads on the back of the 1995, 2000, and 2005 general elections, being the official opposition in both the Dodoma union Parliament (until 2010) and the Zanzibar HRP. Presidential results on Zanzibar have given CCM presidential candidates roughly half of the popular vote. Had these elections been free and fair, CUF would have won—in the estimation of the author—with at least 55–60% of the popular vote.

The Zanzibar multiparty electoral campaigns were, however, consistently marred by low-level violence, manipulation of voter registrations, a

[49] Rawlence (2005: 516–517).

politically partisan electoral commission, fraud, and repression—notably the shooting of protesters after the 2000 elections in the wake of the failed Commonwealth-brokered agreement of June 1999.[50] There was also an informal donor boycott by some Western governments of the Zanzibar government during this period. The CCM Zanzibar and union governments, in order to garner support from the American government and other Western aid donors, sought to conflate anti-CCM sentiment on the Isles with post- "9/11" propaganda that painted CUF as "fundamentalist" and connected to the "Arab" Middle East.[51] Having said this, Western nations, by and large, are primarily concerned with regional stability in Eastern Africa, particularly with regard to trade and investment opportunities, and are not strongly aligned to either CCM or CUF, both of which support liberal reforms.[52]

Negotiations to end the political crisis led to the signing of a *muafaka* (peace accord) in October 2001 between CUF and CCM. Jakaya Kikwete, a Muslim from the mainland, was elected union president in the 2005 general elections, with CCM winning an overwhelming majority in the mainland legislative elections.[53] At his inauguration in 2005, President Kikwete stated that his main priority would be to resolve the tensions on Zanzibar.[54] Amani Karume, son of the assassinated first president, was elected twice as president of Zanzibar between 2000 and 2010. Seeking to placate nationalist sentiment on the Isles, the Karume government adopted a new flag on January 9, 2005, the 41st anniversary of the Zanzibar Revolution. It is based on what was the official flag of Zanzibar from January 29 to April 26, 1964, when the ASP was in power, with the addition of the Union flag in the top corner. The flag was only to be hoisted during official functions that did not involve sovereign nations.

A power arrangement was finally put in place in time for the 2010 elections, after intense domestic and international pressure, constitutional reform, and inter-party reconciliation. In the Zanzibar presidential poll in October 2010, the Zanzibar CCM's Ali Mohammed Shein, a Pemban,

---

[50] Human Rights Watch (2002).

[51] Cameron (2009: 164–165).

[52] Cameron (2009).

[53] After Mkapa, a mainlander, stepped down, Zanzibaris widely expected that the next union president would be a Zanzibari. The CCM union government said that this was not constitutionally guaranteed. The idea of a constitutionally sanctioned rotating presidency between the two parts of the union was mooted in the constitutional review. See Ibrahim (2012).

[54] Jennings (2011: 3–4).

narrowly secured victory over Seif Sharif Hamad. Under the power-sharing agreement, a Government of National Unity (GNU) was established in November 2010 with Shein as Zanzibar president and Hamad as first vice president. Essentially an inter-elite pact, the GNU was widely seen as an effective stabilizing force for reducing political tensions on Zanzibar.[55] While the GNU represented another example of Zanzibari willingness to engage in the reform of the union, despite ongoing economic and political challenges, it was still an open question as to whether the GNU marked the beginning of an end to polarized politics on the islands or only temporarily ameliorated it.[56] Zanzibari nationalists continued to demand having a say on the union during a nationwide constitutional review.[57] The final draft constitution, sent to the union parliament in 2014, dismissed the three-tier union reform, while a scheduled referendum on it was indefinitely postponed.[58] The CCM Dodoma government continued to maintain the status quo on the two-structure union, now over half a century old.

The 2015 elections on the Isles were marred by electoral irregularities, culminating in the sudden cancellation of the Isles' poll, showing once again that both CCM governments remain willing to employ extra-constitutional means to block the CUF from becoming the ruling party in Zanzibar.[59] With the CUF boycotting, the March 2016 re-run saw President Shein receive more than 90% of the presidential vote for the Isles' president. In the HRP, the ruling party gained something of a monopoly of the legislature with only 3 out of 87 seats going to minor parties and the rest to the Zanzibar CCM (elected, nominated, reserved).[60] The union authorities did not intervene which revealed once again that, despite the relative autonomy of CCM Zanzibar, CCM Dodoma remained in charge of what happens on the Isles.[61]

[55] Bakari and Makulilo (2012: 195–218) and Matheson (2012: 594–596).

[56] Babieya (2011: 94).

[57] Ibrahim (2012).

[58] Anyimadu (2016).

[59] While President Shein rejected the election results on the Isles, he also accepted on the same day, at the same polling stations, the voting results for the union presidential and legislative elections (Branson 2016; Throup 2016).

[60] In the 2010–2015 HRP, CCM had a total of 48 seats and CUF 33, plus the Attorney General, for a total of 82 seats (ZRG 2016).

[61] Brown (2010: 628–629).

The CCM union government is politically entrenched on the mainland, and rural Tanzania is its bastion. CUF was one of the four member parties of a political coalition known as *Umoja wa Katiba ya Wananchi* (UKAWA, the Coalition of Defenders of the People's Constitution), the other three being the centrist *Chama cha Demokrasia na Maendeleo* (CHADEMA, Party for Democracy and Progress) (the strongest party on the mainland), the social democratic National Convention for Construction and Reform (NCCR)-*Mageuzi*, and the National League for Democracy (NLD). The votes in the Dodoma National Assembly (*Bunge*) delivered an overwhelming victory to CCM in 2015, with the ruling party winning 252 of 364 seats (elected and appointed), while CHADAMA won 70, and CUF won 42 seats (elected and appointed).[62] John Magufuli, the new union president, won with almost 60% of the presidential vote.[63] CCM is now Africa's longest ruling party.

The union government will continue to respect the union arrangement in its current form and not make any moves to annex Zanzibar. While Zanzibar is certainly a potentially viable independent nation-state, its geographical proximity to the mainland, coupled with a politically divided population, and the backing of CCM by Western powers (perhaps a "better the devil you know" attitude), suggests that the political forces in favor of an independent Zanzibar are at present unable to significantly change the union status quo in the absence of a broader political consensus in the URT. The stage is therefore set for ongoing political tensions on the Isles for the foreseeable future.

Political Polarization and Stasis

A casual observer of Zanzibar's politics could be excused for thinking that the Isles are stuck in a time warp going back to politics just before and after the 1964 Zanzibar Revolution. However, a central difference in the contemporary period is the basis of opposition against the union. CUF's base is broader than either of the defunct parties of the past, the ZNP and ASP. CUF's key constituency comes from Pemba, but the party draws significant support throughout Zanzibar from its wider appeals to Islam, nationalism, and disillusionment with CCM Zanzibar's economic policies.

---

[62] Brewin (2016). NCCR-*Mageuzi* won a seat as did a newer left-leaning party called Alliance for Change and Transparency (ACT).

[63] John Magufuli, the new union President, won with almost 60% of the vote. Edward Lowassa, his chief rival under the UKAWA banner, and a recent defector from the CCM old guard, garnered close to 40% of the vote.

In the 2010 elections, CUF increased its share of the seats in the HRP compared to the 2005 results, including on Unguja. Unionist support on Zanzibar remains strongest in the rural areas of Unguja and among the Christian mainlander community. In recent years, this appears to be slowly eroding in urban Zanzibar constituencies such as Kiembe Samaki and Kikwajuni.[64]

Demographic shifts that have further blurred the Arab-African divide (which was never all that clear) also mark a change in the political landscape.[65,66] A high rate of intermarriage throughout Zanzibar mitigates against racial and ethnic identities becoming powerful independent political factors, despite the leadership in both parties branding one another in ethnically charged ways.[67]

Yet one must be cautious in positing too instrumentalist an interpretation of ethnicity because the extent to which those victimized by past political injustices pass on their recollections in the language of race and ethnicity is difficult to discern. Unionists and nationalists are locked in struggles over historical interpretation of race, revolution, the union, contrasting "golden ages," belonging, and competing moral claims. Neither side is able to supersede the political worldview of the other.[68] It is not enough, however, to analyze these narratives only through their own frames of reference. Inter-elite discourse needs to be understood through the political economy of the revolutionary legacy in its *totality* in order to get at the material interests of those who benefit from promoting them.

One could argue that contested memories allow CCM leaders to sidestep the party's checkered post-revolutionary economic history,[69] easing the shift from socialism to its current neo-liberal position. Zanzibari nationalists ensconced in predominantly free-market thinking have likewise become accommodated to neo-liberal restructuring.

---

[64] Chauvin (2015).

[65] Brown (2010).

[66] Many youth, for instance, belong to the post-revolution generation and are more concerned with employment than history lessons. See G. Cameron (2002a).

[67] Brown (2010: 629, 631).

[68] Fouere (2012: 672–689), Glassman (2011: 298–299), and Myers (2000: 429–448).

[69] Recent work on elite narratives and memory is sound but requires greater engagement with critical political economy to give a better picture of the ways in which material forces articulate with public narratives. See Fouere (2012), Loimeir (2006), and Myers (2000).

The degree to which the phenomenon of contested memory may have fuelled pre-revolutionary political identities in Zanzibar society is not clear. Yet significant lack of economic development would appear to be the primary driver of general discontent with the union. I recall the almost millenarian belief among many Pemban villagers living in grinding poverty in the 1990s that a CUF victory would herald the dawn of a better life.[70] A recent study on Pemba affirms the author's earlier work, which argued that the ethnic factor in Zanzibari politics is largely a creation of the CCM (i.e., that CUF is "Arab" and/or "fundamentalist").[71] That this political discontent is not just confined to the anti-CCM bastion of Pemba is revealed in recent ethnographic research on Jongowe, on Tumbatu Island off of Unguja. Villagers there have few expectations that conventional politics will make a positive difference in their lives.[72] Roughly 70% of Zanzibaris still derive their livelihoods from agriculture and natural resource activities.[73]

Zanzibar's economic indicators are at best mixed. While the Zanzibar government raised the producer price for cloves and connected Pemba to the national electrical grid in 2010, the economy remains vulnerable to fluctuations in tourism, foreign investment, clove prices, food imports, and energy costs.[74] Similarly, recent economic growth on mainland Tanzania was accompanied by only a slight reduction in poverty.[75] Life remains very hard for the majority of Zanzibaris and many migrate to the mainland in search of work. Conversely, mainlanders—albeit in smaller numbers—often migrate in search of work as marginal hawkers in Zanzibar's tourist sector or as business investors in the coastal resorts. On the surface, these migratory flows appear to point to greater bottom-up integration of the union's two political entities, but in the current economic conditions, they contribute to social tensions on the islands around a perceived Christian mainlander influx.

---

[70] Cameron (2004b: 103–119).

[71] Matheson (2012).

[72] Dean (2013: 31–32).

[73] An "investor-led" agricultural strategy is now promoted by the Zanzibar government as the main strategy to tackle the monumental and historical challenges facing agriculture. See Zanzibar Revolutionary Government (2009).

[74] Brown (2010).

[75] van Buren (2011: 6).

The perception that the larger political entity seeks to economically exploit Zanzibar gets expressed in references to "Arabness," the Swahili language, and Islam.[76] One can argue that the rise of Islam as a political factor in Zanzibar in the early 2000s was fuelled by the Isles' economic malaise and the blocked political aspirations of increasingly desperate Zanzibaris.[77,78] Islamists have called for increased local control of the economy, reflecting Zanzibari nationalist concerns about outsiders running roughshod over Zanzibar through uncontrolled tourism, and about the close alignment of the CCM political class to Western governments and investors. It is common for Zanzibaris of all walks of life to contrast the Isles' limited economic base—tourism, cloves, and the Zanzibar port—with Tanzania's huge and comparatively resource-endowed land mass.[79] Political narratives that delink political identity formation from political economy risk simplifying anti-unionism on Zanzibar as some mixture of a regional, ethno-racial, and/or religious conflict that is endemic to a "third-world" African country mired in a failed nation-building project.[80]

CONCLUSION

Zanzibar was a culturally dynamic and independent political entity before becoming a protectorate of Great Britain. Zanzibar's central role as a trade *entrepot* along the East African littoral was to a large degree forged by Omani colonization. But the tragic by-product of Zanzibar's history was the legacy of an underdeveloped colonial economy marred by racial and class cleavages. These seemingly intractable social and political fractures precipitated the Zanzibar Revolution and the subsequent union in 1964. The ASP welcomed the union but jealously guarded the internal autonomy granted by the 1964 Articles of Union. Although the union government

---

[76] Cameron (2002a).

[77] Cameron (2009: 172).

[78] Signs of the emergence of political Islam on Zanzibar were discernible in the early 1990s with political liberalization and the decline in the legitimacy of the old radical nationalist system, a trend perhaps not unlike other contexts, including in Arab North Africa. Religious schisms have also become apparent in recent years between Christian and Moslem communities on the mainland itself over the perceived hegemony of the former in politics and the economy. See G. C. van de Bruinhorst (2009: 127–150).

[79] Cameron (2002a: 313–330).

[80] Burgess (2010b: 429–450).

by and large respected Zanzibar's autonomy, there were encroachments on important jurisdictional areas in 1977.

The ASP-CCM regimes had a narrow phase of legitimacy during the Cold War—and the economic challenges were formidable—but in the end, the government's structuralist economic policies failed to deliver on the promises of revolutionary change. Furthermore, union government repression of nationalist forces resisting constitutional centralization, coupled with economic challenges, contributed to the emergence of CUF during the multiparty era. CUF demanded a return to a three-government structure, as envisioned in the 1964 Articles of Union. The subsequent electoral war of attrition from 1995 culminated in the GNU in 2010, which delivered some improved governance for Zanzibaris. However, the 2015 electoral debacle allowed the CCM Zanzibar regime a free hand in governing, but has opened up a political vacuum in Zanzibar.

Throughout its history, the union garnered support among many Zanzibaris on both Unguja and Pemba, including at key junctures. These junctures included the rural socialist campaigns, the ASP-TANU merger, Mwinyi's liberal reforms, the rise of Seif Sharif Hamad, competitive party election participation, the proposed three-government structure, and more recently, the GNU power sharing arrangement. Yet underdevelopment, coupled with an unwillingness to open up meaningful political space for nationalist forces on the Isles, continues to test the legitimacy of the union. The recalcitrance of the ruling party towards both the democratization of the Isles' politics and union reform, as seen in 2015, coupled with a just political governance and effective economic policymaking, led to the emergence of various political identities (Pemban regionalism, Zanzibar *patria*, political Islam) as a defensive reaction against an increasingly untenable status quo. The CCM state itself is to a great extent anchored to an essentialized past.

Finally, it is easy not to consider the revolutionary legacy in its totality when charting an alternative future. There is an urgent need to more forcefully confront the lessons of the union's 50-year history in order to make sense of a free market paradigm that forecloses the possibility of balanced agricultural development, industrialization, and the satisfaction of basic mass needs.[81] Presently, Zanzibar appears to be shifting away from productionist forms of accumulation to greater integration into the regional and

---

[81] Maghimbi et al. (2011).

world economies, with all that this potentially portends for ordinary Zanzibaris. The 1964 Zanzibar Revolution and the union were part of a world historical moment during which "third-world" national liberation movements burst onto the political stage.[82] This tide has now receded, leaving the Western state system globally dominant for now.

But world historical moments are just that, and it behooves those seeking a new dispensation to re-think the role of structuralist policies, the degree of state centralization, and mass democracy if there is to be any movement out of peripheral capitalist underdevelopment. The popular basis for the union, therefore, is inextricably bound to its historical record and to whether political leaderships, be they in Dodoma or Zanzibar City, or both, can chart alternative development models that truly make a positive difference in the lives of the people of Zanzibar.

REFERENCES

Anyimadu, A. (2016, September 5). Politics and development in Tanzania. Shifting the status quo. Africa Program, Chatham House. Retrieved from https://www.chathamhouse.org/sites/files/chathamhouse/publications/research/2016-03-18-politics-development-tanzania-anyimadu_1.pdf. Accessed 3 Jan 2017.

Ayany, S. G. (1970). *A history of Zanzibar: A study in constitutional development 1934–1964.* Nairobi: East African Literature Bureau.

Babeiya, E. (2011). Multiparty elections and party support in Tanzania. *Journal of Asian and African Studies, 47*(1), 83–100.

Babu, A. M. (1991). The 1964 Revolution: Lumpen or vanguard? In A. Sheriff & E. Ferguson (Eds.), *Zanzibar under colonial rule* (pp. 220–248). London: James Currey.

Bakari, M. A. (2001). *The democratisation process in Zanzibar: A retarded transition.* Hamburg: Institute of African Affairs.

Bakari, M. A., & Makulilo, A. (2012). Beyond polarity in Zanzibar? The 'silent' referendum and the government of national unity. *Journal of Contemporary African Studies, 30*(2), 195–218.

Branson, N. (2016, January). Elections on Zanzibar: An exercise in futility. Africa Research Institute. Retrieved from http://www.africaresearchinstitute.org/newsite/blog/elections-on-zanzibar-an-exercise-in-futility. Accessed 10 Jan 2010.

Brewin, D. (2016, May 1). Zanzibar election re-run. Tanzanian Affairs. Retrieved from https://www.tzaffairs.org/2016/05/zanzibar-election-re-run. Accessed 7 Jan 2017.

Brown, A. (2010). Political tensions in Zanzibar: Echoes from the revolution? *Canadian Journal of Development Studies, 30*(3–4), 615–633.

---

[82] Skocpol (1979: 3).

Burgess, T. G. (2010a). *Race, revolution, and the struggle for human rights in Zanzibar: The memoirs of Ali Sultan Issa and Seif Sharif Hamad*. Athens: Ohio University Press.

Burgess, T. G. (2010b). Memories, myths and meanings of the Zanzibari Revolution. In T. Falola & R. C. Njoku (Eds.), *War and peace in Africa* (pp. 429–450). Durham: Carolina Academic Press.

Cameron, G. (2002a). Zanzibar's turbulent transition. *Review of African Political Economy, 92*, 313–330.

Cameron, G. (2002b). *Protest and cooperation in post-revolutionary Zanzibar*. PhD dissertation, University of London.

Cameron, G. (2004a). Authoritarian federalism in the dock: A historical comparison between the Ethiopia-Eritrea Federation and the Tanganyika-Zanzibar Union. *Journal of Eritrean Studies, 3*(1), 1–25.

Cameron, G. (2004b). Political violence, ethnicity and the agrarian question in Zanzibar. In P. Caplan & F. Topan (Eds.), *Swahili modernities culture, politics, and identity on the East Coast of Africa* (pp. 103–119). Trenton: Africa World Press.

Cameron, G. (2009). Narratives of democracy and dominance in Zanzibar. In K. Larsen (Ed.), *Knowledge, renewal and religion repositioning and changing ideological and material circumstances among the Swahili on the East African Coast* (pp. 151–176). Uppsala: The Nordic Africa Institute.

Campbell, H., & Stein, H. (1991). *The IMF and Tanzania: The dynamics of liberalization*. Harare: SAPES Trust.

Chauvin, M. (2015, August). Electoral shenanigans in Zanzibar: A sign of CCM desperation? Africa Research Institute. Retrieved from http://www.africaresearchinstitute.org/blog/electoral-shenanigans-in-zanzibar-a-sign-of-ccm-desperation. Accessed 12 Nov 2015.

Clayton, A. (1981). *The Zanzibar revolution and its aftermath*. London: Hurst and Co. Ltd.

Dean, E. (2013). 'The backbone of the village': Gender, development, and traditional authority in rural Zanzibar. *Journal of Contemporary African Studies, 31*(1), 18–36.

Flint, J. (1963). The wider background to partition and colonial occupation. In R. Olivier & G. Mathew (Eds.), *History of East Africa* (Vol. 1, pp. 352–390). Oxford: Clarendon Press.

Fouere, M. (2012). Reinterpreting revolutionary Zanzibar in the media today: The case of Dira newspaper. *Journal of Eastern African Studies, 6*(4), 672–689.

Freeman-Grenville, G. S. P. (1963). The coast, 1498–1840. In R. Olivier & G. Mathew (Eds.), *History of East Africa* (Vol. 1, pp. 129–168). Oxford: Clarendon Press.

Glassman, J. (2011). *War of words, war of stones. Racial thought and violence in colonial Zanzibar*. Bloomington: Indiana University Press.

Gray, J. M. (1963). Zanzibar and the coastal belt 1840–1884. In R. Olivier & G. Mathew (Eds.), *History of East Africa* (Vol. 1, pp. 212–251). Oxford: Clarendon Press.

Human Rights Watch. (2002, April). The bullets were raining. *The January 2001 attack on peaceful demonstrators in Zanzibar, 14*(3), 1–45.

Ibrahim, I. (2012). Union and constitutional review. In *Zanzibari Yetu Haki ya Kuwa Mzanzibari (Our Zanzibar the rights of being a Zanzibari)*. www.zanzibariyetu.wordpress.com. Accessed 1 Oct 2013.

Jennings, M. (2011). Recent history of Tanzania essay. In I. Frame (Ed.), *Africa south of the Sahara* (pp. 1–28). London: Routledge.

Jjuuko, F., & Muruiuki, G. (2010). *Federation within federation: The Tanzania union experience and the East African integration process, Eastern Africa Centre for Constitutional Development*. Kampala: Fountain Publishers.

Jumbe, A. (1994). *The partner-ship Tanganyika – Zanzibar union: 30 Turbulent Years*. Dar es Salaam: Amana Publishers.

Lofchie, M. (1965). *Zanzibar background to revolution*. London: Oxford University Press.

Loimeier, R. (2006). Memories of revolution patterns of interpretation of the 1964 revolution in Zanzibar. (English version). For German language original version see Memories of revolution: Zur deutungsgeschichte einer revolution (Sansibar 1964). *Africa Spectrum, 41*, 175–197.

Maghimbi, S., Razack, B., Lokini, B., & Senga M.A. (2011). The agrarian question in Tanzania? A state of the art paper. *Current African Issues, 45*. Uppsala: Nordiska Africa institutet, and University of Dar es Salaam.

Maliyamkono, T. L. (2000). Zanzibar's financial benefits from the union. In T. L. Maliyamkono (Ed.), *The political plight of Zanzibar* (pp. 213–244). Dar es Salaam: Tema Publishers.

Mapuri, O. (1996). *The 1964 revolution achievements and prospects*. Dar es Salaam: Tanzania Publishing House.

Martin, E. B. (1978). *Zanzibar tradition and revolution*. London: Hamish Hamilton.

Matheson, A. (2012). Maridhiano: Zanzibar's remarkable reconciliation and government of national unity. *Journal of Eastern African Studies, 6*(4), 591–612.

McHenry, D. (1994). *Limited choices: The political struggle for socialism in Tanzania*. Boulder: Lynne Rienner.

Myers, G. A. (2000). Narrative representations of revolutionary Zanzibar. *Journal of Historical Geography, 26*(3), 429–448.

Okello, J. (1973). *Revolution in Zanzibar*. Nairobi: East African Publishing House.

Othman, H., & Mlimuka, A. (1990). Zanzibar's presidential elections. In H. Othman, I. Bavu, & M. Okema (Eds.), *Tanzania democracy in transition* (pp. 58–65). Dar es Salaam: Dar es Salaam University Press.

Rawlence, B. (2005). Briefing the Zanzibar elections. *African Affairs, 104*(416), 515–523.

Shao, I. F. (1993). *The political economy of land reform in Zanzibar.* Dar es Salaam: Dar es Salaam University Press.

Sheriff, A. (1987). *Slaves, spices and ivory in Zanzibar integration of an East African commercial empire into the world economy, 1770–1873.* London: James Currey.

Sheriff, A. (1991). The peasantry under imperialism. In A. Sheriff & E. Ferguson (Eds.), *Zanzibar under colonial rule* (pp. 109–140). London: James Currey.

Shivji, I. (1990). *The legal foundations of the union in Tanzania's union and Zanzibar constitutions.* Dar es Salaam: Dar es Salaam University Press.

Skocpol, T. (1979). *States and social revolutions: A comparative analysis of France, Russia, & China.* Cambridge: Cambridge University Press.

Speller, I. (2007). An African Cuba? Britain and the Zanzibar Revolution, 1964. *The Journal of Imperial and Commonwealth History, 35*(2), 283–301.

Throup, D. (2016, March 18). The political crisis in Zanzibar. Centre for Strategic and International Studies. https://www.csis.org/analysis/politicalcrisis-zanzibar. Accessed 16 Aug 2016.

van Buren, L. (2011). Recent history of Tanzania essay. In I. Frame (Ed.), *Africa south of the Sahara* (pp. 1–28). London: Routledge.

van de Bruinhorst, G. C. (2009). Siku ya Arafa and the Idd el-Hajj: Knowledge, ritual and renewal in Tanzania. In K. Larsen (Ed.), *Knowledge, renewal and religion repositioning and changing ideological and material circumstances among the Swahili on the East African Coast* (pp. 127–150). Uppsala: The Nordic Africa Institute.

Wilson, A. (1989). *US foreign policy and revolution: The creation of Tanzania.* London: Pluto Press.

Zanzibar Revolutionary Government. (2009). Zanzibar agricultural transformation for sustainable development, 2010–2020. Retrieved from http://www.gafspfund.org. Accessed 15 Jan 2017.

Zanzibar Revolutionary Government. (2016). House of representatives. Retrieved from http://www.zanzibarassembly.go.tz/new-members.php. Accessed 3 May 2017.

Zeller, W., & Melber, H. (2018). United in separation? Lozi secessionism in Zambia and Namibia. In L. De Vries, P. Englebert, & M. Schomerus (Eds.), *Secessionism in African politics: Aspiration, grievance, performance, disenchantment.* New York: Palgrave.

CHAPTER 8

The Front(s) for the Liberation of Cabinda in Angola: A Phantom Insurgency

Joseph Figueira Martin

INTRODUCTION

For nearly 43 years, a conflict has festered in Angola's Cabinda exclave[1] amidst relative media silence and international indifference. Formerly known as the Portuguese Congo, this boomerang-shaped territory, wedged between the Republic of Congo (RoC) and the Democratic Republic of Congo (DRC), is home to one of the least-known yet most protracted insurgencies on the African continent: the Front for the Liberation of the Enclave of Cabinda (FLEC).

Liberation movement turned separatist group, the FLEC has continually defied history. Though various other Bakongo movements have, to

---

[1] Though often referred to as an "enclave," Cabinda is technically an exclave since it is entirely separated from Angola, and its territory borders two sovereign countries. This chapter adopts this correct terminology except when referring to the official names of Cabindan separatist movements.

J. F. Martin (✉)
African Parks Network, Johannesburg, South Africa

© The Author(s) 2019
L. de Vries et al. (eds.), *Secessionism in African Politics*,
Palgrave Series in African Borderlands Studies,
https://doi.org/10.1007/978-3-319-90206-7_8

207

varying degrees, fought for independence of the Kongo region,[2] the FLEC is unique as the only one that has consistently struggled for the independence of Cabinda as a nation. Nowadays confined to the jungle interior of the exclave deep within the Mayombe Forest from where it wages hit-and-run attacks against the Angolan Armed Forces (FAA), the FLEC is often dismissed by the Angolan government as a spent force and a "relic of the past," operated by governments in exile working from the comfort of remote European capitals.

As of late, regular flare-ups have been reported from the exclave, where FLEC rebels have reportedly killed close to 200 FAA soldiers between early 2016 and mid-2017. While it is difficult to confirm the veracity of these claims given the lack of access to the exclave, many believe the FLEC is still "alive and kicking" despite shrinking military capabilities.[3] At the very least, the government's continued brutal crackdown on peaceful expressions of separatist sentiment, including arbitrary arrests and the disappearance of civil society activists, indicates that Luanda remains wary of popular support for self-determination in Cabinda.

Attempts at reaching negotiated settlements have systematically failed, partly due to the Angolan regime's ability to co-opt and play factions against one another but also because the movement is historically prone to factionalism. Indeed, plagued by fragmentation since inception, the FLEC has produced a bewildering array of offshoots. While the two most famous movements are the FLEC-Forças Armadas de Cabinda (FAC) and the FLEC-Renovada, it is estimated that some 50 different groups, both armed and pacifist, have had some type of association with the FLEC over the past 50 years.

---

[2] The Kongo region straddles Republic of Congo (RoC), Democratic Republic of Congo (DRC), and Angola. Independence movements historically active in this region include, but are not limited to, the NTO-BAKO (the Angolan chapter of Alliance des Bakongo (ABAKO), independence movement turned ruling party in the then Belgian Congo), the Ngwizako Ngwizani a Kongo (NGWIZAKO), an alliance of former Kongo royalists, the Patriotic Front for the independence of the Portuguese Kongo (FPIKP), which resulted from the merger of a section of NTO-BAKO and NGWIZAKO; the Nso Progressive Union, the Progressive African Party (PPA), the National Union Progressive of Angola (UPRONA) and the Angolan Nationalist Cartel (CNA). See Pereira (2004) and Pélissier (1969). More recent movements, such as Bundu Dia Kongo (BDK) movement in DRC, have also advocated for restoration of the old Kongo Kingdom.

[3] Reuters (2016).

THE CURSE OF HISTORY

Faced with competing French and Dutch ambitions in the early phase of European colonization,[4] Portugal initially tried to anchor its own aspirations by entering into protectorate treaties with three chiefdoms north of the Congo River; these form present-day Cabinda.[5] The chiefdoms—Ngoyo, Kakongo, and Loango—had emancipated themselves from the Kongo Kingdom some centuries before.[6] The protectorate treaties enabled progressive annexation by Portugal, with local rulers trading their sovereignty in return for "protection" against rival European and regional powers. Ahead of the Berlin Conference, which dismantled the Kongo Kingdom and redistributed different parts to Belgium, France, and Portugal,[7] these treaties effectively cemented Portuguese grip on the

---

[4] Between 1640 and 1648, the Dutch controlled the territory but were then driven out by the Portuguese. In 1702, French and English navies clashed off the coast of Cabinda. The construction of an English fortress on the coast led to military intervention by Portugal in 1722. As French sailors and Catholic priests began settling in the area some decades later, the Portuguese decided to build a fortress in order to prevent further military incursions, but this led to the sending of a French expedition in 1769. Defeated and decimated en masse by malaria, the Portuguese then fled. It wasn't until the signing of the Convention of Madrid in 1786 that Portugal's rights to that territory were formally recognised in exchange for freedom of trade and slave trade for the other European powers.

[5] According to Shawn McCormick (1992), "Present-day Cabinda lies within the boundaries of the former kingdoms of Loango, Kakongo, and Ngoyo, all three of which were in existence when the first Portuguese traders arrived in the late 15th century. These ethnic groups were linguistically and culturally related to the Kongo kingdom (which extended from areas of what is now southern Gabon to northern Angola). At one time Kongo vassals, the three kingdoms had become nominally independent by the end of the sixteenth century. Three subethnic groups—the Kakongo, Vili, and Woyo—reside along the coastal region; these had relatively extensive contact with the Portuguese. Another three—the Lindi, Sundi, and Yombe—dominate the Mayombe interior; they dealt more with the French and Belgians in what are now Congo and Zaire."

[6] "According to local legend, Cabinda gained some autonomy from the kingdom during a turbulent period in the history of the royal family. A powerful Bakongo queen, Muam Poenha, angered the king and was therefore expelled from the court at Mbanza Kongo. She fled with her triplets to the kingdom's Ngoyo principality and married a local nobleman. When he had calmed down, the Kongo king divided up part of his territory between the triplets, and one of these areas, Ngoyo, later became Cabinda" (*Washington Post* 2001). In addition, according to local tradition, the Loango, Kakongo, and Ngoyo shared a common ancient ancestress named Nguunu. (McCormick 1992).

[7] In 1665, Portugal allied with a nobleman in the south of the Kongo Kingdom to crush the royal troops in Mbwila. The King Antonio I, also called Nvita a Nkanga, was decapitated and the country was subsequently divided into several kingdoms subject to Portugal. The

territories. Most notably, between 1883 and 1884, the Portuguese crown signed the Chinfuma and Chicamba treaties with the princes and notables of Cabinda, and in February 1885, the Treaty of Simulambuco, which formally conferred the status of Portuguese protectorate to Cabinda.

The signing of the Simulambuco Treaty constituted a watershed for the Cabindan independence struggle.[8] Although the Treaty was essentially a Portuguese ruse aimed at securing territory north of the Congo River, for Cabindans, it came to consolidate the foundation of their identity as it enshrined the protectorate status of the exclave, which had now attained a special position entirely separate from the Angolan colony, with its territory bordering two sovereign countries.

However, Cabinda's special status proved to hold little weight with the administration in Lisbon, which, amidst the chaos that prevailed during the decolonization wars, would quickly recast the exclave's status and allow for its inclusion in greater Angola. In addition, regional dynamics played an equally crucial role in the forging of Cabindan identity. Indeed, the birth of FLEC cannot be analyzed in isolation of the context of national fervor prevalent across the wider region at that time. Following the death of the *Manikongo* Dom Pedro VII in 1954, which sparked a struggle for succession between various contenders to the throne of Mbanza Kongo, various ethno-nationalist liberation movements started springing up across the region.[9]

Kongo Kingdom was thus largely defunct by the time the Conference of Berlin was held (Commission des recours aux réfugiés 2004).

[8] Whilst the Portuguese Constitutions of 1826 and 1836 had enshrined claims to Cabinda as a "Portuguese possession," Article 1 of the Portuguese constitution of 1933 de facto consolidated the legal foundation to Cabinda's territorial status as an exclave of Angola. In reality, however, Cabinda was to remain governed as a separate entity until 1956, when it came under the geographic remit of the governor of Luanda.

[9] Supported by the various branches of the Congolese aristocracy, 12 contenders—7 in the Portuguese colony of Angola, and 5 in the Belgian colony of Congo-Kinshasa—competed for the symbolic throne of Mbanza Kongo, the capital of the kingdom renamed São Salvador during the Portuguese occupation. Many Baptists in São Salvador supported a "progressive" candidate, Dom Manuel Kidita, the nephew of the *Manikongo* Manuel Kiditu (1912–1915), whilst another traditionalist group, centred around Matadi in Congo-Kinshasa, rooted for a candidate supported by the Catholic Church and the Portuguese Empire. Dozens of other movements sprang up and dissipated following the collapse of the Kongo Kingdom, including the Bakongo Alliance (ABAKO) of Joseph Kasa-Vubu, future President of Congo-Kinshasa, and the Union of the Populations of Northern Angola (UPNA), led by Holden Roberto.

In this context, the discovery of oil in the 1950s changed the stakes radically,[10] as movements such as the Popular Movement for Liberation of Angola (MPLA) and the National Liberation Front for the Liberation of Angola (FNLA) became bent on taking control of the exclave. In 1966, Gulf Oil, whose rights were later acquired by Chevron, discovered substantial oil reserves offshore. A decade later, Gulf Oil was pumping 150,000 barrels a day from these fields. Cabinda, the London Times noted in 1975, "had an income from oil taxes and royalties (all from the Gulf Oil Company's concession) of $450 million a year."[11] The discovery of oil, supported by regional and international powers that looked covetously at Cabinda's natural resources, would thus forever dash Cabindan independence hopes, as the FLEC's various branches rapidly became pawns in the regional struggle for control of the exclave. As a result, the FLEC has been frequently dismissed as just another rent-seeking militia, fighting only to take advantage of the exclave's vast oil and mineral resources. As we shall see below, however, separatist sentiment pre-dated the discovery of oil by at least a decade.

A Tumultuous Birth

In the 1950s, several organizations began to canvass among migrant Cabindan populations in Congo-Kinshasa and Congo-Brazzaville in order to garner popular support for their brethren living under the yoke of Portuguese colonialism. The *Communauté Cabindaise* (COMCABI), founded in Leopoldville in 1948, as well as its sister organization *Associação dos Originários do Enclave of Cabinda* (AOECA), brought together Congolese and Cabindan residents of the border regions with a view to providing humanitarian aid to Cabindans. With the help of Joseph Kasa-Vubu and Fulbert Youlou, respectively, the first presidents of Congo-Kinshasa and Congo-Brazzaville, COMCABI and AOECA notables eventually came together to form the *Associação dos Residentes do Enclave de Cabinda* (AREC) in 1959, which in turn became the first Cabindan movement to openly call for independence.

---

[10] Original concession rights to Block Zero were granted in 1957, and exploration began soon afterwards. In 1962, large quantities of oil were found in shallow waters, just 10–25 yards from what was then the village of Malembo on the Cabinda coast. Production started in 1968, and since then Block Zero has produced in excess of two billion barrels of oil, which acted as a catalyst for takeover by various other movements.

[11] Times (August 4, 1975).

In 1960, under the impetus of Luis Ranque Franque, a descendant of nineteenth-century Cabindan barons, AREC was then renamed Movement for the Liberation of the Enclave of Cabinda (MLEC). However, the MLEC was perceived as representative of a thin coastal elite—the Woyos—and consequently did not enjoy support of other ethnic groups present in the interior of the exclave, namely the Lindi and the Yombe. As a result, the following year saw the birth of two new movements in neighboring Congo-Brazzaville: the Cabinda National Union Action Committee (CAUNC), led by Henriques Tiago Nzita, a Lindi; and the Mayombe Alliance (ALIAMA), led by Eduardo Sozinho, a Yombe.[12]

It was not until 1963 that the MLEC, CAUNC, and ALIAMA reconciled their differences in Pointe-Noire, under the auspices of Fulbert Youlou and Leon Mba, the first president of Gabon, and came together to form the FLEC. However, this newly formed alliance would soon be thwarted by leadership disputes, primarily between FLEC's President Ranque Franque and Vice President Nzita Tiago. Following the toppling of Youlou just a few weeks after the birth of the FLEC, and the subsequent installment of Alphonse Massamba-Débat, an MPLA sympathizer, the FLEC was forced to leave Congo. Using Congo as a refuge, the MPLA then began to launch military incursions into Cabinda in 1964, but soon encountered hostility not only from coastal members of FLEC who were living near the town of Tshiowa but also from peasants in the Mayombe forest, whose region near the Congo frontier MPLA guerrillas had to cross.

From then onwards, FLEC split into a "pro-American" faction based in Kinshasa and led by Ranque Franque, and a "pro-French" one based in Brazzaville and led by Tiago Nzita. Emulating the FNLA, the FLEC-Ranque Franque established a government in exile in the border town of Tshela in Zaire in January 1967. Reflecting earlier divisions, however, the faction headed by Nzita decided to create its own Cabindan Revolutionary Committee (CRC) in Pointe-Noire. At the time, given that Portuguese authorities were more worried about the FNLA and MPLA's activities,

---

[12] The Yombe (also spelled Iombe) of the mountain forests of Cabinda, are a subgroup of the larger Bakongo ethnic group but were not part of the ancient kingdoms of Loango, Kakongo, or Ngoyo. That part of the Yombe living in Congo did join with the Congolese Bakongo in the Alliance of Bakongo (ABAKO) during the period of party formation in the Belgian Congo, but the Cabindan Yombe (and other Kikongo-speaking groups in the exclave), relatively remote geographically and culturally from the Bakongo of Angola proper, showed no solidarity with the latter. Instead, in 1961, the Yombe formed a Cabindan separatist movement, the Alliance of Mayombe (ALIAMA) (Collelo 1991).

they tolerated and sometimes even encouraged the activities of the FLEC-Ranque Franque, but Nzita was perceived as dangerous given his staunchly anti-Portuguese rhetoric, and the Portuguese incarcerated him.

Six months later, in September 1968, Congo-Brazzaville's President Alphonse Massamba-Débat was forced to resign. The advent of a progressive regime under the aegis of Marien Ngouabi in Congo-Brazzaville marked a major event in the evolution of FLEC. The US National Security Council (NSC) believed that "President Ngouabi would like to see Cabinda established as an independent state under a leadership influenced by and beholden to the Congo," and that "eventually...this could lead to a political union between the Congo and Cabinda."[13] As would become evident some years later, the United States clearly wanted to safeguard their interests in Cabinda. In 1975, Secretary of Defense James R. Schlesinger went as far as suggesting to President Ford that the United States should seek to "encourage the disintegration of Angola, as Cabinda in the clutches of Mobutu would mean far greater security of the petroleum resources."[14]

Aborted Independence

By the early 1970s, the FLEC's political activities were virtually at a standstill, until the Carnation Revolution in Portugal in April 1974 enabled the establishment of a proper armed wing for the first time in the history of the movement. Two months after the revolution, Nzita was released from prison and obtained authorization from the Portuguese governor of Cabinda, Themudu Barata, to open a FLEC representation in Tshiowa. Lacking an army of its own, the FLEC called on former *Tropas Especiais*—indigenous soldiers who had fought under the Portuguese against the MPLA in the exclave—to help them take control of Cabinda. Led by the French mercenary Jean Kay, the *Tropas Especiais* could be seen patrolling the streets of Cabinda City by late 1974.

Seeing the ever-increasing amount of oil being pumped off the coast of Cabinda, France had started to take a keen interest in the exclave and decided to encourage the emergence of a new FLEC in Congo-Brazzaville to counter US interests. In June 1974, the FLEC Rouge emerged in Pointe-Noire under the leadership of José Auguste Tchioufou, a former deputy director of Elf-ERAP, a branch of the French oil company Elf-

[13] Gleijeses (2011: 263).
[14] US National Security Council Meeting Minutes on Angola (1975: 7).

Aquitaine. In August 1974, Congo-Brazzaville's President Ngouabi authorized the deployment of FLEC Rouge in Cabinda; Tchioufou was proclaimed "President of Free Cabinda" upon his arrival in Tshiowa. During his inauguration speech, Tchioufou declared French to be the official language of Free Cabinda, but when invited by the local population to translate his speech into Portuguese and the local Kikongo known as Fiote, the unable Tchioufou was booed and chased off by the crowd.

The MPLA, with the blessing of Portugal, quickly reacted. MPLA guerrillas descended onto Tshiowa, seizing a number of key installations as the Portuguese soldiers looked on. The FLEC retreated to Congo-Brazzaville, leaving the MPLA in control of the city. The FLEC Rouge, for its part, rapidly collapsed, as a faction led by Ranque Franque decided to move closer to Congo-Kinshasa's President Mobutu. This disintegration, however, did not stop President Ngouabi from continuing to refer to Cabinda as an autonomous country, which in the eyes of MPLA leader Agostinho Neto was "the most eloquent proof that the Congo had not renounced its claim to Cabinda."[15]

However, Cabinda was also too rich a prize for Mobutu to forgo; in July 1975, Mobutu called for a referendum on the future of the exclave. Then-President Lopes of Congo-Brazzaville concurred, stating "Cabinda exists as a reality and is historically and geographically different from Angola."[16] Gabon, Uganda, and the Central African Republic had all previously expressed support for or recognition of the FLEC, though the majority of members of the Organisation for African Unity (OAU) remained firmly opposed to the Cabindan separatists on the grounds that it would encourage separatist movements elsewhere.[17]

Despite the lack of OAU support, Mobutu set about organizing a small army under the leadership of Ranque Franque near bordering Tshela in Congo-Kinshasa. Reportedly some 800–2000 Cabinda guerrillas were being trained in the forests of Congo-Kinshasa, about 100 km from the Cabindan border. On November 2, 1975, Mobutu ordered the deployment of nearly 2000 troops—three battalions of the FLEC led by Ranque Franque and the elite Kamanyola troops of the Zairian Armed Forces (FAZ)—under the command of some 150 French and American mercenaries. However, the invasion sponsored by Mobutu failed, and a week later,

[15] Gleijeses (2011: 262).
[16] Gomes Porto (2003: 4).
[17] Forbes Global Magazine (2002).

on November 11, 1975, the MPLA triumphantly proclaimed the independence of the People's Republic of Angola in Luanda. For their part, the FNLA and National Union for the Total Independence of Angola (UNITA) proclaimed the Democratic Republic of Angola in Huambo. But while Congo-Brazzaville and Congo-Kinshasa officially supported the January 1975 Alvor agreement that recognized the independence of Angola and declared Cabinda to be "an integral and inalienable part of Angola,"[18] the two neighbors were quick to recall Cabindans' right to self-determination and continued supporting their respective FLECs: the FLEC Rouge in Congo-Brazzaville and the FLEC-Ranque Franque in Congo-Kinshasa.

The Alvor agreement further accentuated divisions within the FLEC, with Nzita insisting on the need to train the Cabindan youth (the *juventude cabindesa*) as a fighting force to counter the MPLA, while in Pointe-Noire the FLEC Rouge was trying to restructure itself under the leadership of a former Congolese Prime Minister Alfred Raoul. For some months, Colonel Jean da Costa of the French External Documentation and Counter-intelligence Service was busy training FLEC Rouge troops in camps in Gabon, but their efforts were cut short because of President Ngouabi's own aspirations. Indeed, as opposed to Angola, which was in the throes of civil war, Ngouabi was more concerned that a fallout with Congo-Kinshasa could spell the end of his regime. Aware of the risk of a confrontation, Ngouabi accordingly decided to ban all FLEC activities on Congolese soil.

Now the only remaining sponsor of the FLEC in the region, Mobutu again tried in 1976 to annex Cabinda by relying on Holden Roberto's FNLA troops, but these were defeated by the People's Armed Forces of Liberation of Angola (FAPLA) and the Cuban army. As the Zairean copper industry depended heavily on the Benguela railway linking the port of Lobito with the rail network of Katanga province and Zambia, Mobutu was reluctantly forced to enter into negotiations with the MPLA. On May 20, 1976, Mobutu signed an agreement to cease hostilities with Angola and guarantee continued access to its ports on the Atlantic. However, tensions between Congo-Kinshasa and Angola would continue to escalate given the continued presence of FNLA, UNITA, and FLEC separatists on Congolese soil.

[18] Alvor Agreement (1975: Article 3).

THINGS FALL APART

As independence euphoria dissipated, the FLEC—deprived of its regional support—tried to capture headlines by launching an attack against a cantonment of FAPLA forces in Sanda Masala, in the north of the exclave, in May 1976. Once again, a succession of military setbacks revived tensions within the movement, and the FLEC split into new factions in 1977.

At this stage, the Nzita faction, although present in Tshiowa, was only one of the many factions of the FLEC. Indeed, following the assassination of Ngouabi in March 1977, the Military Committee of the party now headed Congo-Brazzaville; the committee's two main leaders, Joachim Yhombi Opango and Denis Sassou-Nguesso, were respectively President and Minister of Defence. The new Congolese military regime launched a policy of rapprochement with the communist bloc. On the orders of Sassou, a raid was organized and more than 400 Cabindans were made prisoners and incarcerated at the Pointe-Noire air base under the supervision of Cuban soldiers. Perceived as responsible for these setbacks, FLEC military executives then turned on Nzita and founded a new organization: the Military Command for the Liberation of Cabinda (CMLC), headed by Marcelino Luemba Tubi. For the first time in the history of the FLEC, armed infighting then ensued, opposing Nzita's faction (by now known as FLEC-FAC of the Black FLEC) and the CMLC in fratricidal combat that left several hundred dead.

The CMLC then appointed a Yombe, François-Xavier Lubota, as Prime Minister in exile to oversee lobbying efforts abroad. Lubota soon found himself accused of trying to promote a cult of personality, and also because of his ties to South Korea's Moon sect, which provided him with logistical support, including the training of CMLC members in camps in the World Anti-Communist League in South Korea. Lubota was also accused of surrounding himself mainly with members of his Yombe ethnic group, which caused the CMLC to break up into yet more factions, including FLEC-Lubota (also known as *FLEC Jaune*, or Yellow FLEC) and the FLEC-Military Position (FLEC-PM), founded in 1983 in the refugee camp of Kimbianga in Congo-Kinshasa.

For its part, Nzita's FLEC-FAC also suffered a new split following the creation of the Front for National Liberation of the Cabinda Enclave (FLNEC) led by Bonifacio Zanga Mambo, one of Nzita's military commanders. The FLEC-Ranque Franque, now known as FLEC-original (FLEC-O), continued its diplomatic efforts across the region, including in

Kampala where in 1975, it proclaimed the independence of Cabinda during an OAU summit. A few months later, Nzita (FLEC-FAC) did the same, announcing the formation of a Cabindan government in exile based in Paris.

The Lure of Criminality

During the 1980s, the strains of the conflict were apparent everywhere; the separatist movement was divided into at least four factions, while the civil war in Angola was in full swing. Against this precarious backdrop, the exclave again roused the interest of regional and international powers. Some combatants within the FLEC, tired of the armed struggle but aware that the protection of the exclave remained one of the MPLA's strategic priorities, sought a rapprochement with UNITA and South Africa. With South African logistical assistance, UNITA established a Cabindan combat unit, called UNIFLEC (or FLEC-UNITA), to target oil installations in the exclave. Notable actions included the bombing of an oil pipeline near Tshiowa that killed nine people in July 1984, as well as the downing of a Chevron helicopter and the sabotaging of several oil pipelines the following year. On May 19, 1985, a South African commando also attempted an attack on the oil storage tanks at Chevron's Malongo base but failed in the face of FAPLA's fierce resistance backed by Cuban troops.[19] Ironically, Cuban troops found themselves defending US oil interests against UNITA incursions and South African commandos, who themselves were backed by the US government.

From the FLEC's point of view, sabotaging oil pipelines and destroying foreign property presented a dilemma—although it was an effective way of pressuring the government and Chevron, such acts of sabotage generally came to the detriment of the population. Nevertheless, in the early 1990s, the targeting of foreign companies became visibly more pronounced. In October 1990, the FLEC kidnapped a US oil worker employed by Chevron. In March and April 1992, militants attacked a number of vehicles belonging to Chevron, and in May of that year, launched a mortar attack against a police station during which 25 shells hit a nearby Chevron facility. A few months later, the FLEC also attacked a convoy of vehicles belonging to a US company. UNITA, for its part, attempted to take control of the exclave on several occasions but was met with fierce resistance by FAPLA and Cuban troops each time. Worried about the rapid

[19] Reed (2009: 67).

deterioration of the situation, Edward DeJarnette, Head of the US liaison office in Angola at the time, warned UNITA leader Jonas Savimbi that if Cabinda's oil production were to be disrupted, the United States would cut off all support to UNITA. Without further ado, UNITA stopped targeting the exclave's oil facilities.

It was in this context that new dissident factions, such as the National Union for the Liberation of Cabinda (UNALEC) and the Movement of Resistance for the Total Independence of Cabinda (MRITC), were created in 1985. Led by Afonso Massanga, former head of the FLEC's South Military Zone, UNALEC rejected any negotiations with Luanda but following a disagreement with the co-founder of the movement Bernardo Conde, Massanga decided to form the MRITC. Echoing UNITA, the MRITC advocated for the "total" independence of the enclave, and outright rejected any possibility of negotiating autonomy with the Angolan government.[20]

At the end of the 1970s, when the armed struggle was being waged by at least four independent military organizations (FLEC-FAC, CMLC, FLEC-Lubota, UNALEC/MRITC, FLEC-PM), confronting each other as well as Angolan and Cuban troops, kidnapping became the preferred modus operandi of the movement. On November 29, 1994, FLEC-R kidnapped two Polish expatriates; in January 1997, three South Africans and a national of São Tomé and Príncipe were abducted by FLEC-FAC; in February 1997, FLEC-R also abducted two employees of the Malaysian company Inwangsa SDN-timber. These kidnapping campaigns had a clear objective: FLEC saw it as a means of ensuring financial wherewithal but above all as a way of garnering international attention. At the same time, however, this strategy also accentuated fragmentation within the separatist movement. In 1992, the formation of yet another group, the FLEC-Democratic (FLEC-D) and its armed wing, the National Armed Forces of Cabinda (FANCA) was announced, creating even more confusion among international observers. Under the leadership of Yumba-di-Tshibuka, one of Nzita's former commanders, the FLEC-D was widely perceived to have been created for the sole purpose of recovering money from ransoms.

---

[20] Telephonic interview with Afonso Massanga, April 2016. The same year, another movement, the National Union for the Liberation of Cabinda (UNLC), led by Luis Carneiro Gimby, was born in Gabon. Also called FLEC-UNLC or FLEC-Union, this movement sponsored by Gabonese President Omar Bongo engaged in negotiations with the Angolan government around a project of autonomy, which caused it to be dismissed as traitor by other tendencies of the FLEC (SEM 1998). UNLC was, however, seen as one of the most credible movements of its time as it was genuinely interested in seeking a negotiated solution to the Cabindan problem (Mabeko-Tali 2001).

DIALECTICS OF NEGOTIATED SETTLEMENTS

In the early 1990s, FLEC guerrillas fell into oblivion. In 1991, Cuban soldiers had left Angola, and South African troops had withdrawn from Namibia. In accordance with the Bicesse peace agreement, Angola's first direct elections since independence were held on September 9 and 30, 1992. Voter participation in Cabinda, however, was estimated at a feeble rate between 7 and 12% in what seems to have been the result of the FLEC's call for electoral boycott.[21] Given the international context of normalization of relations with Angola that followed the Bicesse agreement, some FLEC leaders decided to reconvert into political movements, such as François-Xavier Lubota with his Movement for the Rally of the Cabinda People (MRPC).

At the initiative of the Angolan government, a meeting was held in Lisbon in November 1991 to bring together various unarmed FLEC factions, culminating in the formation of a Supreme Coordination Council (FLEC-CSC). But without the support of the politico-military movements active on the ground, the CSC was condemned to be a stillborn political entity. In 1992, Ranque Franque (exiled in Canada since the late 1970s) tried to reconnect with the Angolan government. To the displeasure of Nzita Tiago, he was ceremoniously welcomed to Luanda by the Angolan head of state, José Eduardo dos Santos. Ranque Franque then agreed to the government's proposal to grant "special status" to the exclave, as inspired by the advanced autonomy of the Portuguese islands of the Azores and Madeira. Because of this compromise, a timid rapprochement occurred: FLEC-Franque was allowed to open a representation in Tshiowa under the name of "FLEC interior."

The prospect of a negotiated settlement to the Cabinda issue prompted several Cabindan movements to come together in an attempt to speak with one voice. In 1996, a second alliance, the Forum of Cabindan Nationalists (FONAC), was formed with a view to negotiate with the Angolan government. The alliance comprised Nzita's FLEC-FAC, Tibúrcio's FLEC-R, Ranque Franque's FLEC "Originel," the Democratic Cabindan Front (FDC) led by Norbet Itoula and François-Xavier Lubota,[22]

---

[21] Musila (2015).

[22] The case of Francisco Xavier Lubota (chairman) and Norbert Itoula (secretary-general) is probably the most caricatural of the dialectical relationship between the Cabinda issue and the two Congos. This unlikely alliance of Lusophones and Francophones also contributed to disagreement, and seems to have been the main cause in the split of the FDC. Culturally and intellectually, Norbert Itoula and Francisco Xavier Lubota grew up in different linguistic and

UNALEC of Conde, MRITC of Massanga, UNLC of Ngimbi Carneiro, Menga's RDPC, and the Cabindan Independence Committee (CIC) led by Belchior Taty.

A third and final attempt to reunite Cabindan factions took place ten years later in the Netherlands. In 2004, in Helvoirt, FLEC-FAC, FLEC-R, and FDC decided to join the Cabinda Forum for Dialogue (FCD) in order to negotiate with the Angolan government. Contrary to prior movements, the FCD included representatives of civil society and clergy such as the president of the Mpalabanda association, Agostinho Chicaia, and Father Raul Tati. With support from Cabinda's Catholic clergy, the FCD platform created the *Nkoto Likanda*—the National Council of the People of Cabinda (CNPC)—and a new military structure, the Unified Armed Forces of Cabinda (FACU). The FDC platform also agreed to enter into negotiations with the Angolan government about the proposed Memorandum of Understanding for Peace and Reconciliation, also known as the Namibe Agreement.

Throughout these attempts at peaceful settlement, however, the Angolan government maintained separate negotiation tracks with rival separatist movements, such as the FLEC-R, who met with the Angolan Government in Namibia in 1995, culminating into a truce of four months. In April 1996, the Angolan authorities had also begun to negotiate with the FLEC-FAC under the aegis of Omar Bongo of Gabon and his Foreign Minister Jean Ping. This co-optation tactic was further pursued in 2004 when, after the signing of the Helvoirt Agreement, FCD Secretary General Antonio Bento Bembe was arrested by Interpol in the Netherlands for his alleged involvement in the abduction in 1990 of the US citizen and employee of Chevron, Brent Swan. Finding itself in a position of strength, Luanda presented Bembe as instrumental toward signing the 2006 Namibe Agreement. In response, FCD President Nzita rejected the agreement, expelled Bembe from the FCD, and announced the full-scale resumption of hostilities by the FACU.

---

cultural universes. The former was a pure product of the Congolese intelligentsia and university, an activist of the Congolese student movements in the 1960s and 1970s, notably UGEEC, while the bulk of the combatants of the movement were Portuguese (Mabeko-Tali 2001).

UNENDING REPRESSION

Following the end of the civil war in 2002, the regional context became extremely unfavorable to Cabindan separatism. The fall of the Mobutu regime in 1997 and the end of the civil war in Congo-Brazzaville had essentially deprived the separatists of their traditional supporters. Following the takeover of Kinshasa by the Alliance of Democratic Forces for Liberation (AFDL) in December 1997, several FLEC leaders, among them José Tibúrcio Zinga Luemba of FLEC-R and Emmanuel Nzita of FLEC-FAC, were arrested by Laurent-Désiré Kabila's security forces.

On the other side of the Congo River, the end of the civil war and the repossession of power by Sassou-Nguesso forced the FDC to dismantle its bases in Congo-Brazzaville, which meant losing the support of the Pan-African Union for Social Democracy (UPADS)'s militias of Pascal Lissouba. The FLEC-R, who had previously engaged with UNITA alongside the UPADS troops, was also summoned to leave the country.

The death of UNITA leader Jonas Savimbi in February 2002 constituted yet another blow to Cabindan separatism. While his assassination led to the end of the Angolan civil war, it also allowed the MPLA to redirect its military efforts on the exclave. That same year, it launched Operation Vassoura in order to "pacify Cabinda by force."[23] More than 50,000 FAAs were deployed in the exclave where FLEC numbers likely amounted to less than 2000. The FAA stormed traditional strongholds of FLEC-R in the south, as well as the headquarters of the FLEC-FAC in Kungo-Shonzo, in the process wiping entire villages off the map.

THE EMERGENCE OF CABINDAN CIVIL SOCIETY NIPPED IN THE BUD

After the 2002 elections and the general opening of political space that followed, civil society organizations started sprouting up across Angola. For the first time in Cabinda, the local population was able to express their grievances through nonviolent means. In the aftermath of repeated military setbacks, the armed struggle no longer seemed a realistic option for the many FLEC leaders who had been forced into exile. Some decided to turn to civil society and in July 2003, with the support of the Open Society Foundation, a conference was held in Chiloango to bring together all the

---

[23] Reed (2009: 147).

political, military, and social movements in Cabinda. Chaired by Father Jorge Casimiro Congo, one of the most vocal opponents of the state-sponsored Episcopal Conference of Angola and São Tomé (CEAST), the conference resulted in the creation of the Mpalabanda Civic Association (*Mpalabanda—Associação cívica de Cabinda*). But Mpalabanda soon came to be perceived as a dangerous nuisance by the regime due to its reports detailing human rights abuses committed by the FAA but also by the FLEC, in Cabinda.[24]

Even if it purported to be apolitical, Mpalabanda was undoubtedly "the symbol of a new form of resistance."[25] By placing itself above the quarrels that had come to characterize the FLEC, it quickly gained a large following across the exclave. In an attempt to refute claims that it feared Mpalabanda, the government initially allowed a demonstration to be held in Tshiowa in July 2004. However, when tens of thousands turned out to flood the streets of Tshiowa, sporting slogans such as "the people want peace" and "dialogue now," the government quickly backtracked on its opening-up policy. In June 2006, it decided to ban Mpalabanda altogether on grounds that some of its leaders had links with the FLEC. Ever since, the government has pursued its policy of repression against Cabindan civil society, as evidenced by the repeated arrests of former Mpalabanda leaders such as José Francisco Luemba, Belchior Lanso Tanti, and José Zefarino Pauti in 2010,[26] and Marcos Mavungo in March 2015.[27]

Following the banning of Mpalabanda, the church effectively became the last peaceful vehicle for channeling political grievances. In 2005, as Bishop Dom Paulino Fernandes Madeca was preparing to retire, the Diocese of Luanda appointed the Angolan bishop Dom Filomeno do Nascimento Vieira Dias, a cousin of one the most faithful advisors to President Dos Santos: General Manuel Hélder Vieira Dias, also known as "Kopelipa." As a result, a power struggle ensued within the clergy of

---

[24] Comissão ad hoc para os direitos humanos em Cabinda and Open Society, "Terror em Cabinda. 1o Relatório sobre a violação dos direitos humanos no território," Cabinda, Luanda, December 2002, and "2o Relatório: Cabinda 2003—Um ano de terror," Cabinda, 2003; Mpalabanda associação cívica de Cabinda and Open Society, "3o Relatório sobre a situação dos direitos humanos em Cabinda—Cabinda, o Reino da Impunidade 2004," Cabinda, January 30, 2005, and "4o Relatório sobre a situação dos Cabinda—Cabinda entre a verdade e a manipulação 2005," Cabinda, April 4, 2006.

[25] Mabeko-Tali (2008).

[26] Reuters (2010) and Agence France Presse (2010).

[27] Amnesty International (2015).

Cabinda: demonstrators gathered in front of the Church *Imaculada Conceição* to demand the appointment of a native of the exclave, but security forces rapidly dispersed the crowd. The administrator of the diocese of Cabinda, Father Eugénio Dal Corso, also retaliated by demanding the suspension of Father Congo and the closure of his church. In the years that followed, the two factions continued challenging each other for control of the Catholic masses in Cabinda, respectively, Father Congo's followers based at the São Tiago church in Tshiowa, and the *Imaculada Conceição* Church of Bishop Vieira Dias, commonly referred to as "the defunct Catholic Church." This situation continued until Pope Francis in December 2014 appointed Vieira Dias as archbishop of Luanda, the country's foremost ecclesiastical authority. To this day, no substitute has been appointed to the Diocese of Cabinda.

From Separatism to "Terrorism?"

In early 2010, the situation in Cabinda briefly recaptured the international community's attention. As Angola was preparing to host the continent's African Cup of Nations, the FLEC attacked one of the buses carrying the national team of Togo in Massabi, near the border with Congo-Brazzaville. The incident caused three deaths in the Togolese team, and provoked international outcry. Rodrigues Mingas, a former FLEC executive and descendant of Cabinda royalty, claimed the attack on behalf of a movement that had ceased to exist since the 1990s, the FLEC-PM. Another movement, the Front for the Liberation of the State of Cabinda (also known as FLEC-Lopes), who had been active in the 1990s and known for having distributed Cabindan "identity cards" within the diaspora, also resurfaced and claimed the attack from Paris. FLEC-FAC, for its part, denied any involvement and pointed the finger at Angolan intelligence services.

In response, the government launched an all-out repression, leading incursions into Congo-Brazzaville and Congo-Kinshasa in order to neutralize members of the FLEC. It also arrested numerous representatives of civil society associated with the Mpalabanda organization. Since then, FAA operations in the DRC and Congo-Brazzaville have continued. In November 2012, FAA elements led an incursion into the Mabunduka forest, in the Territory of Tshela. These operations eventually provoked a diplomatic incident between Luanda and Brazzaville, when in 2013, in the district of Kimongo, Congolese soldiers were taken hostage by the FAA and led over to the Angolan side.

Barely four years after the falling out that followed the Namibe-agreement crisis, a new split took place within FLEC-FAC. In July 2010, Chief of Staff Estanislau Boma and Vice President Alexandre Tati, disobeyed FLEC-FAC's historic leader Nzita and traveled to Luanda in order to declare the end of the conflict. Nzita immediately retaliated by expelling Alexandre Tati, Estanislau Boma, José Veras, and Carlos Moses—the four protagonists who constituted the backbone of the FLEC's armed wing. Tellingly, this split illustrated a new divide within the FLEC, that is to say between a "European" FLEC, under the leadership of Nzita, with factions established in France, Belgium, the Netherlands, Switzerland, and Portugal, and an "African" FLEC, propelled by the four expelled protagonists, with its armed presence in Cabinda.[28]

Meanwhile, targeted repression of the FLEC across borders continued. In March 2011, the FAA were accused of the killing of Gabriel Nhemba "Pirilampo," Nzita's Chief of Staff, as well as that of Commander Mauricio Sabata two weeks later.[29] This dealt a serious blow to the movement as Pirilampo and Sabata were two of the highest-ranking FLEC operatives in Cabinda, and it is clear that the FLEC struggled to overcome this as rebel activity remained at an all-time low until 2016.

A Resurgent FLEC?

Since early 2016, the FLEC has been capturing headlines with its regular communiqués, claiming the killing of FAA soldiers in the exclave, as well as an alleged raid on an oil platform in May 2016. According to their claims, as many as 200 FAA soldiers have been killed since then, but FLEC has offered no proof to support this claim. As a result, some have expressed skepticism given the lack of evidence as well as the fact that there are no family associations calling for soldiers' bodies to be repatriated—let alone the government's repeated rebuttals.

Indeed, several incidents have cast doubt on the movement's claims, including the publication in late 2016 of a photo of military insignia as proof that FAA soldiers had been killed, when that same photo had in fact

---

[28] This diasporization was further illustrated by the creation of new movements outside of Angola, such as the Movement for the Rally of the Cabinda People and its Sovereignty (MRPCS, Congo-Kinshasa), and the Front for the Liberation of the Enclave of Kabinda (FLEK, the Netherlands). But unlike FLEC-FAC, none of these movements seem to have an operational presence in the exclave.

[29] RFI Português (2011) and VOA Português (2010).

been circulating several months before.[30] Likewise, the authenticity of pictures purporting to show four captured policemen in May 2017 has been dismissed as a fake given that the policemen's faces were not clearly visible—suggesting that the FLEC was using locals posing in stolen police uniforms in order to advance their propaganda.[31] This in turn has prompted several analysts to label the FLEC's representatives in Europe as "keyboard rebels," who for lack of an effective military force on the ground have resorted to waging a "cyber-war" by making dubious claims in the media and on the Internet.

CONCLUSION

Plagued by fragmentation and relentless repression at the hands of Angolan security forces, the FLEC's fortunes have waxed and waned over the years. Cabindan nationalist sentiment first surged with the outbreak of the armed struggle against Portugal in 1961, again with the April 1974 Carnation Revolution that resulted in Angola's independence, and following the signing of the MPLA-UNITA peace agreement in 2002. However, the regime's reluctance to engage in peace talks, coupled with efforts at co-opting the different branches of this highly fractious movement, have permanently crippled any future attempt at negotiation.

While it is difficult to assess the movement's future—especially in light of Nzita's death in June 2016—what is certain is that continued political marginalization and lack of access to basic social services in the exclave will continue to fuel the yearning for self-determination in the years to come. In light of this, and given that the regional context is poised to undergo radical change in the next decade, the FLEC could well find new life, and become a powerful force to be reckoned with in the years ahead.

REFERENCES

Agence France Presse. (2010, January 14). Angola: Trois arrestations au Cabinda. *Agence France Presse.*

Almeida, H. (2010, January 17). Angola arrests a third rights activist in Cabinda. *Reuters.*

---

[30] Club-k.net (2016).
[31] Diario de Noticias (2017).

Amnesty International. (2015, September 15). Angola: Conviction of José Marcos Mavungo a Blatant Violation of Freedom of Expression. https://www.amnesty. org/en/latest/news/2015/09/angola-conviction-of-jose-marcos-mavungo-a-blatant-violationof-freedom-of-expression/

Club-k.net. (2016). FLEC exibe galões de soldados das FAA abatidos na região de Buco-Zau. http://club-k.net/~clubknet/index.php?option=com_content&view=article&id=26356&lang=pt

Collelo, T. (1991). *Angola: A country study* (pp. 33–34). Washington, DC: Library of Congress.

Commission des recours aux réfugiés. (2004, August 26). Les indépendantistes dans l'impasse. Commission des recours aux réfugiés, Centre d'information géopolitique. Retrieved from http://www.commission-refugies.fr/IMG/pdf/Angola_-_les_independantistes_dans_l_impasse_au_Cabinda.pdf

Cropley, E. (2016, June 24). Rebels alive and kicking in Angolan petro-province, oil workers say. *Reuters*.

de Alvor, Acordo. (1975). Retrieved from http://www1.ci.uc.pt/cd25a/wikka. php?wakka=descon21

de Noticias, Diario. (2017, May 16). Polícia angolana nega que FLEC tenha feito agentes reféns em Cabinda. *Diario de Noticias*.

Forbes Global Magazine. (2002, February 18). Angola's tormented path to petro-diamond led growth. *Forbes Global Magazine*.

Gleijeses, P. (2011). *Conflicting missions: Havana, Washington, and Africa, 1959–1976*. Chapel Hill: University of North Carolina.

Gomes Porto, J. (2003). *Cabinda. Notes on a soon-to-be-forgotten war*. ISS paper 77. Pretoria: Institute for Security Studies.

Mabeko-Tali, J. M. (2001). La question de Cabinda: séparatismes éclatés, habiletés luandaises et conflits en Afrique centrale. *Lusotopie, 8*, 49–62.

Mabeko-Tali, J. M. (2008). Entre économie rentière et violence politico-militaire. La question cabindaise et le processus de paix angolais. *Politique africaine, 110*, 15–16.

McCormick, S. (1992, June). Angola in transition: The Cabinda factor. *CSIS Africa Notes*, 1–8.

Musila, C. (2015). L'Enclave angolaise de Cabinda: Un conflit ancien au parfum de pétrole. Irenees. Fiche d'analyse Irénées. Retrieved from http://www.irenees.net/bdf_fiche-analyse-1048_fr.html

Pélissier, R. (1969). Nationalismes en Angola. *Revue Française de Science Politique, 19*(6), 1187–1215.

Pereira, L. N. N. (2004). *Os Bakongo de Angola: Religião, política e parentesco num bairro de Luanda*. São Paulo: Universidade de São Paulo.

Pinto Machado, I. (2011, March 11). Pirilampo' líder militar da FLEC/FAC encontrado morto no Congo Brazzaville. *RFI Português*.

Reed, K. (2009). *Crude existence. Environment and the politics of oil in Northern Angola.* Berkeley: University of California Press.

State Secretariat for Migration. (1988, February 1). Angola – Feuilles d'information sur les pays 1 February 1998: http://www.refworld.org/docid/466fc3562.html

Switzerland: State Secretariat for Migration (SEM). (1988, February 1). Angola – Feuilles d'information sur les pays. http://www.refworld.org/docid/466fc3562.html

US National Security Council Meeting Minutes on Angola. (1975, June 27). Retrieved from http://digitalarchive.wilsoncenter.org/document/118161.pdf?v=e0a6710f35195df7a9313d22a0f52b77

VOA Português. (2010, March 21). Cabinda: Mais um general da FLEC-FAC morto em emboscada das FAA. *VOA Português.*

Washington Post. (2001, May). Cabinda: History – Scramble for Cabinda. *The Washington Post.* Retrieved from http://www.washingtonpost.com/wp-adv/specialsales/spotlight/angola/article11.html

CHAPTER 9

Against the Grain: Somaliland's Secession from Somalia

Markus Virgil Hoehne

INTRODUCTION

A key question raised in the literature on secessionism is under what circumstances it occurs.[1] Often secessionist endeavors are understood as following cost-benefit calculations. Who profits or loses from secession—on the side of both the secessionist movement and the parent state?[2] The position that secessionist claims essentially involve a bargain between certain "minority groups" and the center is a variation of this cost-benefit approach. Jenne et al. argue that "if the minority believes it enjoys significant strategic leverage against the center such that, if challenged, it can withstand an organized military attack, it is more likely to advance extreme demands as means of obtaining greater concessions from the state."[3] Englebert and Hummel find an explanation for Africa's "secessionist

[1] Hechter (1992: 267), Horowitz (1992), Bartkus (1999) and Jenne et al. (2007).
[2] Bartkus (1999).
[3] Jenne et al. (2007: 541).

M. V. Hoehne (✉)
Institute of Social Anthropology, University of Leipzig, Leipzig, Germany
e-mail: markus.hoehne@uni-leipzig.de

© The Author(s) 2019   229
L. de Vries et al. (eds.), *Secessionism in African Politics,*
Palgrave Series in African Borderlands Studies,
https://doi.org/10.1007/978-3-319-90206-7_9

deficit" in a cost-benefit analysis, too. They argue that regional leaders weigh up potential rewards—such as at least partial control of institutions of the central state—against the cost, particularly the absence of international recognition, concluding that in most African cases, this weighing of options results in seeking a greater share within the existing nation state.[4]

This chapter presents a case that goes against the grain of these dominant perspectives on secession. I argue that Somaliland's secession from Somalia—or, as some would have it, the dissolution of the voluntary union between British Somaliland (Northwestern Somalia) and Italian Somalia (from Northeastern to Southern Somalia)—did not follow careful cost-benefit calculations. It also did not involve the bargaining of a minority with a majority in power or a center. Rather, the unilateral declaration of independence of Somaliland on May 18, 1991, was, firstly, the unforeseen result of an anti-regime struggle, which in its latest phase, turned genocidal with the regime singling out one particular group, the Isaaq, for mass killing. This provided the basis for claims among many Isaaq, who were organized in the guerrilla front Somali National Movement (SNM), for independence from "the killers." Once the SNM had taken control of Northwestern Somalia (for reasons not related to secessionist but to civil war dynamics), the grievances of many Isaaq turned into forceful demands for independence.

Secondly, the final decision to secede was triggered by security considerations in the context of a state falling apart. Jenne et al. describe this case as extremely rare.[5] After the Somali regime in Mogadishu had been toppled, guerrillas in the south began to fight over power and economic resources. Supporters of the SNM, along with others in the northwest, sensed that new threats for their security could emerge from Mogadishu. Somaliland's independence was declared to distance the region from the ensuing chaos in Southern Somalia.[6]

To sum up my argument: secession in this particular case was an unintended consequence of anti-regime struggle and collapse of the parent state. Calculations of what secession actually means started only after independence had been declared. Even more astonishing about Somaliland is that, although it lacks international recognition, it has been functioning as

---

[4] Englebert and Hummel (2005: 412).

[5] Jenne et al. (2007: 544).

[6] Schoiswohl (2004).

a relatively stable de facto state since the 1990s.[7] It also continued its politically precarious existence over more than two decades despite not being economically viable. People and the state in Somaliland depend on support from outside, by the diaspora, external donors and (more recently) some private investments. The exploration of oil and other natural resources in the region—sometimes mentioned as explanation for the secession[8]—is a recent phenomenon that up to 2017 had not yet yielded tangible results. Somaliland faces the military opposition of Puntland as well as of local clan militias, and the ignorance of Somalia and most other recognized countries.[9] Therefore, neither "power hunger" nor "greed" explains this case of secession. Most people in Somaliland are still waiting for political recognition and substantial economic benefits. But despite the challenges of "doing it alone,"[10] Somalilanders are determined to continue on their chosen path toward sovereign statehood. This chapter analyzes the factors influencing this ongoing process.

A "Pre-history" of Somaliland

During the colonial period, the Somali peninsula was divided among Great Britain, Italy, France, and the Ethiopian Empire. The British became independent on June 26, 1960; five days later, on July 1, 1960, Italian Somalia followed. On the same day, both territories merged to form the Somali Republic. After a brief democratic period, characterized by internal problems of legal and administrative integration, corruption, and clannism,[11] a group of military and police officers led by General Mohamed Siad Barre toppled the democratically elected government of Somalia in

---

[7] According to Pegg (1998: 4) de facto states "feature long-term, effective, and popularly supported organized political leaderships that provide governmental services to a given population in a defined territorial area. They seek international recognition and view themselves as capable of meeting the obligations of sovereign statehood. They are, however, unable to secure widespread juridical recognition and therefore function outside the boundaries of international legitimacy."

[8] Anderson and Browne (2011).

[9] Although I focus on Somaliland, I will present some points on the neighboring region of Puntland in Northeastern Somalia because its opposition to Somaliland's secession contributes to stabilizing it.

[10] Prunier (1998).

[11] In Somali society, groups belonging together by patrilineal descent cooperate or compete with regard to sharing resources. Besides descent, co-residence and adoption also provide a social basis for group-belonging, particularly in Central and Southern Somalia.

October 1969. The new rulers initiated social and economic reforms and built up the military and security forces of the country. In 1977, Somalia attacked Ethiopia, which was weakened after the fall of Emperor Haile Selassi (1974), in an attempt to integrate the Somali-inhabited Ogaden Region into the Somali Republic.[12] The Ogaden War ended in early 1978 with a devastating defeat of the Somali national army. This weakened the regime of President Barre and dealt a blow to pan-Somalism (the idea to unite all Somalis in the Horn under one rule).

Soon, disgruntled military officers and others who felt marginalized rose against the dictatorship. With the Somali Salvation Democratic Front (SSDF) and the SNM, armed guerrilla movements emerged that aimed at overthrowing the government in Mogadishu. The SSDF was predominantly a Majeerteen movement. Members of this clan resided in Northeastern Somalia (today's Puntland). Isaaq dominated the SNM with their clan territories located in the northwest (today's Somaliland). Ethiopia hosted both guerrilla fronts. The SSDF was materially supported by Ethiopia, South Yemen, and Libya with the SNM receiving some military aid from South Yemen. Yet most of the SNM's resources came from the local Isaaq population and their diaspora in the Arab peninsula and Europe.[13] The SSDF dissolved in 1985 owing to internal problems and conflicts with the Ethiopian patron.

The SNM continued its struggle. Following a peace agreement between Mogadishu and Addis Ababa in early 1988, the SNM was forced to enter Somalia. In late May 1988, the guerrillas occupied Hargeysa and Bur'o, the two main towns in Northwestern Somalia. The Somali government reacted by bombing these towns. Thousands of civilians died; hundreds of thousands fled. President Barre, who was supported by the United States and the West during the 1980s, clung to power by distributing resources and weapons among his followers. Many of these were patrilineal relatives of the president.[14] By manipulating Somali clans against each other, Barre contributed to the disintegration of Somalia.

This was why the Dir and Darood/Harti clans in the Northern Somalia sided with the government, fighting bitterly against the Isaaq and their

---

[12] See Vaughan (2018) in this volume.

[13] Reno (2003: 21–23) and Bradbury (2008: 70).

[14] Barre was Marehan. His mother was Ogadeen. An important companion of the president, Ahmed Suleban Dafle, a son-in-law of Barre and high government official, was Dhulbahante. Their clans provided the backbone of the regime.

SNM in the region.[15] Various new clan-based guerrilla movements were established in the south in the late 1980s, and finally the Barre's government was overthrown in January 1991. Fear and hatred between clan groups and the lack of agreement between the various guerrilla movements led to new violence and the complete collapse of the state in Somalia, followed by international intervention in Southern Somalia and internal territorial reorganization in the north.[16]

SECESSION WITHOUT PREPARATION

The SNM controlled much of the northwest in early 1991. But instead of fighting against those clans that had been supporting the government until the end, the SNM proposed peace negotiations. After a series of smaller preparatory meetings, a large conference (*shir* in Somali) was held in Bur'o in May 1991, at which guerrilla commanders, traditional authorities, and clan representatives participated. The SNM leadership was not in favor of secession; the guerrilla leaders wanted to change the political system of Somalia, not split the country. However, the rank and file of the movement was in favor of the secession. They remembered the devastation of the civil war and particularly the harsh measures that previous Somali government had taken against the civilians in the northwest.

Also, the news from Mogadishu was worrisome. The capital was on the verge of descending into violent chaos.[17] Against this backdrop, massive demonstrations took place around the meeting in Bur'o; everybody was armed. The SNM leadership and the delegates from the non-Isaaq clans were compelled to declare the independence of the Republic of Somaliland on May 18, 1991.[18] The declaration happened in a rush and without careful consideration of the possible consequences.[19] The political leadership and wider population in Southern Somalia did not accept this step. However, caught up in civil war and warlordism, there was not much they could do. The international community, led by the UN, was concerned with bringing stability to Mogadishu and the south; the developments in the northwest were largely ignored.

---

[15] Lewis (1994: 165) and Hoehne (2011: 316).
[16] Compagnon (1992).
[17] Bryden (2004b) and Bradbury (2008: 80–83).
[18] Drysdale (1992: 25).
[19] Bradbury (2008: 82–83).

The most decisive feature of Somaliland at this point was its claimed territory: the republic was declared in accordance with the borders of the former British Protectorate. Notably, the SNM did not control the Eastern regions of this territory where the Dhulbahante and Warsangeli resided. This was where—later on—the conflict between Somaliland and Puntland would unfold, which gave Somaliland the chance to advance with state formation. Still, in 1991, the leaders of all major patrilineal descent groups from all over the northwest—including those that had opposed the SNM and had sided with the previous government until the end—agreed to make peace. A two-year interim government led by the SNM was established.

It did not succeed in bringing law and order to the newly declared state. Lack of state revenue, destruction of infrastructure, high numbers of armed militias, and splits within the SNM made effective government impossible. Several local peace conferences were held, and at a new "national" clan conference in Borama in early 1993, a peace and a national charter were adopted. The national charter functioned as a provisional constitution for Somaliland. It separated the executive, legislative, and judicial branches of the government, and introduced a bicameral parliament, consisting of a House of Elders (*Golaha Guurtida*, commonly shortened to *Guurti*) and a House of Representatives (*Golaha Wakiilada*). Thereby, a hybrid political order was founded that incorporated "traditional" and "modern" elements of governance.[20]

The experienced Isaaq politician, Mohamed Haji Ibrahim Egal, was elected as the new president for a two-year term. He had not been part of the SNM struggle. Nevertheless, as an elder statesman, he enjoyed respect. Egal had been the head of Somaliland before its unification with the Italian-administered Somali lands and Somalia's last prime minister before the 1969 coup. His Isaaq/Habar Awal clan held key economic positions in the northwest, giving him financial backing to implement policies. Abdurahman Aw Ali Tolwaa, a SNM commander and member of the Gadabuursi clan, became vice president. The Boorama conference established the political framework of the country for the coming years.[21] It also marked the moment at which the SNM, a victorious guerrilla movement,

---

[20] For a critical evaluation of this hybrid political order and its later developments in Somaliland, see Hoehne (2018).

[21] Bradbury (2008: 98).

voluntarily gave up power and allowed a civilian regime to take over. This was an unprecedented move in the whole of sub-Saharan Africa.

New conflict followed the Boorama conference. After Abdurahman Tuur, the previous SNM-chairman and president of Somaliland, had lost his position, the Gerhajis alliance—himself and other influential personalities from the clans Habar Yoonis and Idagale—abandoned the secessionist project and turned to the south, joining the warlord government of Mohamed Farah Aideed in Mogadishu. They also mingled with the UN, which had sent a massive "humanitarian" intervention force named United Nations Operation in Somalia (UNOSOM) to Southern Somalia in 1992. The UN wanted to extend operations into Somaliland, which Egal and his administration refused.

Also, Idagalle militias that controlled the airport of Hargeysa (located in their clan territory) refused the new government access. After the port of Berbera, the airport was the Somaliland's second most important economic and political asset as gateway for goods and people, including representatives of international NGOs. The Idagalle militias collected taxes at the airport and refused to share these with the government. The more the government threatened the Idagalle militias, the more the Gerhajis alliance backed the militias.[22] Fighting erupted when government troops set out to seize Hargeysa Airport, and quickly spread to Hargeysa town and Bur'o.[23] From mid-1994 to mid-1995, both towns experienced sporadic violence and civil unrest, alternated with periods of tense stalemate. Hundreds were killed and tens of thousands fled the towns temporarily.

These events, however, concerned only a part of the polity of Somaliland. The Isaaq clans in the Sanaag region in the northeast as well as the non-Isaaq clans in the west and east remained at peace. They also remained without any state administration. Governance was exercised locally, by traditional authorities and other community leaders (e.g., former military or police officers, sheikhs, and teachers). From the mid-1990s onward, such local governance was increasingly influenced by the diaspora, whose financial remittances helped to rebuild infrastructure like schools or to pay for incidentals, such as fuel for transport or food during local peace meetings (but also arms and ammunition, in case of need).[24]

---

[22] Eikenberg (1995).

[23] While Hargeysa was at that time mainly inhabited by Idagalle in the south and Habar Awal in the north, Bur'o was dominated by Habar Je'lo and Habar Yoonis. The former sided with the Egal administration; the latter fought against them.

[24] Terlinden (2008) and Hoehne (2011).

CONSTRUCTION OF AN IMAGINED (TRANSNATIONAL) COMMUNITY[25]

A key feature of every state, new or old, is that it must possess a distinctive political identity. In Somaliland, President Egal was able to take important steps toward identity and state formation. The mid-1990s conflicts in which he was involved are usually perceived as setbacks on the way to a stable Somaliland. But one can argue that they helped stabilize the emerging state: they allowed Egal to do away with rivals within the government and among other powerful clans, giving him a chance to emerge as an uncontested leader.[26]

Egal's economic networks were also a deciding factor. He stemmed from a wealthy merchant family and had good relations with his clan's business class. Since his Habar Awal/Esa Muuse sub-clan controlled the port of Berbera, Egal was able to raise substantial funds for some of the most basic tasks of the state: paying salaries to administrators and the armed forces and demobilizing clan militias. The Habar Awal business community financed the introduction of a new currency, the Somaliland Shilling, in 1994. By early 1995, it had become legal tender in Western and Central Somaliland, up to the city of Bur'o.[27]

The government started to tax the *qaad* trade,[28] imports and exports at the port of Berbera and the airport of Hargeysa (once it had taken control over it in 1997), and businesses in the country's center and west. The administration in the capital, the armed forces, and corruption consumed this moderate state revenue. Thus, the only real service provided by the government, usually in cooperation with local traditional authorities, was security in Central Somaliland. In the more peripheral regions of the country, Hargeysa's authority was minimal.[29]

A final national *shir* was held in Hargeysa from October 1996 to February 1997. It marked the end of large-scale fighting in Central Somaliland. In contrast to the previous conferences in Bur'o and Boorama, the government and the incumbent president (whose term of office had been extended previously by the *Guurti* owing to the fighting in Hargeysa

---

[25] Anderson (1983).

[26] Balthasar (2013).

[27] East of Bur'o the old Somali Shilling continued to be used because the economic ties to the rest of Somalia were strong there.

[28] Qaad is a mild stimulant. It is imported from Ethiopia into Somaliland; see Hansen (2010).

[29] Bradbury (1997).

and Bur'o) clearly dominated. Egal put pressure on the elders and delegates that were to elect a new president.[30] In February 1997, Egal was reelected as president of Somaliland for a five-year term. Dahir Rayale Kahin, a Gadabuursi, became the new vice president. The Hargeysa conference also approved a new interim constitution that represented a compromise between Egal's wish for a strong executive and the preference of many delegates for a parliamentary democracy.

The Hargeysa conference enabled Somaliland to move forward with political, economic, and social reconstruction. Within the government, civilians and bureaucrats successively replaced the former SNM cadres.[31] Isaaq politicians, who had served in the Barre administration, came to power again in Somaliland. Gradually, the government in Hargeysa expanded its authority in terms of general administration and the control of key economic resources; it also reached out to the northeastern peripheries around Erigabo, the capital of Sanaag region. Still, Somaliland was extremely poor, and official state revenue was for many years not above 20 million USD per year.[32] Most government salaries, including that of security forces, barely covered basic needs.

After other attempts to rebuild Somalia had failed, the UN and other international actors gradually recognized Somaliland as the most peaceful zone within Somalia, and by 2002, some 44% of the 150 million USD annual aid program for Somalia was being allocated to Somaliland.[33] Official development assistance (ODA) for Somalia totaled 1.3 billion USD in 2016. Financial remittances from the diaspora had started to flow from the mid-1990s onward, ensuring the survival of many people of Somaliland. It is difficult to estimate the sum of remittances going to all of Somalia, but in 2009, it was thought that it was between USD 500 million and one billion. A 2013 estimate put remittances to Somalia at at least 1.2 billion USD annually. It is safe to assume that generally, around one-third of that annual financial influx (in aid and the remittances) went to Somaliland.[34]

---

[30] Bradbury (2008: 126).

[31] It is interesting to note that, although most people in Somaliland attribute much importance to Islam, and Somaliland officially is an Islamic state, religious leaders did not play a very visible role in state formation.

[32] Until 2009, the official annual state-budget increased to 50 million USD. In 2010, this jumped to 100 million USD, largely through anti-corruption measures and intensified taxation. In 2014, the budget stood at 220 million USD.

[33] Bradbury (2008: 157; 236–237) and Lindley (2006: 5).

[34] Menkhaus (2009), Hammond (2013) and Aid Coordination Unit Office of Prime Minister Federal Republic of Somalia (2017).

Somaliland as an imagined community gradually gained traction through the establishment of Radio Hargeysa (1991), the foundation of daily newspapers, such as Jamhuuriya and Haatuf (through the 1990s and early 2000s), the introduction of the Somaliland Shilling as national currency (1994), the introduction of a national flag and anthem (1996), the development of a Somaliland school curriculum (from 1997 onward), and the erection of national and civil war monuments (from 2001 onward). All of these elements facilitated the development of a common political identity. They added weight to the country's de facto statehood, along with the political institutions created in Boorama in 1993 and developed further afterwards.

However, these developments were largely confined to Somaliland's core. This covers the western and central regions of the polity and is home mainly to Dir and Isaaq groups. Many authors dealing with Somaliland ignore the heterogeneity of the historical experiences and political orientations of the people residing in the region.[35] Even in the center of the polity, an influential minority continued to resent the definitive secession from Somalia and the "death" of the vision of "Greater Somalia."[36] The death of Greater Somalia is part of the dominant narrative of the secessionist state. It is also expressed in the Somaliland flag: the small five-pointed star in its center refers to the larger star in the Somali flag. In the Somali flag, the star is white and each of its points symbolizes a Somali territory that had to, in the eyes of Somali postcolonial leaders, be integrated in the Somali nation state (the Ogadeen in Eastern Ethiopia, Northwestern Kenya, parts of Djibouti, British Somaliland, and the Italian Somali territories).

Yet, only British Somaliland and the Italian Somali territories had united in 1960. And even their unity had failed—in the eyes of Somaliland supporters—in the late 1980s, which led to the secession of Somaliland 1991. Therefore, the little star in the Somaliland flag is black—standing for the death of the Greater Somalia vision.

Beyond Somaliland's core, political consensus remained fragile. People could agree on peace but particularly members of the Dhulbahante and Warsangeli clans in the eastern regions (Sool, Sanaag, and parts of Togdheer) kept away from the idea of an independent Somaliland. At least

[35] See for instance, Bradbury (2008) and Walls (2014) for interesting but one-sided (center-oriented) accounts of Somaliland's history and politics.
[36] Interview, anonymous, Hargeysa (2003).

this was the situation in the early 2000s when I started my field research in the area. Consulting sources written closer to that time, it becomes obvious that the question of who actually supported secession is complicated to answer. Compagnon stresses that also non-Isaaq groups favored independence because of a feeling of marginalization by Mogadishu—an issue particularly for the Gadabuursi who had waited in vain throughout the 1980s for a road and other infrastructure allowing them to build their economy.[37] Moreover, the Dhulbahante and Warsangeli were apparently shocked by the extent of clan-cleansing taking place in Mogadishu in 1991—led by the Hawiye—to which many Darood fell victim.[38] Compagnon suggests that non-Isaaq, too, found the idea of separating from a rebel government in Mogadishu controlled by Hawiye militiamen attractive—particularly because the Mogadishu government at that time targeted Darood for allegedly supporting the fallen dictator Barre.[39]

Yet, within Dhulbahante and Warsangeli, there always had been an influential section that from early on had opposed secession. Anti-secessionist Dhulbahante organized "counter-conferences" to the Somaliland conferences in Boorama (1993) and Hargeysa (1997) in Bo'ame (in Sool region). At these conferences, attendants opted for local self-governance as long as Somalia was in turmoil.[40] From the early 2000s onward, resistance of these groups against the administration in Hargeysa became more pronounced; eventually taking a military turn. This means that while core Somaliland became stable and peaceful some ten years after the unilateral declaration of independence from Somalia, its extensive eastern margins (which cover roughly 30% of the state territory and are home to around 20% of the population) were not integrated.

The members of these oppositional groups felt politically and economically marginalized by Hargeysa. Moreover, the non-Isaaq clans had clearly experienced Somali history in a different way from most of the Isaaq. For the former, the monuments, holidays, and other symbols of Somaliland frequently did not instigate "heroic" memories or a sense of togetherness. Rather, they stood for the defeat of the values and visions that many had upheld until 1991 and continued to believe in even though political pragmatism had dictated some concessions to the Isaaq majority and the overwhelming firepower of the SNM.

---

[37] Compagnon (1993: 13–14).
[38] Kapteijns (2013).
[39] Compagnon (1993: 14).
[40] Hoehne (2015: 54–55).

This fostered a counter-political identity aimed at sabotaging the secessionist move of Somaliland and toward securing Somali unity. Nonetheless, it can be argued that exactly this opposition to Somaliland's independence in the eastern regions provided the government in Hargeysa and its supporters with the "relevant other" against whom aspirations to statehood and distinct political identity were furthered.

The Formation of Puntland as Somaliland's Rival

The anti-secessionist position of the Dhulbahante and Warsangeli gained an institutional basis in Puntland.[41] Puntland was established in Northeastern Somalia in 1998 as an (autonomous) regional administration. The dominant clan in the region was Majeerteen. Their old guerrilla movement SSDF, having been dissolved in 1985, had regrouped in 1991; in cooperation with local traditional authorities,they had set out to control the northeast of collapsed Somalia. Throughout the 1990s, representatives of the SSDF had participated in several conferences dedicated to rebuilding Somalia. When these did not yield tangible results, the people and political leaders in the northeast decided to create their own administration. They called for a clan conference, similar to the ones held previously in Somaliland.

The *shir* that eventually led to the establishment of Puntland took place in Garowe between May and August 1998. Genealogy formed the basis for this new polity. Those attending the meeting were descendants of Sheekh Abdurahman Ismael al Jabarti, the founding father of the Darood clan family. Many belonged to the Harti clan-collective within Darood. Particularly Dhulbahante and Warsangeli from Eastern Somaliland played an important role in this *shir* as allies of certain factions within Majeerteen.[42]

On August 1, 1998, the State of Puntland was officially declared, with Colonel Abdulahi Yusuf, the former SSDF leader, as founding president and Garowe as its capital. The Charter of the State of Puntland, which functioned as the polity's preliminary constitution (new constitutions have been adopted in 2001 and 2012), followed "the pattern of the Boorama National Charter, which formalized the birth of Somaliland."[43] Generally

---

[41] Bryden (1999).

[42] Battera (1999), Doornbos (2000), Farah (2001), Somalia; Farah (2004).

[43] Battera (1999: 4).

speaking, Puntland mimicked Somaliland.[44] By embracing clans and traditional authorities and by accepting a kind of "minimal state" whose main
task was to provide security (in cooperation with elders) and open up for
private (transnational) investments and international (humanitarian)
engagement, Somaliland provided a matrix for a successful Somali (post-
dictatorial) state. In contrast to Somaliland, however, the role of traditional
authorities in politics was not institutionalized in the parliament. The elders
played important—albeit ad hoc—roles in Puntland's national politics.

A further difference was the difference in political aims. Puntland did not
declare independence from Somalia, instead aspiring to a united but federal
Somalia. Presenting itself as administering all Harti clans in the north,
Puntland—at least on paper—cut the Dhulbahante and Warsangeli territories out of Somaliland. It thereby undermined the former colonial borders
claimed by the government in Hargeysa as eastern border of Somaliland.

The ensuing conflict between Somaliland and Puntland can be understood as pitting a territorial against a genealogical principle of statehood.
Somaliland claims the land (the former British territory) while Puntland
claims the people (the descendants of Harti and some other Darood
groups). More generally, this conflict is about the question of Somali unity
versus return to (ex-colonial) partition. Somaliland claims that its secession does not violate the colonial boundaries and therefore respects Article
3(3) of the Charter of the Organisation of African Unity (OAU) (1963),
that enshrines a country's borders at its moment of independence. This
has been reiterated in Article 4 of the Constitutive Act of African Union
(AU) (2000). In contrast, Puntland argues that the border between British
and Italian Somali territories in the north was dissolved in 1960. The
Somali Republic joined the OAU in 1963 as one state, and this unity
needs to be safeguarded.

From 2002 to 2018, Somaliland troops clashed several times with
Puntland forces and clan militias in the contested borderlands. In the
course of events, Somaliland managed to gain a militarily superior position
that enhanced the degree of state control Hargeysa could exert in the
peripheral eastern regions (particularly in the Sool region). Over the years,
military control was complemented by administrative services and moderate development initiatives. This enhanced the acceptance for Hargeysa's
rule in the area, despite the fact that most locals still preferred Somali unity
over secession.

[44] Hoehne (2009).

DEMOCRATIZATION AND DEVELOPMENT IN SOMALILAND

During the second term of President Egal, the government developed a new constitution, finally putting it to vote in a public referendum in May 2001. In its first article, the constitution confirmed Somaliland's independence. The referendum happened at a decisive moment for Somaliland, because for the first time in a decade, Somalia seemed to get back on its feet. At a 2000 conference in Arta, Djibouti, the Transitional National Government (TNG) for Somalia had been established. The government of Somaliland had refused to participate at that conference. Once the TNG had been installed, it soon received international backing. The fear was that Somaliland, as an unrecognized entity, could lose out against a slowly recovering Somalia. Against this backdrop, the referendum was essentially a vote about Somaliland's continued independence. In all, 97% of voters—about 1.18 million people according to official sources—approved the constitution. International observers evaluated the referendum positively, even if they were not numerous enough to report authoritatively from throughout the country.[45]

The number of 1.18 million ballots cast is suspicious. It is unlikely there were this many eligible voters, considering that various estimates by international NGOs and UN organizations up until 2000 indicated that only between one and two million people lived in Somaliland.[46] In the local government elections of 2002, only 420,067 valid votes were counted.[47] In the 2005 parliamentary elections, 674,907 ballots were cast.[48] Both of these elections were conducted in basically the same areas and among the same constituencies as the referendum but were more effectively monitored. In Sool, Eastern Sanaag and Southern Togdheer in particular, where Dhulbahante and Warsangeli are dominant, not many people registered for the referendum in 2001. It was almost exclusively Isaaq who voted pro-independence in the referendum. Since this group constitutes roughly two-thirds of the population of Somaliland, the 97% approval meant in fact that around 65% of all eligible voters confirmed the constitution and therefore the independence of the country.[49] While this satisfied the criteria

---

[45] Bryden (2004a: 178).
[46] Bradbury (2008: 160).
[47] Abokor et al. (2003: 30).
[48] International Republican Institute (2005: 27).
[49] This argument was also made by the Ministry of Foreign Affairs (2002: 10).

of "formal" democracy, it added to the already existing tensions between those accepting and those rejecting the idea of secession.

The next steps were to introduce political parties and prepare local government elections. While this process was ongoing, Egal died while on a medical visit to South Africa on May 5, 2002. Vice President Kahin took over for the remainder of the term. The first democratic elections were held on December 15, 2002, in which six political organizations competed for seats in local governments. The three parties with the most votes in various regions were Ururka Demoqraadiga Ummada Bahowdey (UDUB), Kulmiye, and Ururka Caddaaladda iyo Daryeelka (UCID). Subsequently, they became the national parties that would shape Somaliland's politics for the coming years.[50]

UDUB, the party of the incumbent president, had the most votes and became the ruling party; the other two parties formed the opposition. The first democratic presidential elections were held on April 14, 2003. Kahin won by a minimal margin of about 80 votes. Kulmiye, the leading opposition party, contested the result. The Supreme Court ruled in Kahin's favor and his challengers accepted the judgment, bowing to increasing public pressure demanding the preservation of peace and order. In parliamentary elections on September 29, 2005, the UDUB won the largest single share. Kulmiye and UCID together formed an opposition holding almost 60% of the seats in the House of Representatives.[51] Therefore, the president had lost control over parts of the parliament, the Lower House, and sought to govern against it with the help of the Guurti (the Upper House). Both the presidential and parliamentary elections were deemed reasonably free and fair by international election observers.[52] Notably, the parliamentary elections only concerned the Lower House of Parliament while the members of the Guurti remain unelected up until today (2017).[53]

External actors viewed the political developments in core-Somaliland in the early 2000s increasingly positively. While states and international organizations carefully avoided any move that could be interpreted as political recognition, engagement from outside in the humanitarian sector grew exponentially. Somaliland soon was deemed the "better Somalia" since Somalia's TNG had turned out to be a failure. Puntland also had its own

---

[50] Article 9 of the Constitution of Somaliland provides that not more than three national parties must exist in Somaliland. This was a measure against clan factionalism.

[51] Interpeace (2006: 44).

[52] Terlinden and Ibrahim (2008).

[53] There is an ongoing debate around the reformation of the Guurti; see IRIN (2013); for a critical assessment of the Guurti's performance, see Hoehne (2018).

problems. Between 2001 and 2003, it was ravaged by political instability that triggered episodes of civil war after President Yusuf had refused to step down after his term had ended. A counter-president was elected by a group of elders, but Abdullahi Yusuf mobilized his clansmen and forced the opponent away.

Multilateral organizations such as the European Union (EU), numerous international NGOs such as Danish Refugee Council (DRC), and UN agencies such as United Nations Development Program (UNDP), who had tended to work on Somalia and Somaliland from their Nairobi headquarters, set up offices in Hargeysa. From there, they coordinated projects all over Somalia, making central Somaliland a development hub. The organizations profited from the peace and the developing infrastructure particularly in Hargeysa (where increasingly diaspora actors invested and shopping malls and other businesses were established), furthering developments through renting houses and cars, employing locals, consuming "luxury" goods, and creating a market for fast and reliable Internet.

The political identity of Somalilanders matured. When I started my field research in 2002, I hardly ever encountered anyone in daily life who would refer to themselves as "Somalilander." Regardless of patrilineal belonging, people would say: "I am Somali." Many would stress that all Somalis had the same language, the same religion, and the same culture. A few years later, around 2010, I realized that self-identification as Somalilander had become more prevalent, particularly among the younger generation in central Somaliland.[54] This indicates that political identities emerge slowly and are related to various factors such as the creation of an imagined community through print media, monuments, and public celebrations. Also, a new generation had come of age: those who were born in the region from the late 1980s onwards did not know Somalia before its 1991 collapse. For them, it was quite normal to accept Somaliland as their homeland, unless their parents or close social contacts would socialize them differently (and of course, there were people cultivating a nostalgia for "Somalia," even in what I call core-Somaliland).

In the mid-2000s, the feeling that Somaliland had matured into a real state and deserved recognition was not only shared among Somalilanders

---

[54] These statements are based on my long-term observations during frequent visits to Somaliland between 2002 and 2017.

themselves but also gained track internationally.[55] It compared favorably to the rest of Somalia as well as to other established states in the region. There was Eritrea, which after 2000, had turned into a ruthless dictatorship incarcerating the younger generation in endless "national service." Ethiopia had in 2005 violently repressed and aborted the first democratic elections in decades. Kenya reputation for corruption and tribalism had grown worse after the deadly 2007 elections. In comparison, Somaliland was an island of largely homegrown peace, stability, and democracy. Additionally, it exhibited moderate economic development instigated mainly by diasporic investors and foreign aid. It was paradoxical that collapsed Somalia was kept alive as "state on paper," while de facto working Somaliland was officially ignored.[56] A South-African observer close to the administration in Hargeysa had devised the clever nickname for Somaliland as "Africa's best kept secret."[57]

Despite the impressive peace-building and democratization successes of Somaliland, problems remained. In everyday political life, clan politics continued within the parties and, therefore, within all government institutions, including the cabinet and parliament.[58] Leading positions were divided among members of different patrilineal descent groups. In the absence of ideological differences between the three parties, the mobilization of party supporters also followed clan lines.[59] This brought about the unfinished status of democracy that characterizes Somaliland today (2018).

Stability and peace in Somaliland were most successfully established in the core areas between Bur'o, Hargeysa, Berbera, and Boorama. The extensive eastern margins of the country had not participated in the democratic transformation, and the authority of the central government was

[55] While people, according to my observations, could voice diverging opinions about Somaliland and Somalia in casual conversations in Hargeysa in the early 2000s, this has become a more sensitive issue recently, probably after the attacks of Al Shabaab in Hargeysa in October 2008—yet it would be misleading to think that the change of sentiment regarding political self-identification was related to only one event.

[56] In 2005, the government in Hargeysa submitted an official request for membership to the African Union (AU). It remained without official answer; International Crisis Group (2006: 1).

[57] Jhazbhay (2003), Shinn (2002), Sanchez Bermudez (2004) and Roethke (2011).

[58] Ciabarri (2008).

[59] This did not mean that "pure clanism" reigned and that one party was controlled and supported by only one clan. Within each party, all the clans had their share. It did mean, however, that positions within the government and the parties were awarded on the basis of clans rather than individual merit or individuals being elected.

weak there. Over the years, representation of Dhulbahante and Warsangeli in the Somaliland government diminished.[60] Puntland took the opportunity to advance into the contested borderlands; eventually, armed conflict broke out. In retrospect, it becomes clear that this conflict, which in the short term undermined stability in Somaliland, contributed to the expansion of Hargeysa's authority into the east and the stabilization of the secessionist state.

SOMALILAND AND PUNTLAND

Until the death of President Egal, neither the government in Hargeysa nor the government of Puntland had seriously engaged in the Harti-peripheries, with Puntland not having acted on its claim to the area. It is likely that a silent diplomatic agreement between Somaliland's Egal and Puntland's Yusuf existed that helped to avoid costly military clashes in the contested borderlands. On the ground, locals took up nominal positions for either administration, getting a salary either from Hargeysa or Garowe. Yet, everyday politics were in the hands of non-state actors—mainly traditional authorities—from the various local lineages, following customary rules and being concerned with matters of peace and economic survival. Some Dhulbahante and Warsangeli elites sat in the respective centers as ministers, vice ministers, speakers of parliament, parliamentarians, and high-ranking military and police officers. The logic behind this double positioning was that, by serving both governments, local communities doubled their income and maintained political influence in both camps.[61]

After Egal's death, however, President Kahin visited Lasanod, capital of the Sool region, on December 7, 2002. This visit triggered a shoot-out between Somaliland and Puntland troops in the town. Initially, both sides retreated.[62] In December 2003, Puntland police forces used a violent conflict between two Dhulbahante lineages to intervene and occupy the town. Somaliland reacted by sending its army to the region.[63] A frontline was established, but no massive clashes erupted. External events soon escalated the conflict. On October 10, 2004, Puntland's President Yusuf was elected

---

[60] Hansen and Bradbury (2007).

[61] The monthly salary of an ordinary Somaliland or Puntland soldier was not more than 40–50 USD in the early 2000s. Higher positions, for example, as minister, came along with more income and additional job opportunities for bodyguards and drivers.

[62] Hoehne (2006).

[63] Republican (2004).

as president of Somalia at an internationally backed peace conference for Somalia in Kenya. The hope was that the Transitional Federal Government (TFG) under its strong leader, who had good relations with the emerging regional superpower Ethiopia, would bring peace and stability to Mogadishu and Southern Somalia.

In his first announcements as Somali president, Yusuf emphasized that he would work for the integrity and unity of Somalia. The government in Hargeysa and its supporters understood this as threat to the existence of Somaliland. On October 29, 2004, the armies of Somaliland and Puntland clashed some 30 km west of Lasanod. Dozens of soldiers were killed or wounded on both sides. The clash did not bring about any decisive result. Lasanod remained under Puntland's control. The public in core Somaliland was now alert as it had become clear that, after more than a decade of ignoring the problems in Eastern Somaliland, the issue of state control in the area had to be taken on.

The situation remained tense, but for some years, no further fighting occurred in the contested borderland. Soon after its installment, Yusuf's TFG got caught up in fighting against the Islamic courts and Islamist militants in Southern Somalia. Between 2006 and 2008, the Somali national army engaged with Al Shabaab and Hizbul Islam, both effective militias that soon controlled large parts of Southern and Central Somalia. Thousands of Majeerteen soldiers from Puntland were fighting in the Somali army during this time; the Somali army was supported by Ethiopian intervention troops, and from February 2007 onwards, AU "peacekeepers."

People in Puntland elected as new President Mahamoud Muuse Hirsi (also known as Adde Muuse), a Majeerteen military officer, in January 2005. He took a weak stance on the confrontation with Somaliland. When Puntland's Minister of the Interior, who was a senior Dhulbahante politician, fell out with President Muuse in mid-2007, the tide turned in Somaliland's favor. The former Puntland minister went to Hargeysa and eventually led Somaliland's troops to attack Lasanod. The Puntland forces retreated and only some local militias resisted the attack. By November 2007, Somaliland controlled Lasanod.[64]

Ethiopia approved this change of power: it was concerned about militant Islamists infiltrating eastern Ethiopia via Lasanod and more broadly security along Ethiopia's borders with Somaliland and Puntland.[65] Another concern of the Ethiopian government was that fighters of the Ogaden

---

[64] Hoehne (2007).
[65] Interview, Ahmed Mahamoud Warsame (2010).

National Liberation Front (ONLF), who were part of the Darood clan family, could retreat into Dhulbahante to reorganize.[66] Reacting to Somaliland's occupation, thousands of people initially fled Lasanod. Many returned after several months when the situation had calmed down.

But Lasanod and the whole Dhulbahante lands remained a conflict hotspot for years to come. While the tension between Somaliland and Puntland had initially looked like a threat to Somaliland, it became an opportunity, offering the government in Hargeysa a chance to continue with state-building. Subsequent Puntland administrations under President Abdurrahman Mohamed Mohamud Faroole (2009–2014) and President Abdiweli Mohamed Ali Gaas (2014–) continued to fail to take decisive steps toward recapturing Lasanod, therefore undermining "Harti-solidarity" and inadvertently supporting Somaliland's state-building efforts. Puntland was effectively reduced to "Majeerteenya;" Somaliland expanded.

SOMALILAND 2007–2018

The decade from 2007 and 2018 was one of internal challenges for Somaliland. Kahin's administration was facing growing internal opposition and external criticism. Between 2008 and 2010, it reacted heavy-handedly against journalists reporting on a corruption scandal involving the president's wife and against a group of Somaliland intellectuals, seeking to set up a new political party.[67] A disastrous election process meant that both President Kahin and the *Guurti*, firm allies of the president, lost much of its legitimacy.

According to the constitution of Somaliland, presidential elections had to take place in March 2008, yet neither the administration nor the opposition had taken the necessary steps to hold them. The National Electoral Commission (NEC) did not work effectively. The Somaliland parties and NEC opted for a sophisticated biometric registration system using fingerprinting and photo card identification, against the explicit advice of the donors and Interpeace (an international NGO involved in the process).[68] This process was both ambitious and highly symbolic—for the first time,

---

[66] Interview, anonymous informant (2011).

[67] Human Rights Watch (2009).

[68] Most of the resources were provided by the EC, DfID/UK, USAID, SIDA Sweden, Norway, DANIDA/Denmark; together, these organizations form the Democratization Program Steering Committee.

all citizens of Somaliland would be able to receive a document identifying them as "Somalilander."

The registration process started in October 2008, proceeding relatively quickly from Western to Eastern Somaliland despite a host of logistical problems. It then came to a sudden halt when Somaliland and Puntland were shaken by five suicide-bomb attacks on October 29, 2008. In Hargeysa, the presidential palace, the UNDP compound and the Ethiopian liaison office were attacked while two offices of the Puntland Intelligence Service were bombed in Bosaso. More than 20 people were killed and about 30 injured. It was commonly suspected that the perpetrators were closely related to the extremists of Al Shabaab in Southern Somalia, who had supporters in the north. The Islamists—wanting to establish a strong, united, and Islamic state of Somalia—opposed Somaliland's independence.[69]

Voter registration in Somaliland eventually proceeded. Soon after the process was concluded, it became obvious that massive over-registration had happened. The newspapers reported that about 1.4 million registrations were counted of which more than 50% had registered without fingerprints.[70] Certain locations in Somaliland could be easily identified as strongholds of the UDUB, Kulmiye, or UCID, respectively. It was clear that the purpose of multiple registrations, particularly in Booroma, Hargeysa, Bur'o, and surrounding areas, was to increase the voting powers of the different party cum clan constituencies. The resolution of the ensuing political crisis was complicated. No party leader wanted to lose his extra votes.

In early March 2009, the *Guurti* extended the president's term for a second time. It referred to provisions in the constitution concerning the "security situation" (article 83 [5]), which arguably did not apply in the context. This delay, which many believed to be unconstitutional, caused rising tensions in Somaliland. When opposition parties called for demonstrations, the administration regularly declared these illegal, accusing opposition leaders of undermining the peace and stability of Somaliland. Armed police and the military were deployed in the major cities to control the situation.[71] Nonetheless, demonstrations took place and at least one

---

[69] Hoehne (2008: 13–15).

[70] In the parliamentary elections of 2005, during which ink was used to prevent multiple voting, only about 674,000 voters were counted.

[71] Author's observations, Hargeysa (2009).

person died when the police opened fire on demonstrators in Hargeysa on September 12, 2009.

On September 25, 2009, the *Guurti* extended the president's and vice president's terms again "until one month after holding the presidential elections," without fixing a date for these elections. Elections were finally held on June 2010. The opposition candidate Ahmed Mohamed Mahamoud Silanyo, chairman of the Kulmiye party, won. Despite the political wrangling that preceded it, the second peaceful presidential elections that led to a change of power in Somaliland were generally seen as indicator of the continuing democratization of the country. Still, one lasting negative effect of the election crisis 2008–2010 was that the *Guurti* had lost much credibility. In 2011, a Somaliland think tank published a study focused on the extension of the presidential term by the Guurti.[72] According to this report,

Most respondents believe that though the Guurti has played a crucial positive role both during the SNM struggle and the early years of the establishment of Somaliland, their political impartiality is under question particularly relating to the process of extending the term of the incumbent president. Critics maintain that the Guurti is no longer relevant in managing conflict between the competing political actors, because it has itself become a party in ongoing political disputes. This politicization has begun to undermine the Guurti's credibility as an honest neutral broker in managing the conflicts between competing political actors.[73]

Under President Silanyo, the conflict in the eastern regions erupted again. In 2009, diaspora actors, traditional authorities, and others belonging to the Dhulbahante clan residing in Sool and Southern Togdheer (in the area around the town Buuhoodle) founded a new movement called Sool, Sanaag, and Cayn (SSC).[74] The aims of this clan militia were to evict

---

[72] The report is based on qualitative research. The respondents were politicians, lawyers, judges, civil society activists, and members of local think tanks. A total of 80 people were interviewed in Hargeysa; Somaliland Non State Actors Forum (SONSAF 2011: 16–17).

[73] SONSAF (2011: 31).

[74] Cayn (with an Arabic ع at the beginning) refers to the name of an area which is rich in wells and therefore important in the context of pastoral nomadic economy. This area is located in Togdheer region and has been taken over, in the first half of the twentieth century, by Isaaq nomads. The Dhulbahante previously grazing their herds in this area have been pushed further south. Therefore, the name Cayn reminds many Dhulbahante of this loss of resources and fits with their general feeling of marginalization by the Isaaq who dominate in Somaliland.

the Somaliland forces from Lasanod and its surroundings, to stabilize security in the SSC regions, to work for the development of these regions, and to secure direct access to international aid. Hargeysa and Garowe were motivated to establish these militias to pursue monopolization of aid and economic development in the respective centers of Somaliland and Puntland. The SSC opposition to Puntland was also caused by the lack of will of the government in Garowe to recapture Lasanod after Somaliland's takeover in 2007.

Still, the main enemy of the SSC was the Somaliland army in the area. SSC and Somaliland forces clashed several times in the countryside between Bur'o and Buuhoodle in late 2010 and early 2011. After internal splits, the SSC lost support among Dhulbahante. It was succeeded by the administration of the Khaatumo State of Somalia that was declared at a clan conference in Taleh, a small town in the Sool region, in January 2012. The Khaatumo administration said it operated under the federal constitution of Somalia. It established a basic government structure with three rotating presidents, representing the three main branches of the Dhulbahante clan, and each leading the administration for six months.

The armed forces of the Khaatumo State consisted of some professional soldiers (previously trained in the armies of Somalia, Somaliland, or Puntland) and nomadic fighters. Financial support, from which arms and ammunition were bought, came from the diaspora. Between January 2012 and March 2013, Somaliland troops and Khaatumo militias clashed in parts of the Sool region. Lack of military success and disagreements within the Dhulbahante clan eventually led to the collapse of the Khaatumo administration. In August 2014, Ali Khalif Galaydh was elected as the new president by a small group of Dhulbahante. He proved incapable of mobilizing the wider clan again and eventually entered peace negotiations with the government of Somaliland, which as of mid-2017 are ongoing.

Like the Dhulbahante, the Warsangeli also resided in the contested borderlands between Somaliland and Puntland. They positioned themselves more carefully, maintaining relatively good ties with the governments in both Hargeysa and Garowe. From 2006 onward, however, conflict with the Puntland government over the extraction of natural resources in the Galgala Mountains west of Bosaso (which are Warsangeli territory) caused instability. Islamist extremists related to Al Shabaab in Southern Somalia used this instability, as well as the strategic location in the mountains opposite of the Arabian Peninsula, to establish a small dépendance in the Galgala Mountains. Fighting involved mainly Al

Shabaab and Puntland forces. The vast majority of people in Somaliland remained unaffected by this conflict at the northeasternmost margins of their country. In Erigabo, the capital of Sanaag region, one could hear reports of small groups of Al Shabaab fighters transcending the nearby countryside.[75]

An additional challenge for Somaliland emerged when in August 2012, a new—and this time permanent—government for Somalia was established in Mogadishu; it soon received recognition by the international community. Lead by the British, who had taken on Somalia as one of their major foreign policy projects, international donor countries pledged considerable financial and other support for Somalia, aimed at defeating Al Shabaab and rebuilding the state. Carried by the euphoria about a possible end of Somalia's crisis, many international actors (NGOs as well as multilateral or UN bodies) turned their backs on Somaliland and transferred their offices from Hargeysa to Mogadishu (where, because of security concerns, they still reside in barracks on the ground of the highly secured Mogadishu International Airport). Many ordinary people in core-Somaliland perceived this as betrayal. Having delivered peace and stability, they had not been rewarded the political price they had longed for: official recognition.

Despite these turbulences, President Silanyo's government made progress on key domestic issues. The Ministry of Finances quadrupled the budget from around 50 million USD in 2009 to around 220 million USD in 2014.[76] This happened largely through more effective taxation and through encouraging foreign direct investments. In the system, the government strived to standardize the school curricula and invested in teacher education. However, probably all of the better-quality education at all levels available in Somaliland has come about through private investments, often initiated and/or sustained by diasporic actors, and through development assistance.

In 2010, the Ministry of Planning produced a comprehensive development plan for the country, based on critical analysis of the status quo. The plan formed the basis for effective aid coordination. Remarkably, the "centenary" project of the road between Bur'o and Erigabo, which crosses some 300 km of semi-desert, has been partly completed with the financial help from the Somaliland diaspora. Most recently, in early 2017, negotia-

---

[75] Hoehne (2014).
[76] Somaliland: Study on SL Government Budgets from 2010 to 2017. http://www.somalilandpress.com/somalilandstudy-sl-government-budgets-2010-2017/

tions concluded over extensive investments by the United Arab Emirates (UAE) in Somaliland; the port of Berbera has now been leased to Dubai Port World for 30 years and will be enlarged, and UAE now have a military base near Berbera.

These investments will considerably increase the state's budget in the coming years, but they have also attracted massive critique inside and outside of Somaliland about the lack of transparency negotiations that involved mainly President Silanyo's close family. Allegations of corruption have been made. People asked about the implication of a UAE military base on Somaliland's soil, given that UAE is currently involved in the war in Yemen. Despite growing disappointment with President Silanyo and his government, whose official term ended in June 2015 and has since has been extended (again by the *Guurti*, partly being forced by drought and ensuing famine in the region in 2016), people in Somaliland continue on their path of de facto statehood. In November 2017, presidential elections were held in Somaliland. The candidate of Kulmiye, called Muse Bihi, won the election. The opposition party Wadani, founded in 2012, contested the results but after some negotiations, a peaceful electoral process was concluded.[77] The political modus operandi that facilitates the difficulat political journey of Somaliland has two key features: it is crisis-driven and focused on finding solutions "just-in-time" for whatever crisis emerges.

CONCLUSION

The case of the Republic of Somaliland is instructive in several regards. It casts doubt on the cost-benefit calculations that dominate the literature on secessionism in general and in Africa in particular. It highlights the contingent nature of secession and shows that despite any immediate economic or political benefits, people may carry on with a secessionist endeavor against considerable odds over two decades. The declaration of independence in 1991 happened in a haste and was the result of two main factors: first, the changing dynamics of war in Northern Somalia in the late 1980s, in which the Isaaq were singled out for systematic persecution by the government in Mogadishu and then emerged as the militarily dominant group in the region; second, the protracted state collapse in Somalia.

The idea to separate became popular among many Isaaq because living under the former regime had been traumatic,[78] resonating with the literature that stresses violence and repression as important factors influencing

---

[77] Pegg and Walls (2018).
[78] Bradbury (2008).

secessionist dynamics.[79] The region's colonial history provided those favoring secession with a matrix or fallback option. The claim to independence in accordance with the borders of the British protectorate let the secession in the eyes of its supporters appear as a "dissolution" of two formerly independent states that had voluntarily united in 1960. Somalilanders would argue that the split in 1991 therefore did not violate the Charter of the OAU (succeeded by the AU), which protected the borders inhabited upon independence.

It is often assumed that secession has to be economically advantageous, but the separation of Northwestern Somalia from Somalia in 1991 isolated one of the resource-poorest regions from the rest country. The Somaliland case seems to confirm Horowitz's observation that "secessionist regions are disproportionately ill-favored in resources and per-capita income."[80] Southern Somalia is rich in agricultural resources; the north is mostly barren semi-desert. Northern urban infrastructure had been ravaged by decades of marginalization and years of civil war. The only viable economic sectors of the region were pastoral nomadism and trade. Both sectors were essentially mobile, cross-border activities that did not require seclusion (achieved through secession) to thrive. To the contrary, fewer borders might be more beneficial to them.

In 1991, natural resources were not yet an issue (and barely are today). Therefore, the economic argument that secessionist dynamics unfold when a regionally dominant group can monopolize viable local resources is not applicable here.[81] Generous remittances from the diaspora could not substitute for local resources, because in the early 1990s, the volume of remittances sent back to Somaliland was small. The existing Isaaq diasporas in the Arab peninsula and Europe had previously spent their money on supporting the SNM. The hundreds of thousands of new refugees from the region who resided in Ethiopia did not have the means to act as a financially relevant diaspora. And even those who had fled to Europe and North America in the late 1980s and early 1990s needed years to establish themselves in order to substantially invest back home. In sum, from an economic point of view, Somaliland's secession did not pay at all during the first decade of the state's existence, and only moderately afterwards.

---

[79] Horowitz (192: 122), Hechter (1992: 122) and Bartkus (1999: 79–86).
[80] Horowitz (1992: 120).
[81] Collier and Hoeffler (2002: 7).

Internationally, Somaliland initially had no friends. The international community poured massive resources into Mogadishu and Southern Somalia during the joint UN/US intervention between 1992 and 1995, criticizing the Somaliland government for its separatist stance.[82] Political and military leaders (including those from Somaliland), who participated in the externally driven endeavors to rebuild Somalia, reaped political and material benefits. Thus, elites would have had considerable incentives to avoid or abandon secession. Yet, with the exception of the Garhajis elites in 1994 and a few others, the Isaaq elites who guided the most populous group in Somaliland stayed committed to establishing their own state.

What, then, were the benefits of Somaliland's secession? The main benefit in 1991 was a degree of security and peace. However, even this considerable benefit did not materialize immediately. Somaliland was not drawn into the Southern Somali chaos, but it still took many years before it became peaceful. Only from 1997 onward did Somaliland really emerge as a stable de facto state that attracted some diaspora investments and international aid, which provided its residents with a future in the form of education and job opportunities. Therefore, it can be argued that extraversion, the term Bayart uses to describe active African participation in creating and maintaining a dependent position,[83] came into play in Somaliland only several years after independence had been declared.[84]

Somaliland's secession is unique in sub-Saharan Africa: most other secessions were either not successful or were backed by outside forces. Eight factors, in my view, helped Somaliland's development against the grain.

First, a certain culture of independence prevailed among Northern Somali pastoral nomads, used to surviving on their own. John Drysdale captured this in his characterization of northern Somalis as "stoics without pillows."[85]

Second, and somewhat paradoxically, the staggering resource-poorness of Somaliland was a blessing. It is safe to assume that, had Somaliland had valuables like oil or plantations, this would have, in the extremely violence-ridden and unstable early 1990s, led to warlordism.

---

[82] Bradbury (2008: 152).

[83] Bayart (2000).

[84] Extraversion refers to the strategy of political leaders of states to generate external resources (in the form of aid, loans, investments, etc.) to manage their countries and compensate for domestic weaknesses. Tull explains: "At the core of the extraversion strategy are efforts by African government elites to access these resources and thereby capitalize on their foreign dependency," Tull (2011: 8).

[85] Drysdale (2000).

Third, the absence of international interventions throughout the 1990s gave people in Somaliland time to experiment with a political system suitable to their segmentary social order. No one burdened the participants at Somaliland's peace conferences with foreign agendas that disregarded local values, as it often happens, particularly when the power differences between the actors are significant.

This facilitated, fourth, the establishment of a hybrid political order in which Somali "traditions" were combined with the European "tradition" of "modern" statehood. Within this hybrid order, consensus was sought on matters of war and peace and concerning the further political developments. This gave political decisions a considerable weight in the (male-dominated) Somali cosmos, where strength resides in (extended) families.

Fifth, the coming of age of a new generation of young Somalilanders who had grown up without memories of the old Somalia awarded Somaliland a certain "biological" reality. Over the decades, it became the country of birth of many.

Sixth, the constant strive for international recognition forced the Hargeysa government and its supporters to live up to what they perceived were the minimal expectations of Western governments (as the main donors) regarding "real" states. This involved respect for human rights, democracy, and peacefulness. Once these conditions were met, many believed that recognition would be granted (particularly in the early 2000s). In the absence of recognition, the idea that peacefulness and democracy had to be cultivated in order to not become like the rest of Somalia served as a point of reference for Somalilanders, even if domestic political confusion had become quite threatening at certain moments in time (e.g., in 2009 and 2010).

A related seventh and decisive factor was the protracted state collapse in the south that served as a strong warning to people in Somaliland (including those who did not favor an independent Somaliland) of what could happen if they gave up the minimal consensus about peace. The absence of stable state structures in Somalia made it impossible for Somaliland dissidents keen to unite Somalia to find serious negotiation partners in Mogadishu. Thus, Somaliland became like an orphan that had to fend for itself. This strengthened its survival skills.

An eighth and final factor is the armed confrontation with Puntland and oppositional clan militias in the east that contributed to Somaliland's development as a successful de facto state, which also cements its secession. Competing with the neighboring power and with local militias wanting to undermine Somaliland, the Hargeysa government was compelled to enforce its territorial claims and gain control of the border demarcating the state territory. This happened particularly in the Dhulbahante areas where, from the Somaliland perspective, Tilley's dictum that "war makes states" held true. Yet, it needs to be noted that not only war but also stable and effective administration and some development aid channeled from Hargeysa to the east helped to finally integrate people in Lasanod and surroundings into Somaliland.

The installation of a new government in Mogadishu in August 2012 and again in February 2017 changed the situation of Somaliland considerably. In contrast to Sudan/South Sudan,[86] where an international stance fostered the split of Sudan into two countries, the international community remains interested in a united Somali parent state. But this renewed focus on the south and continued ignoring of Somaliland by the international community is, after a brief period of shock in 2012, strengthening the secessionist attitude among Somalilanders. Somaliland remains an entity to be reckoned with.

References

Abokor, A., Bradbury, M., Hoyland, P., Kibble, S., & Ossiya, D. (2003). *Very much a Somaliland-run election. A report of the Somaliland local elections of December 2002.* London: CIIR Publications.

Aid Coordination Unit Office of Prime Minister Federal Republic of Somalia. (2017). *Aid flows in Somalia: Analysis of aid flow data.* Retrieved from https://reliefweb.int/report/somalia/aid-flows-somalia-analysis-aid-flow-data-april-2017

Anderson, B. (1983). *Imagined communities: Reflections on the origin and spread of nationalism.* London: Verso.

Anderson, D. M., & Browne, A. J. (2011). The politics of oil in eastern Africa. *Journal of Eastern African Studies, 5*(2), 369–410.

Balthasar, D. (2013). Somaliland's best kept secret: Shrewd politics and war projects as means of state-making. *Journal of Eastern African Studies, 7*(2), 218–238.

Bartkus, V. O. (1999). *Dynamics of secession.* Cambridge: Cambridge University Press.

Battera, F. (1999). *Remarks on the 1998 charter of the Puntland state of Somalia* (Working paper). United Nations Development Office for Somalia.

Bayart, J. F. (2000). Africa in the world: A history of extraversion. *African Affairs, 99*(395), 217–267.

---

[86] For an insightful comparative discussion of the case of Somaliland and the one of South Sudan, see Berekteab (2012).

Berekteab, R. (2012). *Self-determination and secessionism in Somaliland and South Sudan: Challenges to postcolonial state-building* (NAI discussion paper 75). Uppsala.

Bradbury, M. (1997). *Somaliland. CIIR country report.* London: Catholic Institute for International Relations.

Bradbury, M. (2008). *Becoming Somaliland.* London: James Currey.

Bryden, M. (1999). New hope for Somalia? The building block approach. *Review of African Political Economy, 26*(79), 134–140.

Bryden, M. (2004a). A state-within-a-failed-state: Is Somaliland headed for recognition or reunification? In P. Kingston & I. S. Spears (Eds.), *States-within-states: Incipient political entities in the post-Cold War era* (pp. 167–188). New York: Palgrave Macmillan.

Bryden, M. (2004b). Somalia and Somaliland: Envisioning a dialogue on the question of Somali unity. *African Security Review, 13*(2), 23–33.

Ciabarri, L. (2008). No representation without redistribution: Somaliland plural authorities, the search for a state and the 2005 parliamentary elections. In A. Bellagamba & G. Klute (Eds.), *Beside the state: Emergent powers in contemporary Africa* (pp. 55–73). Cologne: Ruediger Koeppe.

Collier, P., & Hoeffler, A. (2002). *The political economy of secession.* Washington, DC: World Bank.

Compagnon, D. (1992). Political decay in Somalia: From personal rule to warlordism. *Refuge, 12*(5), 8–13.

Compagnon, D. (1993). Somaliland, un ordre politique en gestation? *Politique africaine, 50*, 9–20.

Doornbos, M. (2000). When is a state a state? Exploring Puntland. In P. Konings, W. van Binsbergen, & G. Hesseling (Eds.), *Trajectoires de libération en Afrique contemporaire* (pp. 125–139). Paris: Karthala.

Drysdale, J. (1992). *Somaliland: The anatomy of secession.* London: Haan Associates Publishing.

Drysdale, J. (2000). *Stoics without pillows. A way forward for the Somalilands.* London: HAAN.

Eikenberg, K. (1995). Somaliland: Der konflikt in Hargeysa. *Informationen zum Horn von Afrika, 1*, 7–8.

Englebert, P., & Hummel, R. (2005). Let's stick together: Understanding Africa's secessionist deficit. *African Affairs, 104*(416), 399–427.

Farah, A. Y. (2001). Somalia: Modern history and the end of the 1990s. In War-Torn Societies Project (Ed.), *Rebuilding Somalia: Issues and possibilities for Puntland* (pp. 7–29). London: HAAN.

Farah, A. Y. (2004). *Troubled transition in Puntland state of Somalia (PSS), 1998–2001* (Unpublished manuscript). Nairobi: UNDP Resource Centre.

Hammond, L. (2013). *Family ties: Remittances and livelihoods support in Puntland and Somaliland*. Report commissioned by the Food Security and Nutrition Analysis Unit for Somalia.

Hansen, P. (2010). The ambiguity of khat in Somaliland. *Journal of Ethnopharmacology, 132*(3), 590–599.

Hansen, S. J., & Bradbury, M. (2007). Somaliland: A new democracy in the Horn of Africa? *Review of African Political Economy, 3*(113), 461–476.

Hechter, M. (1992). The dynamics of secession. *Acta Sociologica, 35,* 267–283.

Hoehne, M. V. (2006). Political identity, emerging state structures and conflict in northern Somalia. *Journal of Modern African Studies, 44*(3), 397–414.

Hoehne, M. V. (2007). *Puntland and Somaliland clashing in Northern Somalia: Who cuts the Gordian knot?* Retrieved from http://hornofafrica.ssrc.org/Hoehne

Hoehne, M. V. (2008). *Somalia: Update on the current situation (2006–2008)*. Bern: Schweizerische Flüchtlingshilfe SFH.

Hoehne, M. V. (2009). Mimesis and mimicry in dynamics of state and identity formation in northern Somalia. *Africa, 79*(2), 252–281.

Hoehne, M. V. (2011). Not born as a de facto state: Somaliland's complicated state formation. In R. Sharamo & B. Mesfin (Eds.), *Regional security in the post-Cold War Horn of Africa* (pp. 309–346). Pretoria: ISS.

Hoehne, M. V. (2014). Resource conflict and militant Islamism in the Golis Mountains in northern Somalia (2006–2012). *Review of African Political Economy, 41*(141), 358–373.

Hoehne, M. V. (2015). *Between Somaliland and Puntland: Marginalization, militarization and conflicting political visions*. Nairobi: Rift Valley Institute.

Hoehne, M. V. (2018). One country, two systems: Hybrid political orders (HPOs) and legal and political friction in Somaliland. In O. Zenker & M. V. Hoehne (Eds.), *The state and the paradox of customary law in Africa* (pp. 184–212). London: Routledge.

Horowitz, D. L. (1992). Irredentas and secessions: Adjacent phenomena, neglected connections. *International Journal of Comparative Sociology, 33*(1–2), 118–130.

Human Rights Watch. (2009). *Hostages to peace. Threats to human rights and democracy in Somaliland*. Retrieved from http://www.hrw.org/sites/default/files/reports/somaliland0709web.pdf

International Crisis Group. (2006). Somaliland: Time for African union leadership. *Africa Report, 110*. Retrieved from https://www.crisisgroup.org/africa/horn-africa/somalia/somaliland-time-african-union-leadership

International Republican Institute. (2005). *Somaliland: September 29, 2005 parliamentary elections assessment report*. Washington, DC: IRI.

Interpeace. (2006). *A vote for peace. How Somaliland successfully hosted its first parliamentary elections in 35 years.* Retrieved from http://www.interpeace. org/publications/cat_view/8-publications/12-somali-region?start=25

IRIN. (2013). *Debating reform of Somaliland's house of elders.* Retrieved from http://www.irinnews.org/news/(2013)/07/18/debating-reform-somaliland percentE2 percent80 percent99s-house-elders

Jenne, E. K., Saidman, S. M., & Lowe, W. (2007). Separatism as bargaining posture: The role of leverage in minority radicalization. *Journal of Peace Research, 44*(5), 539–558.

Jhazbhay, I. (2003). Somaliland: Africa's best kept secret, a challenge to the international community? *African Security Review, 12*(4), 77–82.

Kapteijns, L. (2013). *Clan cleansing in Somalia the ruinous legacy of 1991.* Pennsylvania: Pennsylvania University Press.

Lewis, I. M. (1994). *Blood and bone. The call of kinship in Somali society.* Lawrenceville: Red Sea Press.

Lindley, A. (2006). *Migrant remittances in the context of crisis in Somali society. A case study of Hargeisa.* London: Overseas Development Institute.

Menkhaus, K. (2009). The role and impact of the Somali diaspora in peacebuilding, governance and development. In R. Bardouille, M. Ndulo, & M. Grieco (Eds.), *Africa's finances: The role of remittances* (pp. 187–202). Newcastle: Oxford Scholars Publications.

Ministry of Foreign Affairs. (2002). *The case of Somaliland's international recognition as an independent state.* Hargeysa: Ministry of Foreign Affairs.

Pegg, S. (1998). *International society and the de facto state.* Aldershot: Ashgate.

Pegg, S., & Walls, M. (2018). Back on track? Somaliland after its 2017 presidential election. *African Affairs, 117*(467), 326–337.

Prunier, G. (1998). Somaliland goes it alone. *Current History, 97*(619), 225.

Reno, W. (2003). *Somalia and survival in the shadow of the global economy* (Queen Elisabeth House working paper no. 100). Oxford: University of Oxford.

Republican, issue 304, 17–23 July (2004).

Roethke, P. (2011). The right to secede under international law: The case of Somaliland. *Journal of International Service, 20*(2), 35–47.

Sanchez Bermudez, M. (2004). *Somaliland: Time for recognition.* Unpublished MA thesis. Irish Centre For Human Rights.

Schoiswohl, M. (2004). *Status and (human rights) obligations of non-recognized de facto regimes in international law: The case of Somaliland.* Leiden/Boston: Martinus Nijhoff Publishers.

Shinn, D. H. (2002). Somaliland: The little country that could. *CSIS Africa Notes, 9*, 1–7.

Somaliland Non State Actors Forum (SONSAF). (2011). *Somaliland elections review report,* 2011. Retrieved from http://www.somalilandlaw.com/ SOMALILAND_ELECTIONS_REVIEW_(2011).pdf

Terlinden, U. (2008). Emerging governance in Somaliland: A perspective from below. In E. M. Bruchhaus & M. M. Sommer (Eds.), *Hot spot Horn of Africa revisited* (pp. 51–67). Hamburg: Lit Verlag.

Terlinden, U., & Ibrahim, M. (2008). Making peace, rebuilding institutions: Somaliland – A success story? In A. Harneit-Sievers & D. Spilker (Eds.), *Promoting democracy under conditions of state fragility – Volume 2: Somalia.* Nairobi: Heinrich Böll Stiftung.

Tull, D. (2011). *Weak states and successful elites: Extraversion strategies in Africa.* SWP Research Paper 9. Retrieved from https://www.swp-berlin.org/fileadmin/contents/products/research_papers/(2011)_RP09_tll_ks.pdf

Vaughan, S. (2018). Ethiopia, Somalia and the Ogaden: Still the running sore at the heart of the Horn of Africa. In L. de Vries, P. Englebert, & M. Schomerus (Eds.), *Secessionism in African politics: Aspiration, grievance, performance, disenchantment.* New York: Palgrave.

Walls, M. (2014). *A Somali nation state: History, culture and Somaliland's political transition.* Pisa: Ponte Invisible.

PART III

Performance: Secessionism as Politics by Other Means

The Mouvement des Forces Démocratiques de Casamance: The Illusion of Separatism in Senegal?

Vincent Foucher

Introduction

On December 26, 1982, the Mouvement des Forces Démocratiques de Casamance (MFDC) voiced for the first time its demand for the independence of Casamance, the southern region of Senegal. This demand launched the longest, currently running violent conflict in Africa. The MFDC can thus lay claim to having led Africa's second "secessionist moment"[1] of the 1980s, after the first secessionist phase of the 1960s. Over the years, the Casamance conflict has killed several thousand people. It has been a discrete conflict though, with low-intensity violence and little of the extreme brutality that has made some African wars infamous. A peace process has been dragging on since 1991 and violence has waned. Over the past ten years, separatist guerrillas have been involved only in a

[1] Englebert and Hummel (2005: 421).

V. Foucher (✉)
Les Afriques dans le Monde, Centre National de la Recherche
Scientifique - Sciences-Po Bordeaux, Pessac, France
e-mail: v.foucher@sciencespobordeaux.fr

© The Author(s) 2019
L. de Vries et al. (eds.), *Secessionism in African Politics*,
Palgrave Series in African Borderlands Studies,
https://doi.org/10.1007/978-3-319-90206-7_10

handful of incidents. Has it all been an "illusory" separatism, as Englebert[2] puts it, a bargaining chip for local elites trying to renegotiate the terms of their incorporation to the Senegalese state and appropriate local institutions? Can this hypothesis be reconciled with the duration of the conflict?

To answer these questions, this chapter by and large follows the chronology, partly because so much is, in our times, in Casamance and elsewhere, about history: history lived and told, history forgotten and remembered, history discussed and disputed. As much as a history of Casamance, the first part provides a history of *the idea* of Casamance, how it was formed and transformed, up to the point when it could become the basis for a popular demand for separation. The second part discusses the "rest of the story," the complex interactions between the MFDC, the state, the communities, and the sub-regional environment since 1982.

Far from being the manifestation of an eternal essence, Casamançais separatism is the late-1970s recombination of an earlier elite regionalism with a sense of ethnic Diola identity. A key factor in this buildup has been the existence and influence of a literati class among the Diola, with its difficulties and debates about nation-statehood. This explains both the strong commitment of many separatists and the subdued character of the conflict, for the Senegalese state has been able to remain open to the Diola, making clear that the separatist option was just one of the many ways for Casamance to be.

A History of the Idea of Casamance

Nationalism, as Anderson and Gellner have both shown, is embedded in a specific form of historical consciousness.[3] This first part thus tries to give a sense of history of Casamance as it has been written by academics but also as it has been taken up (and re-crafted) from the late 1970s by the separatist narrative. Casamançais separatism is best understood as an essentialist recast of a tradition of elite regionalism by a larger and less dominant group, the growing number of Diola literati. In this social segment, where life choices and chances had been so much about the state, a weakening of that state stimulated reflections on history, statehood, and citizenship. Casamançais separatism is one such reflection, an attempt to imagine, with reference to the past, what a "proper" nation-state could look like.

[2] Englebert (2009: 156).
[3] Anderson (1991 [1983]) and Gellner (1983).

A HISTORY OF DIFFERENCE AND RESISTANCE?

As many current African political entities, neither Casamance nor Senegal had any pre-colonial existence: their borders were drawn in the nineteenth century through struggles and deals involving European powers and a host of African entities, from aristocratic states with slave armies to federations of villages. Before the arrival of the Europeans in the late fifteenth century, the area comprised between the Senegal River valley and current-day Guinea was the western march of the Mali Empire. Mali was a polycentric area over which Malinke rituals, trade networks, and language acted as fragile cement. The societies of the Atlantic Coast strove to escape tributary dependency. New nodes of power formed in the territories that now make North Senegal, while much of current-day Casamance was connected to another node, that of Kaabu, centered on the northeast of current-day Guinea-Bissau.[4] While Malinke and Fula ethnic identities have dominated Middle and Upper Casamance, respectively, an indication of a connection to the networks of Sahelian West Africa and the Malinke world, the swamps and forests of Lower Casamance lent themselves well to groups that kept a greater distance from Kaabunke influences. From the nineteenth century, these groups, which, unlike the Fula and Malinke, were entirely absent from North Senegal, were by and large subsumed by French ethnography under the exo-ethnonym of Diola, which they have since adopted.[5]

Until the late nineteenth century, it was the Portuguese who were most active along the Casamance river, which they named after one of the nearby kingdoms, that of the king (*mansa* in Malinke) of Kasa, a tributary of Kaabu. In 1645, they created the trade post of Ziguinchor. But they did not exert sovereignty over substantial tracts of land along the Casamance river in the seventeenth and eighteenth centuries. In the early nineteenth century, traders and administrators of the French colony of Senegal, then a scattering of trade posts along the coast of what is now North Senegal, started to look elsewhere. To the French coming from the

---

[4] On the Kaabu, see Barry (1988); and Lopes (1999). The author acknowledges the feedback on previous drafts of Séverine Awenengo, Mark Deets, Jean-Claude Marut, Marie-Emmanuelle Pommerolle, and Jordi Tomàs, as well as the comments of the anonymous reviewers.

[5] Portuguese ethnography used the ethnonym "Felupos," still in use in Guinea Bissau.

arid Senegalese north, Casamance and its better rainfalls and forests seemed to offer exciting opportunities, especially Lower Casamance and its productive indigenous rice cultivation and rubber trees. Thus was born the theme of Casamance as a wealthy area, a potential breadbasket for the rest of Senegal. France negotiated treaties of "alliance" and "protection" and built trade posts in Carabane and Sédhiou. They cut a deal with Portugal in 1886, taking over Ziguinchor but did not incorporate the British Gambia. As a result, while part of the colony of Senegal, Casamance was separated from it by The Gambia. Certainly, then as now, to those that look at a map and those that experience the crossing of The Gambia on the way to North Senegal, this outstanding geographical oddity has played a part in making separation thinkable.[6]

By the end of the nineteenth century, France set out to administer the Casamance river valley. This was not easy, particularly with the Diola of Lower Casamance, among whom social hierarchy then was limited and there were no strong, obvious elites to co-opt. Initial attempts to designate North Senegalese (*nordiste*) or Malinke colonial auxiliaries as administrative chiefs were not conclusive. The locals that were subsequently recruited struggled to establish credibility beyond their own village, oscillating between passivity and ruthlessness.[7] In the colony of Senegal, it was only among the Diola that French pressure on resources and manpower led to revolts during World War I.[8] During World War II, a handful of Diola villages revolted again, and the French suspected a young Diola prophetess, Aline Sitoé Diatta, who had established an influential rain cult. She was deported to, and died in, Timbuktu. What seems to have been a mistake on the part of the French lived on: in the 1970s, Aline Sitoé emerged as a symbol of resistance by both Senegalese leftist nationalists and Casamançais separatists.[9]

To the French officials, the Diola were "animist" and "primitive," a forest people without state and writing—not high on their Senegambian

---

[6] Defenders of a Casamançais difference note that Casamançais used to say "I am going to Senegal" when travelling from Casamance to Dakar (and some still do today), their adversaries point out that people from the Senegal river valley or Eastern Senegal say the same and have not asked for independence.

[7] Méguelle (2013).

[8] Roche (1985 [1976]).

[9] See Toliver-Diallo (2005); and Baum (2016).

civilizational ladder. Most of the Muslim and Christian auxiliaries of the French, often *nordiste* ethnic Wolof familiar with the European mores, were no less prejudiced. So Casamance was special in the mind of the French administration: its high development potential of course but also its strange geography, its remoteness, and Diola "culture" (though that culture was only one of several present in Casamance). On a number of occasions, French officials and traders called on the authorities to grant some autonomy, or even separation from Senegal.[10] But French policy never went beyond specific administrative structures at one moment or another: military administration, yes, or an *administrateur supérieur* devoted to Casamance, between the *commandants de cercle* and the governor of Senegal.

The Catholic Church too was thinking hard about Casamance, with more positive connotations. In the nineteenth century, operating from a North Senegal that was Islamizing fast, it began looking to the promising "animist" Diola of Lower Casamance. While critical of Diola "paganism," missionaries construed the image of moral and harmonious rural communities prone to convert to Catholicism. In 1939, Casamance was turned into an apostolic prefecture, separate from the vicariate of Dakar, and placed under the direction of one of the very first African bishops. This was an indication of the region's position in the imagination of the Church. That apostolic prefecture extended much further east than the administration's Casamance and included what are now the regions of Tambacounda and Kédougou, and their tiny animist groups, which were also "interesting" to the Church.

It is precisely this extended Casamance, "from the Atlantic to the Falémé river," that the leading separatist ideologue of the 1980s, a Diola Catholic priest, Father Augustin Diamacoune Senghor, came to adopt in his elaboration of Casamançais nationalism.[11] As many thinkers of Casamance, Church officials tended to talk of Casamance as a whole while often actually meaning the Diola-populated Lower Casamance.[12] The

---

[10] Lambert (1998; 589–591); Awenengo Dalberto (2005).

[11] Marut (2010: 58).

[12] Indeed, nowadays, it is the Kasa, the southwestern portion of Lower Casamance where Islam is the least strong and where traditional Diola religious institutions are at their strongest, which is seen as the real Casamance, a process which Marut (2005: 315) has aptly called a double reduction.

Church was eventually frustrated in its hopes, for in the late nineteenth and early twentieth century, many Diola brought back Islam from their time as migrant laborers on the groundnut fields of the Muslim Malinke in the British Gambia.[13] Today, the Catholics are a minority in Casamance, even among the Diola. The resentment of the Casamançais Catholic circles vis-à-vis the eventual triumph of Islam, which they perceived as backed by the colonial and postcolonial state, fed the construction of a Casamançais difference by the MFDC, though this must not be taken to mean that the separatist conflict is over religion.[14]

Another influence in early debates over Casamance was the "Portuguese" Mestizo elite of Ziguinchor. Initially unhappy with the French takeover, they were keen to gain autonomy for their city (rather than for Casamance) from the North Senegalese urban centers. Along with resident metropolitan French and a few Africans blessed with formal education or colonial favor, they enjoyed full citizenship, as opposed to the bulk of African *sujets*, who were subjected to a derogatory judicial code and to forced labor. Ziguinchor's *citoyens* petitioned and obtained from the administration a degree of autonomy for their municipality as early as 1907.[15]

The history of Casamance is thus one of late incorporation in the colony of Senegal. Unlike North Senegal, where contacts had been going on for centuries, Casamance had few points of connection to the French in the early colonial era. The Diola area stood out on this count, for in Middle and Upper Casamance, there were Fula and Malinke Muslim leaders with whom France eventually worked out deals. With the Diola, unmediated first encounters were often difficult.

Colonial perceptions of Casamançais difference, those of administrators, missionaries, and *nordiste* auxiliaries, formalized by locally influential French scholars such as historian Christian Roche and anthropologist

---

[13] Mark (1978).

[14] Contrary to what hasty analysts have argued, neither Casamance nor Lower Casamance host a majority of Catholic (and/or followers of a traditional African religion): just like in North Senegal, Muslims have long been a majority in Casamance, even among the Diola. No matter Father Diamacoune's leadership, the MFDC is a religious mix, just like Casamance itself, and has never declared itself against Islam. What is true is that Lower Casamance hosts one of the most significant Catholic (and "animist") minorities in Senegal. Foucher (2003).

[15] Trincaz (1984: 43).

Louis-Vincent Thomas,[16] have fed separatist intellectuals. Occasionally subverting the stigma, they have produced an essentialist narrative of difference, insisting the pre-colonial history and cultures of Casamance and North Senegal had little in common—a judgment that is as disputable as the reverse position.[17] They too have given a central part to the Diola, highlighting their egalitarian, acephalous culture, claiming that unlike most *nordiste* groups, they had no hierarchies (which is open to debate), had always refused to take part in the slave trade (which is wrong), and had always resisted conquest (which is too general).[18] The image of the self-reliant, moral, and fiercely independent Diola peasant has been the founding vignette of Casamançais nationalism. It has made a structural pair with a damning stereotype of the *nordistes* as disrespectful and lazy liars and profiteers, only too ready to collaborate with invaders.

As an echo of the inspiration it found in classificatory colonial ethnography, Casamançais nationalism claims to take root in nature itself. It draws a strong contrast between the pristine environment of Casamance as supposedly preserved by the Diola, the strong rainfalls, lush forests, and prosperous rice fields of its Guinean climate, and the desolate Sahel taken to typify North Senegal—supposedly the victim of its greedy inhabitants.[19] Separatist discourse has also been looking for, and unsurprisingly, finding,

---

[16] See Thomas (1958–1959) and C. Roche (1985 [1976]). Thomas' structuro-functionalism lends itself well to essentialism. Roche was the head of the Ziguinchor lycée in the early 1970s and his 1976 book on the conquest and resistance of Casamance has been a major source for the MFDC, providing some of its favorite quotes, such as Governor General Van Vollenhoven's complaint in 1917: "We are not the masters of Lower Casamance. We are only tolerated there."

[17] For a sample of MFDC discourse, see the commented separatist text in Darbon (1985).

[18] On slavery in pre-colonial Diola society, see Linares (1987) and Baum (1999). According to Baum, the acephalousness of Diola society noted from the nineteenth century could be the product of the fracturing of more hierarchical structures. The current existence of sets of villages falling under the ritual purview of certain "priests-kings" could be a vestige of these structures.

[19] The expression "Casamance naturelle" has been in wide use in the Senegalese parlance, especially since the division of the administrative region of Casamance in two and then three units (Ziguinchor and Kolda in 1984, and then Sédhiou in 2008). It testifies to the persistence, even in pro-Senegalese thought, of the sense of a Casamançais difference steeped in the natural environment.

validation in colonial history itself, claiming (wrongly) that France had administered Casamance separately from the colony of Senegal.[20]

The idea of a radical discontinuity between Lower Casamance and North Senegal has been central in the scholarly debate on Casamançais separatism. Darbon (1988) has thus identified the Diola's acephalous political culture as a cause for lasting connection problems. Diop and Diouf as well as Gasser have insisted that given the centrality of the "Islamo-Wolof model" in Senegal, the powerful combination of maraboutic Islam and business networks typical of the Wolof core that have dominated North Senegal and mediated with the state from the colonial times, the Diola are structurally on the losing end of statehood.[21] More recently, Boone has argued that the early colonial pattern of "administrative occupation," an authoritarian, unmediated, and unresponsive state, has endured in Lower Casamance, and is the reason for separatism.[22] There is no doubt that the experience of the state in Lower Casamance has been specific. But it would be a mistake to focus exclusively on the early days of the French presence: in the late colonial era, an educated Diola elite developed, operating in the Senegalese framework while developing a regionalist sensibility.

After 1945: Triumph of the Évolués and Birth of an Enduring Regionalist Sensibility

World War II was a political turning point as it saw the emancipation of the *sujets* in colonial Senegal. Until then, politics had been dominated by the minority African *citoyens* from the *Quatre Communes*, the four old sites of French presence in North Senegal—Dakar, Gorée, Saint-Louis, and Rufisque. The moderate Socialist Section Française de l'Internationale Ouvrière (SFIO) had been hegemonic. After 1945, provinces throughout Senegal took to defending their share against the *Quatre Communes*.

---

[20] In the framework of the OAU charter, the MFDC's claim makes sense: if indeed colonial borders are the basis for postcolonial states, it is important to be able to argue that Casamance and Senegal were separate in the colonial era. But Englebert and Hummel (2005: 419–420) are probably right in assuming that the colonial "evidence" is mobilized primarily to the benefit of an internal audience.

[21] Diop and Diouf (1990) and Gasser (2000).

[22] Boone (2003).

Among the Diola, a particularly large and influential new class of literati led this process.

Indeed, after the war, the young Diola became particularly interested in formal education. This seems to have to do with the intense "modernist anxiety" typical of those latecomers in colonial society analyzed in the neighboring Guinea by McGovern[23]: the communities that are construed as particularly primitive by the colonial power and that occupy the bottom of the colonial hierarchy of ethnic groups, such as the Loma in Guinea and the Diola in Senegal. These communities are "the Other's Other"—the other of the "civilized" indigenes of the *Quatre Communes* or the Muslim *nordistes*, in this instance, themselves already the other of the French. They can become particularly keen to catch up.[24]

In Lower Casamance, with the Catholic Church and the late colonial state at the ready to help, formal education offered relatively accessible opportunities. As early as 1955, about 10% of school classes in Senegal were found in Lower Casamance, which amounted to only about 5% of the population. Thirty years later, the region of Ziguinchor would have a 100% gross primary education rate, while the national average would be less than 60%.[25] This signifies an educational revolution, and it is perhaps here—rather than in the supposedly acephalous Diola political culture—where the real, or most politically relevant, difference of Lower Casamance lies.

In the booming 1950s cities of North Senegal, the arrival of the aspiring *évolués* from the "pagan" forests was not always easy. On their part, there was desire and resentment. And on the part of many *nordistes*, there were (and indeed still are) more or less negative stereotypes—the Diola as bizarre, rough, and somewhat threatening pagan primitives far removed from the Franco-Islamo-Wolof urbanity elaborated in the *Quatre Communes*.[26] There were cases of discrimination, humiliation, and contempt. But the 1950s were overall times of expansion, equalization, and

[23] McGovern (2013).

[24] It is remarkable that the one Diola community that had taken the lead in conversion to Islam and groundnut cultivation, the Buluf subgroup, also led the way in education and, later, in support for separatism.

[25] Foucher (2011: 88).

[26] Tomàs (2010: 155) gives a modern-day example of the persisting nordiste sense of centrality: a nordiste soldier reproaches an old Diola with having a bizarre Diola name, instead of a « classic » (to him), Muslim one....

Africanization of the colonial service, and many of the first Diola *évolués* made decent careers as state functionaries. They converted many Diola to what Anderson has called the secular "pilgrimages" of the state, the circulation in a new uniform nationalized space for formal education and state employment.[27]

The *évolués* became major influences in the villages, bringing new cultural practices (ballroom dancing, football, and theater) and taking care of *développement*: they raised funds and labor and lobbied the authorities to build new classes, taught summer schools, organized health centers, and kindergarten. They also tried to fight ritual female genital mutilation and the migration of young Diola women to Dakar.[28] Diola women had been engaged in urban employment for some time, usually as maids for the nascent bourgeoisie. Migration allowed them to escape the patriarchal order, assert autonomy, marry "out" or never quite, which was a situation deemed abject by the dignified *évolués*. But the latter's reservations had little impact, for the women were able to embed migration in the village communities. Still, the concern about female migration has remained a feature of Diola *évolué* thought, and grew more acute when the new Diola masculinity was called into question by the crisis of the Senegalese state pilgrimages.[29]

After 1945, the aspiring *évolués* throughout Senegal found their man: Léopold Sédar Senghor, a young ethnic Serer *nordiste* intellectual born a *sujet*.[30] In October 1948, he left the SFIO to create the Bloc Démocratique Sénégalais (BDS). He allied with the elites of former *sujets*, including a leading Diola *évolué*, Emile Badiane, who created in 1949 the MFDC, from which the current separatist movement draws its name.[31] The first MFDC fought not for separation but for proper political representation of Casamance in the new Senegalese public sphere, which meant that

---

[27] Anderson (1991).

[28] On female Diola migration, see among others Lambert (1999).

[29] Lambert (1999) and Foucher (2005).

[30] The homonymy with Father Diamacoune Senghor is a coincidence.

[31] Separatist history insists that the MFDC was created in March 1947, a date repeated since by most scholars. Séverine Awenengo, the most seasoned specialist of the late colonial Casamance, convincingly defends 1949. Perhaps the separatists were keen to establish that the first MFDC had been created before Senghor's BDS, and to allow for the inclusion in its history of a little-known figure, Victor Diatta, a Diola évolué mysteriously murdered in Dakar in 1948 and whom they see as an early martyr of their cause.

Casamançais should hold political office for Casamance instead of people identified to *Quatre Communes*.[32] In fact, it was SFIO adversaries of the MFDC that were the first Africans to voice the idea of separation of Casamance, in a desperate attempt to make up for their growing irrelevance in the region.[33]

In 1950, the MFDC formalized its alliance with the BDS. At the 1951 and 1952 elections, the BDS crushed the SFIO in Casamance as well as in the rest of Senegal except in, predictably, *Quatre Communes*. But Senghor's cooperation with the French authorities, his choice to get some Metropolitan French or *nordiste* allies elected on the "safe" Casamance lists, and his pressuring to merge the MFDC into the BDS progressively frustrated the younger left-leaning Casamance *évolués*.[34] In June 1955, those within the MFDC who insisted it should remain autonomous from BDS created a Mouvement Autonome de Casamance (MAC). The MAC picked Assane Seck as its leader, a young Casamançais academic with *nordiste* origins. MAC and SFIO joined forces for the 1956 elections, making some inroads in the city of Ziguinchor but losing badly in the region as a whole.

In 1958, when all French African territories were called to a referendum on immediate independence or participation in a community of states around France, the colonial administration and some Casamançais politicians discussed a separation of Casamance from Senegal should the Senegalese majority go for independence.[35] This eventuality remained unexplored, for Senegal voted a massive "yes" to the French community.[36]

---

[32] The distinction seems to have been a question of degree, for some Casamançais of known nordiste origin, like Ibou Diallo (born in Sédhiou in a family hailing from Saint-Louis), were MFDC figures, while others fought it.

[33] Amadou Lamine Daffé, a citoyen and SFIO leader from Sédhiou, suggested the separation of Casamance to the Senegalese Territorial Assembly in 1948. The idea was rejected and Daffé disappeared from politics. Daffé, a former policeman and a trader, has the profile to be the missing link between French and African reflections on a separation of Casamance. See Awenengo (2005) and Manga (2012).

[34] In 1954, under pressure from the young radicals, MFDC went for "affiliation" to BDS instead of the "integration" proposed by Badiane. But it stopped de facto to function as a separate entity.

[35] Awenengo (2005).

[36] Separatists have alleged that the "No" vote won a majority in Casamance, a claim taken up by hasty researchers. The "No" won only 2.2% of the votes in Senegal as a whole, and 7.4% in Casamance. It was concentrated in the city of Ziguinchor and its surroundings, but it did make some progress beyond.

While the episode does not necessarily testify to a strong Casamançais sense of difference from Senegal, it does show that a line existed that French officials could use. One has to note, however, that the French also broached the idea of separation with the autochthonous leaders of the Dakar peninsula. This secret plan was abandoned with little difficulty; the Casamançais figures involved did not mention it any further.[37]

It was from the anti-French side that the notion of a separation of Casamance was remobilized in the 1960s and early 1970s. In Casamance, as elsewhere in Senegal, the younger *évolués* were impatient with Senghor. Some supported Assane Seck, who now stood for the Parti de la Renaissance Africaine-Sénégal (PRA-S). Left-wing critics of Senghor looked to Sékou Touré, who had led neighboring French Guinea to independence in 1958 and supported the left-wing guerrilla of *Partido* Africano para a Independência da Guiné e Cabo Verde (PAIGC) in Portuguese Guinea, a tiny territory set between his own Guinea and Senegal. Touré's ambition, enmity toward Senghor, enthusiasm for African unity and leftist politics combined in talks of a fusion between the two Guineas and Casamance in a "Grande Guinée." In the 1960s and 1970s, there were a variety of discussions in elite leftist circles over a fusion of Casamance with The Gambia and/or the Guineas.[38]

The regionalist sensitivity remained, kept alive by former PRA-S figures, some of whom had rallied in 1966 Senghor's party (then called Union Progressiste Sénégalaise, UPS) that had absorbed all other legal parties. As early as 1970, a set of Casamançais literati around Mamadou Salim Cissé, a teacher at the Ziguinchor *lycée*, embarked on the creation of a new party, Sunu Gaal ("our canoe" in Wolof). Combining leftism with a sense of the interests of Casamance, they denounced the north-south "distomia."[39] They called not for separation but for equitable development between the

---

[37] Awenengo (forthcoming). It is probably confused memories of this episode that have come up in Father Diamacoune's hitherto undocumented claims that Badiane signed in 1960, a contract with Léopold Sédar Senghor to stay with Senegal, a contract he claims came to term in 1980. See introduction to Father Diamacoune in the following paragraphs.

[38] Awenengo (forthcoming).

[39] Centre des Archives Diplomatiques de Nantes, Fonds Dakar Ambassade 655, lettre manuscrite, Ziguinchor, le 2 novembre 1970, du Consul à Ziguinchor, Parandel, à Monsieur le Conseiller.

different regions.[40] Senghor was suspicious of Sunu Gaal's Casamançais roots and refused recognition. In 1974, the Sunu Gaal activists met with a *nordiste* lawyer, Abdoulaye Wade, also from the suppressed left. Together, they founded the Parti Démocratique Sénégalais (PDS), which became the first legal alternative party in Senegal since 1966.

A historically informed perspective thus shows that the Diola have not remained unconnected to the state. In fact, from World War II, they have engaged it more intensely than many communities in Senegal. This has been a key factor behind the particular strength of regionalism in Casamance since the late 1940s. The *évolués*, dependent on the state for education and employment, had expectations, a sense of common destiny, networks, and the "equipment" for politicization. Many were concerned with the imposition of non-Casamançais politicians in Casamance. Many were looking at Senegal primarily through its capital Dakar—often knowing the city from personal experience—and felt that Casamance was lagging behind. While they deployed a touchy sense of entitlement, they did not then seem interested in separation. In fact, it was the French who had first formulated the possibility of separation, an idea that then looked like a tactical move and did not quite capture imaginations in Casamance.

THE LATE 1970S: FROM REGIONALISM TO SEPARATISM

It was only in the late 1970s that Casamançais regionalism, under the influence of a wide array of forces, transformed into a separatist nationalism. The transformation happened under the guidance of a Diola core; the growing difficulties encountered by Diola *évolués* in their pilgrimages toward the state were a key element in this.

The 1970s were a time of trouble for Senegal. The ambitious developmental state dependent on dwindling groundnut exports could not cope with demographic growth and the mounting *demande sociale*. The exploration of alternative avenues for growth (through oil or improved rice cultivation) in Casamance produced little more than higher expectations and disappointment. There was a sense that pressure on local resources was growing along with frustration with the fact that *nordiste* migrants were coming to Casamance who were better equipped to profit through better access to capital and expertise in the retail trade, tourism, or fishing industries.

[40] Interview, founding member of Sunu Gaal, Dakar 2012–2013.

Some Casamançais denounced the "plunder" of Casamançais forests and rivers by *nordistes*. While Ziguinchor and portions of the coast were undergoing expropriations in the name of development, local officials, many of them *nordistes*, made things worse by giving kin and clients access to land. There were protests in Ziguinchor and around the seaside resort of Cap Skirring. A student strike at the Ziguinchor *lycée* in 1979–1980 witnessed civilians challenging police forces as well as the powerful public intervention of the Usana, pan-Diola female associations affiliated to pre-colonial Diola religion.

All this resonated with issues of political representation. The death of Badiane in 1972 and the resignation in 1980 of Senghor,[41] who was still viewed positively in rural Lower Casamance, did not help. The democratization initiated in 1974 had an impact too—Casamance is one of the early examples where democratization had an affinity with rising debates over autochthony.[42] There were intense factional struggles within the ruling UPS (which became Parti Socialiste, PS in 1976). The old PS Mestizo elites of Ziguinchor engaged in a bitter fight within the PS over the municipality in 1977, denouncing the new PS mayor, Mamadou Abdoulaye Sy—born in Ziguinchor from a *nordiste* Toucouleur father and a Diola mother—as a stranger. But the Mestizo were a dwindling demographic group and a losing force. More significantly, some of Sy's adversaries within PS used the autochthony argument to try and build a base among the growing number of Diola who were settling in Ziguinchor.

The late 1970s also witnessed the development of opposition parties. The opposition PDS was influential in Casamance, thanks to Sunu Gaal, and they too denounced the local authorities in Ziguinchor as strangers. There was no shortage of grievances in Casamance, and particularly in Ziguinchor, but it was almost exclusively Diola who came out in support of separation from Senegal. This has to do with that group's social and political history. As the 1970s went by, the Senegalese state proved increasingly unable to cater to their aspirations. To reduce education spending the state cut funding for boarding schools. These had hitherto been essential for the education of young Diola with limited connections in North Senegal. And the state could not provide civil service

---

[41] He resigned in December 1980 handing over power to his Prime Minister, Abdou Diouf.

[42] Bayart et al. (2001). Indeed, the democratization of the 1950s had had a comparable effect.

jobs for the growing number of educated Diola. For the Diola, who had collectively bet so much on education, this was terrible news.

Among the Diola migrant networks in Dakar and in France, separation began being debated seriously. In 1979, a number of Diola *évolués* based in France created the association Esukolal ("our place" in Diola). Among them, Mamadou Sané Nkrumah stood out: born in 1939, his quest for education had led him to France in 1967, having finished high school. A clerk at a Paris-based engineering school, he was involved in left-wing politics. From January 1981, Esukolal edited five issues of a journal, *Kelumak* ("the palaver tree" in Diola). It included educational material, an echo of the village summer schools. But it was primarily a celebration of Diola values, history, and heroes, and expressed a desire to rejuvenate Diola society and control female migration. It drew inspiration from the Catholic ethnography, then influenced by the theology of *inculturation*, which insisted the Church engage with traditional institutions and practices rather than fight them. The concomitant development of a cultural tourism that placed a high value on Diola identity played a part, too.

Esukolal reached out to Dakar and Casamance. In April 1982, on a visit to Casamance, Sané met with a number of PS and PDS politicians opposed to the local authorities, including Sanoune Bodian, a young Diola schoolteacher and PS supporter active in the land protests. He also met Father Diamacoune Senghor. Born in Casamance in 1928 and ordained in 1956, Diamacoune was a leading figure in the Catholic celebration of the Diola and their values, and ran a program on the local radio. He was also involved in local struggles, particularly in the defense of students.

Esukolal was gaining ground. In June 1982, it created a section in Dakar, and Mamadou Diémé, a cousin of Sané and technician at an academic institution, took over as the manager of *Kelumak*. More meetings were held in Ziguinchor, under the cover of the supporters of Casa Sport, the local football team. In the words of a participant:

> The Casa [Sport], it was just a cover. There, they woke the people up, they woke the history of Casamance up. Even in [post-colonial] schools, the history of Casamance would not be taught. But [in the colonial era] there were songs dedicated to Casamance that were sung at school, but these songs were forbidden [by the post-colonial state]. The Senegalese were coming here, to do just whatever they pleased, with the mayor here, a *nordiste*. That was what they talked about in the meetings.[43]

[43] Interview, MFDC militant, Ziguinchor (2000).

Plans were made to demonstrate in Ziguinchor. Despite the preventive arrest of most leaders, several hundred protesters assembled in a suburb of Ziguinchor on December 26, 1982. Unarmed, they reached the city center and flew a white flag at the governor's office. Leaflets calling for independence and the return of Aline Sitoé circulated. Only a few people were wounded. But on December 6, 1983, three *gendarmes* were killed during an intervention in an MFDC meeting near Ziguinchor. On December 18, 1983, militants marched again in Ziguinchor, this time with hunting rifles and machetes. It turned into a street battle, with possibly more than a hundred persons killed.

From the late 1970s, the idea of Casamance was dramatically recast: in lieu of the old *évolué* elites who had done well and had allied with Senghor, a younger generation of literati stood up, large in numbers and embittered. They recombined Casamançais elite regionalism with a culturalist discourse centered on the celebration of Diola identity and tradition. They owed too much to the earlier regionalist sensibility to drop Casamance as a reference altogether and focus on a purely Diola framing of the issue.[44] They were critical of the old *évolué* generation, the "Casamanqués" (a Diamacoune pun on the French "Casamançais manqués," failed Casamançais), accused of being sellouts. This discourse found powerful echoes in what were troubled times for the population of Ziguinchor and for the Diola *évolués*. In the quest for development and a responsive state, the defense of the representation of Casamance no longer sufficed. A separation from Senegal, founded on a sense of radical difference and a celebration of Diola identity, offered an alternative to those who felt they had none left.

SEPARATISM, THE STATE, AND THE COMMUNITIES SINCE 1983

It remains to be seen what has happened to the idea of Casamance after its violent entry on stage and how it has held up as the fundamental idea underpinning such a prolonged, but often discrete, struggle. This section gives a brief narrative of war and peace in the region and will then

---

[44] Lambert (1998: 587) hypothesizes that the MFDC insists that it is a Casamançais, not a Diola movement because of "an underlying distinction in African political ideology between nationalism and ethnicity," the former "modern" and good and the latter "backward" and bad. One could add that the MFDC cares for modernity precisely because it is a movement of the évolués.

discuss the dynamics within the MFDC and the attitude of the Senegalese state. The balance of forces, the lack of international support for the MFDC and the risks and costs of offensives for both sides all explain something of the peculiar turn of this conflict. But that turn owes a lot to the persisting ambivalence of Diola society itself vis-à-vis the separatist project and to the Senegalese state's capacity to play on this ambivalence.

A Brief History of War and Peace

In the face of repression, some militants took refuge in the forests between Ziguinchor and the Guinea-Bissau border. Armed with only bows and rifles, they remained on the defensive for years. Only in April 1990 did the MFDC's armed wing, Atika ("warrior" in Diola) launch its first assault, killing two customs officers by the Gambian border. More attacks on security forces and civil servants followed, as well as armed robberies against shops and passenger vehicles. Security forces came down hard, as Amnesty International noted in a series of reports.[45]

But the authorities also reached out, and on March 29, 1991, a ceasefire was signed. Negotiations in Guinea-Bissau failed, leading to a rift within the MFDC. Its senior military leader, Sidy Badji, and the guerrillas operating along the Gambian border (the recently created "Front Nord") honored the ceasefire, while "Front Sud" under Léopold Sagna resumed operations along the Guinea-Bissau border. Thousands of civilians took refuge beyond the borders or in the suburbs of Ziguinchor. Front Nord would stay out of the conflict for almost a decade, keeping its zone of control and weapons and receiving assistance for "development" from Dakar.

In April 1993, Diamacoune called for a ceasefire and asked for France's arbitration regarding the colonial boundaries of Casamance, leading the way to yet another shaky agreement on July 8, 1993. Because of his controversial contacts with state officials, Léopold Sagna was deposed by younger radical fighters, among whom emerged Salif Sadio as a leader. On December 21, a France-designated expert released a report that went against Diamacoune's claims that colonial Casamance had been administered separately from Senegal.[46] From 1995 to 1998, the southern front was rocked by violence, with significant losses for the Senegalese army.

---

[45] Amnesty International, La torture au Sénégal: Le cas de la Casamance, 23 May 1990.
[46] Charpy's report is accessible in Charpy (1994).

Front Sud fought Front Nord along the Gambian border. Calls for cease-fire and state initiatives for dialogue, reliant on MFDC moderates, failed. Front Sud witnessed growing tensions between Sadio's hardliners and others closer to Diamacoune.

When a conflict broke out in Guinea-Bissau between President Nino Vieira and his armed forces chief of staff General Ansumana Mané in June 1998, Senegal rushed to the defense of Vieira while Front Sud sent fighters to support Mané.[47] Mané prevailed in March 1999, and Front Sud intensified operations along both the Gambian and Bissau-Guinean borders. Mediation efforts opened the way for talks in The Gambia from June 1999 (the "Banjul process"), but the more radical Sané and Sadio were not involved and violence did not abate.

The election of Abdoulaye Wade as president of Senegal in March 2000, in one of the first democratic handovers of power in postcolonial Africa, was a game changer. Wade, who had committed to solving the conflict in 100 days, made drastic choices. He called into question past arrangements with Front Nord, forbid outside mediation efforts and tried to open direct routes to Front Sud. He cultivated Guinea-Bissau's new president, Kumba Yalá, who had tense relationships with Sadio's patron in Bissau, General Mané. With the killing of Mané in a conflict with Yalá in November 2000, Senegal secured a strong alliance in Bissau. The Bissau-Guinean army, with material support from Senegal, backed MFDC moderates against Sadio. In 2001, they captured his base in Kassolol. Many MFDC fighters died in this conflict, including Sagna himself, replaced by César Badiate. In 2006, Badiate and Bissau-Guinean troops launched a final assault on Sadio, who was forced to take refuge by the Gambian border.

The threat of the Bissau-Guinean army and Senegal's financial support tied Badiate to honoring a de facto ceasefire, but the Gambian border area went up in flames. An attempt by Gambian President Yahya Jammeh to reorganize the MFDC around Front Nord moderates in June 2001 only exposed their infighting. This was a step in a spectacular escalation between Wade and Jammeh, with Jammeh accusing Wade and Front Nord of involvement in a March 2006 failed coup attempt in The Gambia. Front Nord was torn apart: some rallied to Sadio and others to Badiate.

---

[47] Mané's coup was related to Casamance, for Mané rebelled because President Nino Vieira, who had become a close partner of Senegal, was under pressure to curb the arms trade to the MFDC, and blamed it on him.

Those were violent times in Northern Casamance. Wade had quickly dropped his policy of refusing mediation. A host of actors, NGOs, and politicians embarked on unequally serious mediation attempts and Senegalese money was finding its way to certain MFDC factions to broker local ceasefires. The moderates signed a peace agreement in December 2004, and more meetings followed. The death of Diamacoune in January 2007 left the MFDC even more rudderless. Sadio remained along the Gambian border with Jammeh's sympathy. As for Front Sud, it saw a new radical faction emerge in 2009, under Ousmane Gnantang Diatta. MFDC factionalism, which did lead to instances of localized, low-intensity violence, has continued ever since.

In the March 2012 presidential elections in which Macky Sall defeated Wade, Casamance was a major issue. Sall tried to mend bridges with Jammeh and committed himself to "real" negotiations, accepting an Italian Catholic organization, Sant'Egidio, as a facilitator.[48] For the first time ever, Sadio's faction entered into preliminary discussions, though real negotiations seem still a distant possibility. The downfall of Jammeh after the elections in The Gambia in 2016 and his replacement by new authorities very close to Senegal—all events in which Senegalese authorities played no small part—leaves Sadio in a more precarious situation than ever. There are now Senegalese troops on Gambian soil, and the long-awaited bridge on the Gambia river, a powerful symbol of the connection between Dakar and the Casamance, is finally being built. It remains to be seen whether this mounting pressure can push the MFDC to reunite. There have been a number of attacks—essentially on civilians—in 2018 by the other factions of the MFDC, which have supply issues and are vexed at Macky Sall's decision to focus negotiations on Sadio, but it is doubtful they can escalate.[49]

WEAKNESS AND RESILIENCE OF THE MFDC GUERRILLAS

Having fought—for three decades—a state that never collapsed and an army of relatively good standing, the MFDC has proven to be both weak and resilient. Protected by landmines and earthworks and drawing on the experience of veterans from the French and Senegalese army such as Badji and Sagna, the MFDC's guerrillas have kept control of forested areas

[48] Another nongovernmental organization, the Center for Humanitarian Dialogue, tried all the while to reach out to the other factions with Dakar's blessing, but failed.

[49] Badiate has a good relationship with the Front Nord moderates and has been mending bridges with Gnantang's faction, now led by Kompas Diatta. During the first semester of 2013, the Front Nord witnessed the creation of another faction led by Paul Ouloukassine Diatta.

between the tarmac roads crossing Lower Casamance and the borders with The Gambia and Guinea-Bissau. They have also been adept at hit-and-run operations elsewhere. Yet despite a number of attempts, they were never able to take control of the region's cities of Ziguinchor, Oussouye, and Bignona. This mix of weakness and resilience can largely be explained by the organizational history of the movement itself (Foucher 2007b).

The first thing of note is that the turn to arms was not planned but improvised by militants on the run. The movement fed on the desire of many to take revenge and protect themselves from state repression, which seemed to validate the MFDC's discourse about the ill treatment of Casamance. Separatists embarked on campaigns to spread the word and grow rural roots—tapes and tracts circulated and meetings were organized.[50] This discourse had concrete accents: the MFDC was offering prospects, talking of the positions and advantages that early supporters might obtain after independence. Some parents encouraged their children to join for that reason. Many took the 1991 ceasefire as a sign that the MFDC was indeed going somewhere.

The absence of planning meant that Atika started out with neither significant armament nor a resource base. While the 1990 offensive had to make do with a one-shot delivery of automatic weapons by Mauritania, which had had a run-in with Senegal in April 1989, international assistance to the separatists has remained scarce. Dakar has always been suspicious of its two small neighbors, The Gambia and Guinea-Bissau, both hosting Diola minorities. And it is true that the border areas have been essential for the guerrillas, which depend on refugees in both countries.[51] There have been moments of tension, for instance, when Senegalese and Bissau-Guinean troops exchanged fire over a border issue in 1990, or when Jammeh, himself a Diola, accused Dakar of involvement in a coup attempt against him in 2006.

Yet Banjul and Bissau realize Senegal's strength and have had a complex, transactional approach to the Casamance conflict.[52] In fact, Wade was able to clientelize the army of fragile Guinea-Bissau and have it put

[50] For a transcription of a rare mid-1980s recorded MFDC propaganda session, see Gasser (2000).

[51] See, respectively Evans and Ray (2012); and V. Foucher (2013).

[52] Senegal is a giant relative to its neighbors. It covers about 200,000 km2, Guinea-Bissau only 36,000, and the Gambia 11,300. Senegal counted 12.8 million inhabitants in 2011, Gambia 1.7 million inhabitants in 2008, and Guinea-Bissau 1.5 million in 2009.

pressure on the refugees, forcing Front Sud into a quasi-ceasefire.[53] Jammeh, president of the less fragile Gambia until his downfall in 2017, played a complex game of tension and appeasement with Dakar, often acting as a facilitator and knowing not to go too far.

With little foreign assistance, the MFDC had to improvise an economic base. Through the 1980s, activists practiced fundraising/requisition/banditry in the communities and fundraising in the diaspora. As time went by, stable frontlines were drawn. Front Sud, in collaboration with the refugees in Guinea-Bissau, exploited the abandoned lands, producing cannabis, palm oil and palm wine, game, and cashew nuts. Banditry against village shops and passenger vehicles was frequent. By the Gambian border, sustained violence came only after 2000, and the exodus of civilians was limited. Guerrillas there were established among communities, living off the taxation of the lively border trade with The Gambia, a country famous for its cheap consumer goods and demand for agricultural products such as milk, palm oil, charcoal, timber, and cannabis.[54]

Banditry became significant there, too, in the 2000s. For the guerrillas, life has been better nearer the Gambian border, possibly helping to make separatism an option for young Diola men with no better prospects. Fighters tend to marry much younger than other males, to take but one indication of their relative prosperity. This has allowed Atika to renew its troops somewhat, bringing in younger, more rural, less-educated men. But overall this has made for a war economy with low profits, limiting the MFDC's capacity to maintain and equip a large body of troops. Some guerrillas move between the bush and civilian life according to the situation on the ground. Estimates of the number of combatants are thus wild guesses, but at present, the various groups together probably count a few hundred active fighters in all.

This decentralized economy and the incapacity of the external wing and the internal political wing to durably finance the guerrillas have done much to fragment the MFDC. It has also fed the fighters' populist critique of the "politicals," held to be living abroad or in Ziguinchor in comfortable conditions (and sometimes indeed in Senegal's pay). It has allowed

[53] Instability in Guinea-Bissau has occasionally called Senegal's influence into question, and the emergence of Gnantang's more radical faction in 2009 may have had something to do with the killing of Dakar's favorite partners in Bissau.

[54] Indeed, some sources insist that cannabis producers in the Djibidione area did much to convince the MFDC to establish a base in their area, to keep the Senegalese security forces at bay.

the different military camps to keep away from one another, nourishing divisions. Radicals used to be content to consider as sellouts all those who had agreed to formal and informal ceasefires. While those adhering to informal ceasefires have indeed often benefited from state monies, they mention the movement's lack of resources, its weak offensive capability, tough living conditions in the bush, and the absence of prospects for independence as the real reasons for their restraint.

The war has so far not affected the fundamental Diola-ness of the MFDC, though some factions have with for now limited success tried to extend activities to the region of Kolda.[55] This may be because the MFDC owes so much to the history experienced and "written" by the Diola *évolués*. The state's criticism of the movement's ethnocentrism and its Diola-targeted repression may have contributed, too. While activists keep insisting on the MFDC's multi-ethnicity, one is still hard pressed to find its significant non-Diola figures.[56] As for the war itself, it has kept to what are now the administrative regions of Ziguinchor and Sédhiou, the area of Diola settlement.

A final trait resulting from the movement's organizational specificity is that the guerrillas have been embedded in certain communities. This has been a factor of resilience, while forcing the fighters to listen to civilian voices and "behave." There have been notable episodes of violence and abuse, including several massacres, against non-Casamançais civilians in the 1990s and early 2000s, resulting in their displacement. Over the same period, civilians associated with the state—chiefs or civil servants for instance—were often targeted. At times, civilians trying to collect wood or cashew nuts on MFDC-controlled territory have been attacked, sometimes gruesomely.[57] But by and large, Casamance guerrillas have abstained from the extreme abuses observed in many African conflicts: campaigns of rape or mutilation, or the use of child soldiers or sex slaves. Though "living with someone who has a weapon is never a good thing," guerrillas are

---

[55] There are indications that some Fula youth have joined though.

[56] One of the few names that come to mind is that of the now defunct military leader Vieux Faye, a Diola-ized Serer born by the Guinea-Bissau border. Some MFDC electronic communications are signed with patronyms identified with non-Diola groups, but these could be pseudonyms (http://www.members.tripod/casamance).

[57] The most notable massacres include those perpetrated in Pointe Saint-Georges and Cap Skirring in 1992, and in Bélaye and Niahoump in 2001. Each incident saw the death of a dozen or a few dozen people.

not a big cause for concern in many of the communities among which they are settled.[58] This special link has played a part in moderating the MFDC, especially when the Senegalese state proved able to maintain and even revamp its links with the population.

THE SENEGALESE STATE: STILL STANDING

Reactions of the Senegalese state have been a major variable in the MFDC's destiny. While there was no lack of repression, it is remarkable that dialogue was engaged and reforms made very early. As early as 1983, a new generation of Diola cadres was promoted and a review of land disputes launched. Casamance became a testing ground for decentralization. Following reports by Amnesty International, efforts were made in terms of human rights. Yet the real turning point came when Wade stuck to a cautious, less aggressive use of the military, which was rather well symbolized by his decision to designate a Diola as a minister of the Armed Forces.

More important still is that the separatists could never call into question the survival of the state, nor its existing connections to the Diola. The Diola have been a massive presence in Dakar and other *nordiste* cities since the 1960s, and the war and its damages to the regional economy have probably led more Diola north. While there were some investigations and arrests among the Diola diaspora, the state did not let this escalate into systematic discrimination. It made sure for instance that, while the Senegalese press maintained a loyalist stand, it did not feed the hatred against the Diola. Overall, the Diola were able to keep experiencing "Senegality," study, come to Dakar, marry outside of their community, serve in the army, and so forth. While many North Senegalese stick to the stereotype that all Diola are rebels (indeed, this is frequent joke when a *nordiste* meets a Diola), the debate over separation has been running within Diola society itself, with many embracing, or at least bearing with, Senegal as their country.[59]

---

[58] Interview, female civilian resident of a Front Nord controlled area, district of Bignona (2004) and personal communication from Rudolf (2013).

[59] Lambert (1998) and Foucher (2011). Tomàs (2010) notes that the MFDC had difficulties getting purchase in areas of the Diola subregion of Huluf because people there bore with Senegal but had little interest in an alternative. Interestingly, that sub-region was long one of the least affected by the "modernist anxiety."

Since Wade's time, as the economy has recovered and donors have grown more supportive, the state has been able to revamp the old dreams of "development" in Casamance. There have been a lot of unfulfilled promises, but a public university was opened in Ziguinchor, as were many new schools and high schools in villages. Civil service has recruited and improved wages and conditions. An effort has been made at rural electrification. No surprise, then, that between this and the lull in the conflict, President Wade fared well in Casamance in all elections, including in the election that resulted in his defeat in 2012. The MFDC has been losing some of its relevance in a country that has been feeling a bit better, in a region whose economy has been upset by the conflict and where many have been experiencing Senegal as something relatively positive. NGOs and local associations, buoyed by the boost in aid, have been busy "developing" Casamance and creating links with the guerrillas to secure access and negotiate local ceasefires.

Efforts have not infrequently taken a cultural form, with some actors drawing on international and government support to mount symbolic counterattacks. With different degrees of sincerity, authenticity, and impact, initiatives have insisted on the ethnic variety of Casamance or have pointed to the mythical kinship between the Diola and the North Senegalese Serer. Casamançais icons have been included in the Senegalese pantheon and community institutions drawn into the peace process.[60] The priest-kings, typical of certain Diola groups, have come to be recognized and courted by the state and politicians, being treated somewhat as equivalents of the marabouts of North Senegal. These efforts have called into question both the idea of a radical Casamançais difference from North Senegal and that of the unanimity of the people of Casamance behind separatism. Rather more than a cause of the lull, these efforts have been the language in which the mounting popular sentiment that the conflict should end and that Senegal was not such a bad option found expression.

The debate is present among the fighters themselves, even among the most radical groups. Militants are struggling with their faith, hope, and commitment to an independent Casamance; the sustainability and relative lack of danger of armed militancy; lack of prospects for victory; and the

---

[60] On the uses of and controversies around the Serer-Diola kinship, see de Jong (2005); and Smith (2010, chap. 10 & 11); on the Usana and other traditional religious institutions, see Foucher (2007a).

vagueness of alternatives. While most affirm their separatist belief in the company of fellow separatists, many express doubts in private. Some ask outside interlocutors for advice, or even for a way out.[61]

The state's revival since 2000 has boosted its structural sense of superiority. There are indeed reasons to believe that Dakar is tempted to push its advantage and count on the decay of the MFDC and waning of its popular support, instead of engaging in uncertain and uneasy negotiations.[62]

CONCLUSION

The history of Casamance is a history of late inclusion into the Senegalese ensemble; this did much to construe the Casamançais and particularly the Diola as an Other in the Senegalese space. But some integration did take place, especially after World War II. The Senegalese state and the cities of North Senegal became meaningful loci for the Diola, thanks to education, migration, and public employment. Precisely because the Senegalese state was meaningful, its faltering in the late 1970s made many Diola rethink about statehood seriously. Some came to the conclusion that a separate state was best. The force of the separatist resentment and the sincerity of the commitment of many of its supporters mirrored how powerful the dream was that the Senegalese state stimulated among the Diola. Incidentally, the case of Casamance confirms the connection that exists between nationalism and the experience (good and bad) of the secular pilgrimages organized by the state. Formal education is a process with huge moral and material consequences.

In an exercise in selective history writing, separatists built on networks of Diola literati well-equipped to receive a new nationalist project, infusing a tradition of elite regionalism with a new sense of difference nourished by Diola culturalism. This explains why some local elites have associated with the MFDC in one way or another. But the second MFDC, the separatist MFDC, was never of the elites. It is in part the result of turning education into a mass product—and with that devaluing it. The leaders of the separatist MFDC were, logically enough, clerks, schoolteachers, and a Catholic priest.

---

[61] An experience repeatedly made by the author of the present text, and humanitarian workers and journalists.
[62] Marut (2010: chap. 7).

A movement from below, the MFDC has operated with a millenarian sincerity—a belief that fundamental social change will happen—that may not find an easy answer in institutional reform. Attempts by Casamançais elites to promote decentralization and autonomy as solutions have been seen as self-serving by Senegalese officials but also by MFDC. The defense of Casamançais identity has been endowed with a post-political capacity to redress wrongs, incarnate justice into the world, and create a seamless community. With the ambiguity of all things millenarian, Casamançais identity has been tasked to satisfy the material hopes of the Diola *évolués* and their families. Personal gain and collective hopes are not easily distinguished in these situations. The almost obsessive nationalist passion with which some militants still talk after 30 years is too strong to be discarded as illusory. This explains why the MFDC has not quite stopped while the local elites have been keen for it to do so.

The MFDC's roots also explain why it has been forced to hear the voices of the Diola communities. Since these communities, after the initial shock of violence, by and large worked out that Senegal was still providing an alley for much of their moral and material aspirations, the separatist cause has been locked in impossibility. The balance of forces is now more than ever in Senegal's favor, but there are still uncertainties: will Senegal engage at last in credible negotiations? Could the unpredictable internal politics of The Gambia and Guinea-Bissau affect the balance of forces in Casamance? Can separatism get purchase beyond its Diola core? Can the state sustain its essentially economic approach to the situation? How will all this affect the sense of Casamançais identity in the new generations with access to higher education, whether it be at the University of Ziguinchor or in the growing international Diola diaspora? A new wave of Casamançais separatism, while unlikely, cannot be ruled out altogether.

References

Anderson, B. (1991). *Imagined communities. Reflections on the origin and spread of nationalism.* London: Verso.

Awenengo Dalberto, S. (2005). *Les Joola, la Casamance et l'État (1890–2004). L'identisation joola au Sénégal.* Doctoral dissertation, Université Paris VII.

Awenengo Dalberto, S. (forthcoming). Hidden debates about the status of Casamance in the decolonization process: Regionalism, territorialism and federalism at a crossroads in Senegal. In S. Awenengo Dalberto & C. Lefèvre (Eds.), *Tracing uncertainty: Boundaries, territoriality and decolonization in Africa.*

Barry, B. (1988). *La Sénégambie du XVe au XIXe siècle. Traite négrière, islam et conquête colonial.* Paris: L'Harmattan.

Baum, R. M. (1999). *Shrines of the slave-trade. Diola religion and society in pre-colonial Senegambia.* Oxford: Oxford University Press.

Baum, R. M. (2016). *West Africa's women of God: Alinesitoué and the Diola prophetic tradition.* Indiana University Press.

Bayart, J.-F., Geschiere, P., & Nyamnjoh, F. (2001). Autochtonie, démocratie et citoyenneté en Afrique. *Critique internationale, 10,* 177–194.

Boone, C. (2003). *Political topographies of the African state. Territorial authority and institutional choice.* Cambridge: Cambridge University Press.

Charpy, J. (1994). Casamance et Sénégal au temps de la colonisation française. In F.-G. Barbier-Wiesser (Ed.), *Comprendre la Casamance. Chronique d'une intégration contrastée* (pp. 475–500). Paris: Karthala.

Darbon, D. (1985). La voix de la Casamance... une parole diola. *Politique Africaine, 18,* 125–138.

Darbon, D. (1988). *L'administration et le paysan en Casamance.* Paris: Pédone.

de Jong, F. (2005). A joking nation: Conflict resolution in Senegal. *Canadian Journal of African Studies, 39*(2), 389–413.

Diop, M. C., & Diouf, M. (1990). *Le Sénégal sous Abdou Diouf. Etat et société.* Paris: Karthala.

Englebert, P. (2009). *Africa: Unity, sovereignty and sorrow.* Boulder: Lynne Rienner.

Englebert, P., & Hummel, R. (2005). Let's stick together: Understanding Africa's secessionist deficit. *African Affairs, 104*(416), 399–427.

Evans, M., & Ray, C. (2012). Uncertain ground: The Gambia and the Casamance conflict. In A. Saine, E. Cessay, & E. Sall (Eds.), *State and society in the Gambia since independence 1965–2012.* Trenton: Africa World Press.

Foucher, V. (2003). Church and nation: The Catholic contribution to war and peace in Casamance. *Le Fait Missionnaire, 13,* 7–40.

Foucher, V. (2005). Les relations hommes-femmes et la formation de l'identité casamançaise. *Cahiers d'études africaines, 178,* 431–455.

Foucher, V. (2007a). Tradition africaine' et résolution des conflits. Un exemple sénégalais. *Politix, 80,* 59–80.

Foucher, V. (2007b). Senegal. The resilient weakness of Casamançais separatists. In K. Dunn & M. Boas (Eds.), *African guerrillas. Raging against the machine* (pp. 171–197). Boulder: Lynne Rienner.

Foucher, V. (2011). On the matter (and materiality) of the nation: Interpreting Casamance's unresolved separatist struggle. *Studies in Ethnicity and Nationalism, 11*(1), 82–103.

Foucher, V. (2013). Wade's Senegal and its relations with Guinea-Bissau: Brother, patron or regional hegemon? Johannesburg: South African Institute of International Affairs, Occasional Paper 132.

Gasser, G. (2000). *'Manger ou s'en aller':* Le conflit ethnorégional casamançais et l'État sénégalais. PhD dissertation, Université de Montréal.

Gellner, E. (1983). *Nations and nationalism.* Ithaca: Cornell University Press.

Lambert, M. C. (1998). Violence and the war of words: Ethnicity v. nationalism in the Casamance. *Africa, 68*(4), 585–602.

Lambert, M. C. (1999). Have Jola women found a way to resist patriarchy with commodities? (Senegal, West Africa). *Political and Legal Anthropology Review, 22*(1), 85–93.

Linares, O. (1987). Deferring to trade in slaves: The Jola of Casamance, Senegal, in historical perspective. *History in Africa, 14,* 113–139.

Lopes, C. (1999). *Kaabunke: Espaço, territorio e poder na Guine-Bissau, Gambia e Casamance pre-coloniais.* Lisbon: Comissão Nacional para as Comemoracões dos Descobrimentos Portuguêses.

Manga, M. L. (2012). *La Casamance dans l'histoire contemporaine du Sénégal.* Paris: L'Harmattan.

Mark, P. (1978). Urban migration, cash cropping and calamity: The spread of Islam among the Diola of Boulouf (Senegal), 1900–1940. *African Studies Review, 21*(2), 1–14.

Marut. (2005). Marut's is Jean-Claude Marut, La question de Casamance (Sénégal). Une analyse géopolitique, thèse de doctorat, Paris, Université de Paris 8, 1999.

Marut, J.-C. (2010). *Le conflit de Casamance. Ce que disent les armes.* Paris: Karthala.

McGovern, M. (2013). *Unmasking the state. Making Guinea modern.* Chicago: Chicago University Press.

Méguelle, P. (2013). *Chefferie coloniale et égalitarisme diola. Les difficultés de la politique indigène de la France en basse-Casamance (Sénégal), 1828–1923.* Paris: L'Harmattan.

Roche, C. (1976). *Histoire de la Casamance. Conquête et résistance (1850–1920).* Paris: Karthala.

Smith, E. (2010). *Des arts de faire société: parentés à plaisanteries et constructions identitaires en Afrique de l'Ouest (Sénégal).* Doctoral dissertation, Institut d'Etudes Politiques de Paris.

Thomas, L.-V. (1958). *Les Diola, essai d'analyse fonctionnelle sur une population de Basse-Casamance.* Dakar: IFAN.

Toliver-Diallo, W. (2005). 'The woman who was more than a man': Making Aline Sitoe Diatta into a national heroine in Senegal. *Canadian Journal of African Studies, 39*(2), 338–360.

Tomàs, J. (2010). Casamance: el particularismo inquietante. In J. Tomàs (Ed.), *Secesionismo en África* (pp. 129–166). Barcelona: Bellaterra.

Trincaz, P.-X. (1984). *Colonisation et régionalisme: Ziguinchor en Casamance.* Paris: Orstom.

CHAPTER 11

United in Separation? Lozi Secessionism in Zambia and Namibia

Wolfgang Zeller and Henning Melber

INTRODUCTION

The Lozi-Barotse[1] kingdom was colonized and partitioned by Britain, Germany, and Portugal from the late nineteenth century onwards. Its political and economic heartland along the floodplains of the upper Zambezi fell under British rule in 1890. Until Zambian independence in

---

[1] The terms Lozi and Barotse are synonymous.

W. Zeller (✉)
Centre of African Studies, University of Edinburgh, Edinburgh, UK
e-mail: wolfgang.zeller@ed.ac.uk

H. Melber
Nordic Africa Institute, Uppsala, Sweden

Department of Political Sciences, University of Pretoria, Pretoria, South Africa

Centre for Africa Studies, University of the Free State in Bloemfontein, Bloemfontein, South Africa

Centre for Commonwealth Studies/School for Advanced Study, University of London, London, UK
e-mail: Henning.Melber@nai.uu.se

© The Author(s) 2019
L. de Vries et al. (eds.), *Secessionism in African Politics*,
Palgrave Series in African Borderlands Studies,
https://doi.org/10.1007/978-3-319-90206-7_11

293

1964, the territory was administered under the name Barotseland as a more or less integral part of the colony of Northern Rhodesia. In 1969, Barotseland was renamed the Western Province of Zambia. The German— and after 1914, British—and South African-ruled part of the former Lozi kingdom became the Caprivi Region of Namibia at independence in 1990. In August 2013, the Namibian government announced a name change to Zambezi Region.

Western Province and the Zambezi Region have more in common than their shared language Lozi, their pre-colonial Lozi history, and the Zambezi River, which demarcates most of the shared border of the two sovereign states of which they are part. Both areas have given rise to separatist movements. Short-lived incidents of militant secessionist action have constituted major national crises in both postcolonial Zambia and Namibia. This chapter compares the cases of Lozi separatism.

In the run-up to Zambian independence, the British government, the Lozi leadership, and the Zambian transitional government signed the 1964 Barotseland Agreement. The treaty spelled out the terms under which Barotseland would be incorporated into the Republic of Zambia. It was to be a province with far-reaching autonomy and special powers for the *Litunga* (the Lozi King) and his elaborate administrative apparatus of *induna* (headmen) assembling in various *kuta* (formal decision-making councils of headmen) on regional and local levels under the heading of the Barotse Royal Establishment (BRE).

In 1969, Zambia's ruling United National Independence Party (UNIP) under President Kenneth Kaunda decreed to change the name of the territory to Western Province. Since Kaunda's government had also reversed most of the special regulations in the 1964 agreement soon after Zambia's independence, the Lozi leadership was perturbed. Kaunda's actions found some support among the younger generation of Lozi migrants who had left Barotseland to work in the mines and urban centers of Southern Africa and who had adopted the Zambian nationalist stance represented by Kaunda's UNIP.

From the BRE's point of view, however, Kaunda's moves were an open abrogation of a legally binding treaty, causing irreparable damage to the good faith in which they had voluntarily signed the 1964 agreement. Since then, the Lozi leadership has consistently demanded more political autonomy and the reinstatement of the 1964 agreement. That itself is not a secessionist demand. However, politically radical minority groups among the Lozi have openly argued for the secession of Barotseland/Western

Province from Zambia as a measure of last resort. The majority of the Lozi leadership, including their radical factions, explicitly wish for Barotseland to secede peacefully. The Lozi argument has consistently been legalistic: they insist on the contractual facts (and their own interpretation) of the 1964 agreement. But the secessionist claim has also been underlined by, so far, two instances of crisis within the mainstream of the BRE, reaching all the way to its most senior councilor *Ngambela*.[2]

In the Caprivi Region, a secessionist movement gained momentum in the mid-1990s, and on August 2, 1999, a radical core group launched an armed attack against Namibian government installations in Caprivi. The movement's mastermind, Mishake Muyongo—along with other leading members—belongs to a lineage of regional headmen originally appointed by *Litunga* Lewanika in the 1880s to administer this peripheral but strategically important former province of the Lozi kingdom. As one aspect of their self-legitimization, Muyongo and his associates have consistently highlighted what they call cultural and historical differences of the ethnic groups inhabiting the rest of Namibia. They make this point especially regarding the Oshivambo-speaking majority, which constitutes the bedrock support for Namibia's ruling party, the former liberation movement South West African People Organisation (SWAPO).[3]

The Caprivi secessionists thus used implicit references to Lozi history for their own political ends. They did not succeed in establishing an independent state of Caprivi; the Namibian security forces quickly and violently crushed rather pedestrian actions of August 1999. The secessionist leaders have since died, fled into exile, or been put on trial for high treason in Namibian court cases bogged down by endless technicalities. But the issues that drove Caprivi secessionism have continued to stir debate and political confrontation in Namibia. Fifteen people died due to combat action during the Caprivi secessionist attacks in August 1999;[4] detention deaths during the ensuing trials exceeded this number. The attacks constitute Namibia's most severe national political post-independence crisis, leading to the first and only declaration of a state of emergency.

---

[2] In the Lozi administrative hierarchy the *Ngambela* is the most senior councilor who communicates decisions between the *Litunga* and the *khuta*, as well as the public. In obvious relation to the Westminster Model, he is often referred to as "Prime Minister."

[3] United Democratic Party (2005).

[4] The exact number is disputed but this is the verifiable minimum number of casualties.

Two Stories: Comparing the Western Province and Caprivi Region

Size and population in Zambia's Western Province is roughly ten times that of Namibia's Caprivi, but both are home to a similar share of the nation's overall population. Both territories are geostrategically and socio-economically important to their countries, regarding particularly access to transport, water, timber, and arable land. The following table usefully compares and gauges the respective national significance.[5]

Overview

	Lozi area in km²	Lozi % of national area	Lozi population	Lozi % of national population
Western Province/former Barotseland (Zambia)	126,386	16.8%	881,524	6.8%
Caprivi Region (Namibia)	14,785	1.8%	90,100	4.2%

Is Lozi separatism in Zambia and Namibia evidence that a people divided by colonial boundary- and state making has, in the postcolonial period, reunited to oppose enclosure of its ancestral lands by two independent states? Are both separatist movements at least partially motivated by a shared wish to reestablish the greater Lozi kingdom? We do not think so, which is why we feel that a comparison is valuable. Both cases have precolonial roots in the former Lozi kingdom. They share the experience of being partitioned—from different colonial powers but by the same boundary—and of indirect rule through hierarchically organized Lozi-speaking authorities in the area. The borderland population continues to have close kinship ties today.

Yet in our view, supposedly deep-rooted ethnic or tribal identities and grievances, which are often cited as reasons for the radicalization of political opposition in Africa,[6] do not offer an adequate framework to understand and compare separatism in these two parts of the former Lozi kingdom. We identify four major differences that offer an explanation why—despite their shared roots—the two separatist movements have not developed a united cause of pan-Lozi nationalism.

[5] WP: 2010 Zambia national census; Caprivi: 2011 Population and Housing Census.
[6] Cf. Lemarchand (1972) and Eifert et al. (2010).

1. Differences in status of what is now Western Province and the Caprivi/Zambezi Region in the pre-colonial period of the Lozi kingdom and the consolidation of this difference by colonial boundary making and administration.
2. Differences in times and circumstances of the processes of decolonization in Zambia and Namibia, and related to these, differences in secessionists' claims of "betrayal" by their respective postcolonial governments.
3. Differences in regional and national politics in the postcolonial era for each case with different roles of the local actors in or vis-à-vis the central state.
4. Differences in the way the postcolonial state authorities in both countries have reacted to expressions of separatist agendas at different times.

Those with a separatist agenda on both sides have never united behind a pan-Lozi secessionist cause because they involve descendants of rather different people arguing over fundamentally different issues at different times and under different circumstances. The two cases we examine tell two distinct stories of opposition against postcolonial state formation, despite shared roots in one single case of pre-colonial African statehood.

In both cases, central actors of the respective secessionist movements derive some or most of their legitimacy from claims to represent traditional authority. We give some background on the relevance of these claims; a detailed debate on traditional authority in general or in Caprivi and Western Province can be found in the literature.[7] Our use of the term "traditional" throughout this chapter incorporates the element of creative (re)invention of so-called tradition by actors with vested interests; this also means that these actors expressively understand themselves as both representing continuity of the past and as being able to evolve and adapt in the present.[8]

This chapter first outlines the historical processes through which the Lozi kingdom was partitioned and gradually transformed into Barotseland and the Caprivi Strip during the colonial period. We then examine how decolonization planted the seeds of Lozi separatism in Western Province and the secessionist movement in Caprivi, and how both evolved after

[7] cf. Zeller (2007a, b, 2009, 2010) and Melber (2009).
[8] Hobsbawm and Ranger (1983), Mamdani (1996) and Forrest (2004).

Zambia's and Namibia's independence. The final section traces the initial thawing and renewed freezing of relations between successive central governments and separatists in the Zambian case. For Namibia, it looks at the aftermath of the 1999 attacks, Caprivi's 2002 unrecognized declaration of secession from Namibia, the high treason trial, and further contestations that continue until today.

THE BIRTH OF THE KINGDOM IN THE FLOODPLAIN

Territories outside Zambia's Western Province, in particular, Western Angola and Northeastern Namibia, have previously been under the waxing and waning rule of Bulozi (the Lozi kingdom) to a considerable though varying extent. Lozi oral history and current scholarship locate the origins of their ancestors among the Luyi people of the Katanga Region of present-day Democratic Republic of Congo (DRC). From there, a seventeenth- to eighteenth-century migration led the Luyi groups to the upper Zambezi's fertile floodplains, which could support a relatively high population density. Through military defeat and assimilation of other population groups living in the floodplain and its hinterlands, the kingdom gradually grew into a complex patchwork of intermarried kinship and language groups. Some were masters; some were servants with varying degrees of status and loyalty to one or several competing Luyana power centers in the floodplains. From there, the Luyana kings steered an increasingly sophisticated political economy through an elaborate network of senior chiefs and their councilors.[9]

An invasion by the Kololo people reached the Luyana kingdom in the early 1840s, resulting in political and cultural cross-fertilization from which the root of the Lozi kingdom and its lingua franca Silozi emerged. After the demise of the Kololo in the 1860s, Bulozi remained in turmoil for the next two decades. In 1884, however, Lubosi Lewanika, born into one of the Luyana royal lineages, emerged as a strong and ruthless leader. Having killed his main rivals, Lewanika embarked on an elaborate project of administrative reforms and careful crafting of a unified Lozi nation and state—with himself as the sole, centralized, and sovereign *Litunga*.[10]

Trade, tribute, slave labor, and raids on the kingdom's peripheral groups could not sustain the cost of the sprawling administrative system

---

[9] Mainga (1973), Caplan (1970), Gluckman (1959), Trollope (1937: 19) and Flint (2003).
[10] Gluckman (1955, 1965). See also Sumbwa (2000).

and royal grandeur for long. By the late 1880s, Barotse royalty increasingly relied on goods, revenue, and skills acquired from European traders, frontiersmen, and missionaries in exchange for hides, ivory, and the granting of permanent settlements.[11] Bulozi's volatile southern provinces Sesheke and Linyanti gained importance as a gateway for the Lozis engaging the Europeans and their entrepreneurial, technological, and military resources.[12] Lewanika's administrative arrangements to secure these strategic areas were robust: he placed allies into important towns. In Linyanti, inside what is today the Caprivi/Zambezi Region, tried and tested ally Simataa Kabende Mamili was in charge; Mwandi in Western Province's Sesheke District was given to his son Letia.

Engaging the Europeans: British and German Interests in Bulozi

Following the counsel of French missionary Francois Coillard, on June 27, 1890, Lewanika signed a treaty with Frank Lochner, an agent of Cecil Rhodes' British South Africa Company (BSAC). The so-called Lochner Concession was later amended by several follow-up contracts with more lenient conditions than the BSAC offered any other indigenous rulers in what is present-day Zambia.[13] Bulozi became a British protectorate exempted from white settlement and with a large degree of autonomy in administration and taxation.[14] BSAC's resources were thinly spread across Southern Africa, and diplomacy was a more realistic strategy than coercion. Rather than regarding it as a colonial yoke, Lozis today consider *Litunga* Lewanika's alliance with the British a mature voluntary decision that provided a degree of internal stability that Bulozi had not seen during most of the nineteenth century.[15] However, Lewanika did enter into an irreversible process, gradually trading the kingdom's sovereignty for political-military protection by the British.[16] Between 1890 and 1893, Anglo-German and Anglo-Portuguese contracts in effect truncated Lewanika's territory, initially without the *Litunga* knowing.

[11] Caplan (1970) and Mainga (1973: 139).
[12] Flint (2003: 402–410), Mainga (1973: 132f) and Gluckman (1941: 96).
[13] Caplan (1969).
[14] Mainga Bull (1995: 5).
[15] Flint (2004: 119).
[16] Mainga (1973: 171).

On July 1, 1890, only four days after the Lochner Concession, the British and German governments signed the Helgoland-Zanzibar Treaty, which provided for an "access corridor to the Zambezi"[17] for Germany's colony *Deutsch Südwest Afrika* (DSWA).[18] Seeking Zambezi access was motivated by German ambitions to establish a viable transport connection from the protectorate of DSWA via the interior of Southern Africa to the German territories in East Africa. The so-called Caprivi Strip (named after the German chancellor in office at the time) is one of the most recognizable legacies of colonial boundary drawing in Africa.

DSWA needed water and labor resources, which seemed available in great abundance via the access corridor. Reality soon grounded such colonial fantasies. The distance and terrain between the established German outposts and the Zambezi were simply too challenging. Lewanika's appointees—Mamili and Letia—continued to administer and extract tribute for themselves and the *Litunga*. After an arduous three-months' journey through the Kalahari desert, Hauptmann Kurt Streitwolf finally hoisted the German flag in February 1909 by a place he named "Schuckmannsburg"—after DSWA's governor at the time.[19] To his superiors, Streitwolf reported Caprivi had no valuable minerals and a dangerous climate for European settlement, but moderate potential as a labor reserve, albeit restricted by the difficult transport access.[20]

Like the Germans, BSAC initially had only speculative interests and limited administrative muscle in their part of the Lozi kingdom. The company's main objective was to maintain order in a large territory with minimal financial input.[21] The first decade of mutual engagement by the Lozi and the British consolidated the power of Lewanika's inner circle and his administrative setup, resulting in increased political stability in the Bulozi heartland and considerable material wealth for its ruling elites. The Lozi leadership did not passively receive power projected outward by the British colonial system but creatively engaged the colonizers for their own personal advantage. More fundamental changes were to come, however.

---

[17] Anglo-German agreement of 1890, Article III. 2.

[18] The English name of the document is "Anglo-German Agreement of 1890."

[19] The population of the area referred to the place as "Luhonono" and in August 2013, the Namibian government announced that this would replace "Schuckmannsburg" as its official name.

[20] Streitwolf (1911: 229–234).

[21] Mainga Bull (1995: 5), Mainga (1973: 161) and Caplan (1970: 74–118).

From Remote Hinterlands to Labor Reserves

BSAC considered Barotseland unsuitable for white settlement. Its key assets were a large native labor force with potential for tax revenue. The Lozi leadership was willing to cooperate and strong enough to control an ethnically diverse range of people through feudalistic power and ownership structures. In 1903, BSAC divided Barotseland into five districts with resident District Commissioners commanding an armed native police force of ca. 600 men. In the following years, they formally abolished slavery and introduced a hut tax. Lewanika grudgingly settled for a 10% share of the revenue, a small portion of which would trickle down to lower-level chiefs at his own discretion.[22]

The material base of the Lozi elites thus shifted from direct extraction of tribute and labor to monetary income allocated to them by the British authorities. The broader Lozi population had to find sources to earn cash income. The conditions were set for labor migration, and by the early 1910s, thousands of Lozi men were working in mines, on commercial farms, and on the railway lines in Rhodesia and South Africa.[23] Lozi royalty increasingly adapted to the luxuries and etiquette of a European lifestyle, as their offsprings were educated in missionary schools and groomed to take their place in the bureaucracy of indirect rule.[24] In 1911, BSAC amalgamated the existing territories of Barotseland-North-Western-Rhodesia with Northern-Eastern-Rhodesia to establish the protectorate of Northern Rhodesia. Barotseland's relative administrative autonomy continued, but BSAC kept the province as a largely rural native reserve to extract taxes and labor for industrial production, and—from 1914 onwards—for the war effort in East Africa.[25]

Upon his arrival in the Caprivi Strip, Hauptmann Streitwolf's most delicate task was to set up a functioning administration with minimal resources in this large and remote territory. He eventually managed to convince the population that they were now under the protection of the German Kaiser and no longer required to deliver labor or tribute to the Lozi leadership on the other side of the Zambezi.[26] Inspired by the British system of indirect rule, the German resident confirmed Chief Mamili as

---

[22] Caplan (1970: 86f).
[23] Van Horn (1977: 164) and Gluckman (1941: 164).
[24] Mainga (1973: 206).
[25] Mainga Bull (1995: 6).
[26] Streitwolf (1911: 110).

the representative leader of the inhabitants of the western parts of Caprivi, mainly the Mafwe people and several associated—but importantly rather distinct—groups.[27]

Streitwolf then oversaw the appointment of Chief Chikamatondo as a caretaker for the eastern parts inhabited by the Masubiya people. The affirmation of the Mafwe chieftaincy and the creation of the Masubiya chieftaincy broke the existing chain of command and allegiance between the previously subordinate peoples in Caprivi and their Lozi overlords. These events affirmed the partitioning of Bulozi along the colonial boundary from a mere line on maps to a fact of daily life. Chiefs Chikamatondo and Mamili had seized the opportunity to safely dissociate themselves from Lozi rule and build their own power base. Apart from this legacy, effective to this day, the results of German colonial rule in Caprivi are rather modest. On September 21, 1914, the commanding officer at Schuckmannsburg surrendered to advancing British forces, ending the brief period of Germany's actual administration of the Caprivi Strip.

After Lewanika's death in 1916, his son Yeta III became *Litunga*, a position he held until 1945. BSAC's rule in Barotseland ended in 1924, when the Colonial Office took over the administration of the British Protectorate Northern Rhodesia. After intensive lobbying by Yeta III, Barotseland was granted special status and officially declared a protectorate within a protectorate.[28] As large-scale industrial mining took off in the copperbelt in the late 1920s, the economic center of gravity within Northern Rhodesia shifted further away from Barotseland and contract labor migration increased.

In the late 1920s, the Witwatersrand Native Labor Association (WNLA) and other labor bureaus were hiring thousands of men who worked and lived in ethnically segregated communities in all major mining centers of South Africa and the Rhodesias. In some districts, Lozi speakers amounted to as much as half of all able-bodied men.[29] In 1936, the Barotse Native Authority (BNA) was established with a treasury and far-reaching responsibilities in the fields of land and natural resource management, jurisdiction, and law enforcement. Owing to its considerable administrative

---

[27] Two of these groups claimed autonomous chieftaincies in the post-independence period and their official recognition by the South West African People Organisation (SWAPO) government infuriated the core leadership of the Mafwe.

[28] Mainga Bull (1995: 6).

[29] Caplan (1970: 145).

capability, the powers of the BNA were greater than those granted to any other Native Authority within Northern Rhodesia; this remained unchanged until the end of the British colonial period.

The Conference of Versailles brought the Caprivi Strip, along with the rest of South West Africa (SWA), under the League of Nations Mandate handed to South Africa. Between 1919 and 1939, responsibility for the administration of all or parts of Caprivi was passed back and forth several times between South Africa, SWA, Bechuanaland, and Northern Rhodesia. This indicates both low priority and the continuing difficulties to access the territory during that period.

However, the League of Nations continued to consider Caprivi as part of SWA. In 1937, a new administrative center was established near the Zambezi's Katima Mulilo rapids. In 1939, administration of the eastern Caprivi Strip was once again transferred, this time to South Africa. The strategic location of the strip in the heart of Southern Africa was central to Pretoria's interests at the outbreak of the Second World War.[30] Caprivi was declared a Native Reserve, and from 1940, the South African Defense Force (SADF) used the first airfield at Katima Mulilo for training, while WNLA used its own aircraft to transport Caprivi men to the mines near Johannesburg.

Caprivi remained inaccessible over land from the other parts of SWA until the mid-1960s. The government in Pretoria considered the Caprivi Strip as unsuitable for white settlement, sought to minimize expenditure, encouraged labor migration, and implemented its policies via indirect rule through the Mafwe and Masubiya chieftaincies under the supervision of one white government officer. The borderland population throughout this period maintained close relations across the Zambezi, and elder residents today recall that the border was virtually open. As in Barotseland—and in contrast to SWA—the language of schooling in Caprivi was English. Both provinces worshipped in Silozi and ran their clocks on the same time zone as the surrounding British colonies in South Africa: one hour ahead of SWA. Like Barotseland, Caprivi's status as a remote province administered through special arrangements was thus consolidated.

---

[30] Kangumu (2000, 2011).

WHAT KIND OF INDEPENDENCE? SOUTH AFRICAN BANTUSTAN AND ZAMBIAN PROVINCE

The Federation of Rhodesia and Nyasaland was imposed in 1953 against the expressed opinions of the majority of its black population. Under the leadership of the highly controversial *Litunga* Mwanawina, a son of Lewanika, the Lozi leadership gave its lukewarm support for the federal scheme.[31] In return, Barotseland's special status as a protectorate was further entrenched by an Order in Council of the British Government.[32]

By the late 1950s, the Lozi leadership had become accustomed to actively cultivating their self-image of Barotseland as an independent state. This stance was nevertheless increasingly irreconcilable with the realities of Zambia's approaching independence and rising black African nationalist sentiments. Educated Lozis and labor migrants had become politically sensitized and openly questioned the sole authority of the *Litunga* and his leadership apparatus, which was reeling from internal succession disputes at the time.

Conservative British forces meanwhile regarded sustaining the Lozi leadership as the solution to stave off popular demands for black self-rule in the colony.[33] Under these circumstances, nationalist forces gained the political upper hand in Barotseland in the run-up to independence. Educated Lozi candidates of Kenneth Kaunda's UNIP overwhelmingly defeated the Barotse National Party sponsored by *Litunga* Mwanawina in three successive elections in 1962, 1963, and 1964.[34]

The weakened Lozi leadership embarked on a two-pronged strategy: they focused on securing the autonomy of Barotseland within an independent Zambia, while secretly attempting to strike deals with old allies in sympathetic colonial administrations in South Africa, Rhodesia, Portugal, and France. In an attempt to increase BNA's revenue base, *Litunga* Mwanawina's nephew, Lubita, was sent to Johannesburg to negotiate a raise in WNLA's attestation fee for Lozi workers. WNLA was at the time annually recruiting 5000–6000 Lozi men to work in the Rand mines. Lubita also conducted negotiations in March 1964 at Katima Mulilo with

---

[31] Caplan (1970: 168ff).
[32] Mainga Bull (1995: 9) and Caplan (1968: 346f).
[33] Caplan (1968: 350f) and Mulford (1967: 212ff).
[34] Sumbwa (2000).

representatives of South Africa's Verwoerd government over military and financial assistance to "free" Barotseland from Zambia.[35]

What looks like an attempt to create a Barotseland Bantustan—probably including Caprivi, and thus reuniting a large share of the Lozi kingdom—did not become a reality. Instead, the Lozi leadership accepted the incorporation of Barotseland into the independent state of Zambia under the terms of the Barotseland Agreement 1964. This document was the result of three-party negotiations between the BNA, the British, and Northern Rhodesian governments. It was signed in London on May 18 of that year by UNIP's President Kenneth Kaunda, *Litunga* Mwanawina, and Secretary of State for Commonwealth Relations, Duncan Sandys.

UNIP promised to recognize Barotseland's special status beyond Zambian independence and to preserve the *Litunga's* powers to make laws for a wide range of regional and local government matters in Barotseland. These included land and natural resource management, the judiciary, and finances. The Barotseland Agreement 1964 was, however, not formally enshrined in the new republic's constitution and therefore technically an inferior legal document.[36] In the months before Zambian independence, Kaunda gave written and verbal assurances that his government had "no wish to interfere with the day to day running of the internal affairs of Barotseland."[37] Yet, after independence on October 24, 1964, the UNIP government no longer concealed its intention to do away with what they regarded as a reactionary colonial anachronism.[38]

The BRE was then—and is still today—an elaborate and vast network of chiefs from the various Lozi royal lineages and their bodies of senior advisers with duties in specific resorts like land management, jurisprudence, and ceremonial affairs. It is an administrative system using all the signature elements and symbols of state bureaucracy: stationery and flags, uniforms and administrative buildings, written permits and formal meetings held in official languages,[39] security forces and official holidays.

The ruling UNIP party's strong electorate and their nationalization of the copper mining industry provided the muscle to strip the Lozi leadership of much of their formal fiscal and administrative powers. The British

[35] Caplan (1968: 355).

[36] Mainga Bull (1995: 12).

[37] Kenneth Kaunda in a speech at Lealui on August 6, 1964, cited in Sumbwa (2000, 114).

[38] Caplan (1968: 356).

[39] Silozi is used for regular administrative proceedings, Siluyana for royal and ceremonial affairs.

Parliament briefly debated the abrogation of the agreement in December 1966, but the position of the Labor government at the time was "once a country becomes independent these matters become issues for its own internal decision."[40] By 1969, all major institutions of Barotse administration were either dismantled or had their funding streams rerouted through Lusaka. The salaries of the *Litunga* and the royal family were now paid by the president's office. Kaunda's administration also prohibited all further recruitment by WNLA in Bulozi. With its two-thirds majority in parliament, UNIP, in 1969, amended the constitution to cancel the 1964 agreement and rename "Barotseland" as "Western Province." Fast-paced development in the Copperbelt, Lusaka, and along the Tanzania-Zambia Railway Authority (TAZARA) train route to Dar es Salaam were shifting Zambia's economic and political centers of gravity further away from the Zambezi. Cash-crop plantations and other "white elephant" projects introduced by the central government in Western Province were incompatible with the floodplain ecosystem and became bogged down in the day-to-day resistance against government policy by Lozi administrators.[41]

In some sense, the situation for Western Province under UNIP was not unlike the earlier relationship between BSAC and the Lozi leadership. UNIP did little to develop the area, while a small group of high-ranking and well-educated Lozis was receiving state salaries and appointments to ministerial positions or parastatal companies, sufficient to discourage them from full-blown opposition to central government.

A marked difference, however, lay in the role of Lozi "tradition" and "culture." The British authorities had carefully sustained and reinvented ideas and administrative practices of pre-colonial Lozi authority to maintain social stability as part of indirect rule in Barotseland.[42] The Zambian government sought to relocate and isolate Lozi authorities from the realm of everyday administration into a sphere of depoliticized "folklore." This project was never completed. In the absence of efficient state structures, the Lozi system of administration continued to play a central role in many aspects of daily life in Western Province, in particular, the management of land and its natural resources. The controversy over the 1964 agreement remained unresolved.

---

[40] MP Mrs. Judith Hart http://www.theyworkforyou.com/debates/?id=1966-12-13a. 227.9&s=barotse#g229.4.

[41] Flint (2004: 167f).

[42] Cf. Hobsbawm and Ranger (1983).

By 1964, domestic and international pressure was mounting on the South African regime to extend development and greater administrative and political autonomy to its black population. For Caprivi, the Odendaal Commission[43] recommended a roadmap toward a self-governing homeland; with great financial input, Pretoria began to implement ambitious development plans.

As Zambia gained independence, Katima Mulilo became the fast-growing designated seat of a future Caprivi Bantustan government. These plans were not unopposed. The Caprivi African National Union (CANU) had formed in 1963 with the purpose of achieving self-government for the Caprivi Strip. Like their fellow Lozi speakers from Barotseland, many of the early CANU members had formed ideas of black emancipation while abroad as migrant laborers or on education programs. Not surprisingly, the apartheid authorities closely watched CANU's activities. Its first president, Brendan Kangongolo Simbwaye, was arrested in 1964 and disappeared in 1972 under dubious circumstances.[44]

Another leading figure of CANU was Albert Mishake Muyongo, a prominent young member of the Mafwe royal family and direct descendant of Simataa Mamili.[45] Following Simbwaye's arrest and a bloody crackdown on a CANU meeting at Katima Mulilo, Muyongo and other CANU activists fled to Tanzania and Zambia. In November 1964, they met with Sam Nujoma and other leading members of SWAPO in Dar es Salaam and discovered they were fighting for a common cause: independence from white minority rule for the territory of the former German colony DSWA. Muyongo agreed to a SWAPO-CANU merger and thereafter held various positions in SWAPO before he was expelled in 1980.[46]

The internal politics within SWAPO in exile were at the time strongly driven by (not unfounded) fears of assassinations and covert operations by South African and other security and intelligence agencies. SWAPO had originally emerged from the Ovamboland People's Organization (OPO),

---

[43] In 1963 the South African government published the Report of the Commission of Enquiry into South West African Affairs, commonly known as the Odendaal Report after its chairman, Fox Odendaal. Its official purpose was to make recommendations on the best ways to promote the socioeconomic development of Namibia's black majority population, but it is widely regarded as an attempt to fend off anti-Apartheid critics.

[44] Flint (2004: 174) and Kangumu (2011: 214 ff).

[45] Fisch (1999: 42).

[46] Muyongo served as SWAPO Representative in Zambia (1964–1965), Educational Secretary (1966–1970), and Vice President (1970–80).

a contract worker-based movement. This northern, most densely populated part of SWA was home to more than half of the country's total population. External threats and inner pressure from a younger generation of
militant activists joining the organization in exile challenged SWAPO's
established leadership from the early 1970s onwards. The organization's
inner circle developed mistrust against non-Ovambo members.

Muyongo became one of many victims of the liberation struggle's
internal power politics. He nowadays maintains that he and SWAPO
President Sam Nujoma on November 5, 1964, signed a document formally sealing the SWAPO-CANU merger on condition that Caprivi would
be granted either special political status or complete autonomy after
Namibia's independence.[47] Muyongo claims to have a copy of what could
be called the "Caprivi 1964 Agreement" but says he will only produce it
"when time spells for the right opportunity."[48] SWAPO disputes this
claim; neither side has produced conclusive evidence. According to the
website of the secessionist movement, the document contains, among
others, the following clause: "At the attainment of independence, the people of the Caprivi must be asked whether they want to join Namibia or
remain independent."[49] This contested issue became a key reference point
in the allegations of betrayal made by the Caprivi secessionist movement
in the late 1990s.

Despite emerging political opposition, the apartheid regime's push for
development in Caprivi continued through the 1960s with significant
projects in all sectors of public service and infrastructure. The strip finally
became accessible by road; in 1969, postal and telegraph services were
directly connected to South Africa. The East Caprivi homeland was finally
inaugurated in 1972, while the western part of the strip between the
Mashi and Kavango rivers was declared a nature reserve. Four years later,
the Caprivi Bantustan was granted self-government and its name changed
to "Lozi." A government was formed, complete with a constitution, regulations for Lozi citizenship, a national anthem, and a state flag depicting
two elephants. These were supposed to symbolize the Legislative Council
consisting of the Mafwe and Masubiya chiefs, their *Ngambelas*, and ten

---

[47] United Democratic Party (2005) and Flint (2004: 188).
[48] http://www.caprivivision.com/who-has-the-power-to-revive-canu/.
[49] Caprivi Freedom (2013).

councilors each.[50] The council's de facto powers were limited: all important funding and policy decisions were made in Pretoria.

The apartheid regime's political and military strategic concerns shaped the developmental change rolling over Caprivi from 1964 onwards from the outset. These strategic concerns came to take center stage after SWAPO's military wing launched a guerilla insurgency in Caprivi in the late 1960s. South Africa responded with a heavy buildup of military installations and troops. By the late 1970s, the rear bases and main operations of SWAPO's guerrilla war had shifted to Southern Angola.

Although Caprivi remained strategically relevant, the apartheid regime's ability to sustain the costly efforts introduced during the 1960s decreased, as the security-driven development paradigm lost its momentum. Governmental services in Caprivi diminished and Pretoria transferred the administration of Caprivi back to SWA in 1980 when legislation established a three-tier system of local, regional, and central "ethnic" government. After elections, Caprivi's Second-Tier Legislative Assembly was composed equally of Masubiya and Mafwe councilors. A rift over the supposedly rotating chairmanship soon emerged between the two sides. Although it was settled in court shortly before Namibian independence, ethnic animosities in Caprivi were to continue.[51]

In 1989, a negotiated settlement between the United Nations (UN), the South African government, and SWAPO paved the way for Namibia's independence on March 21, 1990.[52] In the first free elections in November 1989, SWAPO emerged as the strongest party with 57% of the overall votes, while the Democratic Turnhalle Alliance (DTA) received 29%. DTW had been established in the 1980s as an umbrella for black political organizations with the blessings of the apartheid authorities. Mishake Muyongo, who had returned from exile in 1985, formed the United Democratic Party (UDP) and soon afterwards merged it with DTA. He thus became a DTA member of Namibia's first independent parliament.

Zambia, on the other hand, had since December 1972 experienced its second republic, triggered by a constitutional amendment act declaring a one-party state under UNIP. In 1991, when the end of the Second Republic ended, Zambia's economy contracted by more than 30%,[53] due

---

[50] South Africa (1964).
[51] Fosse (1996) and Kangumu (2011).
[52] Cf. Melber and Saunders (2007).
[53] Virtual Zambia (2008).

to gross mismanagement of the copper industry and a dramatic fall in the world price of copper. During this period, Zambia also supported liberation movements throughout Southern Africa and consequently lost its access to the ports of Durban and Maputo.

Zambia took major loans from commercial banks overseas and the World Bank, defaulting in the mid-1980s. Banks and donors pressured the Zambian government to reintroduce multiparty democracy and implement a Structural Adjustment Program (SAP). Attempts to follow suit met with internal opposition and the deteriorating economic situation led to food riots. As UNIP's power was waning in the late 1980s, Kaunda made several attempts to appease the Lozi leadership. In 1988, he appointed *Litunga* Ilute to the Central Committee of UNIP. Yet this and other moves in the run-up to the multiparty elections of 1991 failed to secure Kaunda the necessary votes to win the elections.

CALLS TO ARMS: RISING SEPARATISM IN THE 1990s

The winner of Zambia's 1991 parliamentary elections, the Movement for Multiparty Democracy (MMD), announced in its campaign manifesto: "We are committed to a policy whereby traditional rulers regain the enjoyment of their traditional powers. The institution of chieftaincy shall be given its rightful and respectable role, drawing support from government."[54] After years of Kaunda's dogmatic rejection of traditional leaders' role in government, they were reemerging as important players in rural and national governance during the presidency of MMD's Fredrick Chiluba. The reformed 1996 constitution created a national House of Chiefs to act as "advisory body" to the government.

President Chiluba also secured the support of selected individual chiefs (and their voting subjects) through the distribution of personal gifts in the form of cars and cash.[55] An overwhelming majority of the Lozi electorate had voted for Chiluba and MMD in 1991. Party campaigners had led the Lozi leadership and broader population to believe that an at least partial restoration of the 1964 agreement would be conceivable under their government.[56] These expectations were thoroughly disappointing. In early 1993, the MMD government officially recognized an Nkoya chief in

---

[54] MMD (1991).
[55] Times of Zambia (January 31, 2009).
[56] Englebert (2005: 29–59) and Sumbwa (2000: 115f).

Kaoma, considered by BRE a renegade province trying to break away from the Lozi umbrella.[57]

During the same period, the fallout from SAPs and a general breakdown of public services throughout the country were sorely felt in Western Province. Zambia experienced political turmoil as the Chiluba government persecuted a senior member of the Lozi royal family on dubious high treason charges. In early 1995, parliament passed a new law aimed to strip BRE of its power to allocate land. Despite the 1969 Land Act, BRE had never ceased to execute this function and continued to extract a significant part of its revenue from it.[58]

Already in July 1993, some 5000 Lozis had assembled at the *Litunga's* residence, demanding to challenge the Zambian government in court with the aim to secede the province based on the 1964 agreement. President Chiluba had refused to enter into dialogue and instead promised to crush any uprising. In July 1995, tensions came to a head when the presidential motorcade was blocked by stone-throwing Lozis upon a visit to Mongu, the capital of Western Province. In preparation against expected government retaliation, Lozis from all districts followed a ritual call to arms and formed a militia to protect their *Litunga*.[59]

During ensuing raids, state security forces seized rocket launchers, antiaircraft guns, hand grenades, and land mines from radical Lozi separatists. Government alleged these had been obtained from UNITA (*União Nacional para a Independência Total de Angola* National Union for the Total Independence of Angola) forces in neighboring Angola.[60] The Lozi leadership reacted by convening a Barotse National Conference (BNC) in November 1995. The BNC is the highest decision-making body of BRE and only convened on extraordinary occasions. It passed a resolution demanding government recognize the 1964 agreement and incorporated it into the constitution. The resolution text further threatened "if the government continues to be obstinate, the people of the Barotse shall have the right to self-determination by reverting to the original status of Barotseland before 1964."[61]

Importantly, BRE and its highly trained lawyers did not directly threaten with secession but pointed out that they were considering their options. Despite the clash between BRE and the MMD government, neither side

---

[57] Mainga Bull (1995: 8) and Sumbwa (2000: 116).
[58] Sumbwa (2000: 117).
[59] Sumbwa (2000: 119f).
[60] Minorities at Risk (2009).
[61] Barotse National Conference (1995).

implemented their threats in full. Government did not give in to Lozi demands regarding the 1964 agreement, but the implementation of the Land Act remained superficial. BRE did not renege on its demands for the restoration of the 1964 agreement but did not proceed to challenge the MMD government in court either.

While claiming that Barotseland had a right to secede from Zambia, BRE publicly rejected the idea of pursuing the secessionist option by force. *Litunga* Ilute Yeta stated "we shall not secede from Zambia," while simultaneously denouncing the government for its "perpetual enslavement of Barotseland."[62] The *Litunga* and his *Ngambela* distanced themselves publicly from demands made by more outspoken agitators for Lozi separatism. They instead chose to ally with their former enemy, endorsing Kaunda and UNIP in the 1996 elections.

Some junior Lozi royals and associated activists continued to take a more radical stance but eventually toned down their rhetoric as the political climate cooled off once again. Among these, Prince Akashambatwa Mbikusita-Lewanika, who in 1996 contested the Zambian presidential elections on a moderately separatist platform, publicly endorsed the Caprivi separatists' cause in 1999. Possible direct links or material support for Muyongo's movement had not been credibly established, however, and seemed never to be part of the BRE's public rhetoric.[63]

In the run-up to Namibian independence, expectations of rapid economic change as a dividend of the end of apartheid were high among the black majority population. In the first elections in 1989, the Namibian population voted the SWAPO party to power with a strong majority in most regions except Caprivi. Here, DTA held on to a (slowly shrinking) majority vote in all elections until the 1998 local authority elections.

Mishake Muyongo had become the party's leader in 1992 and in 1994 ran for president against Sam Nujoma.[64] Caprivi was Muyongo's personal power base, where a group of educated and politically active Caprivi men gathered around the veteran politician. Many of them had spent their formative years in training and employment for Caprivi's apartheid-era administration. For them, Namibian independence was

[62] The Post (1994) and Englebert (2005).

[63] Englebert (2005). Compare with Mbikusita-Lewanika (2001) and Barotse Patriotic Front (2004).

[64] Muyongo was the Democratic Turnhalle Alliance (DTA) Vice President from 1987 until 1992 and DTA President from 1992 to 1999. http://www.klausdierks.com/Biographies/Biographies_M.html. Accessed June 30, 2008.

yet to deliver the material and symbolic benefits they had experienced during the Bantustan period.

Muyongo's support in Caprivi was, however, roughly split along the region's ethnic divide that Streitwolf's recognition of two chieftaincies had helped create and that regional politics during the Bantustan period had deepened[65]: the Mafwe under their chief Bwima Mamili, a cousin of Mishake Muyongo, were largely voting DTA, while the Masubiya generally supported SWAPO. In the post-independence climate of competition for scarce opportunities within Caprivi, the existing rift soon broke out more openly and turned violent.[66] Mafwe residents alleged that the distribution of government employment and other benefits unfairly favored the Masubiya population and other supporters of the ruling party from outside of Caprivi.[67] Muyongo and his followers claimed that "tribalist" attitudes among the core leadership and voters of SWAPO, as well as post-independence politics in Caprivi, were the continuation of the Ovambo dominance Muyongo and others allegedly had experienced in exile.[68] The politics of the independence struggle thus continued.

Another contested issue emerged soon after independence: the recognition of chiefs in Caprivi by the SWAPO government. Streitwolf's administrative arrangement based on separate Mafwe and Masubiya chieftaincies had functioned continuously since 1909. In the case of the Masubiya, a rather coherent identity and internal hierarchy had been constructed and continues to exist to the present day. The Mafwe chieftaincy was less homogenous from the start. Several groups with more or less clearly pronounced ideas of a separate identity traced their existence back to the times before 1909.[69]

In August 1992, a Mafwe breakaway faction unilaterally elected its own chief. Violent confrontations soon took on a party-political dimension as the SWAPO government officially recognized the new Mayeyi chieftaincy. Eager to beat the main national opposition leader's party on his home ground, SWAPO ran a powerful campaign in Katima Mulilo in the 1998

---

[65] As Soiri (2001: 200) notes, it is difficult to establish whether politics entered into ethnicity or vice versa.

[66] Fosse (1996: 165–168) and Flint (2004: 244–266).

[67] Fosse (1996: 165).

[68] Fisch (1999: 20).

[69] Compare with Streitwolf (1911: 126).

local authority elections and overturned DTA's previous majority.[70] Muyongo alleged irregularities but failed to take legal action.

Instead, he and his supporters questioned the inclusion of Caprivi in the Namibian state formation project and began to openly identify with an alternative: the idea of a separate and sovereign Caprivi state within the borders of the earlier Bantustan. While Muyongo's own statements never indicated a wish for this state to become part of a resurrected Lozi kingdom,[71] the Lozi heritage provided a powerful background in terms of which secessionists could label alleged "Ovambo invaders" as "foreigners." Leading members of the secessionist movement had been educated and groomed for careers in the administration of the Caprivi Bantustan. Both the kingdom's and the Bantustan's lingering histories appear to have provided fertile ground for the secessionists' ideas to take root at a time when the Namibian state formation project had not yielded the results they desired.

After the 1998 election defeat, these ideas ripened and led to organized action. Namibian security forces discovered a training camp of the newly formed Caprivi Liberation Army (CLA) in a Mafwe-dominated area of Caprivi near the Botswana border later that year. The largely Oshivambo-speaking security force used heavy-handed methods on the civilian population in the surrounding region in their search for suspected members and sympathizers of the CLA. Allegedly escaping torture, rape and intimidation, some 2500 people subsequently fled to Botswana where they found shelter in the Dukwe refugee camp. Mafwe Chief Bwima Mamili as well as Mishake Muyongo and Caprivi Governor John Mabuku were among them.

Mamili and Muyongo were soon transferred to Denmark as political refugees under United Nations High Commissioner for Refugees (UNHCR) protection, while several hundred others were voluntarily repatriated to Namibia in the following months. A majority remained in Botswana and a hard core of several dozen CLA members managed to regroup on the Angolan and Zambian territory. On August 2, 1999, they launched poorly coordinated armed attacks on government installations, such as the national broadcaster's station and airport in Katima Mulilo. Although caught completely by surprise, the Namibian army and police quickly regained control.

---

[70] Soiri (2001: 201).
[71] See also Flint (2003: 427).

In total, 15 casualties (Namibian security forces, rebels, and civilians) were officially recorded. President Nujoma declared a state of emergency for the region, which lasted three weeks. Namibian state security forces were pursuing and interrogating suspect secessionist sympathizers throughout Caprivi. Hundreds of arrests were made within and outside Namibian territory, involving torture and unauthorized extradition in several cases.[72] The Caprivi secession had failed, and the radical core members of the movement were either dead, in exile, or in custody. But while the new millennium in some respects brought a new deal to both the Namibian and Zambian parts of the former Lozi kingdom, the grievances which underpinned separatism in both areas did not simply go away.

CONTESTATION CONTINUES

On May 13, 2004, a new road bridge across the Zambezi at Katima Mulilo closed the last gap in a 2524-km-long asphalt route called the "Walvis Bay-Ndola-Lubumbashi Corridor (WBNLC)", connecting DRCs Katanga Province and Zambia's Copperbelt with Namibia's seaport of Walvis Bay. Foreign donors largely financed the bridge and refurbished sections of the TCC but gave the governments of Zambia and Namibia an opportunity to showcase their commitment to bringing economic development to the rural provinces following the separatist incidents of the previous decade. The new infrastructure and investment opportunities provided the backdrop for a political rapprochement between BRE and the new MMD administration of Chiluba's successor Levy Mwanawasa during his period in office (2002–2008).[73] But the SWAPO government of Namibia still showed no signs of compromising its tough stance against the Caprivi secessionists.

CAPRIVI/ZAMBEZI

After their arrest in the aftermath of the August 1999 attacks, more than 140 imprisoned Caprivi secessionists were charged with high treason and 274 other counts. Among the accused was a remarkable portion of teachers and other educated former civil servants. The authorities initially refused to provide legal aid for the accused, but the Namibian Supreme Court ruled in mid-2002 that they were entitled to adequate legal

---

[72] Amnesty International (2003a).
[73] cf. Zeller (2007b, 2010).

representation at the expense of the state. The treason trial finally opened in 2004, and after numerous delays, the prosecution closed its case in mid-2013. The delay in judicial procedures collides with Article 12(1)(b) of Namibia's constitution, which stipulates that trials should "take place within a reasonable time, failing which the accused shall be released." Several bail applications by some of the accused—motivated by deteriorating health conditions and the need for special medical treatment—were refused. During the trial, the number of prisoners who died in detention exceeded the death toll during the attacks.

In early August 2003, Amnesty International published a report criticizing the treatment of the detainees.[74] It expressed deep concern that the violation of pre-trial rights of the accused might undermine their right to a fair hearing as defined in the UN International Covenant on Civil and Political Rights and the African Charter on Human and Peoples' Rights. Amnesty also observed violations against the UN Convention against Torture and Other Cruel, Inhuman, or Degrading Treatment or Punishment as well as the failure of the authorities to investigate and prosecute allegations of torture. The report was concerned over the misuse of the "common purpose" doctrine under which all the defendants were charged with high treason, murder, and sedition. Amnesty called on the Namibian authorities "to immediately and unconditionally release all prisoners of conscience and ensure that the remaining defendants are tried in a fair manner."[75]

The Namibian government continued with the uncompromising full prosecution of the accused. It has shown no willingness to address the political root causes of the separatist attempt, treating it as a law and order issue. The SWAPO government's method of trying to eliminate political challenges through declaring them illegal is also evident in their decision to ban, with effect as of September 1, 2006, the revived UDP that promotes self-rule in Caprivi.[76]

In February 2013, 43 high treason defendants had been dismissed due to lack of evidence. The acquitted have launched legal action, suing the government for compensation amounting close to 1.2 billion NAD in total.[77] Of the 143 accused, only 132 were charged, 12 were released prior

---

[74] Amnesty International (2003a).
[75] Amnesty International (2003b).
[76] afrolNews/IRIN (2006).
[77] *The Namibian*, February 12, 2013 and Menges (2013).

to the opening of the trial in 2003, and another one in August 2012. Twenty-two accused died while in custody, 10 among these between their arrest and the opening of the trial. Of the remaining defendants, 13 identified as ringleaders refused to recognize the court's jurisdiction and this move has further prolonged court procedures, some of which are still ongoing at the time of writing (May 2018).[78]

Since the trial started, the secessionists' agenda of a separate Caprivian State made occasional headlines in the Namibian press.[79] The main trial finally ended with a verdict on December 8, 2015. Of the remaining defendants, around 30 were found guilty and received long jail sentences, while most others had their charges dismissed. Many of them had by that time spent up to 16 years in prison. The judge harshly criticized the police for using torture to force those arrested to implicate others and to confess. Since then, several among those found not guilty have laid charges against the Namibian state and made claims for compensation.

Refugees who had been living in the Dukwe camp in Botswana since the late 1990s were gradually returning to Namibia with the assistance of both the UNHCR and the Namibian government. But despite appeals by the Namibian Commissioner for Refugees, close to 1000 refugees were at the end of 2013 still reluctant to accept the offer and preferred to stay in Dukwe.[80] Until mid-2016, the repatriation process proceeded slowly and with interruptions. It was marred by suspicions among those who had fled that upon return they might be punished. By 2017, some 900 refugees remained in the Dukwe camp, Namibia's state budget for 2017–2018 allocating more than 10 million NAD for their repatriation.[81] A few

---

[78] Analysis Africa (2013). The overall figures slightly differ according to sources and cannot be verified beyond any doubt. As the report also concludes: "Many have been tortured, and the state now faces potentially huge civil claims from the 43 men set free by the court after spending 13 years in jail." See also *The Namibian* of February 2, 2002, and of June 16, 2007, reporting on the claims of some of the accused to be "Caprivians" and not "Namibians » and hence refusing to accept the jurisdiction of the Namibian courts.

[79] Examples include a pro-secessionist opinion piece published in Caprivi Vision 1 September 2005, and the controversy over the revival and subsequent banning of the United Democratic Party (UDP) (*The Namibian*, July 28, 2006, and September 8, 2006; *Allgemeine Zeitung*, September 4, 2006; *New Era*, September 4–5, 2006). Caprivi separatists claim that this (hitherto undisclosed) document proves that the 1964 Caprivi African National Union (CANU)-SWAPO merger was agreed on the condition that Caprivi would become an independent state separate from Namibia (*The Namibian*, January 24, 2007), the reinstallment of CANU by locals and the repeated public claims by accused and acquitted high treason suspects that Caprivi is historically "not part of Namibia" (*The Namibian*, February 2, 2005; January 17, 2007, April 17, 2007, and June 14, 2007, respectively).

[80] Sankwasa (2013).

[81] Sasman (2017).

political asylum seekers were living in Australia, Canada, Denmark, Sweden, and the United States. Some of them were informed that the government was only willing to provide returnees a home without prosecution for Namibian refugees registered with the UNHCR in their host countries—not for asylum seekers.[82]

Mishake Muyongo continues—from his Danish exile home on the outskirts of Copenhagen—to execute leadership as president of the UPD through a virtual, albeit distant presence. This includes annual New Year messages on the party's website, including appeals to continue the "struggle to liberate the Caprivi Strip."[83] In recent years, others have increasingly taken on the task of speaking for the UDP, notably members of a group of exiles now resident in Canada.

Although it has been declared illegal, UDP remains active in Caprivi. It now explicitly denies having a secessionist agenda and currently demands:

1. political dialogue between Namibian President Pohamba and UDP President Muyongo;
2. unconditional release of all Caprivi political prisoners; and
3. a referendum on the Caprivi political dispute (without any specific definition of "the dispute" or the nature of the "referendum").

It insists on using only peaceful means and emphasizes its wish to "prevent the recurring of 2nd August 1999."[84] In April 2012, UDP activists planned a demonstration in Katima Mulilo with the aim to hand a petition stating the above demands to the Caprivi Governor. The petition also made reference to the shared historical roots of Caprivi and Barotseland, claiming that both became part of their respective countries without the consent of their inhabitants. It did not, however, argue for a reunited Lozi kingdom. The Namibian authorities categorically denied permission for the planned demonstrations and demands.[85]

The internal logic of a former guerrilla movement organized through a military hierarchy and chain of command and its fear of enemy infiltration still appear to be central to the way many of Namibia's ruling party mem-

---

[82] Namibian Sun (2013).

[83] http://www.caprivifreedom.com/news.i?cmd=view&nid=1198.

[84] http://www.caprivifreedom.com/news.i?cmd=view&nid=1185; see also www.caprivi-concernedgroup.com.

[85] http://geocurrents.info/news-map/war-and-strife-news/continuing-tension-in-namibias-caprivi-strip#ixzz2VXa0UJv5; http://www.thevillager.com.na/news_article.php?id=1439&title=Caprivi%20rises%20%20again.

bers work and think today.[86] Two and half decades after independence, a widespread unofficial understanding of national leadership, all the way down to party foot soldiers, is that the SWAPO party, the Namibian government, and the Namibian state are identical and indivisible. According to the official paradigm, SWAPO has "brought democracy"[87] as well as "development and progress"[88] to Namibia, and any form of opposition is undermining the "peace and unity" needed for the nation-building project to continue.

Consistent with this logic is the SWAPO government's announcement in August 2013 to rename the Caprivi region "Zambezi." While the responsible government minister described the decision as an articulation of "the wishes of the people," there was significant though not unanimous opposition within the region against the name change.[89] This is consistent with findings that, across ethnic, political, and generational lines within the region, "Caprivian" exists as a category of self-definition that also includes a sense of being "different," though not necessarily separate, from the rest of Namibia.[90] The name change accordingly struck many as an offensive external imposition. A newly formed "concerned group" alleged at a press conference in Katima Mulilo on August 20 that the name change "is destined to destroy our identity and history."[91] Similar concerns and objections were raised in this and similar letters to the local print media:

> Being a Caprivian is our identity, culture, and way of life; it is who we are as a people sharing similar cultural norms and social values. ...The word Caprivian is what unites the...tribes of the Caprivi. This is similar to the Ovawambo, though they are amongst themselves OvaKwanyama, OvaNdonga, OvaMbalantu etc. They find unity and pride in being commonly known as Ovawambo.[92]

---

[86] The ruling party's handling of the SWAPO detainee issue and the National Society for Human Rights and, the emergence of opposition parties Congress of Democrats and Rally for Democracy and Progress are prominent examples.

[87] Reader's Letter (2008). *The Namibian*, accessed at: http://www.namibian.com.na/2008/March/letters/08ED201395.html.

[88] The Namibian (2008). See also "Pohamba at political rally." 2008. *The Namibian*, accessed at: http://www.namibian.com.na/2008/February/national/08EB20FA4F.html.

[89] Mutenda (2013).

[90] Guijarro (2013).

[91] Sanzila (2013).

[92] Ngoshi (2013).

An opinion article observed that "the people of Caprivi accepted that name as part of their collective historical memory and remembrance; its colonial origin notwithstanding." It claimed that colonial history is part of the country's collective history: "One cannot just erase it by using tippex" and "'Caprivi' will remain a contested territory."[93] An editorial in a local weekly suspected "that the reasons for changing the name Caprivi have less to do with its colonial roots than the symbolism it holds for secessionist sympathies in the region."[94]

BAROTSELAND/WESTERN PROVINCE

After his election in 2002, Zambia's president, Mwanawasa, earned back the majority of Lozi votes for his MMD party by directing investments and warm rhetoric toward Western Province. The thawing of relations between Zambia's central government and BRE was commented on in 2004 by Inyambo Yeta, a direct descendant of Lewanika and senior Lozi chief of one of the seven administrative subunits of BRE. Yeta was at the time vice chairman of Zambia's Constitutional Reform Commission, as well as chairman of the Zambian House of Chiefs, and had been appointed to both positions by the president:

> President Mwanawasa [...] is a personal friend of mine. We both are lawyers. That does not necessarily mean that there is recognition of the institution I represent. The minute you get a chief who is not in good books with the president, he will be just ignoring the Royal Establishment and say: "Oh no, those people there, we don't have any time for them."[95]

Yeta's assessment proved to be accurate. The National Constitutional Conference set up by Mwanawasa rejected the submission by BRE to reinstate the 1964 agreement.[96] Following Mwanawasa's death in office in 2008, relations under his successor, MMD's Rupiah Banda, returned to confrontational. On January 14, 2011, the first violent clashes since 1995 occurred between Lozi activists and security forces in the provincial capital Mongu, resulting in two deaths and numerous injuries. One hundred and twenty persons were arrested on treason charges and jailed for up to nine

---

[93] Kaure (2013).
[94] The Windhoek Observer (2013).
[95] Interview, Inyambo Yeta (2005).
[96] http://www.postzambia.com/post-read_article.php?articleId=25516.

months. Among them was the 92-year-old former *Ngambela*, Maxwell Mututwa, who died soon after his release from prison.[97] Lozis, both radical and moderate, were outraged, but on February 10, Chief Yeta led a high-powered Lozi delegation to meet with President Banda to assure him that BRE had no intention to secede from Zambia, stressing that the 1964 agreement was not a secessionist issue but one of negotiated terms of integration.[98]

Michael Sata and his Patriotic Front (PF) party won Zambia's 2011 elections and Lozi activists allege that, while on the campaign trail in Western Province, Sata promised to restore the 1964 agreement if elected. Once in power, however, the president rejected the findings of a commission that had investigated the January 2011 riots and recommended the restoration of the 1964 agreement. Echoing the crisis of the mid-1990s, Lozis accused Sata of "consciously calculated electoral deception."[99]

On March 26 and 27, 2012, some 2000 delegates attended a BNC at Limulunga. Their resolution stated: "Barotseland is now free to pursue its own self-determination and destiny. We are committed to a peaceful disengagement with the Zambian government."[100] The conference resolution declared that they accepted successive Zambian government's consistent failure to heed the 1964 agreement. But since Barotseland had only become part of Zambia on the conditions stipulated in this document, Barotseland was in fact not seceding but merely confirming the nonexistence of a union between the two. The establishment of a Barotse government, including defense forces, ministries, and various other bodies, was also decided, and soon thereafter a mushrooming of websites and pages on Facebook and other social media indicated that these decisions had at least some results in the virtual world.

While the conference could hardly have taken place without it being tolerated by *Litunga* Lubosi Imwiko II (in power since 2000), the royal palace soon started taking a different line. The *Ngambela* who had presided over the 2012 Barotse National Conference, Clement Wainyae Sinyinda, resigned his position in November 2012, citing lack of protection from the office of the *Litunga*. He was arrested on treason charges on

[97] http://www.postzambia.com/post-read_article.php?articleId=21897.

[98] http://www.postzambia.com/post-read_article.php?articleId=18135.

[99] http://www.ukzambians.co.uk/home/2012/02/28/president-satas-reaction-to-barotse-report-a-u-turn-or-a-consciously-calculated-electoral-deception/?695d7100.

[100] http://www.barotseland.info/Freedom_Resolution_2012.htm.

April 14, 2013, the same day President Sata visited the *Litunga* at his residence. The *Litunga* was accused of treachery and openly threatened with regicide by hardline secessionists, a highly unusual but not unprecedented event in Lozi history.

These and other developments have exposed existing rifts between different factions within BRE and a number of separatist groups in Western Province. Many of these differences have deep roots and echo the pre-colonial diversity and internal divisions of the Lozi kingdom. For a large share of the non-Lozi Zambian public, these developments merely affirmed the widely held opinion that the Lozis in Western Province are tribalists living in their own imagined past of lost glory, and that their internal and separatist politics are fundamentally premodern and cannot be taken seriously. Still, the political grievances and the seasoned Lozi lawyers who express them through legally sophisticated language are not likely to go away.

CONCLUSION

We have found no evidence to suggest that the cases of Lozi separatism in Namibia and Zambia are in any meaningful way directly linked beyond a few isolated expressions of mutual solidarity in the past. There has been no ethnically motivated pan-Lozi separatist cause since independence of either country. While the two cases are related through their shared historical roots, we have argued that the trajectories and aims of separatists in both countries are fundamentally different in a number of aspects that allow for fruitful comparison.

Today's Zambian Western Province includes the historical centers of the Lozi kingdom's power, while the area of Namibia's Caprivi was in the pre-colonial period, a peripheral and at times volatile province of Bulozi. Although Lewanika had established more firm control over Caprivi, the area's population had at best a weak allegiance to the kingdom. When closer ties became a possibility in 1909, Caprivi residents were happy to dissociate from Lozi power—especially since the maintenance of daily relations across the colonial border was, at least initially, not impeded. Separate administrative arrangements for the rest of the colonial period consolidated these differences.

With the negotiated processes of decolonization in Zambia and the armed liberation struggle for Namibia decades apart, the different circumstances have resulted in different separatist claims of "betrayal" and goals aiming toward the establishment of a more autonomous, self-governing authority. The factual status of the two 1964 agreements—the Barotseland Agreement and the somewhat mythical Caprivi Agreement between SWAPO and CANU—is hardly comparable: the Barotseland agreement is a fully established, detailed legal document bearing the signatures of the former colonial power and the leader of Zambia's incoming postcolonial government. The Caprivi Agreement's existence is unproven, and it can at best be considered a disputed anecdotal footnote of the liberation struggle; it is quite possibly an invention of historical facts that serves vested interest.

The declared primary objective of Lozis in Zambia, apart from statements made by radical factions or at the height of severe tensions, has not been secession but the inclusion of Barotseland/Western Province in Zambia as a semi-autonomous region with special privileges. This ambition is not far fetched. In contrast, the Caprivi secessionists' goal to liberate their territory and create their own sovereign state was highly unrealistic, considering size, location, and resources of the area. Its lack of realism was underscored by the fact that a considerable share of the population within the former Caprivi (as of August 2013 the Zambezi Region) clearly supports the Namibian government and its firm stance against the secessionists. Yet even among those, as the protest against the new name of the region seems to suggest, are many who have identified with being "Caprivians."

The cases examined in this chapter contain strong elements of national, regional, and interpersonal political issues that have nothing to do with separatism being played out on a national stage. The postcolonial politics of recognizing traditional leaders, the Mafwe-Masubiya dispute, and Muyongo's own personal history are as much part of the Caprivi secessionist story as Zambian party politics, the factional infighting within BRE, and competition within the spectrum of more radical advocates for secession are elements and drivers of the Barotseland issue. While these make comparison between the two cases interesting, these issues do not unite the two movements behind a common cause.

Finally, there are important differences in the way the postcolonial state authorities in both countries have reacted to expressions of separatist agendas. Although the Zambian Barotseland case has elements of violent confrontation, both central government and BRE have so far always allowed room for negotiation. The overall more tranquil manner in which the Barotseland issue has been argued by BRE and handled by all central governments so far is consistent with Zambia's peacefully negotiated independence transition and postcolonial history. The inverse assessment of the same facts, of course, would be that the issue at hand never seems to get settled one way or the other.

In contrast, Namibia's SWAPO government reacted to the secessionists with harsh coercion that left no room for negotiation. This, and the judicial debacle of the excessively long high treason trials, has raised questions as to how committed SWAPO is to rule of law and democratic process. SWAPO's way of dealing with the Caprivi secession has ultimately led to the same result as in the Zambian case: the issues at hand never appear to fully go away and instead keep poisoning the political climate on a local, regional, and national level in both countries.

This last point motivates us to add to our analysis a note of caution. From various other cases of political dispute and indeed secessionism in Africa (and elsewhere), it is evident that historical facts are a rather fluid commodity. Collective memory, the interpretation of facts, and even the claims over their existence can change significantly over time. Although happening against a background of simmering discontent, the sporadic occurrence of acute separatist action in Zambia's Western Province and the Namibian Caprivi/Zambezi region have so far been largely out of sync. But if the socioeconomic causes as well as the handling of the political issues by both the Namibian and Zambian central governments were to aggravate grievances in both regions *simultaneously* at some point in the future, a pan-Lozi separatist cause may well become articulated.

Who is likely to articulate it? Judging from past events in both cases, the spokespeople would likely be educated persons with affiliations to what is left of the Lozi system of "traditional" authority who have been cut out of the deals that have led their fellow—or rival—compatriots to buy into supporting the central state. Lozi separatists would need to mobilize sufficient support among disenchanted youths to back their argument with any significant concrete action. If the socioeconomic situation in both regions does not tangibly improve, there should be no shortage of disenchanted youth, especially if access to and control over the local natural resource base would promise a better living.

Are they likely to succeed? We do not think so, if success is defined as seceding. But if those who articulate the secessionist argument see a chance that this may force the central state authorities to stop ignoring them, then getting noticed may well be a good enough reason to keep the secessionist demand and mobilization on their agenda.

References

Afrol News/IRIN. (2006). *Caprivi political party declared illegal.* Retrieved from http://www.afrol.com/articles/21239

Amnesty International. (2003a). *Namibia. Justice delayed is justice denied. The Caprivi treason trial.* Amnesty International, report reference AFR 42/001/2003.

Amnesty International. (2003b). *Namibia: Authorities must ensure a fair trial for Caprivi defendants.* Amnesty International, report reference AFR 42/005/2003.

Analysis Africa. (2013). *Caprivi secession trial still haunts Namibia.* Retrieved from http://analysisafrica.com/reports/caprivi-secession-trial-still-haunts-namibia/#.Ucr2CqxjEuJ

Barotse National Conference. (1995). *Resolutions of the Barotse National Conference Lealui.* Lusaka, Zambia, November 3–4, 1995.

Barotse Patriotic Front. (2004). Submission to the Constitutional Review Commission.

Caplan, G. L. (1968). Barotseland, the secessionist challenge to Zambia. *Journal of Modern African Studies, 6*(3), 343–360.

Caplan, G. L. (1969). Barotseland's scramble for protection. *Journal of African History, x*(2), 277–294.

Caplan, G. L. (1970). *The elites of Barotseland 1878–1969: A political history of Zambia's Western Province.* London: C. Hurst & Co.

Caprivi Freedom. (2013). History. Retrieved from http://www.caprivifreedom.com/history.i

Eifert, B., Miguel, E., & Posner, D. N. (2010). Political competition and ethnic identification in Africa. *American Journal of Political Science, 54*(2), 494–510.

Englebert, P. (2005). Compliance and defiance to national integration in Barotseland and Casamance. *Afrika Spektrum, 39*(1), 29–59.

Fisch, M. (1999). *The secessionist movement in the Caprivi: A historical perspective.* Windhoek: Namibia Scientific Society.

Flint, L. (2003). State-building in Central Southern Africa: Citizenship and subjectivity in Barotseland and Caprivi. *Journal of African Historical Studies, 36*(2), 393–428.

Flint, L. (2004). *Historical constructions of postcolonial citizenship and subjectivity: The case of the Lozi peoples of southern Central Africa.* Unpublished PhD thesis, University of Birmingham.

Forrest, J. B. (2004). *Subnationalism in Africa: Ethnicity, alliances, and politics.* Boulder: Lynne Rienner.

Fosse, L. J. (1996). Negotiating the nation in local terms. *Ethnicity and nationalism in eastern Caprivi, Namibia.* Master's thesis, Department and Museum of Anthropology, University of Oslo.

Gluckman, M. (1941). *Economy of the central Barotse plain*. Livingstone: Rhodes-Livingstone Institute.

Gluckman, M. (1955). *The judicial process among the Barotse of northern Rhodesia*. Manchester: Manchester University Press.

Gluckman, M. (1959). The Lozi of Barotseland in Northwestern Rhodesia. In E. Colson & M. Gluckman (Eds.), *Seven tribes of British Central Africa* (pp. 1–93). Manchester: Manchester University Press.

Gluckman, M. (1965). *The ideas in Barotse jurisprudence*. New Haven: Yale University Press.

Guijarro, E. M. (2013). An independent Caprivi: A madness of the few, a partial collective yearning or a realistic possibility? Citizen perspectives on Caprivian secession. *Journal of Southern African Studies, 39*(2), 337–352.

Hobsbawm, E., & Ranger, T. (Eds.). (1983). *The invention of tradition*. Cambridge: Cambridge University Press.

Kangumu, B. (2000). *A forgotten corner of Namibia: Aspects of the history of the Caprivi strip, c. 1939-1980*. Master's thesis, University of Cape Town.

Kangumu, B. (2011). *Contesting Caprivi a history of colonial isolation and regional nationalism in Namibia*. Basel: Basler Afrika Bibliographien.

Kaure, A. T. (2013, August 23). There was once a region. *The Namibian*.

Lemarchand, R. (1972). Political clientelism and ethnicity in tropical Africa: Competing solidarities in nation-building. *The American Political Sciences Review, 66*(1), 68–90.

Mainga Bull, M. (1973). *Bulozi under the Luyana kings*. Upper Saddle River: Prentice Hall.

Mainga Bull, M. (1995). *The 1964 Barotseland Agreement in Historical Perspective*. Livingstone: Institute of Economic Studies.

Mamdani, M. (1996). *Citizen and subject: Contemporary Africa and the legacy of late colonialism*. Princeton: Princeton University Press.

Mbikusita-Lewanika, A. (2001). *Barotseland: Bastion of resistance*. Paper presented at conference Interrogating the New Political Culture in Southern Africa, Harare, 13–15 June, 2001.

Melber, H. (2009). One Namibia, one nation? The Caprivi as a contested territory. *Journal of Contemporary African Studies, 27*(4), 463–481.

Melber, H., & Saunders, C. (2007). Conflict mediation in decolonisation: Namibia's transition to independence. *Africa Spectrum, 42*(1), 73–94.

Menges, W. (2013, December 19). Treason accused sue for N$ 1,2 billion. *The Namibian*.

Minorities at Risk. (2009). Assessment for Lozi in Zambia. Retrieved from http://www.cidcm.umd.edu/mar/assessment.asp?groupId=55102

Movement for Multi-Party Democracy. (1991). *The MMD manifesto*. MMD: Lusaka.

Mulford, D. C. (1967). *Zambia. The politics of independence 1957–1964.* Oxford: Oxford University Press.

Mutenda, M. (2013, August 15). Namibia: Zambezi name fuels heated debate. *New Era.*

Namibian Sun. (2013, November 25). Blow for Caprivian exiles' home return. *Namibian Sun.*

Ngoshi, M. K. (2013, August 23). Caprivians in the Zambezi region. *The Namibian.*

Sankwasa, F. (2013, November 19). Govt wants to entice refugees back. *Namibian Sun.*

Sanzila, G. (2013, August 21). Zambezi name still causing waves. *New Era.*

Sasman, C. (2017, April 21). Muyongo speaks out. *Namibian Sun.*

Soiri, I. (2001). SWAPO wins, apathy rules: The Namibian 1998 local authority elections. In M. Cowen & L. Laakso (Eds.), *Multi-party elections in Africa* (pp. 187–216). London: James Currey.

South Africa. (1964). Report of the commission into SWA affairs, 1962–3, Pretoria.

Streitwolf, K. (1911). *Der Caprivizipfel.* Berlin: Süsserott.

Sumbwa, N. (2000). Traditionalism, democracy and political participation: The case of Western Province, Zambia. *African Study Monographs, 21*(3), 105–146.

The Namibian. (2008, April 1). Pohamba at power line opening. *The Namibian.*

The Windhoek Observer. (2013, August 22). What's in a name? *The Windhoek Observer.*

Trollope, W. E. (1937). Inspection tour 1937. *National Archives of Namibia, 2267,* A503/1-7.

United Democratic Party. (2005). *Caprivi Zipfel: The controversial strip.* Retrieved from http://www.caprivifreedom.com/history.i?cmd=view&hid=23

Van Horn, L. (1977). The agricultural history of Barotseland, 1840–1964. In R. Palmer & N. Parsons (Eds.), *The roots of rural society in Central and Southern Africa* (pp. 144–169). London: Heinemann.

Virtual Zambia. (2008). *The economic history of Zambia.* Retrieved from http://www.bized.co.uk/virtual/dc/back/econ.htm

Zeller, W. (2007a). Chiefs, policing and vigilantes: 'Cleaning up' the Caprivi borderland of Namibia. In L. Buur & H. M. Kyed (Eds.), *State recognition and democratization in sub-Saharan Africa: A new dawn for traditional authorities?* (pp. 79–104). New York: Palgrave.

Zeller, W. (2007b). 'Now we are a town': Chiefs, investors, and the state in Zambia's Western Province. In L. Buur & H. M. Kyed (Eds.), *State recognition and democratization in sub-Saharan Africa: A new dawn for traditional authorities?* (pp. 209–231). New York: Palgrave.

Zeller, W. (2009). Danger and opportunity in Katima Mulilo: A Namibian border boomtown at transnational crossroads. *Journal of Southern African Studies, 35*(1), 133–154.

Zeller, W. (2010). Neither arbitrary nor artificial: Lozi chiefs and the making of the Namibia-Zambia borderland. *Journal of Borderlands Studies, 25*(2), 6–21.

INTERVIEWS

Dr. Stephen Muliokela, Director Golden Valley Agricultural Research Trust, Lusaka, June 4, 2004.

Mr. Marcus Ndebele, market trader, Mwandi, May 25, 2004.

Mr. Namukolo Mukutu, former Permanent Secretary for Agriculture, Lusaka, 4 June 2004.

Mr. Sibeso Yeta, Mwandi, May 20, 2004.

Mr. Wally Herbst, Mwandi, May 24, 2004.

Mrs Fiona Dixon-Thompson, Mwandi, May 24, 2004.

Munukayumbwa Mulumemui, BRE Induna Omei for Sesheke District, Mwandi, May 21, 2004.

Dominik Sandema, BRE Induna Anasambala for Sesheke District, Mwandi, June 11, 2004.

Senior Chief Inyambo Yeta, BRE chief for Sesheke District, Mwandi, June 14, 2004.

CHAPTER 12

Biafra and Secessionism in Nigeria: An Instrument of Political Bargaining

Johannes Harnischfeger

INTRODUCTION

Nigeria has a long history of secessionism, beginning around 1950 when it became clear that the country would eventually gain independence from Great Britain. These early calls for secession did not come from marginal groups but from Nigeria's largest ethnic conglomerate. The Hausa-Fulani dominated the Northern Region—which comprised 79% of Nigeria's landmass and about 55% of its population—but lagged behind in economic development as well as political and administrative representation. Northern Muslim elites had little Western education; very few were in the federal civil service. Leading Hausa-Fulani politicians feared that Christians from the south would control the new independent government, threatening to secede if the north was not given a high degree of autonomy. The threat worked and the colonial administration, fearing the country's breakup, granted major concessions. In addition, the British helped the Hausa-

J. Harnischfeger (✉)
University of Frankfurt, Frankfurt, Germany

University of Cologne, Cologne, Germany
e-mail: Lotje.devries@wur.nl

© The Author(s) 2019
L. de Vries et al. (eds.), *Secessionism in African Politics*,
Palgrave Series in African Borderlands Studies,
https://doi.org/10.1007/978-3-319-90206-7_12

Fulani elites gain control of the central government at independence in 1960. Thus Hausa-Fulani politicians came to dominate Nigerian politics for nearly four decades, under civilian as well as military regimes.

Northern hegemony provoked calls for secession in the south, first among the Yoruba, the dominant ethnic group in Southwest Nigeria. After the central administration had placed Yorubaland under a state of emergency and installed a compliant regional government, protesters rioted in 1965, calling for an independent Yoruba republic. In 1966, the center of secessionist agitation shifted to the southeast, which was dominated by the Igbo.

Initially, the Igbo had shown no interest in secessionism or regional autonomy. During the colonial period, many had moved from their densely populated home territory to settle in other parts of Nigeria. They advocated a strong unitary government that would protect the rights of ethnic minorities in all parts of the country. But in 1966, following a military coup and countercoup, thousands of Igbo were killed in the north and about a million fled back to their original home areas. Igbo leaders subsequently demanded far-reaching autonomy for the Eastern Region, including the right to control its own army. When they could not reach an agreement with the federal government, they made true their threat to secede when Chukwuemeka Odumegwu Ojukwu, the Eastern Region's military governor, proclaimed a sovereign Republic of Biafra on May 30, 1967.

With the defeat of the Biafra "rebels" in 1970, after a 30-month civil war, secessionism in Nigeria was dead for more than two decades. When it re-emerged, it followed the existing pattern of confrontation between the three major ethnic groups: the Yoruba who—according to a census in 1952–1953—formed 17% of the population, the Igbo with 18%, and the Hausa-Fulani with 28%.[1] The new wave of secessionism was triggered by a political crisis in 1993 when Nigeria's Northern rulers annulled the results of a presidential election, which a Yoruba candidate had won. To pressure the central government, Yoruba leaders called for far-reaching autonomy, and if necessary, secession. They mobilized a militia that in

---

[1] The census of 1952–1953 (whose main results were reprinted in Coleman [1986: 15]) gave separate figures for the Hausa (18%) and the Fulani (10%). In the nineteenth century, when the Fulani toppled the Hausa kings, they formed a distinct stratum of conquerors, but most of them gradually adopted the language and often the culture of the numerically dominant Hausa. Thus, it has become common to talk of the "Hausa-Fulani," although in northeast Nigeria and parts of the Middle Belt, Hausa and Fulani often prefer to live in separate settlements.

1998 began to attack members of the Hausa-Fulani diaspora living in Lagos and other Yoruba cities. Although Yoruba politicians threatened to secede if the central government did not give in, they had no interest in breaking away from Nigeria because this would have cut them off from their main source of income, the oil revenues. Their aim was to topple a brutal, exclusivist regime, dominated by their rivals.

Ethnic militancy evidently paid off. Threatened with the prospect of a civil war, the military regime embarked on a transition to civilian rule and arranged for a Christian Yoruba to become president. This power shift to the south in 1999 was neither the result of a democratic decision nor of a power-sharing arrangement. Nigeria's fractured elites have never agreed on a formula to let the presidency rotate. Instead, they have resorted to ethnic and religious violence in order to intimidate their rivals and gain access to power.

Inspired by the success of Yoruba separatism, Igbo activists subsequently formed a liberation movement that campaigned for a new Biafra. Despite their radical rhetoric, they were less interested in secession than in pressurizing other Nigerians into making an Igbo president. Separatism also recurred among the Hausa-Fulani, but here it was defined in religious not in ethnic terms. By introducing a strict form of Shari'a in 12 states of the "Far North," Muslims made it clear that they wanted to regulate their affairs autonomously, without interference from infidels. Yet again, they did not want to break the federation and forgo their share of the oil revenues. The Shari'a campaign, which led to bloody clashes between Muslims and Christians in 2000 and 2001, rather served as a brutal reminder to the Yoruba president not to marginalize the north.

Ethnic minorities in the Niger Delta, where Nigeria's oil wealth is produced, have also called for autonomy, in particular for control of "their" natural resources, but they are too fragmented to aspire to a common independent state. The situation is similar in the Middle Belt, between the Muslim north and the Christian south, where hundreds of small ethnic groups coexist. Representatives of these groups have often claimed ethnic self-determination, above all, the right to control their ancestral land and to restrict the influx of "settlers." But like the minorities in the Niger Delta, they need a strong federal government that protects them from possible domination by Nigeria's large ethnic groups.

I analyze the emergence of two main types of secessionisms: based on ethnic self-determination in the south and on religious autonomy in the north. The main focus, however, is on Igbo secessionism because it succeeded in establishing an independent state from 1967 to 1970. The civil war that forced the Igbo back into the Nigerian federation claimed the lives of about one million people, most of them Biafrans. Thirty years later, separatism has risen again and a Movement for the Actualisation of a Sovereign State of Biafra (MASSOB), formed in 1999, has found widespread support among the Igbo. The renewed wish to secede, among the Igbo and other groups, articulates a long-standing and deep disillusionment with Nigerian democracy, and it shows that Muslims and Christians, northerners, and southerners are "fed up with one another."[2]

A breakup of the country would, of course, harm all parts of the federation. Thus, the political elites in Igboland and Yorubaland as well as in the Far North do not seriously pursue secession; they try to use ethnic and religious militancy in order to blackmail the central government. At the same time, they seem to have only limited influence over the angry young men who call for a new Biafra or an Islamic caliphate. As the present Boko Haram insurgency demonstrates, militants who feel that they have nothing to lose may escalate the violence until the hated federation falls apart.

In the following five sections of my chapter, I outline and analyze the main political ruptures and transformations that gave rise to calls for secession in Nigeria. The first section explores the emergence of separatism in the 1950s, when regional elites negotiated under British tutelage the constitutional basis for an independent republic. The second section describes the failure of the First Republic and the descent into civil war in the late 1960s. In the third section, I give a brief survey of attempts by Nigeria's military rulers to defuse ethno-religious conflicts through constitutional engineering in the 1970s and 1980s. Fourth section deals with the re-emergence of secessionism after 1993, when it became obvious that successive military regimes had no intention of balancing ethnic and religious interests. In the concluding section, I examine more closely the MASSOB, the main separatist organization in Igboland today.

---

[2] Weekly Trust, January 14, 2000, quoted in Iliffe (2011: 186).

THE ROOTS OF SECESSIONISM IN PRE-INDEPENDENCE NIGERIA

Nigeria's strong separatist tendencies have often been attributed to the "extreme cultural diversity"[3] of its population. The northern savannah city states of Hausaland and the empire of Kanem-Bornu around Lake Chad have been in contact with the Islamic world of the Mediterranean and the Middle East for a thousand years. Their rulers became Muslims, but they tolerated the "pagan" religions of their subjects and often participated in un-Islamic rituals. Against this "ungodly" behavior, a Fulani preacher called Usman dan Fodio proclaimed a jihad in 1804, which found support among Fulani pastoralists and parts of the Hausa population.

The jihadists toppled the "corrupt" Hausa kings, replaced them with a Fulani aristocracy, and established the Caliphate of Sokoto, an alliance of some 40 emirates that covered large parts of today's Northern Nigeria and extended into the north of Cameroon. As the Fulani rulers formed just a small minority in the conquered areas, they legitimized their supremacy in religious terms, presenting themselves as custodians of a pure form of Islam. Religion alone created a feeling of togetherness that could transcend ethnic loyalties and hold the disparate empire together. However, at its periphery, the caliphate did not establish an Islamic administration but raided for slaves. In order to escape these raids, many groups fled to the Jos Plateau, the Muri Mountains, and other impassable areas where they preserved their independence throughout the nineteenth century. When British colonialism arrived, many of them converted to Christianity in order to distance themselves from the advancing Hausa-Fulani culture.

Further south, the Fulani warriors and their Hausa allies conquered parts of Yorubaland and transformed them into an emirate, yet their expansion toward the coast was stopped in 1840, so that most Yoruba kingdoms preserved their independence. Today, half of the Yoruba population is Muslim while the other half is Christian, with the traditional religion having retained much influence. Yoruba Muslims tend to be more tolerant and secular-minded than their coreligionists in the north. Since most families are religiously mixed, Yoruba have been anxious to avoid a religious polarization.

In the southeast, people had no direct contact with the Fulani emirates and with Islamic culture. Igbo-speaking groups in the tropical rainforest

[3] Joseph (1999: 362).

lived in hundreds of autonomous village federations without any overarching political or religious institutions. A sense of common ethnic identity only emerged in colonial times, under the influence of Western-educated elites. Today, Igbo identity is not so much defined by their ancestral traditions (which were quite diverse) but by Christianity, which began to spread with the colonial conquest.

When the British government took possession of the vast territory between Lagos and Sokoto, it did little to bridge the "enormous cultural distance between north and south."[4] From 1900 to 1914, the Northern and Southern Provinces were administered separately as two protectorates. When they were amalgamated, it was mainly to balance their budgets because the Northern administration ran a deficit and had to be subsidized, while the Southern administration generated a surplus.[5] With their amalgamation, customs frontiers were abolished, the railway system was unified, and the currency standardized.

Yet otherwise the Northern and Southern Provinces remained under two distinct bureaucracies with, writes Coleman, "The only bond of political unity...the person of Sir Frederick Lugard, the new governor-general."[6] In the north, British rule preserved the emirates and their Fulani nobility, and it codified the prevalent legal system, the Shari'a. Hausa was retained as the language of administration, while English was used in the south. Since the authority of the emirs rested largely on their religious legitimacy, the British were anxious to seal off the emirate areas from Christian-Western influences. For decades, Christian missionaries were not allowed to operate in the emirate regions, so they concentrated their activities on the south and on those "pagan" areas of the Middle Belt that had not been conquered by the Fulani. Mission work was accompanied by establishing schools and hospitals; thus, the Christianized areas acquired a lead in Western education. In 1957, merely 185,000 children in the north attended primary school; in the south the number stood at 2,343,000.[7] Thanks to their educational advantage, southerners were in a far better position to gain jobs in the colonial administration and in other parts of the modern sector. Many Igbo, Yoruba, Edo, and Ibibio found employment in the north. But the British authorities, averse to rapid

[4] Diamond (1988: 48).
[5] Falola and Heaton (2008: 116–117).
[6] Coleman (1986: 46).
[7] Coleman (1986: 134).

change, sought to contain the cultural, political, and economic impact of the migrants. Southerners in the north were not allowed to buy land; they had to live in segregated areas, and the Shari'a laws—enforced by the colonial authorities—did not permit them to marry Muslim women.

The south, though much smaller in size, was split into the Western and Eastern Provinces (called Regions from 1951) in 1939, with the River Niger as boundary. The Igbo in the East were more than any other large group, argues Ottenberg, "receptive to culture change, and most willing to accept Western ways."[8] Although mission schools had come late (Igboland had only been pacified by the end of World War I), the Igbo pursued Western education so vigorously that they caught up with their main rivals, the Yoruba, in the late 1940s.[9] At about the same time, they began to dominate the nationalist movement that was going to replace the colonial government.

The controlling position of Nnamdi Azikiwe and other Igbo in the National Council of Nigeria and the Cameroons (NCNC) prompted a young Yoruba intellectual, Obafemi Awolowo, to form a regional party in 1951, with the explicit aim of mobilizing Yoruba voters and gaining control of the west. While the NCNC demanded a unitary government, the Action Group (AG) propagated ethnic autonomy and called for the right of secession to be included in the constitution.[10] In 1955, some AG members actually threatened to secede, after Igbo and Hausa-Fulani politicians rejected the demand to re-incorporate the federal capital Lagos, traditionally a Yoruba town, into the Western Region.[11]

Anticolonial political parties that sought to take over the state apparatus from the British had emerged among the Western-educated elites in Lagos and other southern cities. These parties were led by Igbo and Yoruba politicians who paid little attention to the interests of the north, assuming, Coleman writes, "that the so-called backward north could be manipulated at will."[12] The traditional rulers of the Islamic north only began to organize themselves into a political party when Nigeria's transition to independence had already set in, and they were facing the first election in 1951. Their Northern Peoples' Congress (NPC) was a purely regional party,

---

[8] Ottenberg (2006: 179).
[9] Coleman (1986: 333).
[10] Lynn (2001).
[11] Nnoli (1980: 160) and Sklar (1983: 134–135).
[12] Coleman (1986: 352).

controlled by the emirs and their officials in the "native administration."[13] In the early 1950s, the political prospects of the Hausa-Fulani elite looked grim. Executive positions in the state machinery were filled by an educated elite, and it looked as if European criteria alone would define who was considered educated. Young Nigerians who had learned English in the mission schools now held the key to success, while all forms of Islamic learning had been devalued.

The NPC sought to delay the transition to independence, hoping to improve their competitive position. If southern hegemony could not be averted, separation looked like a better option. In 1950, when delegates from the north and south met for the first time to discuss constitutional reforms, the Emirs of Zaria and Katsina threatened to lead the whole Northern Region out of Nigeria.[14] In 1953, after NPC delegates had been abused by a crowd in the streets of Lagos, the Premier of the Northern Region called the creation of Nigeria in 1914 a "mistake," and the Northern House of Assembly passed a motion that called for separation from the South in all matters except defense, external affairs, and customs.[15] The British considered secession a real possibility,[16] so they granted the NPC far-reaching concessions, thereby encouraging northern intransigence: "secession, as so often in these years, was the threat the North was prepared to use to get its way."[17] The NPC had two key demands: first, give the regions more autonomy, including control over the police and the judiciary. Second, maintain the Northern Region as the largest political unit in the federation, with more than half of Nigeria's population and more than half of the seats in the federal parliament.

The British gave in to these demands, against the protests of Christian Middle Belters, whose political party, the United Middle Belt Congress, demanded a separate region for the minorities in order to break free from Hausa-Fulani hegemony. Although a government commission, instituted in 1956 to enquire into the fears of the minorities, found evidence of

[13] The Fulani aristocracy did maintain its control over the party apparatus into the postcolonial era. In 1961, when elections were held for the Northern Region's parliament, 40% of the elect were members of royal families, a further 28% belonged to other noble families, and only 2% were descendants of slaves (Whitaker 1970: 322), although slaves had comprised between 25 and 50% of the emirates' population (Lovejoy 1986: 240).

[14] Tamuno (1970: 568) and Coleman (1986: 362).

[15] Sklar (1983: 128, 132) and Lynn (2001).

[16] Lynn (2001).

[17] Lynn (2001) and Njoku (2002: 250).

discrimination against them, the British administration resisted any partitioning of the north. It accepted that NPC leaders sought to maintain the north's numerical advantage as "the sole defense against political and economic domination by the South."[18]

When northern politicians were given control over the regional government in 1954, they began to purge their administration of all southerners. This policy was popular in all parts of the north, including the Middle Belt, because a good number of mission-educated Middle Belters now occupied posts vacated by southerners. With its Northernization policy, the NPC acted as champion of an all-inclusive regional solidarity, true to the party motto "One North: One People—irrespective of Religion, Rank or Tribe."

After independence, however, when Hausa-Fulani politicians gained control of the federal government and tightened their grip on the Northern Region, they sidelined the minorities and cracked down on opposition parties. In 1963, the Premier of the Northern Region, Ahmadu Bello, a direct descendant of Usman dan Fodio, embarked on an Islamization campaign to consolidate Hausa-Fulani hegemony in the potentially seditious Middle Belt.[19]

From Independence to Civil War

With British help, the NPC emerged as the strongest party in the federal elections of 1959 with only eight seats short of an absolute majority. Yet, its leaders were still afraid of losing out. While the NPC negotiated with the Igbo-dominated NCNC to form a coalition government, they also held meetings with representatives of neighboring Chad in order to be prepared for secession, incase conflicts with the south escalated.[20] At the time of Nigeria's independence in 1960, northerners held barely 1% of all positions in the federal administration.[21] Yet once in control of central government, northerners lowered the entry qualifications of the civil service and thus improved their own job opportunities.

Together with their Igbo allies, northerners also sought to destroy the main opposition party, Awolowo's Action Group. Its leaders were arrested

[18] Sharwood-Smith: Recollections of British Administration, 1969, quoted in Diamond (1988: 29).

[19] Paden (1986: 566–569).

[20] Lynn (2001).

[21] Diamond (1988: 27).

in 1962, and the Western Region was placed under a state of emergency. The regional elections in 1965 were "fraudulent and brutal confrontations"[22] that disempowered the population in the west. From a Yoruba perspective, Nigeria had turned into a colonial power, and its security forces, writes Diamond, acted like an "army of occupation."[23] Democracy seemed only possible if the Yoruba shook off the Hausa-Fulani yoke. Violent protests and a secessionist mood made the Western Region ungovernable. Other parts of the federation remained calm, but the Igbo (and other groups) were disaffected as well. After NPC politicians had installed a docile government in the west, they no longer needed their allies in the east and began turning against their NCNC coalition partner. In December 1965, the premier of the Eastern Region threatened with secession, and on January 15, 1966, some young army officers (six Igbo and one Yoruba) staged a coup, which was greeted in most places with joy or cautious approval.

The new head of state, however, antagonized large sections of the population when he surrounded himself with Igbo advisers, fueling suspicions that the coup had actually been an Igbo takeover. On May 24, 1966, General Ironsi abolished the Regional structure and decreed a unitary state with a centralized administration. Every observer immediately recognized that this would strengthen Igbo influence in the state apparatus. The Northernization policy, which had benefited the "indigenous" population in the Northern Region, would be reversed, and "strangers" from the south would regain control of the local administration. A few days after the announcement of the decree, riots broke out against Igbo living in the north. Two months later, on July 28, 1966, Northern officers killed General Ironsi.

The coup plotters, led by Lieutenant Colonel Murtalla Mohammed, had initially aimed for secession. At the army headquarters in Lagos, they had hoisted a flag that heralded a Republic of the North. The soldiers, however, were divided. The majority of the rank-and-file, recruited from Christian and "traditionalist" groups in the Middle Belt, had little interest in joining a Republic of the North. Under the rule of the NPC, the minorities had been repressed and marginalized. With the July coup, they suddenly found themselves at the center of power. Their spokesman, Lieutenant Colonel Gowon—who was a Christian Angas—fought vigorously to preserve the federation. He had the support of the British High Commission and of

---

[22] Diamond (1988: 41).
[23] Obafemi Awolowo, quoted in St. Jorre (1972: 109).

high-ranking officials in the federal administration, the so-called techno-crats. As the dominant faction within the army, Gowon and his Middle Belt followers forged an alliance with Muslim soldiers and politicians from the Far North, yet he pressured them to accept a constitutional change: the federation had to be restructured to give the minorities autonomy. The old regions, inherited from the colonial regime, were to be replaced by 12 states. Of the six states planned for the north, Hausa-Fulani would domi-nate only three, with other regions encompassing ethnic minorities.

To protect these minority states, Gowon insisted that there be a strong federal center. This set him on a collision course with the military gover-nor of the Eastern Region, where the July coup had not succeeded. Colonel Ojukwu, an Igbo, called for a looser association: a confederation of regions with their own security forces and with the right to veto deci-sions at the center. He argued that easterners could not trust the army command in Lagos because it had not been able or willing to stop the riots against the Igbo. Between May and October 1966, thousands of Igbo (and some other easterners) had been killed in the north, and about a mil-lion had fled to their home region.

At a conference in Aburi, Ghana, on January 4–5, 1967, Gowon gave in to most of Ojukwu's demands and accepted a confederate solution, but on his return to Lagos, he reneged and insisted that sovereignty must remain with the central government. Yoruba politicians, who had little influence in the army, were reluctant to support Gowon's regime. On May 1, 1967, Awolowo announced that the Western Region would leave the federation in case the east pulled out.[24] Nigeria seemed to be at the verge of collapse. On May 30, 1967, Ojukwu declared secession and the found-ing of the Republic of Biafra on May 30, 1967.

Awolowo did not follow. Federal troops occupied the Western Region, whereas in the East Igbo officers had brought local army units under their control. Moreover, Awolowo realized that he was now dealing with a dif-ferent class of northern rulers: less monolithic and with a strong represen-tation of Middle Belt minorities pursuing a political agenda similar to his own. So he joined Gowon's government and campaigned against Biafra. The rebels, he said, had "committed a crime and must be punished."[25] Part of the "punishment" was an economic blockade against the east. Federal troops invaded the Region on July 6, 1967, cutting off Biafra

[24] Kirk-Greene (1971: 415).
[25] Cronje (1972: 116).

from its seaports and stopping food supply into the densely populated enclave. Trying to starve the Biafrans into submission, the Gowon regime ruled out any compromise: "This war must be fought to the finish."[26]

The Biafran troops were poorly armed and vastly outnumbered. By October 1968, 15 months after the Nigerian invasion, all major cities had been lost and Biafra was reduced to a quarter of its original territory. This was a stretch of land less than 200 km long and 50–100 km wide. In Biafra's middle was an airstrip where up to 40 planes landed each night loaded with arms and food aid.[27] Biafra's leader Ojukwu had no chance of military victory. At his troops' defeat in January 1970, about a million people had died,[28] many of them civilians who had been starved to death.

Why did Ojukwu not surrender when the suffering of his people became unbearable? His only hope lay with the international community, which had to be swayed by humanitarian considerations to intervene on behalf of the secessionists: "Our aim all along has been to delay the enemy until the world conscience can effectively be aroused against genocide."[29] Biafran propaganda, backed by a public relations firm in Geneva, tried to convince the world that the Igbo were fighting a desperate war of survival against a regime of mass murderers that would annihilate them if they surrendered.[30]

News of the hunger blockade led to a wave of protests in Europe and North America. Public opinion was largely pro-Biafran, supporting Ojukwu's call for a ceasefire and a negotiated settlement, yet diplomatically Biafra remained almost completely isolated. Western governments, the Soviet Union, the Organisation of African Unity (OAU), and the Arab world, all sided with Nigeria. It looked as if Biafra was confronted with an "international conspiracy,"[31] as Ojukwu himself phrased it, which defied all religious and ideological antagonisms. The only open support came in

[26] Obafemi Awolowo, Vice Chairman of Nigeria's Federal Executive Council, quoted in Cronje (1972: 115).

[27] Harneit-Sievers (1992: 281) and St. Jorre (1972: 75).

[28] Estimates vary considerably. The only way to obtain reliable figures would have been to take a sample of regions in Southeast Nigeria and inquire about the number of casualties. Harneit-Sievers (1992: 285) found that in his research area about 10% of the population had died as a consequence of the war. If figures in other regions were similar, then the assumption of about one million casualties would be realistic.

[29] Odumegwu Ojukwu, in a speech on September 25, 1968, published in Ojukwu (1981: 353).

[30] Stremlau (1977: 109–177, 320–321, 328) and Gould (2012: 73–79, 139–148).

[31] Odumegwu Ojukwu, quoted in Obi and Nwosu (1997).

the form of relief from the International Red Cross, Caritas, and the World Council of Churches; four African countries (Tanzania, Gabon, Cote d'Ivoire, and Zambia) accorded international recognition to Biafra. There was also some covert support: the French government supplied weapons, though only belatedly and not in large enough quantities for the encircled Biafrans to repel the Nigerian army.[32]

The International Committee of the Red Cross spoke of "the gravest emergency" it had handled since the World War II.[33] For the first time, dozens of religious and secular aid agencies came together and coordinated their operations. Although the Nigerian government vehemently protested against their interference, humanitarian organizations such as Caritas, Oxfam, and Médecins sans Frontières insisted that they had a right to intervene on behalf of the suffering civilians, even if it meant breaking international law.[34] However, the food they delivered was not enough to prevent mass starvation. Though their intervention was meant to avert a humanitarian catastrophe, it may have had the opposite effect. It did nothing to solve the conflict but prolonged the war and thus the suffering of the Biafran population.[35]

CONSTITUTIONAL REFORMS UNDER MILITARY RULE

A few months after the Biafra war, Igbo began moving back to the northern and western parts of the country where most of them could reclaim their properties. Today, there are probably millions of Igbo living in the north, as there are millions in the west, spread into the remotest villages. The oil boom of the 1970s helped to reintegrate them economically, but politically they remained second-class citizens. The federal government had promised at the end of the war that there would be "no victors, no vanquished;" Nigerians were to forget the enmities of the past and make a new start. However, the victors made sure that Igbo did not rise to top positions in the army and that they had little access to political decision-making. This was tolerable for a while but became a severe handicap in the 1980s, when communal conflicts intensified and state authorities in the north did not adequately protect the Igbo diaspora.

---

[32] St. Jorre (1972: 323), Cronje (1972: 323), and Stremlau (1977: 224–233).
[33] St. Jorre (1972: 209).
[34] Pérouse de Montclos (2009: 70).
[35] Pérouse de Montclos (2009: 69, 70, 75) and Gould (2012: 134).

After General Gowon was toppled in 1975, the new military leadership designed a transition program to bring the country back to democratic rule. Nigeria's new federal structure, with 12 states created in 1967 (increased to 19 states in 1976, 21 in 1987, 30 in 1991, and 36 since 1996), seemed better suited to manage ethnic diversity than the tripolar structure of the First Republic. It defused tensions between the Hausa-Fulani, Igbo, and Yoruba, and it better accommodated ethnic minorities. A constitutional conference in 1977–1978 added consociational elements to this federal structure. Proportional representation of ethnic groups was introduced for the cabinet and other federal institutions. A new electoral system favored broad-based multiethnic parties.[36] Political scientists such as Diamond lauded Nigeria's return to civilian rule as "one of the most imaginative and carefully designed transitions ever staged."[37] Yet when the Second Republic started in 1979, it took a similar turn as the first. The National Party of Nigeria, a kind of successor to the NPC, emerged as the strongest force and formed a coalition with the Igbo-dominated Nigerian Peoples Party. The new republic was as short-lived as the old. After four years in office, the government of Shehu Shagari had been so discredited by corruption and election rigging that people celebrated in the streets when the army took over and arrested hundreds of politicians.

While the army saw itself as the guardian of Nigerian unity, northern officers controlled it through an alliance with the Hausa-Fulani elite. Despite their nationalist rhetoric, these officers did not help negotiate a settlement between rival sections of the country. President Ibrahim Babangida (1985–1993) and his successor Sani Abacha (1993–1998) designed ambitious transition programs and promised to place Nigeria's next democracy on a solid basis. But they did not honor their own rules, announcing and then postponing elections or allowing new political parties and then banning them. Thus, they destroyed all institutions that could have mediated between competing elite factions and stabilized power-sharing arrangements.[38]

After much delay, the presidential elections for the Third Republic were finally held on June 12, 1993. When it emerged that Moshood Abiola, a Yoruba Muslim, had defeated the Northern candidate, General Babangida declared the largely free and fair election void. Had all civilian politicians

[36] Bach (2006: 66–68).
[37] Diamond (1988: 2).
[38] Diamond (1995: 461).

accepted the election results, they could have prevented the military regime from aborting the transition to democracy. However, most politicians in the north supported the annulment of the election. Even the highest religious authority, the Sultan of Sokoto, collaborated with the military in betraying the victorious candidate, although Abiola was the Vice President for Nigeria's Supreme Council of Islamic Affairs.[39]

In the end, the Yoruba campaigned almost alone to have Abiola sworn in as president. In Lagos and other cities of Yorubaland, the population went on strike, but elsewhere in Nigeria, people had little interest in fighting for a Yoruba president. An overwhelming majority of the Hausa-Fulani elite preferred a military regime, however brutal, to a democratic government headed by a Yoruba president, supporting the Abacha regime and rejecting accommodating their rivals in the south. Abiola, the election winner, was kept in jail without trial until he died in 1998 under mysterious circumstances.

ETHNIC AND RELIGIOUS MOBILIZATION

The trauma of the annulled election gave rise to a wave of separatism.[40] Why should the Yoruba share a polity with people who excluded them from ruling it? Many Yoruba intellectuals, disillusioned with multiethnic democracy, found ethnic nationalism a better means of confronting the military regime.[41] The threat to secede was more effective than the campaign for democracy.

The sudden death of Abacha in 1998 weakened the military regime. A militia called Oodua People's Congress (OPC) used this to demanded autonomy for Yorubaland, killing hundreds of Hausa-Fulani "settlers": living in Lagos and other Yoruba cities. In retaliation, Hausa-Fulani attacked the Yoruba minority in the Far North, forcing tens of thousands to flee. Yet the OPC, with the backing of Yoruba politicians, intellectuals, and traditional rulers, did not stop its violence against the Hausa; it even escalated the conflict by burning dozens of trucks meant to transport petrol to the north. The Yoruba activists knew that the army was too demoralized and divided to fight an insurgency in Lagos. And they were confident

---

[39] Kalu (2002: 671, 681–682).

[40] The re-emergence of separatism after more than 20 years was also inspired by changes in global attitudes toward secessionism, see Englebert (2009: 181–188).

[41] Sklar (2004: 43).

that Yorubaland would survive, if mutual killings and ethnic cleansing led to a breakup of the federation.

Yorubaland is not as densely populated as Igboland, and it has direct access to the sea. Moreover, about 60% of Nigeria's industrial activity is concentrated in the region around Lagos.[42] Since the military rulers knew that a Yoruba Republic was a realistic option and that secession would probably lead to the disintegration of the whole federation, the OPC blackmail worked—even though Yoruba nationalists had no real interest in breaking away from Nigeria. Their aim was autonomy within a restructured federation.[43] At the height of the confrontation with the military regime in 1998, many protesters called for a break with the federation, but for the political establishment, including the OPC leaders, secession was according to one of the OPC factions, just a "last option"[44] in case the government ignored their demands.

Another factor that led to the dissolution of military rule and a power shift to the south was the rebellion in the Niger Delta. Since 1956, when oil production in the Delta started, Nigeria's government has earned about one trillion US dollars in oil revenues, yet most people in the oil-producing areas live in poverty, facing pollution and a decaying infrastructure. Peaceful protests did not impress the federal authorities; politicians in Abuja, Nigeria's capital since 1991, only began to make concessions when militants occupied oil platforms and blew up pipelines. In 1998 liberation movements in the Delta shut down one-third of the oil production, forcing the federal government to increase the share of oil rents paid directly to the oil-producing states from 3 to 13%.

As in Yorubaland, the activists were organized on an ethnic basis, as Ijaw National Congress, Urhobo National Assembly or Movement for the Survival of the Ogoni People. Their call for ethnic autonomy and resource control proved an effective means of mobilizing people, but it did not unite the Delta population; it rather fuelled local rivalries.[45] So-called oil-producing communities that received payments from oil companies and the federal government did not want to share their revenues with other communities that had no oil fields of their own. Moreover, represen-

---

[42] Economist Intelligence Unit (2007: 37).
[43] cf. "The Yoruba Agenda" (2005: 2).
[44] Gani Adams, leader of the more militant OPC faction, in Wale Adebanwi (2005: 344).
[45] Nwajiaku (2005).

tatives of small ethnic groups accused the numerically dominant Ijaw of "using the *Egbesu Boys* to acquire oil rich lands belonging to others."[46]

Thus, the various liberation movements did not merge into a multiethnic secessionist organization fighting for a common Niger Delta republic. The most prominent campaigner for minority rights, Ken Saro-Wiwa, demanded self-determination for his Ogoni people and control over "their" oil fields, but he did not fight for secession. He suggested that there should be "one Hausa state, one Tiv state, Idoma state, Ijaw state, one Ogoni state,"[47] but he wanted these states, which would be very uneven in size, to be balanced and kept in check through a federation. The reasoning was that only the Nigerian government could protect minorities from a possible hegemony of their Igbo and Yoruba neighbors, and from intercommunal conflicts within the Delta population.

With the increase of ethnic militancy in 1998, Nigeria looked, according to Joseph, as if it was on "the brink of warfare."[48] To avoid disintegration, the army command decided to return the country to democracy and to hand over the presidency to a southerner. This decision was, however, not the result of a power-sharing agreement. The generals in the Provisional Ruling Council took all major decisions, in close consultation with Ibrahim Babangida and other eminent persons from the north. They decreed a constitution that had not been discussed with southern politicians. It contained none of the power-sharing arrangements suggested by Igbo and Yoruba politicians, such as the creation of six geopolitical zones and the rotation of the presidency between them.

Although the generals and their northern allies resolved to give the presidential office to a Yoruba, they did not allow Yoruba politicians to nominate the candidates. Instead, it was decided in closed-door meetings—without Yoruba politicians present—who was to become the first president of the Fourth Republic. The generals needed a Yoruba who was not anti-north, and they settled on Olusegun Obasanjo, a retired four-star general who had the reputation of being "detribalized." Obasanjo was duly elected in April 1999, but it was the money and influence of Babangida and other former generals that had paved his way. Obasanjo later admitted

---

[46] Akaruese (2003: 223).

[47] Ken Saro-Wiwa, "We Will Defend Our Oil with Our Blood," quoted in Ogoni's Agonies: Ken Saro-Wiwa and the Crisis in Nigeria, ed. Abdul-Rasheed Na'Allah (Trenton/Asmara: Africa World Press 1998: 357).

[48] Joseph (1999: 364).

that he signed a secret—but not formal—agreement before becoming presidential candidate. It probably included a provision to serve for one term only and then return the office to the north.[49,50]

Within two months of assuming office, Obasanjo ordered the retirement of 200 high-ranking army officers, most of them from the Islamic north.[51] This "betrayal" changed the balance of power. Without control over the army, northern politicians could no longer determine the course of the transformation they had initiated, and they did not possess the economic means to put pressure on their adversaries. Their only chance of extracting concessions was to threaten their opponents with massive damage, and the most formidable weapon at their disposal was the campaign, which started soon after Obasanjo's inauguration on May 29, 1999. Shari'a was an efficient bargaining chip[52] for political blackmail because it could have extremely dangerous consequences.

When the governors of some Northern states announced the introduction of a strictly orthodox form of Islamic law, everyone knew that this would spark religious riots. Since the early 1980s, clashes between Christians and Muslims in the cities of the north had claimed thousands of lives. With the Shari'a controversy, conflicts in Kano, Kaduna, and Jos were rekindled, provoking the worst massacres since the Biafra War. In February and May 2000, endless convoys of Igbo and Yoruba refugees were heading south.

Professor Ben Nwabueze, a constitutional lawyer, called the introduction of Shari'a "tantamount...to an act of secession."[53] Mood of many Muslims in the north was indeed secessionist. Governor Ahmed Sani, whose administration in Zamfara State had been the first to pass Shari'a legislation, dreamt of a "new caliphatic order."[54] He plastered posters throughout the capital, informing visitors that Nigeria's constitution had been suspended and that "God's Law is Supreme."[55] However, political reason dictated that the federation should be preserved. Without the transfer of oil money from the south, the whole north, including its politi-

---

[49] Campbell (2011, XV: 84).

[50] Obasanjo maintains he had not signed a formal agreement, a claim disputed by his counterparts from the North.

[51] Iliffe (2011: 183).

[52] Harnischfeger (2008: 126–134) and Mazrui (2001).

[53] Maier (2000: 180) and Nwabueze (2001: 25).

[54] Mustapha (2004: 270).

[55] Maier (2000: 180).

cal class, would be impoverished. Moreover, the rich and mighty had little interest in subordinating their life to Shari'a, so the divine rules were applied half-heartedly at best.

However, the elites were not the only actors in the Shari'a drama. Groups of Islamic militants emerged, disenchanted with the state-decreed Islamization. For social rebels who do not share the luxurious life of the elite, oil is of minor importance. They despise the emirs and governors who engage in Nigerian politics in order to make money. A federation with infidels seemed to pollute the community of the faithful; therefore, militant groups did not feel bound to informal agreements with the Christian minority. In 2004, Islamic rebels—called Taliban by the media— attacked rural police stations and local government buildings. They raised flags inscribed with "Afghanistan" and began to impose a pure form of Islamic life on local peasants. In order to dislodge them from their lairs at the border to Cameroon and Niger, the army deployed heavy artillery.[56]

The security forces were not able to suppress this insurrection. While the initial Taliban had just a few hundred members, successor group Boko Haram now has thousands of fighters operating all over Northern Nigeria. Its leaders hold that genuine Shari'a can only be practiced in an Islamic state. In order to live according to their faith, Muslims have to either break free from Nigeria, or they have to convert Christians by force.[57] In January 2012, Boko Haram gave all southerners an ultimatum to leave the north, that is, the former Northern Region, including the Middle Belt, which northern Muslims regard as their sphere as influence.[58] At the same time, the group called on all Muslims to "fight for the restoration of the Caliphate of Usman Danfodio which the white man fought and fragmented."[59] This call was directed, among others, against the Islamic establishment in the north that had been accused of betraying the legacy of pre-colonial Islam.

Although political and religious leaders still refer to Usman dan Fodio as role model of a religious reformer and depict the Caliphate as the culmination of Islamic civilization, they do not care about the divine justice that the jihadist leader propagated. Against this hypocrisy, the rebels were simply demanding what Muslim politicians had promised but failed to

[56] Oshunkeye (2004: 22–26) and Adzegeh (2004: 22–25).
[57] Crisis Group (2010).
[58] Idris (2012b).
[59] Abul Qaqa, spokesman of Boko Haram, in Idiris (2012: 5).

deliver. In an Islamic state strictly based on Shari'a, the immutable law of God would be the yardstick by which all segments of the society—rich and poor—are judged. Thus the arrogant elite would be integrated into a moral community in which rulers and ruled are united by a shared culture, as they had been during the mythical beginnings of Islam.

The Promised Land: A New Biafra

The Shari'a campaign heightened the insecurity of Igbo Christians living in the north. It reinforced their exclusion as a minority of "settlers" from a "host" society that increasingly defined itself as Islamic. At the height of the crisis, when scores of Igbo fled the north, the governors of the five Igbo states warned that they would have to reassess "the continued existence of Nigeria."[60] Igbo separatism re-emerged in response to the Shari'a threat, but it was also inspired by the partial success of the separatist campaign in southwest Nigeria. OPC militants had forced the generals to hand over power to a Yoruba president in order to "compensate" the Yoruba for having been "robbed" of the presidency in 1993. For the Igbo, who also claimed "compensation" for the wrongs they had suffered, it looked as if the threat of secession had paid off.

The main secessionist organization in Igboland, the MASSOB, was formed in November 1999, a few months before the Shari'a campaign gained momentum. MASSOB's founder, Ralph Uwazuruike, had been a member of the ruling People's Democratic Party (PDP). He had supported Obasanjo during his 1999 election campaign but was soon disappointed with Obasanjo's policies. When making federal appointments, the Yoruba president had not given the Igbo consideration, even though 70% of Igbo had voted for him.[61] Obasanjo thus continued the marginalization of the Igbo. When his two terms as president ended, he chose a northerner—not an Igbo—as his successor.

MASSOB leader Uwazuruike had predicted that the Igbo would never be allowed to rule Nigeria, even if they waited for another 40 years; thus it was better to part ways.[62] His campaign for secession was not taken seriously at first. It looked like a one-man-show, but when hundreds of Igbo died in Shari'a clashes, MASSOB became the most popular political orga-

---

[60] Ojewale (2000: 16).
[61] Uwazuruike (2000: 16, 13).
[62] Ogunro (2004: 28).

nization in Igboland, among intellectuals as well as among ordinary people.[63] MASSOB assured its followers that Biafra could be achieved without a war, through a strategy of nonviolence and passive resistance. The Igbo should gradually opt out of Nigeria and establish their own political structures in a long 25-stage process.

MASSOB has already introduced a new currency, the Biafra Pound (in 2005), although it has not gained acceptance; it opened a Biafra House in Washington, DC in 2001, started issuing Biafran passports in 2009, and it has been broadcasting news through its radio station Voice of Biafra since 2001. At the height of its secessionist campaign (between 2000 and 2004), the old separatist flag was hoisted throughout Igboland, and MASSOB activists patrolled the streets in the blue uniforms of the former Biafra police. However, the separatist policemen did not carry arms, as they were not meant to fight criminals. The group of MASSOB activists posing as Biafra police was actually a bizarre masquerade meant to impress politicians from other parts of Nigeria.

By displaying more and more symbols of national sovereignty, they were trying to give the impression that Igboland was in fact drifting toward secession. For Igbo nationalists, this was the only way to force politicians of other ethnic groups to pay attention to the plight of the Igbo. Having been excluded for decades from ruling the country, most Igbo felt that successive governments, civilian or military, had failed to protect them against communal violence and discrimination. The best way to right these wrongs seemed to be for an Igbo to become president and bring the Igbo back into the mainstream of Nigerian politics. The wish to have an Igbo ruling Nigeria did not fit with MASSOB's call for a new Biafra; however, the organization indicated at times that it would forego secession, once the Igbo were no longer excluded from the highest office. Before the elections of 2003, MASSOB activists demonstrated under the slogan: "Igbo Presidency 2003 or Biafra."[64]

When MASSOB organized a stay-at-home strike against the federation on August 26, 2004, the strike was followed in all parts of Igboland. A later stay-at-home strike, on June 8, 2013, met with less success, but in 2004, Igbo traders kept their shops closed even in Lagos and Kano. This does not mean that they had all joined the fight for Biafra. Most Igbo assumed that the federal government would not allow them to secede

---

[63] Anthony (2002: 241).
[64] Uba Aham, "Crushing Biafra," The News, February 7, 2005, 18 (photo).

because their territory is too close to the Niger Delta and its oil fields. And even if Biafra could be achieved, it is not desirable to many, in particular to those Igbo who are living as traders and artisans in other parts of the country. In case of secession, millions of them would have to abandon their investments and return to their overpopulated homeland. They participated in the strike because it gave them an opportunity to vent their anger, yet they have no genuine interest in secession, not even in a looser (con)federation.

It seems that it is a consensus that Igbo interests will be best protected by a unitary government strong enough to guarantee that citizens in all parts of the country are treated equally.[65] Other Nigerians are, of course, aware that the Igbo would suffer the greatest losses if the federation broke apart, so the campaign for Biafra is often dismissed as an empty threat, leaving the Igbo with little bargaining power. They are the first to be attacked and driven away when communal clashes erupt in the North, but they have always returned.

MASSOB has not taken up arms to fight for independence, but its strategy of nonviolence did not save its members from state persecution. The federal government banned the organization, deploying anti-riot police and army units that killed many MASSOB members. Igbo governors and other office holders could do little to protect the group. Since they had sworn loyalty to the Nigerian state, they could not openly support a secessionist movement. However, although Igbo elders have focused their activities on a campaign for Igbo presidency and distanced themselves from separatism, they had an ambiguous attitude toward their radical youth. The elders resented MASSOB's uncompromising stance because it made them look like traitors who collaborated with federal authorities merely for personal gain. At the same time, the elders tried to profit from the radicalism of their boys. In order to put pressure on the federal government, they needed the menacing scenario of a separatist agitation, which would only subside if the rest of Nigeria listened to Igbo demands.

---

[65] When assessing the pros and cons of secession, there is no rift between Igbo living in the Nigerian diaspora and those in Igboland. Both dislike Nigeria but know that they would be worse off without it. MASSOB's campaign for a new Biafra has its most ardent followers among the urban poor, mostly young men who have not experienced the horrors of the war. Moreover, it draws financial and intellectual support from Igbo émigrés in America and Europe who would not bear the costs of civil war: "the flame of a new Biafra is burning with a greater passion abroad" ("Aftermath of Biafra Conference in USA", 9).

The agitation for Biafra has drawn much of its support from the urban poor, especially from young men who have not experienced the horrors of the war. Nationalist politics is attractive to them because it can be used, among others, to bring popular pressure to bear on the Igbo elite. Fighting for a common national interest presupposes "unity of mind, thoughts and aspiration for the entire Igbo race."[66] Igbo leaders are expected to close ranks, set their personal interests aside, and devote their political activities to the welfare of the people. Without such a commitment to a common cause, the opinion is that they will always use their positions within the state apparatus to enrich themselves and betray their constituency.

Patriotism requires a culture of self-sacrifice; it sets standards of morality that can be invoked against politicians who sell out Igbo interests. After campaigning for more than a decade, Igbo politicians have not come closer to an Igbo presidency. When the elections of 2011 approached, they realized that no Igbo candidate could mobilize significant support among non-Igbo. The main contest was between ex-General Buhari, a Fulani Muslim, and the incumbent President Goodluck Jonathan, a Christian from the Niger Delta. Buhari had earned respect throughout Nigeria through his tough stance against corruption, but he had also been at the forefront of the Shari'a campaign. Therefore, Igbo politicians decided, almost unanimously, to back the Christian candidate. The radicals in MASSOB performed a similar shift. They dropped their opposition to participating in presidential elections and supported, though without much fanfare, Goodluck Jonathan.

Although separatist agitation has not achieved its aims, it has had a profound effect on Igbo self-perception. It has revived memories of the Biafra "genocide" and highlighted the discrimination that the Igbo had to suffer ever since, warning them that an "unrepentant" Nigeria is still determined "to stamp out our people from the face of the earth."[67] Moreover, nationalist discourses have given a religious meaning to their suffering. This religious dimension was already present in the 1960s when the Biafra conflict evolved. The secessionists saw the Muslims in the north as their main adversaries and hoped for support from neighboring peoples, who were largely Christian. However, the vast majority of non-Igbo Christians joined the northerners in their fight against Biafra. For the beleaguered Igbo, this was a betrayal: Christian Yoruba, Tiv, and Berom

---

[66] Obinna Uzoh, a politician from Anambra, "It Is Our Turn," Newswatch, April 1, 2002, 31.
[67] Uwazuruike (2003: 10).

had abandoned the cause of Christianity by siding with the Muslim "jihad-ists." Europeans who visited Igboland in those years found a widespread "self-consciousness of a Christian state facing a Muslim *jihad*."[68] Biafra's leader, General Ojukwu, declared in 1968: "Biafra is a Christian Country, we believe in the ability of the Almighty God to come to the aid of the oppressed and give us victory as he gave to young David over Goliath."[69]

The reference to David and Goliath placed the struggle for Igbo self-determination in the context of Biblical mythology, but it also pointed to contemporary events and indicated a strong tendency to identify with the modern Jewish nation. Just a week after Biafra had declared its independence, the Six-Day War broke out in the Middle East and Israel defeated its Arab neighbors, whose armies were larger and better equipped. Igbo nationalists have interpreted the "liberation of Jerusalem"[70] by Israeli soldiers in June 1967 as fulfillment of a divine promise. God's chosen people, the ancient Hebrews, had been despised and persecuted, put under a foreign yoke, and scattered among distant peoples. However, God had promised to raise their descendants above other nations. For modern-day Jews, this prophecy seemed to have come true. Just a few years after they had almost been annihilated, the survivors of the Holocaust had mustered the strength to establish their own state. Igbo patriots marvel at the way Jewish settlers turned an arid stretch of land into an intensely cultivated, prosperous country; they are fascinated by the military might of Israel—attractive because it gives its citizens security in a hostile environment. Although Israel's population is far outnumbered by its Muslim neighbors, its citizens do not, in Igbo interpretation, have to bow. The Igbo, by contrast, have to endure discrimination, particularly in the diaspora of northern Nigeria.

Many Igbo believe that they are "living in the midst of enemies,"[71] a fate that they considered to be shared with the Jews. In addition, they assume that Jews and Igbo have been hated for the same reasons: both nations are more gifted than others, and its members have often been blessed by economic success. The Igbo stereotype is that both people have attracted envy due to their achievements in trade, academia, and other professions. Thus, the "Igbophobia" of non-Igbo appears to Igbo be rooted in an inferiority complex; it is "born out of the fear of the higher

---

[68] Walls (1978: 212).
[69] Odumegwu Ojukwu, quoted in Okorocha (1987: 117).
[70] Alaezi (1999: 16, 141).
[71] Uwazuruike (2002: 42).

ingenuity, higher industry, higher wisdom and higher intellectual power of Ndigbo [Igbo people]."[72]

Jews and Igbo seem to be related not only by common historical experiences but also by common traits of culture and personality. One way of explaining this congruence is to assume a common origin. The idea that the ancestors of the Igbo were Jews who migrated to present-day Nigeria in Biblical times has become so popular that it "pervades oral historical accounts," writes Harneit-Sievers,[73] Identifying with a faraway people that seems destined to attract hostility may help the Igbo to reflect on the trauma of the civil war. However, this narrative alienates the Igbo from other Nigerians and makes forming long-term alliances difficult. Such alliances, however, would be the only means for the Igbo to gain a more significant role in Nigerian politics.[74]

CONCLUSION

Nigeria's Fourth Republic has proven more durable than its predecessors, partly due to its first president Obasanjo. The former general depoliticized the army and distributed the oil resources more or less evenly among the 36 states. Although he rigged the elections and selected his own successor, he kept political competition open by handing the presidential office to a Muslim from the north. This 2007 power shift to the north was not the result of an agreement among the political elites; Igbo and other southerners strongly resented it. Likewise in 2011, when a southerner became president, riots broke out in the north. Competition for the highest office tends to be violent because those losing out cannot expect to be given a fair chance at the next elections.

Nigeria's democracy has never worked. When northern politicians came to dominate the first independent government in 1960, they were determined to stay in power by all means. They rigged elections, falsified census figures, imposed emergency rule, and called in the army. The only way to oust them was by mobilizing ethnic militias and threatening with secession, as Yoruba politicians did. They found support from activists in the Niger Delta who by disrupting oil production forced the regime to

[72] "Editorial," (*News Service*) 2002, 13; cf. The Voice of Igbo Israel (2009).
[73] Harneit-Sievers (2006: 22).
[74] Harnischfeger (2011).

compromise—according to the motto that those in power will only listen to you if you can cause trouble.

However, the capacity to wreak havoc is unevenly distributed among Nigeria's regions and ethnic groups. Igboland has no oil pipelines and flow stations that militants could attack. If they chose to demolish infrastructure, the Igbo would only be able to destroy their own government buildings and schools, power lines, and bridges. But who in Abuja would care? Moreover, they would not dare to attack the Hausa-Fulani diaspora in Igboland, as Yoruba militiamen did in Lagos. Millions of Igbo live in northern cities, while just a few Hausa-Fulani reside in Igboland. If mutual killings escalated, Igbo would lose out—just as they did in 1966, when they were driven away.

Igbo secessionists define autonomy in ethnic terms, yet religion is also an important part of their national identity. They tend to see themselves as a bulwark of Christianity (and Western modernity), beleaguered by an expansionist Hausa-Fulani Islam. This ethno-religious discourse favors an exclusivist understanding of Christianity, focusing on the idea that the Igbo are a chosen people—closer to God than others—with an experience not unlike that of Old Testament Jews. Thus, Igbo and Hausa-Fulani tend to identify with global religious forces, but this is not an option for the Yoruba who are evenly divided between Muslims and Christians.

Yet among Yoruba nationalists, religion is important. New members recruited into the OPC—the main autonomist movement—have to pledge loyalty to one of their ancestral deities: Ogun, Shango, or Osun. Orthodox Islam and Christianity view such "idolatry" as a violation of the most basic religious obligation. This is exactly what this initiation ritual seeks to achieve. Religious bonds have served as a link for a section of Yoruba Muslims that since the early 1960s has split from the mainstream Yoruba politics in favor of an alliance with Hausa-Fulani leaders. Thus, swearing an oath to Yoruba deities requires that candidates place their ethnic solidarity above religious links. Most Yoruba Muslims did not join the project of religious renewal through Shari'a, which meant that their coreligionists in the north accused them of not taking their faith seriously. Both sides are aware, however, that the call for a strict form of Islam is not meant to bring peace to Yorubaland. Any attempt to Islamize state and society continues to set Muslims and Christians against each other and to weaken Yoruba influence within the federation.

Since Nigeria's politicians do not respect the present constitution, it has been suggested that a national conference be convened and a new political order negotiated. Delegates would have to reach a consensus on a broad range of contentious issues: how to share power and natural resources, how to protect the rights of ethnic and religious minorities, and how to define the relationship between "settlers" and "indigenes." Chances for agreement on a major reform are slim, given that rival segments of the political elites pursue divergent aims and interests. Since the 1950s, they have failed to agree on a constitution; the rift between them has only widened.

Most northern Muslims reject ethnic autonomy, favoring religious or regional self-determination. They seek to reform society using the laws of Islam, which are the same all over the world. Yet the incomplete and selective form of Shari'a that Muslim governors imposed in the 12 states of the Far North has led to widespread disillusionment; a large part of the population believes that genuine Shari'a is the only way out of corruption and social decline. In their dealings with non-Muslims, the faithful have to accept compromises. Political arrangements that contradict their faith at variance will not command much loyalty. Christians and Muslims are thus losing a sense of a shared moral and legal conviction on which a common polity can be built.

Ethnic nationalism in the south has also enhanced mistrust. The Igbo, who have felt sidelined since the lost war, tend to blame others for their woes. Their perception of themselves as a people like the Jews—"living in the midst of enemies"[75]—has reinforced the tendency to renounce their Nigerian citizenship and call again for secession. The MASSOB has deepened the Igbo's sense of alienation, but it has not enabled them to break free from what they resent. They are trapped, writes Nwabueze in a "country characterized...by mutual antagonism and antipathy between its various peoples."[76]

Although Nigeria's political elites cannot agree under which rules they might govern a united state, they will continue to muddle through. They have too much to lose. Without the oil money that accounts for 85% of government income,[77] public administrations in most parts of Nigeria would collapse. All actors are aware that an orderly, consensual breakup of the federation is unlikely. Nigerians do not have common rules on how to draw new boundaries and how to treat ethnic and religious minorities. Thus a division of the country would be, as Nigerian writer Wole Soyinka put it, "extremely messy."[78]

[75] Uwazuruike (2002: 42).
[76] Nwabueze (2001: 25).
[77] "Signs of Life" (2010).
[78] "Sahara Reporters" (2012).

REFERENCES

Abdul-Rasheed Na'Allah. (1998). *Ogoni's agonies: Ken Saro-Wiwa and the crisis in Nigeria*. Trenton/Asmara: Africa World Press.

Adebanwi, W. (2005). The carpenter's revolt: Youth, violence and the reinvention of culture in Nigeria. *Journal of Modern African Studies, 43*(3), 339–365.

Adzegeh, S. (2004, October 11). The routing of the Talibans. *Newswatch*.

Aham, U. (2005, February 7). Crushing Biafra. *The News*.

Akaruese, L. (2003). Beyond ethnic militias: Re-constructing the Nigerian state. In T. Babawale (Ed.), *Urban violence, ethnic militias and the challenge of democratic consolidation in Nigeria* (pp. 212–227). Lagos: Malthouse.

Alaezi, O. (1999). *Ibos: Hebrew exiles from Israel. Amazing facts and revelations*. Aba: Onzy Publications.

Anthony, D. A. (2002). *Poison and medicine: Ethnicity, power, and violence in a Nigerian city, 1966 to 1986*. Portsmouth/Oxford/Cape Town: Heinemann/James Currey/David Philip.

Bach, D. (2006). Inching towards a country without a state: Prebandalism, violence and state betrayal in Nigeria. In C. Clapham & G. Mills (Eds.), *Big African states* (pp. 63–96). Johannesburg: Wits University Press.

Campbell, J. (2011). *Nigeria: Dancing on the brink*. Lanham: Rowman & Littlefield.

Coleman, J. S. (1986). *Nigeria: Background to nationalism*. Benin City/Katrineholm: Broburg & Wiström.

Crisis Group. (2010). *Northern Nigeria: Background to conflict*. Africa Report N° 168. Retrieved from http://crisisgroup.org/~/media/Files/africa/west-africa/nigeria/168Northern Nigeria-Background to Conflict.ashx

Cronje, S. (1972). *The world and Nigeria: The diplomatic history of the Biafran War 1967–1970*. London: Sidgwick & Jackson.

De St. Jorre, J. (1972). *The Nigerian civil war*. London: Hodder and Stoughton.

Diamond, L. (1988). *Class, ethnicity and democracy in Nigeria: The failure of the first republic*. Syracuse: Syracuse University Press.

Diamond, L. (1995). Nigeria: The uncivic society and the descent into praetorianism. In L. Diamond et al. (Eds.), *Politics in developing countries: Comparing experiences with democracy* (pp. 416–491). Boulder/London: Lynne Rienner.

Economist. (2010, March 31). Signs of life. *Economist*. Retrieved from http://www.economist.com/node/15825790

Economist Intelligence Unit. (2007). *Nigeria: Country profile*. London: EIU.

Englebert, P. (2009). *Africa: Unity, sovereignty, and sorrow*. Boulder/London: Lynne Rienner.

Falola, T., & Heaton, M. M. (2008). *A history of Nigeria*. Cambridge: Cambridge University Press.

Gould, M. (2012). *The struggle for modern Nigeria: The Biafran War 1967–1970.* London/New York: Tauris.

Harneit-Sievers, A. (1992). Nigeria: Der Sezessionskrieg um Biafra. Keine Sieger, keine Besiegten – Eine Afrikanische Erfolgsgeschichte? In R. Hofmeier & V. Matthies (Eds.), *Vergessene Kriege in Afrika* (pp. 277–318). Göttingen: Lamuv.

Harneit-Sievers, A. (2006). *Constructions of belonging: Igbo communities and the Nigerian state in the twentieth century.* Rochester: University of Rochester Press.

Harnischfeger, J. (2008). *Democratization and Islamic law: The Sharia conflict in Nigeria.* Frankfurt/New York: Campus.

Harnischfeger, J. (2011). *Igbo nationalism and Biafra.* Retrieved from http://afrikanistik-online.de/archiv/(2011)/(3042)

Idris, H. (2012, March 21). Boko Haram says no more talks with FG. *Daily Trust.* Retrieved from http://allafrica.com/stories/201203210120.html. Accessed 11 May 2018.

Idris, H. (2012, January 2). Boko Haram: State of emergency meant to attack Muslims. *Daily Trust.* Retrieved from http://allafrica.com/stories/201201030834.html. Accessed 11 May 2018.

Iliffe, J. (2011). *Obasanjo, Nigeria and the world.* Woodbridge/Suffolk: James Currey.

Joseph, R. (1999). Autocracy, violence, and ethnomilitary rule in Nigeria. In R. Joseph (Ed.), *State, conflict, and democracy in Africa* (pp. 359–373). Boulder/London: Lynne Rienner.

Kalu, O. U. (2002). The religious dimension of the legitimacy crisis, 1993–1998. In T. Falola (Ed.), *Nigeria in the twentieth century* (pp. 667–685). Durham: Carolina Academic Press.

Kirk-Greene, A. H. M. (1971). *Crisis and conflict in Nigeria: A documentary sourcebook 1966–1969* (Vol. 1. January 1966–July 1967). London: Oxford University Press.

Lovejoy, P. E. (1986). Problems of Slave Control in the Sokoto Caliphate. In P. E. Lovejoy (Ed.), *Africans in bondage: studies in slavery and the slave trade. Essays in honor of Philip D. Curtin* (pp. 235–272). Wisconsin: University of Wisconsin Press.

Lynn, M. (2001). Introduction. In M. Lynn (Ed.), *Nigeria. Part 1: Managing political reform 1943–1953* (pp. XXXV–XCIII). London: Stationary Office.

Maier, K. (2000). *This house has fallen: Midnight in Nigeria.* New York: Public Affairs.

Mazrui, A. A. (2001, April 14). *Shariacracy and federal models in the era of globalization: Nigeria in comparative perspective.* Paper presented at conference restoration of Shariah in Nigeria: Challenges and benefits, London. Retrieved from http://sharia2001.nmnonline.net/mazrui paper.htm

Mustapha, A. R. (2004). Ethnicity & the politics of democratization in Nigeria. In B. Berman et al. (Eds.), *Ethnicity & democracy in Africa* (pp. 257–275). Oxford: James Currey.

News Service [Enugu]. Editorial. (2002, February).

Njoku, R. C. (2002). An endless cycle of secessionism: Intellectuals and separatist movements in Nigeria. In B. Coppieters & M. Huysseune (Eds.), *Secession, history and the social sciences* (pp. 249–274). Brussels: Brussels University Press.

Nnoli, O. (1980). *Ethnic politics in Nigeria*. Enugu: Fourth Dimension.

Nwabueze, B. (2001, January 15). Igbo Kwenu! *Tell*.

Nwajiaku, K. (2005). Between discourse and reality: The politics of oil and Ijaw ethnic nationalism in the Niger Delta. *Cahiers d'Études Africaines, 45*(2), 457–496.

Obi, C., & Nwosu, M. (1997, June 2). Why we lost. *The Source*.

Ogunro, J. (2004, December 20). Nothing works in Nigeria. *Insider Weekly*.

Ojewale, O. (2000, October 23). Their stand on Nigeria. *Newswatch*. Retrieved from http://allafrica.com/stories/200010250118.html. Accessed 11 May 2018.

Ojukwu, C. O. (1981). *Biafra: Selected speeches of C. Odumegwu Ojukwu, general of the people's army. With diaries of events*. New York: Harper & Row.

Okorocha, C. C. (1987). *The meaning of religious conversion in Africa: The case of the Igbo of Nigeria*. Aldershot: Avebury.

Oshunkeye, S. (2004, April 26). On Taliban. *Tell*.

Ottenberg, S. (2006). Ibo receptivity to change. In T. Falola (Ed.), *Igbo: Religion, social life and other essays by Simon Ottenberg* (pp. 179–194). Trenton/Asmara: Africa World Press.

Paden, J. N. (1986). *Ahmadu Bello: Sardauna of Sokoto. Values and leadership in Nigeria*. Zaria: Hudahuda Publishing.

Pérouse de Montclos, M.-A. (2009). Humanitarian aid and the Biafra War: Lessons not learned. *Africa Development, 34*(1), 69–82.

Sahara Reporters. (2012, February 7). *Interview: Wole Soyinka: Next phase of Boko Haram terrorism*. Retrieved from http://saharareporters.com/interview/interview-wole-soyinka-next-phase-boko-haram-terrorism-thenews. Accessed 15 May 2012.

Sklar, R. L. (1983). *Nigerian political parties: Power in an emergent African nation*. New York/London/Lagos/Enugu: NOK Publishers International.

Sklar, R. L. (2004). Unity or regionalism: The nationalities question. In R. I. Rotberg (Ed.), *Crafting the new Nigeria: Confronting the challenges* (pp. 39–59). Boulder/London: Lynne Rienner.

Stremlau, J. F. (1977). *The international politics of the Nigerian Civil War 1967–1970*. Princeton: Princeton University Press.

Tamuno, T. N. (1970). Separatist agitations in Nigeria since 1914. *Journal of Modern African Studies, 8*(4), 563–584.

The Voice of Igbo Israel. (2009). *What are responsible for Igbo and Jewish higher intelligence?* Retrieved from http://igboisrael.blogspot.com

The Yoruba Agenda. (2005). n.p. Retrieved from http://www.nigerianmuse. com/20101011091938zg/sections/general-articles/the-yoruba-agenda-of-january-2005/

Uwazuruike, R. (2000, April 17). I will bury Nigeria. *The News.* Retrieved from http://allafrica.com/stories/200004100237.html. Accessed 11 May 2018.

Uwazuruike, R. (2002, January 7). Nobody can stop Biafra. *The News.*

Uwazuruike, R. (2003). Biafra: Our reason, our tactics. *Body & Soul, 3*(3).

Walls, A. F. (1978). Religion and the press in 'the enclave' in the Nigerian Civil War. In E. Fasholé-Luke et al. (Eds.), *Christianity in independent Africa* (pp. 207–215). Bloomington/London: Collings.

Whitaker, C. S. (1970). *The politics of tradition: Continuity and change in northern Nigeria 1946–1966.* Princeton: Princeton University Press.

CHAPTER 13

Katanga's Secessionism in the Democratic Republic of Congo

Miles Larmer and Erik Kennes

INTRODUCTION

The Democratic Republic of the Congo (DRC) was *the* formative case of secessionism in postcolonial Africa. The secession of Katanga on 11 July 1960, 11 days after Congo achieved independence from Belgium, provided the exemplary warning of the dangers of the principle of self-determination. The perception (based on considerable evidence) that Katangese secessionism was largely the product of external manipulation

M. Larmer
University of Oxford, Oxford, UK

Department of Historical and Heritage Studies, University of Pretoria, Pretoria, South Africa
e-mail: miles.larmer@history.ox.ac.uk

E. Kennes (✉)
Institut Supérieur d'Etudes Sociales, Lubumbashi, Democratic Republic of the Congo

Institute for Development Policy and Management, University of Antwerp, Antwerp, Belgium

Africa Museum, Tervuren, Belgium

© The Author(s) 2019   361
L. de Vries et al. (eds.), *Secessionism in African Politics*,
Palgrave Series in African Borderlands Studies,
https://doi.org/10.1007/978-3-319-90206-7_13

by interests hostile to independent Africa was the primary influence on the Organisation of African Unity's 1963 acceptance of colonial borders as the sole basis for postindependence states.

However, understanding of the Katangese secession has arguably been hampered by this historical importance. The hatred directed toward Katanga and its Western supporters has petrified historical understanding into a caricatured battle between the saintly Congolese Prime Minister Patrice Lumumba and the sinner, Katangese President Moïse Tshombe. Even today, Katanga is widely understood, exclusively or primarily, as the result of outside manipulation; Ludo de Witte's otherwise exemplary investigation of the assassination of Lumumba suggests: "Officially, power was held by Africans in secessionist Katanga. In fact, Belgians were pulling all the strings."[1]

While the secession was undeniably enabled and shaped by colonial settlers, mining capital, and the Belgian military, this chapter explains that the worldview of autochthonous African elites in Southern Katanga, in particular, their hostility to Kasaian in-migration, was crucial to the secessionist project—and remains an important element in Katangese politics today.

Furthermore, the related tendency to treat Katanga as a negative aberration within an otherwise largely coherent Congolese nation-state, in which nationalism is conflated with Lumumbism, is entirely at odds with the evidence. Across Congo, ethnic and political leaders sought to mobilize support and achieve their aims through initiatives that implicitly or explicitly challenged the authority of the Congolese state to govern the territory to which it laid claim. The Lumumbist unitary project was beset by ethnically based alternatives led by charismatic local leaders and by subnational challenges rooted in the regional structures imposed by colonialism. Such projects drew on mythico-historical notions of origin and belonging for purposes of legitimation. These were then influenced and complicated by the reconstruction of ethnic identities as a result of cultural and socioeconomic changes during the colonial period. Like Katanga, they drew on external support from within and outside Africa; indeed, many African governments, while in principle rejecting secession or declared autonomy, provided political and military support to projects that undermined the authority of Leopoldville over Eastern Congo.

At times, during President Mobutu's authoritarian rule (1965–1997), it appeared that his centralizing authority had overcome this tendency to separation. In fact, it was only contained under an increasingly ineffective

---

[1] De Witte (2001: xxi).

canopy of patrimony and repression. During the Congo wars of the late 1990s and early 2000s, a real national unity was achieved in confronting a common Rwandan enemy, but the price was considerable violence against those Congolese who were of Rwandan ethnicity. Today, any discussion regarding political decentralization in the Kivus is considered to be playing into the hands of Rwanda, but those involved in entrepreneurial economic activity effectively sidestep the increasingly absent central state.

Meanwhile, autonomist tendencies in former Katanga and Kongo-Central have more recently reasserted themselves, as disaffection has grown with Kinshasa's inability to govern effectively or to distribute state patronage to the east of the country.[2] It is nevertheless undeniable that none of these tendencies or initiatives has reached the point of outright secession that occurred in Katanga. In this chapter, we explore the Katangese secession simultaneously with the wider relationship between the central state and regional autonomous dynamics in Congo.

REGIONAL DIFFERENCE AND DIVERGENCE IN PRE-COLONIAL AND COLONIAL CONGO

When, in the 1890s, agents of the Belgian King Leopold II gained effective control of the Congo Basin territory, it had no shared history that could provide the basis for a collective sense of identity.[3] The highly disparate societies of Central Africa included major "kingdoms" with relatively complex centralized administration (most notably, the Kongo, Lunda, Luba, and Kuba), the subject peoples of these major polities, and also relatively nonhierarchical local communities. These societies had experienced considerable flux over the preceding three centuries, as changing relations with each other and with the opportunities and threats provided by international trade had waxed and waned. In Katanga, the once powerful Lunda kingdom had, in the seventeenth century, utilized Atlantic trading routes to become one of the dominant political forces in Central Africa. By the late nineteenth century, the kingdom was a shadow of its former

---

[2] Some existing provinces, including Katanga, were partitioned in 2015. Bas-Congo was renamed Kongo-Central at the time.

[3] Jan Vansina argued in the late 1960s that similarities in the culture of Congolese societies provided the basis for the potential development of a "general Congolese culture" (1967: 150–1). Importantly, he suggests that a degree of pre-colonial Katangese unity was achieved by the adoption of Luba political principles by the Lunda (223).

self, undermined by societies with links to the increasingly important Indian Ocean trade (the Yeke) and by the self-assertion of their historic subject peoples (the Tshokwe), who had by the time of colonial annexation gained control of valuable trading routes. By marrying into each of the main societies in which he claimed authority, Msiri (the Yeke ruler) established a short-lived pre-colonial pan-Katangese political system.[4]

All this was of little interest to King Leopold, whose Congo fiefdom served until 1908 for the extraction of natural resources. There was great unevenness in the exploitation of this vast and disparate territory. Katanga was, from the start, governed in a distinctive way that reflected the colonial state's weakness and its mineral wealth and which protected its peoples from the worst excesses of forced labor for which Leopold's Congo was notorious. The region was formally ruled between 1900 and 1910 by the *Comité Spécial du Katanga* (CSK), which was dominated by mining companies, most notably the *Union Minière du Haut Katanga* (UMHK). The CSK had quasi-state powers, including the right to raise an armed police force. Following the Belgian state's takeover of the Congo, Katanga was overseen by a Vice-Governor General, the only province to be governed in this way. In the 1920s, Belgian settlers in Katanga chafed at interference from the Congolese capital Leopoldville, and the centralization of power in 1933 provided an important basis for later autonomist/secessionist demands, first among discontented settlers and later among indigenous elites.[5]

The exceptional nature of Katanga was reinforced by the successful exploitation of its mineral wealth. By 1923, Congo was the world's third largest producer of copper, but mineral exports had little impact in the territory as a whole. Southern Katanga was, as a socioeconomic entity, integrated more into Southern Africa than into the wider Belgian Congo: its railroads and supply routes initially ran southwards to Durban (South Africa), Lobito (Angola), and Lourenço Marques, today's Maputo (Mozambique). No tarred road connected Katanga to the capital in Leopoldville, which could for many decades be reached more quickly by rail and ferry via Cape Town than over land. Katanga was, however, not only divided from the rest of the Congo; it was itself a divided territory: the

[4] Leclercq (1926).

[5] Some pro-secessionist Katangese genuinely believed Katanga was independent before 1933. See, for example, interview with ex-National Front for Liberation of the Congo (FLNC) General Mwepu, Kinshasa, 13 July 2008; Interview with ex-FLNC Colonel Vincent de Paul Nguz, Kinshasa, 11 December 2013; Matuka (2009), and Kennes and Larmer (2016: 24, 185–186).

Northern Luba-dominated part of the province was essentially rural, with substantially less mining activity.[6] With the opening of the railway to Port Francqui in 1936, the Kasai province supplied food to Katanga's mines, but the railway also brought increasing numbers of Kasai migrant workers to Katanga and, with them, profound political consequences for the future.

More generally, the identities of African societies were reshaped by their particular relationships with colonialism and the mining economy. The subsequent Katangese secessionist project revolved around the projection of supposedly essentialist ethnic identities that had been culturally and geographically reconstructed by their interaction with colonialism. Both Lunda and Yeke, having been conquered by regional opponents (respectively, the Tshokwe and Sanga), were reconstructed in territories that made it impossible for them to replicate their pre-colonial authority. The Congolese Lunda, divided by the tri-border with Northern Rhodesia and Angola, were thereby cutoff from historic external markets and were reduced to selling agricultural produce to mining centers, while avoiding dangerous and low-paid employment.

The Kasai Luba, who had historically lived within smaller chieftaincies, were (partly as a result) increasingly perceived—via Belgian ethnic stereotyping but also self-identification—as positively attuned to individual advancement via missionary education and migrant labor. They were accordingly recruited and promoted to increasingly senior positions in the mines and other workplaces.[7] The potential political consequences of the stabilization of migrant labor in Southern Katanga's mining towns from the late 1920s were not seriously considered. Unlike in British colonies, which experienced later labor stabilization, urbanization was not linked to the breakdown of chiefly authority and the advancement of "modern" political rights.

DECOLONIZATION, NATIONALISM, AND ITS DISCONTENTS

As elsewhere in sub-Saharan Africa, the political and economic effects of World War II were a watershed for the expression of Congolese anti-colonial discontent. The *Kitawala* (Watchtower) messianic movement,

---

[6] Some parts of Northern Katanga along the railway were part of "UMHK Katanga"; the urban center of Kamina fell within the territory of the Katanga Luba chief, the Kasongo Niembo, who would support the Katangese secession.

[7] Jewsiewicki (1989: 324–349).

which emerged in the 1920s, provided radical spiritual explanations for European domination and the devastating effects of the 1930s depression.[8] Separately, the December 1941 Katanga mineworkers' strike reflected discontent with the failure of wages to keep pace with wartime inflation; its brutal military suppression led to circa 100 deaths, with 74 others shot and wounded.[9] Although labor unrest continued to 1943, in contrast to British and French-ruled Africa, it was not addressed by the formalization of labor representation.[10]

There is little evidence to support Nzongola-Ntajala's assertion that these strikes reflected Congolese nationalist awakening.[11] The 1944 soldiers' insurrection in both Kasai and Katanga did, however, advance demands that more closely resembled anti-colonial manifestos elsewhere (compare, e.g., Foucher's chapter on Casamance in this book).[12] In Luluabourg (today's Kananga) in 1944, évolués petitioned the Governor General to consider their interests as a "kind of native bourgeoisie... [deserving]...a particular protection from the government, sheltering them from certain masses or treatment which may apply to an ignorant or backward mass."[13] Many évolués conceived of emancipation as amounting to the transfer of power to themselves, as the rightful heirs of colonial power.[14]

These expressions of anti-colonial discontent, articulating the concerns and aspirations of a particular section of an economically and culturally diverse territory, had the potential (as elsewhere in Africa) to coalesce into a more representative nationalist movement. Their general failure to do so certainly reflected the structural difficulties of establishing a coherent national identity across Congo's vast spaces, across uneven socioeconomic conditions, and between diverse communities but above all, Belgium's unwillingness to seriously contemplate meaningful political change. The granting of limited civil rights to évolués following the Luluabourg protests presented only a distant prospect of political advancement. Compared to most of British and French-ruled Africa, Belgium made little prepara-

---

[8] Higginson (1992: 55–80).

[9] Higginson (1989: 172–194), Perrings (1979: 225–7), and Bustin (1975: 141).

[10] For the British and French African experience, see Frederick Cooper (1996); for Congo, see Georges Nzongola-Ntajala (2002: 76).

[11] Nzongola-Ntajala (2002: 53).

[12] Foucher (2018). See also Higginson (1992: 53), and Fetter (1969: 269–277).

[13] Reprinted in Rubbens (1945: 128–9); quoted in Young (2003: 414–427).

[14] The term évolué was a formal colonial category of registered "civilized" Congolese Africans.

tion for Congolese decolonization.[15] New initiatives to address African welfare and development were not introduced with a significant grasp of the political changes that might follow from such developments. Most importantly, the ban on all political parties that remained in place until 1957 severely limited the organized expression of proto-nationalist politics.

In Katanga, however, the social context was somewhat different. The mining industry's social policy, encouraging the permanent settlement of miners' families in a pioneering model of gendered domesticity, created new mining towns that bore little resemblance to the rest of the country.[16] Katanga's mines also brought a particularly high European presence, amounting to 2.08% of the province's population at independence, by far the highest in Congo; these would play an important role in shaping the secession.[17] By 1959, 36% of Katanga's population earned their living as waged employees. Katanga's mineral production was 75% of the Congolese total and earned 50% of the colony's income.[18]

In Congo more generally, the extraordinary level of rural-urban migration was as much a reflection of rural poverty and the brutality of agricultural policies as it was of urban opportunity. While Congo's urban population doubled between 1940 and 1950, the African population of the Katangese capital Elisabethville nearly quadrupled in the same period, from 27,000 to 99,000.[19] There was little sense of a shared Congolese identity linking the distant towns of Leopoldville (today's Kinshasa), Stanleyville (Kisangani), and Elisabethville (Lubumbashi); in each, the political aspirations of migrant communities were expressed within self-help cultural associations established on ethnic lines. Such associations were not inherently antagonistic to more overtly Congolese nationalist political consciousness, but the ban on political parties meant they provided the sole legal basis for the assertion of cultural and political identity. The process of establishing "modern" African political organizations tended in practice to heighten ethnic self-awareness.

Late-colonial Congo also provided few opportunities for individual self-advancement. In Katanga, however, an emergent Southern Katangese

---

[15] Cooper (1996).
[16] Brion and Moreau (2006: 275–6).
[17] Gerard-Libois (1966: 3).
[18] Gérard-Libois (1966: 5).
[19] Bustin (1975: 160).

economic elite, often aristocratic in origin but utilizing individual wealth to escape the confines of tribal authority, began to assert itself. Foremost among them was Joseph Kapenda Tshombe, the wealthiest and most prominent Lunda businessman.[20] Such men benefited from the booming mining economy but as entrepreneurs rather than as workers. In the late 1950s, however, Lunda elites became anxious about rising political expression among other ethnic groups. The Lunda, one of the largest ethnic groups in Katanga, made up only 6.3% of the population of Elisabethville in 1957, compared to 22% in Kasai Luba and 18% in Katanga Luba—the same applied in other southern urban towns.[21]

Lunda prestige was initially unthreatened by Kasai Luba migrant workers carrying out low-status manual labor; now, however, they were asserting new rights. In December 1957, the first elections in Katanga's urban centers led to the election of nonindigenous mayors, three of whom were Kasai Luba. This event, revealing with shocking clarity the potential marginalization of the indigenous population in a new political environment dominated by modernist practices such as electoral democracy, created a new urgency among those that would go on to articulate secessionist and anti-Kasaian sentiment.

In the late 1950s, the Belgian authorities made belated reforms that raised the prospect of self-rule. Indigenous chiefs asserted their authority through recourse to historical rights, as did many peripheral kingdoms in late-colonial Africa at the moment of independence (e.g., the Lozi in Zambia).[22] In January 1959, the Lunda king, the Mwaant Yav, wrote to the Belgian authorities "in the name of the Lunda Empire, one of the most important demographic groups in Katanga whose sphere of customary authority extends beyond the boundaries of Congo [into] Angola and [Northern] Rhodesia." He attacked the "unforgivable aberration" of "considering the opinions which emanate from the urban centers as representing the general feeling of this province."[23]

---

[20] Notwithstanding his family's claims of association with the Mwaant Yav, the Lunda emperor, Joseph Kapenda, was primarily a social climber who used the new possibilities made available by the money economy to enrich himself and achieve a social position not otherwise available to him.

[21] Bustin (1975: 176–7).

[22] This phenomenon has been most successfully analyzed in West Africa: see, for example, Allman (1993). See also Zeller and Melber (2018).

[23] Communication by the Mwaant Yav, 31 January 1959, cited in (Bustin 1975: 189).

The authorities were surprised to discover the enduring extent of the Mwaant Yav's authority in these territories and his recent visits to both Angola and Northern Rhodesia to play his traditional role in Lunda ceremonies.[24] By 1959, the term "Lunda empire" had become politically ubiquitous in Lunda aristocratic and political discourse. As Bustin identifies, anthropological studies "supplied the Mwaant Yaav and his entourage with a good deal of the theoretical and scientific ammunition they needed to enhance the credibility of the imperial concept."[25] The ability of the Mwaant Yav to articulate a political dispensation based on the pre-colonial Lunda kingdom was, notwithstanding its apparent impracticality and difference from Katanga-wide state identification, an important element of secessionist thinking.

What distinguished Katanga from the many places where such claims failed to translate into overt secessionism was, of course, its extraordinary mineral wealth; in this sense, political economy played a vital role in shaping what cultural ideas could be converted into a credible political project. It was, as is well known, the global value of Katanga's minerals that underwrote the secession. Yet, mineral wealth was not simply an external factor; local elites believed this indigenous wealth was in danger of being exploited by another group of outsiders, namely the poorer peoples and provinces of Congo.[26] The visible expression of this danger was Kasai migration to urban Katanga and the growing political mobilization of this "foreign" population. This led in 1958 to the formation of the *Groupement des associations de l'empire lunda* (Gassomel), an explicitly autochthonous cultural association which, as its name suggests, looked back nostalgically to what was now characterized as the "Lunda Empire." Gassomel's most prominent leader, Moïse Tshombe, Lunda aristocrat and the mission-educated son of Kapenda Tshombe, personally symbolized the problematic alliance between educated elites and chiefly authority.[27]

But Gassomel's Lunda base was too narrow to act as an effective political vehicle in the emergent electoral context. In Katanga, an alliance of indigenous ethnic leaders formed the *Confédération des Associations Tribales du Katanga* (Conakat) in October 1958. The introduction of

[24] Bustin (1975: 189).

[25] Bustin (1975: 193).

[26] In this sense, Katanga's rejection of Congo resembled the refusal of Ivorian leaders to remain within a reconstructed postcolonial version of French West Africa.

[27] Tshombe's uncle Gaston Mushidi succeeded to the Mwaant Yav title in 1963, establishing the domination of the Lunda kingship by the Tshombe family until the present day.

universal suffrage in January 1959 caused consternation to ethnic associations and stimulated further construction of political alliances between them. In February 1959, Conakat leader Godefroid Munongo (a pensions clerk, and brother of the Yeke chief) wrote to Governor André Schöller to express the party's concerns:

> The native Katangans have good reason to wonder if the authorities did not accord permanent residence permits to the people from Kasai in our towns so that the natives [of Kasai] can, because of their ever-increasing numbers, crush those from Katanga.[28]

This distrust had strong foundations: notoriously, Governor Jean Paelinck had, during his 1956 investiture, spoken in Tshiluba of "You Kasaians, who live in the Katanga,... I, for my part, will not forsake you.... Ask me for what you need and you will get it."[29] Given Conakat's apparently pro-European stance during the secession, it is vital to recall its earlier anger at the perceived overt support of colonial officials and the Catholic Church for the supposedly enterprising Kasai Luba.[30] In his seminal article "Katangais où es-tu?" Alexis Kishiba expressed fear of an imminent transfer of power from the Belgian colonizer directly to those of Kasaian origin: "Katangan.... If you don't say anything, a language will be imposed on you and it will not necessarily be a language from the Katanga Province."[31] Such fears found overt political expression in July 1959 when Conakat was transformed into a political party claiming to represent all Katangese peoples, at which point Tshombe took over as its leader.[32] The Conakat Manifesto declared it was in favor of a federal system "in which the reins of command will have to be in the hands of authentic Katangese."[33]

THE ROAD TO SECESSION, 1959–1960

It is thus important to recognize that Conakat's leaders conceived of Katanga as a project rooted in the self-determination of Katanga's indigenous populations. This was not exceptional within Congo: most new

---

[28] Quoted in Bustin (1975: 181).
[29] Cited in Lemarchand (1964: 237). Schöller, who replaced Paelinck as Governor in September 1958, would himself go on to support Conakat.
[30] Lemarchand (1964: 237–8).
[31] Katanga, Elisabethville, 1 February 1958.
[32] Bustin (1975: 180).
[33] L'Essor du Congo, 26 May 1959; quoted in (Bustin 1975: 181).

political parties had their roots in ethnically based cultural associations and openly articulated ethno-regional concerns. An instructive comparison can be drawn with the *Alliance des Bakongo* (ABAKO), the militant party led by Congo's first president Joseph Kasavubu, whose demand for immediate self-government did not prevent it from articulating specifically Bakongo interests. Lumumba's *Mouvement National Congolais* (MNC/L) sought to establish itself as the basis of political life across the whole of the Congo. However, many MNC/L leaders favored a more federal system, and the party had little choice but to engage in overtly tribal politics, for example, in supporting the Lulua against Albert Kalonji's pro-Luba MNC/K faction in South Kasai. In 1959, the sudden emergence of indigenous political power exacerbated tensions between the Lulua and Luba: a state of emergency was declared in August 1959, the Luba leader Kalonji was arrested, and tens of thousands of Luba were displaced.[34]

In Katanga, the MNC/L allied closely with the more radical wing of Jason Sendwe's Lubakat (as the Luba from Katanga are known), giving Lumumba's party a distinctly ethnic partiality in the conflict between autochthons and incomers. The dominant presence of the MNC/L, itself led primarily by Luba figures, at the congress of Congolese political parties held in April 1959 at Luluabourg, confirmed the perceived subordination of Katanga after independence and suggested this would be under an MNC/L-led, Kasai Luba-dominated government. This contributed, Lemarchand suggests, to the alliance into which Conakat entered with the settler organization Union Katangaise the following month.[35]

This temporary alliance placed Conakat on the same side as some overt white supremacists, undermining the party's relations with federally minded parties, such as ABAKO, at the Roundtable meeting held in Brussels in January 1960 to determine Congo's future.[36] Settler representatives were, however, less influential than Belgian metropolitan and intellectual thinkers. Tshombe was highly dependent on Belgian advisers such as George Thyssens (who would draft the declaration of Katangese independence) and René Clemens (who wrote the Katangese constitution).[37] In addition, the local directors of the UMHK, fearing likely political interference in its operations from a postindependence Leopoldville government, assiduously developed relationships with Katangese political leaders.[38]

[34] Lemarchand (1964: 208–9).
[35] Lemarchand (1964: 238).
[36] Gerard-Libois (1966: 22–5).
[37] Colvin (1968: 18–19).
[38] Brion and Moreau (2006: 310–311).

Conakat also received political support from the British-ruled Central African Federation; this reflected links between white settlers on both sides of the Rhodesian-Katangese border but also the linkages of mining economy and infrastructure that had existed since the late nineteenth century and which found expression in Tanganyika Concessions' (TANKS) share in UMHK. British members of the UMHK board were part of a powerful British pro-Katanga lobby, which feared that rapid decolonization might place strategic areas of Africa into the hands of radical and Soviet-aligned governments.[39] The proposal that Katanga might join the Federation was widely discussed in the right-wing British press in March 1960; federal leader Roy Welensky publicly speculated about incorporating Katanga into a reconstructed Central African state.[40] During the secession, Welensky, having failed to persuade Britain to permit the deployment of Federal troops in support of Tshombe, allowed the Federation to become a major recruiting ground for mercenary forces.[41] Portuguese-controlled Angola was an equally important (though less public) ally, providing an important conduit for arm supplies and an outlet for its mineral exports. Katanga's relations with allies across Congo's borders were thus an important factor in making the secession possible.

Despite its dependency on white-controlled capital and territory, Conakat asserted a particular vision that both promoted an autonomous Katanga rooted in indigeneity *and* rejected settler claims to dominate the same space. Conakat leader Evariste Kimba sought "to demonstrate to the settlers that Katanga was not a desert before the arrival of the Europeans and that this province could not be made to serve...as a region for massive European settlement."[42] Godefroid Munongo, who well understood the power of historical myth-making in contemporary nation-building, offered a similar critique:

> To serve certain political designs, people have pretended that the Katanga did not exist, that it was a construction of the colonizers. This is to deny that when the first white explorers discovered the part of Africa called Katanga they found three monarchies [i.e., Lunda, Luba, and Yeke] which were not only bound by family, economic and social links but – and this is by far the most important – their historic destiny had been linked for centuries.[43]

[39] Hughes (2003: 505–756).

[40] Daily Express (London), 2 March 1960, cited in Gérard-Libois (1966: 53–56).

[41] Hughes (2003: 604–6); cf. James (1996).

[42] Gérard-Libois (1966: 17).

[43] G. Munongo, *Comment est. né le nationalisme katangais*, Elisabethville, 16 June 1962 (mimeo), cited in Lemarchand (unpublished manuscript).

These monarchies, with their history as powerful trading and raiding empires, provided the mythico-historical basis for a Katangese state that could ensure the retention of Katanga's wealth among its indigenous communities. This, it should be stressed, necessitated a very partial reading of Katanga's past. It was not, however, qualitatively different to those articulated by nationalist parties elsewhere in Africa, seeking to present particularist political projects (often rooted in ambiguous readings of African history) as unproblematic representations of coherent national identities.

As a Luba, Kimba's imagined "Katanga" stretched out to encompass the former Luba kingdom. It was certainly possible for the Katanga Luba to be included in the secessionist project, since many shared these anti-Kasaian sentiments (although they were much more pronounced in urban Luba areas such as Kamina). In the case of Katanga, however, such constructions proved, despite the support of Luba chief Kasongo Niembo Jerome Ndaie, to be politically unacceptable for his rival Jason Sendwe's Balubakat, the political party that came to represent the Katanga Luba. Personal enmity between Tshombe and Sendwe, combined with the structural division between the urbanized south and largely rural north, drove Balubakat to form the "Cartel" with other pro-unitary parties in November 1959.[44]

As independence approached, political competition spilled out into ethnic clashes between autochthonous groups and Kasai Luba in Katanga's southern towns. Rioting occurred in January and March 1960, as each party prepared for the May 1960 elections that paved the way for independence. In those elections, Conakat won 8 of the 16 national assembly seats for Katanga, and 25 of 60 provincial seats, securing 32% of the vote, a lower percentage than the Cartel. Conakat, however, constructed a broader coalition of support, establishing a bloc of 38 of the 60 provincial seats.[45] Balubakat claimed electoral fraud and refused to take its seats, leaving its Northern Katangese supporters unrepresented. Katanga's ethnic and economic divide had now taken political form and would soon become the basis of a military conflict. René Lemarchand concluded that one factor (alongside settler and Belgian metropolitan interests) explaining Katanga's claim to self-determination, was:

---

[44] Lemarchand (1964: 241–2).
[45] Gérard-Libois (1966: 63–65).

the sense of economic grievance which permeates the attitude of the so-called genuine Katangese towards the inhabitants of the other provinces. ... regional differences in the distribution of economic resources operated to aggravate latent tensions among ethnic groups, so that economic stratification tended to coincide with tribal divisions. In a sense, therefore, tribal antagonisms must be viewed as symptoms of economic grievances. The fact that the Conakat succeeded in rallying the support of otherwise unrelated tribal entities (Bayeke, Lunda, Batabwa, etc.) suggests indeed that these grievances were an important source of solidarity among its members.[46]

Conakat leaders came close to declaring Katangese independence in the weeks before Congolese independence in June 1960. It was, however, the profound instability of independent Congo, reflecting the frustration of soldiers seeking postcolonial advancement parallel with that achieved by civilian politicians, which provided the opportunity to declare an independent Katanga. The mutiny of Force Publique (FP) soldiers prompted thousands of European residents to flee. Given the dependence of both government and the economy (particularly the mining industry) on Europeans, Belgium, settler representatives, and Conakat leaders presented the potential collapse of economy and society as the result of left-wing agitation and a justification for action.

Following Lumumba's replacement of Emile Janssens as the commander of the now renamed Congolese National Army (ANC) with the Kasaian Victor Lundula, and Lumumba's refusal to accept Belgium's "offer" of military intervention, elements of the divided Belgian government threw their weight behind an accelerated effort to secure its mineral and strategic interests via secession. Accordingly, on 11 July, Conakat declared independence in the following terms:

> Throughout the Congo and particularly in Katanga and in Leopoldville province, we see a tactic of disorganization and terror at work, a tactic which we have seen in...many countries now under Communist dictatorship... Katanga cannot bow to such proceedings. ...Under these circumstances, and before the dangers we would bring down upon us by prolonging our submission to the arbitrary will and Communistic intentions of the central government, the Katangese government has decided to proclaim the independence of Katanga.

[46] Lemarchand (1962: 415).

THIS INDEPENDENCE IS TOTAL. However, the Katangese government, to which Belgium has just granted the assistance of its own troops to
protect human life, calls upon Belgium to join with Katanga in close economic community. Katanga calls upon Belgium to continue its technical,
financial, and military support. It calls upon her to assist in reestablishing
order and public safety.[47]

In order to secure chiefly support, Conakat had previously argued for a
prominent role for chiefs in the postindependence political system, and
this was formalized with the establishment of a Grand Council of 20 chiefs
as part of the Katangese constitution promulgated in August 1960; 10
chiefs, including the Mwaant Yav, were appointed as Ministers of State.
None of this, however, translated into practical political authority over the
new state itself; while those chiefs who had been loyal to the colonial order
and who sought to maintain their influence were granted substantial
autonomy in their own areas, control over mineral wealth and the levers of
power remained in the hands of Conakat's leaders.

Conakat's leaders were adept in their symbolic performance of a new
nation-state. As in Congo and elsewhere across the continent, Katanga
produced its own national anthem, flew its own flag, issued its own
stamps, and broadcast its own radio programs. It sought diplomatic relations with other states and, notwithstanding the rebuffing of these
efforts, continued to correspond with what it regarded as its equals as a
fully fledged state.

If these claims to statehood only partially masked its material and
structural weaknesses and contradictions, then this was equally true, not
only of Congo as a whole but also of many African states engaged in the
process of making nations from above during this period. Behind the
more performative aspects of Katangese nationhood, however, Conakat
leaders sought to retain a monopoly over taxation revenue, primarily
generated by the province's vast mining industry, and a similar monopoly over armed force. It is well known that *Union Minière* underwrote
and partly shaped the secession, redirecting the taxation it had previously paid to the colonial state to the Elisabethville government. Despite
this support, *Société Générale,* with many other assets to protect, was
divided over its support for an independent state.[48] Although dozens of

[47] Translated from Gérard-Libois (1966: 328).
[48] Brion and Moreau (2006: 316–8).

Belgian officers rallied to support the secessionist state, bringing significant material with them, Katanga also established an indigenous rank-and-file army of its own.[49]

SECESSIONISM IN SOUTH KASAI, 1960–1962

As in Katanga, other parts of the new Congolese nation-state, experiencing political tensions that arose in significant part from the reconstruction of ethnic identity during colonialism, sought to address their problems by secessionist initiatives. South Kasai was, like Katanga, both rich in minerals (primarily diamonds) and had experienced ethnic conflict and political tension between local and Leopoldville-based political leaders in the run-up to independence. On 14 June 1960, former MNC leader Albert Kalonji unilaterally proclaimed a "Federal State of South Kasai."

Kalonji claimed (less convincingly than his Katangese counterparts) aristocratic credentials and ruled overtly in the interests of his Luba ethnic group, opposed to Lumumba's support of their ethnic opponents the Lulua. Following Congolese independence, Kalonji and his fellow leaders worked closely with Katanga's rulers and established what briefly amounted to a secessionist alliance. On 8 August, Kalonji declared the autonomy of what was now known as the "Mining State of South Kasai," with its capital at Bakwanga (today's Mbuji-Mayi) and with Kalonji as its president. However, South Kasai lacked both Katanga's economic significance and the consequent level of Belgian military support; its geographical position also made South Kasai far more vulnerable to attacks by the Congolese armed forces; their brutal operation in September 1960, characterized by UN Secretary-General Dag Hammarskjöld as "genocide," had the unintended effect of increasing Kalonji's legitimacy.

Kalonji (unlike his Katangese counterparts) saw little need to maintain a veneer of modern political practice. He appointed himself "Mulopwe" (Emperor) of South Kasai in April 1961, despite his demonstrably false claim to this title. Joseph Mobutu, chief-in-staff of the Congolese army, mounted a bloody four-month campaign that led to thousands of civilian deaths and ended the secession in December. Kalonji escaped from prison and managed to briefly revive his government in 1962. However, in com-

[49] The extent of this Belgian support should not be exaggerated: only a handful of Belgian officers were in Katanga in July–August 1960 and a total of 177 served there during the secession.

parison with Katanga, the narrower ethnic basis of South Kasaian identity, its limited armed capacity, and its lack of external support made it a much less realistic prospect for sustained secession.

THE CONGO CRISIS, 1960–1963

Although secessionist Katanga received limited and temporary support from Belgium, the United States and other Western powers quickly rallied against the secession. In the run-up to independence, State Department officials argued that "a united Congo would enable the West to compete more advantageously with the [Communist] Bloc than a fragmented Congo which would…offer the Bloc an especially fertile ground for penetration."[50] The United States' aim was a central government sufficiently broad to claim national representation and sufficiently stable to protect Western interests and guard against communist infiltration.

American backing was crucial to the United Nations' (UNs) support of Congolese unity and its call for the withdrawal of Belgian forces. At Lumumba's request, it dispatched a peacekeeping force; by the end of July 1960, 8400 UN troops were in Congo.[51] However, the UN Security Council, while resolving that "the entry of the United Nations Force into the province of Katanga is necessary," simultaneously affirmed that "the United Nations Force in the Congo will not be a party to…any internal conflict…."[52] UN Special Representative Ralph Bunche became convinced that UN entry into Katanga would involve confrontation with its new armed forces and would therefore breach the Security Council resolution.[53] This "failure" by the UN prompted a frustrated Lumumba to seek support from the Eastern Bloc. This led in turn to Lumumba's conflict with President Kasavubu, Lumumba's removal from office in September 1960, and ultimately his murder in January 1961 at the hands of Belgian soldiers and Katangese leaders.

---

[50] US State Department archives (hereafter USSD), RG59, E3111 (Bureau of African Affairs), Box 8, File 14.4., "Communism, 1960–1," Hugh S. Cumming, Jr. to The Secretary, Intelligence Note: "Prospects for Communist Inroads in the Belgian Congo under Alternative Conditions of Unity or Fragmentation," n.d. but c.16 June 1960.

[51] Hoskyns (1965: 158–9).

[52] Resolution adopted in 886th Session of UN Security Council, 9 August 1960, Appendix II, Gérard-Libois (1966: 330).

[53] For Hammarskjöld's report to the UN, see NAUK FO/371/146775, "Congo, 1960," UK UN Mission to FO, 6 August 1960.

The UN's fateful decision involved a successful bluff on Katanga's part, given the barely trained army it was still bringing into existence.[54] In early 1961, Belgian officials organized the transfer of hundreds of Belgian volunteers (and those of other nationalities) to fight in Katanga.[55, 56] Former FP troops based in Elisabethville were disarmed, and only those of Katangese origin or residence were retained for the new force. They were supplemented with volunteers from Southern Katangese communities, as well as Baluba warriors recruited by the pro-secession Luba chief, the Kasongo Niembo.

The new army was immediately mobilized in Northern Katanga. Despite Conakat's claim to represent all of Katanga, the subsequent sub-secession of Northern Katangese areas and the formation of the Northern Lualaba province in October 1960, under Balubakat control and allied to the Congolese government, demonstrated the failure to integrate much of Northern Katanga into the secessionist project—it was in the Balubakat forces that a young Laurent Kabila, himself of Northern Katangese origin, cut his teeth as a military commander. One of the ironies of the Katangese secession was its mirroring of the unwillingness of the Leopoldville authorities (and African nationalists generally) to recognize that considerable cultural and socioeconomic diversity provided a legitimate basis for self-determination. Katanga's successful military operations placed its gendarmerie in occupation of what amounted to a foreign territory, which it brought under its control but failed to convince of its political legitimacy.[57] This failure revealed the profound contradictions inherent in the Katangese state project, closely resembling similar contradictions and tensions inherent in many nationalist projects in Africa, most obviously that of Congo itself, that sought to carve nation states out of ambiguous his-

[54] Hoskyns (1965: 163).

[55] US State Dept archives, RG59, E3111 (Bureau of African Affairs), Box 8, file 17.2 "Internal Research Reports, Jan-Jun 1963," Hare to Elting, 2 February 1961, "Belgian Assistance to the Congo."

[56] Belgium never officially recognized Katanga as an independent state and its actions were motivated, not by active enthusiasm for the secessionist project but rather to defend Belgium's control and/or influence over Katanga's mining industry against a potentially radical Central Congolese government.

[57] On the history of the Katangese Gendarmes and its successive transformations until 2006, see Kennes and Larmer (2016).

torical claims and territories of highly uneven socioeconomic development and "differential modernization."[58]

In early 1961, the Western powers sought to reconcile the Leopoldville and Elisabethville governments. The United States initially agreed with Belgium and Britain that the secession should not be ended forcibly; this reflected its desire to protect Katanga's strategic mineral assets and to ensure peaceful reintegration into a Western-oriented Congo. Moïse Tshombe engaged in lengthy negotiations that, it was hoped, would bring Conakat into a Leopoldville unity government as a pro-Western bulwark against the rebel Lumumbist "government" in Stanleyville.[59] At the Tananarive Conference of March 1961, Tshombe conceded independence in exchange for a confederation of autonomous Congo states.[60] Agreement foundered, however, on two issues central to the secessionist project: the distribution of UMHK-derived taxation revenue and control over Katangese military forces.

Once news of Lumumba's assassination became public, Belgium increasingly sought to secure its interests via the now pro-Western Leopoldville government and gradually withdrew support to the Katangese state. While Belgium consistently resisted UN efforts to forcibly reincorporate Katanga, it equally sought to pressure Tshombe to accept the inevitability of reintegration, take up a position in the Leopoldville government, and negotiate a peaceful settlement. Relations between Elisabethville and Brussels, never as fulsome as sometimes suggested, markedly deteriorated— indeed, Conakat leaders, whose movement was founded on a perception of pro-Kasaian Belgian bias (see above), believed Belgium had betrayed their cause and looked on its subsequent diplomatic efforts with suspicion.[61] The official Belgian position, which itself changed when the Gaston Eyskens government fell in April 1961, should not be equated with the still powerful pro-Katanga lobby in Brussels, the UMHK, nor that of many senior Belgian political and military figures who continued to pro-

---

[58] Young (1976: 175).

[59] After Lumumba was deposed as Congolese Prime Minister, his deputy Antoine Gizenga established a rival Congolese government in Stanleyville; supported by Lumumbist forces, this government was overthrown by Armée Nationale Congolaise (ANC) forces in January 1962.

[60] Colvin (1968: 56–7); Centre de Recherche et d'Information Socio-Politiques (1962).

[61] Evidence of this fractious relationship can be found in the telexes sent from Belgium's consul in Elisabethville to the Foreign Ministry in Brussels during the secession: Belgian Ministry of Foreign Affairs Archives Diplomatique, File refs Nr 14,333, 17,138, and 17,139.

vide considerable backing to the secession.[62] What is clear is that if Katanga had been overwhelmingly an externally dependent project, the state and its manifestations would have collapsed, instead of surviving for nearly two more years.

Congolese frustration over unending negotiations led to Tshombe and Kimba's detention in April 1961, following talks at Coquilhatville. The Katangese leaders were released in June, having signed an accord agreeing to unify Congo and Katanga's political structures, finances, diplomatic representation, and armed forces.[63] However, the Katangese assembly refused to ratify an agreement that was made, it was claimed, under duress. Tshombe's apparently inconsistent approach to negotiations reflected both his personal opportunism and his restricted room to maneuver.[64]

Following the international outcry after Lumumba's murder, a far stronger UNSC resolution 161 authorized "all appropriate measures" to "prevent the occurrence of civil war in the Congo, including…the use of force, if necessary, in the last resort." The resolution, backed by the Congolese government, empowered UN forces to detain and repatriate foreign officials and advisors. The UN's attempt to bring reinforcements into Elisabethville led to clashes with Katangese forces. Tshombe skillfully whipped up popular anger against UN action, with a civilian mob attacking UN symbols.[65] UN forces nevertheless advanced to take key positions in Northern Katanga and, by August 1961, 338 "mercenaries" and 443 Belgian "political advisors" had been detained and expelled.[66] It was widely believed that such measures would result in the collapse of both the Katangese economy and military. In fact, the Forces Armeés Katangaises did not collapse as was widely predicted. Some returned to their positions in unofficial guise, others were replaced by a new, more wholly mercenary officer class, but military discipline was also maintained by newly promoted Katangese officers.

---

[62] Katanga's Minister of Finance, Jean-Baptiste Kibwe, made financial demands on UMHK and its subsidiary companies during the secession that belied his government's reputation as the "tool" of the mining company. See, for example, UMHK archives, Box file 102, Assemblée Générale, 24 May 1962, Interpellations, 2.

[63] Gérard-Libois (1966: 188).

[64] USSD, RG59, E3111 (Bureau of African Affairs), Box 8, File 14.3, "The Katanga Question," J. Wayne Fredericks to Robert C. Good, "Neutralizing extremist Congo political elements as a prelude to Katanga reintegration and political consensus," 7 May 1962.

[65] Colvin (1968: 57).

[66] Young (1965: 340).

The US-sponsored Cyrille Adoula government, which took office in August 1961, proved a more formidable opponent for Katanga. Tshombe accused the United States of using the Congo crisis as a way for American financiers and capitalists to gain control of Katangese copper.[67] Katanga's failure to cooperate led the UN to launch "Operation Rumpunch" in August 1961, during which it prematurely proclaimed the end of the secession. In September, "Operation Morthor" again sought to capture the remaining foreign advisors and to implement arrest warrants for Katangese leaders issued by the Adoula government. Tshombe temporarily fled to Northern Rhodesia (an important rear base for the secession during this period), from where he urged resistance, and Irish UN forces suffered a humiliating defeat in Jadotville (today's Likasi).[68] UN Secretary-General Hammarskjöld's attempt to negotiate personally with Tshombe led to the former's death in a plane crash.[69] After these reversals, the UN agreed to a ceasefire on disadvantageous terms.

In November, however, Security Council resolution 169 called for the UN to "take vigorous action, including the use of the requisite measure of force, if necessary" to remove foreign personnel. A new operation in December 1961, causing significant casualties on both sides, gave the UN control of strategic positions in Elisabethville and grounded the Katangese air force. Simultaneously, the ANC advanced into Northern Katanga, while violence against the Kasaian civilian population of Southern Katangese towns forced many into UN-organized refugee camps. In the Kitona agreement with Adoula of 22 December 1961, Tshombe conceded the principle of Congolese unity, the need to place Katangese forces under central government control, and the participation of Conakat in the national Congolese parliament. Tshombe nevertheless succeeded in delaying the end of the secession for another year through drawn-out negotiations with the Congolese central government.

---

[67] USSD, RG59, E3111 (Bureau of African Affairs), Box 6, File 1.D/1.1. The President (Tshombe), 1961 and 1963, J. Wayne Fredericks to Mr. McGhee, "Tshombe's Political Orientation," 12 July 1962.

[68] Various accounts suggest assistance from the Central African Federation in moving Tshombe's gold reserves and in assisting his retreat to Northern Rhodesia Hughes (2003: 611–12).

[69] Notwithstanding numerous official enquiries that have concluded that the plane crash was not caused by foul play, considerable suspicion still surrounds Hammarskjöld's death: see most recently, Susan Williams (2011).

From May 1962, Belgium and the United States agreed that regional stability depended on resolving the crisis and worked together to bring an end to the secession.[70] Negotiations were periodically undermined by fighting between the Katangese gendarmerie and ANC, which advanced further into Katanga. Negotiations now revolved around the peace plan proposed by the new UN Secretary-General, U Thant. The Thant Plan sought to secure Katangese reintegration into the Central Congolese state on the basis of a notably federal division of powers between central and provincial administrations. Mineral revenue would be divided equally between the central government and the province that produced it.[71]

The Leopoldville government, while paying lip service to the Thant Plan, took offensive military action that provided Tshombe with an excuse for inaction. The UN's lengthy, troubled, and expensive operation in Congo, largely underwritten by the United States, was increasingly regarded as unsustainable. Facing the withdrawal of some member state forces but benefiting from increased US military backing, the UN sought to bring matters to a head. Amidst rising tension, a UN helicopter was shot down on 24 December 1962. Five days later, Tshombe's refusal to remove roadblocks led the UN to end the secession by force in a surprisingly swift operation.[72] The Katangese government formally ended the secession on 14 January 1963.[73]

UNITY AND DIVISION IN CONGO

It was in the interests of the international community to present the Katangese secession as the singular exception to an otherwise unified Congolese state. Yet it was only the presence of UN forces that enabled this illusion to be maintained. It should be recalled that the weakness of the Central Congolese state was such that two alternative Congolese governments existed throughout the early 1960s, with Lumumbists establishing a capital in the eastern city of Stanleyville after Lumumba's ousting. This was not an act of secession, since the Stanleyville regime claimed sovereignty over the entire country in the name of the murdered prime

---

[70] USSD, RG59, E3111 (Bureau of African Affairs, Box 7, File 5.2 "Conferences," William Brubeck to McGeorge Bundy, "Our Congo Policy after the London Talks," 21 May 1962).

[71] "Le Plan Thant pour la reintegration du Katanga" (1963: 12–17).

[72] Gérard-Libois (1966: 273).

[73] Gérard-Libois (1966: 275).

minister and strongly opposed the secessions of South Kasai and Katanga; yet its effect was certainly to undermine the fragile authority of the Leopoldville government.

With the scheduled withdrawal of UN troops in mid-1964, further rebellions broke out in the far west (Kwilu) and much of the east of Congo, demonstrating the inability of the Congolese state and its armed forces to ensure even a facade of national unity. This is not to suggest that the eastern Mulelist rebellion, which continued in a limited form until Mulele's death in 1968, was intentionally regional: rather, its aim of a second and "real" independence reflected the enduring weakness and widely perceived illegitimacy of the central government; a majority of Congolese territory was not under the control of the Leopoldville government in mid-1964. This rebellion was forcibly ended in November with the entry into Stanleyville of Belgian paratroopers, now utilized by the Leopoldville government and supported by the United States.

However, the remnants of the eastern rebellion continued for many years. As in Katanga, the rebels' capacity depended on external military and political support: the Stanleyville government was supported by most left-leaning African states and received Chinese weaponry. The loss of this support was crucial to the gradual weakening and suppression of the remaining pockets of rebellion in 1965–1966. By 1967, a small part of the Fizi area of Southern Kivu remained in rebel hands and remained so throughout the Mobutu era. Laurent Kabila's Popular Revolutionary Party (PRP) forces were able to maintain control of Fizi because of limited support from neighboring Tanzania. Fizi was, in contrast to mineral-rich Katanga, arguably allowed to remain "liberated" because it offered no apparent threat to the Congo/Zaire state. Nevertheless, Kabila retained some standing with radical Southern African leaders in Tanzania and Angola. This arguably provided the basis for his leadership in the successful operations of the Alliance des Forces Démocratiques pour la Libération du Zaïre (AFDL) that overthrew Mobutu in 1997 and installed Kabila as Congolese president.[74]

Given the potential for autonomism in Eastern Congo, it is instructive to consider why, in contrast to Katanga, it did not embark onto fully fledged secessionism following independence. The Kivus possessed an important settler population (though smaller and less well politically connected than that in Katanga); the Banyamulenge served as a potential uni-

[74] Kennes (2003).

fying enemy, and a strong regional economy provided the basis for self-sufficiency but was based on agriculture rather than mining and was therefore less amenable to control by the weak Congolese state of its revenue. The Kivus had a history of powerful pre-colonial "kingdoms," and in some areas nostalgia for the "Grand Kivu" province that existed for much of the colonial (1933–1962) and Mobutu (1966–1988) periods, but there was no attempt to mobilize these as the basis for a secessionist project.[75] The Kivus also had a stronger presence of the unitary MNC/L and a lower degree of politicization; the absence of powerful mining capital; and a lack of support from neighboring states (Rwanda-Urundi had not then achieved independence).

Mobutu and After: Centralization and Regionalism in Congo, 1965–1997

When Joseph Mobutu came to power in a 1965 coupwith strong support from the United States, it was because he and his army appeared to be the only force capable of unifying a nation-state in constant danger of fragmentation. Mobutu's popular vilification of civilian politicians provided him with the breathing space to impose what became, over time, a highly centralized regime, in which authority was concentrated in Kinshasa and increasingly embodied in Mobutu as an individual. Many politicians previously engaged in autonomist or secessionist movements recognized that all political power and personal wealth now flowed from the center and sought for themselves a (usually precarious) position in the Mobutu-appointed hierarchy.

Mobutu ensured that state revenues were first accumulated in Leopoldville and then distributed to the provinces. While little benefit accrued to ordinary people, the political elite and those who aspired to join it recognized that there was no alternative to participation in Mobutu's patrimonial system. The re-imposition of the centralized colonial provinces of the 1930s in 1966 largely restored the system in place under colonialism. For much of Mobutu's period in office, senior provincial officials were appointed to areas where they were ethnic "strangers," ostensibly to promote national togetherness but in practice to prevent such leaders constructing a political base in their locality.

---

[75] For the belief in the notion of reviving "Grand Kivu" see Thomas Turner (2007: 78).

It initially appeared that Mobutu's New Regime had succeeded in achieving a fuller and more sustainable integration of Zaire.[76] However, its foundation was an authoritarian centralism that ruthlessly suppressed any hint of renewed regional identification. Katanga was the only region where significant internal rebellion, fueled by external support from Katangese rebels, required the mobilization of Congolese forces, heavily supported by Western military intervention.[77] Mobutu's initial success rested on a system of patronage that in turn depended on mining-led economic growth and external credit. When this foundered with the economic crisis of the mid-1970s, the patrimonial state became increasingly predatory on its own citizens. Because the central state still lacked the means to extract wealth on a sustainable basis, its capacity to control outlying regions decreased.[78] Mobutu made a virtue of this necessity, encouraging state officials to generate local revenue on an ad hoc basis (termed *débrouillez-vous*—help yourselves) and played off ethnic groups against each other in order to stay in office.

In Shaba (the renamed Katanga province), the appointment of Kyungu wa Kyumwanza as governor in 1990 re-awakened anti-Kasaian sentiment, together with the first revival of a desire of autonomy for Katanga. In September 1992, tens of thousands of Kasaian Luba residents in Shaba were deported to Kasai; this removed from Katanga many supporters of the opposition *Union pour la Démocratie et le Progrès Social* (UDPS). In sharp contrast to UMHK's support of Conakat, Kyungu's project helped bring the mining industry to its knees. Meanwhile, Kasai demonstrated its autonomy from the central state by refusing to adopt new Zairian banknotes in 1993, in an attempt to defend its diamond mining economy.

Mobutu's removal from power in 1997 did little to address these underlying problems. The fact that Laurent Kabila's *Alliance des Forces Démocratiques pour la Libération du Congo-Zaïre* (AFDL) came to power through the agency of Rwanda further illustrated the inability of Congolese opposition forces to act on an effective national basis. It arguably required the subsequent attack by Rwanda, Uganda, and Burundi on Kabila in

---

[76] Young (1994: 247–263) and Young and Turner (1985: 60–63).
[77] For the Shaba rebellions of 1977 and 1978, see Larmer (2013: 89–108).
[78] De Boeck (1996: 75–105).

1998 to rally most Congolese into national unity.[79] While the Kivus have, under the presidency of Joseph Kabila (since 2001), been strongly unified and opposed to federalism (viewed as opening the door to Rwandan domination), other parts of Congo again expressed autonomous tendencies.

As in the pre-independence period, cultural associations, in the context of limited democratization and a central state unable to defend rights and provide basic services, came into conflict with that state when demanding federalist decentralization. In 2008, supporters of *Bundu dia Kongo*, a Kongo cultural association that evoked the ABAKO of 1959–1961, clashed with the police—at least a hundred of its supporters were shot dead.[80] Frustration at the nonresponsiveness of the Congolese state to economic and/or ethno-regional concerns, particularly in border areas (Bas-Congo, Ituri, the Kivus, and Southern Katanga, among others), periodically finds expression in demands for extreme autonomy and (less frequently) outright secession. In March 2013, the Mai-Mai guerillas known as "Ba Kata Katanga" (cutoff Katanga) briefly occupied the central square of Lubumbashi and demanded the independence of Katanga. They raised the flag of the Katangese state of the early 1960s to consciously express a link to their predecessors.[81]

During this period, the population of Katanga was arguably more united than in the early 1960s in rejecting the perceived illegitimacy of Kinshasa's authority. Cross-border support for Katanga's political elite, so important during the secession, is replicated in the singular figure of then Katangese Governor Moïse Katumbi, whose strong links with Zambia's political elite have been important to his political success. Yet the practical capacity of any new autonomist initiative is undermined by the perception that politicians of Katangese origin, Kabila *père et fils* have been central to national political life for more than a decade. Whereas a potentially intrusive Central Congolese state was a cause of the secessionist project of 1960–1963, Joseph Kabila is in many respects an absentee president, whose lack of visibility (except on television during election campaigns)

---

[79] The complexities of the two Congo wars cannot be seriously examined here. Among the wealth of literature on the Congo wars, the most useful studies of this question are Lemarchand (2009), Reyntjens (2010), and Prunier (2009). See also the volumes of *Cahiers Africains* published during this period, by authors including Kennes, J.-C. Willame and G. De Villiers among others.

[80] MONUC (2012).

[81] http://radiookapi.net/actualite/2013/03/23/lubumbashi-le-calme-est-revenu-apres-la-reddition-des-miliciens-bakata-katanga-la-monusco/ (last accessed 03/24/13).

mirrors the continuing ineffectiveness of the Congolese state to play any positive role in the lives of its subjects.

The contemporary Congolese ruling elite does, however, share with its Lumumbist predecessors an unwillingness to recognize regionally specific identities and an insistence on a centralist state. When Governor Moïse Katumbi and his ally Kyungu wa Kumwanza expressed in December 2014, their ambition to challenge Joseph Kabila by refusing his project for an unconstitutional third presidential mandate, the Katanga province was again brought under central control. Paradoxically this was disguised as a further decentralization: the 2006 constitutional provision to subdivide the provinces in smaller units was implemented but only by ensuring that the newly created provincial governments and assemblies were closely controlled by the presidential majority ruled from Kinshasa.

Although the operation turned 6 of the former 11 provinces into 21 new ones, its main objective was to break Katanga's tendency toward autonomy by subdividing it into four smaller units largely corresponding to former districts (Haut-Katanga, Lualaba, Haut-Lomami, Tanganyika). As a result, four new political spaces were created but with a very limited room for proper initiative and few resources. The destitution by the provincial assemblies of two of the four new governors in 2017 expressed the shallow ground on which the new provincial institutions were resting. The strong presence of security forces in ex-Katanga and the high level of repression against any opposition forces, especially when linked to Katumbi, prevent the development of autonomist tendencies for the new provinces centered around specific cultural identities.[82] It is presently unclear to what extent the former Katangese identity may have room for revival in the future, undoubtedly depending on the emergence of a new leadership.

Conclusion

Few Congolese see all-out secession or the dismantling of the state as the solution to their problems.[83] Despite the instructive recent example of South Sudanese independence, and the partial relaxation of the reification of colonial borders by the African Union that it reflects,[84] the road

---

[82] There may be a limited exception for the Lunda in Lualaba province, but this cannot be detailed here.

[83] Herbst and Mills (2009).

[84] See also Byrne and Englebert (2018) in this volume.

to full independence is a rocky and unpredictable one, requiring a highly unusual and quite specific set of factors to be in place for it to stand any chance of success.

This focuses our attention on the very particular circumstances that made the declaration of secession in Katanga a feasible political project. The common assertion of political rights in late-colonial Congo via ethno-regional associations, and the paucity of planning for self-rule by Belgium, made adherence to a common national identity for all Congo's peoples a minority position among aspirant rulers. The particular processes of socio-economic change in Southern Katanga—the mining industry and the influx of Kasaian migrant labor—both stimulated the anxieties that led to secession and provided the economic (mining revenue) and political resources (UMHK and Belgian elite support) that made it possible.

The context of the Cold War enabled Conakat to utilize a powerful anti-communist rhetoric that won it significant external political support. This external support was essential in turning the claims by chiefs to pre-colonial authority, and the anxieties of conservative elites regarding modernization and immigration, into a feasible state-based project. The reverse is, however, equally the case: Katanga could not have existed, nor sustained itself, without significant pre-colonial integration among the "kingdoms of the savannah" (Luba-Lunda and Yeke) and the ability of late-colonial African leaders to construct legitimacy and a cohesive political project out of the changes wrought by twentieth-century colonial capitalism.

REFERENCES

Allman, J. (1993). *The quills of the porcupine: Asante nationalism in an emergent Ghana*. Madison: University of Wisconsin Press.

Brion, R., & Moreau, J. L. (2006). *De la mine à Mars: La genèse d'Umicore*. Tielt: Lannoo.

Bustin, E. (1975). *Lunda under Belgian rule*. Cambridge, MA: Harvard University Press.

Byrne, H., & Englebert, P. (2018). Shifting grounds for African secessionism? In L. de Vries, P. Englebert, & M. Schomerus (Eds.), *Secessionism in African politics: Aspiration, grievance, performance, disenchantment*. New York: Palgrave.

Centre de Recherche et d'Information Socio-Politiques. (1962). *Congo 1961*. Brussels: CRISP.

Colvin, I. (1968). *The rise and fall of Moïse Tshombe*. London: Leslie Frewin Publishers.

Cooper, F. (1996). *Decolonization and African society: The labour question in French and British Africa*. Cambridge: Cambridge University Press.

De Boeck, F. (1996). Post-colonialism, power and identity. In R. Werbner & T. Ranger (Eds.), *Post-colonial identities in Africa* (pp. 75–105). London: Zed Books.

De Witte, L. (2001). *The assassination of Patrice Lumumba*. London/New York: Verso.

Fetter, B. S. (1969). The Luluabourg revolt at Elisabethville. *African Historical Studies, 2*, 269–277.

Foucher, V. (2018). The Mouvement des Forces Démocratiques de Casamance: The illusion of separatism in Senegal? In L. de Vries, P. Englebert, & M. Schomerus (Eds.), *Secessionism in African politics: Aspiration, grievance, performance, disenchantment*. New York: Palgrave.

Gérard-Libois, J. (1966). *Katanga secession*. Madison: University of Wisconsin Press.

Herbst, J., & Mills, G. (2009). There is no Congo. *Foreign Policy, 18*. Retrieved from http://www.foreignpolicy.com/articles/(2009)/03/17/there_is_no_congo

Higginson, J. (1989). *A working-class in the making: Belgian colonial labor policy, private enterprise, and the African mineworker, 1907–1951*. Madison: University of Wisconsin Press.

Higginson, J. (1992). Liberating the captives: Independent watchtower as an avatar of colonial revolt in southern Africa and Katanga, 1908–1941. *Journal of Social History, 26*(1), 55–80.

Hoskyns, C. (1965). *Congo since independence, January 1960–December 1960*. Oxford: Oxford University Press.

Hughes, M. (2003). Fighting for white rule in Africa: The Central African Federation, Katanga, and the Congo crisis, 1958–1965. *International History Review, 25*(3), 505–756.

James, A. (1996). *Britain and the Congo crisis, 1960–63*. Basingstoke: Macmillan.

Jewsiewicki, B. (1989). The formation of the political culture of ethnicity in the Belgian Congo. In L. Vail (Ed.), *The creation of tribalism in southern Africa*. Oxford: James Currey.

Kennes, E. (2003). *Essai biographique sur Laurent Désiré Kabila*. Paris: L'Harmattan.

Kennes, E., & Larmer, M. (2016). *The Katangese gendarmes and war in Central Africa. Fighting their way home*. Bloomington: Indiana University Press.

Larmer, M. (2013). Local conflicts in a transnational war: The Katangese gendarmes and the Shaba wars of 1977–78. *Cold War History, 31*(1), 89–108.

Leclercq, J. J. (1926). *Aux chutes du Zambèze: du Cap au Katanga*. Paris: P. Roger.

Lemarchand, R. (1962). The limits of self-determination: The case of the Katanga secession. *American Political Science Review, 56*, 404–416.

Lemarchand, R. (1964). *Political awakening in the Belgian Congo*. Berkeley: University of California Press.

Lemarchand, R. (2009). *The dynamics of violence in Central Africa*. Philadelphia: University of Pennsylvania Press.

Lemarchand, R. Katanga: Background to secession. unpublished manuscript.

Matuka Manuna Tshitshi, S. (2009, May 5). Guide de Corak (Coordination d'organisation du referendum d'autdétermination du Katanga). Lubumbashi.

MONUC Human Rights Division. (2012). Special inquiry into the Bas Congo events of February and March. Retrieved from https://reliefweb.int/report/democratic-republic-congo/drc-special-inquiry-bascongo-events-february-and-march-2008

n.a. (1963). Le Plan Thant pour la reintegration du Katanga. *Etudes Congolais, 4*, 12–17.

Nzongola-Ntalaja, G. (2002). *The Congo from Leopold to Kabila: A people's history*. London: Zed Books.

Perrings, C. (1979). *Black mineworkers in Central Africa*. London: Heinemann.

Prunier, G. (2009). *From genocide to continental war: The Congolese conflict and the crisis of contemporary Africa*. London: C. Hurst & Co.

Reyntjens, F. (2010). *The Great African War: Congo and regional geopolitics, 1996–2006*. Cambridge: Cambridge University Press.

Rubbens, A. (Ed.). (1945). *Dettes de Guerre*. (n.p.): Elisabethville.

Turner, T. (2007). *The Congo wars: Conflict, myth and reality*. London: Zed Books.

Vansina, J. (1967). *Introduction à l'ethnographie du Congo*. Kinshasa: Université Lovanium Kinshasa.

Williams, S. (2011). *Who killed Hammarskjöld? The UN, the Cold War and white supremacy in Africa*. London: Hurst & Co.

Young, C. (1965). *Politics in the Congo*. Princeton: Princeton University Press.

Young, C. (1976). *The politics of cultural pluralism*. Madison: University of Wisconsin Press.

Young, C. (1994). Zaire: The shattered illusion of the integral state. *Journal of Modern African Studies, 32*, 247–263.

Young, C. (2003). Zaire: The shattered illusion of the integral state. In J. D. Le Sueur (Ed.), *The decolonization reader* (pp. 414–427). New York: Routledge.

Young, C., & Turner, T. (1985). *The rise and decline of the Zairian state*. Madison: University of Wisconsin Press.

Zeller, W., & Melber, H. (2018). United in separation? Lozi secessionism in Zambia and Namibia. In L. De Vries, P. Englebert, & M. Schomerus (Eds.), *Secessionism in African politics: Aspiration, grievance, performance, disenchantment*. New York: Palgrave.

Archival Sources

Belgian Ministry of Foreign Affairs Archives Diplomatique, File refs Nr 14333, 17138 and 17139.

UK national archives. (TNA), FO/371/146775, 'Congo, 1960', UK UN Mission to FO, 6 August (1960).

UMHK archives., Box file 102, Assemblée Générale, 24 May (1962), Interpellations, 2.

US State Department archives. (USSD), RG59, E3111 (Bureau of African Affairs), Boxes 6 – 8, various documents.

PART IV

Disenchantment: The Aftermath of Success

"We Didn't Fight for This": The Pitfalls of State- and Nation-Building in Eritrea

Alexandra Dias and Sara Dorman

INTRODUCTION

Eritrea gained independence in May 1991 with the overthrowing of Ethiopia's Derg by the combined forces of the Eritrean People's Liberation Front (EPLF) and the Tigray People's Liberation Front/Ethiopian People's Revolutionary Democratic Front (TPLF/EPRDF).[1] An April 1993 referendum formalized and further legitimized the independent state's claim to sovereignty, but few doubted the state's reality at that point. This near-universal acclaim was a far cry from the period after World War II when Eritrea had a legal existence but no international recognition

---

[1] Styan (1996: 80).

A. Dias (✉)
Department of Political Studies of Nova, University of Lisbon, Lisbon, Portugal

Portuguese Institute of International Relations, University of Lisbon, Lisbon, Portugal
e-mail: alexandradias@fcsh.unl.pt

S. Dorman
University of Edinburgh, Edinburgh, UK

© The Author(s) 2019
L. de Vries et al. (eds.), *Secessionism in African Politics,*
Palgrave Series in African Borderlands Studies,
https://doi.org/10.1007/978-3-319-90206-7_14

of that status. This tension between the claims to statehood and recognition of its legitimate existence shaped the struggle for independent statehood and continues to influence state formation, political terrain, and international relations in complex ways.

The international community's failure to recognize Eritrea's claim to self-determination after Italy's defeat in World War II resulted in a three-decades-long war for independence that led to 65,000 military[2] and between 150,000 and 250,000 civilian deaths.[3] But the struggle was not just tragically destructive of lives and human potential. It also shaped cultures and norms, created a transnational diaspora, and formed international alliances.

This chapter first considers the international response vis-à-vis Eritrea's claim for self-determination and independent statehood. It then focuses on the war for independence and the success of Eritrea's separatist insurgency in order to understand the legacy of this period to the process of state and nation formation in Eritrea. In the second part, the chapter examines the political project of state- and nation-building of the ruling party, the EPLF/People's Front for Democracy and Justice (PFDJ), and its implications for domestic and international relations. Despite the president's rhetoric of constructive engagement, the increasingly authoritarian path and the mutation of the principle of self-reliance have isolated the EPLF/PFDJ in the domestic, regional, and global political arenas. Eritrea's formal sovereignty is no longer in doubt, but its anomalous and fraught relations with neighbors and an international system that scorned it continue to shape the country's domestic and international policies.

Claiming Self-Determination and Independent Statehood

Eritrea's route to independent statehood was neither straightforward nor simple. Unlike the better-known liberation insurgencies of the 1960s and 1970s, Eritrea's quest for independence was not from European colonial or minority rule. It sought to free itself from inclusion in the expansive Ethiopian state, with the experience of European colonialism providing the basis for its independence claim. Other liberation movements had to convince the international community that they were the sole representative of an oppressed people; the leaders of the Eritrean struggle had to

[2] Pool (1998: 19).
[3] Jacquin-Berdal and Aida Mengistu (2006: 97).

prove the world that their oppressed nation existed and then position themselves as legitimate representatives of it.

We speak of a "separatist insurgency" occurring in Eritrea as it sought to have its right to self-determination recognized after the abrogation of the Ethio-Eritrean Federation (1952–1962). While some reject the idea of Eritrean independence being described as secession—on the grounds that its incorporation into Ethiopia was illegitimate—it may be that it instead can be seen as a case originating in a distinctively African pattern of secession, whereby colonial boundaries and experiences serve as a claim to legitimate grounds for sovereignty. The struggle for that legitimation also contributed to the building of that independent state.

Ultimately, Eritrea successfully claimed independence by presenting the nation as a former Italian colony (1890–1936)—similar to the narratives with which Western Sahara, Somaliland, Zanzibar, and Namibia have sought to frame their nationhood and claims to sovereignty.[4] Eritrea's successful liberation stood in marked contrast to earlier claims to the territory's nationhood, which had been dismissed as that of a primarily Muslim clique supported by Arab countries. Ethiopia's powerful presence and strategic allies in the immediate post-war period made it impossible for nationalists to garner international support.[5]

After the defeat of Italy in the Horn of Africa and ten years of British mandate rule, Ethiopia skillfully presented its claims over Eritrea and took it into its territorial sway, fully incorporating it in 1962. Eritrea's position—on the margins of one of Africa's great powers and with strategic importance to the global superpowers during the Cold War—meant the struggle for sovereignty involved internal nation-building and defeat of the controlling power as well as defying powerful international norms and interests. The forceful incorporation of Eritrea as the 14th Governorate of Ethiopia triggered dissent and armed opposition in Eritrea, but the Organisation of African Unity's (OAU) and the United Nations' (UN) silence and acquiescence with Ethiopia's policy left Eritrea isolated in the regional and global political arenas. Iyob notes that this isolation had benefits as well as costs for Eritrean nationalists. One benefit was Eritrea's emphasis on self-reliance and popular mobilization that was necessitated by its relative marginalization in international and regional communities.

---

[4] See Porges (2018), Hoehne (2018), Cameron (2018), and Zeller and Melber (2018) in this volume.

[5] Iyob (1995: 53).

But the primary cost was the subsequent absence of regional and international legitimacy, exacerbated by Ethiopia's diplomatic effectiveness in isolating the conflict.[6]

Ethiopia's claim to "reunification with Eritrea" coupled with its standing in Africa and internationally as an anti-colonial power obstructed the OAU's usual practice of recognizing independence following colonial rule.[7] Eritrea's case thus shows the limitations in the OAU's definition of the right to self-determination. African nationalism equated the principle of self-determination with freedom from European colonialism.[8] Rather than presenting a challenge to the *uti possidetis* norm that colonial borders are respected, Eritrea's claim for independence reinforced it. The separatist insurgency asserted the legitimacy of Eritrea's claim to self-determination on the basis of its past as an Italian colony (1890–1941).[9] Eritrea claimed that its right to self-determination should be recognized on the same basis as that of other ex-African colonies. However, Eritrea's trajectory was *sui generis* because the country from which it sought to separate had remained independent throughout the colonial period, and Ethiopia's territorial claim over Eritrea remained powerful.[10] The alliance between the EPLF and the TPLF/EPRDF against the Derg was important during Eritrea's final steps toward international recognition. The rump state's prompt recognition of Eritrea's claim for independent statehood facilitated the process of international recognition.[11] Eritrea's insurgency is often described as one of the most disciplined and effective African insurgencies.[12] It succeeded in forging a nation and successfully challenged and transformed international norms.

The Emergence of a National Identity

Eritrea's trajectory as a distinct entity started with the colonial partition of Africa. In the Horn of Africa, this process differed from sub-Saharan Africa because the Ethiopian empire played a role, along with the major European powers, in the partition of territory.[13]

[6] Iyob (1995: 17).
[7] Pool (1979: 45).
[8] Mayall (1990).
[9] Jacquin-Berdal (2002: 86).
[10] Halliday and Molyneux (1981) and Prunier (2007).
[11] Pool (1998: 19).
[12] Clapham (1998: 6).
[13] Clapham (2017: 3).

When Ethiopia defeated the invading Italian Army at the historical battle of Adwa (1896) and Italy was forced to shelve its plan to expand further south of the Mereb River, the territories' trajectories diverged. The peoples who lived north and south of the river Mereb, especially those based in the Ethiopian region of Tigray, continued to cross the border to inter-marry, visit relatives, attend weddings and funerals, worship, seek employment, trade, and search for pasture and water.[14] The creation of the Italian colony did not prevent groups now separated by the border from continuing with their daily lives, including contact with their kin across the border. But the period of Italian colonial rule did transform Eritrean society and contributed to the creation of a sense of difference among groups within Eritrea with regard to their neighbors in what came to be Ethiopia.[15]

According to Jacquin-Berdal, the Italian colonial authorities left a minimal form of modern education, and the numerous missions of various Christian denominations may have contributed to the creation of a sense of "Eritrean-ness." Schools, and in particular history lessons, played an important role in this: the textbooks used by Catholic missions depicted Eritrea as a cohesive entity. Mission-educated Eritreans thus acquired a unitary conception of Eritrea and of its particular history as distinct from other countries in the region. These textbooks contained maps of Eritrea that visually supported the formation of an imagined community.[16]

Italy also introduced important economic changes. Opportunities beyond the traditional sector of agriculture became available, with consequences for the previous semifeudal relations that had characterized the socioeconomic organization of society, particularly in the highlands.[17] For some lowland groups, the development of a cash economy, the availability of alternative economic opportunities, and the new forms of production associated with colonialism, in both Eritrea and Sudan, contributed to their process of emancipation from serfdom.[18] Unsurprisingly, such groups were not keen to experience reunification with Ethiopia.[19]

Italy also changed land tenure from a lineage-based system to one based on residence. In addition, Italy issued land grants in order to stimulate

---

[14] Abbay (1997) and Smidt (2010).
[15] Smidt (2010) and Abbay (1998).
[16] Jacquin-Berdal (2000: 59).
[17] Pool (2001: 14–15).
[18] Jacquin-Berdal (2002: 89).
[19] Pool (2001: 45).

Italians to relocate to Eritrea. This policy bore fruit. Between 1886 and 1930, only 5000 Italians had relocated. By 1941, the number had risen to 70,000.[20] Italian investment in the industrial sector in Eritrea did transform the predominantly rural and traditional society, leading to the emergence of a significant urban class.[21] During Italy's occupation of Ethiopia (1935–1941), Asmara remained its main commercial and economic center—even if Addis Ababa was the titular capital of the Italian East African Empire—nourishing a sophisticated self-image when compared to its Ethiopian rival.

Following Italy's defeat during World War II, Britain administered the ex-Italian colony until Eritrea's future was determined. The period of British Administration (1941–1952) politicized Eritreans around a nationalist project. The British Administration enhanced the educational system and established political parties.[22] Under the British Administration, all primary school books were in Tigrinya. Arabic textbooks were also obtained from Egypt and Sudan; however, Arabic was never widespread enough to become a second official language.[23] According to Pool, this period was accompanied by a politicization of religion.[24] The British plan to partition Eritrea between Sudan and Ethiopia became an important rallying point for the emerging Eritrean nationalist movement. An agreement between British Foreign Secretary Bevin and Italian Foreign Minister Sforza unified the new political elite around the cause of preserving Eritrea's territorial integrity.[25]

The United Nations Resolution 390 A (V) of 1952 established Eritrea's status as an autonomous region within the Federation with Ethiopia. However, the progressive deterioration of the federal arrangements and Ethiopia's final abrogation of the Federation sparked dissent and contributed to the emergence of the armed struggle. But at this stage, nationalist aspirations were mostly articulated by Eritrea's educated elites.[26] Mobilizing support across various groups became the main challenge and aim of the insurgent movements during the war for independence. Ethiopia's forceful reaction to the insurgency and the targeting

---

[20] Joireman (2000: 70–86).
[21] Jacquin-Berdal and Mengistu (2006: 90).
[22] Jacquin-Berdal (2002: 98).
[23] Jacquin-Berdal (2000: 61).
[24] Pool (2001: 39).
[25] Jacquin-Berdal (2002: 63), Pool (2001: 39), and Kibreab (2008).
[26] Jacquin-Berdal and Mengistu (2006: 91).

of civilians in both the low- and highlands during the war played a decisive role in the acceptance and legitimacy of the insurgency among large sections of the society.[27]

Secession as Nation-Building and Liberation Politics

Eritrea provides an archetypal example of how liberation movements need to be simultaneously inward-looking and externally focused. How a movement responds to those pressures is instructive for our understanding. This section examines the Eritrean insurgency and, in particular, the range of strategies deployed to attain independence. The various movements defined their political projects in ways that reflected the main cleavages of Eritrean society. These social divisions also shaped the mobilization of support for each political party and movement. To understand the trajectory of the different insurgent movements, we explore the emergence of political parties during the period of British administration and how this contributed to the emergence and maturation of the insurgent movements.

First, it must be understood that independence and national identity were by no means an automatic outcome of Eritrea's colonial experience. As is common in Africa, Eritrea's colonial boundaries separated it from ethnically contiguous areas, and migration to Eritrea from Ethiopia was common.[28] Following Italy's defeat by British-led Allied forces in 1941, the Four Powers Commission of Investigation visited the ex-Italian colony between November 8, 1947, and January 3, 1948, and the population was divided. According to the British and American delegates, 44.8% favored union with Ethiopia, while Italian and French delegates placed the number at 47.83%.[29] The remainder, that is, a small majority, was thought to favor independence—yet there was a perception that those favoring independence were primarily Muslim and thus the Great Powers did not see independence as a viable option for Eritrea's future.

Islam's role in the articulation of nationalist aspirations at the onset of resistance to Ethiopia should come as no surprise. In Ethiopia, Islam was portrayed as the religion of oppressed peoples, whereas Orthodox Christianity was seen as the establishment religion. Eritreans opposing Ethiopia's increasing breaches to their autonomy within the Federation

[27] Ibid: 91 and Marchal (1993: 22).
[28] Joireman (2000: 76).
[29] Iyob (1995: 63).

articulated their demands and mobilized support around religious solidarity, particularly to subvert the authority of Ethiopia. The daily consequences of the war on civilians paved the way for the extension of support to combatants engaged in the war for independence.[30]

The period of British Administration proved crucial for the emergence of political parties with an Islamist orientation. As Miran showed, "The foundation of the pro-Independence Muslim League (1946) in Keren rallied many ethnically and linguistically diverse Eritrean Muslims under the banner of Islam, making religious identity an essential component of nationalist aspirations."[31] The Muslim League thus opposed reunification with Ethiopia, while the Unionists were an alliance between Ethiopian nationalist groups with influence in Eritrea and the Orthodox Church's leadership in Eritrea.[32] Other non-Muslim political parties, namely the Liberal Progressive Party, also favored independence over the union with Ethiopia. Some Muslim groups, however, joined the unionists. Religious and political orientation, therefore, were not synonymous.

By 1958, the deterioration of the Federation triggered the creation of the Eritrean Liberation Movement (ELM) by a group of mostly young and educated Eritreans exiled in Sudan.[33] However, the movement did not thrive. The Eritrean Liberation Front (ELF) was created in Egypt in 1960. In 1961, ELF combatants carried the first demonstrations of forceful resistance to the Ethiopian presence in Eritrea. Although the ELF was more organized than the ELM, it rallied support along religious and ethnic cleavages and was supported by the Muslim groups of the lowlands. According to Prunier, in 1966, Orthodox Christians joined the separatist insurgency. However, the ELF and in particular, one of its leaders, Osman Saleh Sabe, continued to follow sectarian politics and presented the Eritrean fight as an Arab cause.[34]

Between 1969 and 1970, the ELF was marred by internal strife. Prunier argues that the old central core of the ELF was eliminating young Christian recruits.[35] Others have claimed that the ELF factions targeted Afar combatants who had joined their ranks.[36] Both Christian

---

[30] Marchal (1993: 22).
[31] Miran (2005: 204).
[32] Pool (2001: 39).
[33] Prunier (2007: 339) and Jacquin-Berdal and Mengistu (2006: 91).
[34] Prunier (2007: 340) and Pool (2001: 21).
[35] Prunier (2007).
[36] Yasin (2008).

and Muslim combatants who disapproved of this policy left the ELF and created the splinter faction known as the ELF-Popular Liberation Forces (PLF). Tension between these factions culminated in the ELF's February 1972 attack against the ELF-PLF.

The most serious crisis within the separatist insurgency took place in 1973, and its legacy still resonates.[37] The leadership faced opposition from the *menqa* faction, comprised of ultra-leftist former university students. Pool and Gaim Kibreab diverge on the interpretation of the crisis. According to Pool, Solomon Woldemariam's faction of fighters from the Akele Guzai province sought to overcome their lack of representation within the new leadership, which was dominated by fighters from Hamasien.[38] According to Gaim Kibreab, the *menqa* faction was a reform movement wanting to advance the combatants' rights vis-à-vis the leadership, rendering the latter accountable, and to prevent abuse of civilians by the combatants.[39] Kibreab further challenges Pool's account on the basis that Solomon Woldemariam was from Hamasien and not Akele Guzai, and that he switched sides from an alliance with the leaders of the *menqa* to Issaias Afewerki's faction.[40] Ultimately, this shift was paramount in the weakening and dismembering of the 1973 movement.[41] The factional strife lasted until 1974, threatening the insurgency's ultimate aim. The fragmentation of the ELF and the hostility against Christian recruits paved the way for the creation of the EPLF in the 1970s.[42,43]

A further challenge occurred in the aftermath of the 1977–1978 war between Ethiopia and Somalia. The Ethiopian National Defense Forces emerged victoriously and well equipped with Soviet armaments. As they

[37] Iyob (1995: 116–17), Pool (2001: 76, 86), Connell (2001: 352–53; 2005b: 85–90).

[38] Pool (2001: 76).

[39] Kibreab (2008: 256).

[40] The ELF created Five Divisions and distributed its forces according to regional and ethnic affiliations. These Divisions had forces stationed in the following provinces: (1) Barka and Gash, (2) Senhit and Sahel; (3) Akele-Guzay and Seray; (4) Semhar and Denkel, and (5) Hamasien in Anderbrhan WeldeGiorgis (2014: 123–24). Isaias, upon return from China, was sent as political commissar of the Fifth Division back to his province of origin: Hamasien in Plaut (2016: 107).

[41] Kibreab (2008: 247–248).

[42] Plaut (2016: 12).

[43] According to Anderberhan Wolde Giorgis, the EPLF emerged in 1973 as the result of the union of three of the dissident factions of the ELF that regrouped to annihilate the ELF-Revolutionary Council. The ELF-RC was finally pushed out of Eritrea into Eastern Sudan in 1981 through coordinated EPLF and TPLF's action (2014: 127–128).

intensified their counterinsurgency operations in Northern Ethiopia's Tigray region and Eritrea, the ELF and the EPLF were forced to withdraw. The ELF combatants went into Sudan; the EPLF sought refuge within Eritrea and in the Sahel.

During the war for independence, Muslim groups were not unified in support for the insurgency movements. The ELF leadership was dominated by Western Muslims: Beni Amer, Tigre, and to a lesser extent the Nara.[44] The Afar, who profess Islam as well and are concentrated in Eastern Eritrea, did not embrace the war for independence as their own cause, even if some joined the separatist insurgency. Based in three states in the Horn of Africa, Eritrea's independence was not the Afar's central aim, as their traditional homeland cuts across sovereign boundaries.[45] Other borderland groups, such as the Kunama in Western Eritrea, were also at odds with the separatist insurgency's aims.[46] The strife between the movements suggests that while religion played a role in the emergence of the nationalist movement, a more nuanced understanding is needed beyond the divide between ethnic and at times regional allegiances that superseded both religious and the emerging national solidarity. Indeed, Muslims and Christians fought for independence,[47] and the former's marginalization in the post-independence political dispensation created grievances among the Muslim groups.[48]

While fighting Ethiopian hegemony, the separatist insurgency's real challenge was to create a nationalism that could subsume existing religious ethnic and regional cleavages and present a convincing alternative both domestically and internationally. The EPLF's emphasis on unity, secularism, and reform succeeded to a great extent, but these pressures shaped its understanding of political power and its own role in leading Eritreans to victory. Throughout this period, the EPLF was thus engaged in a discursive struggle with the international media, academics, and the international system. The conflict was thus fought on three fronts—a military conflict with Ethiopia, a battle for hearts and minds at home but also a battle for international legitimacy and recognition abroad—all of which shaped the regime's identity and expectations.

[44] Yasin (2008: 57).
[45] Dias (2008: 77–82).
[46] Plaut (2016: 13) states that some Kunama, as well as Afar, supported unity with Ethiopia.
[47] Pool (2001: 53).
[48] Schlee (2014: 34).

POST-SECESSION NATION- AND STATE-BUILDING

Upon independence in 1993, the EPLF's nationalist credentials and its long-held belief that Eritrea was a viable political and economic independent unit were put to the test. In its bid to transform the movement into a political party, the 1994 EPLF Congress changed the former liberation movement's name to the PFDJ. The EPLF/PFDJ continued to perceive religious, ethnic, and regional solidarity as a hindrance to state- and nation-building. Although the ruling party officially recognizes freedom of religion, in practice, it has restricted this right for all but the four government-approved religions: Orthodox Christians, Muslims, Catholics, and the Evangelical Church of Eritrea.

After independence, the ruling party officially recognized nine ethnic groups: the Afar, the Bilen, the Hadareb, the Kunama, the Nara, the Rashaida, the Saho, the Tigre, and the Tigrinya.[49] In terms of political representation, the constitution, ratified in 1997, recognizes provisions for an elected national assembly. However, Eritrea has held no elections since independence, and the constitutional provisions agreed in 1997 have not been implemented. Ethnic minorities' access to political office is limited and closely related to participation in the war for independence; few were on the PFDJ's Executive Council or served on the Central Council. Some senior government and party officials were members of minority groups, such as the Tigre, and the head of the Navy is an Afar.[50] Indeed, the official recognition of ethnic groups has implications at the level of the national education policy and in radio broadcasting. Elementary students are required to learn their mother tongue, as well as Tigrinya and/or Arabic. The mother-tongue policy was a form of social engineering that emphasized the slogan "one state, one nation, and many languages."[51] This policy stands in contrast with the Ethiopian insistence on Amharic as the dominant language of instruction before 1991. However, despite the Eritrean government's rhetoric of oneness, Tigrinya seems to be privileged in terms of number of elementary schools over other languages.

As this suggests, post-secession nation-building has maintained elements of the liberation struggle but has also faced new challenges. Three interconnected themes weave through post-independence policies: identity,

---

[49] Jacquin-Berdal and Mengistu (2006: 88–89).
[50] US Department of State (2011b: 21).
[51] Woldemikael (2003: 122).

self-reliance, and service. The first task of the post-independence state was to define its people. Eritrean nationality was defined transnationally, as befitted the dispersed state. Rules defined in the first proclamation of citizenship by the provisional Government of Eritrea (PGE) in 1992 aimed to embrace a population dispersed territorially, attributing Eritrean nationality via matrilineal and/or patrilineal descent or naturalization. Those who registered to vote for the referendum, both within Eritrea and abroad, were issued identity cards. The criteria for acquiring Eritrean citizenship were birth, naturalization, and/or adoption. "Any person born to a father or mother of Eritrean origin in Eritrea or abroad" was entitled to become an Eritrean citizen and to acquire voting rights, regardless of the country of residence.[52]

This conception of nationhood granted equal rights to those living in Eritrea and outside. If the host country allowed dual nationality, the Eritrean conception of nationhood posed no problems. However, this definition potentially created ambiguity for those qualified to acquire Eritrean citizenship but who also had acquired citizenship in a state that allowed only single nationality. This concerned those of Eritrean origin who held Ethiopian citizenship. The PGE's conception created a pan-Eritrean identity with a transnational component,[53] reinforcing the diaspora's links to the homeland but also recognizing of their financial and moral support during the struggle.[54] Nevertheless, within a few years of independence, identity became contested with the reciprocal expulsions of Ethiopians of Eritrean origin and Eritreans from Ethiopia at the outbreak of hostilities in 1998.[55]

Identity was not just an outward-looking issue, as it figured in internal policies as well. With Eritrean identity and nationhood being defined in terms of colonial territoriality,[56] the PFDJ redesigned local government and the administrative units to reflect the new multi-ethnic national identity. In dramatic contrast to Ethiopia's ethnic federalism, regional boundaries were redrawn to form the new administrative units (*zobas*) that cut across ethnic units. The PFDJ state-building project was aimed at "erasing regional identities, i.e. loyalty to one's region and the village."[57] During the

---

[52] Iyob (2000: 663, 671).
[53] Iyob (2000: 664).
[54] Bernal (2004: 11).
[55] Koser (2003: 112).
[56] Clapham (2006: 25).
[57] Conrad (2006: 261).

war for independence, accusations of sectarianism and regional allegiance had proved highly destructive for factions within the insurgent movement.[58] The creation of multi-ethnic administrative regions was pursued in order to prevent the emergence of territorially based ethnic opposition.[59] However, as Conrad claims, this attempt to erase regional identities created resentment and seems to have "contributed to a growing disengagement from the national project and reinforced deep-seated local and regional affiliations."[60] Schlee argues that in the PFDJ's political project, ethnicity as well as religious affiliations (Muslim and Christian) were disregarded in the official self-image but were present in the political power play.[61]

Education policy was a central element in the PFDJ's political project of nation-building both before and after independence.[62] After its victory in 1991, the EPLF used this to transmit a definition of Eritrean national identity in which "the war for independence had become the founding myth."[63] The teaching and learning of languages and history seem to confirm the state's monopoly of the educational system and its central role in the PFDJ state- and nation-building project. During the border war, any divergence from the PJDF narrative of the war for independence and the historical obligation to defend this hard-won achievement was viewed as an act of treason. Conrad suggests that this perception was shared both domestically and among the diaspora communities.[64] This should be understood against the backdrop of the government's trend to conflate the identity of the nationalist movement and its political manifestation, the PFDJ, to a point that they were "near indistinguishable from that of the state."[65] Indeed, the PFDJ has been "positing itself as the sole interpreter of national destiny."[66] However, opposition to the PFDJ's narrative of the war for independence has emerged, particularly after the 1998–2000 war.[67] While the PFDJ had defined June 20 as a public holiday to pay tribute to the martyrs of the state of Eritrea, the former ELF (RC) celebrate Martyr's Day on December 1.[68]

---

[58] Kibreab (2008: 228).
[59] Fouad Makki (1996: 484).
[60] Conrad (2006: 261).
[61] Schlee (2014: 34).
[62] Reid (2009c), Eritrean Centre for Strategic Studies (2010), and Jacquin-Berdal (2000: 65).
[63] Jacquin-Berdal (2000: 67).
[64] Conrad (2006: 251).
[65] Dorman (2005: 207).
[66] Reid (2009c: 211).
[67] Dorman (2005: 203–222).
[68] Conrad (2006: 260).

Militarization and Mobilization

During the war for independence, the principle of self-reliance was critical for EPLF's success in developing strong local control based on local legitimacy, far beyond that of other liberation movements.[69] In the absence of recognition in the regional and global political arenas, the EPLF was successful in mobilizing the support of Eritrea's society, both internally among the rural groups and among the Eritrean diaspora, with tangible and practical effects in the liberated areas. Through its organizational efficiency and discipline, the EPLF was able to deliver social services among the rural groups in the areas under its effective territorial control.[70] The EPLF started the land system's reform with community leaders, established learning centers, and organized public sessions in order to inform the population of its goals and intentions. The EPLF also established medical units in the areas under its control.[71]

Since independence, spending has been disproportionately high in the defense sector, with much less money going to health services, confirming the PFDJ break with its previous policies of services delivery. The 2008 Global Militarization Index classified Eritrea as the most militarized country in the world: the government spent 20% of its GDP on the armed forces, with a meager 3.7% going to public health services.[72] Since 2007, no data has been made available to allow an understanding of Eritrea's current degree of militarization.[73]

The EPLF's practice of organizing public sessions to mobilize support has been abandoned. After the two-year border war with Ethiopia and the 2001 crisis, public space for discussion has been closed. During 2001, a group of politicians and ex-combatants close to the president voiced their disapproval and criticism over domestic- and foreign-policy matters in a public letter. The bones of contention were the delay in the implementation of the constitution and the conduct of the 1998–2000 border war with Ethiopia. As a consequence of the public letter, the majority of the G-15 members were imprisoned and held incommunicado during the period 2001 to 2018.[74] Opposition to the PFDJ's political project of state-

---

[69] Englebert (2007: 59).
[70] Iyob (1995: 119).
[71] Pool (2001: 81).
[72] Heinke (2009: 20).
[73] BICC (2012).
[74] Connell (2005a, b) and Human Rights Watch (2011, 2012).

and nation-building or to President Isaias Afewerki is equated with treason to the Eritrean state and results in detention and imprisonment without trial.[75] This is not a rupture with past practices but instead reflects past failures to accommodate peaceful changes of leadership.

Instead, self-reliance has bridged notions of autonomy from external forces with mobilization internally. A key component of this, linked to both education and nation-building, has been national service for youth. As proclaimed in 1995, national service stipulated 18 months mandatory military service for all citizens: six months military training followed by 12 months national service. The state's continuous demand for extended conscription has contributed to the widening of the generational divide between those ex-combatants from the war for independence and those who fought in the 1998–2000 war.[76] Those who fought in the border war are either still serving in the military or at civilian jobs on a pecuniary wage.[77]

National service conscripts tend to be engaged in development work within the *warsay-yikealo* initiative.[78] This initiative aims to bring together the *warsay* (those recruited to the new Eritrean army after Independence) and the *yikealo* (the ex-combatants from the liberation war).[79] From the government's perspective, Sawa is understood as the military training center par excellence and also as the "national finishing school."[80] The national military center has contributed to the construction of a new myth of the Sawa Tigers, in distinction to the draft dodgers portrayed as the "Coca-Cola generation" for their unwillingness to sacrifice for the nation and for their poor display of patriotism.[81]

However, the length of service prevents many from developing careers and families, and the fact that some of those undergoing compulsory military service were deployed to PFDJ-linked corporations generated much political discontent.[82] Magnus Treiber's ethnographic research powerfully

---

[75] Connell (2005a, b), Human Rights Watch (2009), Rawlence (2009), and Tronvoll (2009).

[76] Reid (2005: 474).

[77] Dorman (2005: 211) and United States Department of State (2011a, b: 29).

[78] Dorman (2004) and Reid (2009c).

[79] Conrad (2006: 260, 267).

[80] Reid (2005: 479).

[81] Conrad (2006: 267).

[82] Dorman (2005: 214) and United States Department of State (2011a, b: 29).

portrays the sense of alienation and anomie experienced by youth who see no future in Eritrea.[83]

Significantly, the unusual and privileged link with diaspora formations has granted the EPLF/PFDJ significant resources from the conditional extraction of a 2% tax on their income. In the war for independence, this contribution was voluntary, but after the 1998–2000 war, it became a condition to acquire any official documentation in their handlings with the state, and not even diaspora citizens are safely exempted from other nation-building duties, as is described in the following section.

ASYLUM AND EXILE

The conflation of citizenship and service with the pressures of nation-building has led to substantial refugee flows from Eritrea to neighboring countries and further afield. Figure 14.1 shows that many Eritreans are choosing the exit option

While asylum applications increased even during the border war with Ethiopia, the most significant increase came between 2004 and 2016. The peak in 2002 was due to the United Nations High Commissioner for Refugees' (UNHCR) announcement that Eritrean refugees in Sudan would no longer benefit from refugee status after December 31, 2002.[84] In 2011, the number of Eritreans placing new asylum claims was still high, at 14,172.[85, 86] Reports of Eritreans held hostage in the Sinai and fleeing across the Mediterranean in unsafe boats have dominated news coverage.[87] The Eritrean government came under increasing pressure to halt the flow. At the end of 2014, the EPLF/PFDJ stated that national service would resort back to the 18-month period and reassured that civic or government posting of recruits would be discontinued. The numbers of new asylum applicants for 2015 and 2016 contradict the notion that these measures restored commitment to the PFDJ's political project. On the

[83] Treiber (2009).

[84] Dias (2008: 198).

[85] UNHCR (2012).

[86] The decrease in 2011 in the total number of applicants was accompanied by a steady rise in new applicants in Ethiopia, which reached 54,900 (see Fig. 14.2). The independence of South Sudan and its impact in the relations between Eritrea and Sudan it is not negligible as Eritrea lost leverage. Indeed, Eritrea's relations with Sudan have been volatile.

[87] Human Rights Watch (2014).

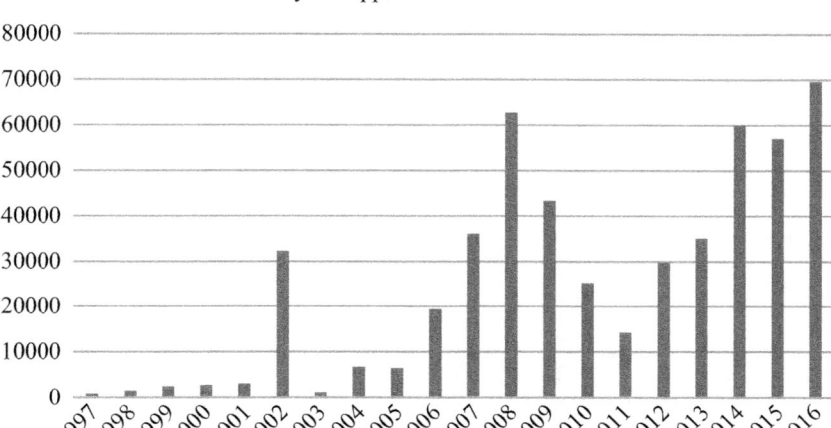

Fig. 14.1 Eritrean asylum applicants globally. (Adapted from Dias (2008: 198) and updated with data from UNHCR (2007: 10; 2008: 16; 2009: 18; 2010: 43; 2011: 43; 2012: 27; 2013: 29; 2014: 31; 2015: 42; 2016: 14))

contrary, a growing proportion of Eritreans are opting for exile in face of the increasingly authoritarian path pursued by the PFDJ. After 60,000 new applicants in 2014, the number stood at almost 70,000 in 2016.[88]

In the United Kingdom, with the number of Eritreans seeking asylum rising, Eritrea was among the top seven asylum-seeker-producing countries. Recently, this number has dropped—in sharp contrast to other European countries, such as Germany and Italy.[89,90]

Figure 14.2 shows that the number of asylum applicants in Ethiopia originating from Eritrea has continued to grow, illustrating a disjuncture between the portrayal of Ethiopia and the TPLF as the greatest threat to Eritreans, and Eritrean citizens' perceptions of the neighboring country.

[88] 69,600. The total number of Eritrean refugees was 407,500 in 2015. In 2016, the number rose to 459,400 UNHCR (2016: 15).

[89] UK Home Office (2010).

[90] In 2015, the number of Eritrean applicants in the mentioned European countries was: 700 in Italy, 3800 in the United Kingdom, and 10,900 in Germany. In 2016, the increase was remarkable with 7400 new applicants in Italy and 18,900 in Germany, as well as the stunning decrease in the United Kingdom to only 1300 UNHCR (2015: 38; 2016: 40–41).

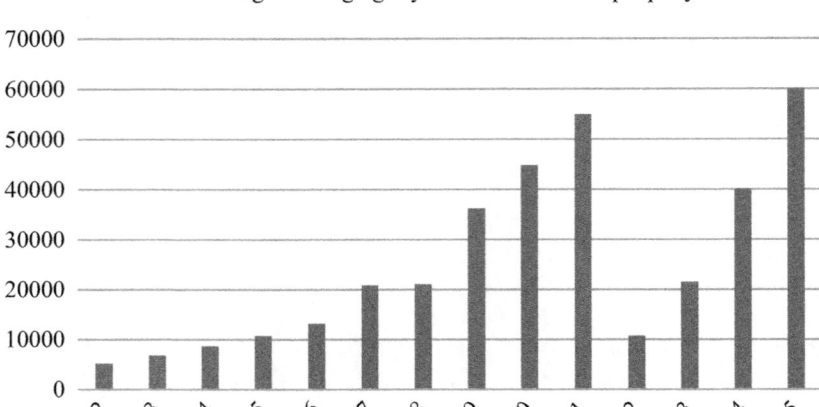

Eritreans arriving and lodging asylum claims in Ethiopia per year

Fig. 14.2 Asylum applicants from Eritrea in Ethiopia per year. (Source: Adapted from Dias (2008: 198) and updated with data from UNHCR 2011 up to 2016. By the end of 2016, Eritrean refugees (in 2016 the number of Eritrean refugees was 459,400 mostly located in Ethiopia (165,600), Sudan (103,200), Germany (30,000), Israel (27,800), Switzerland (26,300), and Sweden (26,000) (UNHCR 2016: 15)) in Ethiopia amounted to 165,600 (the UNHCR had not published data of new claims lodged in Ethiopia during 2016 (UNHCR 2016: 15)))

The number of new applicants, both in general terms and in Ethiopia, has been on the rise for consecutive years, particularly since 2012.

The sharp increase in Eritrean refugees has not gone unnoticed: in 2015, UNHCR published a landmark report with evidence on the PFDJ's authoritarian and repressive measures, including torture, forced labor equated to slave labor, instances of rape, and sex without consent, as well as several other human rights' abuses and violations.[91]

The PFDJ's political project of nation-building fails to mobilize support, as it is more life denying than life affirming. Beyond exiting, the authoritarian leanings of the regime have triggered other manifestations of passive resistance. Those within the compulsory military service age group who remain in Eritrea have developed subtle ways of voicing their dissatisfaction and dissent, through jokes or self-destructive strategies of

[91] OHCHR (2015).

avoidance.[92] This points to subtle changes in the Eritrean political land-scape, including disengagement from the state.[93]

GROWING ISOLATION IN REGIONAL AND GLOBAL POLITICAL ARENAS

Self-reliance had proved a winning principle during the liberation war, but post-independence has had wider and problematic domestic and regional implications. To a certain extent, the current isolationist path reflects a transposition into foreign policy-making of one of the cornerstones of the separatist insurgency; the principle and strategy of self-reliance dictates that only Eritrea can be trusted to protect Eritrea's interests. Suspicion of neighbors and their interests and a tendency to rely on military rather than diplomatic responses to problems has led to a number of border disputes and conflicts with wider implications in the regional political arena. Since 1991, Eritrea has been involved in border disputes with Sudan (1994); Yemen (1995); Djibouti (1996, 2008); and Ethiopia, escalating into full-scale war (1998–2000). Eritrea's tendency to settle territorial disputes by force is related to the Eritrean leadership's perception of being threatened within the volatile Horn of Africa region. Reid argues:

Eritrea does not trust anyone; and the powerful concept of "historical betrayal" permeates the nation's image of itself. ...The concept of "Eritrea alone against the world", misunderstood and abused, now forms a core component of the moral code with which Eritrea deals with close neigh-bors and the "international community" alike.[94]

The 1998–2000 border war with Ethiopia was a critical turning point—with domestic and regional ramifications—in the PFDJ's political project of state- and nation-building. The ramifications of the 1998–2000 war in the domestic political arena suggest that citizens see that their government has failed to vindicate its democratic credentials through open and fair elections; this failure weighs more heavily than nationalist credentials asserted on the battlefield. The war had repercussions on regional alliances and spillover effects for ongoing conflicts in Sudan and in Somalia. Eritrea and Ethiopia shaped their regional foreign policies as power politics under

---

[92] Bozzini (2013) and Treiber (2009).
[93] Reid (2009c: 211).
[94] Reid (2005: 483).

the motto: "if your neighbor is your natural enemy the power on the other side of your neighbor is your natural ally."[95]

Ethiopia supported Eritrean armed opposition movements based in Sudan or in Ethiopia.[96] Eritrea supported Ethiopian armed opposition movements based in Somalia, Kenya, and on its territory.[97] Eritrea's interference in Somalia's internal affairs since the rise of the Islamic Courts Union in 2006 can only be understood against this background. Ethiopia's forceful intervention in support of Somalia's Transitional Federal Government of President Abdullahi Youssuf (December 2006–January 2009) meant that Eritrea provide support for those opposing Youssuf.

On April 2007, Eritrea terminated its membership from the Inter-Governmental Authority on Development (IGAD) because IGAD had endorsed Ethiopia's occupation of Somalia.[98] After the dismemberment of the Islamic Courts Union by the combined offensive of the Ethiopia-backed Transitional Federal Government in Somalia, Eritrea offered exile to former Islamic Courts Union members, namely to the Chairman of the Shura (Consultative Council) Sheikh Hassan Dahir Aweys, who has been on the US list of terrorists since November 2001 and was designated a terrorist under United Nations Security Council (UNSC) Resolution 1267.[99] Eritrea's defiance of the TFG's legitimacy, its support for former members of the Islamic Courts Union, and support—including alleged arms deliveries—for the militant Islamist group al-Shabaab brought Eritrea close to being included in the US list of states sponsoring terrorism in 2008.[100]

Eritrea again resorted to force to settle a territorial dispute with Djibouti in 2008.[101] Military buildup along the common border led to skirmishes between the armed forces of the two states in June 2008. To date, Eritrea has failed to comply with the UNSC Resolution 1862 (2009), ordering the parties to withdraw to positions held before June 10, 2008. The border skirmishes between Eritrea and Djibouti have further eroded Eritrea's regional and global political legitimacy. The UNSC classified Eritrea's position as "utter intransigence." Eritrea's justification was that it is not occupying Djibouti's national territory, linking its

[95] Martin Wight cited in Bull and Holbraad (2004: 157).
[96] Africa Confidential (2011).
[97] Cliffe (2005).
[98] Sudan Tribune (2007) and Eritrea Ministry of Information (2007).
[99] US Department of State (2008).
[100] *The Telegraph* April (2009).
[101] Connell (2009a).

position to Ethiopia's failure to comply with the 2002 EEBC decision, arguing that Ethiopia still occupies Eritrea's sovereign territory without any international reprisals.[102]

The IGAD member-states and the African Union (AU) have criticized Eritrea's support for the militant Islamist insurgency in Somalia. Eritrea's alleged support to al-Shabaab has allowed the insurgency to continue unabated at critical moments when the group was more vulnerable.[103] The African consensus on Eritrea's role in the Somalia crisis since December 2006 has culminated in an unprecedented move. Through the AU Peace and Security Council, member-states unanimously requested that the United Nations Security Council impose sanctions on Eritrea for its support for the militant Islamist insurgency in Somalia, arguing that Eritrea's foreign policy vis-à-vis Somalia was compromising both the legitimate government and the AU Mission in Somalia (AMISOM) and contributing to further destabilization in the Horn of Africa.

The UNSC Resolution 1907 of December 23, 2009, authorized sanctions on Eritrea. In response, Eritrea positioned itself as regional bulwark against external forces. The president claimed that under no circumstances is any breach to sovereignty acceptable, hence the resolution was "totally unacceptable."[104] President Isaias Afewerki's position vis-à-vis extraregional actors, the AU, IGAD, and the UN, thus seems to reflect a "need to preserve intact sovereignty as the key source of regime legitimacy."[105]

Plaut considers Eritrea a minor state in a strategic location,[106] thus it is not surprising that Isaias Afewerki has twice tried to use Eritrea's strategic location as a resource and to the regime's advantage. His first attempt was trying to host the US Combined Joint Task Force for the Horn of Africa (CJTF-HOA). Eritrea was unsuccessful; the US base now sits on Djibouti's coast. Since 2015, Yemen's civil war means that Eritrea's Assab and Massawa ports, as well as some of the Hanish Islands under Eritrea's sovereign jurisdiction, are now a resource of strategic value usable to make allies of those with an interest in the Yemeni civil war: Saudi Arabia and the

---

[102] Eritrea Ministry of Foreign Affairs (2009) and Eritrean Center for Strategic Studies (2010).
[103] UN Security Council (2013).
[104] Eritrean Center for Strategic Studies (2010).
[105] Alden (2010: 14, 17).
[106] Plaut (2016: 101).

United Arab Emirates. This move has curtailed Eritrea's isolation and given the regime the financial resources needed for its survival.[107]

CONCLUSION

The trajectory of Eritrea's insurgent movements during the independence war has shaped the deepening crisis of the PFDJ state- and nation-building project, with both domestic and international implications. The highly centralized authority within the EPLF did not easily accommodate dissent or challenges to leadership. These characteristics became more problematic once independence could no longer be used to justify curtailing domestic challenges to the EPLF's leadership. The setbacks of the EPLF/PFDJ's political project in the domestic, regional, and global political arenas have significantly eroded the domestic and international legitimacy the movement had enjoyed at the time of independence.

Once, the EPLF had been lauded as one of the most disciplined, efficient, and highly organized separatist movements. Its hold on power is now mainly sustained through the methods of an authoritarian regime that suppresses its own citizens. The failures of the former guerilla fighters to transform into state builders, and of the separatist insurgency to become a democratic political party, have cost the EPLF the legitimacy they had enjoyed and earned through the war for independence.

Yet, we ought not reduce our gaze to the trajectory of the liberation war and the individuals who played leading roles in the struggle. The power relations between the states in the Horn also condition these responses and interactions in complex ways. These are states formed primarily by colonial penetration and also by indigenous responses to state formation.[108] The region has long exhibited different trends than the rest of the continent, with greater rates of boundary challenges, secessionist and irredentist pressures, and interstate wars.[109] Eritrea remains tightly enmeshed in these contested regional political dynamics that shaped its difficult birth.

It seems unlikely that the PFDJ is able or willing to introduce changes that might enhance its domestic legitimacy and create public space either

---

[107] Plaut (2016: 83–85), De Waal (2015: 153), and Clapham (2017: 140).

[108] See Vaughan (2018) and Hoehne (2018) in this volume.

[109] See also Byrne and Englebert (2018) in this volume on how much cases involving Ethiopia change statistics on secessionist trends in Africa.

for opposition parties to flourish or for any peaceful change of leadership to occur. In the face of severe constraints placed on Eritrean citizens, neither those who remain in Eritrea nor those in the diaspora have been able to influence domestic politics.

In light of these facts, it is no wonder that exit is an attractive option. De Waal argues that younger Eritreans just want to run away and that the majority is disengaged from political debates: "most just want a life."[110] Eritrea stands among the top countries producing asylum-seekers. Although allegiance to Eritrean national identity does not seem to have waned, Eritrean citizenship is unattractive.[111] Furthermore, while the liberation war positively consolidated a sense of Eritrean-ness, the costs of the 1998–2000 war and continuous militarism have subsequently undermined the legitimacy of the regime. As a consequence, for some, national identity may start to unravel, while for others it has intensified, either in defense of the regime or as an outcome of the shared tragic experience since Eritrea's independence.[112]

Yet few question the state's right to exist or the Eritrean state's survival in a post-Afewerki era.[113] Eritreans who are able to voice their discontent say, "we didn't fight for this."[114] They thus reaffirm both their commitment to the struggle and their deep concern for the future of their country.

REFERENCES

Abbay, A. (1997). The trans-Mereb past in the present. *Journal of Modern African Studies, 35*, 321–334.

Abbay, A. (1998). *Identity jilted, or, re-imagining identity? The divergent paths of the Eritrean and Tigrayan nationalist struggles.* Lawrenceville: Red Sea Press.

Africa Confidential. (2011, April). The Anti-Asmara Campaign. *Africa Confidential, 250–300.*

---

[110] De Waal (2015: 154).

[111] Reid (2009a) An interview with a diaspora member and a former fighter confirms that in addition to leaving the country, more recently, those who make it to the United Kingdom seem uninterested in politics. The interviewee stated that "I don't know what they have done to our youth. They are broken. They just care about living their lives." Interview conducted by AM Dias, London, October 2015.

[112] Clapham (2017: 136) In this respect, Clapham and the authors of the present chapter disagree entirely with De Waal's statement that the Eritrean state is at risk of disintegration "when its founder-owner dies or is removed" De Waal (2015: 154).

[113] Clapham (2017: 135).

[114] Interview, group, conducted by AM Dias, London (2007).

Alden, C. (2010). A pariah in our midst: Regional organisations and the problematic of western-designated pariah regimes – The cases of SADC/Zimbabwe and ASEAN/MYANMAR. In Crisis State Research Centre (Ed.), *Working paper no. 73 – Regional and global axes of conflict*. London: LSE.

Andebrhan, W. G. (2014). *Eritrea at a crossroads: A narrative of triumph, betrayal and hope*. Houston: Strategic Book Publishing and Rights Co.

Bernal, V. (2004). Eritrea goes global: Reflections on nationalism in a transnational era. *Cultural Anthropology, 19*, 3–25.

Bonn International Centre for Conversion. (2012). *Update: Bicc's global militarization index Gmi 2012*. Bonn: BICC. Retrieved from http://www.bicc.de/old-site/uploads/gmi/pdf/Update_GMI_2012%20Fact%20Sheet_e.pdf

Bozzini, D. (2013). The catch-22 of resistance: Jokes and the political imagination of Eritrean conscripts. *Africa Today, 60*(2), 39–64.

Bull, H., & Holbraad, C. (Eds.). (2004). *Power politics/Martin Wight*. New York/London: Continuum.

Byrne, H., & Englebert, P. (2018). Shifting grounds for African secessionism? In L. de Vries, P. Englebert, & M. Schomerus (Eds.), *Secessionism in African politics: Aspiration, grievance, performance, disenchantment*. New York: Palgrave.

Cameron, G. (2018). Zanzibar in the Tanzania Union. In L. de Vries, P. Englebert, & M. Schomerus (Eds.), *Secessionism in African politics: Aspiration, grievance, performance, disenchantment*. New York: Palgrave.

Clapham, C. (1998). *African guerrillas*. Fountain: James Currey.

Clapham, C. (2006). Ethiopia. In C. Clapham, J. Herbst, & G. Mills (Eds.), *Big African states* (pp. 17–38). Johannesburg: Wits University Press.

Clapham, C. (2017). *Horn of Africa: State formation and decay*. London: Hurst & Company.

Cliffe, L. (2005). Regional implications of the Eritrea-Ethiopia War. In D. Jacquin-Berdal & M. Plaut (Eds.), *Unfinished business: Eritrea and Ethiopia at war* (pp. 151–168). Trenton/Asmara: Red Sea Press.

Connell, D. (2001). Inside the EPLF: The origins of the 'People's Party' & its role in the liberation of Eritrea. *Review of African Political Economy, 89*, 345–364.

Connell, D. (2005a). *Conversations with Eritrean political prisoners*. Trenton/Asmara: Red Sea Press.

Connell, D. (2005b). Eritrea: On a slow fuse. In R. I. Rotberg (Ed.), *Battling terrorism in the Horn of Africa* (pp. 64–92). Cambridge, MA/Washington, DC: World Peace Foundation & Brookings Institution Press.

Connell, D. (2009a). The EPLF/PFDJ experience: How it shapes Eritrea's regional strategy. In R. Reid (Ed.), *Eritrea's external relations: Understanding its regional role and foreign policy* (pp. 22–44). London: Chatham House.

Connell, D. (2009b). Eritrea and the United States: Towards a new US policy. In R. Reid (Ed.), *Eritrea's external relations: Understanding its regional role and foreign policy* (pp. 131–149). London: Chatham House.

Conrad, B. (2006). Out of the 'memory hole': Alternative narratives of the Eritrean revolution in the diaspora. *Afrika Spectrum, 41*, 249–271.

de Waal, A. (2015). *The real politics of the Horn of Africa.* Cambridge/Malden: Polity Press.

Dias, A. M. (2008). *An inter-state war in the post-cold war era: Eritrea-Ethiopia 1998–2000* (Unpublished PhD thesis). Department of International Relations, London School of Economics and Political Science, London.

Dorman, S. R. (2004). Past the Kalashnikov: Youth, politics and the state in Eritrea. In J. Abbink & I. van Kessel (Eds.), *Vanguard or vandals? Youth, politics and conflict in Africa* (pp. 189–204). Leiden: Brill Academic Publishers.

Dorman, S. R. (2005). Narratives of nationalism in Eritrea: Research and revisionism. *Nations and Nationalism, 11*, 203–222.

Englebert, P. (2007). Whither the separatist motive? In M. Boas & K. C. Dunn (Eds.), *African guerrillas: Raging against the machine.* Boulder/London: Lynne Rienner Publishers.

Eritrea Ministry of Foreign Affairs. (2009, January 15). UNSC Resolution 1862 2009 defies the rule of law.

Eritrea Ministry of Information. (2007). Eritrea suspends membership in IGAD. Retrieved from http://www.shabait.com

Eritrean Center for Strategic Studies. (2010, December). Interview with H.E. President Isaias Afwerki. Retrieved from http://ecss-online.com/category/interviews/

Halliday, F., & Molyneux, M. (1981). *The Ethiopian Revolution.* London: Verso.

Heinke, S. (2009). *BICC annual report 2008/2009.* Bonn: Bonn International Center for Conversion BICC.

Hoehne, M. V. (2018). Against the grain: Somaliland's secession from Somalia. In L. de Vries, P. Englebert, & M. Schomerus (Eds.), *Secessionism in African politics: Aspiration, grievance, performance, disenchantment.* New York: Palgrave.

Human Rights Watch. (2009). Service for life: State repression and indefinite conscription in Eritrea. https://www.hrw.org/report/2009/04/16/service-life/state-repression-and-indefinite-conscription-eritrea

Human Rights Watch. (2011). *Ten long years: A briefing on Eritrea's missing political prisoners.* New York: Human Rights Watch. Retrieved from http://www.hrw.org/reports/(2011)/09/22/ten-long-years-0

Human Rights Watch. (2012). *World report 2012: Eritrea.* New York: Human Rights Watch. http://www.hrw.org/sites/default/files/related_material/eritrea_(2012).pdf

Human Rights Watch. (2014, February 11). *"I wanted to lie down and die" Trafficking and torture of Eritreans in Sudan and Egypt.* New York: Human Rights Watch. https://www.hrw.org/report/2014/02/11/i-wanted-lie-down-and-die/trafficking-and-torture-eritreans-sudan-and-egypt

Iyob, R. (1995). *The Eritrean struggle for independence: Domination, resistance, nationalism 1941–1993.* Cambridge: Cambridge University Press.

Iyob, R. (2000). The Ethiopian-Eritrean conflict: Diasporic vs. Hegemonic States in the Horn of Africa, 1991–2000. *Journal of Modern African Studies, 38*(4), 659–682.

Jacquin- Berdal, D. (2000). State and war in the formation of Eritrean national identity. In S. O. Vandersluis (Ed.), *The state and identity construction in international relations.* London: Macmillan Press.

Jacquin-Berdal, D. (2002). *Nationalism and ethnicity in the Horn of Africa: A critique of the ethnic interpretation.* Lewiston/Queenston/Lampeter: Edwin Mellen Press.

Jacquin-Berdal, D., & Mengistu, A. (2006). Nationalism and identity in Ethiopia and Eritrea: Building multiethnic states. In D. A. Bekoe (Ed.), *East Africa and the Horn: Confronting challenges to good governance.* Boulder/London: Lynne Rienner.

Joireman, S. F. (2000). *Property rights and political development in Ethiopia and Eritrea: 1941–74.* Oxford/Athens: James Currey/Ohio University Press.

Kibreab, G. (2008). Menqaé: A reform or a destructive movement? In G. Kibreab (Ed.), *Critical reflections on the Eritrean War of independence: Social capital, associational life, religion, ethnicity and sowing seeds of dictatorship.* Trenton/Asmara: Red Sea Press.

Koser, K. (2003). Mobilizing new African diasporas: An Eritrean case study. In K. Koser (Ed.), *New African diasporas.* London/New York: Routledge/Taylor and Francis Group.

Makki, F. (1996). Nationalism, state formation and the public sphere: Eritrea 1991–96. *Review of African Political Economy, 23*, 475–497.

Marchal, R. (1993). L'après-Mengistu dans la Corne de L'afrique: Une stabilisation impossible? *Cultures & Conflicts, 8*, 40–63. Retrieved from http://www.conflits.org/document529.html

Mayall, J. (1990). *Nationalism and international society.* Cambridge: Cambridge University Press.

Miran, J. (2005). A historical overview of Islam in Eritrea. *Die Welt des Islams, 45*, 177–215.

OHCHR. (2015). *Commission of inquiry on human rights in Eritrea.* Geneva: OHCHR. Retrieved from http://www.ohchr.org/EN/HRBodies/HRC/CoIEritrea/Pages/ReportCoIEritrea.aspx

Plaut, M. (2016). *Understanding Eritrea: Inside Africa's most repressive state.* London: Hurst & Company.

Pool, D. (1979). *Eritrea: Africa's longest war.* London: Anti-Slavery Society.

Pool, D. (1998). The Eritrean People's Liberation Front. In C. Clapham (Ed.), *African guerrillas.* Fountain: James Currey.

Pool, D. (2001). *From guerrillas to government: The Eritrean People's Liberation Front.* Oxford/Athens: J. Currey/Ohio University Press.

Porges, M. (2018). Western Sahara and Morocco: Complexities of resistance and analysis. In L. de Vries, P. Englebert, & M. Schomerus (Eds.), *Secessionism in African politics: Aspiration, grievance, performance, disenchantment.* New York: Palgrave.

Prunier, G. (2007). La question érythréenne. In G. Prunier (Ed.), *L'Éthiopie contemporaine* (pp. 329–347). Addis Abeba/Paris: CFEE/Karthala.

Rawlence, B. (2009). Eritrea: Slender land, giant prison. Retrieved from www.opendemocracy.net

Reid, R. (2005). Caught in the headlights of history: Eritrea, the EPLF and the postwar nation state. *Journal of Modern African Studies, 43,* 467–488.

Reid, R. (2009a). *Eritrea's external relations: Understanding its regional role and foreign policy.* London: Chatham House.

Reid, R. (2009c). The politics of silence: Interpreting apparent stasis in contemporary Eritrea. *Review of African Political Economy, 36*(120), 209–221.

Schlee, G. (2014). Regional political history and the production of diasporas. In L. Laakso & P. Hautaniemi (Eds.), *Diasporas, development and peacemaking in the Horn of Africa* (pp. 28–50). London: Zed Books.

Smidt, W. G. C. (2010). The Tigrinnya-speakers across the borders: Discourses of unity and separation in ethnohistorical context. In D. Feyissa & M. Hoehne (Eds.), *Borders and borderlands as resources in the Horn of Africa* (pp. 61–83). Suffolk/New York: James Currey.

Styan, D. (1996). Eritrea 1993: The end of the beginning. In T. Allen (Ed.), *In search of cool ground: War, flight and homecoming in northeast Africa.* London/Trenton: James Currey/Africa World Press.

Tronvoll, K. (2009). *The lasting struggle for freedom in Eritrea.* Oslo: Oslo Centre for Peace and Human Rights.

UN Security Council. (2013). Report of the monitoring group on Somalia and Eritrea pursuant to the Security Council resolution 2060. Eritrea. S/2013/440.

United Nations High Commissioner for Refugees. (2007). *2006 global trends: Refugees, asylum-seekers, returnees, internally displaced and stateless persons.* Retrieved from http://www.unhcr.org/statistics/

United Nations High Commissioner for Refugees. (2008). *2007 statistical yearbook: Trends in displacement, protection and solutions.* Geneva: UNHCR. Retrieved from http://www.unhcr.org/statistics/

United Nations High Commissioner for Refugees. (2009). *2008 global trends: Refugees, asylum-seekers, returnees, internally displaced and stateless persons.* Geneva: UNHCR. Retrieved from http://www.unhcr.org/4a375c426.html

United Nations High Commissioner for Refugees. (2010). *2009 statistical yearbook.* Geneva: UNHCR. Retrieved from http://www.unhcr.org/statistics/

United Nations High Commissioner for Refugees. (2011). *2010 statistical year-book*. Geneva: UNHCR. Retrieved from http://www.unhcr.org/statistics/

United Nations High Commissioner for Refugees. (2012). *2011 global trends: A year of crises*. Geneva: UNHCR.

United Nations High Commissioner for Refugees. (2013). *2012 global trends: Displacement the new twenty-first century challenge*. Geneva: UNHCR. Retrieved from http://www.unhcr.org/statistics/country/51bacb0f9/unhcr-global-trends-(2012).html

United Nations High Commissioner for Refugees. (2014). *2013 global trends: War's human cost*. Geneva: UNHCR. Retrieved from http://www.unhcr.org/statistics/country/5399a14f9/unhcr-global-trends-(2013).html

United Nations High Commissioner for Refugees. (2015). *2014 global trends: World at war*. Geneva: UNHCR. Retrieved from http://www.unhcr.org/statistics/country/556725e69/unhcr-global-trends-(2014).html

United Nations High Commissioner for Refugees. (2016). *2015 Global trends: Forced displacement in 2015*. Geneva: UNHCR. Retrieved from http://www.unhcr.org/statistics/unhcrstats/576408cd7/unhcr-global-trends-(2015).html

United Nations High Commissioner for Refugees. (2017). *2016 global trends: Forced displacement in 2016*. Geneva: UNHCR. Retrieved from http://www.unhcr.org/dach/wp-content/uploads/sites/27/(2017)/06/(2016)_Global_Trends_WEB-embargoed.pdf

United States Department of State. (2011a). *2010 human rights report on Eritrea*. Washington, DC: Department of State. Retrieved from http://www.state.gov/g/drl/rls/hrrpt/(2010)/af/154345.html

United States Department of State. (2011b). *Country reports on human rights practices for 2011: Eritrea*. Washington, DC: Department of State. Retrieved from http://www.state.gov/documents/organization/186404.pdf

Vaughan, S. (2018). Ethiopia, Somalia and the Ogaden: Still the running sore at the heart of the Horn of Africa? In L. de Vries, P. Englebert, & M. Schomerus (Eds.), *Secessionism in African politics: Aspiration, grievance, performance, disenchantment*. New York: Palgrave.

Woldemikael, T. M. (2003). Language, education, and public policy in Eritrea. *African Studies Review, 46*(1), 117–136.

Yasin, M. (2008). Political history of the Afar in Ethiopia and Eritrea. *Afrika Spectrum, 42*, 39–65.

Zeller, W., & Melber, H. (2018). United in separation? Lozi secessionism in Zambia and Namibia. In L. de Vries, P. Englebert, & M. Schomerus (Eds.), *Secessionism in African politics: Aspiration, grievance, performance, disenchantment*. New York: Palgrave.

CHAPTER 15

A State of Contradiction: Sudan's Unity Goes South

Mareike Schomerus and Lotje de Vries

Introduction

On July 9, 2011, the new national anthem of the Republic of South Sudan was officially sung for the first time. For many South Sudanese, this was the day when a historical error—the retention of southern Sudan within Sudan at the latter's independence from British/Egyptian colonial rule in 1956—was corrected at last after 98.8% of South Sudanese citizens had officially voted in favor of secession.[1] It seemed as if, finally, a contradiction had been cleared up.

That contradiction had become acute in the decade leading up to South Sudan's independence. South Sudan's long-standing demand for self-determination had, during this time, been coupled with a commitment in

---

[1] Southern Sudan Referendum Commission (2011) and Connell (1995: 588).

M. Schomerus
Overseas Development Institute, London, UK

L. de Vries (✉)
Wageningen University & Research, De Bilt, Utrecht, The Netherlands
e-mail: Lotje.devries@wur.nl

© The Author(s) 2019
L. de Vries et al. (eds.), *Secessionism in African Politics*,
Palgrave Series in African Borderlands Studies,
https://doi.org/10.1007/978-3-319-90206-7_15

423

the Comprehensive Peace Agreement (CPA) of 2005 to Sudan's unity. This commitment—on paper—sat parallel to an ever-growing discourse that presented secession as the only possible option. South Sudan's declaration of independence, however, set up another inconsistency within the broader context of African secessionism: it was supported—albeit not always openly and not as the only option for a peaceful Sudan—by a broader international community from both within and beyond Africa. This support, as Byrne and Englebert elaborate in this volume, marked a decisive shift in the international stance on secessionism in Africa.[2]

The glorious independence celebrations were soon forgotten: less than three years after the vote for secession, in July 2013, a major political crisis developed, turning into civil war in December that same year. It seemed a contradiction: how had the state whose birth had been so celebrated by so many—at home and abroad—turned ugly so quickly? With hindsight, had this turn for the worse been inevitable? Had it been catalyzed by everyone's willingness to overlook South Sudan's many contradictions? Or had the government of the new nation committed to bringing everyone in line—violently if necessary—to avoid future contradictions in an evolving pluralist political landscape?

To explore these questions, we approach South Sudan's path to secession largely chronologically from pre-colonial times. We show how during colonial rule, England's contradictory ambitions for the southern part of the Sudan laid the seeds for the later claim for self-determination. We scrutinize the history of South Sudan's rebel movement and now governing party, the Sudan People's Liberation Movement/Army (SPLM/A), following its transition from a liberation movement with a political vision for all of Sudan that rarely referred to self-determination, to the political party that ruled semi-autonomous southern Sudan with an exclusive focus on secession. The same rebel group (and later political party) pursued, on the one hand, southern secession and, on the other hand, a democratic and inclusive greater Sudan. We link the consequences of these contradictions to the current situation in South Sudan. In the last part of the chapter, we show how the CPA—yet again enshrining the same contradictory agenda—stimulated the support for secession within both southern Sudan and the international community.

These multiple contradictions were compounded into different peace initiatives, principles, and agreements that allowed for all parties involved

[2] Byrne and Englebert (2018).

to muddle through, rather than to pull out of, a process in discontent. National and international actors committed to the peace process focused on technical matters, while leaving political contradictions—including their own, notably on secession in Africa—untouched. This ultimately left no other option than to facilitate the referendum and acknowledge its outcome despite international principles against it.

METHOD

We draw on our extensive qualitative research conducted since 2006/2007. In combining many interviews, conversations, and observations into a coherent narrative of South Sudan's move toward independence, we lose some of the nuanced contradictions that are at the heart of the South Sudanese experience; at times, our chapter, in its succinctness, might read as if we are suggesting that the political and military leadership had a clearly articulated consensus on South Sudan's future. Yet neither South Sudan's leaders nor the many different international actors were clear or unified on many of the issues discussed here. These many different experiences and expectations, however, were then streamlined into what looked like a determined and planned move toward independence. The many underlying contradictions—and the many different voices that spoke about these—disappeared in this process, which is possibly one of the reasons why today South Sudan's political space has narrowed dramatically.

THE SOUTHERN QUEST FOR SELF-DETERMINATION, UNITY, AND SECESSION

Sudan's two civil wars (1955–1972 and 1983–2005) were fought largely between the central Khartoum government and southern rebels. However, these wars were only a continuation of the country's previous violent history—which, as Wassara argues, constitutes political phenomena that ultimately helped to construct a notion of a distinct South Sudan.[3] Pre-colonial governance patterns of southern exploitation continued into Sudanese independence when Britain withdrew without securing southern interests.[4] In the mid-nineteenth century, the Egyptian empire had reached as far south as the Great Lakes, with Egypt exploiting the territory of today's South Sudan

---

[3] Wassara (2015).
[4] Johnson (2003a: xviii–xix).

for ivory and slaves. The slave trade, argues Woodward, crucially shaped "the region's historic self-perception."[5] The trade contributed to further animosity between the predominantly Arab and Islamic north and the patchwork of African tribes in the south. Between 1881 and 1898, Sudan was ruled from Khartoum by al-Mahdi; his reach into the south was limited, but the exploitation of southern resources, including slaves, further contributed to alienation between the northern and southern parts of Sudan.

After the Anglo-Sudan War of the late nineteenth century, the British Foreign Office administered Sudan as an Anglo-Egyptian Condominium between 1899 and 1955, although in practice there was little to distinguish the administration of this territory from other British colonies. From the early days of the Condominium, the British had an interest in limiting Egyptian and northern Sudanese influence in the south, including the spread of Islam.[6] To save administrative costs while still advancing this agenda, the British developed their "Southern Policy" from the 1920s onwards, which limited British southern presence by governing through "native administration." The idea was that "the future of the southern Sudan might ultimately lie with the countries of British East Africa, rather than with the Middle East," writes Johnson.[7] English became the language of education, with Christian missionaries the most common teachers.[8]

The British administrators used the 1947 Juba Conference to present a decision taken jointly with the newly emerging Sudanese political elite. Plans were made to integrate southern and northern Sudan; the conference was primarily used to suggest that there was southern support for this step—which generally Southerners felt formalized northern political domination, as evident in the limited political appointments for Southerners.[9] Britain continued to support Sudan's independence as one country, primarily to weaken Egypt—but posed a condition: if Sudan was to gain independence from Britain, it was to implement a federal structure, allowing the south a stronger position. The promise of federalism, argues Deng, meant that Southerners—albeit reluctantly—

[5] Woodward (2011: 6).
[6] Holt and Daly (2000: 119).
[7] Johnson (2003a: 11).
[8] Johnson (2003a: 11–15).
[9] Oduho and Deng list four national political positions as having been given to southerners, while Holt and Daly argue that there were six (Holt and Daly 2000 (5th edition): 139; Oduho and Deng 1963).

supported Sudanese independence, having asked for guarantees.[10] The northern government, however, systematically sabotaged the southern wish for political positions, regional autonomy, and self-determination;[11] Oromo argues that soon after Sudan's independence, the word "federalism" became a "taboo tantamount to subversion."[12]

Upon Sudan's declaration of independence from colonial rule on January 1, 1956, both northern and southern Sudan were unprepared for this new entity, writes Belloni.[13] The signs that this unity was uneasy were clear: the south had already experienced its first mutiny just before Sudan's independence, which was to turn into Sudan's first civil war. Yet Khartoum continued to renege on promises of support for southern development, instead focusing on unifying the country through Arabization and Islamization. Thus, Southerners fought the first civil war—the Anya-Nya I War—with articulated separatist objectives,[14] most notably when, in 1965, the Southern Front National Convention in southern Sudan's Malakal took the decision to firmly put the right to southern self-determination on the agenda in Khartoum. One of the then leaders of the Southern Front recalls that: "The North did not like it, calling the demand for Self-determination 'treason.'"[15]

The first war ended in 1972 with the Addis Ababa peace agreement. The accord stated that the southern non-Islamic areas within the Sudanese state would be constitutionally recognized; the south would be self-administered through the Southern Regional Assembly with a High Executive Council (HEC). That Sudan was to remain one while the south was to receive some autonomy was something of a contradiction. The Anya-Nya rebels had of course sought more, as one veteran recalled in a 2009 interview: "Frankly speaking, we were not satisfied with the Addis Ababa Agreement. It was signed on the basis that Sudan was one, and we did not want that."[16]

Unity and semi-autonomy did not work well together, partly because self-administered southern Sudan had not found a system of governance

---

[10] Deng (2005: 6).

[11] Johnson (2003a: 27) and Oduho and Deng (1963: 25).

[12] Oromo (2015: loc1898).

[13] Belloni (2011: 413).

[14] Rolandsen (2011b).

[15] Malwal (2011: 3).

[16] Interview by Lotje de Vries with the security advisor to the CES Governor, an Anya-Nya veteran, and retired Major General of the Sudan Armed Forces, Juba 2009.

that acknowledged and represented its diverse territory of many people, cultures, and faiths. Southerners had to come "to terms with themselves" was how a commentator of the time described the tension.[17] Internal power struggles and infighting in the Southern Regional Assembly often manifest themselves along ethnic lines.[18] Relations between people from different parts of the south, roughly divided into Equatorian people and Nilotic people, were particularly tense, as groups struggled over recognition of their contributions during the Anya-Nya War and their representation in southern Sudan's administration.[19] Interviewed in 2009, a man from the Bor Dinka people who had worked in the HEC, explained:

> There was a group who said that the Dinkas were running the south—that there were too many of them in Juba. The political situation became rough.... From here, the political talk came up, especially among the Equatorians, led by Joseph Lagu [one of the leaders of the Anya-Nya]. The *kokora* [re-division into ethnic territories in the South] movement started. At the end of the 1970s these talks became too much.[20]

Coming to terms with the southern internal difficulties and contradictions was difficult enough—and made even more challenging by increasingly strained relations with Sudan. Sudan's President Gaafar Nimeiry renounced the Addis Ababa Agreement in 1983 by dissolving the Southern Regional Assembly and establishing three regions: Greater Bahr el-Ghazal, Greater Equatoria, and Greater Upper Nile. His objective was to reduce southern influence on national politics, but the new administrative division strengthened the very same regional identities that were to become hugely important—and continue to be so since South Sudan's independence in 2011.

The break up into regions was one of several steps that contributed to a brewing rebellion. Egypt's and Sudan's joint plans to build a canal to channel the water of southern Sudan's Jonglei swamps to agricultural projects in the north, which Southerners saw as a threat to their livelihoods,

---

[17] Green (2011: 1093).
[18] Green (2011: 1093).
[19] Johnson (2003a: 43).
[20] Interview by Lotje de Vries with member of the Local Government Board, who is from the Dinka Bor area, Juba 2009.

was another.[21] When Chevron discovered oil in the south in 1979, President Nimeiry "effectively annexed the south's main oil wells" by manipulating the borderlines between the northern and southern parts of the country and deciding to transport oil out of the country via northern Sudan's Port Sudan rather than build refineries locally, argues Woodward.[22] Implementing partial *Shari'a* law in the predominantly Christian south was also seen as a great provocation and a renunciation of southern autonomy.

The developments of the late 1970s and early 1980s incited the outbreak of rebellion in 1983, marking the start of a war that was to claim an estimated 2.5 million lives and displace 5 million people.[23] In 1983, the SPLM/A published its first manifesto, which redefined, as Johnson argues, "the so-called 'problem of Southern Sudan' as a more general 'problem of backward areas' in the whole country," being underdevelopment, religious freedom, elitism, and economic hardship.[24] Yet, contrary to the ambitions of the previous Anya-Nya rebellion, the newly established SPLA—in the shape of its overpowering leader John Garang—did not propose that independence from Khartoum was the obvious answer to these problems. In contradiction to the official line, however, the SPLA rank and file seemed to be largely in support of fighting a war to secede.

New Sudan? Independence? Or Just Self-Determination?

In 1983, Garang was an officer in the Sudanese Army in Khartoum. The young man from the town of Kongor in Twic East, Jonglei state, had joined the Anya-Nya movement shortly before the signing of the Addis Ababa Agreement. Like many other young southern rebels, he had then been integrated into the Sudan Armed Forces after the first civil war, allowing him to study for a doctorate in the United States. In May 1983, when soldiers in the army barracks in Bor started a mutiny, he was ordered to travel to his home area to pacify the mutineers. But Garang had already

---

[21] John Garang's doctoral dissertation at the University of Iowa makes a strong argument against the canal on the basis of its expected adverse effect on the Jonglei population Garang de Mabior (1981).

[22] Woodward (2011: 3).

[23] UNMIS (2009).

[24] Johnson (2003a: 63).

been part of the resistance movement, and he joined the rebellion and crossed the border into Ethiopia to establish the SPLA.

The immediate objectives of the armed rebellion were less clear than subsequent narratives might suggest—this contradiction is a huge part of South Sudan's founding myth. That the SPLA for a long time did not have a political wing is testament to its murky political stance and focus on military matters.[25] There is also a crucial difference between a common outsider's view of Sudan's problems and how Garang articulated them. Deng writes, "central to Garang's philosophy was the conviction that the dichotomy between the Arab-Islamic North and the African South is largely fictional."[26]

Instead, the 1983 SPLA manifesto called for a "united, democratic and secular" New Sudan that was founded on unity through its diversity. Garang's idea was that this would mean to include the marginalized periphery, distribute resources equally, honor human rights, and establish the rule of law.[27] The notion of "New Sudan," argues Moro, made sense for marginalized northern Sudanese and had resonance in other countries in Africa, particularly Ethiopia, but less so within the SPLA.[28] Garang—a strong and even dictatorial leader—[29] was able to maintain this position, even if he faced internal disagreement. His leadership of not allowing dissenting voices stood in stark contradiction to his vision of a democratic and inclusive New Sudan. Ayers writes that under Garang, the SPLA worked toward "a Sudan that would be ethnically pluralistic and socially inclusive."[30] However, the emphasis on a united Sudan was also, argues Deng, largely incongruent with the aspirations of most Southerners. It was also seen as utopian because the Sudanese government could never allow it. "In their eyes, it was arrogant and, at best, naïve."[31] It may have been this underestimation of Garang—and his lack of fear of being contradictory—that allowed the SPLA to develop into Sudan's most successful rebel movement.

Despite running the SPLA with an iron first, Garang and his rhetoric of a "New Sudan for all" motivated people in the other marginalized regions

---

[25] Young (2005).
[26] Deng (2005: 6).
[27] Garang de Mabior (1992).
[28] Moro (2015: loc 2174).
[29] Cockett (2010).
[30] Ayers (2010: 162).
[31] Deng (2005: 6).

of Sudan—mainly Blue Nile and the Nuba Mountains—to join the movement. The inclusion of rebels from these areas beyond the south greatly widened the SPLA's reach and influence.

Critics argue, however, that this notion of the SPLA as an inclusive force is revisionist and that Garang's rule was less inclusive than is now claimed. The New Sudan agenda has also been seen as opportunistic, as it allowed the SPLA to get support from Ethiopian leader Haile Mengistu Mariam, who could not back a separatist group while he was fighting Eritrean separatist movements in his own country.[32] That the SPLA coined itself as Marxist largely to ensure Mengistu's backing created another contradiction in a country, where social structures are a long way from being readily interpretable through Marxism. Thus, despite New Sudan being at the heart of Garang's rhetoric, Young writes that New Sudan "never had any resonance among southerners."[33] Southerners, nonetheless, understood the contradictions, according to Deng:

> The fighting men and women in the South took [Garang's rhetoric of New Sudan] as a clever ploy to allay the fears of those opposed to separation within Sudan, the international community and the Organisation of African Unity (later the African Union). Their attitude was reflected in the Dinka saying popular among fighters: "Ke tharku, angicku," "What we are fighting for, we know." While Garang was talking the language of a united Sudan, they were fighting for secession.[34]

The contradiction between pursuing New Sudan and independence came to a head in 1991. Three SPLM/A commanders—Riek Machar, Gordon Kong, and Lam Akol—formed their own movement to explicitly fight for southern independence in defiance of Garang's New Sudan vision. Machar—later the Vice-President of the Republic of South Sudan, whose dismissal in 2013 marked the start of South Sudan's political crisis and the beginning of an armed movement against the government of President Salva Kiir—aptly called his faction the South Sudan Independence Movement.[35] The Khartoum government, ready to cheer

---

[32] Young (2005).
[33] Young (2005: 539).
[34] Deng (2005: 6).
[35] Machar not dated (ca.1996).

on any opponent of Garang, supported this movement with weapons and other resources.

THE CONTRADICTORY PATHS TO PEACE

During most of the 1990s, differences of opinion about what was the best future for southern Sudan fuelled internal southern violence, as different parties fought over that vision. Southern groups committed some of the worst atrocities against southern civilians during the time of the SPLA split; those deeds continue to reverberate in post-independence South Sudan.[36]

The south–south battles were physical as well as ideological, with Garang maintaining his dream of unity in a New Sudan and Machar supporting separation. Nonetheless, the divided SPLA convened for peace talks in Abuja in 1992. Originally, President Babangida of Nigeria had initiated these talks as head of the Organisation of African Unity (OUA)—yet pressures from Khartoum made him extend the invitation in his capacity as president of Nigeria only to avoid giving the impressions that the OAU was officially engaging with secessionist movements.[37]

The Abuja talks were to bring together the two visions for southern Sudan—independence or improvement within New Sudan. Consolidating these two positions seemed possible, since for the first time Garang himself had put a discussion of self-determination on the agenda, presumably because, as Young argues, the loss of Ethiopian support after the fall of the Derg regime in 1991 had made space for this debate.[38] The agenda item "referendum," however, had to be deleted after days of controversy.[39] After several days of negotiation, the two delegations merged into one to develop joint positions.

A surprising outcome of this move—which would have been unlikely had the OAU convened the meeting—was William Nyuon's proposal as head of the delegation of Garang's SPLA (SPLA Torit) to announce secession as the common goal for both SPLA delegations. This move—from discussing self-determination to developing secession as the official goal—

---

[36] In 2013, the then Vice-President Machar initiated a national reconciliation process. President Kiir canceled this project later the same year before dissolving his cabinet, dismissing the Vice-President in July 2013.

[37] Wondu and Lesch (2000: 21).

[38] Young (2007: 8).

[39] Wondu and Lesch (2000: 23).

caught Garang off guard and created tension between leader and dele-gates.[40] It is likely that this pronouncement also alarmed the OAU, which feared that other African countries might follow the example of the SPLA as a separatist rebel movement. In 1993, Eritrea had held its referendum on independence, and there was little appetite in the OAU to see another referendum leading to independence on the continent. Thus, the Abjua talks ended with a number of unclear, somewhat ambiguous, messages.

Thus, when the Intergovernmental Authority on Development (IGAD) in 1994 convened the first round of peace talks between the SPLM/A and the Khartoum government of Sudan, different interests collided. From the OAU's point of view, any concession toward independence was off the table. Machar's forces and other Khartoum-backed militias were still working to a separatist agenda. Garang's SPLM/A needed to respond to interests of his rank and file from the Nuba Mountains and Blue Nile—both parts of northern Sudan—who were alarmed by the suggestion that the south would separate, leaving them exposed to Khartoum's wrath without southern support. To appease Northerners fighting with the Southerners, the SPLM/A aimed for, as Rolandsen writes, "a secular, plu-ralistic Sudan and self-determination for the South."[41] Self-determination was possible also within Garang's notion of a New Sudan. Delinking self-determination from calls for independence made the SPLM/A more inclusive, as it allowed northern supporters of the SPLM/A to join in on the self-determination agenda.[42]

The first round of the IGAD talks produced a Declaration of Principles (DoP) that reflected the continuing tension between changing the broader political system in Sudan and the southern desire to leave this system behind entirely. The DoP states that "the rights of self-determination of the people of South Sudan to determine their future status through a ref-erendum must be affirmed; and…maintaining the unity of the Sudan must be given priority by all the parties involved."[43] That this set up a contradic-tion was not lost on the authors of the DoP, who explicitly did not auto-matically equate self-determination with secession: "Extensive rights of self-administration on the basis of federation, autonomy, etc. to the various

---

[40] Wondu and Lesch (2000: 23).

[41] Rolandsen (2011a: 553).

[42] A detailed discussion on how the principle of self-determination was interpreted in South Sudan, see de Vries and Schomerus (2017a).

[43] GoS/SPLM/A/SPLM/A-United (1994: 2).

peoples of the Sudan must be affirmed."[44] Only if these rights were violated would the next step be taken: "In the absence of the above
principles…the respective people will have the option to determine their
future including independence through a referendum."[45] The main point
of the DoP was that the option of secession was only granted if Sudan did
not change toward being democratic, secular, and inclusive. This means
that self-determination was presented here as the process that would create a government that shared resources and power equally.[46]

Yet during the first round of talks, the Khartoum government's representative, Dr. Ghazi Salauddin el Atabani, returned to Garang's idea of a
New Sudan, emphasizing that independence was not in the cards (and
presenting a widely-held OAU position on the matter):

> Whereas the claim to an independent Southern Sudan was adopted very
> briefly by the Anya-nya rebellion…it has never been an original claim of the
> present SPLA rebellion. On the contrary the SPLA rebel movement has
> been renounced for its unionist claims. Its shift to separatist positions can
> only be seen as a negotiating tactic. Self-determination, alas, separation of
> Southern Sudan is bound to elicit a chain-reaction afflicting the rest of
> Africa.[47,48]

Yet when various southern militias—including militias led by Machar,
but not the SPLA—signed a separate agreement with the Sudanese government, the 1997 Khartoum Peace Agreement, it prominently included
"self-determination exercised through a referendum."[49] Although the
agreement itself is generally considered unsuccessful—the main SPLM/A
was not a signatory, and all signatories quickly violated what had been
agreed—it formed the foundations for later SPLM/A negotiations. What
seems in retrospect to be a huge concession from Khartoum did not
appear so at the time. One of the SPLM/A's then negotiators later argued

---

[44] GoS/SPLM/A/SPLM/A-United (1994: 2).

[45] GoS/SPLM/A/SPLM/A-United (1994: 3).

[46] See Young (2007: 15) and de Vries and Schomerus (2017a).

[47] Nyaba (2000: 165).

[48] During the interim period and the early days of the Republic of South Sudan, the
Organisation of African Unity (OAU's) position was often challenged by southern Sudanese
representatives, who argued that the southern policy of administering southern Sudan separately during colonial times meant that the inviolability of colonial borders did not apply to
South Sudan, since, in practice, it had been treated as a separate entity.

[49] "The Khartoum Peace Agreement, general principle no. 4, 2".

that the Government of Sudan "had not expected [self-determination] to be such an important issue for the southern Sudanese, so it did not seem to the government the concession that it now appears.... Indeed, self-determination was not as important in the mid-1990s to the southern Sudanese as it is now."[50] This shifting perspective on what issues are important is what ultimately allowed the slow move toward the SPLM/A's definite pro-secessionist stance; the continuing reassessment of the matter over the SPLM/A history meant that those wanting to avoid South Sudan's independence rarely had a concrete moment to push back. In addition, independence seemed simply out of reach.

However, in 1995, the National Democratic Alliance (NDA)—an alliance between Sudanese political parties, armed groups, and trade unions that had been formed to oppose President Bashir after he came to power in 1989—signed the Asmara Declaration, which outlined that the country had two choices: either reformed unity—under a federal or confederate system—or southern secession. The SPLM, however, in the Asmara Declaration, voiced its support for a confederation, at least in an undefined interim.[51] That self-determination was equated with a decision on independence was not surprising, considering that the Eritrean government hosted the meeting that produced the declaration.[52] Commentators at the time stressed that for Southerners to execute their right to self-determination, "any informed and rational decision by the people of Southern Sudan will have to be, of necessity, preceded by an effective enlightenment campaign about the true implication of each and every option that will be put before them for a final vote."[53]

Self-determination in the Asmara Declaration was implicitly reduced to a decision on a system of government rather than a process in which people can freely decide on how they want to govern themselves. At the same time, the declaration watered down the principle of self-determination, since territories that fought against Khartoum but were not necessarily interested in being part of an independent south were not granted the same privilege.[54]

[50] Ofuho (2006).
[51] Abdel Salam and de Waal (2001: 214).
[52] See also Johnson (2003b: 104).
[53] Abdel Salam and de Waal (2001: 217).
[54] Johnson (2003b: xii).

As late as 2002, the US position—as expressed in the final report of the US Special Envoy for Peace, John C. Danforth—was that self-determination could not equal independence. This was largely because independence was deemed unachievable, but self-determination could ensure "the right of the people of Southern Sudan to live under a government that respects their religion and culture."[55] The 2002 Kampala Declaration by civil society from the non-southern but SPLA-supporting areas of Blue Nile and the Nuba Mountains also stressed that Sudanese unity was a priority, and that unity would be the way to "work together to create a new democratic Sudan, in which all regions and communities are fairly represented, particularly in view of the fact that the peoples of the two regions are the indigenous peoples of Sudan."[56]

That its allies openly opposed equating self-determination with secession put the SPLM/A into a bind. It started negotiating the Machakos Protocols, the first major step forward toward the final CPA, in Kenya in 2002—again under the auspices of IGAD and again holding a number of contradictory positions simultaneously. There was a furious SPLM/A reaction when delegates realized that the mediator-drafted negotiation text that was supposed to start off the talks did not even mention self-determination.[57] What came out of the Machakos talks were, as Young argues, "very different political waters" with regard to self-determination than the IGAD DoP had proposed: self-determination was no longer assumed to be fulfilled also through the reform of the Sudanese state to a secular democracy that respects human rights but was explicitly equated as a vote "after a transitional period, irrespective of any changes within the central state."[58]

Garang himself, as well as international observers, were reportedly surprised at this outcome. Garang is said to have gone "berserk" when he learned that his deputy Kiir had introduced a language on self-determination that was at odds with Garang's views.[59] As a consequence, Garang dismissed Kiir—but Southerners' "right to self-determination" to be exercised through a vote became enshrined in the 2005 CPA.

---

[55] Danforth (2002: 24).
[56] Nuba Mountains and South Blue Nile Civil Society Forum (2002).
[57] Young (2007: 14).
[58] Young (2007: 15).
[59] Ofuho (2006: 94).

Throughout the negotiations, Garang had shone with his eloquence and his ability to garner international support, particularly from the United States. Since the early 1990s, southern Sudan had been a political cause in the United States, with politicians pursuing an agenda of "compassionate conservatism."[60] The initiative also suited US resource interests in the region, with oil again at the forefront. Thus, the United States, the United Kingdom, and Norway (the so-called Troika) supported the CPA and its promise of self-determination at the end of a six-year interim period, meaning a referendum on whether or not South Sudan was to stay within Sudan with the semi-autonomy that the CPA granted or was to separate.

The CPA also formalized yet again the contradiction that is a characteristic of the SPLM/A's entire history: it stipulated, in addition to the vote on self-determination, that both parties were to "make unity attractive." This was to be done through democratic transformation and inclusive development in all of Sudan. Garang maintained that New Sudan was still an option, but he acknowledged that if political transformation within Sudan were to prove impossible, independence was the only other choice for the south.[61] With this, the SPLM/A—and the international supporters of the CPA—had set up a contradictory agenda that was to cause a range of problems in subsequent years.

THE FAILURE TO "MAKE UNITY ATTRACTIVE" IN SOUTH SUDAN

The "different political waters" were to substantially change South Sudan's path, particularly after Garang died in a helicopter crash in 2005. This happened only weeks after the start of the interim period of the CPA and the swearing in of both the nationwide Government of National Unity (GoNU) and the largely autonomous Government of southern Sudan (GoSS). With Garang's death, the most vocal and credible proponent of New Sudan had gone—and possibly the only person who was able to hold such contradictory agendas simultaneously.

Yet, despite the fact that the CPA provided for self-determination, making unity attractive was also an official commitment in the CPA. Of the international supporters, neither the African Union (AU), the UN, the United States, Norway, nor the United Kingdom wanted to be seen to

---

[60] Cockett (2010).
[61] Johnson (2013: 149).

renege on it.[62] But with Garang gone, representatives of the UN or foreign governments regularly informally stated that support for unity had become lip service, particularly as there were limited signs of political transformation in Khartoum.[63] Long before the referendum, it was clear that neither the SPLM nor northern Sudan's ruling National Congress Party (NCP) was engaging in serious efforts to make unity attractive.[64] At the same time, the SPLM/A was expected to build a credible political party, government institutions, and a professional army. The international community focused its aid efforts on building these institutions in the semi-autonomous south, thus inadvertently fueling the contradiction between making unity attractive while putting everything into place that would allow independence.

During the first three or four years of the CPA's interim period, the secessionist and New Sudan agendas still nominally coexisted within the SPLM/A, also because a small group of SPLM members who had been close to Garang were still very influential. Southern Kordofan, Blue Nile, and Abyei (the so-called three areas), all of which had supported the SPLM/A along the way, faced uncertain futures, and the SPLM's national role in the GoNU was seen as a commitment to the New Sudan. In those first years, the right to self-determination thus included debate over what southern independence might mean for the south, for Southerners living in the north, and for people in the three areas. The SPLM officially confirmed its commitment to Sudanese unity and the New Sudan policy at an SPLM leaders' conference in February 2007 in Yei[65] and also during the second SPLM national convention in May 2008.[66]

But the reality of institution building in semi-autonomous southern Sudan was complicated.[67] Just like the period after the Addis Ababa agreement in the 1970s, the six years of the CPA demonstrated how strained internal cohesion in the south was. The SPLM/A had negotiated for the

---

[62] See also the online debate between John Young and Alex de Waal, (last accessed January 29, 2016), http://sites.tufts.edu/reinventingpeace/2013/05/14/democratization-and-the-failure-of-the-sudan-peace-process/

[63] From 2006–2011, the authors spent more than four years in Sudan between them, during which they regularly discussed the issue with international representatives. See also O'Leary (2012: 509).

[64] See, for example, International Crisis Group (2010).

[65] Rolandsen (2007: 7).

[66] SPLM (2008).

[67] Kalpakian (2008) and de Vries and Justin (2014).

future of all Southerners but without comprehensively taking everybody's interests into account. Old divides such as those between the SPLA and other militias, between elite interests and concerns of ordinary people, and between different ethnic and regional affiliations soon started to resurface.

ELECTIONS AS THE END OF DREAMS
OF SELF-DETERMINATION

The widespread discontent at the failure of the leadership to pursue a southern Sudan that cherished all its people became more and more visible as enthusiasm over the CPA wore off.[68] As Sudan prepared for national elections in 2010, the conduct of the government of southern Sudan and its ruling party, the SPLM, meant that the two milestones—national elections and the referendum—marked a shift from self-determination as a process championing the primacy of the individual will toward the emphasis on the predetermined outcome of secession.[69]

In October 2009, Garang's successor Kiir said that only in an independent South Sudan would southern Sudanese stop being second-class citizens.[70] In late 2010, Kiir publicly announced for the first time that his personal vote in the referendum would be for separation.[71] As the referendum approached, emphasis on unity became subdued, as did any substantial political debate on the advantages and disadvantages of secession. The SPLM/A leadership sacrificed its championing of self-determination as the individual right to decide how they wanted to be governed to push a collective interpretation of self-determination to mean that southern Sudan's political situation could only improve through secession. International actors, keen to see the CPA implemented, had little room to argue against this interpretation, considering they had championed South Sudan's self-determination so strongly.

Numerous analysts and observers questioned the SPLM's actions in its role as patron of the CPA agenda, particularly as security forces were often heavy-handed, which made international observers uneasy and South Sudanese citizens worried.[72] In March 2010, an article in *The East African* claimed:

---

[68] Schomerus and Allen (2010).
[69] de Vries and Schomerus (2017a).
[70] Belloni (2011: 414).
[71] Woodward (2011: 9).
[72] Human Rights Watch (2009) and Kalpakian (2008).

Key Western democracies and institutions...have quietly urged President Salva Kiir's government to go slow on secession. "Independence for the South should be put off for a few more years primarily because of lack of capacity in the South to run a stable and secure state," said a source privy to Western analysis of the evolving situation in Sudan.[73]

For the ruling party, considerations of state capacity were secondary to consolidating power through elections. Thus, the SPLM used the elections—and the credibility given to them by international support during the lead-up and by several monitoring missions during voting—to close down space for genuine political discussion.[74] Two related factors played into this: the SPLM's unwillingness to cede any political power and internal power struggles that translated into hardline external attitudes. In practice, this meant that in the run-up to the elections, any credible and possibly influential opposition, part of which came from within the SPLM, was violently suppressed. Young sums up the methods as follows:

> Freedom of association was limited; non-governmental political parties faced periodic harassment...and the security organs...continued to play a leading role in the state. Thus the elections took place in an environment in which democratic freedom and respect for human rights were limited and political repression was common.[75]

The different international observation missions mentioned arbitrary detention, interference in the polling, fraud, and security forces intimidating candidates of opposition parties as well as voters.[76] As Willis and el Battahani argue, in the south the discretion of the vote was "tarnished by its association with an authoritarian and violent state."[77] When it came to voting, such repression was manifest in the harassment of opposition candidates on their way to the polls, the presence of security forces at the polls—including in the voting booth—and "assisted voting" that left no

[73] Wakabi (2010).

[74] Young (2012) Both authors worked in South Sudan during the elections and witnessed this development.

[75] Young (2012: 136).

[76] International Crisis Group (2010: 8) Again, both authors witnessed these types of incidents.

[77] Willis and el Battahani (2010: 196).

choice but to vote for the SPLM.[78] Voters witnessed outright rigging,[79] uncounted ballots, registering of small children, or voters being told that they would be killed if they did not vote for the preferred SPLM/A candidates.[80]

It was a confusing mélange, true to the contradictions at the heart of South Sudan: the southern government paid lip service to democratic principles by conducting elections. Yet they used these as a means to steer toward a specific goal—creating a political environment that inhibited any influence from beyond the realm of the SPLM. The elections did not meet the international standards, according to observers, but concerns were expressed in a subdued way. The reports of the international election observation missions mentioned a few incidents, especially on the tabulation of the vote,[81] but warning bells did not ring very loudly. To the international community, the fact that general elections were accomplished in the first place was more important than democratic principles. The international focus on logistical and technical questions helped to concentrate on the more important landmark on the southern agenda: getting to the referendum without problems along the way. It was a weirdly apolitical stance on a highly political matter.

International governments and multilateral organizations chose this stance because of the contradiction at the heart of the CPA that had been formulated in order to keep all signatories to the CPA on board to prevent renewed war between Sudan and its south. Yet in another inconsistency, the international commitment to support peace in Sudan through democratic processes allowed the elections to turn into an exercise that cemented, rather than challenged, a problematic political status quo.[82]

On the back of the election experience, and with the leadership's clearly stated preference for secession as the outcome of exercising the right to self-determination, political and technical debates were also silenced in the run-up to the crucial referendum. South Sudan's government prioritized security issues over anything else, and by the summer of 2010, debate on options other than secession was practically nonexistent. It was not openly discussed who would be granted citizenship of a new South Sudan, nor

---

[78] Incidents such as these were observed by the authors, who were both election observers for the Carter Center.

[79] Field report Ayod/Panyagor: December, 2010.

[80] Field report Malakal: December, 2010.

[81] See, for example, Carter Center (2010).

[82] Hemmer (2009).

was it clear how national wealth and debts would be divided. Pastoralist populations used to crossing the border between northern and southern Sudan to graze cattle were left in the dark as to how their movement would be handled in the future. It was not even clear where the border would run and which parts of Abyei and the oil-rich border areas would belong to north or south.[83]

The international community had difficulty finding a way to work with the contradictions laid out in the CPA; simultaneously, international actors also held ambiguous opinions. A stark difference existed, for instance, between what international actors officially said—and their unofficial stance on the issue of Southerners' vote on secession. Informally, international actors often acknowledge that independence was all but certain, yet the official public stance of governments and intergovernmental organizations was to continue to support the democratic principles of the CPA, including making unity attractive.

During the interim period, McNamee argues, the international community "buried its head in the sand until secession was all but inevitable."[84] International actors who expressed hesitations toward secession or doubts over some of its consequences were accused of being allies to Sudan's allies. The international community was caught between its commitment to support democratic governance in the semi-autonomous south, while making unity attractive. The reality that emerged, however, was neither southern democratic governance nor commitment to unity in a democratic transformation process. For international actors, simply focusing on technicalities of the process, with the UN as operational manager, offered a way out.

The SPLM/A, well aware of the muted but widely known international support for independence, thus succeeded to "instrumentalize the state and engage in 'predatory activities,'" as Englebert and Hummel have called the process in other contexts.[85] At the same time, the SPLM/A was aware that the aftermath of the elections had produced divisions that needed attention. In October 2010, the different political parties of the south met in Juba in order to unite their voice. The parties were "calling

---

[83] For an overview of issues of citizenship and cross-border relations in South Sudan's borderlands, see Vaughan, Schomerus, and de Vries (2013).

[84] McNamee (2012: 8).

[85] Englebert and Hummel (2005).

for a timely and transparent conduct of the region's referendum on independence" as well as for "achieving reconciliation in the region."[86]

EXPERIENCING THE REFERENDUM

For the citizens of South Sudan, the year prior to the referendum on self-determination was rather surreal. For many, the referendum process caused disruption, recreating or reinforcing divisions. The referendum experience split people into political classes, with some being able to be engaged in the politics, while others felt distinctly—and deliberately—left out. Many simply feared that an outcome other than independence would inevitably lead to further war with Khartoum. A young man from Juba, updating his Facebook status, summed up his view that voting would need to be accompanied by military preparedness: "Ink your index finger so that you vote on a trigger."[87]

Southern citizens viewed the process with skepticism: the absence of an exchange of political ideas and the reduction of any political criticism to the question of whether someone was pro-unity or pro-separation was worrying to many. During referendum campaigning, representatives of opposition parties were difficult to find; people who wanted to speak to international observers about Sudan's unity did so mainly to point out that they were not able to speak about unity. With political discourse driven largely by local SPLM figures in vocal support of separation and with a firm grip on power and resources, leaving very little room for disagreement or nuance, the question of what kind of power the SPLM would hold after the referendum weighed heavily on peoples' minds. A conversation with a young man in Upper Nile was illustrative of this tension: "Leadership isn't good, actually. Not all are trustworthy. Some are suffering and [the leader] is enjoying himself with the community's resources. Some have good hearts, but not all of them. But it should be better after independence."[88]

A man in Western Bahr el-Ghazal, a state largely controlled by the north during the war, expressed his hope that becoming South Sudan would not just mean transferring to someone else's oppressive leadership. "There is need to make things work after the separation," he explained.

---

[86] Sudan Tribune (2010).
[87] Schomerus fieldwork notes November 2010.
[88] Field report Malakal: December 2010.

"Things have to take shape different from when we were under control of the North." He pointed out that if one tribe tried to dominate everything and everyone, without inclusion, there would be a "problem of power... with the leaders."[89] In Bentiu, community leaders called a meeting for *Nyal payam* to discuss how to avoid such internal conflicts within the SPLM and within the community. Hundreds of people reportedly attended.[90] One of the former "lost boys," now 27 years old, argued that the referendum process had empowered South Sudan's national security apparatus as well as the SPLA; these were two entities he feared.[91]

The CPA had given the south a goal. It had not, however, established processes or even political content beyond the bare bones of the referendum. The CPA seemed to promise that in post-CPA times, political affairs would be conducted in a fair and transparent manner, with citizens genuinely involved in political decision-making. Respondents strongly expressed that they wanted transparent processes for three reasons: to make sure that the referendum result could not be manipulated, to make the result credible, thus assuring that the post-referendum period would be peaceful, and to instill trust that democratic processes were genuine.

One of South Sudan's continuing challenges is its founding narrative: who can lay claim to having fought the war and thus achieved ownership of South Sudan remains a sore issue until today. In a referendum stakeholders' meeting, called to discuss the referendum, political parties leveled accusations against each other. The smaller parties present made clear that in their opinion, the SPLM/A was treating the referendum as though it was its property, deliberately excluding any other party from efforts of campaigning, mobilization, and funding. The result was that the referendum was claimed as an SPLM/A process rather than a joint effort of all Southerners.[92]

Thus many respondents experienced the referendum process—and as a precursor, the elections—as a process of political disenfranchisement. Some felt that their voice in this process was insignificant. This was emphasized by the persistent—and unfounded—rumor that voting in country would not count and that the referendum would be decided with

---

[89] Field report Natabo: November 19, 2010.
[90] Field report, Bentiu: December, 2010.
[91] Field report, Bentiu: December, 2010.
[92] Field report Yambio: November 29, 2010.

out-of-country votes of the diaspora.[93] Many felt so removed from the process that voting had become irrelevant. A group of women in Eastern Equatoria explained that "southern Sudan" for them was only their village, and their only concern was how to survive every day. Only if the referendum could bring development would it be interesting to them, but as it could also bring war, they saw no point in the process, except that it made them feel powerless.[94]

Others felt disenfranchised because their politicians told them what to vote for. This was further exacerbated by the fact that the role of chiefs as identifiers of who was eligible to vote was not transparent and not consistent. How chiefs were chosen to act as identifiers varied greatly across Sudan. Southern populations in some areas, particularly in the north, reported that they did not agree with the choice of chief as their identifier.

Voter registration turnout for the referendum declined by 20% in the south in comparison to the election registration in 2009. There might be a technical reason for this decline: Northerners who had registered in the South during elections were not eligible to vote in the referendum and thus could not register. Lack of clarity about the implications of voting as a Southerner in the north might have contributed to low turnout in the north, as did the smaller number of registration centers compared to the elections. But there may be other explanations: some people at the time pointed out that they did not see the point of voting this time: after all, they had done so in April and nothing had changed. They argued that it was useless for them to vote again, since the elections had not improved the government.

Few people seemed to know what the registration process allowing people to vote in the referendum was about; often, people answered that they were registering for separation. This pointed to a greater issue. The conduct of the referendum process emphasized the ongoing disconnect between high-level politics and the local experience. Lack of understanding, a lack of an open environment for political debate, and a lack of care in educating voters about their choice opened the possibility to manipulate voters rather than allowing them to participate in an open and democratic process in which they can freely make their own informed choice.

[93] This assumption was in no way supported by the rather low out-of-country registration numbers.
[94] Field report Kapoeta: November 2010.

An older woman's concerns in Eastern Equatoria are illustrative. Even though she was illiterate, she wanted to understand the process and her choices. Since she did not yet know which way to vote, she wanted information that would not require her to be able to read. The government had not been forthcoming at all in providing such information, which presumably would have best been dispersed in a public debate outlining the implications of separation and unity. Without proper information, she was afraid that someone might tell her she was voting for one thing and make her vote for something else because she had no means of checking what was written on the paper.[95] Often, in conversations, people asked how they should vote: those inquiring pointed out that they had not been given any information on what either choice actually meant.[96]

Confusion in Warrap State about the meaning of registration was exemplary for the lack of understanding and for the disconnect between the government and its citizens, caused by limited information to voters. The chief of the area had told people that this was a registration to join the SPLA, causing a significant drop in registration. The fact that only people 18 years and older were allowed to register made the SPLA explanation seem credible enough to deter people from putting down their names. It seemed that this misinformation was a deliberate policy to withstand the process based on the fact that the chief felt that the government had neglected his *boma*. The deputy governor had to clarify the situation.[97]

A group of Western Equatorian NCP members put their finger on what they felt was a weakness in voter education. They explained that their CPA partner, the SPLM, was falsely equating the referendum with separation instead of portraying it as a choice between two options. The SPLM, they argued, did not give any option to support unity, although achievements made in the last six years were the work of the GoNU, drawn from the joint effort of the SPLM and NCP.[98] A man from Kuajok, however, referred to the referendum and to politics in general as "the good fight" because it is a "fight of opinions."[99] Yet "the good fight" tended to get lost in the anxieties attached to the referendum process; content and meaning of the referendum were rarely discussed, as its symbolic significance was elevated and the

---

[95] Field report Kapoeta: November 2010.
[96] Field report Raga Town: November 2010.
[97] Field report Pankot: November/December 2010.
[98] Field report Yambio: December 2010.
[99] Field report Gogrial: November/December 2010.

process was portrayed as having only one possible outcome. "Forced Unity Means War," posters throughout Kapoeta town announced.[100]

Additionally, people had experienced how, because of the elections, the SPLM got embroiled in internal strife. A member of the Unity State Assembly who also chaired a commission expressed his worry that Unity's election troubles would be repeated during the referendum, with again mostly internal conflicts in the SPLM being played out.[101] The community, aware of the risks of a replay, organized a well-attended meeting to discuss how various groups could work together both pre- and post-referendum. The suggested solution was to pause local political conflict, leaving their differences behind for the time being in order to pursue a common goal.[102] While this seemed to pacify matters for the time being, it also was clear that many problems would resurface after the referendum.

There was also the issue of Southerners who had been living in the north, sometimes for decades. Now they were asked to return "home." The UN Office for the Coordination of Humanitarian Affairs noted that more than 264,000 Southerners who settled in the north traveled to the south between October 2010 and March 2011.[103] Contrary to what was suggested, this was not a return home: most of the people who traveled southwards to vote in the referendum had never been to the south before. The referendum and subsequent independence thus was not only a moment of liberation but also included personal stories of loss of identity, homes, and loved ones. Sadly, many of the thousands of Southerners who arrived from the north were forced to flee again in the months after the outbreak of December 2013.

On January 9, 2011, exactly six years after the signing of the peace agreement, Southerners in all regions of Sudan, as well as those living abroad, finally exercised their right to self-determination. While the CPA had articulated this as a vote between South Sudan's semi-autonomy within Sudan or secession from the north, the referendum vote did not give such nuance: it was simply a choice of staying with Khartoum or leaving. The Referendum Act stipulated the vote to be valid when at least 60% of those who had registered cast their ballots. This first requirement was easily met: of the 4.8 million registered voters, 4 million went out to vote.

---

[100] Field report Nimule/Magwi: 20 November 2010.
[101] Field report Bentiu, November 2010.
[102] Field report Bentiu, November 2010.
[103] OCHA (2011).

A majority of 50% plus one was sufficient to declare independence, but the official result announced that 98.9% voted for secession.[104] In the local enthusiasm and international relief that followed, little attention was paid to reports of preprinted ballots and extensive occurrences of intimidation.[105] The outcome of nearly 99% in favor of separation was simply celebrated, rather than questioned.

South Sudan's Contradictions

South Sudan's wars were fought over issues of political, economic, and social marginalization. Yet the political path the country has since taken has meant that the grip on power of few is steadily being consolidated. In the six months between the referendum and the declaration of independence, different representatives of civil society and political parties came together to start the process of a constitutional review. The idea was to develop political support beyond the SPLM/A and to jointly decide what principles and system of governance would be enshrined in the new constitution.

This process was, however, sidelined in favor of a transitional constitution that greatly strengthened the powers of the president. In the highly-centralized system of governance, the president has the right to dismiss elected governors, and a state of emergency can be declared without consent from the parliament. Year 2013 marked the visible signs of these new presidential powers.

Salva Kiir dismissed nearly his entire cabinet in July 2013 and replaced the first elected governors with more supportive ones in an attempt to curb opposition. In December 2013, prominent SPLM members—including dismissed Vice-President Machar and Rebecca Garang, widow of the late John Garang—publicly voiced their concerns about the turn the government was taking. They claimed that the president tarnished Garang's ideology of political inclusiveness and instead was turning the SPLM into a political oppressor. Within days after the criticism from among the ranks of the SPLM, the government claimed that Riek Machar had attempted a coup, cracking down violently on the political opposition.[106] Machar fled

---

[104] Belloni (2011: 412).

[105] One of the authors reviewed reports submitted by referendum observers that reported widely on such incidents.

[106] de Vries and Justin (2014).

Juba. The army and other organized forces split: those loyal to the government were brutally fighting those opposed to it.

Five years later, despite an externally imposed power-sharing agreement signed by the two main parties—the SPLM and the SPLM-In Opposition (IO)—and a number of ceasefire agreements, the country is still caught up in a crisis that deeply affects all layers of society without a clear end in sight.[107] The war has forced hundreds of thousands of people to leave their homes and has killed tens of thousands. Civilians have been targeted by both parties to the conflict and have experienced the most brutal violence. The UN Panel of Experts has accused both President Kiir and armed opposition leader Machar of commanding responsibility for atrocities.[108] Despite attempts by IGAD and other international actors to continue a peace process, it remains difficult to imagine how the country might move out of this deep crisis. South Sudan's contradictory history of getting to this point, of first fighting for the rights of citizens to be active political participants and then failing to empower them to be just that, makes it difficult to believe that the next political process could be different.

CONCLUSION

In his first speech as president of a sovereign nation, Salva Kiir said: "Critical to the future of our people and the endeavor to fulfill their aspirations, match their hopes and ambitions, is a government that is democratic, inclusive, and accountable."[109] His government has not lived up to this promise. It is one of many of South Sudan's contradictions.

The fallout of South Sudan's path toward secession is complicated and consists of layers of contradictory experiences, emotions, expectations, and oppression. Citizens have become disillusioned with their experiences of the democratic process. Support for freedom from Khartoum was not necessarily the same as support for the SPLM. Opposition voices continue to articulate concern about the interchangeability of the government of the Republic of South Sudan, its national army, and the SPLM. The violence that started in late 2013 and that continues in various forms until today—with atrocities committed by both government forces and armed rebels—is the ultimate sign that South Sudan's politics are violent, even

[107] de Vries and Schomerus (2017b).
[108] Panel of Experts on South Sudan (2016).
[109] Salva Kiir, speech in Juba, July 9, 2011.

without Khartoum as an enemy. For international actors, who had been so vocal and instrumental in supporting an independent South Sudan, the process has been disillusioning while also highlighting the flaws and limits of international engagement. What has emerged now echoes previous patterns of governance, in which political authority over southern Sudan was never achieved; no political entity has ever been the legitimate representative of all the people of southern Sudan.[110]

South Sudan is a country of many people and cultures and yet was united against a common enemy. It rebelled with the support of the Ethiopian government that was against supporting a secessionist cause. Yet it became Africa's biggest, most successful, and now ultimately disenchanted secessionist story. South Sudan's rebels fought their war on a platform of political inclusion and the right to determine how the country will be governed; yet, the country was ultimately born from a political decision taken by leaders and imposed on a people that would probably have supported its leadership anyway. The country's leading party was fluent in the language of human rights and yet has always violated those rights. It signed a peace agreement that simultaneously supported unity with Khartoum as well as the right to separate from it.

Today, South Sudanese citizens—the majority of whom voted for independence, even if the majority was likely not as absolute as the official numbers suggest—are in an uneasy relationship with their political and military leadership because overwhelming popular support for the secession cause came at the expense of allowing differing voices to be heard. The CPA embodied the SPLM/A's internal division over the secession or unity issue, which created a series of diplomatic and political pitfalls for an international community that supported southern Sudan through the interim period of the CPA. To manage these contradictions, the international community focused on the technical and practical exercises of holding elections and a referendum. Politically sensitive topics were avoided. People involved preferred to be optimistic, insisting on the promise of "starting from scratch," as Connel writes describing the Eritrean experience but conveniently forgetting that a long history of war cannot be wiped blank.[111]

Do these contradictions explain why the SPLM/A successfully maneuvered South Sudan toward independence? Did the many meandering

---

[110] Washburne (2010).
[111] Connell (1995).

paths toward secession allow the breaking of so many principles along the way that all regional and international actors involved simply lost track of the bigger picture? The first five years of South Sudan's independence seem to suggest that what South Sudanese citizens got is not an improvement. This path is not unique to South Sudan: Zambakari argues that failure to meet the challenge of creating plural and inclusive societies is common to the post-colonial experience and is at the heart of much violence in Africa today.[112] This is also a particular challenge for former liberation movements that become governments in situations in which, as Melber argues in relation to Namibia, "the democratic notion is also contested territory...in particular, liberation movements in power tend to deviate from implementing originally declared policy aims."[113]

It is easy to argue that South Sudan did not live up to the promise. But then again, its history also shows that the promise was never as clear as it might have seemed.

REFERENCES

Abdel-Salam, H., & de Waal, A. (2001). *The phoenix state: Civil society and the future of Sudan.* Trenton: Red Sea Press.

Ayers, A. J. (2010). Sudan's uncivil war: The global–Historical constitution of political violence. *Review of African Political Economy, 37*, 153–171.

Belloni, R. (2011). The birth of South Sudan and the challenges of statebuilding. *Ethnopolitics, 10*, 411–429.

Byrne, H., & Englebert, P. (2018). Shifting grounds for African secessionism? In L. de Vries, P. Englebert, & M. Schomerus (Eds.), *Secessionism in African politics: Aspiration, grievance, performance, disenchantment.* New York: Palgrave.

Carter Center. (2010). *Carter Center reports widespread irregularities in Sudan's vote tabulation and strongly urges steps to increase transparency.* Khartoum/ Atlanta: Carter Center.

Cockett, R. (2010). *Sudan: Darfur and the failure of an African state.* New Haven/London: Yale University Press.

Connell, D. (1995). Eritrea: Starting from scratch. *Review of African Political Economy, 66*, 587–592.

Danforth, J. C. (2002). *Report to the President of the United States on the outlook for peace in Sudan.* Washington, DC.

---

[112] Zambakari (2012: 521).
[113] Melber (2003).

de Vries, L., & Justin, P. (2014). Un mode de gouvernement mis en échec: Dynamiques de conflit au Soudan du Sud, au-delà de la crise politique et humanitaire. *Politique Africaine, 135*, 159–175.

de Vries, L., & Schomerus, M. (2017a). Fettered self-determination: South Sudan's narrowed path to secession. *Civil Wars, 19*, 1–20.

de Vries, L., & Schomerus, M. (2017b). South Sudan's civil war will not end with a peace deal. *Peace Review: A Journal of Social Justice, 29*, 1–8.

Deng, F. M. (2005). African renaissance: Towards a New Sudan. *Forced Migration Review, 24*, 6–8.

Englebert, P., & Hummel, R. (2005). Let's stick together: Understanding Africa's secessionist deficit. *African Affairs, 104*, 399–427.

Garang de Mabior, J. (1981). *Identifying, selecting and implementing rural development strategies for socio-economic development in the Jonglei Projects area, southern region, Sudan.* Doctoral thesis, Philosophy Iowa State University.

Garang de Mabior, J. (1992). *The call for democracy in Sudan.* New York: Kegan Paul International.

GoS/SPLM/A/SPLM/A-United. (1994). Retrieved from https://peacemaker. un.org/sites/peacemaker.un.org/files/SD_940520_The%20IGAD%20 Declaration%20of%20principles.pdf

Green, E. (2011). Decentralization and political opposition in contemporary Africa: Evidence from Sudan and Ethiopia. *Democratization, 18*, 1087–1105.

Hemmer, J. (2009). *Ticking the box: Elections in Sudan.* The Hague: Clingendael Netherlands Institute of International Relations.

Holt, P. M., & Daly, M. W. (2000). *A history of the Sudan: From the coming of Islam to the present day.* Harlo: Longman.

Human Rights Watch. (2009). *There is no protection: Insecurity and human rights in southern Sudan.* New York: Human Rights Watch.

International Crisis Group. (2010). *Sudan: Regional perspectives on the prospect of southern independence: Africa Report 159.* Brussels: International Crisis Group.

Johnson, D. H. (2003a). *The root causes of Sudan's civil wars: Peace or truce.* Bloomington: Oxford.

Johnson, D. H. (2003b). *The root causes of Sudan's civil wars.* Currey: Indiana University Press; Oxford/Bloomington/Kampala: Fountain Publishers.

Johnson, D. H. (2013). New Sudan or South Sudan? The multiple meanings of self-determination in Sudan's comprehensive peace agreement. *Civil Wars, 15*, 141–156.

Kalpakian, J. (2008). The narrow prospects of the SPLA/M's transition into a political party in the short term. *South African Journal of International Affairs, 15*, 159–183.

Machar, R. (n.d.). *South Sudan: A history of political domination – A case of self-determination.* Philadelphia: African Studies Center, University of Pennsylvania. Retrieved from http://www.africa.upenn.edu/Hornet/sd_machar.html

Malwal. (2011). *Southern Sudan Referendum Commission (2011)*. Retrieved from https://pachodo.org/latest-newsarticles/pachodo-english-articles/2158-bona-malwal-public-statement

McNamee, T. (2012). The first crack in Africa's map? In *Secession and self-determination after South Sudan* (pp. 1–28). Johannesburg: The Brenthurst Foundation.

Melber, H. (2003). Limits to liberation: An introduction to Namibia's postcolonial political culture. In H. Melber (Ed.), *Re-examining liberation in Namibia: Political culture since independence*. Nordic Africa Institute: Uppsala.

Moro, L. (2015). Second civil war: Creation of the united 'New Sudan'. In R. Bereketeab (Ed.), *Self-determination and secession in Africa: The post-colonial state*. London/New York: Routledge.

Nuba Mountains and South Blue Nile Civil Society Forum. (2002). Kampala declaration of the Nuba Mountains and South Blue Nile Civil Society Forum. Kampala, Uganda.

Nyaba, P. A. (2000). *The politics of liberation in South Sudan. An insider's view*. Kampala: Fountain Publishers.

O'Leary, B. (2012). The federalization of Iraq and the break-up of Sudan. *Government and Opposition, 47*, 481–516.

Oduho, J., & Deng, W. (1963). *The problem of the southern Sudan*. London: Oxford University Press.

Office for the Coordination of Human Affairs. (2011). *Humanitarian update: Return to southern Sudan*. Juba: OCHA. Retrieved from https://www.ecoi.net/en/file/local/1261887/1788_1334004086_1st2011.pdf

Ofuho, C. H. (2006). Negotiating peace: Restarting a moribund process. In P. Dixon & M. Simmons (Eds.), *Peace by piece: Addressing Sudan's conflicts*. London: Conciliation Resources.

Oromo, S. L. (2015). Sudan's first civil war for self-determination. In R. Bereketeab (Ed.), *Self-determination and secession in Africa: The post-colonial state*. London/New York: Routledge.

Panel of Experts on South Sudan. (2016). *Final report of the panel of experts on South Sudan established pursuant to Security Council resolution 2206 (2015)*. New York: Security Council Affairs Division, UN.

Rolandsen, Ø. H. (2007). From guerrilla movement to political party. In *The restructuring of Sudan People's Liberation Movement in three southern states*. Oslo: Centre for the Study of Civil War/International Peace Research Institute.

Rolandsen, Ø. H. (2011a). A quick fix? A retrospective analysis of the Sudan Comprehensive Peace Agreement. *Review of African Political Economy, 38*, 551–564.

Rolandsen, Ø. H. (2011b). A false start: Between war and peace in the southern Sudan, 1956–62. *Journal of African History, 52*, 105–123.

Schomerus, M., & Allen, T. (2010). *Southern Sudan at odds with itself: Dynamics of conflict and predicaments of peace.* London: LSE/DESTIN/Pact Sudan/DfID.

Southern Sudan Referendum Commission. (2011). Results for the referendum of southern Sudan. Retrieved from https://pachodo.org/latest-news-articles/pachodo-english-articles/2158-bona-malwal-public-statement

Sudan People's Liberation Movement. (2008). SPLM manifesto.

Sudan Tribune. (2010, October 18). South Sudan political forces join hands ahead of referendum. *Sudan Tribune.* Retrieved from http://www.sudantribune.com/spip.php?article36641

The Khartoum Peace Agreement. (1997). Retrieved from http://www.incore.ulst.ac.uk/services/cds/agreements/pdf/sudan2.pdf

United Nations Mission in Sudan. (2009). *The background to Sudan's comprehensive peace agreement.* New York/Khartoum: United Nations Mission in Sudan/Information and Communications Technology Division.

Vaughan, C., Schomerus, M., & de Vries, L. (Eds.). (2013). *The borderlands of South Sudan: Authority and identity in contemporary and historical perspectives.* New York: Palgrave Macmillan.

Wakabi. (2010, March 22). Don't break away from Sudan, West tells South. *The East African.* Retrieved from http://www.theeastafrican.co.ke/news/Dont-break-away-from-Sudan-West-tells-South-/2558-883182-qsmeiaz/index.html

Washburne, S. L. (2010). *Legitimacy, identity and conflict: The struggle for political authority in southern Sudan 2005–2010.* Thesis, University of Exeter.

Wassara, S. S. (2015). Political history of Southern Sudan before independence of the Sudan. In R. Bereketeab (Ed.), *Self-determination and secession in Africa: The post-colonial state.* London/New York: Routledge.

Willis, J., & el Battahani, A. (2010). We changed the laws: Electoral practice and malpractice in Sudan since 1953. *African Affairs, 109,* 191–212.

Wondu, S., & Lesch, A. (2000). *Battle for peace in Sudan: An analysis of the Abuja conferences, 1992–1993.* Lanham: University Press of America.

Woodward, P. (2011). Towards two Sudans. *Survival, 53(2),* 5–10.

Young, J. (2005). Garang's legacy to the peace process, the SPLM/A & the south. *Review of African Political Economy, 106,* 535–548.

Young, J. (2007). *Sudan IGAD peace process: An evaluation.* Retrieved from http://www.sudantribune.com/IMG/pdf/Igad_in_Sudan_Peace_Process.pdf

Young, J. (2012). *The fate of Sudan: The origins and consequences of a flawed peace process.* London: Zed Books.

Zambakari, C. (2012). South Sudan: Institutional legacy of colonialism and the making of a new state. *Journal of North African Studies, 17,* 515–532.

CHAPTER 16

Shifting Grounds for African Secessionism?

Heather Byrne and Pierre Englebert

INTRODUCTION

Given the diversity of experiences with secessionism on the continent—ranging from the lack of recognition of postcolonial Somaliland to the near universal endorsement (if not, originally, celebration) of the independence of breakaway South Sudan in 2011—we aim in this concluding chapter to summarize the recent evolution and current state of the right to self-determination and the principle of territorial integrity in Africa. In doing so, we seek to identify doctrinal changes as well as possible contradictions in the practice of states.

Focusing on the post-Cold War period and particularly the years following the adoption of the Sudanese 2005 Comprehensive Peace Agreement (CPA), which paved the way for the independence of South Sudan, we then review the empirical trends in secessionism across the continent to 2015. We do so by focusing first on major conflicts but also by

H. Byrne
Fulbright Fellow, Centre for Policy Research, New Delhi, India

P. Englebert (✉)
Pomona College, Claremont, CA, USA

Senior Fellow, Atlantic Council, Washington, DC, USA
e-mail: penglebert@pomona.edu

© The Author(s) 2019
L. de Vries et al. (eds.), *Secessionism in African Politics*,
Palgrave Series in African Borderlands Studies,
https://doi.org/10.1007/978-3-319-90206-7_16

looking more closely at smaller and more ambiguous movements. As an exercise in summarizing all these instances of African (would-be) secessionism, we present a map of what Africa would look like should all these groups get their wishes.

While we find, by and large, very few tangible effects of the South Sudan precedent on African secessionist activity, we note a significant rise in the coincidence of separatist and Islamist insurgencies and suggest that Islamism might represent a more radical challenge to the postcolonial territorial state in Africa than most other instances of secessionism to date. We conclude with a brief discussion of these different trends.

A Muddled Legal Regime

The parameters of African self-determination are usually construed as leaving little room for nuance or uncertainty. Past existence as a colony is generally seen as the fundamental principle guiding contemporary recognition as a sovereign entity in Africa. This principle was enshrined in UN General Assembly Resolution 1514 (XV)—of 1960—which dissociated the sovereignty of former colonies from their empirical existence[1] and outlawed their territorial reconfiguration, and was reaffirmed on multiple occasions, including in the 1963 Charter of the Organisation of African Unity (OAU), its famous "Cairo Resolution" the following year, and again with the creation of the African Union (AU) in 2000.

In a nutshell, because the African repertoire of international law squeezes the right to self-determination into the straightjacket of territorial integrity and maintenance of boundaries inherited from colonialism, decolonization has been the only legitimate manifestation of African self-determination since the extinction of the struggle against apartheid in South Africa.[2,3] It is no surprise then that most of the salient cases of attempted secessions on the continent have been couched in terms of decolonization or restoration of colonial boundaries, as in Eritrea, Somaliland, or Western Sahara. Some of the groups that could not plausibly make such a claim have tried instead to argue that they enjoyed a particular status under colonial rule from the rest of the country (e.g.,

---

[1] Jackson and Rosberg (1982).

[2] Jackson and Rosberg (1982) and Herbst (1990).

[3] It bears noting that, in adopting such a rule, independent African governments were at least partly reproducing a norm of nineteenth-century European international law, which denied statehood or international legal personality to most indigenous African communities Allott (1974: 112).

Katanga, Casamance, or Cabinda), or some sort of differential treatment (as with Britain's "Southern Policy" in Nigeria or Sudan), but there is no evidence that such a claim was ever successful at stimulating recognition. The case seems thus both simple and closed. In Robert Jackson's piercing formulation, "To be a sovereign state today one needs only to have been a formal colony yesterday."[4]

Yet, as many of the case studies in this book make clear, the behavior of both African and non-African states toward African secessions has been more ambiguous over the years than the principle of maintaining colonially inherited boundaries would suggest. To start with the end, the recognition of the right of South Sudan to secede in the CPA in 2005, and its subsequent accession to sovereignty as an independent state in 2011, shattered Africa's conservative legal record and brought in a considerable degree of confusion as to what makes secession legitimate and what the odds are of recognition. However, while South Sudan has contributed to such confusion, this book amply illustrates that previous practice was already highly contradictory.

Uti Possidetis or Not

The principle that African states must maintain the boundaries they inherited from colonization is known as *uti possidetis* (as you possessed).[5,6] A dominant element of doctrine and state practice in Africa,[7] its original adoption was motivated by the perceived need to protect new and fragile states and prevent attempts at partial independence. With the secession of Katanga from Congo in July 1960, which garnered at least indirect initial support from Belgium, its former colonial ruler, these issues were understandably far from moot for African rulers.

Yet, while the principle is often reaffirmed and hailed as a building block of Africa's international relations, this volume makes clear that *uti possidetis* has been historically unevenly applied and has been particularly called into question in the wake of South Sudan's independence.[8] The

---

[4] Robert Jackson (1990: 17).

[5] Summer (2004: 1790).

[6] It originated with the independence of Latin American countries in the early nineteenth century.

[7] Dugard (2003).

[8] It also suffered exceptions in Latin America, as with the secession of Panama from Colombia in 1903.

principle was first violated, before its enshrinement by the UN and OAU, when Ethiopia attempted to swallow Eritrea in the 1950s, despite having received administration over it as a UN Mandate (Eritrea had been an Italian colony until taken over by the British during World War II). Although it had originally agreed to manage Eritrea through a federation, Ethiopia argued that it had historical relations of political control over the region and forcibly incorporated it into a unitary administration. Eritrea's secession war ensued.[9]

Uti possidetis was then violated by four African countries—Côte d'Ivoire, Gabon, Tanzania, and Zambia—that decided to recognize the secession of Biafra in the late 1960s. While Côte d'Ivoire and Gabon were only too eager to weaken Anglophone Nigeria, Nyerere's Tanzania made the legal argument that the humanitarian obligation to help the Biafran victims of Nigerian repression trumped the principle of territorial integrity (offering, in effect, an early version of the "responsibility-to-protect" [R2P] doctrine, to which we return later).

The next violation took place when Morocco invaded Western Sahara in November 1975, a mere month after the International Court of Justice (ICJ) turned down its claim of historical control over it (a similar one to Ethiopia's over Eritrea). To Morocco's credit, it showed consistency by leaving the OAU upon the Sahrawi Republic's admission in 1984. Incidentally, the ICJ considered whether Western Sahara before Spanish colonization was under Moroccan control or "res nullius" (belonging to no one—in which case the colonial shell would prevail in its subsequent self-determination). The argument that the local population could belong to itself does not seem to have been considered—only external control (in this case, Spanish or Moroccan) seems to provide the ground for sovereignty in Africa's legal regime.[10] The failure of all UN attempts to organize a referendum in Western Sahara (despite the existence of a UN mission with this very purpose), the de facto annexation of two-thirds of its territory by Morocco, and the continued relations of other African states with Morocco, indicate the weak standing of *uti possidetis* as an African norm. The 2017 readmission of Morocco to the AU (after significant diplomatic

[9] Iyob (1997).

[10] As Matthew Porges (2018) makes clear in this volume, however, the International Court of Justice (ICJ) conceded that Morocco had historical personal links of control over local leaders but asserted that these did not constitute territorial sovereignty, a yardstick that would deny sovereignty to almost any pre-colonial African political formation.

and financial efforts over more than a decade by King Mohammed VI toward numerous African states) without a change in either's position on Western Sahara, largely avoided the question of the territory and resulted in both Morocco and the Sahrawi Republic being AU members.

Another rather flagrant violation of *uti possidetis* took place when France chose to retain the island of Mayotte as an overseas territory, as Comoros became independent in 1975. Of course, it is not clear whether *uti possidetis* was binding to France in the first place. Not only did France obviously not sign the OAU treaty, but it also abstained on UN Resolution 1514. Nevertheless, in terms of continental practice, the partial independence of Comoros represented a serious deviation from the norm. The Comoros continue to claim Mayotte, and, as Gregor Dobler tells us in this volume, there have been no fewer than 13 UN General Assembly resolutions condemning France since then. The French tried to boost the legitimacy of their move by holding several referenda in Mayotte. In 1974, 64% of *Mahorais* voted to stay with France; in 1976, the number was 99.4%.[11] This is an unusual practice, however, as there does not seem to exist a right in international law for sub-national groups to opt out of a country through referendum. No other subregion of former colonies ever got a chance to vote on whether it wanted to remain colonized.[12] It is true, however, that French colonies voted in 1958 on whether to remain with France or become independent. That all but Guinea chose then to remain French did not prevent the French from (somewhat forcibly) granting independence to most of them two years later. Mayotte, which became a French Department in 2011, illustrates the arbitrariness of postcolonial sovereignty and the lack of enforceable legal standing of *uti possidetis*.

To some extent, albeit a contrario, the refusal of any country to date to recognize Somaliland as a sovereign state also runs counter to *uti possidetis*. Somaliland was a distinct colony from Somalia. The British negotiated its boundaries with the Italians and the Ethiopians.[13] It reached independence as its own country on June 26, 1960, before uniting by act of parliament with former Italian Somalia on July 1. Since 1991, after three decades of relative persecution by the South and the latter's complete collapse

---

[11] Dobler (2018).

[12] The Southern Cameroons, as UN Mandate, constitute a partial exception. Its population was given the option of joining Nigeria or Cameroon but not of reaching independence alone, in what seems again an apparent case of African communities being deemed unable to belong to themselves.

[13] Hoehne (2018).

following Siad Barré's departure from power, Somaliland has reclaimed its own separate sovereignty but without any recognition. Yet, an independent Somaliland formally conforms to the *uti possidetis* principle and should thus have a right to self-determination as a postcolonial entity. Its lack of recognition contrasts with the experience of Senegal, which was still recognized as a sovereign state when it pulled out of the Mali Federation in August 1960, two months after forming it with then French Sudan (later to become Mali) in a pattern very similar to the unification of Somalia. It is also worth mentioning here that several countries declined to recognize Somaliland because of the Somali government's refusal to do so. It should be noted, however, that many of the same countries, the United States included, did not have similar concerns recognizing Kosovo in 2008 despite Serbia's objection to its secession.[14] Without a doubt, Serbia exercises more significant territorial control over at least parts of Kosovo than Somalia over Somaliland.

However, it is the near universally recognized independence of South Sudan in 2011 that most radically shattered the conventional territorial constraints to the right of self-determination in Africa. As Mareike Schomerus and Lotje De Vries detail in this volume, the notion that South Sudan has a right to self-determination through referendum showed up among some African states for the first time in 1994 and was formalized in the Machakos Protocol between the North and the South in 2002. Apparently, the military stalemate between the two parties and the international support for the South (together with the North's pariah status as a state supporting terrorism after 2001) were sufficient for the southerners to win this significant legal breakthrough. The subsequent endorsement of the right of self-determination by referendum of the South as part of the CPA consecrated this drift and constituted the broader and most explicit departure from *uti possidetis* on the continent since 1960.

It should be noted, however, that the recognition of South Sudan's independence by other countries, not least the United States, is not entirely arbitrary. For sure, it violates *uti possidetis* as it gives sovereignty to a subregion that has no history as a separate colony but differs from the rest of the country mostly on religious and racial grounds, which are not constitutive elements of self-determination in Africa. Yet some argue that the region's sustained and dramatic humanitarian crisis trumped *uti possidetis*. Solomon Dersso, for example, sees in South Sudan a "new human

---

[14] Hilpold (2009).

security-based approach" to the continental tension between *uti possidetis* and self-determination. In his words, South Sudan "represents a case of self-determination through independence that came about as a result of serious human rights violations and denial of the right to participate in public affairs and the running of the country on an equal basis."[15] In other words, the humanitarian catastrophe that 50 years of warfare, 2.5 million deaths, and 5 million displaced have caused might have mitigated the otherwise firm postcolonial contours of *uti possidetis*. Similarly, Terrence McNamee, who believes the recognition of South Sudan is more sui generis than representative of legal evolution, mentions the "length of the struggle," the "sharp racial and religious divide," the "extreme economic hardship" experienced in the South, and the "support of major external players" like the United States, Israel, and Ethiopia.[16] He adds that if there is a situation in which maintaining the territorial status quo might be seen as undermining international security, the international community might consider a new state as a solution.[17] US policy seems to have made room for this reasoning.[18] Schomerus and de Vries also highlight that South Sudan's lack of secessionist direction over the course of its struggle provided limited opportunity to push back on it; inadvertently a confused approach might have helped to reach the goal.[19]

There is no precedent for such an overruling. Recall indeed that a version of this argument was also employed by Tanzania in the late 1960s to justify its recognition of Biafra, which suffered four years of ruthless warfare that caused one million, mostly civilian, deaths. Yet the rest of the international community did not then deem the humanitarian crisis sufficient to warrant recognition (though Johannes Harnischfeger indicates in his chapter that the Ojukwu administration tried to capitalize on the humanitarian situation).[20] The independence of South Sudan might represent once again some application to self-determination of the R2P principle. The connection between secession, self-determination, and R2P is, however, tenuous and far from a historical precedent.[21] Why it was validated

---

[15] Solomon Dersso (2012: 7).
[16] Terrence McNamee (2012: 9).
[17] McNamee (2012: 20).
[18] See ARB (2009: 18168A).
[19] Schomerus and de Vries (2018).
[20] Harnischfeger (2018).
[21] Only in certain circumstances has the recognized principle of self-determination of peoples amounted to the right to secession. Responsible to protect (R2P) itself is not universally

with South Sudan and not with Biafra is unclear. It could be that one million casualties were not sufficient; more likely, the R2P norm evolved and liberalized over the last four decades.[22] At any rate, South Sudan suggests that in cases of prolonged significant suffering and malign administration, subregional peoples might have a humanitarian right to secede.[23] From the point of view of the African system of states, such a doctrinal evolution would have the benefit of keeping secession out of reach of by and large every other African insurgency, given the high threshold of required misery. Many African governments ruthlessly repress their citizens, and many deny them domestic avenues for addressing their grievances, yet, few if any have done so on the scale of Sudan, and most tend not to discriminate regionally or racially in their mistreatment of their citizens.

There is also another way of reading South Sudan's independence that does not represent as much of a legal evolution but fits more squarely with more conservative principles. It relies on what Jure Vidmar calls the "domestic consensus" principle.[24] According to this view, international law is neutral on the question of self-determination of sub-national "peoples" through independence, provided the existing national government agrees to it. This had already been the case with Eritrea in 1991, whose independence had been agreed with the rebels of Ethiopia's Tigray People's Liberation Front (TPLF) before their takeover of Addis Ababa. The participation of Sudan in the CPA and its approval of the referendum extended the application of this principle to South Sudan. In this perspective, which fits more squarely with AU doctrine and with the preservation of sovereignty of African states, South Sudan's independence is legitimate because Khartoum approved of it. In contrast, the government in Mogadishu never approved of Somaliland's independence (neither did

---

applied or accepted internationally and does not directly translate to the "solution" of separation. Given the principle of territorial integrity enshrined in Article 2(7) of the UN Charter, the resistance to humanitarian justification for separation may be subject to greater resistance than humanitarian intervention for state building, and so on. MacFarlane and Sabanadze (2013).

[22] MacFarlane and Sabanadze (2013).

[23] This is not so different from the justification of the secession of the United States in the 1776 Declaration of Independence (US 1776). It was then "self-evident" to Thomas Jefferson that "when a long train of abuses and usurpations, pursuing invariably the same Object evinces a design to reduce them under absolute Despotism, it is [the] right [of mankind], it is their duty, to throw off such Government, and to provide new Guards for their future security."

[24] Jure Vidmar (2011–2012). See also McNamee (2012).

Nigeria with Biafra or Congo with Katanga), making these secessions illegal. Once again, however, this leaves the case of Kosovo as either an illegal outlier or following different rules, apparently not applicable to Africa.[25] One thing the case of South Sudan shows in this respect is that *uti possidetis* does not constrain the behavior of states with respect to their own territory. In other words, it does not prevent an existing state from agreeing to its own partition.[26] But, in that case, is such a decision revocable? Could Sudan now revert its earlier decision and reclaim South Sudan?

In any event, like the earlier precedents that challenged *uti possidetis*, the true lesson from South Sudan is that these principles of international law are of limited importance when push comes to shove. If dominant international actors like the United States want to recognize a new state, they can do so and find reasons to do so, and the rump state as well as the African Union can be made to follow suit.

One final case deserves our attention, although its significance so far falls well short of that of South Sudan. While the Tuareg takeover of much of Malian territory in 2012 (to which we return at more length below) was forcibly overturned by a French military intervention starting in January 2013 and never led to any formal recognition of their "Azawad" republic, the subsequent attitude of the French toward the Tuareg rebels suggests some degree of recognition of their claim and represents a departure from mainstream practice. As they pushed out Islamist insurgents from the North, the French military allied with the *Mouvement National de Libération de l'Azawad* (MNLA) separatist rebels who had taken control of the city of Kidal after the Islamists fled in February. MNLA fighters had originally allied with the Islamists but had lost political control to them by June 2012 and used the French intervention to regain the upper hand in Kidal.

The unusual precedent comes from the fact that the French military, probably dependent on the MNLA for intelligence, declined to take over the town of Kidal (whereas it had reconquered Gao, Timbuktu and other northern towns), limiting its presence to the airport and de facto recognizing the separatist administration of the town, despite the opposition of the Malian government, which the MNLA declared would not be allowed

---

[25] One possible difference with Kosovo is that it was under UN administration since 1999, with the agreement of Yugoslavia, then the holder of sovereignty over it. Yet, Yugoslavia disappeared in the interim, and Serbia claimed the region, which remained under UN administration until its unilateral declaration of independence in 2008 (Hilpold 2009).

[26] Englebert (2013).

into the town.[27,28] France, the former colonial power largely responsible for the very existence of Mali, then pushed for a political settlement between the secessionist rebels and the Malian government, frustrating many Malians.[29] Rejecting the terrorist label the Malian government was trying to put on the MNLA, French President François Hollande announced that while Malian civil administration would be welcomed into town, its military would not.[30] Meanwhile, in Kidal, French officers held regular contact with Mohamed Ag Najim, chief of staff of the MNLA, and in Paris, some influential French politicians received MNLA delegations.[31] As of 2017, and despite the signing of a peace agreement in 2015, the Malian administration had still not successfully re-established itself in the Kidal region and other parts of the North where de facto MNLA control remained amid continued Islamist insurgency.

The precedent of working with and at least de facto recognizing a separatist rebel group suggests a further loosening of the principle of territorial integrity in Africa. It contrasts greatly with France's rejection of the legitimacy of Casamance or Anglophone Cameroon's demands. As the Tuareg chapter in this book makes clear, however, it is not totally in contradiction with France's long-standing sympathy for the Tuaregs, to whom they applied a more beneficial colonial regime (no forced labor, no required Western education) and for whom they created the *Organisation Commune des Régions Sahariennes* (OCRS) in 1957.[32]

LESSONS FOR WOULD-BE AFRICAN SECESSIONISTS

Where does the recent evolution of doctrine, jurisprudence, and practice leave potential and actual African separatists? In this section, we try to sort through the requirements for legal or legitimate secession.

Despite Somaliland's continued setbacks, previous existence as a separate colony remains probably the soundest ground to demand independence in Africa. The strength of this principle is one of the reasons that Western

---

[27] Lotze (2015).

[28] By then, however, the *Mouvement National de Libération de l'Azawad* (MNLA) had toned down its demands from independence to mere autonomy. See "Mali Army Clashes with Separatist MNLA Rebels." *BBC News,* June 5, 2013.

[29] Boutellis (2015).

[30] Lewis (2013).

[31] See Jeune Afrique (2013).

[32] Lecocq and Klute (2018).

Sahara still awaits a UN-sponsored referendum to exercise its self-determination, although it was for all practical purposes annexed by Morocco in the 1980s and has the population of a midsize city. If the Zanzibari were united in their pursuit of independence, they too could probably avail themselves of this principle. It has been written before but it bears repeating: there is genuine hypocrisy and a considerable degree of alienation in the notion that recognition is a function of the colonial plausibility of the claim to self-determination. Such plausibility is in turn a function of some past territorial sovereign status from the perspective of the European state system. Hence, Ethiopia is a state, but Buganda, Ashanti, and Zulu cannot be. This is the postcolonial equivalent of the European notion, exercised in the breakup of Yugoslavia and the Soviet Union, that the federated units of a federal system are imbued with sovereignty but not provinces or other administrative divisions (a principle also challenged by the recognition of Kosovo). In the African case, it is colonial rather than federal status that provides the foundation for sovereignty, even though being colonized is as far from being sovereign as one can be.

Even if a group can make the claim of past colonial existence (and it is hard to see who is left that might be able to make such a claim), there can still be no recognition without the agreement of the rump state. Such agreement seems necessary for the African Union to recognize the secession, and most non-African countries seem to condition their own recognition on such an AU endorsement. Ethiopia formally recognized Eritrea in 1993, and Sudan was the first country to recognize South Sudan in 2011. A contrario, Somalia's refusal to recognize Somaliland has been used by other countries as justification for not recognizing it either. Note, in this respect, that the rules elaborated by the European Union in the context of the breakup of Yugoslavia (that secession was legitimate because Yugoslavia had ceased to exist) somehow were never deemed to apply to Somaliland.[33,34]

As a third prerequisite, few secessionist groups could make a credible claim to sovereignty if they could not demonstrate massive popular support. The organization of a successful pro-independence referendum appears therefore to be a sine qua non. If anything, the pro-independence tsunamis obtained in the 1993 Eritrean (99.83%) and 2011 South Sudanese (98.83%) referenda raised the threshold of acceptable support

[33] Phillips (2012).

[34] One possible implication here is that it might pay for secessionist movements, if they have the capacity, to take over the state at its center then let go of parts.

and put secession further out of reach of most groups (most African sepa-ratist regions have divided populations, with large groups against seces-sion). As mentioned earlier, the French were also careful to organize referendum in Mayotte to legitimize its breakup from Comoros and later its status as a French department (95.4% in 2009).[35]

Even then, a successful referendum might be necessary but is not suf-ficient. Somaliland's constitutional referendum of 2001, which resulted in an official (and possibly inflated, according to Hoehne) 97% support for secession, does not seem to have made a difference.[36] Neither did Anjouan's in 1997 that showed 99.88% for breakup from Comoros.[37] The Sahrawi are still waiting for theirs.[38]

The South Sudan case suggests that only the first of these three condi-tions (postcolonial status) can be amended in circumstances of massive and prolonged humanitarian crisis. Even then, the approval of the rump state (a condition that might be hard to obtain without international pres-sure or takeover of the entire state) and a successful referendum are neces-sary. The implication is that sustained massive violence might help. With recognition coming ex post facto, the South Sudan precedent might bias rebel leaders toward continued warfare and reduce the political costs of civilian casualties, providing incentives for more violence in Africa.

What is unclear is whether a secession must demonstrably lead to a reduction in violence and suffering, and what happens to its status if it does not. Without attempting to assess any "scorecard" of suffering, South Sudan's infancy has been marred with civil war since 2013, and the government declared a war-induced famine in early 2017. Violence, dis-placement, and famine appear to make South Sudan as "brutal" a coun-try[39] as was its status under Sudan. Eritrea too has turned into a political and humanitarian catastrophe, with its citizens escaping *en masse* on dan-gerous migration journeys to Europe and beyond. If humanitarian tragedy led to recognition in South Sudan, should it now be removed? If not, on what legal basis does it endure?

And what if a new country is not economically viable?[40] The need for the breakup state to be able to provide for itself was never apparently made

---

[35] Dobler (2018).
[36] Hoehne (2018).
[37] Dobler (2018).
[38] Porges (2018).
[39] de Vries and Schomerus (2017a: 335).
[40] McNamee (2012: 12).

explicit in the case of South Sudan, but the availability of oil was known to all and thus the country was deemed financially viable. It could be argued that the incentive for potential break-off states to secede rather than strive for autonomy could be reduced if they lacked financial viability as a smaller, independent, and perhaps controversial state, with subsequently less donor support. In other cases, one occasionally hears claims that new small African countries could not survive and therefore should not exist, but we are not aware of any country making this a prerequisite for recognition. As a matter of fact, such a prerequisite would seem to go against UN Resolution 1514—which bans the use of viability criteria in recognizing postcolonial states.[41] Moreover, if this were a requirement for recognition, about half of the continent's countries should be derecognized, as they rely on donors for much of their budgets.

EMPIRICAL TRENDS

Has the evolution of doctrine and state practice corresponded to any empirical trend on the continent? Have some movements seized upon the uncertainties of *uti possidetis* to seek independence? Specifically, has the South Sudan precedent led to any upsurge of secessionist activity? We seek to answer these questions in two stages, looking first at the trend among large-scale secessionist conflicts and then investigating smaller and more ambiguous cases.

TOWARD A MAINSTREAMING OF SECESSIONIST POLITICS

The empirical record suggests that the end of the Cold War led to a resurgence of major secessionist conflicts, that Africa's secessionist moment peaked in the 1990s, and that it has since stabilized at a level higher than during the Cold War, suggesting a relative mainstreaming of secessionism as a mode of political action. As Fig. 16.1 illustrates, there was a significant increase in secessionist conflicts after 1990.[42] However, this trend peaked

---

[41] UN (1960).

[42] Using data from the Peace Research Institute of Oslo (PRIO), Fig. 16.1 includes instances of secessionist conflicts with at least 25 casualties in a year. Eritrea and South Sudan were removed once they achieved independence. Although violence continued in South Sudan, it was no longer secessionist. However, the Sudan People's Liberation Movement (SPLM), coded as non-secessionist by PRIO for the 1983–2004 period, was re-coded as secessionist. The Afar Liberation Front (Ethiopia), Bundu Dia Kongo (Democratic Republic

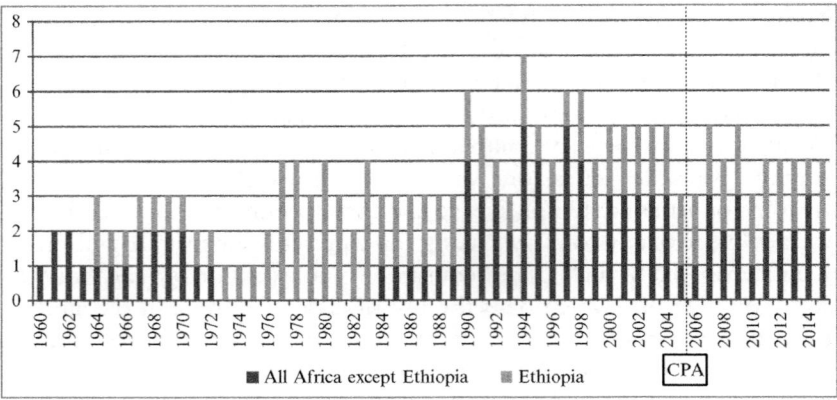

Fig. 16.1   Time trends in Africa's secessionist conflicts

in the late 1990s. The data does not show any measurable positive effect on large-scale secessionist violence across the continent from the CPA or the independence of South Sudan. On the contrary, while secessionist activity in the ten years preceding the CPA averaged five cases a year, it fell to 3.9 in the 2005–2015 period. Nevertheless, because secessionist violence abated in South Sudan after 2005 and the country was removed from the data once it reached independence, the level of secessionist violence after 2005 is broadly similar to that before. In other words, while South Sudan itself might not have had any effect, the average prevalence of secessionism in Africa since 2000 exceeds that in the first three decades of independences.

To be fair, it might be too soon to fully identify any long-term effect of South Sudan's independence, but there is no indication of a significant uptick at this point, which is largely consistent with our earlier discussion of the high threshold set by this precedent. The spread of civil war in South Sudan since 2013 has no doubt tarnished the appeal of the country's experience for other would-be secessionists. It might be safe to say

of the Congo—DRC), and the Niger Delta People's Volunteer Force (Nigeria) were also removed, as their claims are mostly not secessionist (we return to some of them in the subsequent section). We also followed Matthew Porges' argument that Western Sahara is not properly classified as secessionist and did not include it. Somaliland is included each year since 1991 as it is still seeking recognition and effective secession, despite having remained largely free of violence over that period.

that South Sudan changed the rules of recognition at the very margin only and thus did not noticeably affect the calculus of would-be separatist insurgents, who remain unlikely to secede, given the generally low odds of recognition.[43]

Hence, Chadian President Idriss Déby's concern that "we all have a south"[44] might have been exaggerated, as was Qaddafi's 2010 warning that South Sudan was a "disease" that would "spread to all of Africa."[45] Even in Sudan itself, the breakup has not provided additional motivation to existing rebel groups. Darfur's Justice and Equality Movement (JEM), for example, which had announced in 2009 that if South Sudan gained independence it too would pursue a secessionist agenda, has since joined forces with other groups to create the Sudanese Revolutionary Front whose goal is to overthrow the Arab-dominated regime in Khartoum rather than to secede.[46]

The breakup of the Soviet Union and Yugoslavia in 1989–1990 and the recognition of several new states at the time in other regions appear to have exercised a greater stimulus on African secessionists than South Sudan.[47] It is actually around that same period (1994) that the right to self-determination of South Sudan was first affirmed.[48] However, the failure of most secessionist movements to gain recognition, or their decision to settle for less than independence, soon tamed the continental enthusiasm. Nevertheless, it bears stressing that the average level of secessionist violence has increased compared to the period before the Cold War, even after removing South Sudan from the data, which might be related to the somewhat greater ambiguity in rules of recognition brought about by the inconsistent practices of African and non-African states alike. As Table 16.1 shows, the mean level of secessionism, which had greatly increased in the 1990s, fell back in the 2000s but to a level significantly higher than in previous decades, at 2.5 cases a year, not including Ethiopian movements. From 2010 to 2015, this figure decreased to 2.0. Compare this with the levels of the 1970s (0.4) and 1980s (0.6). Speculation on drivers of this higher post-2000 average could include a slight erosion in the idea that

[43] Englebert (2009).

[44] McNamee (2012).

[45] "Gaddafi Warns Sudan Secession Would be Dangerous for Africa." *France 24*, October 10, 2010.

[46] ARB (2012: 19045B).

[47] Englebert and Hummel (2005).

[48] de Vries and Schomerus (2017b).

Table 16.1 Decade averages of African secessionist activity

	All Africa except Ethiopia	Ethiopia
1960s	1.5	0.7
1970s	0.4	1.8
1980s	0.6	2.5
1990s	3.5	1.5
2000s	2.5	2.0
2010–15	2.0	1.8

Source: Based on adjusted PRIO data (see note 42)

Not including Western Sahara

secessionism is an unacceptable or impractical solution to regional griev-ances, thus weakening the principle of territorial integrity after the peak of the 1990s and secession of South Sudan.

Looking more carefully at the specific cases since 1990 sheds some light on the data. The first and most obvious trend is the large amount of seces-sionist conflicts that take place in Ethiopia. On average, since 1990, 46% of all large-scale African secessionist conflicts have involved regions trying to break away from Ethiopia (it was 56% from 1960 to 1989, when Eritrea was still included and the rest of the continent saw significantly fewer such con-flicts). Ogaden and Oromiya are the two regions responsible for this Ethiopian tilt in the data, almost constantly reaching the 25 battle-deaths threshold since the 1970s, though clashes occurred intermittently in the 1960s.

The original bump in secessionism around 1990, however, is interestingly not an Ethiopian affair (see Fig. 16.1, where the peak in the early 1990s remains without including Ethiopian conflicts). As a matter of fact, 1993, which sees the recognition of Eritrea, is one of the few years without any large-scale Ethiopian secessionist conflict. The only active conflict remained in the Ogaden, with local, predominantly Somali, separatists supported by attacks from the Islamic militant group, Al Ittihad Al Islamiya from Somalia. Yet, after the new regime in Addis Ababa started reneging on its promises of federalism and local autonomy, Ogaden and Oromiya returned to warfare and contributed largely to the subsequent higher continental average. The Ogaden National Liberation Front (ONLF) has sustained numerous instances of heavy fighting with the Ethiopian government over the last decade, a violence possibly fueled by the discovery of oil in the region. In Oromiya, however, secessionist conflict, absent from 2012 to 2014, returned in 2015 with several movements continuing to demand independence.

One explanation for the exception of Ethiopia is the fact that it was not only never colonized but also very much acted like a colonial power itself, conquering and trading new territories with European colonizers in the late nineteenth and early twentieth centuries, which is how both Ogaden and Oromiya were acquired under Emperor Menelik II. Unlike the Europeans, however, the data suggest that Ethiopia might still have significant decolonizing to do, as political actors in these regions have sustainably demonstrated a desire to free themselves from Ethiopian control. Ethiopia's unique historical background makes it a highly idiosyncratic case from which only limited continent-wide inference can be drawn.[49]

The other large-scale cases are Senegal's Casamance, which shows up in the data ten different years between 1990 and 2015 (but not between 2004 and 2010); Mali's Tuaregs and their Azawad Republic, with eight instances between 1990 and 2015 (plus two instances among Niger's Tuaregs); Angola's Cabinda with nine observations but none since 2010; Comoros' Anjouan with one year in 1997 (though its secession continued nonviolently until 2002); and Somaliland, whose secession has been effective but unrecognized since 1991. Since each of these has a chapter in this book, we focus mainly here on the most recent developments among these groups, in part, to trace whether South Sudan exerted any influence on their demands and strategies.

The Casamance insurgency has been going on and off since the early 1990s and has been characterized by a long list of poorly implemented peace agreements and a profound tendency toward factionalism within the *Mouvemement des Forces Démocratiques du Sénégal*, MFDC.[50] Although he had threatened to put an end to the conflict in 100 days, President Abdoulaye Wade transferred the problem to his successor Macky Sall in 2012 but was able to avoid large-scale violence after a peace agreement was signed in 2004, until 2010. Yet, the Senegalese army launched an offensive in March 2010, and violence peaked in December 2011, ahead of the presidential elections, with the MFDC rebels killing an estimated 30 Senegalese soldiers. No less than five different wings of the MFDC have representation in Casamance, with the one based in The Gambia probably representing the most hardline faction under Salif Sadio and auguring of continued violence ahead. MFDC factionalism is one of the main reasons this conflict has endured, as peace agreements typically result in the excom-

---

[49] See Englebert (2009: 178–181).
[50] Foucher (2018).

munication of the negotiators and their faction and the resumption of the fight by some splinter group until the next peace accord.

In line with the trend of the argument of the "new wars" literature that stresses the relevance of criminality in post-Cold War civil conflict, there is also a significant amount of banditry now in the region, with some of the same actors as the secessionist conflict. The election of Senegalese President Macky Sall in 2012 led to renewed negotiations, culminating in a ceasefire agreement with MFDC faction leader Salif Sadio on April 30, 2014, which has yet to be broken. This agreement was significant, given Salif Sadio's previous resistance to negotiations, which has served as a hindrance to a successful ceasefire with the highly polarized factions of the MFDC.[51] The recent election of Gambian President Adama Barrow and subsequent ousting of Yahya Jammeh may facilitate a lasting solution to the conflict, given The Gambia's previous history of sheltering refugees and rebels of the Casamance conflict on its southern border.

The other major recent resurgence of secessionist activity is accounted for by the Tuaregs of Northern Mali in 2012. The first wave of Tuareg insurgency had taken place in 1990–1994 and had then largely been placated by promises of autonomy and government jobs. It resurfaced in 2007–2008 as the Malian government started showing signs of decay in its capacity to co-opt and deliver on its commitments. In the 2006 Algiers Accords, Mali had once again pledged to devote resources toward developing the northern region, but little was forthcoming, as had already been the case after the 1991 National Pact. Thus, significant skirmishes took place in 2007 and 2008, but the military weakness of the rebels and the willingness of President Touré to negotiate tamed them. The overthrow of President Qaddafi of Libya in 2011 reactivated the conflict, as it suddenly created a massive imbalance between the rebels, aided by hundreds of heavily armed Tuaregs returning from serving in Qaddafi's military and the Malian army.[52] The fusion of the new fighters with existing groups engendered the MNLA, led by former Libyan colonel Mohamed Majim.[53]

Clashes between the MNLA and Mali's army began in January 2012. Criticism of Bamako's handling of the crisis and a lack of efficacy against the northern insurgents culminated in a military coup in March, but this did not prevent the MNLA and other groups, like the Islamist Ansar Dine

---

[51] Seyferth (2014).
[52] Lotze (2015).
[53] ARB (2012: 19130B).

and the Movement for Unity of Jihad in West Africa (MUJAO), from making rapid territorial progress and taking, in short order, the cities of Gao, Kidal, and Timbuktu, effectively controlling the northern half of the country. In June, the MNLA declared the unilateral independence of the Republic of Azawad, possibly as an effort to fend off the rising influence of the other groups.[54]

Its control over territory rapidly dwindled after that, as Ansar Dine, MUJAO, and al-Qaeda in the Islamic Maghreb (AQIM) asserted their dominance and imposed Shari'a law in the region, largely sending the MNLA on the run.[55] In an implicit assertion that secular politics mattered more to them than independence, the MNLA then offered its services to Bamako against AQIM and its allies in the North, officially renouncing their goal of independence and offering assistance in return for autonomy.[56] The situation then stagnated until MUJAO took the town of Douentza, 800 kilometers north of Bamako, an area not considered part of Azawad, in January 2013, which led to a 4000-strong French military intervention that liberated the entire territory from Islamist rebels, while keeping the MNLA partly in charge of Kidal.[57] A partial French withdrawal was subsequently paired with the deployment of a UN peacekeeping mission. As of 2017, the MNLA remained de facto in control of Kidal, where a weak central government struggled to establish an effective presence.

The enclave of Cabinda, squeezed between Congo-Kinshasa and Congo-Brazzaville, did not witness significant secessionist violence between 2007 and 2016, although the Front for the Liberation of the Enclave of Cabinda (FLEC) remained active. The Angolan army's 2002–2003 offensive largely destroyed FLEC's military forces. Thus, in August 2006, a peace agreement formally establishing a ceasefire was signed between the Angolan government and Antonio Bento Bembe on behalf of the Cabinda Forum for Dialogue (FCD) that had formed two years earlier in an effort to consolidate former FLEC factions. However, Bembe, who represented the FLEC-Renovada faction, was accused by opposing faction leader Nzita Tiago of FLEC-*Forças Armadas de Cabinda*

---

[54] ARB (2012: 19241C).

[55] ARB (2012: 19243AB–19244C).

[56] ARB (2012: 19353A).

[57] Several African states also participated in the military operations, first among being Chad, which sent 2000 troops.

and others of having no authority to make such an agreement, which stipulated the demilitarization of FLEC's military in exchange for amnesty for separatist violence from the past 30 years.[58] The agreement also included the recognition that Angola and Cabinda were "a united and indivisible nation."

However, lack of solidarity among FLEC factions resulted in the continuation of low-scale activity. FLEC-FAC maintains their exiled faction in Paris under Tiago.[59] An attack on Togo's national football team and an Angolan military vehicle by Cabinda separatists in 2010 provoked a clampdown on Cabinda natives and the arrests of two human rights activists: a lawyer and a priest.[60] In April 2012, Angola offered to participate in peace talks with the remaining separatist activists.[61] Yet, after a brief respite, notably in the wake of South Sudanese independence, in February 2016, FLEC announced the resumption of the use of violence to advance their separatist agenda, and attacks on government forces intensified after the death of the group's founder, Nzita Tiago, in June 2016.[62]

It does not appear from this brief overview that the CPA or the actual independence of South Sudan had any particular effect on these larger insurgencies. These movements all by and large took off in the early 1990s. One reason they have been ongoing for so long seems to be the failure of peace agreements to hold, largely because of factionalism within the rebel movements and because governments do not typically deliver on their commitments, whether out of bad will or incompetence.

It is worth noting, however, that the years since 2011, and particularly 2013, have seen some resurgence of Katangese secessionism, as noted by Larmer and Kennes in this volume, although the specific goals and motivations of the actors involved remain murky, and domestic politics seem more relevant at this point than any hypothetical link with South Sudan.[63] In February 2011, the Katangese separatist flag was raised at a UN base by attackers who clashed with government forces for three hours. In August, gunmen displaying Katangese red and white headbands attacked Luano

---

[58] "Angola Signs Deal with Cabindans." *BBC News,* August 1, 2006.
[59] "Cabindan Separatists in Exile Deny End to Conflict." *IRIN News,* July 22, 2010.
[60] ARB (2010: 18234AB, 18630C).
[61] ARB (2012: 19238A).
[62] Buchanan (2017).
[63] Larmer and Kenner (2018).

Airport in Lubumbashi, killing three government troops.[64] Another attack of the airport took place in December 2012.

The situation escalated in February 2013, as a militia called Bakata Katanga—"cut Katanga off"—first perpetrated exactions in the region of Lubumbashi, then briefly invaded the city of Lubumbashi and raised the secessionist flag downtown before being violently pushed back by government forces at the cost of 35 casualties.[65] Although these events would be the first instances of violent secessionism in the province since the 1960s (there were rebellions in the 1970s and 1980s, but they were not secessionist), observers suggest that they are more likely to be warnings to the incumbent regime from some Katanga politicians opposed to further decentralization of their province.

Below the Radar: Insights from Smaller and Ambiguous Cases

While there are relatively few fully fledged secessionist conflicts in Africa, there is a multitude of smaller movements that at times make secessionist demands or at least voice claims to autonomy. What has been the evolution of practice among these movements, particularly since the CPA? For one, it is worth noting that they have not generally become more violent. In other words, the South Sudan precedent has not so far triggered an upsurge of violence among African secessionists eager for recognition, which suggests that the threshold of humanitarian recognition might indeed have been set too high for it to become an incentive to violence elsewhere. Mali's Tuaregs are a possible exception here, but their increased use of violence in 2012 actually resulted largely from the breakdown of the Libyan regime and the return of Tuaregs serving as foreign fighters for Qaddafi.[66] Moreover, most of the violence after the initial stage of the conflict came from Islamist insurgents/invaders rather than from the MLNA.

Elsewhere, the CPA might have boosted a more legalistic evolution, as it appears that more and more movements call for a referendum or seem committed to holding one, in contrast to earlier continental practice when rebels did not bother to ascertain or demonstrate popular support. This trend predates both the CPA and the 2011 South Sudan referendum, but

---

[64] ARB (2011: 18733A).

[65] "Militants Target Katanga," *Africa Confidential* 54(5), March 1, 2013.

[66] Lotze (2015).

the latter seems to have accelerated it and given smaller groups a lifeline of sorts to validate their claims.

Looking at cases over time, the development of a referendum norm appears clearly, although that does not mean referenda are necessarily held in each case. Eritrea had one in 1993; the Southern Cameroons National Council has been demanding one since 1995[67]; Anjouan held one in October 1997 on independence (99.88% in favor) and in 2000 on a federal solution (defeated); Somaliland held one in 2001; the French had one in Mayotte as recently as 2009 (on the status of Department for the island); South Sudan's took place in 2011; the ONLF demanded in 2012 that the Ethiopian government commit to a referendum on secession within 15 years (a right the Ethiopian constitution grants—but the request was turned down); the MNLA tried to organize one online on its web page in 2012,[68] although no results were published, and the overall effort looked rather amateurish; the POLISARIO Front still demands and awaits its many-times promised one since the Spanish first voiced the intent to do so in 1974 (it remains insistent on a referendum offering the options of autonomy and independence for Western Sahara, while Morocco appears only willing to offer regional autonomy); the Association for Islamic Mobilization and Propagation (UAMSHO) demanded a referendum in 2012 on the separation of Zanzibar from Tanzania[69]; and, finally, a *Coordination pour le Référendum pour l'Autodétermination du Katanga* called for a referendum on Katangese independence in 2012 while the then speaker of the provincial assembly, Gabriel Kyungu wa Kumwanza, collected 300,000 signatures petitioning for greater autonomy and the application of a constitutional clause for a greater share of the province's revenue.[70]

What would the map of Africa look like if all these smaller secessionist movements successfully held referenda and obtained recognition, in addition to the larger violent ones discussed in the previous section? Without suggesting any endorsement of their claims, we present such a map here,

---

[67] In 2012, some borderland Nigerian communities, including the Efiks in Bakassi, announced their support of Southern Cameroon's independence and formed an association that allegedly planned to apply to the UN for a self-determination referendum. See *ARB* 2012, 19443A.

[68] www.mnlamov.net.

[69] ARB (2012: 19321A).

[70] Since then, the central government broke Katanga down into four provinces and, as of 2017, Kyungu had fallen from assembly speaker to hounded opposition member.

Fig. 16.2 The secessionist's map of Africa. (Crescents indicate movements with Islamist component)

including some additional smaller and more ambiguous movements not discussed in this book, such as Buganda (the crescents indicate movements that have an Islamist component, an issue the next sections turns to) (Fig. 16.2).

ISLAMISM AND SECESSIONISM: TWO PEAS OUT OF THE SAME POD?

A careful reading of the cases in this book and the empirical evidence from the last few years indicates that, while there might have been at best a mild mainstreaming of secessionism as political action, a deeper and more radical evolution might be taking place with the increased coincidence of

Islamic fundamentalist and secessionist rebellions in several regions of the continent. This connection is first and foremost ideological, yet it also has considerable practical and even accidental dimensions. We try to make preliminary sense of it in this final section and assess its impact on the future of secessionism on the continent.

ISLAMISM AS A SECESSIONIST IDEOLOGY

Ideologically, the fundamentalist Islamist project can be construed as one of legal separation from the Western state, whether through takeover, conversion, or possibly territorial separation. Few Islamists directly entertain the notion of territorial secession (as was made clear, e.g., when Mali's *Movement for Unity and Jihad in West Africa* [MUJAO] declared their intent to take over and Islamicize the entire country rather than satisfying themselves with Azawad), yet their agenda at least implied legal separation from the existing political order and was thus consistent with secession. Compared to most nonreligious secessionist movements, especially those that embrace the postcolonial mold, Islamist fundamentalism represents a much more radical questioning of the imported Western state and acquires credibility, in part because of its potential to generate external support from international Islamist movements such as the Islamic State and al-Qaeda or from rich supporters such as Saudi Wahhabists.

In its political ramifications, Islam offers the idea of a unified state for Ummah, the supranational commonwealth of the believers. The Caliphate is the embodiment of the Islamic state, functioning along the precepts of Shari'a. Historically, the Caliphate had a limited effective reach, but the idea of a potential unifying caliph representing the political descent of Mohammed remained powerful until its extinction at the end of the Ottoman Empire in the early twentieth century. The restoration of the Caliphate by uniting worldwide Muslim populations has considerable appeal, and the re-establishment of a united government of Muslims is allegedly one of al-Qaeda's objectives. The rise of Islamic State, to which Nigeria's Boko has pledged allegiance, has seen a concurrent aspiration to restore a transnational caliphate.[71] Although such lofty goals are beyond the reach of the common variety of African and other secessionists, they provide a useful narrative that can sustain separatist conflicts and provide

---

[71] It must be noted, however, that these pledges may be instrumental rather than sincere.

legitimacy to alternative political forms such as local pre-colonial Muslim states (e.g., the Sokoto Caliphate in Nigeria or the Zanzibar Sultanate).

As a result, Islamist separatism is particularly radical, threatening as it does the very existence of the Western postcolonial state in Muslim areas and the very political project it represents. While common secessionism aims at multiplying the number of Western-inspired states, Islamism seeks to abolish them. Moreover, by addressing deeper issues of political order such as corruption, Islamist separatism also makes moral claims that challenge the modus operandi of the African state and can have great appeal in areas of widespread youth unemployment and alienation.

At a more practical level, the correlation between secessionism and Islamism is also somewhat accidental, as they both thrive in similar environments and tend therefore to find themselves in proximity to each other in Muslim areas. Zones of lawlessness and trafficking that are also historically Muslim, like much of the Sahara and parts of the East Coast, lend themselves to both separatism and Islamic extremism. The increase in such lawlessness in the wake of post-1990 state failures, the rising importance of drugs, weapons, and migrant trafficking, and these regions' oil potential have contributed to raising their relative political importance and heightened the potential returns for local insurgents, irrespective of their specific goals. Groups like the Tuareg, for example, have found multiple economic opportunities in such environments and been associated with both secular and religious political movements. By letting loose the multiple militias that existed under his patronage, the fall of Libya's Qaddafi in 2011 gave renewed vigor to groups that had existed in the region for some time and brought about new actors and resources, multiplying the region's lethal potential.

Case Studies

Several chapters in this volume offer considerable evidence of the rise of Islamist separatism. Reading them together gives one a sense of the scope of this new development and suggests it might be one of the furthest-reaching trends in African secessionism. Unlike more benign cases of postcolonial separatism, Islamist insurgents appear like poorer candidates for dilution into networks of neopatrimonial co-optation and might thus herald a structural shift in the politics of African countries with Muslim populations.

Nigeria, with its long history of both religious and secessionist conflicts, offers one of the most salient cases. Although the Igbo and Delta regions of the South are the ones best known for separatism, together with an occasional outburst by Yoruba groups such as the Odua People's Congress, it is the North that has provided the crucible for Islamist separatism. It bears repeating that the Sokoto Caliphate, which derives from Usman Dan Fodio's Fulani Jihad against the Haussa kingdoms in the early nineteenth century,[72] was a powerful and spreading political system at the advent of British colonialism, one in which indirect rule was largely preserved and which remained active in independence politics (Ahmadu Bello, the premier of the northern region from 1954 to 1966, was a high-ranking member of the Caliphate).[73]

The adoption of Shari'a by 13 northern states in 1999, after Obasanjo, a born-again Christian southerner, assumed the Nigerian presidency, represented thus a form of separatism "tantamount to an act of secession" according to a Nigerian constitutional scholar quoted by Harnischfeger in his chapter. In many ways, it was an act of treason, rejecting crucial parts of the federal constitution. It is no coincidence that the governor of Zamfara State, the first to adopt Shari'a, called for a "new caliphatic order."[74] However, the lack of serious religious commitment of the corrupt northern governors led younger and more radical Muslims to create Boko Haram around 2004 (first called "Taliban"), which is opposed to all things Western and, as such, to the Nigerian state too. While Shari'a adoption was an elite political move aimed at weakening the new president, Boko Haram is more of a grass-root militant effort. Although it has not historically presented itself as a secessionist movement, its goals include the dissolution of Nigeria as it exists now, and it is increasingly associated with separatist goals. According to Boko Haram, "genuine Shari'a can only be practiced in an Islamic state,"[75] which implies breaking free of Nigeria or converting all Christians. *Africa Research Bulletin* notes that Boko Haram wants "to restore the Islamic state that once existed [in northern Nigeria] and was 'destroyed' by British colonialists."[76,77] In 2015,

---

[72] Loimeier (2007).

[73] Harnischfeger (2018).

[74] Harnischfeger (2018).

[75] Harnischfeger (2018).

[76] ARB (2012: 19318A).

[77] For other interpretations of Boko Haram as separatist, see Pflanz (2012) and Walker (2012).

Boko Haram pledged allegiance to the Islamic State, furthering the narrative of the restoration of a broader caliphate.

Zanzibar and Coastal Kenya offer a similar case, albeit at much lower levels of violence. Yet, the region's pre-colonial political history as an Islamic state carries the same type of narrative as in Northern Nigeria. Zanzibar, and the strip of coastal mainland it controlled in today's Tanzania and Kenya, was part of the Sultanate of Oman until 1856, when it became its own sultanate under British tutelage. In 1890, both the islands and the coastal strip became a British protectorate. The Tanganyika part of the strip was subsequently purchased by the Germans and merged with Tanganyika, while the Kenyan part remained a distinct British protectorate (as opposed to Kenya, which was a colony) until 1961.[78]

The sultan was quickly evicted from Tanzanian politics during the "Zanzibar revolution" of 1964, which reinforced pro-union political actors on the island for decades to come, as detailed in Greg Cameron's chapter.[79] Unlike several other African countries, the federal merging of Tanganyika and Zanzibar was not sidestepped by unitary politics, despite some such tendencies in the 1970s. Thus, Zanzibar retained a considerable degree of autonomy and a preferential position in the federation, given its small size, which largely prevented the rise of significant secessionism despite a continuous undercurrent of separatist discourse in island politics. The fact that Julius Nyerere's successor in 1985, Ali Hassan Mwinyi, was Muslim and Zanzibari probably helped. Yet, there were limits to this autonomy, as the island discovered when it was prevented from joining the Organization of Islamic Conference in 1993.[80]

Here too, however, as in many other parts of the world, Islamism's influence has been rising since the outset of the twenty-first century. While traditional island parties have largely made peace with the union, an Islamic group called UAMSHO has demanded a referendum to leave the union because of its secular status, and its activities have involved small riots and the burning of churches.[81,82] In Kenya, the grievances of coastal communities, of which some but not all are Arab and Muslims, have found a voice since 2005 in the Mombasa Republican Council (MRC), which

[78] Lofchie (2015).
[79] Cameron (2018).
[80] Cameron (2018).
[81] *ARB* (2012: 19321A, 19465C).
[82] The 1964 union of Tanganyika and Zanzibar was never submitted to a referendum but resulted from an agreement among elites.

occasionally demands secession for the strip. The sultanate provides a convenient historical narrative, which connects loosely with Muslim rule (in 1961, religious protections were extended to the Muslim community). As Willis and Gona suggest, there have been claims that MRC could be linked to al-Shabaab, though they make it clear that it is broader than that.[83] Kenyan officials themselves claim that the MRC is infiltrated by fighters from al-Shabaab.[84] There are also concerns that the MRC might be funded by Sudan to retaliate for Kenyan support for South Sudan, as well as by some member states of the Arab League, concerned at increased collaboration between Ethiopia, South Sudan, and Kenya.[85] The Kenyan government has taken the MRC threat seriously and has cracked down on its militants after cases of violence linked to the MRC increased, along with rising fears within security circles that the movement would plan to disrupt school examinations as well as voting in March 2013.

The MRC partly relies on the past colonial existence argument, and as such is a very conventional African secessionist movement, reminiscent of Barotseland or Anglophone Cameroon in its invocation of alleged past treaties with the British (and in its appeals to the Queen). But the MRC also reawakens the pre-colonial notion of the sultanate, its Arab and Muslim roots, and as such represents a more radical challenge to postcolonial Africa. It is no coincidence in this respect that the movement seems to develop around 2005 (about the same time as UAMSHO in Zanzibar), at a moment when Islamic counter-narratives to Western domination spread around the world. While no caliphate, the Zanzibari Sultanate offers an alternative, Muslim and pre-Western, blueprint for political order.

Although they cannot rely on an equally powerful pre-colonial narrative, the Tuaregs of Mali provide another particularly interesting case of overlapping Islamist and separatist conflicts and logics. While the Tuareg rebellion had been going on and off since the early 1990s, the fall of the Qaddafi regime in Libya in 2011 changed its dynamics. Over the years, a significant portion of young unemployed Tuareg men had migrated to Libya, where some were incorporated into Qaddafi's military. When Qaddafi was killed, about 2000–4000 of these fighters made the trek back to Northern Mali with heavy equipment (including truck-mounted rocket

---

[83] Willis and Gona (2013).
[84] ARB (2012: 19458AB).
[85] ARB (2012: 19351BC).

launchers) and ammunition and a comparative advantage in violence. *Jeune Afrique* describes them as "part-drug traffickers, part-rebels, some-time-Islamists, and often opportunists."[86] As discussed earlier, they set up the MNLA and allied with Ansar Dine, a relatively new 300-strong Islamic fundamentalist group with links to al-Qaeda in the Islamic Maghreb (AQIM). They quickly overpowered Mali's anemic military and captured the cities of Kidal, Gao, and Timbuktu, eventually controlling the northern half of Mali's territory. They issued a unilateral declaration of independence of Azawad in April 2012. However, two months later, they by and large lost control of these towns to Ansar Dine and another group, the (MUJAO), which sought to impose Shari'a in the region.

In the case of Mali, however, the coincidence of Islamist and separatist insurgencies does not imply that the Islamists also necessarily entertained secessionist aims. Their goal seems to have been more ambiguous. At times, they claimed to seek total control of Mali, if only as a first step toward a regional Islamic state. Ansar Dine was quoted as being against Azawad independence and "rebellions not in the name of Islam," and that they were "against the division of Mali" and wanted the application of Shari'a law in both the North and the South.[87] It installed Shari'a law in the cities and villages under its control and openly claimed ties to AQIM. There is also some evidence that it received help from Boko Haram militants in the control of the city of Gao, suggesting broader regional collaboration among Islamist groups.[88] For a while, an Islamist separatist state appeared possible, as a merger deal was allegedly signed between MNLA and Ansar Dine in 2012 in Gao with the goal of turning their territory into an Islamist state. Colonel Bouna Ag Attayoub, an MNLA commander in Timbuktu, told BBC "the Islamic Republic of Azawad is now an independent sovereign state."[89] However, an MNLA spokesman later said the agreement with Ansar Dine would provide for a secular republic.[90] It is apparently the question of implementing Shari'a that led to a break up between these two factions and pushed the MNLA to eventually ally with the French in their reclaiming of the territory from Ansar Dine and MUJOA.

[86] ARB (2012: 19130AB).
[87] ARB (2012: 19243A; 19316C).
[88] ARB (2012: 19244B).
[89] ARB (2012:19277BC).
[90] ARB (2012: 19278A).

Other cases with an Islamist dimension include Ogaden, a Somali Muslim region in Christian-dominated Ethiopia. As Sarah Vaughan's chapter makes clear, two Islamic organizations were established in the region in 1991: the Ogaden Islamic Union and the Islamic Solidarity Party-Western Somalia-Ogaden. The former professed Wahabbism and aimed at "imposing an Islamist state over all of Somali-inhabited East Africa."[91] It was also active in Somalia and might have been part of the Islamic Courts after 1997. The latter was led by a founder of the Ogaden separatist insurgency, the ONLF. As Sarah Vaughan notes, Sheikh Ibrahim Abdella, the ONLF leader "known for his sophisticated Islamic education [and] strong religious views" returned from exile in Saudi Arabia in 1992 and contributed to the resurgence of Ogadeni separatism.[92] In another example of the ambiguity of territorial goals of Islamist separatists, the Wahhabist group is said to want an Islamist state over the whole of Somali area (which covers all or part of five countries). In this case, Ogaden would be a mere stepping stone, in another example of the more radical restructuring of state forms in Africa promoted by Islamist insurgents.

In Western Sahara too, the old Algerian-inspired republican and socialist emphasis of the POLISARIO movement has been challenged by the rising Islamist influence in the region, which was vividly illustrated by the kidnapping of foreign aid workers in a Sahrawi refugee camp in 2011. The UN envoy to the region worried in 2012 that the current stalemate on the referendum would increase the region's vulnerability to the growing presence of Islamist extremists and militants in the Sahara.[93]

Finally, the chapter on Eritrea suggested that Islam played a role in the articulation of "nationalist aspirations" during the secession war. Islam was antiestablishment and clashed with Ethiopia's Christianity. In the end, however, Islam was downplayed as a building block of Eritrea in favor of the postcolonial narrative, which proved a successful move.[94]

At any rate, the correlation of Islamic extremist and separatist goals among African insurgencies is a new development. A study of secessionism ten years ago would have hardly noticed the Islamic extremism connection. It might represent an important dimension of the future of secessionism on the continent and one that will not be as easy to dissolve in the postcolonial container as previous secessionist waves.

---

[91]Vaughan (2018).
[92]Vaughan (2018).
[93]ARB (2012: 19478C–19479AB).
[94]Iyob (1997).

Conclusion

In some regions of Africa, secessionism continues, more than five decades after independence, to provide a powerful and appealing narrative to marginalized political communities and their elites. By and large, however, its translation into sustained military campaign for independence and sovereignty remains rare. The early 1990s saw an increase in secessionist conflicts, but the limited avenues for recognition subsequently slowed its momentum. Only Eritrea came out of it recognized as a new state.

The later recognition of South Sudan as a sovereign state, despite its lack of specific colonial status, seemed to provide a dramatic departure from previous practice and to open up renewed opportunities for African secessionists. Yet, as we showed in this chapter, South Sudan neither constitutes such a dramatic shift from previous practice nor has it apparently led so far to renewed secessionist activism on the continent. It has, however, possibly contributed to a relative mainstreaming of secessionist goals and a new culture of the referendum, which, if anything, promotes a more legalistic and democratic approach to separatism on the continent.

Possibly more compelling and of far-reaching consequences have been the progressive development of an apparent association between secessionism and Islamism, at least in the Sahara and on the East Coast. This observation, highlighting a genuinely novel trend as far as we can tell, comes out as a direct contribution of the chapters in this book. Thus, while many secessionist movements calling for sovereignty based on more or less contrived readings of *uti possidetis* within the postcolonial paradigm seem to be running out of steam, Islamist separatism is both a dynamic ideology and an effective mobilizer of combatants. Whatever its own limitations and inherent dangers to individuals and communities, it addresses head-on the intrinsic failures of the African postcolonial state to bring welfare, opportunities, and emancipation to its citizens and is therefore sure to sustain considerable appeal in the years to come.

References

Africa Confidential. (2013, March 1). Militants target Katanga. *Africa Confidential, 54*(5). p.9

Africa Research Bulletins. (2009–2012). Political, social, and cultural series, January 2009–December 2012. *Africa Research Bulletin, 45*(12) to *49*(11).

Allott, A. (1974). The changing legal status of boundaries in Africa: A diachronic view. In K. Bingham (Ed.), *Foreign relations of African states* (pp. 111–126). London: Butterworth.

BBC News. (2006, August 1). Angola signs deal with Cabindans. *BBC News.* http://news.bbc.co.uk/2/hi/africa/5236230.stm

BBC News. (2013, June 5). Mali army clashes with separatist MNLA rebels. *BBC News.* https://www.bbc.com/news/av/world-africa-22791147/mali-army-clashes-with-separatist-mnla-rebels

Boutellis, A. (2015). Can the UN stabilize Mali? Towards a UN stabilization doctrine? *Stability: International Journal of Security & Development, 4*(1), 1–16.

Buchanan. (2017, February 13). Angola: Who are the FLEC rebels calling for election boycott in oil-rich Cabinda? *International Business Times.* https://www.ibtimes.co.uk/angola-who-are-flec-rebels-calling-election-boycott-oil-rich-cabinda-1606198

Cameron, G. (2018). Zanzibar in the Tanzania Union. In L. de Vries, P. Englebert, & M. Schomerus (Eds.), *Secessionism in African politics: Aspiration, grievance, performance, disenchantment.* New York: Palgrave.

De Vries, L., & Schomerus, M. (2017a). South Sudan's Civil War will not end with a peace deal. *Peace Review: A Journal of Social Justice, 29,* 333–340.

De Vries, L., & Schomerus, M. (2017b). Fettered self-determination: South Sudan's narrowed path to secession. *Civil Wars, 19*(1), 1–20.

Dersso, S. (2012, February). International law and the self-determination of South Sudan. *Institute for Security Studies,* Paper 231.

Dobler, G. (2018). Anjouan and secessionism in the Comoros: Internal dynamics, external decisions. In L. de Vries, P. Englebert, & M. Schomerus (Eds.), *Secessionism in African politics: Aspiration, grievance, performance, disenchantment.* New York: Palgrave.

Dugard, J. (2003). A legal basis for secession – Relevant principles and rules. In J. Dahlitz (Ed.), *Secession and international law: Conflict avoidance, regional appraisals* (pp. 89–96). The Hague: Asser Press.

Englebert, P. (2009). *Africa: Unity, sovereignty and sorrow.* Boulder: Lynne Rienner Publishers.

Englebert, P. (2013). Separatism in Africa. In J. Hentz (Ed.), *African security handbook* (pp. 147–156). London: Routledge.

Englebert, P., & Hummel, R. (2005). Let's stick together: Understanding Africa's secessionist deficit. *African Affairs, 104*(416), 399–427.

Foucher, V. (2018). The mouvement des forces démocratiques de Casamance: The illusion of separatism in Senegal? In L. de Vries, P. Englebert, & M. Schomerus (Eds.), *Secessionism in African politics: Aspiration, grievance, performance, disenchantment.* New York: Palgrave.

France 24. (2010, October 10). Gaddafi warns Sudan secession would be dangerous for Africa. *France 24.* http://www.france24.com/en/20101010-muammar-gaddafi-sudan-secession-danger-africa-libya/

Harnischfeger, J. (2018). Biafra and secessionism in Nigeria: An instrument of political bargaining. In L. de Vries, P. Englebert, & M. Schomerus (Eds.), *Secessionism in African politics: Aspiration, grievance, performance, disenchantment.* New York: Palgrave.

Herbst, J. (1990). War and the state in Africa. *International Security, 14*(4), 117–139.

Hilpold, P. (2009). The Kosovo case and international law: Looking for applicable theories. *Chinese Journal of International Law, 8*(1), 47–61.

Hoehne, M. V. (2018). Against the grain: Somaliland's secession from Somalia. In L. de Vries, P. Englebert, & M. Schomerus (Eds.), *Secessionism in African politics: Aspiration, grievance, performance, disenchantment.* New York: Palgrave.

IRIN News. (2010, July 22). Cabindan separatists in exile deny end to conflict. *IRIN News.* http://www.irinnews.org/news/2010/07/22/cabindan-separatists-exile-deny-end-conflict

Iyob, R. (1997). *The Eritrean struggle for independence: Domination, resistance, nationalism, 1941–1993.* Cambridge: Cambridge University Press.

Jackson, R. H. (1990). *Quasi-states: Sovereignty, international relations and the third world.* Cambridge: Cambridge University Press.

Jackson, R., & Rosberg, C. (1982). Why Africa's weak states persist: The empirical and the juridical in statehood. *World Politics, 35*(1), 1–24.

Jeune Afrique. No. (2733), 26 May–1 June (2013).

Larmer, M., & Kenner, E. (2018). Katanga's secessionism in the Democratic Republic of Congo. In L. de Vries, P. Englebert, & M. Schomerus (Eds.), *Secessionism in African politics: Aspiration, grievance, performance, disenchantment.* New York: Palgrave.

Lecocq, B., & Klute, G. (2018). Tuareg separatism in Mali and Niger. In L. de Vries, P. Englebert, & M. Schomerus (Eds.), *Secessionism in African politics: Aspiration, grievance, performance, disenchantment.* New York: Palgrave.

Lewis. (2013, May 19). After crushing Mali Islamists, France pushes deal with Tuaregs. *Reuters.* https://www.reuters.com/article/us-mali-crisis/after-crushing-mali-islamists-france-pushes-deal-with-tuaregs-idUS-BRE94I06420130519

Lofchie, M. F. (2015). *Zanzibar: Background to the revolution.* Princeton: Princeton University Press.

Loimeier, R. (2007). Nigeria: The quest for a viable religious option. In W. F. S. Miles (Ed.), *Political Islam in West Africa: State-society relations transformed* (pp. 43–72). Boulder: Lynne Rienner.

Lotze, W. (2015). United Nations multidimensional integrated stabilization mission in Mali. In J. A. Koops, N. Macqueen, T. Tardy, & P. D. Williams (Eds.), *The Oxford handbook of United Nations peacekeeping operations* (pp. 854–864). Oxford: Oxford University Press.

MacFarlane, N., & Sabanadze, N. (2013). Sovereignty and self-determination: Where are we? *Journal of Global Policy Analysis, 68*(4), 609–627.

McNamee, T. (2012). *The first crack in Africa's map? Secession and self determination after South Sudan.* Johannesburg: Brenthurst Foundation Discussion paper 2012/01.

Pflanz. (2012, January 22). Fresh attacks kill nine in Northern Nigeria as police hunt Boko Haram bombers. *Telegraph.* https://www.telegraph.co.uk/news/worldnews/africaandindianocean/nigeria/9030752/Fresh-attacks-kill-nine-in-northern-Nigeria-as-police-hunt-Boko-Haram-bombers.html

Phillips, D. (2012). *Liberating Kosovo: Coercive diplomacy and U.S. intervention.* Cambridge: MIT Press.

Porges, M. (2018). Western Sahara and Morocco: Complexities of resistance and analysis. In L. de Vries, P. Englebert, & M. Schomerus (Eds.), *Secessionism in African politics: Aspiration, grievance, performance, disenchantment.* New York: Palgrave.

Schomerus, M., & de Vries, L. (2018). A state of contradiction: Sudan's unity goes south. In L. de Vries, P. Englebert, & M. Schomerus (Eds.), *Secessionism in African politics: Aspiration, grievance, performance, disenchantment.* New York: Palgrave.

Seyferth, D. (2014, July 9). Senegal: An end to one of Africa's longest civil conflicts? *Atlantic Council.*

Summer, B. T. (2004). Territorial disputes at the International Court of Justice. *Duke Law Journal, 53*(6), 1779–1812.

United Nations General Assembly. (1960, December 14). Declaration on the granting of independence to colonial countries and peoples. A/RES/(1514) (XV).

Vaughan, S. (2018). Ethiopia, Somalia and the Ogaden: Still the running sore at the heart of the Horn of Africa. In L. de Vries, P. Englebert, & M. Schomerus (Eds.), *Secessionism in African politics: Aspiration, grievance, performance, disenchantment.* New York: Palgrave.

Vidmar, J. (2012). South Sudan and the international legal framework governing the emergence and delimitation of new states. *Texas International Law Journal, 47,* 541–560.

Walker, A. (2012, May 30). What is Boko Haram? *United States Institute of Peace.*

Willis, J., & Gona, G. (2013). Pwani C Kenya? Memory, documents and secessionist politics in coastal Kenya. *African Affairs, 112*(446), 48–71.

Index[1]

[1] Note: Page numbers followed by 'n' refer to notes.

© The Author(s) 2019
L. de Vries et al. (eds.), *Secessionism in African Politics*,
Palgrave Series in African Borderlands Studies,
https://doi.org/10.1007/978-3-319-90206-7

Printed by Printforce, the Netherlands